P9-DVA-896

Contents

Introduction: How to Read Critically   1

Why Read Critically   2
How to Read Critically   3
Sample Essay for Analysis   3

A No-Fault Holocaust   3

John Leo

> *Keeping a Journal on What You Read   5*
> *Annotate What You Read   6*
> *Outline What You Read   9*
> *Summarize What You Read   11*
> *Question What You Read   12*
> *Analyze What You Read   14*

1 Fashion and Flesh: The Images We Project   22

The Beefcaking of America   24

Jill Neimark

A "seismic shift" in gender roles is turning men into objects of desire, a role traditionally held by women.

Three for the Stripes   33

Michael Fitzpatrick (student essay)

"People from the inner city as I know it, myself included, have made fashion more than a fashion statement. In our isolation from the mainstream, we've made it a statement of identity, of who we are."

iii

Sample Ads and Study Questions 127

Mercedes-Benz
Smirnoff
Wonderbra
Clif Bar
Diesel
Don Diegos
Airwalk
Milk
AT&T
U.S. Army

---

3 Television: Friend or Foe? 148

Sex and Today's Single-Minded Sitcoms 151
Nancy Hass

Since 1970, television has lost its innocence in a big, and often boring, way. Can't anyone look elsewhere for laughs?

TV Talk Shows: Freak Parades 157
Charles Oliver

Daytime talk shows bring the carnival sideshow to America's living rooms.

Watching the Eyewitless News 162
Elayne Rapping

"When you turn on the news, whether at home or in an airport or Holiday Inn in some totally strange locale, you see a predictable, comforting spectacle."

The Problem with Black T.V. 168
Frederick L. McKissack Jr.

"Blacks are increasingly pigeonholed in simpleminded comedies."

Gays, Lesbians, and the Media: The Slow Road to Acceptance 174
Barbara Raab

"Why, when there are gay characters in movies, sitcoms, talk shows, and soap operas, are there not openly gay and lesbian TV anchorpeople and news reporters?"

In Defense of Prime Time 182
Martha Bayles

Television's best shows give us morality plays of everyday life.

Into the Heart of Darkness 185
Terrence Rafferty

The X-Files and *Millennium* are tapping into our collective unconscious—and forcing us to confront our greatest fears.

Sequencing Assignments: Making New Connections   565

Rhetorical Contents

PROCESS ANALYSIS
Step-by-Step Explanation of How Something Operates

COMPARISON AND CONTRAST
Examining Similarities

HUMOR AND SATIRE
Making Us Laugh While We Think

Preface

The *Contemporary Reader* you are holding may be a sixth edition, but in many ways, it is an entirely new book. True, the basic recipe that has made this text one of the most widely used composition readers over its previous five editions is the same: At its core, *The Contemporary Reader* remains a collection of well-written, provocative readings that students can relate to—readings that, by talking about the time and culture of which we are all a part, inspire thought, stimulate classroom discussion, and serve as writing models. However, this sixth edition contains a lot that's fresh and new. In it, you will find eight new chapter topics. The four carryover topics from the previous edition have a sharper focus. Of the 94 readings, only 4 are from the fifth edition; the other 90 are new to this edition.

Why a 95 percent overhaul? The answer is in the title: this is a truly *contemporary* reader. Topics date quickly and lose their appeal, while new and fascinating issues are surfacing all the time in our culture. In just three years, there have been dramatic changes in almost every aspect of our lives. That's why of the 94 readings in this text, 75 have been written since 1996.

The Contemporary Reader is contemporary in more than just the selections. Because this book is about writing as much as it is about reading, we have designed the apparatus according to the latest and most effective rhetorical theory and practice. Thus, all of the rhetorical apparatus is new, including a new introduction on critical reading, new group projects after each reading selection, and new Sequencing Assignments at the end of the book. We think this is our best effort yet, and we hope it serves you well.

New Chapter Topics

A glance at the twelve chapter themes—eight of which are completely new to this edition—will give you a good idea of the breadth of coverage (boldface highlights the chapter topics that are new).

1 **Fashion and Flesh: The Images We Project**
2 Advertising: Feeding Our Fantasies
3 Television: Friend or Foe?
4 **Gender Battles on the Big Screen**
5 **Pop Icons**

I chose these themes because they seemed to best reflect the wide spectrum of forces that affect all of us and because they begin to define what life is like in contemporary American culture. Most importantly, they seem to capture the conflicts and paradoxes that make American culture unique. For ours is a culture caught up with images from fashion and advertising, from television and movie screens. We are a people who at once hanker for up-to-the-minute trends as well as nostalgia. We are as much a culture steeped in traditional values and identities as we are one that constantly re-defines itself in response to alternate lifestyles and subcultures. We are both determined traditionalists and unique individualists.

Issue-Focused Chapter Topics

While these chapters appear to cover vast territories, each tightly focuses on specific issues so as not to sprawl and lose purpose. For instance, instead of a diffuse collection of essays on gender issues, Chapter 4, "Gender Battles on the Big Screen," explores how movies reflect and create the images of men and women that make up our fantasies. Likewise, Chapter 9, "The Family in Flux," contains pieces that re-examine the definition of "family" to show how the traditional definition has changed in America in light of the growing number of divorces, step-families, same-sex marriages, single-parent households, and extended multi-generational families.

A Closer Look at Chapter Themes

The twelve thematic chapters are organized to progress from the world of popular culture to the individual's place within it, ending with a look at what the next century might hold for all of us.

The first five chapters focus on the visual forces in our popular culture that forge our behavior—the areas which may influence us the most. Chapter 1, for instance, looks at how caught up we can be in finding the right look—the brand-name shoe, the latest fad (e.g., body piercing), and the impossible ideal. Chapter 2 explores how advertising so craftily capitalizes on our fantasies—including those previewed in Chapter 1. Chapter 3 considers the good and bad aspects of television—how some shows fill primetime with mindless, tasteless nonsense, while others demonstrate the medium's potential for intelligence and sophistication. Chapter 4 continues the discussion of the power of the media by examining important gender issues in Hollywood and current movies. This naturally segues into Chapter 5 and a discussion of individuals (both alive and dead) whom our culture has elevated to icon status—figures such as Michael Jordan, Princess Diana, Selena, and even Barbie.

Chapters 6 and 7 turn to the ever changing racial and ethnic face of millennial America. Here we link the theme of identity begun in the first five chapters to considerations of heritage, prejudice, and the politics of language. Chapter 8, "Democracy, Community, and Cyberspace," explores the use and abuse of the Net—as a research tool, a social hangout, a political forum, a shopping mall—issues that are proving to have a profound affect on community and culture.

Chapter 9 moves from community to family—in particular the redefinition of the American family unit. Chapter 10, "Young and Criminal" focuses on juvenile crime and looks for connections between the disturbing increase in crimes committed by children and the changes in our culture discussed in previous chapters. Chapter 11, "Work: What's in It for Me?" addresses concerns all college students (traditional and returning) must eventually face: What does getting or having a job mean? What do I want from it? Are money and success the same thing? Am I my career? The final chapter, "Into the Future: America in the Twenty-First Century," raises a wide variety of concerns for all of us as we look across the millennial threshold—the economy, privacy and the Internet, and genetic engineering, to name a few.

More Variety and More Genres in the Readings

In addition to updating 96 percent of the readings, we've infused this edition with more variety and more genres than in any edition of *The Contemporary Reader* thus far. Expository writing comes in all shapes and modes, and as readers, we are exposed to many different genres of writing every day. We read our morning newspaper and find examples of objective reportage, opinionated columnists, satirical editorials, movie reviews, and a lot more. Students read academic articles, personal narratives, position papers, and various political arguments, just to mention a few. *The Contemporary Reader* reflects this variety by including newspaper columns, editorials, feature stories, op-ed essays, letters to the editor, memoirs, autobiographical musings, personal diaries, descriptive narratives, academic articles, movie reviews, eulogies, pointed arguments, humorous satires, and interviews. In an effort to introduce students to other genres of writing, we have also included short fiction and a poetry.

New Pro/Con Debates

Essays on controversial topics have always been a popular special feature of *The Contemporary Reader*. In this edition, we have included for the first time five pairs of essays at the end of select chapters that go head-to-head on some hot issues: the language of advertising (truth or manipulation); television (never watch it or be selective); gay marriage (for and against); punishing juvenile criminals as adults (for and against); and two intensely opposed reviews of the popular, and to some, benchmark movie about black male/female relationships, *Waiting to Exhale*. While few issues can be reduced to a black-or-white either/or stand, these pro/con pieces, while providing shades of gray, will inspire students to join the different debates and defend or challenge either position. Beginning writers need to appreciate opposing views in order to explore the subtleties of various positions.

New Advertisements

The chapter on advertising, one of the most popular in the previous edition, has been completely updated with ten new ads. Each ad in Chapter 2, "Advertising: Feeding Our Fantasies" is accompanied by specific questions to help students closely analyze how advertising—and the particular ad at issue—affects us. The questions should spark lively class discussions about the art and craft of advertising. But even beyond that, they encourage students to increase their "visual literacy" as much as their verbal reading powers by closely focusing on particular print ads and making new associations and discoveries.

New Student Essays

In addition to new writings by many respected and award-winning writers, this collection contains three carefully chosen essays by student writers. Our hope is that students will be inspired by these thought-provoking, intriguing, and well-written essays composed by Michael Fitzpatrick, Lynn Dornink, and Chana Schoenberger.

Humor

There is no reason why the writing experience should not be fun, nor is there any reason why writing models cannot be entertaining. As you will discover, many of the selections, even some with a serious purpose, are quite funny. Included here are essays by Pulitzer Prize winning humorist Dave Barry and standup comic Paula Poundstone.

New Rhetorical Features

While we are hopeful that the essays here are stimulating and fun, we can't lose sight of the fact that our greater objective is to help students become better writers. Therefore, the readings are accompanied by exercises and activities to spur thoughtful response and reflection. This text is full of innovative tools to help students develop their writing skills.

New Introduction to Critical Reading

The premise of *The Contemporary Reader* is that good writing grows out of good thinking, and good thinking grows out of good reading. Therefore, the text begins with a new specially tabbed introduction How to Read Critically which discusses what critical reading is, how to do it with step-by-step guidelines, and how it helps readers become better writers. The Introduction illustrates the process in a detailed sample analysis of a 1997 essay, "A No-Fault Holocaust" by *U.S. News & World Report* columnist John Leo. The sample analysis prepares students for the readings that follow and the writing they will generate. Students sharpen their response to another's writing so that they can better respond to their own.

New Group Projects

Being an active part of a community involves working together—getting to know people whose identities, values, ideals, gender, race, ethnicity, socio-economic stratum, and educational experiences are different. In an effort to develop students' skill for working and learning together, and to encourage them to move beyond the classroom and into the community, Group Projects accompany each reading. These exercises emphasize collaborative writing—from brainstorming to invention to problem solving to writing to peer editing. They also encourage students to get out of the classroom and beyond the text—to search the Internet, research, and talk to people in their communities—to explore further what they've read.

New Sequencing Assignments

At the end of the book, in a new tabbed unit are Sequencing Assignments: Making New Connections. What distinguishes these assignments from those following each selection is that sequenced questions ask students to move back and forth among selections from different chapters, their own experience, the experiences of their classmates, and their own writing. In each sequence, students prepare a collection (a journal or portfolio) of their own casual writing materials to return to when developing formal essays. Not only do students benefit from accumulating a body of their own writing, but circling back helps them gauge their progress.

Although the three sequences in this unit approach a range of contemporary topics, they are also quite distinct from each other. The first sequence, Reflections on the Personal, emphasizes personal experiences; the second, Images of Power, focuses on popular culture; and the third, "The Politics of Language," is politically oriented. Each sequence can stand alone, but their effect can be seen as cumulative: The narrative emphasis in Sequence 1 is incorporated into the next two sequences; the need to define terms is emphasized in Sequence 2 but is part of both other sequences; and Sequence 3 asks for a persuasive argument or essay on a controversial subject.

Revised Study Apparatus

Each of the twelve chapters has an introduction outlining the rationale behind the selections and some previews of what to expect. Likewise, each reading selection is preceded by a headnote containing thematic and biographic information as well as clues to writing techniques and strategies.

Each selection is followed by a series of review questions. Exploring the Text questions cover thoughts, themes, and rhetorical strategies—questions designed to help students think analytically about the content and form of the essays. Each essay is also followed by Writing Assignments that suggest how students might relate the essays to other selections and to their own experience. These assignments also suggest research projects that take students into the library, out into their communities, and onto the Internet. These two sets of exercises are followed by the new group projects exercises discussed earlier.

Rhetorical Contents

While the book is thematically organized, some instructors prefer to organize their writing courses according to rhetorical strategies. Therefore, as in past editions, we offer a Rhetorical Contents that groups essays according to particular writing strategies.

Supplements

World Wide Web Site

A new World Wide Web site at <http://longman.awl.com/goshgarian> has been developed to accompany this edition of *The Contemporary Reader*. Features of the site include additional on-line readings for each chapter and apparatus to accompany each of these new readings; chapter summaries and objectives; a collection of links for each chapter that provide additional information on the chapter's issues; and guidelines for doing research on popular culture topics.

Instructor's Manual

The Instructor's Manual, which is available to adopters, includes suggested responses to all the questions in the text.

Acknowledgments

Many people behind the scenes deserve much acknowledgment and gratitude. It would be impossible to thank all of them, but there are some for whose help I am particularly grateful. First, I would like to thank all the instructors and students who used the first five editions of *The Contemporary Reader*. Their continued support has made this latest edition possible. Also I would like to thank those instructors who spent hours answering lengthy questionnaires on the effectiveness of the essays and who supplied many helpful comments and suggestions in the preparation of this new edition. They are: Bob Baron, Mesa Community College; Mattie Collins, Angelina College; Richard Edmunds, Yuba College; Charles French, Lehigh University; Paul Heilker, Virginia Tech University; Robert Hokom, San Juan College; Kathleen Iudicello, The George Washington University and Estrella Mountain

Community College; Jo-Ann Mapson, Orange Coast College; Margaret Dietz Meyer, Ithaca College; Cindy Moore, University of Louisville; E. Suzanne Owens, Lorain County Community College; Anne Reagan, Moraine Valley Community College; Nedra Reynolds, University of Rhode Island; Leaf Seligman, University of New Hampshire; Frank Sesso, Rogers University; Rosemarie Spight, Fresno City College; George Staley, Portland Community College; and Pauline Uchmanowicz, SUNY-New Paltz.

My thanks goes out to Lynn Dornick, Kathryn Goodfellow, Deanne Harper, Jeanne Phoenix Laurel, Matthew Noonan, and Joyce Tesar for their good suggestions and expert assistance in writing the study apparatus for the essays. I am also very grateful to Charles O'Neill for updating his fine and popular essay, "The Language of Advertising," specially for this edition.

Very special thanks to the people of Addison Wesley Longman, especially Anne Smith and Lynn Huddon, my editors, and Sharon Balbos, my ever-efficient Development Editor who often gave me the push I needed.

Finally, thanks again to my wife Kathleen for her keen insight, her many hours of assistance, and her encouragement.

Gary Goshgarian

Introduction: How to Read Critically

Whenever you read a magazine article, newspaper editorial, or piece of advertising and find yourself questioning the authors' claims, you are exercising the basics of critical reading. You are looking beneath the surface of words and thinking about their meaning and significance. And subconsciously you are asking the authors questions such as:

- What did you mean by that?
- Can you back up that statement?
- How do you define that term?
- How did you draw that conclusion?
- Do all the experts agree?
- Isn't this evidence dated?
- So what?
- What is your point?
- Why do we need to know this?

You are making statements such as:

- That's not true.
- You're contradicting yourself.
- I see your point, but I don't agree.
- That's not a good choice of words.
- You're jumping to conclusions.
- Good point. I never thought of that.
- That was nicely stated.
- This is an extreme view.

Whether conscious or unconscious, such responses indicate that you are thinking critically about what you read. You are weighing claims, asking for definitions, evaluating information, looking for proof, questioning assumptions, and making judgments. In short, you are processing another person's words, rather than just taking them in.

Why Read Critically?

When you read critically you think critically. That means that instead of blindly accepting what's written on a page, you separate yourself from the text and decide for yourself what is or is not important, logical, or right. You do so because you bring to your reading your own perspective, experience, education, and personal values, as well as your powers of comprehension and analysis.

Critical reading is an active process of discovery. You discover an author's view on a subject, you enter into a dialogue with the author, you discover the strengths and weaknesses of the author's thesis or argument, and you decide if you agree or disagree with the author's views. The end result is that you have a better understanding of the issue and the author. By asking the author questions and analyzing where the author stands with respect to other experiences or views of the issue—including your own—you actively enter into a dialogue or a debate. You seek out the truth on your own instead of accepting at face value what somebody else says.

In reality, that is how truth and meaning are achieved—through interplay. Experience teaches us that knowledge and truth are not static entities but the byproducts of struggle and dialogue—of asking tough questions. We witness this phenomenon all the time, recreated in the media through dialogue and conflict. We've recognized it over the years as a force of social change. Consider, for example, how since the 1950s our culture has changed its attitudes with regard to race and its concepts of success, kinship, social groups, and class. Or consider how dialogue and conflict have changed social attitudes regarding gender: Were it not for people questioning rigid old conventions, most women would still be bound to the laundry and the kitchen stove.

The point is that critical reading is an active and reactive process—one that sharpens your focus on a subject and your ability to absorb information and ideas while encouraging you to question accepted norms, views, and myths. And that is both healthy and laudable, for it is the basis of social evolution.

Critical reading also helps you become a better writer, because critical reading is the first step to critical writing. Good writers look at another's writing the way a carpenter looks at a house: They study the fine details and how those details connect and create the whole. Likewise, they consider the particular slants and strategies of appeal. Good writers always have a clear sense of their audience, such as their readers' racial makeup, gender, and educational background; their political and/or religious persuasions; and their values, prejudices, and assumptions toward life. Knowing one's audience helps writers determine nearly every aspect of the writing process: the kind of language to use, the writing style (casual or formal, humorous or serious, technical or philosophical), the particular slant to take (appealing to the reader's reason, emotions, ethics, or a combination of these), what emphasis to give the essay, the type of evidence to offer, and the kinds of authorities to cite.

It's the same with critical reading. The better you become at analyzing and reacting to another's written work, the better you will analyze and react to your own.

You will ask yourself: Is it logical? Do my points come across clearly? Are my examples solid enough? Is this the best wording? Is my conclusion persuasive? Do I have a clear sense of my audience? What appeal strategy did I take—to logic, emotions, or ethics? In short, critical reading will help you to evaluate your own writing, thereby making you both a better reader and a better writer.

While you may already employ many strategies of critical reading, this book will offer you some techniques to make you an even better critical reader.

How to Read Critically

Use these six proven basic steps to help you read critically:

- Keep a journal of what you read
- Annotate what you read
- Outline what you read
- Summarize what you read
- Question what you read
- Analyze what you read

To demonstrate just how these techniques work, let's apply them to a sample essay. Reprinted below is the essay "A No-fault Holocaust" by John Leo taken from his column in *U.S. News & World Report,* first published in the July 21, 1997, issue. I chose this piece because, like all the pieces in this book, it focuses on contemporary cultural issues. In addition, Leo raises some serious questions about the attitudes and values of American students such as yourself.

Sample Essay for Analysis

A No-Fault Holocaust

John Leo

1 In 20 years of college teaching, Prof. Robert Simon has never met a student who denied that the Holocaust happened. What he sees quite often, though, is worse: students who acknowledge the fact of the Holocaust but can't bring themselves to say that killing millions of people is wrong. Simon reports that 10 to 20 percent of his students think this way. Usually they deplore what the Nazis did, but their disapproval is expressed as a matter of taste or personal preference, not moral judgment. "Of course I dislike the Nazis," one student told Simon, "but who is to say they are morally wrong?"

2 Overdosing on nonjudgmentalism is a growing problem in the schools. Two disturbing articles in the *Chronicle of Higher Education* say that some students are

unwilling to oppose large moral horrors, including human sacrifice, ethnic cleansing, and slavery, because they think that no one has the right to criticize the moral views of another group or culture.

3   One of the articles is by Simon, who teaches philosophy at Hamilton College in Clinton, N.Y. The other is by Kay Haugaard, a freelance writer who teaches creative writing at Pasadena City College in California. Haugaard writes that her current students have a lot of trouble expressing any moral reservations or objections about human sacrifice. The subject came up when she taught her class Shirley Jackson's *The Lottery,* a short story about a small American farm town where one person is killed each year to make the crops grow. In the tale, a woman is ritually stoned to death by her husband, her 12-year-old daughter, and her 4-year-old son.

4   Haugaard has been teaching since 1970. Until recently, she says, "Jackson's message about blind conformity always spoke to my students' sense of right and wrong." No longer, apparently. A class discussion of human sacrifice yielded no moral comments, even under Haugaard's persistent questioning. One male said the ritual killing in *The Lottery* "almost seems a need." Asked if she believed in human sacrifice, a woman said, "I really don't know. If it was a religion of long standing. . . ." Haugaard writes: "I was stunned. This was the woman who wrote so passionately of saving the whales, of concern for the rain forests, of her rescue and tender care of a stray dog."

5   **The Aztecs did it.** Both writers believe multiculturalism has played a role in spreading the vapors of nonjudgmentalism. Haugaard quotes a woman in her class, a "50-something red-headed nurse," who says, "I teach a course for our hospital personnel in multicultural understanding, and if it is part of a person's culture, we are taught not to judge. . . ." Simon says we should "welcome diversity rather than fear it" but says his students often think they are so locked into their own group perspectives of ethnicity, race, and gender that moral judgment is impossible, even in the face of great evils.

6   In the new multicultural canon, human sacrifice is hard to condemn, because the Aztecs practiced it. In fact, however, this nonjudgmental stance is not held consistently. Japanese whaling and the genital cutting of girls in Africa are criticized all the time by white multiculturalists. Christina Hoff Sommers, author and professor of philosophy at Clark University in Massachusetts, says that students who can't bring themselves to condemn the Holocaust will often say flatly that treating humans as superior to dogs and rodents is immoral. Moral shrugging may be on the rise, but old-fashioned and rigorous moral criticism is alive and well on certain selected issues: smoking, environmentalism, women's rights, animal rights.

7   Sommers points beyond multiculturalism to a general problem of so many students coming to college "dogmatically committed to a moral relativism that offers them no grounds to think" about cheating, stealing, and other moral issues. Simon calls this "absolutophobia"—the unwillingness to say that some behavior is just plain wrong. Many trends feed this fashionable phobia. Postmodern theory on campuses denies the existence of any objective truth: All we can have are clashing perspectives, not true moral knowledge. The pop-therapeutic culture has pushed nonjudgmentalism very hard. Intellectual laziness and the simple fear of unpleasantness

are also factors. By saying that one opinion or moral stance is as good as another, we can draw attention to our own tolerance, avoid antagonizing others, and get on with our careers.

8   The "values clarification" programs in the schools surely should come in for some lumps, too. Based on the principle that teachers should not indoctrinate other people's children, they leave the creation of values up to each student. Values emerge as personal preferences, equally as unsuited for criticism or argument as personal decisions on pop music or clothes.

9   But the wheel is turning now, and "values clarification" is giving way to "character education," and the paralyzing fear of indoctrinating children is gradually fading. The search is on for a teachable consensus rooted in simple decency and respect. As a spur to shaping it, we might discuss a culture so morally confused that students are showing up at colleges reluctant to say anything negative about mass slaughter.

Keeping a Journal on What You Read

Unlike writing an essay or a paper, keeping a journal is a personal exploration in which you develop your own ideas without set rules. It is a process of recording impressions and exploring feelings and ideas. It is an opportunity to write without restrictions or judgment. You don't have to worry about breaking the rules—because in a journal, anything goes.

Reserve a special notebook just for your journal—not one you use for class notes or homework. Also, date your entries and include the titles of the articles to which you are responding. Eventually, by the end of the semester, you should have a substantial number of pages to review so you can see how your ideas and writing style have developed over time.

What do you include in your journal? While it may serve as a means to understanding an essay you're assigned, you are not required to write only about the essay itself. Perhaps the essay reminds you of something in your personal experience. Maybe it triggered an opinion you didn't know you had. Or perhaps you wish to explore a particular phrase or idea presented by the author.

Some students may find keeping a journal difficult because it is so personal. They may feel as if they're exposing their feelings too much. Or they may feel uncomfortable thinking that someone else—a teacher or another student—may read their writing. But such apprehensions shouldn't prevent you from exploring your impressions and feelings. Just don't record anything that you wouldn't what your teacher or classmates to read; or if you do, keep your journal private.

Reprinted below is one student's journal entry on our sample essay:

"A No-Fault Holocaust," by John Leo, *U.S. News & World Report*, July 21, 1997.

Leo groups all college students by what a few seem to think. Prof. Simon says that 10–20 percent of his students don't want to pass moral judgment. That doesn't seem very specific. Also, what type of class is this? If it's philosophy, the students are supposed to raise questions. If history, why is he asking for moral judgments anyway?

The Holocaust was a terrible tragedy, and I'm pretty sure all my friends feel this way too. As far as morality is concerned, it is immoral to kill innocent people. The Jews were innocent people, slaughtered because another group didn't like them. This is obviously immoral.

Leo paints college students as a bunch of insensitive, uncaring kids who don't give a damn. Even worse, he seems to think that we feel if an ancient culture did something awful, we are more likely to think it was cool and not judge them for it. Like what he says about human sacrifice and the Aztecs. WHO made such a claim? He doesn't say—just that students feel this way. WHICH students???? Not me. Not my friends. In fact, I think few people would actually come out and say human sacrifice is OK because the Aztecs practiced it. This is unfair.

This guy seems to think students have no values and we need to be taught them. Well, I think he should focus on the positive. On the flip side of his argument, at least 80 percent of students DO feel the Holocaust was morally wrong. His other statements are not supported in the rest of the essay—it is just his opinion framed to make students seem uncaring. Most college students I know are caring, moral, honest people. There are a few bad apples in the basket, but that doesn't make the whole basket bad.

Annotate What You Read

It is a good idea to underline (or highlight) key passages and make marginal notes when reading an essay. (If you don't own the publication in which the essay appears, or choose not to mark it up, make a photocopy of the piece and annotate that.) I recommend annotating on the second or third reading, once you've gotten a handle on the essay's general ideas.

There are no specific guidelines for annotation. Use whatever technique suits you best, but keep in mind that in annotating a piece of writing, you are engaging in a dialogue with the author. As in any meaningful dialogue, you hear things you may not have known, things that may be interesting and exciting to you, things that you may agree or disagree with, or things that give you cause to ponder. The other side of the dialogue, of course, is your response. In annotating a piece of writing, that response takes the form of underlining (or highlighting) key passages and jotting comments in the margin. Such comments can take the form of full sentences or some shorthand codes. Sometimes "Why?" or "True" or "NO!" will be enough to help you respond to a writer's position or claim. If you come across a word or reference that is unfamiliar to you, underline or circle it. Once you've located the main thesis or claim, highlight or underline it and jot down "CLAIM" or "THESIS" in the margin.

Below is the Leo essay reproduced in its entirety with sample annotations.

1   In 20 years of college teaching, Prof. Robert Simon has never met a student who denied that the Holocaust happened. What he sees quite often, though, is worse: students who acknowledge the fact of the Holocaust but can't bring themselves to say that killing millions of people is wrong. Simon reports that <u>10 to 20 percent of his students think this way.</u> Usually they deplore what the Nazis did, but their disapproval is expressed as a matter of taste or personal preference, not moral judgment. "Of course I dislike the Nazis," one student told Simon, "but who is to say they are morally wrong?"

Over what period of time? 20 years?

2   Overdosing on nonjudgmentalism is a growing problem in the schools. Two disturbing articles in the *Chronicle of Higher Education* say that (some) students are unwilling to oppose large moral horrors, including human sacrifice, ethnic cleansing, and slavery, because they think that no one has the right to criticize the moral views of another group or culture.

Some isn't a total or a trend!

3   One of the articles is by Simon, who teaches philosophy at Hamilton College in Clinton, N.Y. The other is by Kay Haugaard, a freelance writer who teaches creative writing at Pasadena City College in California. Haugaard writes that her current students have a lot of trouble expressing any moral reservations or objections about human sacrifice. The subject came up when she taught her class Shirley Jackson's *The Lottery,* a short

story about a small American farm town where one person is killed each year to make the crops grow. In the
tale, a woman is ritually stoned to death by her husband,
her 12-year-old daughter, and her 4-year-old son.

Wow! Get this story

4   Haugaard has been teaching since 1970. Until recently, she says, "Jackson's message about blind conformity always spoke to my students' sense of right and
wrong." No longer, apparently. A class discussion of human sacrifice yielded no moral comments, even under
Haugaard's persistent questioning. One male said the ritual killing in *The Lottery* "almost seems a need." Asked
if she believed in human sacrifice, a woman said, "I really don't know. If it was a religion of long standing. . . ."
Haugaard writes: "I was stunned. This was the woman
who wrote so passionately of saving the whales, of concern for the rain forests, of her rescue and tender care of
a stray dog."

Makes assumption

5   **The Aztecs did it.** Both writers believe multiculturalism has played a role in spreading the vapors of nonjudgmentalism. Haugaard quotes a woman in her class, a
"50-something red-headed nurse," who says, "I teach a
course for our hospital personnel in multicultural understanding, and if it is part of a person's culture, we are
taught not to judge. . . ." Simon says we should "welcome diversity rather than fear it" but says his students
often think they are so locked into their own group perspectives of ethnicity, race, and gender that moral judgment is impossible, even in the face of great evils.

Key point

6   In the new multicultural canon, human sacrifice is
hard to condemn, because the Aztecs practiced it. In fact,
however, this nonjudgmental stance is not held consistently. Japanese whaling and the genital cutting of girls
in Africa are criticized all the time by white multiculturalists. Christina Hoff Sommers, author and professor of
philosophy at Clark University in Massachusetts, says
that students who can't bring themselves to condemn the
Holocaust will often say flatly that treating humans as
superior to dogs and rodents is immoral. Moral shrugging may be on the rise, but old-fashioned and rigorous

Qualify this statement!

moral criticism is alive and well on <u>certain selected is-</u>
<u>sues: smoking, environmentalism, women's rights, ani-</u>
<u>mal rights.</u>

\ Aren't these moral
/ issues too?

7   Sommers points beyond multiculturalism to a general problem of so many students coming to college
<u>"(dogmatically)</u> committed to a moral relativism that of-
fers them no grounds to think" about cheating, stealing,
and other moral issues. Simon calls this "absolutopho-
<u>bia"</u>—the unwillingness to say that some behavior is just
plain wrong. Many trends feed this fashionable phobia.
<u>Postmodern theory</u> on campuses denies the existence of
any objective truth: All we can have are clashing perspectives, not true moral knowledge. The pop-therapeutic culture has pushed nonjudgmentalism very hard. Intellectual laziness and the simple fear of unpleasantness
are also factors. By saying that one opinion or moral
stance is as good as another, <u>we can draw attention to our</u>
<u>own tolerance,</u> avoid antagonizing others, and get on
with our careers.

Meaning?

— Discuss in journal

, Look up

\ But isn't tolerance
/ a good thing?

8   The "values clarification" programs in the schools
surely should come in for some lumps, too. <u>Based on the</u>
<u>principle that teachers should not indoctrinate other peo-</u>
<u>ple's children, they leave the creation of values up to</u>
<u>each student.</u> Values emerge as personal preferences,
equally as unsuited for criticism or argument as personal
decisions on pop music or clothes.

\ True. But should
> teachers teach
/ values?

— How so?

9   But the wheel is turning now, and <u>"values clarifica-</u>
<u>tion"</u> is giving way to "character education," and the par-
alyzing fear of indoctrinating children is gradually fading. <u>The search is on for a teachable consensus rooted in</u>
simple decency and respect. As a spur to shaping it, we
might discuss <u>a culture so morally confused</u> that students
are showing up at colleges reluctant to say anything negative about mass slaughter.

— Who is searching?

> Which culture? Ours?

Outline What You Read

Briefly outlining an essay is a good way to see how writers structure their ideas.
When you physically diagram the thesis statement, claims, and supporting evidence,
you can better assess the quality of the writing and decide how convincing it is. You

may already be familiar with detailed, formal essay outlines where structure is broken down into main ideas and subsections. However, for our purposes here, I suggest a brief and concise breakdown of an essay's components. This is done by simply jotting down a one-sentence summary of each paragraph. Sometimes brief paragraphs elaborating the same point can be lumped together:

- Point 1
- Point 2
- Point 3
- Point 4
- Point 5
- Point 6, etc.

Even though such outlines may seem rather primitive, they demonstrate at a glance how the various parts of an essay are connected—that is, the organization and sequence of ideas.

Below is a sentence outline of "A No-Fault Holocaust":

<u>Point 1:</u> Unlike their predecessors, today's university students are unwilling to make moral judgments. Professor Robert Simon notes that students are hesitant to morally condemn incidents such as the Holocaust.

    <u>Point 2:</u> This "nonjudgmentalism" is based on the supposition that no one has the right to morally judge another person. They believe that they cannot morally condemn another group or culture.

    <u>Point 3:</u> Kay Haugaard, a creative writing teacher, says Shirley Jackson's story "The Lottery" used to appeal to students' moral sense of right and wrong, but does not any more.

    <u>Point 4:</u> Refusal to make a moral determination is not consistent. While students seem unwilling to morally judge human sacrifice, they criticize whaling, female mutilation, animal experimentation, rain forest depletion, and smoking.

    <u>Point 5:</u> Two professors (Simon and Haugaard) attribute this nonjudgmentalism to the growing influence of multiculturalism. Students believe that their moral beliefs may be culturally specific; therefore, they cannot judge another group or culture's beliefs.

Point 6: Another professor believes that nonjudgmentalism is rooted in intellectual laziness—an attitude promoted by postmodern theory, which maintains that there are no absolutes. Students are reluctant to judge certain behaviors as right or wrong because they don't want to deal with the consequences.

Point 7: Perhaps this unwillingness to make moral judgments stems from a lack of moral training in childhood. Today's teachers are encouraged not to interfere in the development of values and to allow values to emerge as personal preference.

Point 8: The author concludes that "character education" is returning. He urges society to closely examine a youth culture so "morally confused" that students can't—or won't—judge something as straightforward as human genocide.

At this point you should have a fairly good grasp of the author's stand on the issue. Now let's analyze the essay in its parts and as a whole.

Summarize What You Read

Summarizing is perhaps the most important technique to develop for understanding and evaluating what you read. This means boiling the essay down to its main points. In your journal or notebook try to write a brief (about one hundred words) synopsis of the reading in your own words. Note the claim or thesis of the discussion (or argument) and the chief supporting points. It is important to write down these points rather than to highlight them passively with a pen or pencil, because the act of jotting down a summary helps you absorb the argument.

Now let's return to our sample essay. In the brief paragraph below, we offer a summary of Leo's essay, mindful of using our own words rather than the author's to avoid plagiarism. At times, it may be impossible to avoid using the author's own words in a summary, but if you do, remember to use quotation marks.

Today's university students are unwilling to pass moral judgments on issues as seemingly straightforward as the Holocaust. They believe that they don't have the right to morally condemn another group or culture. Supported by the principles of multiculturalism and postmodern theory, students hesitate to judge the behavior of other groups in an effort to exhibit cultural tolerance. Intellectual laziness and personal distancing may also prevent students from forming moral opinions. The author concludes that today's society is "morally confused" and calls for our culture to teach simple decency so that our children can make moral judgments once again.

Although this paragraph seems to do a fairly good job of summarizing Leo's essay, it took a few tries to get it down to under a hundred words. So, don't be too discouraged when trying to summarize a reading on your own.

Question What You Read

Although we break down critical reading into discrete steps, these steps will naturally overlap in the actual process. While reading this essay you were simultaneously summarizing and evaluating Leo's points in your head, perhaps adding your own ideas or even arguing with him. If something strikes you as particularly interesting or insightful, make a mental note. Likewise, if something rubs you the wrong way, argue back. For beginning writers, a good strategy is to convert that automatic mental response into actual note taking

In your journal (or, as suggested below, in the margins of the text), question and challenge the writer. Jot down any points in the essay that do not measure up to your expectations or personal views. Note anything about which you are skeptical. Scratch down any questions you have about the claims, views, or evidence. If some point or conclusion seems forced or unfounded, record it and briefly explain why. The more skeptical and questioning you are, the better a reader you are. Likewise, note what features of the essay impressed you—outstanding points, interesting wording, clever or amusing phrases or allusions, particular references, the general structure of the piece. Record what you learn from the reading and what aspects of the issue you would like to further explore.

Of course, you may not feel qualified to pass judgment on an author's views, especially if the author is a professional writer or an expert on a particular subject. Sometimes the issue discussed might be too technical, or you may not feel informed enough to make critical evaluations. Sometimes a personal narrative may focus on experiences completely alien to you. Nonetheless, you are an intelligent person with an instinct to determine if the writing impresses you or if an argument is sound, logical, and convincing. What you can do in such instances—and another good habit to form—is to think of other views on the issue. If you've read or heard of experiences different from the author's, or arguments with the opposing views, jot them down. Even if you haven't, the essay (if it's an argument) should contain some inference or reference to alternate experiences or opposing views from which you could draw a counterposition.

Let's return to Leo's essay which, technically, is an argument. While it's theoretically possible to question or comment on every sentence in the piece, let's select a couple of key points that may have struck you as presumptuous, overstated, or inconsistent with your own experience.

Paragraph 1: The author states that Professor Robert Simon "reports that 10 to 20 percent of his students" can't make a moral determination about the Holocaust. How did Professor Simon come up with this figure? Did he take a vote? Is he guessing? Did he ask if the students really understood what the Holocaust was all about? Professor Simon was teaching a philosophy class—and many philosophy classes encourage students to explore all points of view before passing judgment. Maybe students were arguing for argument's sake. It's risky to decide how students really feel without some hard data to back up statements.

Paragraph 2: The author cites that two articles in the *Chronicle of Higher Education* say that "some students are unwilling to oppose large moral horrors." *Some* is not all; it isn't even many. The word does not indicate a trend where today's average student is unwilling to decide if mass murder is wrong.

Paragraphs 3 and 4: When discussing student response to the short story "The Lottery," Kay Haugaard comments that "class discussion yielded no moral comments." This assumes that all students contributed to the class discussion. Many students do not participate in class, but they still have opinions. Just because no one made a moral comment does not mean that everyone in the class felt that stoning is morally permissible in some cultures.

Paragraphs 4 and 5: The author cuts off the quotations halfway. What were the full statements? Did the students qualify the beginning of their comments? We don't know because he cited only pieces of their comments.

Paragraph 6: The author determines that "in the new multicultural canon, human sacrifice is hard to condemn, because the Aztecs practiced it." The author, however, does not qualify or explain this statement. Does he mean that we have morally accepted human sacrifice? Why is he linking the acceptance of multiculturalism to the acceptance of human sacrifice? The author may be hard pressed to get students to openly say that human sacrifice is morally acceptable because an ancient civilization did it. And as far as the article goes, no student actually made this statement.

Paragraph 8: The author jumps from students' unwillingness to make moral judgments to the lack of values taught in elementary schools. This shift seems forced.

Paragraph 9: A sweeping statement claims that today's culture is "morally confused." How can he jump from "some" student reluctance to making moral judgments to the ethics of an entire culture? Not all students are showing up at college unwilling to say mass murder is wrong. Without hard statistical data, such a statement is misleading and even demeaning to today's college students.

Analyze What You Read

To analyze something means to break it down into its components, to examine those components closely and evaluate their significance, and to determine how they relate as a whole. In part you already did this by briefly outlining the essay. But there is more, because analyzing what you read involves interpreting and evaluating the points of a discussion or argument as well as its presentation—that is, its language and structure. Ultimately, analyzing an essay after establishing its gist will help you understand what may not be evident at first. A close examination of the author's words takes you beneath the surface and sharpens your understanding of the issue at hand.

While there is no set procedure for analyzing a piece of prose, here are some specific questions you should raise when reading an essay, especially one that is trying to persuade you to change your view.

- What kind of audience is being addressed?
- What are the author's assumptions?
- What are the author's purpose and intentions?
- How well does the author accomplish those purposes?
- How convincing is the evidence presented? Is it sufficient and specific? Relevant? Reliable and not dated? Slanted?

- How good are the sources of the evidence used? Were they based on personal experience, scientific data, or outside authorities?
- Did the author address opposing views on the issue?
- Is the author's perspective persuasive?

What Kind of Audience Is Being Addressed?

Before the first word is written, a good writer considers his or her audience—that is, its age group, gender, ethnic and racial makeup, educational background, and socioeconomic status. Also considered are the values, prejudices, and assumptions the readers hold, as well as their political and religious persuasions. Some writers, including several in this book, write for a "target" audience—readers who share the same interests, opinions, and prejudices. For example, several essays in Chapter 8, "Democracy, Community, and Cyberspace," were written for people familiar with computers and the Internet. Other writers write for a "general" audience. Although general audiences consist of very different people with diversified backgrounds, expectations, and standards, think of them as the people who read *Time, Newsweek,* and your local newspaper. That is, people whose average age is 35, whose educational level is high school plus two years of college, who make up the vast middle class of America, who politically stand in the middle of the road, and whose racial and ethnic origins span the world. You can assume they are generally informed about what is going on in the country, that they have a good comprehension of language and a sense of humor, and that they are willing to listen to new ideas.

Because Leo's essay appeared in his column in *U.S. News & World Report,* he is clearly writing for a "general" audience. A closer look tells us more:

—The language level suggests a general audience with at least a high school education.

—The "kids today" tone suggests an older audience—beyond college age.

—References to college students, academic journals, and campus theories suggest readers who are college educated.

—The particular slant suggests an audience that is proeducation,

What Are the Author's Assumptions?

Having a sense of one's audience leads writers to certain assumptions. If a writer is writing to a general audience as is Leo, then he or she can assume a certain level of awareness about current events, certain values about education and morality, certain nuances of an argument. After going through Leo's essay, one might draw the following conclusions about the author:

—Assumes readers' knowledge of the Holocaust.

—Assumes the audience is as appalled as he is that today's students are unwilling to pass moral judgment on mass murder.

—Assumes readers are willing to make moral judgments themselves.

—Assumes readers understand the principles of multiculturalism and may feel that these principles have gone too far.

—Assumes readers are fed up with the lack of moral instruction in today's public schools and that this deficiency is directly linked to the appearance of morally apathetic students on college campuses.

—Assumes the audience believes in universally held moral values that can be taught in schools.

What Are the Author's Purpose and Intentions?

A writer writes for a purpose beyond wanting to show up in print. Sometimes it is simply expressing how the writer feels about something; sometimes the intention is to convince others to see things in a different light; sometimes the purpose is to persuade readers to change their views or behavior. Of the Leo essay it might be said that the author had the following intentions:

—To convince people of a disturbing trend on college campuses today.

—To urge people to encourage students to divest themselves of intellectual laziness and to think and judge things for themselves.

—To raise public awareness of students' apathy toward the Holocaust.

—To encourage people to demand reform in teaching methods so children are taught moral basics of human decency.

How Well Does the Author Accomplish Those Purposes?

Determining how well an author accomplishes such purposes may seem subjective, but in reality it comes down to how well the case is presented. Is the thesis clear? Is it well laid out or argued? Are the examples sharp and convincing? Is the author's conclusion a logical result of what came before? Back to Leo's essay:

—He offers many examples of the situation; he presents his views clearly, citing scholarly journals; and he quotes educators and students.

—He keeps to the point for most of the essay. A strong message is conveyed well. We know what he is trying to say and how he feels about the issue.

How Convincing Is the Evidence Presented? Is It Sufficient and Specific? Relevant? Reliable and Not Dated? Slanted?

Convincing writing depends on convincing evidence—that is, sufficient and relevant facts along with proper interpretations of facts. Facts are pieces of information that can be verified—such as, statistics, examples, personal experience, expert testimony, and historical details. Proper interpretations of such facts must be logical and supported by relevant data. For instance, it is a fact that the SAT verbal scores in America went up in 1997. One interpretation might be that students are spending more time reading and less time watching television than in the past. But without hard statistics documenting the viewing habits of a sample of students, that interpretation is shaky, the result of a writer jumping to conclusions.

Is the Evidence Sufficient and Specific?　Writers use evidence on a routine basis, but sometimes it may not be sufficient. Sometimes the conclusions reached have too little evidence to be justified. Sometimes writers make hasty generalizations based solely on personal experience as evidence. How much evidence is enough? It's hard to say, but the more specific the details, the more convincing the argument. Instead of generalizations, good writers cite figures, dates, and facts; instead of paraphrases, they quote experts verbatim.

Is the Evidence Relevant?　Good writers select evidence based on how well it supports the point being argued, not on how interesting, novel, or humorous it is. For instance, if you are arguing that Michael Jordan is the greatest living basketball player, you wouldn't mention that he owns a restaurant and has three children; those are facts, but they have nothing to do with Jordan's athletic abilities. Irrelevant evidence distracts readers and weakens an argument.

Is the Evidence Reliable and Not Dated?　Evidence should not be so vague or dated that it fails to support one's claim. For instance, it wouldn't be accurate to say that Candidate Jones fails to support the American worker because 15 years ago she purchased a foreign car. It's her current actions that are more important. Readers expect writers to give them specific enough dates so that they can be verified. A writer supporting animal rights may cite cases of rabbits blinded in drug research, but such tests have been outlawed in the United States for many years. Another may point to medical research that appears to abuse human subjects, but not name the researchers, the place, or the year of such testing. Because readers may have no way of verifying evidence, suspicious claims will weaken an argument.

Is the Evidence Slanted?   Sometimes writers select evidence that supports their case while ignoring evidence that doesn't. Often referred to as "stacking the deck," this practice is unfair and potentially self-defeating for a writer. While some evidence may have merit, an argument will be dismissed if readers discover that evidence was slanted or suppressed. For example, suppose you heard a classmate claim that he would never take a course with Professor Sanchez because she gives surprise quizzes, assigns 50 pages a night, and doesn't grade on a curve. Even if these reasons are true, they may not be the whole truth. You might discover that Professor Sanchez is a dynamic and talented teacher whose classes are stimulating. Withholding that information may make an argument suspect. A better strategy is to acknowledge counterevidence and to confront it—that is, to strive for a balanced presentation by raising views and evidence that may not be supportive of your own.

Now let's take a look at the evidence in Leo's essay:

—Author gives percentages without backing them up—making loose approximations that undermine his argument.

—His use of partial quotations seems suspicious. Appears to be controlling others' words to suit his own purposes.

—He makes many assumptions about students—how they think and why they are unwilling to judge.

—His argument is emotional rather than logical. Likewise, his presentation of the "facts" is clearly one-sided.

—He makes statements without qualifying them, such as "human sacrifice is hard to condemn, because the Aztecs practiced it." Does not explain where this statement comes from, or who actually feels this way.

How Good Are the Sources of the Evidence Used? Were They Based on Personal Experience, Scientific Data, or Outside Authorities?

Writers enlist four basic kinds of evidence to support their views or arguments: personal experience (theirs and others), outside authorities, factual references and examples, and statistics. In your own writing, you'll be encouraged to use combinations of these.

Personal testimony cannot be underestimated. Think of the books you've read or movies you've seen based on word-of-mouth recommendations. (Maybe even the school you're attending!) Personal testimony provides eyewitness accounts not available to you or your readers—and sometimes such accounts are the most persuasive kind of evidence. Suppose you are writing about the rising abuse of alcohol on college campuses. In addition to statistics and hard facts, quoting the experience of a first-year student who nearly died one night from alcohol poisoning would add dramatic impact. While personal observations are useful and valuable, writers must not draw hasty conclusions from them. Because you and a couple of friends are in favor of replacing letter grades with a pass-fail system does not support the claim that the student body at your school is in favor of the conversion.

Outside authorities are people recognized as experts in a given field. The appeal to such authorities is a powerful tool in writing, especially for writers wanting to persuade readers of their views. We hear it all the time: "Scientists have found . . . ," "Scholars inform us that . . . ," "According to his biographer, Abraham Lincoln. . . ." While experts try to be objective and fair-minded, sometimes their testimony is biased. You wouldn't turn to scientists working for tobacco companies for unbiased opinions on lung cancer.

Factual references and examples do as much to inform as to persuade. If somebody wants to sell you something, they'll pour on the details. Think of the television commercials that show sports utility vehicles climbing rocky mountain roads while a narrator lists all the great standard features—permanent four-wheel drive, alloy wheels, second-generation airbags, power brakes, cruise control, etc—or, the cereal "infomercials" in which manufacturers explain how their new Yumm-Os now have 15 percent more fiber to help prevent cancer. While readers may not have the expertise to determine which data are useful, they are often convinced by the sheer weight of the evidence—like courtroom juries judging a case.

Statistics impress people. Saying that 77 percent of your school's student body approves of women in military combat roles is much more persuasive than saying "a lot of people" approve. Why? Because statistics have a no-nonsense authority. Batting averages, polling results, economic indicators, medical and FBI statistics, demographic percentages—they're all reported in numbers. If accurate, they are hard to dispute, although they can be used to mislead. If somebody claims that 139 people on campus protested the appearance of a certain controversial speaker, it would be a distortion of the truth not to mention that another 1,500 attended the talk and gave the speaker a standing ovation. Likewise, the manufacturer who claims that its potato chips are 100 percent cholesterol free misleads the public because no potato chips cooked in vegetable oil contain cholesterol—which is found only in animal fats. That is known as the "bandwagon" use of statistics—that is, appealing to the crowd-pleasing, healthy-eating awareness.

Now let's briefly examine Leo's sources of evidence:

—Author draws much of his material from outside "authorities." One wonders what makes these people authorities on student thinking.

—He cites Prof. Simon's 20 years of experience and the views of 10 to 20 percent of his students.

—He cites Kay Haugaard who has been teaching since 1970 and who refers to two specific students of a class who expressed nonjudgmentalism.

—Personal experience seems stronger in his understanding of multiculturalism than with students. Moreover, his views of multiculturalism seem a bit skewed—for example, his statement about Aztecs.

Did the Author Address Opposing Views on the Issue?

Many of the essays in this book will in varying degrees try to persuade you to agree with the author's position or argument. But, of course, any slant on a topic can have multiple points of view. In developing their ideas, good writers will anticipate different and opposing views. They will cite contrary opinions, maybe even evidence unsupportive of their own position. Not to do so leaves their own stand open to counterattack, as well as to claims of naivete and ignorance. This is particularly damaging when arguing some controversial issue.

Returning to the Leo essay:

—Author says students are unwilling to make judgments because of their perception of the principles of multicultural and postmodern theory.

—Admits that students may feel a "personal" repugnance for the Nazis but are unwilling to condemn them as an entire cultural group.

—Implies that the lack of moral instruction in schools may be changing.

Is the Author's Perspective Persuasive?

Style and content make for a persuasive piece of writing. Important points are how well a paper is composed—the organization, the logic, the quality of thought, the presentation of evidence, the use of language, the tone of discussion—and the details and evidence.

Turning to Leo's essay, we might make the following observations:

—On the surface, he presents his argument well. After a closer reading, however, the argument raises more questions about the author's presentation of the material. He bases his agreement primarily on generalizations. He applies the feelings of "some" to represent an entire group of people—college students.

—Author appears to be "pushing buttons" rather than presenting a well-formed, logical argument. Makes statements without qualifying them. Finally, he reinforces his own preconceived notions about student thinking with generalizations rather than facts.

In the chapters that follow, you will discover almost a hundred different selections, ranging widely across contemporary matters that we hope you will find exciting and thought provoking. Arranged thematically into 12 chapters, the writings represent widely diverse topics—from the right brand-name sneaker to wear, to sex on television sitcoms; from an in-depth look at *The X-Files,* to an appreciation of Princess Diana; from arguments against the use of Native American names and mascots by sports teams, to arguments for prosecuting teenage criminals as adults; from abuse of the Internet, to abuse of genetic engineering. Some of the topics will be familiar; others will be new to you. Regardless of how these issues touch your experience, critical reading and critical writing will open you up to a deeper understanding of our culture and of yourself as a vital member of that culture as we cross the threshold of the twenty-first century.

1
Fashion and Flesh: The Images We Project

Pick up a magazine. Turn on television. View a film. Charging nearly every visual image are the exhortations: Slim down and be sexy! Be thin and find happiness. Get beautiful or handsome and win respect. Wear the right labels and find success.

We live in a society caught up in images of itself—a society seemingly more driven by the cultivation of the body and how we dress it than personal achievement. In fact, so powerful is the influence of images that other terms of self-definition are difficult to distinguish. In this chapter, several writers grapple with questions raised by our cultural occupation with flesh and fashion: Are we our bodies? Can our inner selves transcend the flesh? Do the clothes we wear express the people we want to be? Will I be accepted? Do I look cool? And where does all the body-conscious pressure come from? Some essays in this chapter recount stories of people at war with their bodies—men and women who rely on diet or brand names to subjugate or adorn their flesh. Others are accounts of people rising above the din of fashion's dictates and creating a soul or sense of self that is authentic and rooted in the spirit.

We begin with a report on the contemporary male body. In "The Beefcaking of America," Jill Neimark reports on the results of a recent survey—one indicating that as the ideal of manhood shifts from macho to mellow, the ideal male body image also has changed. While still expected to be muscled and potent, a man's physique should also be sensuous, beautiful in movement, and smooth-skinned. In fact, Neimark points out that men of late are being eyed the way women always have been—as sexual objects and sources of "visual pleasure." The question arises: Will men also become enslaved to regimens of diet and exercise, and to a preoccupation with appearance?

In the next piece, "Three for the Stripes," composition student Michael Fitzpatrick moves the discussion to the inner city. In an insightful personal essay, Fitzpatrick recounts just how powerful fashion statements can be. For the young men of his neighborhood, the correct sneaker label determines status and group solidarity. It can also invite violence. Fitzpatrick's analysis of brand-name identity and survival in the mean streets is a chilling exploration of the connection between consumerism and gang identity. In the next essay, the reverberations of inner-city style rattle a father-son rapport. In "Baggy Clothes Don't Make the Man," Leonard Pitts offers some keen insights on "gansta chic" and the ramifications for those who subscribe to it even when they live in middle-class suburbs.

The next cluster of essays deals with today's prevailing images of female beauty and the fallout—at worse, toxic; at best, debilitating. These essays share a consensus: For women, the cultural expectation of the slender, nymphlike beauty can strangle personal evolution with impossible expectations—expectations that reduce one's life to dieting and self-loathing.

In "The Body Myth," *Vogue* magazine's Rebecca Johnson says that hostility against thin people is at an all-time high, and fashion models are taking the brunt of the criticism. Because of the priority placed on being thin, many are blamed for the high incidence of eating disorders—and unfairly so, argues Johnson. That Johnson's stand in her essay was a controversial one is measured by the large volume of mail the editors of *Vogue* received following her essay's publication. Five of those letters have been reprinted next in the chapter.

The next essay is a sobering look at body image and its links with marketing and advertising. In "Burning Desire to Be Slimmer Is a Slow Suicide," Barbara Brotman examines the collusion between cigarette advertising and young women's craving to be thin. As Brotman sadly reveals, many females take to smoking as a form of weight control, and therein lies a potent marketing tool for the tobacco industry.

In the next essay, "The Eye of the Beholder," Grace Suh gives voice to the minority culture. After a makeover in an upscale department store, the face that stares back from the mirror is unrecognizable to Suh. The metamorphosis executed by the extensive application of various cleansers, paints, and glosses revealed to Suh a side of beauty that isn't so pretty—the obliterating power of the norm.

Another group affected by rigid notions of physical beauty are the disabled. In "The Other Body: Reflections on Difference, Disability and Identity Politics," Ynestra King discusses the underlying rage at a system that makes you feel as if you are your body and that everything else is "window dressing." Not only do the disabled resent traditional norms of "perfection," they are constantly reminded how they represent the fear of being "other" to the nonhandicapped.

The chapter concludes on a lighter note and with a look at a fad that has begun to stick with image-conscious young adults—body piercing. What was once the practice of a minor subculture and an expression of individuality, even rebellion, has become a mainstream trend. In any big mall in America you can find piercing parlors that will, if you wish, riddle your body with holes. But, asks D. James Romero in "Believers in Search of Piercing Insight," is this an expression of personal uniqueness or just another instance of following the herd?

The Beefcaking of America
Jill Neimark

We're all familiar with the image of the lecherous male construction workers catcalling every pretty woman who walks down the street. But what about the spate of recent commercials that feature lusty women ogling various "hunks" as they make deliveries, retrieve cars, or simply stroll by their appreciative female audience? In the following article, Jill Neimark argues that traditional gender roles are undergoing rapid changes, particularly in the way women now regard men as sex objects. Using the results of various surveys, she makes a convincing argument about just how much the attention to flesh has shifted in the last decade.

Neimark is senior editor of *Psychology Today* where this article first appeared in the November/December 1994 issue.

1   John Wayne. A dusty town in the wild West, and our sweaty, windbitten hero with a bit of a beer belly, rumpled clothing, and an air of absolute indifference to his appearance. Slinging his gun and saving the ranch.

2   Marky Mark. Urban billboards and bus depots. A tauntingly insolent beefcake of boy, smooth skinned, clean shaven, with a tight, carved body that's part tough guy, part Greek god.

3   Men don't look like they used to. Think of Fabio. Arnold Schwarzenegger. Or the countless men who, in cologne ads, lie like languid odalisques on sandy beaches. In movies, heartthrobs from Alec Baldwin to Keanu Reeves are seen shirtless, with rippling pecs and lats; on fashion runways male models in skin-tight tanks and jackets unbuttoned to flaunt washboard bellies pace before cheering crowds. Think of the television commercial where a whole bevy of office secretaries rush to a window to watch a stunning hunk of man take off his shirt and drink a Diet Coke.

4   "There's coming to be an acceptance of men as sex objects, men as beautiful," reports fashion arbiter Holly Brubach, style editor for the *New York Times Magazine.* Male mannequins now sport genital bulges and larger chests, and for the first time in window-dressing history, have achieved equality with female mannequins. The male body is even being used to sell cars, no doubt to both men and women: "If the beautiful lines of the new Monte Carlo seem somehow familiar, they should," reads a current ad. "After all, we borrowed them from you." Above the caption, melting photos show the classic waistline of a woman, curving leather, and the sinewy torso of a naked man. A closer look at each photo reveals a masterful blend of male and female images, of shadowy clefts and powerful bulges.

5   I've always loved to look at men. There is power in a certain kind of masculine beauty, and it's a turn on. Am I alone? No, according to the first national survey ever of men's appearance and how they feel about it, collected from *Psychology Today* readers. It turns out that the world indeed is changing, and that there is now a subset of women who themselves are attractive, educated, and financially secure, who care about every aspect of the way their men look. They can choose good-looking men, and they do.

6   Those women, by the way, are currently a minority. Still, all revolutions begin with a band of pioneers. And when I look around at what's happening in the culture, I sense a sea change.

7   [Today] . . . the male body has arrived—not only is it being offered up for scrutiny, it seems to be both hypermasculine and strangely feminine, a new mix that accurately reflects tremendous and ambivalent changes in our culture.

8   What's happening to men's bodies—and how do both men and women feel about it? In [a recent] . . . issue, we asked our readers to help us delineate what seems to be a seismic shift in male body image. Over 1,500 . . . responded with completed questionnaires and comments, which were analyzed in depth by psychiatrist Michael Pertschuk, M.D., and his colleagues. About twice as many women answered as did men, demonstrating women's keen interest in the subject. The answers revealed fascinating shifts and misconceptions:

9 • Men believe their appearance has a greater impact on women than women themselves actually acknowledge. From hairline to penis size, men believe their specific physical features strongly influence their personal acceptability by women.

10 • Women, in general, are quite willing to adapt to their own mate's appearance, accepting features such as baldness or extra weight, even though their ideal male is different. Women tend to like what they've got—whether he is bearded, uncircumcised, short, or otherwise "off" the norm.

11 • A significant subset of women who are financially independent and rate themselves as physically attractive place a high value on male appearance. This new and vocal minority unabashedly declares a strong preference for better-looking men. They also care more about penis size, both width and length.

12 • For both men and women, personality wins hands down: it's what men believe women seek, and indeed, what women say is most important in choosing a partner.

13 • Nonetheless, men still care about their own looks. Though men give top priority to their sense of humor and intelligence, a nice face is a close third, and body build is not far behind. Women give an overall lower significance to men's physical appearance, but height is still an important turn-on for women.

14 • Men are scared of losing their hair, but women are more accepting of baldness in a mate than men realize. Both men and women prefer clean-shaven men—today.

15 • Men are less worried about being overweight than most women, but more concerned about muscle mass—reflecting our cultural ideals of thin women and powerful men. The muscle-bound body build was highly rated by men, while women preferred a medium, lightly muscled build in their ideal males.

16 Curiously enough, there seems to be emerging a single standard of beauty for men today: a hypermasculine, muscled, powerfully shaped body—the Soloflex man. It's an open question whether that standard will become as punishing for men as has women's superthin standard.

17 We are moving away from the old adage: men do, women are. As noted anthropologist David Gilmore, Ph.D., author of *Manhood in the Making,* states, "That dual view will never entirely go away, but now we're reaching some kind of compromise, where there is more choice. Women can choose men who are not rich or successful, but who are beautiful."

What's in a Man?

18 It seems that the whole idea of what it means to be male is molting. Cultural upheavals from the women's movement to the national emphasis on health and fitness have altered our sense of how a man should act and look. The new male is no longer the unquestioned head of the household, in control of the nuclear family if nothing else. Gender parity in the workplace has made inroads: today a man may easily have a female boss. Men's health has been given new emphasis ever since several post-World War II studies found that men were at greater risk of heart disease than women.

19 According to cultural critic Hillel Schwartz, Ph.D., author of *Never Satisfied,* that awareness of men's physical vulnerability led to a new concern with their bodies. Then, in the 1960s, the Kennedy excitement with amateur sports helped kick off a resurgence in exercise and jogging. Of late, the phenomenal rise of self-help groups and popular movements such as Robert Bly's "wild men" has led to a new male awareness of feelings, and growing intolerance of the once typical "tough guy" upbringing. Marks and scars are no longer badges of honor. . . .

20 As ideals of manhood shift, so has the ideal male body. While it is clearly more masculine—well muscled and sexually potent—it is paradoxically feminine as well. Our ideal man is no longer rough and ready, bruised and calloused, but, as Schwartz puts it, "as clean skinned and clear complected as a woman." His body is "no longer stiff and upright, but sinuous and beautiful when it moves. Sinuousness didn't used to be associated with manliness." A sexual object, a source of pure visual pleasure, men are increasingly being looked at in ways women always have.

21 This fascination with male beauty is not entirely new—consider the ancient Greeks, the beautiful boy of the Renaissance, or Elizabethan noblemen parading the court in revealing tights, silks, satins, and jeweled codpieces. Charles Darwin himself popularized the idea of women as selectors of plumed and spectacular male mates. "He was speaking of finches and partridges," explains historian Thomas Laqueur, Ph.D., author of *Making Sex: Body and Gender from the Greeks to Freud* (Harvard University Press, 1990), "but we generalized to humans. It was known as the peacock phenomenon—the notion of the male as the one with plumage." It wasn't until the rise of capitalism and the bourgeoisie that men renounced flagrant beauty and adopted the plain suit as a uniform. During the so-called "great masculine renunciation" men began to associate masculinity with usefulness. Then, notes Laqueur, "gradually women became the bearers of the science of splendor."

22 The consequences of today's shift in male body image is already apparent. The number of men exercising has soared by 30 percent in the last six years alone—8.5 million men now have health club memberships, according to American Sports Data, a research firm. And men spend an average of 90.8 days a year in the club (that's over 2,000 hours). That's nine days a year more than women. . . .

Mirror Mirror: Women Look at Men

23 For both men and women, male personality is regarded as the most significant quality in attracting a mate. In a sense, this flies in the face of our concern with appearance: it lets us know that no matter how enormous our body obsession, both men and women still rate inner beauty as paramount. . . . [I]ntelligence and sense of humor were rated most important, and sexual performance and physical strength least important.

24 However, there are intriguing differences, even misconceptions, between the sexes about the importance of certain physical characteristics. For instance, men believe an attractive face is more important to women than empathy and the ability to talk about feelings. They also put more emphasis on body build than women do. In general, men judge their physique to be more important than women do.

25   Yet appearance is still only a piece of the pie. Women's sexual response to men is more complex than men's to women. "How odd and unsettling an experience it is," comments Brubach, "to look at all these ads of sexy men sprawling on beds and beaches. I think, 'What a nice chest or legs,' but I don't ever feel that this would be enough material for me to have a sexual fantasy. For most of the women I know sex appeal isn't purely about physical appearance."

26   Gilmore agrees. His studies of gender and sexuality in tribal and modern cultures have found that for women, "the male image conveys much more than sexual virility. Male power, wealth, dominance, control over other men—all those inspire a response in women. The pure visual image of the handsome man, the languid beautiful male is attractive. But it does not necessarily connect with inner virility, which also turns women on. What's so interesting about this subject is that men today get a double message: The culture tells them, 'Be successful, be the boss of bosses, and women will fall at your feet.' The media tell them, 'Look like a model, and women will fall at your feet.' "

27   Some women, of course, value male looks very highly. One of the most fascinating survey results was that women who rated themselves as more attractive tended to rank men's facial appearance and sexual performance higher. These women were a little older on average (mean age 38), thinner (only 6 percent met criteria for overweight), and better off financially (almost half earned over $30,000 annually).

28   This is particularly intriguing given the anthropological literature about female mate selection: In most cultures, women seem to choose sexual partners on the basis of a male's ability to protect and provide for a mate and offspring—whether that is a big salary, hunting game, or achievement as a warrior. . . .

29   Attractive, self-sufficient women may place higher value on physical features because they have been reinforced for these attributes. Traditionally, beautiful women have been able to leverage their looks to snare a wealthy and powerful man. Now that some women have greater financial independence, they may use that power to seek a stunning mate.

Twin Peaks—Hair and Height

30   "In America," writes Gilmore in an essay called, "The Beauty of the Beast" (in *The Good Body,* Yale University Press, 1994), "male concern focuses on two main issues: height and hair." What do height and hair symbolize? Raw maleness. Philosophers like Edmund Burke and art historians like Johann Wincklemann conflate the sublime and the masculine—and associate both with greatness, strength, and majesty. "What are height and musculature, after all," Gilmore asks, "but male equivalents of voluptuousness in females? How is height in a male different from bust size in a female? Short men can have terrible problems." And in a culture that eroticizes differences between the sexes, the potent masculinity of a tall male can be appealing.

31   Though many studies indicate that women love a tall man—Hatfield and Sprecher found that women prefer a man at least six inches taller than themselves—male concern with height seems linked to competition with other males as well. "Men are worried about how they appear to other men," notes Gilmore. "I remember boys being mercilessly ridiculed and beaten up for looking effeminate. Size and power were of absolute importance. I knew a fat boy who had a kind of bosom, who was persecuted so relentlessly that he had a nervous breakdown at age 13."

32   No wonder, then, that both men and women in the survey rated a trimmer, taller male as more attractive. However, a striking finding emerged from the data: There was a discrepancy between what women desired and what they would accept in a mate. Women adapt to their own partner's height—in fact, their preferences seem strongly linked to their mate's actual height. As Michael Pertschuk points out, this ability to adapt, to adjust abstract ideals in favor of the real man, showed up again and again among the women in the survey. It seemed to cut across all variables—from height to weight to penis size. It seems that "negative" appearance factors become lost within the greater gestalt of the partner. The woman sees past or through a less-than-ideal feature.

33   Hair, in turn, is another highly valued masculine signpost. Hair is a traditional signal of youth and power, an index of male virility. Hair signals man in his natural, wild state—uncivilized, and somehow more primal and sexual. Not only is hair a potent symbol, it is one that can be easily manipulated—and has been throughout history. As Pertschuk says, "In the early to mid 1800s, men went to jail for wearing beards. By the Civil War era you would be hard-pressed to find a general who was not sporting a beard. This fashion lasted until the turn of the century, when it was replaced by militant 'clean shavenism.' In some Protestant sects, long hair and beards are suspect. Other sects, such as the Jewish Hasidim, are expressly forbidden to cut their beards. In England the antimonarchists wore their hair short, in protest to the long, flowing locks that were approved of by the monarchy."

34   Though it's tempting to look at hair as a concrete reflection of the role of males in society, Pertschuk feels it may be more indicative of rebellion, of setting oneself apart from an existing social order. Boys coming of age in the rebellious 1960s wore their hair long and grew beards in a gesture. The next generation was cleanshaven. The punks dyed their hair fluorescent pinks and greens, spiked it, and shaved their heads in Mohawk designs—a veiled threat, an attempt to upset and defy the existing order.

Body Build: The Muscular Male

35   The showy, muscle-bound heroes of today are a far cry from yesteryear's aristocratic heartthrobs—Cary Grant, John Barrymore. And although Charles Atlas bodybuilding ads pumped up the back pages of magazines and comic books as far back as the 1920s, we are witnessing a new fascination with the perfectly proportioned, tautly muscled male god. "When women swoon over these men," notes Gilmore,

"it's not unlike the response men have when they see a beautiful woman. Men like to be sex objects, too. It's never been acknowledged, because that desire is not considered manly, and the more urgent need is to appear masculine. But studies have shown that men envy women their ability to attract and command the attention based simply on their appearance."

36   This cultural emphasis on a specific male type has a definite dark side—the growing number of men suffering from body image disorders. According to Steven Romano, M.D., Director of the Outpatient Eating Disorders Clinic at New York Hospital/Cornell Medical Center's Westchester Division, "I'm seeing more and more males who have body image disturbances. They are compulsive exercisers, and there are a number of steroid abuses." Another expert calls it "reverse anorexia."

37   "Psychologically, this group is very tied to female anorexics," says Romano. "Just as the anorexic continues to see herself as fat even though she's thin, these males are well muscled but they look in the mirror and see themselves as too thin. They are judging themselves by the ideal projected in the media. I had a 19-year-old walk in who said he had to look like Marky Mark. He would only eat a diet that allowed him to build muscle. These men tend to be straight males who think a well-muscled physique is what women are interested in."

38   Gilmore concurs. In interviewing men about body image, he found "body anxiety is related to appearing unmasculine or effeminate. This obsession especially attaches to body hair, chest development, waist, and hips. Our culture lays considerable stress on a manly physique." . . .

39   Yet male fascination with muscles may have more to do with other men than with women. "Women don't know what goes on in the playing field among boys," insists Gilmore. "It's very cruel. Boys are beaten up if they don't measure up. To be masculine requires a certain musculature."

40   The new male fascination with muscle may indeed hold destructive potential for men—though perhaps less so than the female ideal does for women. Women who starve themselves to reach a cultural ideal of feminine beauty are damaging their physical health; men who exercise and work out at the gym to build muscle may still eat well. Yet if men feel compelled to make over their bodies to achieve difficult aesthetic goals, they may be opening themselves to problems with steroid abuse, musculoskeletal injury, and eating disorders. If weight is a male concern, it has more to do with looking effeminate, puny, and thin than carrying a few excess pounds. . . .

Male Body as Cultural Crucible

41   Our culture has never openly addressed the reason masculine beauty matters so much. There is a long Western tradition merging aesthetics and ethics, stretching back to Plato's belief that the beautiful is good—and in particular, that masculine power is the ideal emblem of our culture. "This moral primacy of male beauty," muses David

Gilmore, "this exaltation of maleness as both heroic and beautiful places a powerful stress on males. Masculinity becomes an apotheosis of national identity. The erotic and social appeal of a virile, handsome, muscular man successfully accomplishing some task is very strong. It's what our culture prizes above all. Men experience deep psychic terror of failing literally to embody national ideals."

42   The pressure on males to measure up to such iconic images has never been adequately examined by anthropologists or by social psychologists. Why? Ironically, says Gilmore, because "men don't talk about it. It would seem narcissistic, and that would seem feminine. It's an old male code—never complain." Yet studies have long shown that the height of males is linked to the attractiveness of their female partners, that handsome men are more successful than short or plain men, and that taller men earn more than short men.

43   Even more important, this male silence has helped drive the sexes apart. "If we could talk about it openly," comments Gilmore, "we could mutually experience the agony of the visual tyranny in our culture. Both men and women experience it in different ways. My own interviews with men between the ages of 30 and 50 have revealed deep-seated concerns about appearance, many in terms that rival the feminine 'beauty trap.' Men's passionate worries struck me as no less poignant than those expressed by women. The male body, like the female's, has become a punishing crucible painfully subjected to the tyranny of a cultural ideal." . . .

44   Contemporary men are experiencing an upheaval in their social role. It is unclear just what it means to be male anymore. The physical limits of the body provide a tangible arena of control and purpose. And so the ideal male body has become more rigidly masculine than ever.

45   At the same time, our willingness to gaze almost brazenly at male flesh, to pursue it as an object of pleasure, is a stark sign that men are joining the ranks of women. They are being looked at. That is inevitable in a culture where a staggering amount of visual information shapes our very existence—from cinema to advertising to television, from children dying in war zones to world leaders showing up on "Larry King Live." . . . This is truly a culture where a picture is worth a thousand words. Men are no longer exempt.

EXPLORING THE TEXT

1. What is Neimark's thesis? Briefly restate her main point in your own words.
2. Neimark argues in paragraph 7 that "the male body . . . seems to be both hypermasculine and strangely feminine." What examples does Neimark offer throughout the essay to support this statement?
3. While arguing that emphasis on male beauty is currently widespread, Neimark also acknowledges that this emphasis is not without historical precedent. List several examples of other cultures or historical periods when male beauty was highly valued according to the author.

4. In the surveys Neimark cites, what misconceptions do men have about what women most want in a man? What is the single most important quality for women in choosing a mate?

5. Neimark argues that a small but growing number of women are very concerned with their male partners' physical appearance. What is her theory about this particular group of women? What characteristics do these women seem to share?

6. In the essay, author David Gilmore is quoted as saying, "In America, male concern focuses on two main issues: height and hair" (paragraph 30). Explain what each of these qualities symbolizes in terms of defining masculinity.

7. According to the essay, what are some of the drawbacks of a renewed emphasis on a sleek and very muscular male build? What is "reverse anorexia"?

8. Gilmore believes that men's concerns about their appearance rival those of women. What is his explanation for why men do not discuss the pain of trying to live up to a cultural ideal?

9. In her closing paragraphs, what does Neimark suggest about how the male body is seen by society? What does she see as largely responsible for this shift?

WRITING ASSIGNMENTS

1. Write a detailed description of your ideal male image (what you desire in a male or what you would most want to look like as a male). Now look back over the essay and compare your man to Neimark's description. How closely does your ideal male resemble the one(s) Neimark describes?

2. Looking back to your experience in high school, write a narrative about the males who were considered most "studly." What qualities made these particular males most desirable and enviable? How much of their appeal was based on physical appearance? How much on something else?

3. Neimark implies throughout her essay that although men are more and more often being seen as sex symbols by women, women still tend to accept and desire men for more than their physical appearance. Write an essay discussing whether you think this is true. Be sure to draw on your own experience for examples to support your point of view.

4. Using yourself or the males you know as an example, list the "beauty products" (such as hair styling products like gel and mousse; hair dye; cologne; skin moisturizer, cleanser, or toner; blemish cover-up or other kinds of makeup; or nail polish) these men use. Write an essay discussing how the trend toward more male beauty products ties into Neimark's article.

GROUP PROJECTS

1. Do your own survey about male appearance. As a group, come up with a list of qualities that can be ranked in order of importance. Qualities could include such things as: intelligence, overall body build, facial features, sense of humor, and physical strength (try to come up with between 8 to 12 characteristics or qualities). Now distribute your poll among men and women on your college campus (try to get at least 15 responses from each gender and make sure that respondents mark whether they are male or female). Tabulate the results, then write up an analysis of your findings to present to the class. (For an interesting comparison, groups may also want to distribute the same list and ask respondents about female characteristics or qualities.)

2. Have everyone in the group buy a copy of a magazine aimed mainly towards men (e.g., *Details, GQ, Esquire*). Different group members may want to focus on different aspects of the magazine—such as ads, articles, fashion layouts, or advice columns. Do the models in the magazine fit Neimark's description of the ideal male as "smooth skinned, clean shaven, with a tight, carved body"? What do the articles suggest men should aspire to look like? How many articles on improving appearance are there? After reading through the magazine, discuss your findings and collaborate on an essay about how this particular text defines the "ideal" male.

3. Working in small groups, arrange to visit a local gym or health club that caters to men and women (although you will be focusing on males for this assignment). Split up and take notes about what kinds of men you see working out there. What patterns of behavior do you see—for example, are there more men working with weights than doing aerobics? Interview club trainers about what male clients most often ask for help with in terms of their workout. Write brief descriptions of male clients' workout attire. Do the men seem as concerned about how they look while they are working out as the women? Why or why not? After your visit, get together and compare notes. Write a report on your findings and present it to the class.

Three for the Stripes
Michael Fitzpatrick

We live in a culture so caught up with image that we judge people by the physical shape they're in, their hairstyle, the clothes they wear, and the labels on their shoes. Likewise, through these we also forge our own identities. The images we project in flesh and fashion are statements about ourselves. In the next essay, Michael Fitzpatrick shifts discussion to brand consciousness. In a personal narrative, he explores the roles that big-name brands of shoes and clothing have played in shaping not only his own identity as a Boston city youth but that of subcultures on the other side of the world.

Fitzpatrick was a student at Northeastern University in Boston when he was asked to write an essay for his freshman English class considering what role popular culture has played in his life. The following is the result of that assignment.

1 I recognize that I am a product of popular culture and am strongly influenced by the consumerism which is its base. I've always liked to stay up-to-date and be one step ahead of the fashion game. But people from the inner city as I know it, myself included, have made fashion more than a fashion statement. In our isolation from the mainstream, we've made it a statement of identity, of who we are. And as I discovered, we are not alone.

2 Back in the mid 1980s when I was in elementary school, I had to wear bo-bos (no-name sneakers). This was really humiliating. Kids used to call my shoes "roach stompers" and "combat boots," and they used to sing: "Bo-bos, they make your feet feel fine. Bo-bos, they cost a dollar ninety-nine." The only kids with status and clout were the ones with name-brand clothing (Adidas, Levis) and name-brand sneakers (Nike, Adidas, Fila). My mother wasn't going to pay 50 dollars for a pair of sneakers, so I had to find a way to get what I wanted. I became a street entrepreneur, selling everything from newspapers to candy and other things that were in popular demand. Name-brand sneakers and clothes were popular culture to me at the time, and I wanted to be down. I wanted to be recognized as a part of hip-hop.

3 These were the days of hip-hop's birth. Urban creativity was booming. I was breakdancing as a 9-year-old, drawing graffiti, beat boxing, and learning to rap. I had bought my first pair of Adidas for five dollars from a booster (a dope fiend who steals and sells clothes and other things to support his habit) and I wanted the full uniform. In these days you were on point if you wore Adidas, Nike, Puma, or even Converse. As hip-hop culture continued to grow, certain brands became more closely identified with hip-hop fashion. Most breakdancers wore sneakers with flat soles, like Shelltoe Adidas, running Nikes, and Pumas. From the early 1980s Adidas was identified with the rappers RUN DMC, who wrote and performed the song "My Adidas." By the end of the 1980s, Nike was fighting it out with Adidas. In Boston, the Nike crew and the Adidas crew literally fought it out on the streets. Kids got beat up and shot. Adidas won because the company was more creative, coming out with flashier products made from simulated snakeskin and patent leather. They also started having celebrities like Dr. J., Patrick Ewing, and RUN DMC advertise for them. Before long, Adidas came to signify keeping it real, and represented not only hip-hop fashion but Boston street life. It might have been an international label, but for us it symbolized the unity in our city's ghetto streets. In the late 1980s, before this style became a widespread trend, if a person was dressed in Adidas and a B-hat along with loose-fitting clothes, he or she was recognized as sharing the same day-to-day hardships and urban struggle.

4   When I started to get my hands on some money—enough to get my own clothes—usually I bought Adidas. It was only common sense since that is what the people I looked up to wore. But once I slipped and bought a pair of Nikes—I thought at the time that the Charles Barkleys looked good. When I went to school the next day everyone stepped on my feet and called me a sucker and a pretty boy. This led to a lot of fights, and I have never bought another pair.

5   But that was not the end of the trouble. On the first day of school each year anyone who expected respect had to look as sharp as a tack. On my first day in sixth grade, I wore a pair of brand-new blue-and-white high-top Adidas Phantoms. At the lunch table, an envious friend who had on old sneakers from the summer repeatedly stepped on my new sneakers, which led to another fight. It was a constant struggle to keep status, and even when you thought you had it, it could be literally stepped on. This was the story behind many newspaper headlines during the late 1980s and early 1990s, as brand-name clothing became a prize possession and kids were held up for 8 Ball leather coats, jewelry, and their expensive Timberland boots.

6   After years of growing up in a fashion-conscious environment, where how you dress is who you are, I excelled at coordinating my outfits and keeping ahead of the game. At one stage I had about 20 pairs of brand new Adidas shoes, and once I started to wear them, I kept them looking new by carrying a toothbrush with me. I'd even travel as far as New York City to get the latest pair of Adidas sneakers before they reached Boston stores. In my neighborhood you couldn't afford to front, or you'd get put in check quickly. So I tried my best to keep it real, from never running from a fight, to never rocking Nikes—only three stripes for me. I still had to fight, but I managed to stay on top by maintaining my status through appearance, demonstrating that I was in control of my life.

7   For a brief time I had to live in Louisville, Kentucky. There, the inner-city youth also related Adidas to hip-hop culture but saw it as a thing of the past. They had switched to Nikes, much like the rest of the country, probably because Nikes had become the most expensive and flashy brand of sneakers in the country and sports superstar Michael Jordan has his own line of Nike clothing.

8   But I wasn't going to cross over. I had to represent my city. I continued to wear only Adidas, and in further representing Boston and myself as an individual in Louisville, I took it to the extreme and occasionally wore Adidas from head to toe. I didn't stop there.

9   There was an event coming up called the Freaknik in Atlanta, Georgia. People from all over the country go to get buck wild and let it all hang out. I went with some friends. We decided to get tattoos. I knew I wanted a tattoo on my arm and my stomach. Feeling homesick and realizing Adidas would never go out of style, at least in Boston, I got a flaming Adidas leaf tattooed over my naval. On my arm I got "Boston killer bees" over the image of a killer bee. This is not a gang name, but the "bee" represented the letter *B* and the letter *B* represents Boston, like on the front of Red Sox caps. Wearing a Red Sox cap in my neighborhood of Boston has nothing to do with being a Red Sox fan—it's all about representing (what we call "reppen").

10   Black nationalist rapper KRS ONE says that African Americans have a strong subconscious sense of homelessness because of the way they arrived in this country and the oppression they have suffered ever since. We like to create styles that represent us in unity and give us a sense of community apart from mainstream nationalism. At the nationwide level, there's hip-hop fashion on the whole, while on the neighborhood level there are particular styles that project a sense of place. For me the place is Grove Hall in Roxbury, and the style is strictly A-dogs, Tim boots, and B-hats, hoodied all up and fatigues. That's "reppen."

11   For years I identified my fashion style with my neighborhood and city. But this past summer I went to South Africa with an organization called Project HIP-HOP (Highways Into the Past–History Organization and Power). Toward the end of our journey, I found myself in Cape Town, where hip-hop culture was very much alive. We held a Project HIP–HOP conference, to get an opportunity to hear how the young people of the Cape Flats (Cape Town's "colored" ghetto) felt about the transformation from apartheid to a democratic government. I was surprised to see so many people show up. It turns out that everyone had thought we were holding a hip-hop show, and they wanted to be part of the action.

12   The first thing that I noticed when I looked around the room was that most people were wearing Adidas gear from head to toe. The second thing that struck me was that they seemed to be in a time warp. They wore Adidas sweat suits, Shelltoe Adidas sneakers, and windbreakers, the way we did when we were break-dancing in the 1980s. The fact is they were still break-dancing and gave us a demonstration later that evening. They were also rapping, and they showed us the graffiti art on their neighborhood walls. It's not like they were out of sync with the new school of hip-hop, but they continued to embrace the old school as well, while we had moved on. To them, hip-hop and the fashion that expressed it were a total way of life.

13   Discovering this identity with hip-hop and Adidas in South Africa made me think about my own assumptions. I had never thought of hip-hop fashion as "oppositional," in the sense that Elizabeth Wilson describes it in her essay "Oppositional Dress." She considers oppositional dress a way of opposing the mainstream. We didn't really think about the mainstream, because we were totally isolated from it in all respects. I didn't even understand how the life of the mainstream that I saw on television could really exist in the cold world that I knew. It wasn't until much later in my life that I got the chance to meet people from different environments. Because we were so cut off at the time from interacting with the larger world, our fashion did not seem to be a political statement.

14   However, looking back on it after my trip to South Africa, I realize that what my neighborhood had in common with the Cape Flats was that both were cut off from the mainstream economy and opportunities. We had to create our own economy (drug trade) and our own forms of expression. It was not, on the surface at least, about "social rebellion against poverty," which Elizabeth Wilson says might have been the case with the "zoot suiters" of the 1940s. We just wanted to do our own thing and have something to feel proud of.

15   But under the surface, perhaps more was going on. Looking back, I can see how poverty bred expression through hip-hop in America and in South Africa. Artists considered gangster rappers most of the time rap about the bad conditions in their communities, like drugs and violence. It was interesting to find that Cape Town's biggest youth gang, that identifies with Adidas hip-hop fashion and controls the drug trade, calls itself the Americans. In different neighborhoods you have the Crazy Americans, the Ugly Americans, and the Young Americans. They say they took those names because America is the biggest gang in the world, and they want to control their neighborhoods like America controls the world.

16   I returned to my neighborhood seeing that we weren't the only ones who identified Adidas with hip-hop culture and much more aware about how mass consumerism and popular culture help to shape our identities and outlook. I now know that I am part of a worldwide subculture that has made an international corporation our symbol—and a lot of money. It is strange that a company that is really mainstream has come to represent communities isolated from the mainstream, with few opportunities to legitimately buy its expensive products and even fewer opportunities to get ahead in the world.

EXPLORING THE TEXT

1. How does Fitzpatrick use his own personal history to trace the growth of brand-name clothing through the mid-1980s to mid-1990s? Do you find the use of personal anecdotes effective?

2. What, according to the author, did Adidas as a brand symbolize in his neighborhood?

3. How did the battle between Nike and Adidas for product shares play out in the street? What problems did the author experience as a result of his clothing choices?

4. In paragraph 6, Fitzpatrick says: "In my neighborhood you couldn't afford to front." Yet much of the rest of the paragraph is about creating a certain image through fashion, something we usually consider as "a front." Do you find these two ideas contradictory? Why or why not?

5. In several places throughout the essay, Fitzpatrick mentions various celebrities who have endorsed either Adidas or Nike products. What role did these endorsements play in the author's eyes?

6. Explain what Fitzpatrick means when he says: "Wearing a Red Sox cap in my neighborhood of Boston has nothing to do with being a Red Sox fan—it's all about representing" (paragraph 9). What, in particular, does he mean by "representing"?

7. How did Fitzpatrick's trip to South Africa broaden his awareness of the political aspects of popular culture? What conclusions does he come to about

the connections between the people he saw in Africa and people in his neighborhood back home?

8. Discuss how you feel about the last line of the essay. Does it strike you as a satisfying idea on which to resolve the essay or does it open new issues that you would like to see explored further?

WRITING ASSIGNMENTS

1. Using Fitzpatrick's essay as a model, write a narrative about your own fashion history. You do not have to focus exclusively on sneakers; discuss any fashions that seem relevant. Like the author, be sure to go beyond describing what you and your friends wore and draw some conclusions about what statements you think these clothes were making about you and about popular culture as a whole (whether you were aware of it at the time or not).

2. Have you ever traveled to another country (or even another state) and suddenly realized something about yourself or your way of life that you were unable to see before the trip? Write a narrative about what you realized, focusing on how your new surroundings helped you to see something that had never been apparent before.

3. At the end of his essay, Fitzpatrick points out the irony of large corporations making a great deal of money off kids who are largely disenfranchised from the economic system they are making rich. Write an essay discussing this issue, focusing particularly on whether you think companies such as Adidas and Nike exploit innercity kids.

GROUP PROJECTS

1. In the latter part of his essay, Fitzpatrick discusses his trip to South Africa and comments on the widespread influence of American popular culture on the youth he saw there. In small groups, do some research on American popular culture's influence throughout the world. For instance, does American rock or rap music dominate the charts in Germany? Brazil? India? How many countries in the world now have McDonald's restaurants? Are Levi's jeans still as popular in Russia as they were in the mid-1980's? Use the Internet as well as current magazines for your research. You may also want to interview some international students for firsthand feedback. Report your findings to the class.

2. Do some research exploring the connection between fashion and music. In the mid-1980's, it was easy to see the widespread influence such performers as Madonna and Michael Jackson had on fashion. In the mid-1990's, Grunge became popular as a fashion statement. What recent clothing trends

have come directly from the music world? Have your group discuss who are currently the most influential groups and/or artists in terms of influencing fashion. Lead the class in a discussion about who they would add to your group's list.

Baggy Clothes Don't Make the Man
Leonard Pitts

As a 13-year-old, did you have battles with your parents over how you dressed? Do you ever look back now and cringe at what you thought were fashionable clothes then? In the following essay, Leonard Pitts laments the popularity of "gangsta chic" among today's youth—his own son included—and argues that "saggin'" is a sad statement reflecting many young black males' need for self-esteem.

Pitts is a syndicated columnist for the *Miami Herald* where this essay first appeared in 1995.

1   Touch your thumb to your forefinger. That's the approximate waist size of my 13-year-old son.

2   Now put your index fingers together so that your arms form a circle in front of you. That's the size of the pants he tried to walk out of the house in the other day—with boxer shorts riding two inches above the belt line, no less.

3   Marlon was, let us say, reluctant to change his gear. His mother and I were obligated to explain—forcefully—that he would go out like this only over our cooling corpses.

4   Ordinarily, I'd support a child's right to make a fashion statement. As the former owner of platform shoes that could be mounted only by stepladder, I lack the moral authority to advise anybody on issues of style and taste.

5   But I draw the line at pants five sizes too big. Because saggin', as it's called, has less to do with fashion than with dressing down to the desolation of inner-city streets.

6   Not that that has stopped the boys in the 'hood—and for that matter, the boys in the 'burbs—from going with the flow. Gangsta chic, the look and style of inner-city thuggery, has seduced not only the children who must live there, but a generation of wannabe gangstas who've never been any closer than their MTV screens.

7   "You look like a little gangsta!" I yelled at my son. My anger surprised me.

8   "You can't judge a book by its cover," he replied, deftly using one of Father's aphorisms to entrap Father. And so Father was forced to sigh and concede that this was an exception.

9   Though it's foolish to draw conclusions about a person based on race, gender, sexual orientation or some other accident of birth, I told him, clothes are another

matter. Clothing reflects a conscious, personal choice. If you see a man in a clown suit, you can reasonably assume him to be a clown. If you see a woman in a business suit, it is not outlandish to think she might be a businesswoman.

10   And if you see a young man in a thug suit, might a person not fairly take that man to be a thug?

11   Yet so many boys rush to that identity. I've lost count of how many white suburban mall rats I've seen slouching through the food court in self-conscious imitation of people they've never met in a place they've never been.

12   A white boy who looks like a thug might—*might*—get the chance to correct that impression. A black boy is unlikely to be afforded even that opportunity. He is, as a comic once said, "born a suspect." In his case, clothes don't so much *make* the man as *mark* him, verifying for people who've never taken time to know him that they were justified in their prejudgment.

13   No, it's not fair; but it is a fact.

14   That's a hell of a thing to explain to a 13-year-old who only wants to be stylish, a child for whom racial politics is a distant noise, faintly discerned.

15   Not that I worry for my boy, mind you. This is, as they say, a phase. He'll make it to manhood OK.

16   But I've seen and know too many other black boys in whom I don't have that confidence. Manhood is a less definite destination for them, a place they search for in violent words, a cool stance, and in the folds of clothes that sag like a flag on a windless day. The words, the stance and the clothes are a way of asserting control, inciting fear, demanding respect and saying what they haven't the words for: I am somebody.

17   And a way of not hearing the whisper of doubt that replies, "No, you are not."

18   Their hurting makes a lousy fashion statement.

EXPLORING THE TEXT

1. Describe how Pitts's son dresses. How does Pitts "read" his son's fashion statement?
2. What seems to be the difference to Pitts between his own youthful taste— "as the former owner of platform shoes that could be mounted only by stepladder" (paragraph 4)—and his son's interest in "gansta chic"?
3. What difference does Pitts see between white kids and black kids when it comes to wearing "saggin' "?
4. Summarize what Pitts is concerned about in paragraph 16.
5. Pitts argues that clothes present a "conscious, personal choice," yet also suggests that young men are dressing this way because it is "cool." Do you see baggy clothes in the same way as Pitts does—that is, as something that represents "thug life"—or simply as an MTV-inspired trend.

WRITING ASSIGNMENTS

1. Using Pitts's piece as a model, write a critique of a current fashion trend on campus or among young teenagers (ages 12 to 15). Be sure to "read" (interpret) this trend for the reader as Pitts does.
2. Two aphorisms are used in this article. The title plays on the cliche "clothes make the man" and Pitts's son counters his father's argument by saying, "Don't judge a book by its cover." Discuss these two sentiments in terms of how you view fashion—that is, do you tend to agree with one more than the other?
3. Discuss why you think "gansta chic," a style that originated with urban African American youth, became so popular with "white suburban mall rats."

GROUP PROJECTS

1. Investigate the connection between music and fashion. Group members' evidence can be drawn from television (MTV may be particularly helpful), magazines, movies, or live musical shows. Discuss what trends you find and write a collaborative essay.
2. Pitts's article focuses on young males. Explore what fashion trends are currently popular among young females. Plan to visit a nearby mall or go to a part of town where teenagers hang out. Have group members take notes on the styles they see girls most often wearing. Report your findings to the class.

The Body Myth
Rebecca Johnson

In this essay below, Rebecca Johnson offers a counterargument to the common belief that women face the often-painful, sometimes dangerous pressure to be thin in today's society. Johnson believes that there is hostility directed toward thin women, particularly models, and that it is based primarily on jealousy. She suggests that critics of slender fashion models should "get over it." It's not surprising that her article produced some lively letters to the editor—both pro and con—published in subsequent issues. On the following pages are five representative letters. Read over the various responses and try to decide where you stand on the issues raised.

Johnson is a contributing editor at *Vogue* magazine where this article first appeared in the September 1996 issue.

Letters to *Vogue*

March 1977

Dear Editor:

The female body is an art in itself, and seeing all the sleek, slim bodies photographed artistically, I find myself wishing that I, too, could look like that. Now I find that I have the ambition to start that all-important diet and begin exercising regularly—THANK YOU!

December 1987

Dear Editor:

While I stand at the [high school] cafeteria salad bar, I see girls drink a pint of chocolate milk and eat a slice of pizza, plus a package of Ho Hos. I have a piece of advice: Hand them a copy of *Vogue* and a full-length mirror. I used them in January 1986 and today I am a healthy 4' 11", 102-pound young woman.

January 1996

Dear Editor:

I have always considered your magazine to be reputable and in good taste, so I was extremely disappointed upon seeing the enclosed picture of one of your models. This woman looks deathly ill from anorexia. *YOU* as a *leader* in the world of fashion have a responsibility to stop portraying sickly thin models as desirable. You have lost one consumer.

March 1996

Dear Editor:

Vogue, Vogue, Vogue, we don't like this!! [accompanying picture of Shalom Harlow in Christian Dior gown]

1   Have you ever noticed that the only acceptable time to say "I hate you" to a friend is when she has lost weight and you haven't? As America gets fatter and fatter—33 percent of us are now officially over our ideal weight—hostility to very thin women, and to images of them, seems to have grown. As recently as ten years ago, readers wrote to thank magazines for presenting an ideal. The relationship between reader and magazine was cozy and hortatory. Today, letters to editors, designers, and even advertisers tremble with outrage over the size of Kate Moss's femur. How dare you promote an image, they ask, so toxic to our fragile self-esteem?

2   Small wonder, then, that the fashion industry is defensive on the issue: "Calvin's going to pass on this one." "Donna's too busy with her IPO to talk." "Norma would

like to talk, but she's on her way to India." *After you; no, after* you. This past spring, one advertiser, the Omega watch company, made headlines when it announced it would suspend advertising in British *Vogue* partly because the company found models like Trish Goff "skeletal," "anorexic," and "extremely distasteful."

3   What's going on here? Have the exigencies of the season—the long, lean line of the new evening dress, the cling of double matte jersey, the androgyny of the man's pant—created demand for a model so thin that she must, by definition be ill? Or worse, a heroin addict? Is the fashion industry, with its constant, restless mandate for something new, in this case a model who doesn't look like whoever came before (curvy Claudia or luscious Cindy), generating higher and higher levels of self-loathing and potentially life-threatening diseases in women? Should fashion spreads that show impossible-to-achieve bodies carry a warning on the bottom of the page: DON'T TRY THIS AT HOME?

4   Once, these were questions answered only with idle speculation. Though cases of anorexia can be traced as far back as the thirteenth century—at least one historian believes that saints Catherine of Siena and Clare of Assisi suffered from it—most scientists and psychiatrists ignored it as a disorder too rare to merit serious study. (The exceptions were followers of Freud, who speculated that the anorexic rejects food because it reminds her of her father's phallus.) However, as I learned when I asked these questions, scientists are now grappling with the sociological and biological roots of anorexia, forever changing how we think of the disease.

5   But let's pull focus, for a moment, to examine what is happening in society at large. Fat, or fear of fat, is not, as it turns out, a feminist issue. It's an issue for everyone. Men and women. Would Al Franken's book be a best-seller had it been called *Rush Limbaugh Is an Idiot* instead of *Rush Limbaugh Is a Big Fat Idiot*? To make an insult stick these days, all you have to do is add *fat.*

6   Even children disdain fat. A study conducted on ten- and eleven-year-olds finds that drawings of people with handicaps, wheelchairs, and missing hands are rated more appealing than drawings of fat people. I tried a similar experience on a friend: "If you had to choose between being 100 pounds overweight and losing your left hand, which would you choose?"

7   "The 100 pounds; I could lose it."

8   "No," I amended the game, "you could never lose it."

9   Pause.

10   "I guess I'd give up my hand."

11   "How about 50 pounds?"

12   "Could I give a few fingers?"

13   Feminists cite this broad-based preference for skinniness as proof of a male-dominated society's tyranny over women's bodies. As a good liberal, I hate to disagree with feminist orthodoxy, but I think they're wrong on this one. To begin with, thinness as an ideal has traditionally accompanied periods of greater freedom for women. It was in the 1920s, when we won the right to vote, that skirt lengths went up and the boyish flapper body came into vogue. You see this in popular culture as

well. In the movies, curves sexualize and humanize, but the formidable careerists—Faye Dunaway in *Network,* Sigourney Weaver in *Working Girl,* and, more recently, Téa Leoni in *Flirting with Disaster*—are tall, skinny, and angular.

14   It would be one thing if it were healthier to be fat than thin. It's not. As far back as 60 years ago, scientists found they could extend the outer limits of a rat's life span 33 percent by placing it on a severe calorie-restricted diet. More recently, scientists at the National Institutes of Health have observed the same phenomenon in preliminary work on monkeys, animals whose DNA differs from ours by less than 2 percent. We've yet to see similar experiments on humans, but in places like Okinawa, Japan, where diets are low in calories but nutritionally sound, the incidence of centenarians is as much as 40 times greater as on other Japanese islands.

15   Nobody is sure why this is, but researchers have observed that the skinny monkeys had a one-degree decrease in body temperature. It's life as a slow roast instead of a fast fry. However it works, it is doubtful that being thin can help very many models live longer; too many of them smoke.

16   I don't go to the gym three times a week and forgo foie gras in order to live longer. I do it to look better. It's just a happy coincidence that vanity and health should go hand in hand—or is it? Could hostility to thinness be nothing more than sublimated envy for the promise of prolonged life? Maybe the art director at his light box picks the shot where Trish Goff looks her thinnest because he's responding to some atavistic knowledge that to be thin is to live longer? Probably not. To him, as to the designer, it's aesthetic. Clothes hang better on thin women. When fat settles in, it renders the body formless, amorphous, like a landscape blanketed in snow. In athletes and very thin people, the endoskeleton, the ligature, and the striae of muscle become visible, reminding us of what a wondrous piece of machinery the human body is.

17   To find a picture visually arresting is one thing; to try to emulate the model by losing weight is something else altogether. The model is chosen for her job precisely because she does not look like you or me. She is selected because she is extreme—extremely young, extremely pretty, and extremely thin. The more so, the better. (Kirsty Hume stands five feet eleven inches and weighs less than 120 pounds. Such a body is, for most women, unattainable.) But now she is criticized for this extremity—not, by the way, for her youth or her beauty. We all get to be young sometime, and we accept that beauty is genetically determined and beyond our control. The model is criticized for her weight because that is something we can change. Her body becomes a rebuke to all women. Don't show us this, the critics complain, because it makes us want to look the same way. In the broadest sense, this leads women to become unhappy with their bodies; in its extreme, it leads to anorexia nervosa. At least that's the conventional wisdom. But is it true?

18   *Anorexic* is a word used so casually and so often that it has come loose from its original, clinical meaning. When I lost twelve pounds on a diet recently, my mother immediately began clucking about anorexia, though I did not meet a single diagnostic criterion for the disease. Besides being significantly under the average weight for a woman her size, a true anorexic is someone who insists on constant weight loss.

This standard alone exempts models like Kate Moss. In the four years that she has been a famous model, her weight has remained steady. She's just a skinny girl.

19   Does making a skinny girl an icon create eating disorders? In the simpleminded pop psychology of books like Naomi Wolf's *The Beauty Myth,* the answer is yes, but those books do a great disservice to women by throwing around false statistics to buttress an ideology of victimhood. When it was originally published, Wolf claimed that 150,000 women a year die from eating disorders, a figure Gloria Steinem repeated in *Revolution from Within.* If that were true, it would mean ten times as many women die from anorexia as die in car wrecks. They don't. (In the paperback edition, Wolf deleted the figure and wrote instead that "there are no reliable statistics.") The American Anorexia/Bulimia Association estimates that 1,000 women die from the disease yearly, but even that seems high. According to the National Center for Health Statistics, only 62 died in 1992. Much more significant are the thousands who die of heart disease and hypertension each year, brought on partly by being overweight. As Howard Shapiro, a New York City diet doctor, says, we shouldn't be angry with Madison Avenue for showing us images of beautiful, thin women; we should be angry with food manufacturers, who mislead consumers by labeling high-calorie foods like jelly beans or bagels "fat-free," or with chain restaurants that serve portions so large they're obscene.

20   Wolf and others place the blame for eating-disorder deaths on the media, but when you talk to clinicians whose sole practice is the treatment of anorexics, they say otherwise. Photographs of models may have some influence on young women with eating disorders, but, says Richard Gordon, Ph.D., author of *Anorexia and Bulimia: Anatomy of a Social Epidemic,* "it's a complex, multidetermined disease. It's too simplistic to say, 'It's the culture.' For an anorexic, the goal of thinness is not to be attractive. It's more about being in control. It comes from family experience, mood disorders. Even sexual abuse can be a factor."

21   "I really don't believe the media play such a big role in it," agrees Susan Ice, M.D., medical director of the Eating Disorders Program at the Belmont Center for Comprehensive Treatment in Philadelphia. "Families of anorexics are always trying to blame someone else, but when I work with anorexics, I don't work with things in the culture. What I try to change are family dynamics and the ways people communicate with one another." Ice goes on to say that the problems usually begin during two key phases of life: early adolescence, when hormonal puberty begins, and late adolescence, when girls leave home and go away to college.

22   Many researchers are beginning to suspect that eating disorders are based more on a biological predisposition toward a personality type rather than societal influences. "This is not a social fad," says Michael Strober, Ph.D., director of the Eating Disorders Program at the University of California in Los Angeles, "this is a serious disease." As scientists in the past decade began to detect genetic influences in such psychiatric disorders as schizophrenia and manic depression, Strober began to wonder if there might not be a similar inherited component to anorexia. Sure enough, his surveys indicated that mothers and sisters of anorexics were ten times more likely to suffer from the disease than members of the general population.

23   Correlation is not causation, but Strober and others began to wonder whether the personality characteristics of an anorexic—inflexibility, persistent self-doubt, extreme perfectionism, obsessiveness, avoidance of novel experiences, the need for sameness in one's life, and general timidity—might be inherited traits. Meanwhile, at the University of Pittsburgh School of Medicine, Walter Kaye, M.D., was trying to isolate what that biological difference might actually be. "Lots of women diet," he says. "Very few end up at 65 pounds. We wondered if there was some special vulnerability that would lead them to lose that weight."

24   Kaye found that anorexics tend to have higher-than-normal levels of the neurotransmitter serotonin in their blood. Since low levels of serotonin have been linked to impulsive and violent behavior, it makes sense that elevated levels would accompany the restrained, inhibited behavior of the anorexic. Now Strober, Kaye, and four other researchers are studying anorexics and their sisters to see if they can isolate a genetic marker.

25   The more I inquired about anorexia and its relationship to a reigning aesthetic, the more abstract the disease came to seem. True, everybody I talked to had an opinion about it, but their opinions all reflected their own interests and biases on the subject. The designers either wouldn't speak or denied it was even an issue. "This is just a made-up story," said Michael Kors. "Everyone is looking for someone to blame." The feminists wildly overstated the case. And the scientists wanted to reduce everything to the double helix of the DNA molecule. What I wanted to hear was the voices of real women. So I arranged to spend an afternoon at the Renfrew Center, an eating-disorders clinic in the heart of a bucolic nature preserve in Philadelphia.

26   Women, mostly young ones, spend an average of three weeks at the center (at around $950 a day). Their time is taken up with therapy, and their meals are closely monitored—everybody must agree to eat a minimum of 1,500 calories a day. I did have one mystery cleared up by the visit. On a bulletin board in the admittance area, somebody had posted a photocopy of a waif-laden Benetton ad. On it were written comments like "These images piss me off—we're trying to get away from this"; "She looks sickly, meek, vulnerable." When I asked about it, I was told that therapists often encourage patients to write letters to the editors of fashion magazines in order to "find their voice." That explains where some of the angry letters are coming from. I couldn't help noticing, however, that the first comment on this list was "I wish I could look like her."

27   I spent most of my time there with three graduates of the program, all of whom were on antidepressants and all of whom still struggled with serious issues of self-esteem. Not that you could tell by looking. They appeared perfectly healthy and were normal weight, though all three instinctively reached for pillows on the couch to cover their stomachs when they sat down. (The director of the center had requested that I not ask them their current weight.) When I asked if any of them thought their problems with food could be traced to the media or images of models, they all answered no, even though when I showed them a photo of Amber Valletta, they agreed that she was "too thin." One woman traced her eating disorder to sexual abuse by her father. Another said she had thrown up her entire life. She got treat-

ment only when her disintegrating marriage caused her to start vomiting—or, as they say at the center, "purging"—five times a day.

28   "Mostly, I blame myself," said Tamia Beeman, a stunning five-foot-ten-inch, 21-year-old brunette who resembles a young Cindy Crawford but who once had a laxative-abuse problem so acute that she ended up in the emergency room a few times for stomach pain. "When I was growing up, my mother was overweight and my father was mean to her about it. In my head, I connected his cruelty to her weight. If I was thin, I thought, nobody would be mean to me."

29   Beeman was supposedly in recovery, but that day she had eaten only one piece of low-fat banana-cream pie and was already beginning to wonder how she would get through a family dinner that evening without eating anything. As she said, " . . . If you're an alcoholic, you never have to pick up a drink again, but when you have an eating disorder, the issue never completely goes away. You've got to eat."

30   As I listened to Beeman talk about her own ambivalent relationship to her looks and her body—"People tell me I'm beautiful. I don't believe it myself, but I need to hear it"—I could hear echoes of the thousands of conversations I have had with my female friends. We are a culture of strivers. Whatever we have, whoever we are, it's never enough. There is always someone at the party who is thinner and prettier. If we seem obsessed, it's because beauty, for women, is the promise of happiness. "Look at how deeply it's written into our culture," says Nancy Friday, who took on the subject in her most recent book, *The Power of Beauty*. "It's even in our fairy tales." When asked if she had any regrets in life, even the great Eleanor Roosevelt answered, "I wish I'd been prettier."

31   If we resent the model on the page, it's because she alone, in the freeze-frame of the moment, is the fairest of them all. (Even if she herself doesn't believe it—as we know from the seemingly disingenuous but de rigueur model quotes "I've never thought I was pretty" or "I was a geek in high school.") The vast majority of us go on to turn our discontent into something positive, like drive, ambition, an M.B.A., or a Ph.D., but the anorexic can't. She converts her angst into the controllable world of calories ingested versus calories expended. It diverts her attention from the larger world to a much smaller one. "I preferred the pain in my stomach," Beeman said, "to the pain of my situation." It seems wrong to hang such a heavy psychic burden on the shoulders (however bony) of this season's model.

Response to "The Body Myth"

The large response to the publication of Rebecca Johnson's "The Body Myth" in the September 1996 *Vogue* showed a clear split between those who thought that Johnson's defense of superthin supermodels was justified and those who thought that it was one more example of "the tyranny of slenderness in our society," as Anna Silver put it. Below is a sampling of those letters published in *Vogue's* "Talkingback" section in December 1996. Where do you stand on the issue?

One can always count on VOGUE for self-exculpating defenses of its politics. I am referring to your article on the use of superthin fashion models ["The Body Myth," by Rebecca Johnson, September], which simplifies the incredibly complex problem of a culture of anorexia by arguing that fashion models are not to blame for eating disorders. No subtle cultural critic would argue that the overpaid but underfed models who grade your pages are directly to blame for an individual woman's eating disorder. As Foucault has argued, power is devious and discreet and is located in innumerable points throughout a culture. In other words, a girl growing up is exposed to a rigid physical standard of beauty not only in your magazine but in the media as a whole. Simultaneously, she is rarely exposed, in VOGUE or in movies or television, to alternative, more realistic images of beauty. One need only consider the vicious media attacks on Alicia Silverstone for gaining weight as evidence of the tyranny of slenderness in our society. VOGUE's knee-jerk response? It's not Kate Moss's fault!

Anna Silver
Decatur, GA

If people think Kate Moss influences females to become anorexic and bulimic, isn't Anna Nicole Smith influencing women to enlarge their breasts? Of course not! Women and young girls who have eating disorders need to search for the root cause of their problem, which isn't other women. We will never find the true cause if we continue to allow society to encourage this ridiculous competition between "real women" and models.

Chantelle M. Jenkins
New York, NY

Rebecca Johnson claims that magazines show emaciated models because people like to see extremes. Then how about using some people with extremely big noses, or who are extremely short, or (God forbid) extremely overweight? But you don't want to show obese individuals, because you think being too fat is an even bigger health problem than being too thin. Aside from the fact that there are significant studies disputing the claim that thin people are healthier or live longer, starving yourself to get thin is certainly not healthy. Furthermore, the reason it's hard to track death rates from eating disorders is that things like "heart failure" are listed on death certificates, not "anorexia nervosa." Telling us not to worry about glorifying emaciation because there are worse problems, such as obesity, is like saying it is OK to show images of people using cocaine because heroin is much worse.

Carolyn Costin, MFCC
The Eating Disorder Center of California and
The Monte Nido Residential Treatment Facility
Malibu, CA

Brava to Rebecca Johnson for her much-needed article "The Body Myth" and Irving Penn's exquisite portraits of three very surreal and very beautiful women. Even in the earliest art forms, the master craftsmen sought figures that embodied extremes of beauty to suit their visions. Today the art form is photography, and the subject has evolved into the slender, angelic supermodel. These women are inspiring, ethereal muses—unreal in their framework and almost too real in their perfection.

Someone should tell your readers that jealousy is very unbecoming. Women should embrace the grace, style, charisma, and modesty of these gorgeous creatures instead of criticizing them for their bodies.

Natasza and Karolina Holowatinc
Edmonton, Alberta

You have finally printed an article that puts all of those annoying, thin-hating, obnoxious, bored people in their places. If it's such a sin to criticize fat people, what gives them the right to criticize those who are thin? As you said in your article, designer clothes just look better on these people. Would a slim-fitting, sleek Armani gown look as attractive to a prospective buyer on a size-16 model? I think not.

A. C.
Newport, RI

EXPLORING THE TEXT

1. According to Johnson's opening paragraphs, how has the public's view of models and fashion magazines changed in the last ten years?
2. Johnson says in paragraph 13, "As a good liberal, I hate to disagree with feminist orthodoxy, but I think they're wrong on this one." List the evidence she offers to support her argument that fashion magazines and the thin models they feature are not causing eating disorders. Which evidence do you find most persuasive? Why?
3. What does Johnson feel are the causes of the current animosity directed at thin women by society?
4. Naomi Wolf and Gloria Steinem have both written best-selling books that criticize the media's depiction of women. Describe how Johnson undercuts these well-known feminists' positions in her article. Do you find her critique effective? Why or why not?
5. Johnson quotes several doctors about the causes of eating disorders. Summarize what each authority says about this issue. How do their comments support Johnson's argument?
6. Summarize what insights Tamie Beeman offers Johnson about eating disorders. How does Beeman's authority on the subject differ from the various doctors' authority? Which form of authority do you find more compelling? Why?

7. Mark the places in the text where Johnson acknowledges the power that beauty holds over us. How does this discussion fit into her argument as a whole?

8. Read over the "Talkingback" letters that appeared after the publication of Johnson's article. List the arguments that best challenge Johnson's thesis. Explain your choices briefly.

9. Natasza and Karolina Holowatinc's letter in "Talkingback" states that "someone should tell your readers that jealousy is very unbecoming." Do you agree with this view? Do you think that people who complain that the fashion industry distorts body image are just jealous?

10. Johnson points out that while few women actually die of weight loss, many women die of diseases perpetuated by obesity. Carolyn Costin's letter challenges Johnson's assertion. Do you agree with Costin or Johnson? How does Costin emphasize her point? Is her letter persuasive? Why?

WRITING ASSIGNMENTS

1. Do you know someone who seems obsessed with food who suffers from an eating disorder? Discuss what you feel were the causes of his or her problem. Do you tend to agree with Johnson that the causes of most eating disorders are complicated and often stem from troubled family relationships? Why or why not?

2. Write your own "Talkingback" letter to *Vogue* in response to Johnson's article. Make sure you respond to a specific point(s) made in the article.

3. Write a response to one of the letters in "Talkingback." Explain why you chose the particular letter you did and what you agree or disagree with and why.

4. In her letter, Anna Silver comments that the media has influenced how girls feel about their bodies. "As Foucault has argued, power is devious and discreet and is located in innumerable points throughout a culture." Write an essay in which you analyze your own feelings about your self-image. What factors do you feel shaped your feelings? What "points" in our culture influenced your development of body consciousness?

GROUP PROJECTS

1. Johnson quotes author Nancy Friday as saying, "Look how deeply it's [beauty] written into our culture. It's even in our fairy tales." Do some investigation into how fairy tales communicate important ideas about female beauty. Pick three or four well-known tales—for example, Cinderella, Snow White, Beauty and the Beast, Rapunzel—so that you can be sure

your audience will be familiar with the basic story. Find the stories and read them, then as a group discuss how the issue of beauty is presented and dealt with in each story. Write up your analysis and present it to the class.

2. Kate Moss and the other "waif" models are often compared to another famously thin model from the sixties—Twiggy. In small groups, do some research on Twiggy (be sure to find some pictures). Did she spark the same kind of controversy as Kate Moss? Discuss how Johnson might have used Twiggy as part of her argument.

3. Try Johnson's experiment on a group of your own friends or classmates. (Choose people who have not read this article). Ask them: "If you had to choose between being 100 pounds overweight and losing your left hand, which would you choose?" (Remind them that they can't lose the weight). You may want to have different members try different amounts of weight as Johnson did. For instance, pose the question to a second group of people using the figure of 50 pounds (or even 35 pounds) overweight. Tabulate your responses and present them to the class.

4. Rebecca Johnson defends the fashion industry's use of very thin models as catering to the public's desire to "see extremes." In her "Talkingback" letter, Costin says that if this were true, the fashion industry should depict models who have extremely large noses or who are extremely obese. With your group, discuss how the public would react to such extremes in modeling. What would motivate our reactions?

Burning Desire to Be Slimmer Is a Slow Suicide
Barbara Brotman

We all know smoking is bad for us. Every day new studies point to smoking as the culprit in yet another health problem. And recently, even the tobacco companies have fessed up to suppressing the grim truth for years. Yet smoking among young white women is at an all-time high and continues to grow. In the following article, Barbara Brotman looks at why young women continue to light up despite all the evidence that smoking is hazardous to their health. Her answer might surprise you.

Brotman is a columnist for the *Chicago Tribune* where this essay first appeared in July 1996.

1 From billboards and magazines, the pretty young women exude beauty and hipness. They grin insouciantly; they polish their nails turtle green. The ad copy neatly connects female cool with the product being sold:

2 "VIRGINIA SLIMS. It's a woman thing."

3   I find myself drawn to the ads, in a morbid sort of way. Sometimes I picture one of the young women with a turtle green oxygen tube in her pert nose. Other times I play mentally with the tag line:

4   "It's a chemo thing."

5   "It's a fatal thing."

6   We should be accustomed to tobacco manufacturers' using sisterhood to try to persuade us to kill ourselves. The practice has a long and sorry history, from the creation of a march in New York's 1929 Easter Parade by debutantes and feminists smoking "torches of freedom" on behalf of Lucky Strikes to the wholesale appropriation of feminism in Virginia Slims' "You've come a long way, baby" campaign.

7   The current ads are an interesting variation on the theme—feminine rather than feminist, but infused with the solidarity of girlfriends.

8   "It's very shrewd," said Carol Boyd, director of the University of Michigan Substance Abuse Research Center, who has examined tobacco marketing to women.

9   The campaign plays on "our backtalk, our talk amongst ourselves," she said, packing a potent message to teenagers about smoking.

10   "They didn't say it's a girl thing; it's a woman thing," she said. "It has to do with growing up, being independent."

11   But regardless of how canny the campaign is, and of the extent to which such marketing affects young people's images of smoking, the continuing popularity of ingesting a known carcinogen remains a mystery.

12   People start smoking voluntarily. They do so with the full knowledge, held by every sentient human in the U.S. past preschool age, that smoking kills.

13   And the demographic group volunteering most frequently for nicotine addiction is white teenage girls.

14   In a 1995 survey on high school smoking, the Centers for Disease Control and Prevention found that 40 percent of white girls had smoked in the previous month. Twenty-one percent were heavy smokers.

15   The rates among white boys and black boys were lower, but they have been increasing like those of white girls. The startling exception is black girls; only 12 percent smoked at all, and just 1 percent were heavy smokers.

16   Why is smoking a white-teenage-girl thing, but not a black-teenage-girl thing?

17   "Black girls may associate smoking with things they don't want to be associated with, an image they don't find appealing," said psychologist Robin Mermelstein, deputy director of the University of Illinois at Chicago's Prevention Research Center, who holds a federal grant to study gender and race differences in tobacco use. "They may see it as interfering with some of their hopes for success."

18   Peer under the rock of young white women's infatuation with cigarettes, and guess what crawls out? Social pressure to be thin, which afflicts white women far more than blacks, who have other ideas of what constitutes beauty.

19   "They said they smoked as a form of weight control," said Boyd, who interviewed the 30 percent of women students in her lecture class who smoked.

20   Between 1960 and 1990, deaths from lung cancer among women increased more than 400 percent. In 1987, lung cancer surpassed breast cancer as the most common form of cancer among women, and the No. 1 cancer killer of women. Be-

tween heart disease, cancer, respiratory diseases and burn deaths, smoking kills more than 142,000 women a year.

21 The ads speak the truth; smoking now is a woman thing.

22 But maybe the battle should be fought on another front. In addition to talking about disease, death and damage to unborn children, maybe we should be talking about why our girls want to be thin so badly that they are willing to risk them.

EXPLORING THE TEXT

1. Discuss how the recent Virginia Slims' ad campaign exploits girls' desires to be grown up and independent.
2. What explanation does Brotman offer for why smoking has rapidly increased among white girls, but not black girls?
3. Discuss how Brotman uses statistics and expert opinion to develop and support her argument.
4. Why do you think Brotman waits until the end of the article to reveal her main point? How does her final revelation about why white girls smoke tie back to the opening anecdote about Virginia Slims, as well as to the title?
5. Describe Brotman's tone in this piece. How does it add to or detract from the article's effectiveness? Explain your answer.

WRITING ASSIGNMENTS

1. Do you agree with Brotman's explanation for why white girls are the fastest growing smoking population? What other reasons can you think of to explain this phenomenon?
2. As Rebecca Johnson points out in the previous essay, many models smoke cigarettes as a way to keep from eating. Barbara Brotman here points out that young white females account for the fastest growing segment of cigarette smokers. Interview several female smokers about their smoking habits and see if they support or dispute the idea that the main reason females smoke is to control their weight.
3. Write a narrative about your own experience with smoking. If you've smoked, why and when did you start? If you've never smoked, why have you avoided the habit? Are you fairly accepting of smoking, or do you find it distasteful?
4. Brotman's piece first appeared as a column in the *Chicago Tribune*. Assume the role of columnist and write your own opinion piece on an issue you feel strongly about. (You may also want to pick an issue that affects young people.) Be sure to back up your opinion with examples as Brotman does.

GROUP PROJECTS

1. Brotman asserts that "people start smoking voluntarily. They do so with the full knowledge, held by every sentient human in the U.S. past preschool age, that smoking kills" (paragraph 12). In recent years, however, several wrongful death lawsuits have been brought against tobacco companies. These lawsuits claim that tobacco companies lied to the public about the addictiveness and dangers of smoking. Using the library or the Web, do some research about some of these lawsuits. Once you have gathered your information, divide your group in half and have them take opposing sides—half in support of tobacco companies, half against. Present a debate to the class on whether tobacco companies should be held responsible in smokers' deaths.

2. In small groups, gather cigarette ads from various magazines. Write up an analysis of the various ways these ads sell their products. For instance, many cigarette ads use images of nature and "clean" colors like blue and green to suggest that smoking is anything but a "filthy habit." What other patterns do you see in these ads? Present your findings to the class.

The Eye of the Beholder
Grace Suh

The notion that cosmetics enhance one's appearances is prone to exaggeration. For example, it's said that a touch of lipstick can transform plain to pretty or a blush of rouge can make the ordinary lovely. In this piece Grace Suh describes her visit to a makeup counter in search of the transformation promised by the "priestesses of beauty." But after the judicious application of ointments, blush, and gloss, the face that greeted Suh in the mirror was one she neither recognized nor liked. The adage that "beauty lies in the eye of the beholder" resonated with new meaning for her.

Suh was born in Seoul, Korea, and was reared in Wisconsin and Chicago. She lives in New York City and works in academic publishing by day and as a poetry editor of the *Asian Pacific American Journal* by night. This article originally appeared in *A. Magazine* in 1992.

1 Several summers ago, on one of those endless August evenings when the sun hangs suspended just above the horizon, I made up my mind to become beautiful.

2 It happened as I walked by one of those mirrored glass-clad office towers, and caught a glimpse of my reflection out of the corner of my eye. The glass on this particular building was green, which might have accounted for the sickly tone of my complexion, but there was no explaining away the limp, ragged hair, the dark circles

under my eyes, the facial blemishes, the shapeless, wrinkled clothes. The overall effect—the whole being greater than the sum of its parts—was one of stark ugliness.

3   I'd come home from college having renounced bourgeois suburban values, like hygiene and grooming. Now, home for the summer, I washed my hair and changed clothes only when I felt like it, and spent most of my time sitting on the lawn eating mini rice cakes and Snickers and reading dogeared back issues of *National Geographic*.

4   But that painfully epiphanous day, standing there on the hot sidewalk, I suddenly understood what my mother had been gently hinting these past months: I was no longer just plain, no longer merely unattractive. No, I had broken the Unsightliness Barrier. I was now UGLY, and aggressively so.

5   And so, in an unusual exertion of will, I resolved to fight back against the forces of entropy. I envisioned it as reclamation work, like scything down a lawn that has grown into meadow, or restoring a damaged fresco. For the first time in ages, I felt elated and hopeful. I nearly sprinted into the nearby Nieman Marcus. As I entered the cool, hushed, dimly lit first floor and saw the gleaming counters lined with vials of magical balm, the priestesses of beauty in their sacred smocks, and the glossy photographic icons of the goddesses themselves—Paulina, Linda, Cindy, Vendella—in a wild, reckless burst of inspiration I thought to myself, Heck, why just okay? Why not BEAUTIFUL?

6   At the Estée Lauder counter, I spied a polished, middle-aged woman whom I hoped might be less imperious than the aloof amazons at the Chanel counter.

7   "Could I help you?" the woman (I thought of her as "Estée") asked.

8   "Yes," I blurted. "I look terrible. I need a complete makeover—skin, face, everything."

9   After a wordless scrutiny of my face, she motioned me to sit down and began. She cleansed my skin with a bright blue mud masque and clear, tingling astringent and then applied a film of moisturizer, working extra amounts into the rough patches. Under the soft pressure of her fingers, I began to relax. From my perch, I happily took in the dizzying, colorful swirl of beautiful women and products all around me. I breathed in the billows of perfume that wafted through the air. I whispered the names of products under my breath like a healing mantra: cooling eye gel, gentle exfoliant, night time neck area reenergizer, moisture recharging intensifier, ultra-hydrating complex, emulsifying immunage. I felt immersed in femininity, intoxicated by beauty.

10   I was flooded with gratitude at the patience and determination with which Estée toiled away at my face, painting on swaths of lip gloss, blush, and foundation. She was not working in vain, I vowed, as I sucked in my cheeks on her command. I would buy all these products. I would use them every day. I studied her gleaming, polished features—her lacquered nails, the glittering mosaic of her eyeshadow, the complex red shimmer of her mouth, her flawless, dewy skin—and tried to imagine myself as impeccably groomed as she.

11   Estée's voice interrupted my reverie, telling me to blot my lips. I stuck the tissue into my mouth and clamped down, watching myself in the mirror. My skin was

a blankly even shade of pale, my cheeks and lips glaringly bright in contrast. My face had a strange plastic sheen, like a mannequin's. I grimaced as Estée applied the second lipstick coat: Was this right? Didn't I look kind of—fake? But she smiled back at me, clearly pleased with her work. I was ashamed of myself: Well, what did I expect? It wasn't like she had anything great to start with.

12   "Now," she announced, "Time for the biggie—Eyes."

13   "Oh. Well, actually, I want to look good and everything, but, I mean, I'm sure you could tell, I'm not really into a complicated beauty routine . . ." My voice faded into a faint giggle.

14   "So?" Estée snapped.

15   "Sooo . . ." I tried again, "I've never really used eye makeup, except, you know, for a little mascara sometimes, and I don't really feel comfortable————"

16   Estée was firm. "Well, the fact is that the eyes are the windows of the face. They're the focal point. An eye routine doesn't have to be complicated, but it's important to emphasize the eyes with some color, or they'll look washed out."

17   I certainly didn't want that. I leaned back again in my chair and closed my eyes.

18   Estée explained as she went: "I'm covering your lids with this champagne color. It's a real versatile base, 'cause it goes with almost any other color you put on top of it." I felt the velvety pad of the applicator sweep over my lids in a soothing rhythm.

19   "Now, being an Oriental, you don't have a lid fold, so I'm going to draw one with this charcoal shadow. Then, I fill in below the line with a lighter charcoal color with a bit of blue in it—frosted midnight—and then above it, on the outsides of your lids, I'm going to apply this plum color. There. Hold on a minute . . . Okay. Open up."

20   I stared at the face in the mirror, at my eyes. The drawn-on fold and dark, heavy shadows distorted and reproportioned my whole face. Not one of the features in the mirror was recognizable, not the waxy white skin or the redrawn crimson lips or the sharp, deep cheekbones, and especially, not the eyes. I felt negated; I had been blotted out and another face drawn in my place. I looked up at Estée, and in that moment I hated her. "I look terrible," I said.

21   Her back stiffened. "What do you mean?" she demanded.

22   "Hideous. I don't even look human. Look at my eyes. You can't even see me!" My voice was hoarse.

23   She looked. After a moment, she straightened up again, "Well, I'll admit, the eye shadow doesn't look great." She began to put away the pencils and brushes, "But at least now you have an eyelid."

24   I told myself that she was a pathetic, middle-aged woman with a boring job and a meaningless life. I had my whole life before me. All she had was the newest Richard Chamberlain miniseries.

25   But it didn't matter. The fact of the matter was that she was pretty, and I was not. Her blue eyes were recessed in an intricate pattern of folds and hollows. Mine bulged out.

26   I bought the skincare system and the foundation and the blush and the lip liner pencil and the lipstick and the primer and the eyeliner and the eyeshadows—all four

colors. The stuff filled a bag the size of a shoebox. It cost a lot. Estée handed me my receipt with a flourish, and I told her, "Thank you."

27   In the mezzanine level washroom, I set my bag down on the counter and scrubbed my face with water and slimy pink soap from the dispenser. I splashed my face with cold water until it felt tight, and dried my raw skin with brown paper towels that scratched.

28   As the sun sank into the Chicago skyline, I boarded the Burlington Northern Commuter for home and found a seat in the corner. I set the shopping bag down beside me, and heaped its gilt boxes and frosted glass bottles into my lap. Looking out the window, I saw that night had fallen. Instead of trees and backyard fences I saw my profile—the same reflection, I realized, that I'd seen hours ago in the side of the green glass office building. I did have eyelids, of course. Just not a fold. I wasn't pretty. But I was familiar and comforting. I was myself.

29   The next stop was mine. I arranged the things carefully back in the rectangular bag, large bottles of toner and moisturizer first, then the short cylinders of masque and scrub and powder, small bottles of foundation and primer, the little logs of pencils and lipstick, then the flat boxed compacts of blush and eyeshadow. The packages fit around each other cleverly, like pieces in a puzzle. The conductor called out, "Fairview Avenue," and I stood up. Hurrying down the aisle, I looked back once at the neatly packed bag on the seat behind me, and jumped out just as the doors were closing shut.

EXPLORING THE TEXT

1. Consider the appropriateness of the title of Suh's essay. Do you recognize the allusion? Can you explain its meaning? How does the title forecast the issues Suh addresses?

2. What experience made Suh decide to become "beautiful"? In this decision, what image of herself was she giving up? How does she envision becoming beautiful?

3. Why does Suh trust the middle-aged woman from the Estée Lauder counter? What goes through her imagination as she undergoes the beauty treatment?

4. Toward the end of the makeover, the beautician applies makeup to Suh's eyelids to make them appear more Caucasian. What words does the beautician use that insult Suh's sense of self and cultural identity? How does Suh respond?

5. Explain Suh's actions upon leaving the store with her makeup kit. What does Suh finally realize about herself? How is the ending a sign of her transformation?

6. How would you describe the author's voice in this essay? What does this voice reveal about the author as a person? Find a paragraph that demon-

strates the tone of her voice. How well does such a tone add to the persuasiveness of the author's argument?

7. Suh uses striking, vivid language in this essay. What particular words and phrases capture her views on her own appearance? Her views of the beautician? Did you find this language effective?

WRITING ASSIGNMENTS

1. Write a brief essay about how you feel about your looks. What changes have you made or would you make if you could? Do you feel social pressure to look any certain way?

2. Powerlessness is a universal feeling when someone takes charge of our bodies or appearance. Explore your own feelings of powerlessness when you had to undergo a physical examination, a haircut, a massage, etc. What messages about your culture, your body, or your appearance was the person in charge conveying to you? In an essay, explore this theme using Suh's techniques of description and dialogue.

3. Write an essay describing a time when you took on "another" identity by wearing very different clothes, makeup, or hair than you normally do. Perhaps you went to a costume party or a very formal affair when you had to look especially "fancy." Or perhaps you have purposefully "dressed down" to go to a bar or club. Did people treat you differently in this new guise? Did you act differently? Was the experience something you enjoyed? Why or why not?

GROUP PROJECTS

1. Arrange a time when your group can visit a makeup counter in a large department store. Takes notes about the products and displays that you see there. If possible, observe someone getting a makeover (someone in your group may even want to volunteer). Compare your experience to Suh's. Did the image of beauty that each cosmetic counter promoted seem similar? Did the salespeople themselves seem to conform to a particular ideal of beauty? Did you feel, like Suh, that many of the faces seen at the cosmetic counter have a "plastic sheen, like a mannequin's"? Report your findings to the class.

2. In her article, Barbara Brotman asserts that white women feel far more pressure to be thin than black women do, that black women "have other ideas of what constitutes beauty." In Suh's essay, her idea of beauty clearly does not match "Estée's" ideas. In small groups, explore the idea that beauty is culturally determined—that is, what one group may find beautiful, another may not. Can you find any evidence that the all-American,

blue-eyed blond image of beauty is changing? Draw on television shows, fashion magazines, and movies for evidence. Report your conclusions to the class.

The Other Body: Reflections on Difference, Disability and Identity Politics
Ynestra King

The way society looks at the disabled has changed a great deal in the last two decades, and almost always for the better. However, for Ynestra King things haven't changed quite enough. She feels that people with disabilities have been ostracized and marginalized in our society and that such prejudice reflects a general uneasiness about the life of the flesh and a fear of death. In the following piece, King writes movingly about her own experience as a disabled woman and her frustration of being seen as "other" throughout her life.
This essay first appeared in the March/April 1993 issue of *Ms.* magazine.

1   Disabled people rarely appear in popular culture. When they do, their disability must be a continuous preoccupation overshadowing all other areas of their character. Disabled people are disabled. That is what they "do." That is what they "are."

2   My own experience with a mobility impairment that is only minorly disfiguring is that one must either be a creature of the disability, or have transcended it entirely. For me, like most disabled people (and this of course depends on relative severity), neither extreme is true. It is an organic, literally embodied fact that will not change— like being a woman. While it may be possible to "do gender," one does not "do disability." But there is an organic base to both conditions that extends far into culture, and the meaning that "nature" has. Unlike being a woman, being disabled is not a socially constructed condition. It is a tragedy of nature, of a kind that will always exist. The very condition of disability provides a vantage point of a certain lived experience in the body, a lifetime of opportunity for the observation of reaction to bodily deviance, a testing ground for reactions to persons who are readily perceived as having something wrong or being different. It is fascinating, maddening, and disorienting. It defies categories of "sickness" and "health," "broken" and "whole." It is in between.

3   Meeting people has an overlay: I know what they notice first is that I am different. And there is the experience of the difference in another person's reaction who meets me sitting down (when the disability is not apparent), and standing up and walking (when the infirmity is obvious). It is especially noticeable when another individual is flirting and flattering, and has an abrupt change in affect when I stand up. I always make sure that I walk around in front of someone before I accept a date, just to save face for both of us. Once the other person perceives the disability, the

switch on the sexual circuit breaker often pops off—the connection is broken. "Chemistry" is over. I have a lifetime of such experiences, and so does every other disabled woman I know.

4   White middle-class people—especially white men—in the so-called First World have the most negative reactions. And I always recognize studied politeness, the attempt to pretend that there's nothing to notice (this is the liberal response— Oh, you're black? I hadn't noticed). Then there's the do-gooder response, where the person falls all over her/himself, insisting on doing everything for you; later they hate you; it's a form of objectification. It conveys to you that that is all they see, rather like a man who can't quit talking with a woman about sex.

5   In the era of identity politics in feminism, disability has not only been an added cross to bear, but an added "identity" to take on—with politically correct positions, presumed instant alliances, caucuses to join, and closets to come out of. For example, I was once dragged across a room to meet someone. My friend, a very politically correct lesbian feminist, said, "She's disabled, too. I thought you'd like to meet her." Rather than argue—what would I say? "I'm not interested in other disabled people," or "This is my night off"? (The truth in that moment was like the truth of this experience in every other moment, complicated and difficult to explain)—I went along to find myself standing before someone strapped in a wheelchair she propels by blowing into a tube with a respirator permanently fastened to the back of the chair. To suggest that our relative experience of disability is something we could casually compare (as other people stand by!) demonstrates the crudity of perception about the complex nature of bodily experience.

6   My infirmity is partial leg paralysis. I can walk anywhere, climb stairs, drive a car, ride a horse, swim, hang-glide, fly a plane, hike in the wilderness, go to jail for my political convictions, travel alone, and operate heavy equipment. I can earn a living, shop, cook, eat as I please, dress myself, wash and iron my own clothes, clean my house. The woman in that wheelchair can do none of these fundamental things, much less the more exotic ones. On a more basic human level I can spontaneously get my clothes off if I decide to make love. Once in bed my lover and I can forget my disability. None of this is true of the woman in the wheelchair. There is no bodily human activity that does not have to be specially negotiated, none in which she is not absolutely "different." It would take a very long time, and a highly nuanced conversation, for us to be able to share experiences as if they were common. The experience of disability for the two of us was more different than my experience is from the daily experience of people who are not considered disabled. So much for disability solidarity.

7   With disability, one is somewhere on a continuum between total bodily dysfunction—or death—and complete physical wholeness. In some way, this probably applies to every living person. So when is it that we call a person "disabled"? When do they become "other"? There are "minor" disabilities that are nonetheless significant for a person's life. Color blindness is one example. But in our culture, color blindness is considered an inconvenience rather than a disability.

8   The ostracization, marginalization, and distorted response to disability are not simply issues of prejudice and denial of civil rights. They reflect attitudes toward

bodily life, an unease in the human skin, an inability to cope with contingency, ambiguity, flux, finitude, and death.

9   Visibly disabled people (like women) in this culture are the scapegoats for resentments of the limitations of organic life. I had polio when I was seven, finishing second grade. I had excelled in everything, and rarely missed school. I had one bad conduct notation—for stomping on the boys' blocks when they wouldn't let me play with them. Although I had leg braces and crutches when I was ready to start school the next year, I wanted desperately to go back and resume as much of the same life as I could. What I was not prepared for was the response of the school system. They insisted that I was now "handicapped" and should go into what they called "special education." This was a program aimed primarily at multiply disabled children, virtually all of whom were mentally retarded as well as physically disabled. It was in a separate wing of another school, and the children were completely segregated from the "normal" children in every aspect of the school day, including lunch and recreational activities. I was fortunate enough to have educated, articulate parents and an especially aggressive mother; she went to the school board and waged a tireless campaign to allow me to come back to my old school on a trial basis—the understanding being that the school could send me to special education if things "didn't work out" in the regular classroom.

10   And so began my career as an "exceptional" disabled person, not like the *other* "others." And I was glad. I didn't want to be associated with those others either. Apart from the objective limitations caused by the polio, the transformation in identity—the difference in worldly reception—was terrifying and embarrassing, and it went far beyond the necessary considerations my limitations required.

11   My experience as "other" is much greater and more painful as a disabled person than as a woman. Maybe the most telling dimension of this knowledge is my observation of the reactions of others over the years, of how deeply afraid people are of being outside the normative appearance (which is getting narrower as capitalism exaggerates partriarchy). It is no longer enough to be thin; one must have ubiquitous muscle definition, nothing loose, flabby, or ill defined, no fuzzy boundaries. And of course, there's the importance of control. Control over aging, bodily processes, weight, fertility, muscle tone, skin quality, and movement. Disabled women, regardless of how thin, are without full bodily control.

12   I see disabled women fight these normative standards in different ways, but never get free of negotiating and renegotiating them. I did it by constructing my life around other values and, to the extent possible, developing erotic attachments to people who had similar values, and for whom my compensations were more than adequate. But at one point, after two disastrous but steamy liaisons with a champion athlete and a dancer (during which my friends pointed out the obvious unkind truth and predicted painful endings), I discovered the worlds I had tried to protect myself from: the disastrous attraction to "others" to complete oneself. I have seen disabled women endure unspeakably horrible relationships because they were so flattered to have such a conventionally attractive individual in tow.

13   And then there's the weight issue. I got fat by refusing to pay attention to my body. Now that I'm slimming down again, my old vanities and insecurities are sur-

facing. The battle of dieting can be especially fraught for disabled women. It is more difficult because exercising is more difficult, as is traveling around to get the proper foods, and then preparing them. But the underlying rage at the system that makes you feel as if you are your body (female, infirm) and that everything else is window dressing—this also undermines the requisite discipline. A tempting response is to resort to an ideal of self as bodiless essence in which the body is completely incidental, and irrelevant.

14   The wish that the body should be irrelevant has been one of my most fervent lifelong wishes. The knowledge that it isn't is my most intense lifelong experience.

15   I have seen other disabled women wear intentionally provocative clothes, like the woman in a wheelchair on my bus route to work. She can barely move. She has a pretty face, and tiny legs she could not possibly walk on. Yet she wears black lace stockings and spike high heels. The other bus occupants smile condescendingly, or pretend not to notice, or whisper in appalled disbelief that this woman could represent herself as having a sexual self. That she could "flaunt" her sexual being violates the code of acceptable appearance for a disabled woman. This woman's apparel is no more far out than that of many other women on our bus—but she refuses to fold up and be a good little asexual handicapped person.

16   The well-intentioned liberal new campaigns around "hire the handicapped" are oppressive in related ways. The Other does not only have to demonstrate her competence on insider terms; she must be better, by way of apologizing for being different and rewarding the insiders for letting her in. And the happy handicapped person, who has had faith placed in her/him, must vindicate "the race" because the politics of tokenism assumes that there are in fact other qualifications than doing the job.

17   This is especially prejudicial in a recession, where there are few social services, where it is "every man for himself." Disabled people inevitably have greater expenses, since assistance must often be paid for privately. In the U.S., public construction of the disabled body is that one either is fully disabled and dysfunctional/unemployable (and therefore eligible for public welfare) or totally on one's own. There is no in-between—the possibility of a little assistance, or exceptions in certain areas. Disabled people on public assistance cannot work or they will lose their benefits. (In the U.S. ideology that shapes public attitudes and public policy, one is either fully dependent or fully autonomous.) But the reality of human and organic life is that everyone is different in some way; there is no such thing as a totally autonomous individual. Yet the mythology of autonomy perpetuates in terrible ways the oppression of the disabled. It also perpetuates misogyny—and the destruction of the planet.

18   It may be that this clear lack of autonomy—this reminder of mortal finitude and contingency and embeddedness of nature and the body—is at the root of the hatred of the disabled. On the continuum of autonomy and dependence, disabled people need help. To need help is to feel humiliated, to have failed. I think this "help" issue must be even harder for men than women. But any disabled person is always negotiating both the provisionality of autonomy and the rigidity of physical norms.

19   From the vantage point of disability, there are some objective and desirable aspects of autonomy. But they have to do with independence. The preferred protocol

is that the attendant or friend perform the task that the disabled person needs done in the way the disabled person *asks it to be done*. Assistance from friends and family is a negotiated process, and often maddening. For that reason most disabled people prefer to live in situations where they can do all the basic functions themselves, with whatever special equipment or built-ins are required.

20   It's a dreadful business, this needing help. And it's more dreadful in the U.S. than in any place in the world, because our heroes are dynamic overcomers of adversity, and there is an inevitable cultural contempt for weakness.

21   Autonomy is on a continuum toward dependency and death. And the idea that dependency could come at any time, that one could die at any time, or be dismembered or disfigured, and still have to live (maybe even *want* to *live*) is unbearable in a context that understands and values autonomy in the way we moderns do.

22   I don't want to depict this experience of unbearability as strictly cultural. The compromising of the human body before its natural time is tragic. It forces terrible hardship on the individual to whom it occurs. But the added overlay of oppression on the disabled is intimately related to the fear of death, and the acknowledgment of our embeddedness in organic nature. We are finite, contingent, dependent creatures by our very nature; we will all eventually die. We will all experience compromises to our physical integrity. The aspiration to human wholeness is an oppressive idealism. Socially, it is deeply infantilizing.

23   It promotes a simplistic view of the human person, a static notion of human life that prevents the maturity and social wisdom that might allow human beings to more fully apprehend the human condition. It marginalizes the "different," those perceived as hopelessly wedded to organic existence—women and the disabled. The New Age "human potential movement"—in the name of maximizing human growth—is one of the worst offenders in obscuring the kind of human growth I am suggesting.

24   I too believe that the potential for human growth and creativity is infinite—but it is not groundless. The common ground for the person—the human body—is a place of shifting sand that can fail us at any time. It can change shape and properties without warning; this is an essential truth of embodied existence.

25   Of all the ways of becoming "other" in our society, disability is the only one that can happen to anyone, in an instant, transforming that person's life and identity forever.

EXPLORING THE TEXT

1. What does King say are the most common responses to her disability? What is particularly disturbing to her about these responses?
2. In paragraph 4 King says, "Then there's the do-gooder response, where the person falls all over her/himself, insisting on doing everything for you; later they hate you; it's a form of objectification." What does the word *objectification* mean? How does the process of objectification relate to hating the handicapped person according to King?

3. In paragraphs 5 and 6 King recounts an incident where a friend introduces her to a woman in a wheelchair with the words, "She's disabled, too. I thought you'd like to meet her." What does this statement reveal about her friend's view of disabilities? How does King feel about the woman in the wheelchair?

4. What does King mean when she refers to herself as "an 'exceptional' disabled person"? What is her attitude toward her own disability?

5. Why are women with disabilities so often seen as asexual according to King? How does King seem to feel about the woman on the bus who dresses provocatively? How do the non-handicapped riders see her?

6. In paragraph 17 King says, "In the U.S., public construction of the disabled body is that one either is fully disabled and dysfunctional/unemployable (and therefore eligible for public welfare) or totally on one's own." What kinds of problems does this polarized view create for people with handicaps? How does it limit their options?

7. Toward the end of the essay in paragraph 23 King says, "The New Age 'human potential movement'—in the name of maximizing human growth—is one of the worst offenders in obscuring the kind of human growth I am suggesting." What does King dislike about the New Age definition of growth? What kind of growth does she want to see?

WRITING ASSIGNMENTS

1. King claims that needing help is "more dreadful in the U.S. than in any place in the world, because our heroes are dynamic overcomers of adversity, and there is an inevitable cultural contempt for weakness" (paragraph 20). List some popular American heroes. Now list what makes these people heroic in society's eyes. Using your hero list as a starting point, write a brief essay agreeing or disagreeing with King's statement.

2. Write an essay about your experience with people with disabilities. Are you close to anyone who is considered disabled? Are you, or have you ever been, disabled? Do you tend to think of those with handicaps as "other"?

3. King suggests that what underlies most people's contempt for those with disabilities is their own fear of dependency or death. What is your greatest fear about your own body? If you were to suffer a major accident that left you paralyzed or blind, how would your life change? Do you find it unpleasant even to imagine these things? Explain.

GROUP PROJECTS

1. In the first sentence of her essay King says, "Disabled people rarely appear in popular culture." In small groups, see if you can find any examples

where they do. For instance, have any recent movies or television shows featured main characters who have handicaps? Can you think of ads that depict people with handicaps? Discuss how visibility in the media—or lack thereof—shapes society's view of the disabled. Write up your conclusions in a brief collaborative essay.

2. To at least some degree, computers have opened up new opportunities for many people who have disabilities—for example, people with mobility problems may be able to work at home by telecommuting, people whose voices have been lost due to paralysis may be able to speak by using computers that are able to generate voices, and chat rooms on the Web offer the opportunity for people with similar disabilities to discuss issues that concern them. Using either the Web or your school's library have group members do some research about how the latest computer technology is changing the way people with handicaps are living their lives. Report your findings to the class.

3. In small groups, do some research about what services your campus offers people with disabilities. For instance, does your campus have a disabilities resource center? What services are offered to blind or deaf students? What organizations offer support to disabled students? If possible, arrange an interview with someone who works at one of these organizations in order to find out details about their services. Write up a report about what you discovered.

Believers in Search of Piercing Insight

D. James Romero

You are no doubt well aware of the body piercing fad sweeping the nation, especially among young people who sport hoops in their ears and studs in their tongues. But did you know that the Victorian Prince Albert "had a genital piercing"? Or that Victorian women "pierced their nipples in acts of sensuality"? Probably not. Most people think of the phenomenon as one that is contemporary and American or as a custom practiced only by "primitive" peoples for ceremonial reasons. In the following article, D. James Romero looks at some of the Western-world history of body piercing, while commenting on what the no-holes-barred fad means to people today.

Romero is a staff writer for the *Los Angeles Times,* where this article first appeared on January 29, 1997.

1   Here we are at the end of a century of scientific and technological advances so vast they may surpass the rest of humankind's history of knowledge—and cutting-edge culture has some of us looking like tribal nomads ready to take some heads: barbells in our eyebrows. Studs in our chins. Hoops in our genitalia.

2   Many in California—this holy mecca of holes—say they pierce their bodies to fully realize their individuality. The body's landscape—for so long adorned with

T-shirts-as-billboards, and clothing-labels-as-advertisements—becomes *their* own. Piercing is a return to flesh as fashion—and a revitalized rite of passage.

3   "If someone's under 18, it's normal behavior to get pierced," asserts pop culture expert Stuart Ewen. "It's when I see 50-year-old guys at the gym with nipple rings that I start to worry."

4   Indeed, there isn't much progressive about piercing anymore. Not when your yuppie uncle has enough hoops in his body to set off airport security. And not when state lawmakers are trying to make a note from Mom mandatory for under-18 piercing.

5   So what is a fashion-wary West Coaster to do?

6   Not to worry. There are youth cults busy at work devising new ways to anger parents and subvert the mainstream's black hole.

7   The cutting edge of piercing's "modern primitive" movement can be found at Nomad Body Piercing Studio in San Francisco. The shop specializes in tribal and ancient piercings such as stretched-out lip holes (piercing the lower lip and stretching the hole), large septum jewelry and low-hanging earlobes.

8   The term "modern primitive" was coined by Fakir Musafar, a '70s pioneer of body modification who now publishes Body Play magazine. The phenomenon took off in 1989 with the publication of "Modern Primitives" (Re/Search), a book that featured photos of ancient and modern body art.

9   "It's a rejection of the modern aesthetic," says Nomad owner Kristian White. "Your body is yours. It's the one thing you have to express yourself with."

10   Extreme piercing can be found in underground pagan and gothic cults, too—sets that hang at L.A. nightclubs such as Sin-a-matic, Stigmata and Coven 13. Reports also abound of underground parties where piercing is performed and rites of pain are demonstrated as performance art.

11   Sexual piercings are the rage in L.A. body art, from the male Prince Albert (apparently, the old chap had a genital piercing—in Victorian times, no less) to the unisex nipple ring. Body Modification E-Zine, an online magazine, surveyed readers and found that half had their nipples pierced.

12   "It's a freaky subculture of people," says West Hollywood piercer Jennifer "Jeff" Middleton, who has square chrome hair, several piercings in her ears and one in her nose.

13   Earlier in the day, she was putting on latex gloves and preparing sterile instruments in a bright, clean second-floor room at the Gauntlet in West Hollywood. Customer Brian Lee had hoops in both ears and a tattoo on his back, so he felt the need to distinguish himself—with a pierced brow. "You want to show off what you're about," he said.

14   It took only about five minutes for Middleton to clean Lee's right eyebrow, mark it, pinch it with forceps and poke an ultra-sharp, inch-long needle through his skin: $30 please. Lee didn't flinch. Middleton explained the eight weeks of tedious healing and cleaning, but Lee just looked in the mirror and smiled when he saw the "barbell" protruding from his head.

15   "It does get trendy," said Lee, a 22-year-old club deejay. "But there will always be a new body part to be pierced."

16   Culture watchers say there is something deeper going on here. The Nomad studio's White says organized religion has relinquished its grip on the minds and bodies of youth so that they may go back to pre-Christian rituals. And professor Ewen, chair of media studies at Hunter College in New York, says it is indeed a rejection of the neat, sleek, modern fashion aesthetic.

17   "This was a culture that was sold on the idea of progress since the turn of the century—clean lines, industrial aesthetic, mass-produced clothes," he says. "There's a sense of meaninglessness in this, so there's a search for meaning—a belief that other ways of life might have more authenticity than ours."

18   It is said that Roman warriors pierced body parts to show how tough they were, while Victorian women, otherwise notoriously chaste, pierced their nipples in acts of sensuality. Body modification has also been a staple of non-Western cultures for thousands of years.

19   But today, as teens and twenty-somethings try to stand out, they face the paradox of modern subculture: More people want it, more people want to make money off it, and rebellion becomes a uniform instead of a torch of individuality.

20   "Body art was an embrace against the packaged self," Ewen says. "Yet any attempt to marginalize one's self provides new grist for the style industries.

21   "The only way to battle it is to find an ideal and stick with it. At that point, you kill off the consumption process. My only solution is to buy five pairs of pants and five sweaters and never wear anything else."

22   Now that's a radical concept.

EXPLORING THE TEXT

1. According to Romero, why do most people get piercings? What evidence does Romero offer to support the idea that piercing has become mainstream?
2. What does the term *modern primitive* mean? Why is the name Nomad particularly appropriate for this "piercing studio"?
3. What explanation does Professor Ewen give for the popularity of piercing? Do you agree or disagree with his explanation?
4. Do you find any details about the history of piercing surprising?
5. How has piercing become a "uniform instead of a torch of individuality"? What is paradoxical about this?

WRITING ASSIGNMENTS

1. Write a brief essay describing how you feel about the subject of piercing. Do you have piercings? If so, why did you have these piercings done? Do you feel piercing is "body art"?
2. Romero points out that "there are youth cults busy at work devising new ways to anger parents and subvert the mainstream's black hole" (paragraph 6). Discuss how every generation searches for a way to rebel, for a way to

    distinguish itself from older generations. What other trends besides piercing do you currently see among young people that are an attempt to do this?

3. Discuss the difficulty of being original in a media-saturated culture such as ours. Do you feel that you know anyone who is "truly unique"? If you do, what qualities make him or her so?

GROUP PROJECTS

1. Have your group conduct some interviews with people who have multiple piercings. (If you don't know anyone personally, go to the student union and look for likely candidates.) Ask people why they chose to undergo piercing and see if you can find any similarities in their responses. Write up a profile of a "typical" piercer and present it to the class.
2. Romero mentions that *Body Modification E-Zine* is an on-line magazine. Have your group look for this magazine, as well as any other magazines or Web sites about piercing. What is your opinion of these magazines? Who seems to be their audience? Do the magazines seem fairly mainstream or do they target an "underground" minority? Write up your findings and present them to the class.

2

Advertising: Feeding Our Fantasies

Advertising is everywhere—television, newspapers, magazines, the Internet, the side of buses, highway billboards; it's printed on T-shirts, hot dogs, postage stamps, and even license plates. It is the driving force of our consumptive economy, accounting for $150 billion worth of commercials and print ads each year (more than the gross national product of many countries in the world) and comprising a quarter of each television hour and the bulk of most newspapers and magazines. It's everywhere people are, and its appeal goes right to the quick of our fantasies: happiness, material wealth, eternal youth, social acceptance, sexual fulfillment, and power. And it does so in carefully selected images and words. It is the most pervasive form of persuasion in America and, perhaps, the single most significant manufacturer of meaning in our consumer society.

And, yet, most of us are so accustomed to advertising that we hear it without listening and see it without looking. But if we stopped to examine how it works, we might be amazed at just how powerful and complex a psychological force it is. This chapter will examine how a simple page in a magazine or a 15-second television spot feeds our fantasies and fears with the sole intention of separating us from our money.

This chapter opens with the double messages we get everyday from our consumer culture: Go spend your money on what you want, and save a buck for when you really need it. As Barbara Ehrenreich explains in "Spend and Save," the first message, the "permissive" one, is the inescapable by-product of advertising. The second, "puritanical" message arises from the core American values of working hard and deferring gratification. What bothers Ehrenreich is not the economic paradox in such messages but their psychological consequences on the consumer.

Underlying Ehrenreich's argument is the idea that advertising has a dumbing-down effect on us, targeting our "childlike, self-centered" impulses to buy, buy, buy. In "But First, a Word from Our Sponsor," James B. Twitchell picks up from that point, saying that our daily life is so saturated with commercial messages that we live in a dumbed-down culture he calls "Adcult." But, as he explains, the fault lies not in the corporate conglomerates that run American media, but in ourselves. If we don't like all the ads, if we see through the hype, then we shouldn't buy into the illusions the ad-makers project at us.

The next piece, "Hey Kids, Buy This!" confirms what parents have long suspected—that Madison Avenue is home of the Antichrist. It used to be that advertisers would try to reach mothers by pitching their toys and cereals to children on Saturday mornings. But as David Leonhardt and Kathleen Kerwin explain, that's all changed. Mom's out of the picture because kids today have more money than their parents did when they were young. And knowing that, advertisers have declared an all-out market assault on today's kids, surrounding them with logos, labels, and ads literally from the day they're born. As the authors point out, what's most depressing is that our market-driven culture teaches kids that the only things of value are those with sales pitches attached "and that self-worth is something you buy at a shopping mall."

One of the most visible and lucrative products in the fashion industry is fragrance. Open any of the trendy magazines and you'll find many pages devoted to perfumes, colognes, and aftershave lotions. Because these products are odors and most print ads don't come with scent strips, creating a winning ad or television commercial is particularly challenging. For as Mary Tannen observes in the next essay, manufacturers must instill in images "the mostly inarticulate desires of fragrance buyers." Of course, such desires are as trendy as colognes. In "Mr. Clean," Tannen takes a look at the most recent trend in men's fragrances—a trend that tries to reflect the fantasy of what the millennial man yearns to be and who the millennial woman yearns to be with.

Speaking of trends, one of the latest is cigar smoking. In spite of all the health scares, cigars have become a national craze—with both men *and* women. There are big, splashy cigar magazines with male and female celebrities on the cover. Cigar bars are cropping up in many big cities. And fancy hotels play host to cigar "smokers" where well-heeled patrons pay hefty prices to eat and drink well and smoke exotic leaves. Curious about the trend, humorist Paula Poundstone investigated the phenomenon for herself. In "Choking on Hype," Poundstone reports on some of the realities she finds behind all the smoke.

According to *Harper's Magazine,* the average American child will have seen over two million commercials by the time he or she is 16 years old. Whether or not that figure applies to you, you've no doubt seen some ads that you just could not stand—ads that were somehow offensive or downright obnoxious. In "Snuggle Bear Must Die!" Pulitzer Prize–winning humor columnist Dave Barry takes a very funny look at some familiar commercials that have turned people off—commercials that are annoying, condescending, and just plain stupid. Commercials that are probably painfully familiar to you.

Finally, our paired oppositions go head-to-head on the persuasive appeal of advertising language. By its nature the language of advertising is a very special language—one that combines words cleverly and methodically to get us to spend our money. On that point the authors of the next two essays agree. But beyond that, their views diverge widely. In the first piece, "With These Words I Can Sell You Anything," language-watcher William Lutz argues that advertisers tyrannically twist simple English words so that they appear to promise just what the consumer wants to hear. Taking a defensive posture in "The Language of Advertising," Charles A. O'Neill, a professional advertiser, admits that the language of ads can be very appealing. With reference to some recent ads, he nonetheless makes a persuasive argument that no ad can force consumers to lay down their money.

We end this chapter with ten recently published magazine ads, each followed by a set of questions to help you analyze how ads work their appeal on us. It is hoped that by inviting you to apply a critical eye, some of the power of advertising might be unraveled and dispelled.

Spend and Save

Barbara Ehrenreich

We live in a society where consumption is a way of life. We live in a country where a shopping mall sits within driving distance from most Americans. Visit one any Saturday and you'll see people like you and me trying to find happiness in a seemingly endless search. Paradoxically, as the material choices increase, so does the acceleration of our rat-race efforts toward impossible fulfillment. In the essay below, Barbara Ehrenreich examines a different kind of consumer choice paradox. Everyday, she says, we are bombarded with two contradictory sets of messages—one that says "Go for it!" and the other that says "Don't!"

Ehrenreich is a widely respected author who writes witty analyses of social and feminist issues. She has worked as a contributing editor at *Ms.* magazine and also writes a column for *Time.* Her essays have appeared in such magazines as *Mother Jones, Nation,* and the *New York Times Sunday Magazine.* Ehrenreich is the author of *Fear of Falling: The Inner Life of the Middle Class* (1989), *The Worst Years of Our Lives: Irreverent Notes from a Decade of Greed* (1990), and *Kipper's Game* (1994), her first novel. Her most recent book is *Blood Rites* (1997), an investigation into the origins of war. This article is an excerpt from an address she gave at the 1993 Family Therapy Networker Symposium.

1   A week or so ago, a billboard appeared a few blocks from my home. It shows a giant dollar bill, so I thought it was going to be something about "buying American," but when I got close enough to see the writing, it said, "Buck the recession, spend a buck." On what? It didn't say. Just get out there and buy. I found this deeply confusing. Wasn't our problem—only 10 minutes ago, historically speaking—that we didn't save enough? (It certainly is *my* problem!) What are we supposed to do? Spend? Save? Spend *and* save?

2   Here's another example that may be familiar to many of you: If I don't pay my credit card bill on time, I get one of those really cold, nasty messages from American Express, or whoever, saying, "You miserable wretch, pay up or die." As soon as I send in the check, another letter comes back saying, in fawning tones, "Ms. Eisenreich, you are one of our most valued customers. How would you like us to increase your credit limit by $2,000?" Well, which am I: value customer or miserable wretch?

3   The paradox is that we get two sets of messages coming at us every day. One is the "permissive" message, saying, "Buy, spend, get it now, indulge yourself," because your wants are also your needs—and you have plenty of needs that you don't even know about because our consumer culture hasn't told you about them yet! The other we could call, for lack of a better word, a "puritanical" message, which says, "Work hard, save, defer gratification, curb your impulses." What are the psychological and social consequences of getting such totally contradictory messages all the time? I think this is what you would call "cognitive dissonance," and the psychological consequence is a pervasive anxiety, upon which the political right has been very adept at mobilizing and building.

4   The puritanical message comes to us from a variety of sources: from school, from church, often from parents, and every so often from political figures when they refer to "traditional values." Hard work, family loyalty, the capacity to defer gratification—these are supposed to be core, American values, the traits that made our country great and so forth.

5   But the permissive message, as I said, comes to us chiefly in the form of advertising, which is a force to which family therapists should perhaps devote more attention. Advertising is inescapable; it is fed to us in dozens of forms and in more and more settings:

- on TV, in movie theaters, in movies themselves (*Die Hard 2* contained 19 paid ads for products featured in it; *Pretty Woman* was, in a way, one long discourse on the joys of shopping);
- in the print media (including in the "advertorials," or ads disguised as articles, which are so common in the fashion magazines);
- over the phone; and there is advertising now even in the schools (through Channel One, which brings kids 12 minutes of news plus two minutes of commercials for, for example, Burger King—during school time).

6   Someone has calculated that by the time an American reaches the age of 40, he or she has been exposed to one million ads. Another estimate is that we have encountered more than 600,000 ads by the time we reach the age of only 18. Now, of course, we don't remember what exactly they said or even what the product was, but the underlying message gets through: That you deserve the best, that you should have it now, and that it's *alright* to indulge yourself—now—because this is a Michelob moment, or because you *prefer* those silky Hanes pantyhose, or because you *deserve* the greater control, sex appeal, or adventure you are going to get from a BMW or Flex shampoo or Merit cigarettes.

7   One of the best—in fact one of the only—books dealing with this paradox was written by Daniel Bell, who pointed out, in 1979, that our consumer-based economy makes two absolutely contradictory psychological demands on its members. On the one hand, you need the "puritanical" values to ensure that people will be good workers and lead orderly, law-abiding lives. On the other hand, you need the "permissive" messages to get people to be good consumers. Bell was disturbed about the permissive side, but acknowledged that "without the hedonism stimulated by mass consumption, the very structure of [our] business enterprises would collapse."

8   The interesting question, which Bell did not explore, has to do with the psychological consequences of the double message we are taking in all the time. In old-fashioned, Freudian terms, the puritanical, or "traditional values," theme is addressed to the superego and demands a personality with a strong enough superego to keep the individual doing unpleasant work at inadequate wages, or to stay in an unhappy marriage, and, in general, to play by the rules.

9   The permissive message, on the other hand, is addressed to the id and tends to endorse a very different kind of personality—one that is childlike, self-centered, impulsive, has a short attention span and is unwilling to defer gratification because

even the most transient desires are experienced as genuine needs. As an illustration, I can't resist citing one of my favorite ads of all time, a 1975 ad from the magazine *Psychology Today.* The caption says, in boldface, "I love me. I'm just a good friend to myself. And I like to do what makes me feel good. Me, myself and I used to sit around, putting things off till tomorrow. Tomorrow we'll buy new ski equipment, and look at new compact cars, and pick up that new camera . . . [But now] I live my dreams today, not tomorrow."

10   So what happens to us as we take in these contradictory messages, as we are, in fact, torn between the contradictory personality types that our society seems to require of us? As I argued in my book, *Fear of Falling,* the result is anxiety, fear, a nameless dread. We want more things, we want to indulge ourselves, and not just because advertising tells us to—who wouldn't want that scuba equipment?

11   But at the same time, a little voice inside us echoes all those puritanical messages and says, "Watch out, don't get sucked in, you'll get into debt—worse still, you'll lose your edge, you'll get soft, you won't be able to make it anymore."

12   In the 1980s, this anxiety was often expressed in Cold War terms. The fear was that we Americans were being softened—that was the word they used—by our affluence and consumer culture, while the Russians, who didn't have TVs or toaster ovens, were supposedly still tough and hard and smart. Johnny couldn't read, but—as another book title from the '50s informed us—Ivan could.

13   But even without Cold War propaganda to reinforce it, the fear of being sucked in and dragged down by the consumer culture is real: American Express is not friendly when you can't pay your bills. And we all know that the path of self-indulgence and consumerism leads pretty quickly to financial ruin—for most of us, anyway—and that, in American society, there isn't much of a safety net to catch you if you fall.

EXPLORING THE TEXT

1. How does Ehrenreich define "cognitive dissonance" (paragraph 3)? How do the two examples that she begins the essay with illustrate this concept? Do you find her examples effective? Why or why not?

2. Ehrenreich claims that "the underlying message" of advertising is "that you deserve the best, that you should have it now, and that it's *all right* to indulge yourself . . . " (paragraph 6). Do you agree that this concept underlies all advertisements? Consider the products Ehrenreich uses as examples in this paragraph. What other goods and services might not sell with the indulge-yourself message? (You may consider some of the ads reproduced at the end of this chapter.) To what other values and beliefs do advertisers typically appeal?

3. Ehrenreich uses several kinds of evidence to support her claims, including anecdotal evidence (examples from her own experience), statistics, and quotes from author Daniel Bell. How does each type of evidence advance her argument? Is any one type more effective than another?

4. Explain the Freudian terms *id* and *superego* that Ehrenreich refers to in paragraphs 8 and 9. How do these concepts relate to her argument?
5. Look at paragraph 9 where Ehrenreich quotes an ad from *Psychology Today*. Why do you think she calls it one of her "favorite ads"? What does this tell you about Ehrenreich's sensibilities?
6. Do you find Ehrenreich's argument about the consequences of these conflicting messages persuasive? Why or why not? Do you agree with her assertion that consumers feel "anxiety, fear, a nameless dread" when faced with paradoxical save/spend messages? From what, according to her, do these feelings arise?
7. Summarize paragraph 12. How does she link Cold War fears to her earlier point about puritanical messages versus permissive messages? Do you find this connection persuasive? Why or why not?

WRITING ASSIGNMENTS

1. Discuss what role credit cards play in the tug of war between spending and saving—for instance, does having access to a credit card change the way you or your friends spend? Have you been solicited with numerous credit card offers? Why might college students be a particularly good target for credit companies?
2. Make a list of ads for low-fat or fat-free products and discuss how they embody puritanical and permissive messages simultaneously. Think of any other current ads that seem to embody both appeals at the same time and list several.
3. Write a brief narrative about a time when you experienced a spending versus saving dilemma. How did you resolve the conflict?

GROUP PROJECTS

1. Working in small groups, see what conclusions you can draw about how your generation's spending and saving habits compare to those of older generations. As a group, develop a short questionnaire (eight to ten questions) that measures people's attitudes about money. Have half the group give the questionnaire to friends and classmates between the ages of 16 and 25. Have the other half give their questionnaires to one or both of their parents. Discuss your findings, then write up a short essay about what your research revealed.
2. Discuss Ehrenreich's idea of permissive versus puritanical messages in other aspects of our society. For instance, "do it" messages about sex, drinking, and cheating can often be found in television shows, movies, and pop and rap music, while schools, government agencies, and religious organizations counter with a "don't do it" message. As a group, brainstorm

some examples of these contradictory messages. Discuss why these battling messages may be particularly confusing for children.

But First, a Word from Our Sponsor
James B. Twitchell

Do you sometimes find yourself paying more attention to the commercials between television programs than to the programs themselves? Do you sometimes feel that there's not a space left in America that isn't being used to sell us something? Most of us do, and James B. Twitchell has a name for this buy-crazy environment: Adcult. Twitchell believes that advertising is inescapable and works to shape our desires and beliefs everywhere we turn. But he does suggest a way to get back at advertisers—especially those who create misleading images for products that are no different from all the competition.

Twitchell is an Alumni Professor of English at the University of Florida and is the author of several books including *Carnival Culture: The Trashing of Taste in America* (1992) and *Adcult USA: The Triumph of Advertising in America* (1996). This article first appeared in the *Wilson Quarterly* in the Summer 1996 issue.

1   Whenever a member of my paunchy fiftysomething set pulls me aside and complains of the dumbing down of American culture, I tell him that if he doesn't like it, he should quit moaning and go buy a lot of Fast-Moving Consumer Goods. And every time he buys soap, toothpaste, beer, gasoline, bread, aspirin, and the like, he should make it a point to buy a different brand. He should implore his friends to do likewise. At the same time, he should quit giving so much money to his kids. That, I'm sorry to say, is his only hope.

2   Here's why. The culture we live in is carried on the back of advertising. Now I mean that literally. If you cannot find commercial support for what you have to say, it will not be transported. Much of what we share, and what we know, and even what we treasure, is carried to us each second in a plasma of electrons, pixels, and ink, underwritten by multinational advertising agencies dedicated to attracting our attention for entirely nonaltruistic reasons. These agencies, gathered up inside worldwide conglomerates with weird, sci-fi names like WPP, Omnicom, Saatchi & Saatchi, Dentsu, and Euro RSCG, are usually collections of established shops linked together to provide "full service" to their global clients. Their service is not moving information or creating entertainment, but buying space and inserting advertising. They essentially rent our concentration to other companies—sponsors—for the dubious purpose of informing us of something that we've longed for all our lives even though we've never heard of it before. Modern selling is not about trading information, as it was in the 19th century, as much as about creating an infotainment culture

with sufficient allure to enable other messages—commercials—to get through. In the spirit of the enterprise, I call this new culture Adcult.

3   Adcult is there when we blink, it's there when we listen, it's there when we touch, it's even there to be smelled in scent strips when we open a magazine. There is barely a space in our culture not already carrying commercial messages. Look anywhere: in schools there is Channel One; in movies there is product placement; ads are in urinals, played on telephone hold, in alphanumeric displays in taxis, sent unannounced to fax machines, inside catalogs, on the video in front of the Stairmaster at the gym, on T-shirts, at the doctor's office, on grocery carts, on parking meters, on tees at golf holes, on inner-city basketball backboards, piped in along with Muzak . . . ad nauseam (and yes, even on airline vomit bags). We have to shake magazines like rag dolls to free up their pages from the "blow-in" inserts and then wrestle out the stapled- or glued-in ones before reading can begin. We now have to fast-forward through some five minutes of advertising that opens rental videotapes. President Bill Clinton's inaugural parade featured a Budweiser float. At the Smithsonian, the Orkin Pest Control Company sponsored an exhibit on exactly what it advertises it kills: insects. No venue is safe. Is there a blockbuster museum show not decorated with corporate logos? The Public Broadcasting Service is littered with "underwriting announcements" that look and sound almost exactly like what PBS claims they are not: commercials.

4   Okay, you get the point. Commercial speech is so powerful that it drowns out all other sounds. But sounds are always conveyed in a medium. The media of modern culture are these: print, sound, pictures, or some combination of each. Invariably, conversations about dumbing down focus on the supposed corruption of these media, as demonstrated by the sophomoric quality of most movies, the fall from the golden age of television, the mindlessness of most best-sellers, and the tarting-up of the news, be it in or on *USA Today, Time,* ABC, or *Inside Edition.* The media make especially convenient whipping boys because they are now all conglomerated into huge worldwide organizations such as Time Warner, General Electric, Viacom, Bertelsmann, and Sony. But, alas, as much fun as it is to blame the media, they have very little to do with the explanation for whatever dumbing down has occurred.

5   The explanation is, I think, more fundamental, more economic in nature. These media are delivered for a price. We have to pay for them, either by spending money or by spending time. Given a choice, we prefer to spend time. We spend our time paying attention to ads, and in exchange we are given infotainment. This trade is central to Adcult. Economists call this "cost externalization." If you want to see it at work, go to McDonald's. You order. You carry your food to the table. You clean up. You pay less. Want to see it elsewhere? Buy gas. Just as the "work" you do at the self-service gas station lowers the price of gas, so consuming ads is the "work" you do that lowers the price of delivering the infotainment. In Adcult, the trade is more complex. True, you are entertained at lower cost, but you are also encultured in the process.

6   So far, so good. The quid pro quo of modern infotainment culture is that if you want it, you'll get it—no matter what it is—as long as there are enough of you who (1) are willing to spend some energy along the way hearing "a word from our spon-

sor" and (2) have sufficient disposable income possibly to buy some of the advertised goods. In Adcult you pay twice: once with the ad and once with the product. So let's look back a step to examine these products because—strange is it may seem—they are at the center of the dumbing down of American culture.

7   Before all else, we must realize that modern advertising is tied primarily to things, and only secondarily to services. Manufacturing both things *and* their meanings is what American culture is all about. If Greece gave the world philosophy, Britain drama, Austria music, Germany politics, and Italy art, then America gave mass-produced objects. "We bring good things to life" is no offhand claim. Most of these "good things" are machine made and hence interchangeable. Such objects, called parity items, constitute most of the stuff that surrounds us, from bottled water to toothpaste to beer to cars. There is really no great difference between Evian and Mountain Spring, Colgate and Crest, Miller and Budweiser, Ford and Chevrolet. Often, the only difference is in the advertising. Advertising is how we talk about these fungible things, how we know their supposed differences, how we recognize them. We don't consume the products as much as we consume the advertising.

8   For some reason, we like it this way. Logically, we should all read *Consumer Reports* and then all buy the most sensible product. But we don't. So why do we waste our energy (and billions of dollars) entertaining fraudulent choice? I don't know. Perhaps just as we drink the advertising, not the beer, we prefer the illusion of choice to the reality of decision. How else to explain the appearance of so much superfluous choice? A decade ago, grocery stores carried about 9,000 items; they now stock about 24,000. Revlon makes 158 shades of lipstick. Crest toothpaste comes in 36 sizes and shapes and flavors. We are even eager to be offered choice where there is none to speak of. AT&T offers "the right choice"; Wendy's asserts that "there is no better choice"; Pepsi is "the choice of a new generation"; Taster's Choice is "the choice for taste." Even advertisers don't understand the phenomenon. Is there a relationship between the number of soft drinks and television channels—about 27? What's going to happen when the information pipe carries 500?

9   I have no idea. But I do know this: human beings like things. We buy things. We like to exchange things. We steal things. We donate things. We live through things. We call these things "goods," as in "goods and services." We do not call them "bads." This sounds simplistic, but it is crucial to understanding the power of Adcult. The still-going-strong Industrial Revolution produces more and more things, not because production is what machines do, and not because nasty capitalists twist their handlebar mustaches and mutter, "More slop for the pigs," but because we are powerfully attracted to the world of things. Advertising, when it's lucky, supercharges some of this attraction.

10   This attraction to the inanimate happens all over the world. Berlin Walls fall because people want things, and they want the culture created by things. China opens its doors not so much because it wants to get out, but because it wants to get things in. We were not suddenly transformed from customers to consumers by wily manufacturers eager to unload a surplus of products. We have created a surfeit of things because we enjoy the process of "getting and spending." The consumption ethic

may have started in the early 1900s, but the desire is ancient. Kings and princes once thought they could solve problems by amassing things. We now join them.

11   The Marxist balderdash of cloistered academics aside, human beings did not suddenly become materialistic. We have always been desirous of things. We have just not had many of them until quite recently, and, in a few generations, we may return to having fewer and fewer. Still, while they last, we enjoy shopping for things and see both the humor and the truth reflected in the aphoristic "born to shop," "shop 'til you drop," and "when the going gets tough, the tough go shopping." Department store windows, whether on the city street or inside a mall, did not appear by magic. We enjoy looking through them to another world. It is voyeurism for capitalists. Our love of things is the *cause* of the Industrial Revolution, not the consequence. We are not only *homo sapiens,* or *homo ludens,* or *homo faber,* but also *homo emptor. . . .*

12   We need not be reminded of what is currently happening to television to realize the direction of the future. MTV, the infomercial, and the home-shopping channels are not flukes but the predictable continuation of this medium. Thanks to the remote-control wand and the coaxial (soon to be fiberoptic) cable, commercials will disappear. They will become the programming. Remember, the first rule of Adcult is this: given the choice between paying money or paying attention, we prefer to pay attention.

13   What all this means is that if you think things are bad now, just wait. There are few gatekeepers left. Most of them reside on Madison Avenue. Just as the carnival barker doesn't care what is behind the tent flap, only how long the line is in front, the poobahs of Adcult care only about who's looking, not what they are looking at. The best-seller lists, the box office, the Nielsens, the various circulation figures for newspapers and magazines, are the meters. They decide what gets through. Little wonder that so much of our popular culture is derivative of itself, that prequels and sequels and spin-offs are the order of the day, that celebrity is central, and that innovation is the cross to the vampire. Adcult is recombinant culture. This is how it has to be if advertisers are to be able to direct their spiels at the appropriate audiences for their products. It's simply too expensive to be any other way.

14   Will Adcult continue? Will there by some new culture to "afflict the comfortable and comfort the afflicted"? Will advertising, in its own terms, lose *it*? Who knows? Certainly, signs of stress are showing. Here are a few: (1) The kids are passing through "prime-branding time" like a rabbit in the python, and as they get older things may settle down. The supposedly ad-proof Generation X may be impossible to reach and advertisers will turn to older audiences by default. (2) The media are so clogged and cluttered that companies may move to other promotional highways, such as direct mail, point-of-purchase displays, and couponing, leaving the traditional avenues targeted at us older folks. (3) Branding, the heart of advertising, may become problematic if generics or store brands become as popular in this country as they have in Europe. After all, the much-vaunted brand extension whereby Coke becomes Diet Coke which becomes Diet Cherry Coke does not always work, as Kodak Floppy Disks, Milky Way Ice Cream, Arm & Hammer antiperspirant, Life Saver Gum, and even EuroDisney have all shown. And (4)—the unthinkable—mass con-

sumption may become too expensive. Advertising can flourish only in times of surplus, and no one can guarantee that our society will always have more than it needs.

15   But by no means am I predicting Adcult's imminent demise. As long as goods
are interchangeable and in surplus quantities, as long as producers are willing to pay
for short-term advantages (especially for new products), and as long as consumers
have plenty of disposable time and money so that they can consume both the ad and
the product, Adcult will remain the dominant meaning-making system of modern
life. I don't think you can roll this tape backwards. Adcult is the application of capitalism to culture: dollars voting. And so I say to my melancholy friends who bemoan the passing of a culture once concerned with the arts and the humanities that
the only way they can change this situation is if they buy more Fast-Moving Consumer Goods, change brands capriciously, and cut the kids' allowances. Good luck.

EXPLORING THE TEXT

1. Twitchell begins his essay with an example about his colleagues complaining about "the dumbing down of America." What does he seem to mean by
   this phrase?
2. How does Twitchell define Adcult? Where are some of the places he says
   Adcult can be found?
3. What does Twitchell point to as the usual causes of the "dumbing down of
   America"? What does Twitchell blame as the main culprit for this phenomenon?
4. What does Twitchell mean when he says, "We don't consume the products
   as much as we consume the advertising"? List several examples of where
   you see this in your own life.
5. Summarize Twitchell's argument about how choice (or the appearance of
   choice) plays a role in consumer behavior.
6. What kinds of evidence does Twitchell offer to support his idea that the human desire for things is not a new phenomenon? Do you find his evidence
   persuasive? Explain your answer.
7. What ideas from the essay does the title help to underscore?
8. Summarize what Twitchell believes the future of Adcult will be (closing
   paragraphs).

WRITING ASSIGNMENTS

1. Twitchell argues that "manufacturing both things *and* their meanings is
   what American culture is all about." Discuss how American culture creates
   meaning for products by choosing a well-known (and well-advertised)
   product and writing an analysis of its image. For instance, what does Mc-
   Donald's *mean*? What values are associated with the name? How does advertising help create, and then reinforce, McDonald's image?

2. Do you agree with Twitchell that "there is really no great difference between Evian and Mountain Spring, Colgate and Crest, Miller and Budweiser, Ford and Chevrolet" and that often the only difference between products is "in the advertising"? Write a narrative about the way your family chooses products. Is your family loyal to certain brand-name products? Which ones?

3. Twitchell argues that the number of choices in products offered to consumers has gotten out of hand. Pick a product—soft drinks, tennis shoes, or pain relievers, for instance—and brainstorm as many kinds or brands of the product as you can. What are the drawbacks, or benefits, of having so much choice?

4. Write an essay discussing how you deal with advertising "bombardment." For instance, do you make it a habit of flipping the channel when ads come on during your favorite television program? Do you tend to look at ads in magazines or quickly page by them? Are there any ads that you do find entertaining or engaging? What about these ads appeals to you?

5. In paragraph 12 Twitchell says: "MTV, the infomercial, and the home-shopping channels are not flukes but the predictable continuation of this medium . . . commercials will disappear. They will become the programming." Expand on Twitchell's idea using MTV, infomercials, or home shopping channels as your examples. Watch one of these channels or programs for an hour or two. Describe their effect on you. Did you find yourself entertained? Did you think about buying things as you watched? Are you as disturbed by the blurring between advertising and entertainment as Twitchell seems to be? Why or why not?

GROUP PROJECTS

1. As a group, use question 3 under "Writing Assignments" to help you create a debate for the class. Have half the group members take the pro side—arguing that so much choice among products is a positive thing—and have the other half take the con side—arguing that so much choice is not beneficial and may even be destructive. (Before presenting you debate to the class, be sure that each side has thought through their arguments and has support for their position.) After the debate, ask the class to vote on which side was more effective.

2. Twitchell argues that advertising has invaded every aspect of our lives and can even be found in such unexpected places as schools and churches. Do some research to see if you can find additional support for Twitchell's theory. Have group members take notes on ads they find in various public places—university classrooms or dormitory lobbies, public transportation, libraries, parks, town commons, sports stadiums, restaurants, etc. What kinds of things are being advertised? What correlation can you find between the ad and the place it appears? Did you find any ads particularly

surprising? (For instance, you don't expect to find ads for alcohol in a university dorm.) Present your findings to the class.

3. Twitchell presents the idea that Americans or American culture is becoming "dumber" without offering some examples to support this claim. Your job is to challenge Twitchell's assertion. Do some research (use the library as well as the Internet) focusing on the current state of education, which often is pointed to as "proof" that American students are less prepared than they were in the past. Think about how statistics on things like declining test scores may not present the whole picture. Also, look for examples of ways in which current students may actually be better prepared for college or the work world than their parents or grandparents. When your research is complete, compose an essay as a group that offers strong evidence to refute Twitchell's claim.

Hey Kids, Buy This!
David Leonhardt and Kathleen Kerwin

There was a time when the only ads aimed at children were slotted between Saturday morning cartoons. But that's all changed, as marketers have discovered this eager and impressionable segment of the population, turning kids into consumers of brand-name products nearly from birth. Children today have more money to spend than previous generations of children and, thus, are very attractive targets for various advertising pitches. As a result, there is an increasing pressure among children to wear, eat, and play with the right brand-name "stuff" in order to win peer approval. Has Madison Avenue gone too far? ask the authors.

David Leonhardt and Kathleen Kerwin are staff writers for *Business Week,* where this article served as the cover story for the June 30, 1997, issue.

1   At 1:58 p.m. on Wednesday, May 5, in Houston's St. Luke's Episcopal Hospital, a consumer was born. Her name was Alyssa J. Nedell, and by the time she went home three days later, some of America's biggest marketers were pursuing her with samples, coupons, and assorted freebies. Procter & Gamble hoped its Pampers brand would win the battle for Alyssa's bottom. Johnson & Johnson offered up a tiny sample of its baby soap. Bristol-Myers Squibb Co. sent along some of its Enfamil baby formula.

2   Like no generation before, Alyssa's enters a consumer culture, surrounded by logos, labels, and ads almost from the moment of birth. As an infant, Alyssa may wear Sesame Street diapers and miniature pro basketball jerseys. By the time she's 20 months old, she will start to recognize some of the thousands of brands flashed in front of her each day. At age 7, if she's anything like the typical kid, she will see

some 20,000 TV commercials a year. By the time she's 12, she will have her own entry in the massive data banks of marketers.

3   Multiply Alyssa by 30 million—the number of babies born in this country since 1990—and you have the largest generation to flood the market since their baby boom parents. More impressive than their numbers, though, is their wealth. The increase in single-parent and dual-earner households means kids are making shopping decisions once left to mom. Combining allowance, earnings, and gifts, kids 14 and under will directly spend an estimated $20 billion this year, and they will influence another $200 billion. No wonder they have become the target of marketing campaigns so sophisticated as to make the kid-aimed pitches of yore look like, well, Mickey Mouse.

4   Forget, for now, the hullabaloo over alcohol and tobacco ads that attract kids well under the age of consent. Yes, the makers of such "sin products" are under fire for the cartoon characters they use to sell their wares, as are trend-setting designers such as Calvin Klein, whose ads feature sexualized waifs barely out of puberty. But what goes on in the name of more legitimate children's fare is far more pervasive— and in many ways just as insidious.

5   Marketers that had long ignored children now systematically pursue them— even when the tykes are years away from being able to buy their products. "Ten years ago, it was cereal, candy, and toys. Today, it's also computers and airlines and hotels and banks," says Julie Halpin, general manager of Saatchi & Saatchi Advertising's Kid Connection division. "A lot of people are turning to a whole segment of the population they haven't been talking to before."

6   Those that have always targeted kids, such as fast-food restaurants and toymakers, have stepped up their pitches, hoping to reach kids earlier and bind them more tightly. Movies, T-shirts, hamburger wrappers, and dolls—all are part of the cross-promotional blitz aimed at convincing kids to spend.

7   Together, the new efforts represent a quantitative and qualitative change in the marketing aimed at children. As any parent who has struggled to find kids' underwear without a licensed cartoon character on it knows, virtually no space is free of logos. And traditional ads have more venues than ever, with a gaggle of new magazines, dozens of Web sites, and entire TV channels aimed at kids. From 1993 to 1996 alone, advertising in kid-specific media grew more than 50 percent, to $1.5 billion, according to *Competitive Media Reporting.*

8   The cumulative effect of initiating our children into a consumerist ethos at an ever earlier age may be profound. As kids drink in the world around them, many of their cultural encounters—from books to movies to TV—have become little more than sales pitches, devoid of any moral beyond a plea for a purchase. Even their classrooms are filled with corporate logos. Instead of transmitting a sense of who we are and what we hold important, today's marketing-driven culture is instilling in them the sense that little exists without a sales pitch attached and that self-worth is something you buy at a shopping mall.

9   "No one ad is so bad," says Mary Pipher, a clinical psychologist and author of *The Shelter of Each Other,* a current best-seller about family life. "But the combina-

tion of 400 ads a day creates in children a combination of narcissism, entitlement, and dissatisfaction.''

Brand Barrage

10   It also can leave parents feeling as if Madison Avenue were raising their kid. Paula Goedert, a tax attorney in Chicago with two sons, ages 15 and 6, has noticed big changes in kids' marketing over the past decade. "Brand awareness has become an incredibly abusive experience—the relentless requests to go to McDonald's, to see movies that are inappropriate for 6-year-olds that are advertised on kids' shows,'' Goedert says.

11   In the end, the barrage may hurt the marketers themselves. Parents and policy-makers are increasingly unnerved by the notion of marketers gathering information about children's preferences and then hiring psychologists to analyze it. In the last year, the federal government has shown a new interest in regulating advertising, be it commercials over the Internet or those for tobacco and alcohol. Meanwhile, some parents, unwilling to expose their children to the unceasing ad blitz, are trying to shield them from consumer culture altogether. "We have deliberately tried to keep Madeline from becoming brand-aware,'' says Nancy Brophy, an Arlington Heights (Ill.) mother of three, including 5-year-old Madeline. "If something's hot, like Beanie Babies or Power Rangers, I'll avoid it.''

12   Marketers, for the most part, say the concerns are overblown—and that critics don't give kids and their parents enough credit. "I have a high regard for the intelligence of kids,'' says Tom Kalinske, president of Knowledge Universe, a new education company, and the former CEO of Sega of America and Mattel Inc. Kalinske and others in the industry believe that kids today are more sophisticated consumers than the generations that preceded them, well able to recognize hype and impervious to crude manipulation. But at least a few worry about the effects of what they do. "As more companies go after kids, the more pressure on kids there will be,'' says Tom Harbeck, Nickelodeon's senior vice-president for marketing.

13   For better or for worse, the marketing barrage has created a generation hypersensitive to the power of brands. For teens, insecure as ever about fitting in, the barrage of brand names offers the irresistible promise of instant cool. The onslaught begins so early—and continues so consistently—that even children who recognize it have trouble putting it aside. "My father always tells me that I could buy two pairs of jeans for what you pay for Calvin Klein,'' laughs Leydiana Reyes, an eighth-grader in Brooklyn, N. Y. "I know that. But I still want Calvin Klein.''

14   Helping to create that lust for brands is a plethora of new ad vehicles. Walt Disney Co. is launching a 24-hour kids' radio network. At Time Warner, *Time, Sports Illustrated,* and *People* have all started or are about to start new editions for kids and teens. In addition, there are Nickelodeon, the Cartoon Network, and a bevy of new girls' magazines.

15   Underlying much of the new kid advertising is an implicit challenge to one of society's basic assumptions: that there is a fundamental difference between kids and grown-ups in judgment and taste. At one time, marketers pitched their children's

wares mainly to parents, who would decide what their kids ate, wore, and played with. To appeal to the immature judgment of children was to take unfair advantage.

Cars, Too

16 But today that reticence is gone. "We're relying on the kid to pester the mom to buy the product, rather than going straight to the mom," says Barbara A. Martino, a vice-president in Grey Advertising Inc.'s 18 & Under division. Why? In part because it's harder for advertisers to eke out domestic sales growth and in part because busy parents no longer act as filters between their kids and the outside world.

17   Kids are being tempted with more than just toys. In an era when children are seen, heard, and catered to as if they were smaller versions of grown-ups, some non-traditional kid marketers are figuring out that the fastest way to mom and dad may well be through junior. In the May issue of *Sports Illustrated For Kids*, which attracts mostly 8- to 14-year-old boys, the inside cover featured a brightly colored two-page spread for the Chevy Venture minivan.

18   This is General Motors' first attempt to woo the group that Karen Francis, the Venture's brand manager, calls "back-seat consumers." Francis is sending the minivan into malls and showing previews of Disney's *Hercules* on a VCR inside. "We're kidding ourselves when we think kids aren't aware of brands," says Francis, adding that even she was surprised by how often parents told her their kids played a tie-breaking role in deciding which car to buy.

19   Marketers of other big-ticket items are also pursuing kids. Delta Airlines Inc. publishes an in-flight magazine for kids, while United Airlines serves McDonald's Happy Meals. Stein Roe & Farnham, Inc., a Chicago money-management firm, runs a mutual fund for child investors consisting largely of favorites such as Disney and Nike Inc. And IBM has teamed up with the National Basketball Assn., hoping sports-crazed kids will sway their parents to choose its Aptiva when they shop for a personal computer.

Marlboro Kids

20 Kid marketers have also recognized the power of nontraditional marketing such as loyalty programs. Last year, PepsiCo launched its enormously successful Pepsi Stuff, which lets customers trade bottle caps for merchandise, including mountain bikes and phone cards. This year, it's aiming the program even more directly at teenagers, increasing the trade-in value of the 20-ounce bottles they favor and using endorsers with kid appeal, such as basketball's Lisa Leslie and baseball's Derek Jeter. "It's more important for us to be successful with teens," says Dave Burwick, vice-president for marketing. "If there are 12 million people out there with our stuff, let's have them be 12 million 18-year-olds."

21   Tobacco companies have also seized on the giveaway programs. Philip Morris Co. denies that Marlboro Gear, largely made up of cowboy-like outerwear, is aimed at teens. To get the gear, participants must mail in a form stating they are over 21.

But Marlboro is now the brand of choice for 60 percent of teen smokers, according to the Centers for Disease Control. Camel has a similar program called Camel Cash, which features Joe Camel on its "dollars." Despite talk of a legal settlement with tobacco companies that could ban such programs, new initiatives that appeal to teens are appearing. U.S. Tobacco Co.'s Skoal brand and Philip Morris' Virginia Slims are both sponsoring rock concert tours.

22   Other tobacco and alcohol ads appeal to even younger kids. Close to 90 percent of 10- to 17-year-olds recognize Joe Camel as a cigarette booster, studies show. The California-based Center on Alcohol Advertising recently found that 9- to 11-year-old children were more apt to recognize the Budweiser frogs and be able to recite the beer's slogan than they were to remember that Tony the Tiger says, "They're grrr-eat." On the fringes, there are even brasher efforts to woo kids with questionable products. A California candy company called Hotlix markets a line of cocktail-flavored lollipops, including a margarita version that comes with salt and a tequila-flavored pop with an edible worm inside of it.

23   Ad campaigns that blur the line between adulthood and childhood are especially troubling—and especially effective—because parents have largely lost their role as "gatekeeper." Just take a look at the grocery-store aisle, where kids are confronted with plenty of messages on their level—literally. Frito Lay Inc. last year rolled out a display called Chip City that allows kids to measure themselves, look a themselves in a funhouse mirror, and press a button to hear Chester Cheetah, spokescharacter for its Chee-tos. Since kids want their chips now, the display includes plenty of one-ounce packages on sale for a quarter.

24   Everywhere, the target is younger. Companies that have already saturated the grade school market are turning toward the crib. Overall sales of licensed sports gear are flat, but the National Football League saw 37 percent growth last year in sales of clothing for tots. Across all lines, sales of licensed products for infants grew 32 percent, to $2.5 billion, in 1996. That means that even before kids can recognize symbols, they are surrounded by the brands that will soon beckon. "Kids are the most pure consumers you could have," says Debra McMahon, a vice-president who follows media for Mercer Management Consulting. "They tend to interpret your ad literally. They are infinitely open."

25   That description fits Nicholas Rouillard, a 9-year-old from Westfield, Mass. The difference between an ad and a TV show is simple, he says: "Commercials are shorter. A commercial is one minute long, but a cartoon can last up to two hours."

26   He's right. The line between the sponsor and the sponsored has all but disappeared. Much of kids' entertainment, featuring characters whose licensed images are immediately stamped on toys, sheets, clothes, even food packages, is almost indistinguishable from the commercials that support it. Amid the media clutter, commercials try to entertain, focusing less on the product and more on creating an image. At the same time, movies and TV shows are more intricately linked to the selling of toys than ever before. Hasbro Inc., for example, helped design the car in Warner Bros.' new *Batman* flick. New, long-term licensing deals between studios and master marketers such as Mattel and McDonald's mean the trend will continue.

Built-in Scripts

27 "Toy companies used to be a font of creativity," says Seth M. Siegel, co-chairman of Beanstalk Group, a licensing company represents the latest craze, Tamagotchi dolls. "Now, what they sell is little more than three-dimensional celluloid." Indeed, Louis Marx Toy Co., the largest in the country back in the 1950s, never signed a single license. Last year, 38 percent of all dollars spent on toys went to licensed toys. Thanks to *Star Wars,* the *Jurassic Park* sequel, *Hercules,* and the next *Batman* installment, that number could near 50 percent this year.

28 The slew of licensed toys leaves less time for imaginative play, and that, too, is causing worries. When toys come with built-in scripts, there's less room for creativity. "You learn flexibility when you play imaginatively. You learn self-control and how to delay impulses," says Dorothy G. Singer, a child psychologist at Yale University and the co-author of *House of Make Believe.* "If the toy comes from TV, a kid tends to follow the story line."

29 Of course, making a toy appeal to a kid isn't as simple as slapping a licensed character on it. Figuring out which hero is the right one brings in the market researchers. "Twenty years ago, you had maybe a dozen companies" researching kids, says Deborah Roedder John, a University of Minnesota professor who specializes in kid marketing, adding that back then she knew practically everybody in the field. "Now, there are many firms out there I've never heard of."

30 Their goal is to know more about children's preferences than even parents do. Researchers host online chats, where kids are more apt to talk openly about personal matters. They hire toddlers to play with new toys and then watch from behind a two-way mirror, often joined by psychologists. Nickelodeon alone surveys 4,000 children every week in its offices, at schools, over the phone, and on the Internet.

31 Thanks in part to recent academic studies, marketers now know more than ever about the child psyche. That has helped them translate the urges and obsessions of different age groups into bigger sales. By limiting the number of each new Beanie Baby and announcing on its Web site which dolls it had discontinued, Ty Inc. in Oak Brook, Ill., for example, cashed in on the desire of 7-year-olds to collect. That urge used to be satisfied by sea shells or baseball cards, back before the latter became an investment opportunity.

Backlash?

32 At the same time, the new research has allowed some companies to shatter long-held assumptions about kids' behavior—such as the belief that female images work with girls but alienate boys. Nickelodeon discovered that kids were changing and didn't hesitate to launch a series of live-action shows with girls as the protagonists. One, *The Secret World of Alex Mack,* now has an audience that is 53 percent male.

33 Some of the new kid marketing draws on more troubling trends. It's no secret that images of sexuality and other forbidden pursuits appeal to many teenagers. And marketers, fighting to be noticed, are increasingly calling upon such symbols. Think

about the current controversy over "heroin chic" images in fashion magazines. Or last year's Calvin Klein campaign that mimicked cheesy child pornography videos. That may have been the most egregious example of sexualizing children in order to sell to them, but it's not unique.

34   If fact, there are already signs of a backlash against the constant marketing assault facing kids. In Massachusetts, the Boston Childern's Museum is running an exhibit that teaches children to understand commercials by allowing them to experiment with lighting and backdrops to change the look of an object. The purpose, says the museum's director of cultural programs, Joanne Rizzi, is "to show the manipulative aspect of commercials." In California, meanwhile, the state government is investigating Anheuser-Busch Cos. Inc.'s new giveaway program—called "Buy the Beer, Get the Gear"—in part out of concern over its appeal on college campuses. And in Washington, the Federal Trade Commission has proposed banning Joe Camel, while Bill Clinton has used the bully pulpit of the White House to chastise alcohol and tobacco companies for targeting kids.

35   None of those efforts, however, is likely to deflect the massive sales machine now directed at children. As long as kids have money to spend, marketers will fight to reach them. "Every 10 years, we begin to ask these questions, and no one has come up with a satisfactory answer," says Minnesota's John. The solution probably lies where it always has: with parents. They will simply have to be more vigilant than ever, knowing that wherever their children go—from day care to the Internet—there's now a marketer close behind.

EXPLORING THE TEXT

1. How does the opening anecdote about Alyssa J. Nedell establish the authors' main point about consumerism among children? Do you find it surprising?
2. Underline all the statistics in paragraphs 1–7. Discuss the authors' use of statistics to support the anecdotal evidence. Do you find one kind of evidence more compelling than another? Why?
3. According to the article, what problems has the brand-name barrage at such an early age created for parents? Is this barrage always effective?
4. Dave Burwick, vice president of marketing for Pepsi-Cola, is quoted as saying, "If there are 12 million people out there with our stuff, let's have them be 12 million 18-year-olds (paragraph 20)." Why does Burwick want teenagers rather than adults as consumers of his product?
5. The authors seem to be particularly critical of how tobacco and alcohol companies have indirectly marketed their products to young people. List several examples from the essay of how these companies sell to kids. What is your opinion on these strategies?
6. How do the observations of the authors of this article parallel those regarding Adcult in James B. Twitchell's piece above ("But First, a Word from Our Sponsor")?

7. What are the authors' final conclusions about the trend toward marketing to children? Do you feel this trend is inevitable and unstoppable or would you like to see the government and/or consumer groups play a more active role in regulating ads and marketing aimed at children?

WRITING ASSIGNMENTS

1. Write an essay discussing your own observations about children's consumption of products. You can draw on your own experience as a child or write about a child you know. Do you feel that brand-name awareness and demand have increased? If so, offer support for your view.

2. Extreme demand for a particular toy, whether Beanie Babies, Tickle Me Elmo dolls, or Power Ranger Action Figures, is often the result of supplies of these toys being limited. Write an essay discussing how the scarcity of certain toys contributes to their "must have" quality. Can you think of any recent examples of parents going crazy trying to get a "hot" but scarce toy for their children? (During the Christmas 1996 season people were placing ads offering Tickle Me Elmo dolls to the highest bidder; some newspapers reported dolls going for as high as $1,500.)

3. Leonhardt and Kerwin suggest that the changing nature of family structure—that is, more than two-income households and more children left on their own—has contributed to kids having more money and parents acting less as "gatekeepers." Write an essay discussing what role you think parents should play in shaping their children's behavior as consumers. Do you feel that restricting television is the key to controlling ad bombardment, or do you see parents' ability to shield their children from these messages as limited?

GROUP PROJECTS

1. In small groups, do some research on how the Internet is used as a marketing tool to sell to children. The article mentions how Ty Inc., makers of Beanie Babies, used their Web site to announce when certain dolls would be discontinued. See if you can find Web sites for other toy or game companies such as Mattel, Hasbro, or Milton Bradley. What do these sites offer? Write up an analysis of how they serve to "entice" children. Report your findings to the class.

2. Assign each group member to watch an hour of television aimed at children—for example, Saturday morning programs, Nickelodeon, or the Cartoon Channel. Jot down the shows that you watch and all the commercials that run during the programs. Once you have compiled your data, do some analysis. How many commercials ran per 15 minutes of programming? Did

you notice any pattern to these commercials? Did any seem particularly manipulative? Did you see examples of tie-ins—for example, a *Flintstones* cartoon followed by an ad for Flintstones vitamins? (To make this project even more interesting, watch these programs with a child. Note his or her responses to what is seen. Did the child seem to be unduly influenced or hypnotized by the ads?)

Mr. Clean
Mary Tannen

In the essay below, beauty columnist Mary Tannen focuses on recent trends for an old and familiar product—men's colognes. In the past, marketers tried to create special appeal for their product by announcing how it made men smell manly or how it won women over. Today, as Tannen observes, the marketing trend is promoting a clean, androgynous, and, above all, safe male image. Tannen ties this trend to several different causes, including some workplace concerns and social fears.

Tannen, a novelist, writes about beauty for the *New York Times Sunday Magazine* where this article first appeared in 1995.

1 Years from now, when historians are analyzing the great male identity crisis of the late 20th century, exploring the text of "Iron John," freeze-framing scenes of Liam Neeson in "Nell," hoping to uncover the inspiration for what was to become the male ideal for the 21st century, I trust they will not overlook the crucial role played by the men's fragrance industry. As the debate and confusion persist over what a man should be, the toilers in ambergris and musk have succeeded in realizing—not in a 200-page tome, or two hours of celluloid, but in the whiff of a scent strip and the flick of a photo, or at best, in a 30-second spot run back to back with breakfast cereal—the archetype for our times: the ideal man, fully formed (if not necessarily fully clothed). It is their unique mandate to cull the mostly inarticulate desires of fragrance buyers and distill them into scent and image. Because at least 50 percent of the customers are women, this creation, this Adonis, must be the hero every man longs to be and every woman longs to be with.

2 This didn't used to be a problem. In the 50's, men wore after-shave, not fragrance; they were all dads who received this after-shave on Father's Day. The captain of a sailing ship was an appropriate image for just about everyone. In the 60's, we began to admit what we'd known all along, that smelling good is linked to being sexually attractive.

3 Annette Green, president of the Fragrance Foundation, says that musk, an odor that the male musk deer secretes to let lady deer know he is willing, first won the affection of the perfume underground in the 60's and began playing a bigger role in commercial fragrances. From the 60's into the 80's, she says, men's scents were "a

little bit of a dirty joke." She cites the Hai Karate ad in which a man kicks his way through life, and women fall at his feet. Now there are fewer "killer colognes" (those emphasizing musk and other odors mimicking the sex glands of animals) and more with the accent on "health food ingredients": citrus, berries, herbs, fruit peels and coriander. Today's "juice," as people in the business call the stuff in the bottle, is likely to be cleaner and greener.

4   In fact, models in ads are so clean they're often sopping wet. The sleeping giant for Davidoff Cool Water has been washed up in the surf. He works out—look at those pecs—but he's also hairless. (Most men in fragrance ads are, which makes them look not only clean but androgynous.) His eyes are closed. Wake him at your pleasure. He is not aggressive.

5   He may channel his aggression into an upscale, noncontact sport. Watch him— in the television spots for Brut Actif Blue by Fabergé—as he skis off a cliff, as he kayaks down a cataract. At the end of the day there is a woman with him, running hand in hand—she's almost leading—and a gorgeous final embrace underwater, so sexy, yet so clean. (The video was field-tested on both men and women—equally.)

6   Our hero is often seen in a loving and equal relationship. See him, in the Calvin Klein Escape for Men photo, damp and dazed, in an old canoe with his female counterpart. Not for him the traditional pose as paddler while she reclines in the prow. The boat is going nowhere. There are no paddles. And how about that stunning, well-moistened couple in the Guy Laroche Horizon ad! He is prone, looking adoringly into her eyes. She is supine, arms modestly folded across her breasts. Their bodies, clean and chaste, extend along the line where earth, sea and sky meet in perfect harmony.

7   Why is our new ideal so squeaky clean? Certainly fear of AIDS has something to do with it. Clinique, introducing a new scent for men, dispenses with the wet model entirely and shows only the interior of his medicine cabinet—an Irving Penn portrait of a glass, a toothbrush, a comb and the luminous bottle. The only copy is the name of the product, Chemistry, which promises sex, but the liquid in the unadorned bottle looks like disinfectant.

8   The ideal of a clean and nonaggressive male also reflects he way we live now. More than ever before, men and women work side by side as equals. Being overtly sexual is not only unacceptable but, in this age of sexual-harassment charges, it is downright dangerous. Men and women (women's daytime fragrances have also been getting lighter, cleaner and more neutral) want to smell pleasant, but they don't want to exude a scent that makes co-workers look around for an empty broom closet where they can satisfy their lust together.

9   The hero for Fahrenheit by Christian Dior stands alone, gazing at the sunset from a dock. He is not naked and wet, but in a business suit. Sea and sky are calm; the storm has passed, passion spent. The fragrance, a yin-yang balance of honeysuckle and hawthorne, sandalwood and cedar, was born before its time, in the 80's, and has been picking up interest ever since. Sixty percent of the buyers are women, but nobody knows if they are wearing it themselves or giving it to men. Men's fragrance has become part of the working wardrobe, and like a good white shirt, is appropriate on either sex.

10   But wait! Just when we are closing the chapter on the neutering of male fragrance, DK Men comes roaring onto our television screen. See his stubbly face
close-up as he puts his racing car through its gears. Feel the pistons pump. Watch
him wipe the sweat from his rough mug. The promotional copy describes the smell
as "Sexy. Fresh. Citrus." But with surprise, un-P.C. ingredients—tobacco and
suede. (Animal skins, O.K.?)

11   The DK man is the brainchild of a famous working couple: Donna Karan and
her husband, Stephen Weiss. No doubt future historians will take this into account
when they try to reconcile the DK man, who is wet (but from his own perspiration),
enveloped in gas fumes (not generally thought to be healthy, or attractive to women)
and has hair on his chest. Maybe D.K. is secure enough in her own power (after all,
she is C.E.O. of her own empire) that she does not feel threatened by testosterone.
"Gravity defied. 24-hour, speed-of-sound sensation. Perpetual, raw and pure."
Yeah! Give it to me, baby!

12   I will leave it to future historians to decide if DK Men is a final cry of regret
over what has been thrown out with the bath water, so to speak—the wild, risky and
unclean part of our natures—or whether it signals a recognition that sex will always
be with us, and when we're feeling secure enough, it's really fun to let 'er rip.

EXPLORING THE TEXT

1. Tannen begins her piece by mentioning several idealized male images. Who
    are Iron John, Liam Neeson, and Adonis? What characteristics do these three
    images share? How do they set the tone for Tannen's discussion?
2. What changes have occurred in men's colognes in the last 40 years? What
    kinds of scents does Tannen say were popular in the fifties and sixties?
    What do the nineties cologne's "health food ingredients" suggest about the
    image men want to present today?
3. Look at paragraphs 4–6. How does Tannen characterize the men in the
    Cool Water, Actif Blue, Escape, and Horizon ads? Do the names of the
    colognes serve to reinforce the images she describes? What is Tannen's
    tone in this section?
4. How does Tannen use the popularity of certain male colognes as a barome-
    ter for changing sexual attitudes? Discuss her assertion that AIDS has
    played a role in producing the clean and nonaggressive male models she
    describes.
5. Do you find Tannen's assertion in paragraph 8 that "Being overtly sexual is
    not only unacceptable but, in this age of sexual-harassment charges, it is
    downright dangerous" persuasive? What kind of evidence does she offer to
    support this claim?
6. How does the example of the ad campaign for DK Men suggest a return to
    previous definitions of masculinity from previous decades? Discuss simi-
    larities between the DK Men ad and the ad for Hai Karate.

7. What does the final paragraph reveal about Tannen's attitude toward the various "clean" ads? What does it reveal about her attitude toward sex? What do you make of her repetition of the word *secure* in the final two paragraphs?

WRITING ASSIGNMENTS

1. Why do you think Tannen chose to focus her discussion on cologne ads? Do you find her choice effective? Why or why not? List several other products' ads that seem especially useful in determining current attitudes toward sex.
2. Tannen argues that current ads for cologne tend to desexualize males. Do you see a similar trend in ads for women's fragrances? Collect two or three perfume ads from a magazine. Write a brief essay about whether these ads support or contradict Tannen's thesis.
3. Discuss the popularity of Calvin Klein's C.K. One, a cologne made for "a man or a woman." What might this advertising campaign suggest about current definitions of masculinity and femininity?

GROUP PROJECTS

1. As a group, investigate the ad campaigns for men's colognes by visiting the fragrance counters in a larger department store. Have different group members take notes on a least three separate colognes. The focus of your investigation should be to determine what images these colognes seem to be trying to create. To that end, be sure to note the name of the product, to describe the design of the bottle, and to describe how the cologne smells— for instance, is it fruity, woodsy, musky, spicy? Is it a strong or light scent? Also take note of any ad paraphernalia on the counter (pictures, cardboard cutouts, free samples, etc.). After your visit, sit down and compare notes. Like Tannen, do you see patterns emerging in terms of how these products are marketed? Write up a report of your investigation to present to the class.
2. Many designers now have their own Web sites that consumers can visit for information about the latest products being offered. Go on-line and to locate a site for designers such as Donna Karan, Calvin Klein, Tommy Hilfiger, and Ralph Lauren. Look for information about the designers' colognes. As a group, discuss the similarities and differences between advertising on a Web site and through more traditional media such as television, magazines or newspapers. Does the Web offer any special advantages? Write a group report about your findings.

3. As a group create an ad campaign for one of the following fictional men's colognes: *Rodeo, Jackhammer,* or *City Swinger.* In order to effectively present your campaign to the class, you will need to write copy for the product, come up with a tag line (a catchy slogan like McDonald's, "You deserve a break today"), and create visual aids.

Choking on Hype
Paula Poundstone

Joe Camel has been put out to pasture, cigarette sponsorship of sporting events has been cut, and tobacco companies are at an all-time low in public opinion. However, there is new smoke on the horizon. In spite of all the anti-smoking campaigns, cigars are on the rise. Yes, what seems a George Burns anachronism has become the latest craze. At any newsstand you'll find glossy cigar magazines with cover shots of sports and movie celebrities—men and women—lighting up. In many cities, trendy bars and restaurants keep their humidors well stocked with rolled leaves. What to some is a public health problem has through crafty hype been elevated to a chic pastime that marketers equate with power and leisure. Curious about all the promise, Paula Poundstone set out to see for herself what all the hubbub was. The title of her piece gives you some idea of what her research turned up.

Poundstone is a popular stand-up comedian who also writes a regular column called "The Poundstone Report" for *Mother Jones* magazine where this piece first appeared in the March/April 1996 issue.

1 Christopher Columbus was the Inspector Clouseau of explorers. Not only had Vikings and Native Americans been here long before he "discovered" America, but he also thought he was somewhere else entirely. No wonder you have to come as far inland as Ohio to find a town named after the guy.

2 Columbus is also credited with taking the idea of smoking back to Europe from here. Could he do nothing right? If Columbus were alive now he would no doubt be part of the tobacco companies' myth machine—the one that maintains that tobacco and cancer have never been conclusively linked and the one that now tells us that cigars are the country's hip new rage.

3 The editor guy at *Mother Jones* asked me to go to some Los Angeles "cigar bars" to see what they were like. First I read several articles on the subject. They all claimed that cigar smoking is sweeping the nation, with the female cigar-smoking population growing the fastest.

4 *Cigar Aficionado* magazine contained an article listing the hottest spots around L.A. to smoke cigars. I couldn't find them. Occasionally I found the venues themselves, but I never found them teeming with patrons. A woman at one of the restaurants said, "We're not a cigar bar, but if we're empty, people can smoke cigars." I

began to put it together: *Cigar Aficionado* might have a vested interest in hyping a cigar craze that doesn't exactly exist.

5   I kept returning to some of the places, figuring I just wasn't going at peak hours. The site of my first successful infiltration was the bar at the swanky Peninsula Hotel. I was truly embarrassed to be there, but I decided I'd blow my investigative cover if I banged my hors d'oeuvre fork on my wine glass and announced, "I think you all look very silly and I'm only here because I have to be." I sat near a gaggle of men struggling with cigars the size of baseball bats wedged in their mouths. They looked like those circus acts who balance chairs on their chins.

6   I wear a leather flight jacket with Glenn Miller on the back. More than one man approached me to ask if I had played with Glenn Miller. I'm 36. Either the lighting in the glamorous cigar bar is not flattering or cigar smokers are not that bright.

7   The cigar smokers I ran across did seem pretentious and stupid, especially the women. I saw one woman choking on a puff. She looked like she was thinking, "This can't possibly be what everyone is doing."

8   I hate women. Instead of reaching our potential, we are tied to the thought that says: "We want to do what men do." That's why tobacco and gun companies target us. Even if cigar smoking were popular, that doesn't mean it'd be a good thing to do. Lynching was popular once, too.

9   I went to Philip Dane's Cigar Lounge in Beverly Hills on two separate occasions. This place is so exclusive that no one was there either time. (I don't know how I got in. I must look as if I made wise investments with my Glenn Miller album royalties.) They had an issue from volume three of *The Cigar Monthly* magazine on the bar. I was wondering how they could publish more than two volumes about cigars when I noticed an article about a place in Louisiana where they make humidors. I realized the magazine was not just about cigars. If it seemed thin, I'm sure it's because they're gearing up for their special collector ashtray issue.

10   *The Cigar Monthly* also had an article by a woman describing how she realized smoking cigars was "something my fiancé and I could enjoy together, something interesting and different." You'd think she would have noticed that they had so little they could enjoy together before they got engaged. They probably went from months of uncomfortable silence to such stimulating conversation as:

11   "Honey, are you puffing?"

12   "Yes, I'm puffing."

13   I don't even date, but I feel safe in counseling that if you see cigar smoking as a beacon of hope for interaction with your fiancé, you've unearthed a fairly severe shortcoming in the relationship. It might be a good time to go back over the guest list for your wedding and eliminate the groom.

14   The hype says that cigar smoking is a way to meet more interesting people and that the variety of cigar colors, shapes, and sizes makes them an interesting topic for conversation. Cupid himself is probably perched high atop the humidor at Hamilton's cigar and wine lounge, inspiring encounters like:

15   "Hey, you smell disgusting and so do I." (Puff, puff.)

16   "Do you come here often?" (Puff, puff.)

17   "Yes, do you?"

18   "Yes, isn't that freaky?"

19   "Your cigar is brown and my cigar is brown. How eerie."

20   "I love the smell of cigars."

21   "Me too, it reminds me of my grandpa just before he died."

22   "Me too!"

23   Crayons also come in different colors, shapes, and sizes. Interesting people (or at least many children) use them. Crayons smell great, and they say "nontoxic" right on the side. Why can't crayon bars be all the rage?

EXPLORING THE TEXT

1. In the first paragraph, how does Poundstone paint Columbus? Why does she compare him to Inspector Clouseau? Discuss how effective you find this as a lead-in to an article about smoking.

2. Look through the first four paragraphs and mark the sentences that most clearly suggest Poundstone's attitude toward smoking and the cigar "craze." How would you characterize this attitude?

3. What does Poundstone's research lead her to conclude about cigar smoking? How does she cast doubt on the cigar magazines' credibility?

4. How does the author's descriptions of the people she met at the cigar bars add to her critique?

5. How does Poundstone characterize herself throughout the article? How does this add to the piece's humor?

6. Do you find Poundstone's first-person account of exploring the cigar "scene" effective prose? Do you think the humor lessens the more serious message about how the tobacco industry attempts to manipulate the public? Why or why not?

WRITING ASSIGNMENTS

1. This article first appeared in *Mother Jones* magazine. Buy a copy of the magazine or take a look at an issue at the library. How would you define the political stance of the magazine? What leads you to this conclusion? Does Poundstone's piece seem compatible with these politics? Why or why not?

2. Discuss the issue of hype in the media. What other media-created crazes can you think of? How does the media, advertising in particular, attempt to make us believe we want and need the latest "hot" product or experience?

3. Imagine you must create an advertising campaign for a soon-to-be-released movie about aliens. Write a press released that will result in maximum hype for your movie.

GROUP PROJECTS

1. You may have noticed that beneath the humor of Poundstone's piece is a fairly strong antismoking message. As a group, investigate antismoking ads (these ads will more likely target cigarettes than cigars). You can gather data by taping television commercials, collecting print ads from magazines, or gathering antismoking pamphlets from around your campus. Once your data is collected, write an essay about the strategies these anti-smoking ads use to combat the images of "coolness" and glamour that smoking ads employ so well.

Snuggle Bear Must Die!
Dave Barry

Have you ever seen a television commercial that rubbed you the wrong way? One you found offensive or irritating or just plain dumb? Sure you have, and so have a lot of other people, including humor columnist Dave Barry who decided to solicit his readers for their most hated commercials. What appears below is a summary of the thousands of replies he received—replies that give Barry a golden opportunity to let loose his wacky sarcasm about some of America's most familiar and obnoxious television spots.

Barry has been described as "America's most preposterous newspaper columnist," a man "incapable of not being funny." He is the author of more than ten books and is a Pulitzer Prize–winning humorist whose column appears in more than 200 publications. His books include *Dave Barry Is Not Making This Up* (1994), *Dave Barry in Cyberspace* (1996), and *Dave Barry's Complete Guide to Guys* (1996). This piece appeared in his column on February 2, 1997.

1 Whew! Do I have a headache! I think I'll take an Extra Strength Bufferin Advil Tylenol with proven cavity fighters, containing more of the lemon-freshened Borax that is recommended by doctors and plaque fighters for those days when I am feeling "not so fresh" in my personal region.

2 I'm feeling this way because I just went through the thousands of letters sent in when I asked readers to tell me which advertisements they don't like. A lot of you *really* hate certain ads, to the point where you fantasize about violence. For example, quite a few people expressed a desire to kill the stuffed bear in the Snuggle fabric-softener ad. "Die, Snuggle Bear, die" is how several put it.

3 Likewise, there was hostility expressed, often by older readers, toward the relentlessly cheerful older couples depicted in the competing commercials for Ensure and Sustacal. These ads suggest that if you drink these products, you will feel "young," which, in these commercials, means "stupid." People were offended by the ad in which the couple actually drinks a toast with Ensure. As Jamie Hagedorn described it:

"One says, 'To your health,' and the other says, 'Uh-uh—to *our* health,' and then they laugh like ninnies. I want to hit them both over the head with a hammer."

4   Some other commercial personalities who aroused hostility were Sally Struthers; the young boy who lectures incessantly about Welch's grape juice; the young people in the Mentos commercials (as Rob Spore put it: "Don't you think those kids should all be sent to military school?"); everybody in all Calvin Klein commercials; the young girl in the Shake 'N Bake commercial—Southerners *really* hate this girl—who, for what seems like hundreds of years, has said, "And I helped!" but pronounces it "An ah hayulpt!"; the smug man in the Geritol commercial who says, "My wife . . . I think I'll keep her!" (the wife smiles, but you just know that one day she will put Liquid Drano in his Ensure); the woman in the Pantene commercial who says, "Please don't hate me because I'm beautiful" (as many readers responded, "OK, how about if we just hate you because you're obnoxious?"); and the Pillsbury Doughboy ("I would sacrifice my microwave to watch him inside on high for 10 hours," wrote Gene Doerfler).

5   Readers are none too fond of the giant Gen X dudes stomping all over the Rocky Mountains in the Coors Light ads. Matt Scott asks: "Will they step on us if we don't buy their beer?" Scott McCullar asks: "What happens when they get a full bladder?" Many people would like Candice Bergen to shut up about the stupid dimes.

6   I am pleased to report that I am not the only person who dislikes the Infiniti Snot—you know, the guy with the dark clothes and the accent, talking about Infiniti cars, as though they were Renaissance art. As Kathleen Schon, speaking for many, put it: "We hate him so much we wouldn't buy one of those even if we could afford it." Speaking of car commercials, here's a bulletin for the Nissan people: Nobody likes the creepy old man. Everybody is afraid when the young boy winds up alone in the barn with him. This ad campaign does not make us want to purchase a Nissan. It makes us want to notify the police.

7   And listen, Chevrolet: People don't mind the first 389 million times they heard Bob Seger wail, "Like a rock!" But it's getting old. And some people wish to know what "genuine Chevrolet" means. As Don Charleston put it: "I intended to buy a genuine Chevy, but I couldn't tell the difference between the 'genuine' and all those counterfeit Chevys out there, so I bought a Ford."

8   But the car-related ads that people hate the most, judging from my survey, are the dealership commercials in which the announcer shouts at you and then, in the last three seconds of the ad, reads, in muted tones, what sounds like the entire US tax code. Hundreds of people wrote to say that they hate these commercials. I should note that one person defended them. His name is George Chapogas, and he is in—of all things—the advertising business. Perhaps by examining this actual excerpt from his letter, we can appreciate the thinking behind the shouting ads:

9   "I write, produce, and *voice* those ads. Make a damn good living doing it, too. Maybe more than you, even. And would you like to know why? Because they move metal, buddy."

10   Thanks, George! I understand now.

11   Well, I'm out of space. Tune in next week, and I'll tell you which commercial the readers hate the most; I'll also discuss repulsive bodily functions in detail. Be

sure to read it! You'll lose weight without dieting, have whiter teeth in two weeks by actually growing your own hair on itching, flaking skin as your family enjoys a delicious meal in only minutes without getting soggy in milk! Although your mileage may vary. Ask a doctor! Or somebody who plays one on TV.

EXPLORING THE TEXT

1. How would you characterize Barry's tone? What assumptions does he seem to make about his audience?
2. Barry lists many ads that people seem to love to hate. Do you see any pattern in the types of ads described?
3. How do the various readers' comments about hated ads contribute to the humor of the article?
4. What does Barry seem to imply about many advertising claims? How does he parody those claims in his article?

WRITING ASSIGNMENTS

1. Interview a few friends and family members and compile your own "most-hated" list. Be sure to ask for specific comments on why they hate these ads in particular. Adding your own comments to those of the people you interview, create your own version of *"Snuggle Bear Must Die!"*
2. Imagine that you are a newspaper critic. Write a critique of Barry's column focusing on how effective you find his humor. Support your argument with evidence from the text.
3. Many of the ads that Barry describes seem to annoy people because they treat consumers as if they were stupid. Discuss an ad that you think takes the opposite tact—that is, one that appeals to the consumer's sophistication and/or intelligence. Do you think there is a risk in being "too intelligent" in advertising?

GROUP PROJECTS

1. Barry solicited letters from people about what commercials they hated, and readers seem to have responded enthusiastically with many examples. Try your own hand at gathering opinions about some current television commercials. As a group, develop a questionnaire that focuses on finding out which commercials people like best, which they like least, and why. Make sure your questions are written so that they avoid a yes or no answer and are open-ended enough so people have an opportunity to explain their answers. Send group members to various locales—the student union, a mall, a coffee shop, any place where a variety of people are gathered. After your

data has been collected, meet and compare notes. Can you find a pattern to the kinds of commercials people seem to hate or like? Did any commercials make *both* the hated and liked list? Write up your findings in a brief report.

2. Had you heard of Dave Barry before you read "*Snuggle Bear Must Die!*"? Is anyone in your group familiar with anything else he has written? Your job is to do some research on Barry and write a brief biography for the class. Go to the library and have each group member research a different aspect of Barry's life. For instance, one person can look into Barry's personal background—where was he born, where did he go to school, does he have any children? Someone else can focus on Barry's output as a writer—how long has he been writing columns, which papers or magazines run his work, has he written any books? A third person might look into what critics have said about Barry. Look for reviews of his work. Has Barry ever won any awards for his writing? After you present your findings to the class, ask them to discuss how this new information affects their response to "Snuggle Bear Must Die!"

3. Paula Poundstone ("Choking on Hype") and Dave Barry are both writers known for their humorous and distinctive voices. Create a dialogue between the two as they "review" several well-known television commercials. Keeping with the spirit of their pieces, choose commercials that strike you as particularly deserving of a satirical approach. (You should also pick ads that everyone in the class will have seen.) See if you can capture the style of each writer as you speak in "his or her" voice. Plan on reading your review aloud to the class.

Pro/Con: The Language of Advertising—Twisting the Truth?

The next two selections represent contrary views of the language of advertisers. In particular, they argue whether or not the linguistic habits of hucksters amount to an irresponsible twisting of the truth. William Lutz says they do, while Charles A. O'Neill argues that they don't.

PRO

With These Words I Can Sell You Anything
William Lutz

Words such as *help* and *virtually*, phrases such as *new and improved* and *acts fast* seem like innocuous weaponry in the arsenal of advertising. But not to William Lutz who analyzes the way such words are used in ads—how they misrepresent, mislead, and deceive consumers.

In this essay, he alerts us to the special power of "weasel words"—those familiar and sneaky little critters that "appear to say one thing when in fact they say the opposite, or nothing at all."

Lutz has been called the George Orwell of the 1990s. Chair of the Committee on Public Doublespeak of the National Council of Teachers of English, Lutz edits the *Quarterly Review of Doublespeak,* a magazine dedicated to the eradication of misleading official statements. He also teaches in the English department at Rutgers University. He is the author of *Doublespeak* (1990), from which this essay was taken.

1 One problem advertisers have when they try to convince you that the product they are pushing is really different from other, similar products is that their claims are subject to some laws. Not a lot of laws, but there are some designed to prevent fraudulent or untruthful claims in advertising. Even during the happy years of non-regulation under President Ronald Reagan, the FTC did crack down on the more blatant abuses in advertising claims. Generally speaking, advertisers have to be careful in what they say in their ads, in the claims they make for the products they advertise. Parity claims are safe because they are legal and supported by a number of court decisions. But beyond parity claims there are weasel words.

2 Advertisers use weasel words to appear to be making a claim for a product when in fact they are making no claim at all. Weasel words get their name from the way weasels eat the eggs they find in the nests of other animals. A weasel will make a small hole in the egg, suck out the insides, then place the egg back in the nest. Only when the egg is examined closely is it found to be hollow. That's the way it is with weasel words in advertising: Examine weasel words closely and you'll find that they're as hollow as any egg sucked by a weasel. Weasel words appear to say one thing when in fact they say the opposite, or nothing at all.

"Help"—The Number One Weasel Word

3 The biggest weasel word used in advertising doublespeak is "help." Now "help" only means to aid or assist, nothing more. It does not mean to conquer, stop, eliminate, solve, heal, cure, or anything else. But once the ad says "help," it can say just about anything after that because "help" qualifies everything coming after it. The trick is that the claim that comes after the weasel word is usually so strong and so dramatic that you forget the word "help" and concentrate only on the dramatic claim. You read into the ad a message that the ad does not contain. More importantly, the advertiser is not responsible for the claim that you read into the ad, even though the advertiser wrote the ad so you would read that claim into it.

4 The next time you see an ad for a cold medicine that promises that it "helps relieve cold symptoms fast," don't rush out to buy it. Ask yourself what this claim is really saying. Remember, "helps" means only that the medicine will aid or assist. What will it aid or assist in doing? Why, "relieve" your cold "symptoms." "Relieve" only means to ease, alleviate, or mitigate, not to stop, end, or cure. Nor does the claim say how much relieving this medicine will do. Nowhere does this ad claim it

will cure anything. In fact, the ad doesn't even claim it will *do* anything at all. The ad only claims that it will aid in relieving (not curing) your cold symptoms, which are probably a runny nose, watery eyes, and a headache. In other words, this medicine probably contains a standard decongestant and some aspirin. By the way, what does "fast" mean? Ten minutes, one hour, one day? What is fast to one person can be very slow to another. Fast is another weasel word.

5   Ad claims using "help" are among the most popular ads. One says, "Helps keep you young looking," but then a lot of things will help keep you young looking, including exercise, rest, good nutrition, and a facelift. More importantly, this ad doesn't say the product will keep you young, only "young *looking*." Someone may look young to one person and old to another.

6   A toothpaste ad says, "Helps prevent cavities," but it doesn't say it will actually prevent cavities. Brushing your teeth regularly, avoiding sugars in foods, and flossing daily will also help prevent cavities. A liquid cleaner ad says, "Helps keep your home germ free," but it doesn't say it actually kills germs, nor does it even specify which germs it might kill.

7   "Help" is such a useful weasel word that it is often combined with other action-verb weasel words such as "fight" and "control." Consider the claim, "Helps control dandruff symptoms with regular use." What does it really say? It will assist in controlling (not eliminating, stopping, ending, or curing) the *symptoms* of dandruff, not the cause of dandruff nor the dandruff itself. What are the symptoms of dandruff? The ad deliberately leaves that undefined, but assume that the symptoms referred to in the ad are the flaking and itching commonly associated with dandruff. But just shampooing with *any* shampoo will temporarily eliminate these symptoms, so this shampoo isn't any different from any other. Finally, in order to benefit from this product, you must use it regularly. What is "regular use"—daily, weekly, hourly? Using another shampoo "regularly" will have the same effect. Nowhere does this advertising claim say this particular shampoo stops, eliminates, or cures dandruff. In fact, this claim says nothing at all, thanks to all the weasel words.

8   Look at ads in magazines and newspapers, listen to ads on radio and television, and you'll find the word "help" in ads for all kinds of products. How often do you read or hear such phrases as "helps stop . . . ," "helps overcome . . . ," "helps eliminate . . . , " "helps you feel . . . ," or "helps you look . . . "? If you start looking for this weasel word in advertising, you'll be amazed at how often it occurs. Analyze the claims in the ads using "help," and you will discover that these ads are really saying nothing.

9   There are plenty of other weasel words used in advertising. In fact, there are so many that to list them all would fill the rest of this book. But, in order to identify the doublespeak of advertising and understand the real meaning of an ad, you have to be aware of the most popular weasel words in advertising today.

Virtually Spotless

10   One of the most powerful weasel word is "virtually," a word so innocent that most people don't pay any attention to it when it is used in an advertising claim. But watch out. "Virtually" is used in advertising claims that appear to make specific,

definite promises when there is no promise. After all, what does "virtually" mean? It means "in essence of effect, although not in fact." Look at that definition again. "Virtually" means *not in fact.* It does *not* mean "almost" or "just about the same as," or anything else. And before you dismiss all this concern over such a small word, remember that small words can have big consequences.

11   In 1971 a federal court rendered its decision on a case brought by a woman who became pregnant while taking birth control pills. She sued the manufacturer, Eli Lilly and Company, for breach of warranty. The woman lost her case. Basing its ruling on a statement in the pamphlet accompanying the pills, which stated that, "When taken as directed, the tables offer virtually 100 percent protection," the court ruled that there was no warranty, expressed or implied, that the pills were absolutely effective. In its ruling, the court pointed out that, according to the *Webster's Third New International Dictionary,* "virtually" means "almost entirely" and clearly does not mean "absolute" (*Whittington* v. *Eli Lilly and Company,* 333 F. Supp. 98). In other words, the Eli Lilly company was really saying that its birth control pill, even when taken as directed, *did not in fact* provide 100 percent protection against pregnancy. But Eli Lilly didn't want to put it that way because then many women might not have bought Lilly's birth control pills.

12   The next time you see the ad that says that this dishwasher detergent "leaves dishes virtually spotless," just remember how advertisers twist the meaning of the weasel word "virtually." You can have lots of spots on your dishes after using this detergent and the ad claim will still be true, because what this claim really means is that this detergent does not *in fact* leave your dishes spotless. Whenever you see or hear an ad claim that uses the word "virtually," just translate that claim into its real meaning. So the television set that is "virtually trouble free" becomes the television set that is not in fact trouble free, the "virtually foolproof operation" of any appliance becomes an operation that is in fact not foolproof, and the product that "virtually never needs service" becomes the product that is not in fact service free.

New and Improved

13 If "new" is the most frequently used word on a product package, "improved" is the second most frequent. In fact, the two words are almost always used together. It seems just about everything sold these days is "new and improved." The next time you're in the supermarket, try counting the number of times you see these words on products. But you'd better do it while you're walking down just one aisle, otherwise you'll need a calculator to keep track of your counting.

14   Just what do these words mean? The use of the word "new" is restricted by regulations, so an advertiser can't just use the word on a product or in an ad without meeting certain requirements. For example, a product is considered new for about six months during a national advertising campaign. If the product is being advertised only in a limited test market area, the word can be used longer, and in some instances has been used for as long as two years.

15   What makes a product "new"? Some products have been around for a long time, yet every once in a while you discover that they are being advertised as "new." Well, an advertiser can call a product new if there has been "a material functional

change" in the product. What is "a material functional change," you ask? Good question. In fact it's such a good question it's being asked all the time. It's up to the manufacturer to prove that the product has undergone such a change. And if the manufacturer isn't challenged on the claim, then there's no one to stop it. Moreover, the change does not have to be an improvement in the product. One manufacturer added an artificial lemon scent to a cleaning product and called it "new and improved," even though the product did not clean any better than without the lemon scent. The manufacturer defended the use of the word "new" on the grounds that the artificial scent changed the chemical formula of the product and therefore constituted "a material functional change."

16 Which brings up the word "improved." When used in advertising, "improved" does not mean "made better." It only means "changed" or "different from before." So, if the detergent maker puts a plastic pour spout on the box of detergent, the product has been "improved," and away we go with a whole new advertising campaign. Or, if the cereal maker adds more fruit or a different kind of fruit to the cereal, there's an improved product. Now you know why manufacturers are constantly making little changes in their products. Whole new advertising campaigns, designed to convince you that the product has been changed for the better, are based on small changes in superficial aspects of a product. The next time you see an ad for an "improved" product, ask yourself what was wrong with the old one. Ask yourself just how "improved" the product is. Finally, you might check to see whether the "improved" version costs more than the unimproved one. After all, someone has to pay for the millions of dollars spent advertising the improved product.

17 Of course, advertisers really like to run ads that claim a product is "new and improved." While what constitutes a "new" product may be subject to some regulation, "improved" is a subjective judgment. A manufacturer changes the shape of its stick deodorant, but the shape doesn't improve the function of the deodorant. That is, changing the shape doesn't affect the deodorizing ability of the deodorant, so the manufacturer calls it "improved." Another manufacturer adds ammonia to its liquid cleaner and calls it "new and improved." Since adding ammonia does affect the cleaning ability of the product, there has been a "material functional change" in the product, and the manufacturer can now call its cleaner "new," and "improved" as well. Now the weasel words "new and improved" are plastered all over the package and are the basis for a multimillion-dollar ad campaign. But after six months the word "new" will have to go, until someone can dream up another change in the product. Perhaps it will be adding color to the liquid, or changing the shape of the package, or maybe adding a new dripless pour spout, or perhaps a———. The "improvements" are endless, and so are the new advertising claims and campaigns.

18 "New" is just too useful and powerful a word in advertising for advertisers to pass it up easily. So they use weasel words that say "new" without really saying it. One of their favorites is "introducing," as in, "Introducing improved Tide," or "Introducing the satin remover." The first is simply saying, here's our improved soap; the second, here's our new advertising campaign for our detergent. Another favorite is "now," as in, "Now there's Sinex," which simply means that Sinex is available. Then there are phrases like "Today's Chevrolet," "Presenting Dristan," and "A fresh

way to start the day." The list is really endless because advertisers are always finding new ways to say "new" without really saying it. If there is a second edition of this book, I'll just call it the "new and improved" edition. Wouldn't you really rather have a "new and improved" edition of this book rather than a "second" edition?

Acts Fast

19 "Acts" and "works" are two popular weasel words in advertising because they bring action to the product and to the advertising claim. When you see the ad for the cough syrup that "Acts on the cough control center," ask yourself what this cough syrup is claiming to do. Well, it's just claiming to "act," to do something, to perform an action. What is it that the cough syrup does? The ad doesn't say. It only claims to perform an action or do something on your "cough control center." By the way, what and where is your "cough control center"? I don't remember learning about that part of the body in human biology class.

20   Ads that use such phrases as "acts fast," "acts against," "acts to prevent," and the like are saying essentially nothing, because "act" is a word empty of any specific meaning. The ads are always careful not to specify exactly what "act" the product performs. Just because a brand of aspirin claims to "act fast" for headache relief doesn't mean this aspirin is any better than any other aspirin. What is the "act" that this aspirin performs? You're never told. Maybe it just dissolves quickly. Since aspirin is a parity product, all aspirin is the same and therefore functions the same.

Works Like Anything Else

21 If you don't find the word "acts" in an ad, you will probably find the weasel word "works." In fact, the two words are almost interchangeable in advertising. Watch out for ads that say a product "works against," "works like," "works for," or "works longer." As with "acts," "works" is the same meaningless verb used to make you think that this product really does something, and maybe even something special or unique. But "works," like "acts," is basically a word empty of any specific meaning.

Like Magic

22 Whenever advertisers want you to stop thinking about the product and to start thinking about something bigger, better, or more attractive than the product, they use that very popular weasel word, "like." The word "like" is the advertiser's equivalent of a magician's use of misdirection. "Like" gets you to ignore the product and concentrate on the claim the advertiser is making about it. "For skin like peaches and cream" claims the ad for a skin cream. What is this ad really claiming? It doesn't say this cream will give you peaches-and-cream skin. There is no verb in this claim, so it doesn't even mention using the product. How is skin ever like "peaches and cream"? Remember, ads must be read literally and exactly, according to the dictionary definition of words. (Remember "virtually" in the Eli Lilly case.) The ad is making absolutely no promise or claim whatsoever for this skin cream. If you think

this cream will give you soft, smooth, youthful-looking skin, you are the one who has read that meaning into the ad.

23   The wine that claims "It's like taking a trip to France" wants you to think about a romantic evening in Paris as you walk along the boulevard after a wonderful meal in an intimate little bistro. Of course, you don't really believe that a wine can take you to France, but the goal of the ad is to get you to think pleasant, romantic thoughts about France and not about how the wine tastes or how expensive it may be. That little word "like" has taken you away from crushed grapes into a world of your own imaginative making. Who knows, maybe the next time you buy wine, you'll think those pleasant thoughts when you see this brand of wine, and you'll buy it. Or, maybe you weren't even thinking about buying wine at all, but now you just might pick up a bottle the next time you're shopping. Ah, the power of "like" in advertising.

24   How about the most famous "like" claim of all, "Winston tastes good like a cigarette should"? Ignoring the grammatical error here, you might want to know what this claim is saying. Whether a cigarette tastes good or bad is a subjective judgment because what tastes good to one person may well taste horrible to another. Not everyone likes fried snails, even if they are called escargot. (*De gustibus non est disputandum,* which was probably the Roman rule for advertising as well as for defending the games in the Colosseum.) There are many people who say all cigarettes taste terrible, other people who say only some cigarettes taste all right, and still others who say all cigarettes taste good. Who's right? Everyone, because taste is a matter of personal judgment.

25   Moreover, note the use of the conditional, "should." The complete claim is, "Winston tastes good like a cigarette should taste." But should cigarettes taste good? Again, this is a matter of personal judgment and probably depends most on one's experiences with smoking. So, the Winston ad is simply saying that Winston cigarettes are just like any other cigarette: Some people like them and some people don't. On that statement, R. J. Reynolds conducted a very successful multimillion-dollar advertising campaign that helped keep Winston the number-two-selling cigarette in the United States, close behind number one, Marlboro.

Can't It Be Up to the Claim?

26   Analyzing ads for doublespeak requires that you pay attention to every word in the ad and determine what each word really means. Advertisers try to wrap their claims in language that sounds concrete, specific, and objective, when in fact the language of advertising is anything but. Your job is to read carefully and listen critically so that when the announcer says that "Crest can be of significant value . . . ," you know immediately that this claim says absolutely nothing. Where is the doublespeak in this ad? Start with the second word.

27   Once again, you have to look at what words really mean, not what you think they mean or what the advertiser wants you to think they mean. The ad for Crest only says that using Crest "can be" of "significant value." What really throws you off in this ad is the brilliant use of "significant." It draws your attention to the word "value" and makes you forget that the ad only claims that Crest "can be." The ad

doesn't say that Crest *is* of value, only that it is "able" or "possible" to be of value, because that's all that "can" means.

28   It's so easy to miss the importance of those little words, "can be." Almost as easy as missing the importance of the words "up to" in an ad. These words are very popular in sales ads. You know, the ones that say, "Up to 50 percent Off!" Now, what does that claim mean? Not much, because the store or manufacturer has to reduce the price of only a few items by 50 percent. Everything else can be reduced a lot less, or not even reduced. Moreover, don't you want to know 50 percent off of what? Is it 50 percent off the "manufacturer's suggested list price," which is the highest possible price? Was the price artificially inflated and then reduced? In other ads, "up to" expresses an ideal situation. The medicine that works "up to ten times faster," the battery that lasts "up to twice as long," and the soap that gets you "up to twice as clean" all are based on ideal situations for using those products, situations in which you can be sure you will never find yourself.

Unfinished Words

29   Unfinished words are a kind of "up to" claim in advertising. The claim that a battery lasts "up to twice as long" usually doesn't finish the comparison—twice as long as what? A birthday candle? A tank of gas? A cheap batter made in a country not noted for its technological achievements? The implication is that the battery last twice as long as batteries made by other battery makers, or twice as long as earlier model batteries made by the advertiser, but the ad doesn't really make these claims. You read these claims into the ad, aided by the visual images the advertiser so carefully provides.

30   Unfinished words depend on you to finish them, to provide the words the advertisers so thoughtfully left out of the ad. Pall Mall cigarettes were once advertised as "A longer finer and milder smoke." The question is, longer, finer, and milder than what? The aspirin that claims it contains "Twice as much of the pain reliever doctors recommend most" doesn't tell you what pain reliever it contains twice as much of. (By the way, it's aspirin. That's right; it just contains twice the amount of aspirin. And how much is twice the amount? Twice of what amount?) Panadol boasts that "nobody reduces fever faster," but, since Panadol is a parity product, this claim simply means that Panadol isn't any better than any other product in its parity class. "You can be sure if it's Westinghouse," you're told, but just exactly what it is you can be sure of is never mentioned. "Magnavox gives you more" doesn't tell you what you get more of. More value? More television? More than they gave you before? It sounds nice, but it means nothing, until you fill in the claim with your own words, the words the advertisers didn't use. Since each of us fills in the claim differently, the ad and the product can become all things to all people, and not promise a single thing.

31   Unfinished words abound in advertising because they appear to promise so much. More importantly, they can be joined with powerful visual images on television to appear to be making significant promises about a product's effectiveness without really making any promises. In a television ad, the aspirin product that

claims fast relief can show a person with a headache taking the product and then, in what appears to be a matter of minutes, claiming complete relief. This visual image is far more powerful than any claim made in unfinished words. Indeed, the visual image completes the unfinished words for you, filling in with pictures what the words leave out. And you thought that ads didn't affect you. What brand of aspirin do you use?

32   Some years ago, Ford's advertisements proclaimed "Ford LTD—700 percent quieter." Now, what do you think Ford was claiming with these unfinished words? What was the Ford LTD quieter than? A Cadillac? A Mercedes Benz? A BMW? Well, when the FTC asked Ford to substantiate this unfinished claim, Ford replied that it meant that the inside of the LTD was 700 percent quieter than the outside. How did you finish those unfinished words when you first read them? Did you even come close to Ford's meaning?

Combining Weasel Words

33 A lot of ads don't fall neatly into one category or another because they use a variety of different devices and words. Different weasel words are often combined to make an ad claim. The claim, "Coffee-Mate gives coffee more body, more flavor," uses Unfinished Words ("more" than what?) and also uses words that have no specific meaning ("body" and "flavor"). Along with "taste" (remember the Winston ad and its claim to taste good), "body" and "flavor" mean nothing because their meaning is entirely subjective. To you, "body" in coffee might mean thick, black, almost bitter coffee, while I might take it to mean a light brown, delicate coffee. Now, if you think you understood that last sentence, read it again, because it said nothing of objective value; it was filled with weasel words of no specific meaning: "thick," "black," "bitter," "light brown," and "delicate." Each of those words has no specific, objective meaning, because each of us can interpret them differently.

34   Try this slogan: "Looks, smells, tastes like ground-roast coffee." So, are you now going to buy Taster's Choice instant coffee because of this ad? "Looks," "smells," and "tastes" are all words with no specific meaning and depend on your interpretation of them for any meaning. Then there's that great weasel word "like," which simply suggests a comparison but does not make the actual connection between the product and the quality. Besides, do you know what "ground-roast" coffee is? I don't, but it sure sounds good. So, out of seven words in this ad, four are definite weasel words, two are quite meaningless, and only one has any clear meaning.

35   Remember the Anacin ad—"Twice as much of the pain reliever doctors recommend most"? There's a whole lot of weaseling going on in this ad. First, what's the pain reliever they're talking about in this ad? Aspirin, of course. In fact, any time you see or hear an ad using those words "pain reliever," you can automatically substitute the word "aspirin" for them. (Makers of acetaminophen and ibuprofen pain relievers are careful in their advertising to identify their products as nonaspirin products.) So, now we know that Anacin has aspirin in it. Moreover, we know that Anacin has twice as much aspirin in it, but we don't know twice as much as what.

Does it have twice as much aspirin as an ordinary aspirin tablet? If so, what is an ordinary aspirin tablet, and how much aspirin does it contain? Twice as much as Excedrin or Bufferin? Twice as much as a chocolate chip cookie? Remember those Unfinished Words and how they lead you on without saying anything.

36   Finally, what about those doctors who are doing all that recommending? Who are they? How many of them are there? What kind of doctors are they? What are their qualifications? Who asked them about recommending pain relievers? What other pain relievers did they recommend? And there are a whole lot more questions about this "poll" of doctors to which I'd like to know the answers, but you get the point. Sometimes, when I call my doctor, she tells me to take two aspirin and call her office in the morning. Is that where Anacin got this ad?

Read the Label, or the Brochure

37 Weasel words aren't just found on television, on the radio, or in newspaper and magazine ads. Just about any language associated with a product will contain the doublespeak of advertising. Remember the Eli Lilly case and the doublespeak on the information sheet that came with the birth control pills. Here's another example.

38   In 1983, the Estée Lauder cosmetics company announced a new product called "Night Repair." A small brochure distributed with the product stated that "Night Repair was scientifically formulated in Estée Lauder's U.S. laboratories as part of the Swiss Age-Controlling Skincare Program. Although only nature controls the aging process, this program helps control the signs of aging and encourages skin to look and feel younger." You might want to read these two sentences again, because they sound great but say nothing.

39   First, note that the product was "scientifically formulated" in the company's laboratories. What does that mean? What constitutes a scientific formulation? You wouldn't expect the company to say that the product was casually, mechanically, or carelessly formulated, or just thrown together one day when the people in the white coats didn't have anything better to do. But the word "scientifically" lends an air of precision and promise that just isn't there.

40   It is the second sentence, however, that's really weasely, both syntactically and semantically. The only factual part of this sentence is the introductory dependent clause—"only nature controls the aging process." Thus, the only fact in the ad is relegated to a dependent clause, a clause dependent on the main clause, which contains no factual or definite information at all and indeed purports to contradict the independent clause. The new "skincare program" (notice it's not a skin cream but a "program") does not claim to stop or even retard the aging process. What, then, does Night Repair, at a price of over $35 (in 1983 dollars) for a .87-ounce bottle do? According to this brochure, nothing. It only "helps," and the brochure does not say how much it helps. Moreover, it only "helps control," and then it only helps control the "*signs* of aging," not the aging itself. Also, it "encourages" skin not to *be* younger but only to "look and feel" younger. The brochure does not say younger than what. Of the sixteen words in the main clause of this second sentence, nine are weasel

words. So, before you spend all that money for Night Repair, or any other cosmetic product, read the words carefully, and then decide if you're getting what you think you're paying for.

Other Tricks of the Trade

41 Advertisers' use of doublespeak is endless. The best way advertisers can make something out of nothing is through words. Although there are a lot of visual images used on television and in magazines and newspapers, every advertiser wants to create that memorable line that will stick in the public consciousness. I am sure pure joy reigned in one advertising agency when a study found that children who were asked to spell the word "relief" promptly and proudly responded "r-o-l-a-i-d-s."

42 The variations, combinations, and permutations of doublespeak used in advertising go and on, running from the use of rhetorical questions ("Wouldn't you really rather have a Buick?" "If you can't trust Prestone, who can you trust?") to flattering you with compliments ("The lady has taste." "We think a cigar smoker is someone special." "You've come a long way baby."). You know, of course, how you're *supposed* to answer those questions, and you know that those compliments are just leading up to the sales pitches for the products. Before you dismiss such tricks of the trade as obvious, however, just remember that all of these statements and questions were part of very successful advertising campaigns.

43 A more subtle approach is the ad that proclaims a supposedly unique quality for a product, a quality that really isn't unique. "If it doesn't say Goodyear, it can't be polyglas." Sounds good, doesn't it? Polyglas is available only from Goodyear because Goodyear copyrighted that trade name. Any other tire manufacturer could make exactly the same tire but could not call it "polyglas," because that would be copyright infringement. "Polyglas" is simply Goodyear's name for its fiberglass-reinforced tire.

44 Since we like to think of ourselves as living in a technologically advanced country, science and technology have a great appeal in selling products. Advertisers are quick to use scientific doublespeak to push their products. There are all kinds of elixirs, additives, scientific potions, and mysterious mixtures added to all kinds of products. Gasoline contains "HTA," "F–130," "Platformate," and other chemical-sounding additives, but nowhere does an advertisement give any real information about the additive.

45 Shampoo, deodorant, mouthwash, cold medicine, sleeping pills, and any number of other products all seem to contain some special chemical ingredient that allows them to work wonders. "Certs contains a sparkling drop of Retsyn." So what? What's "Retsyn"? What's it do? What's so special about it? When they don't have a secret ingredient in their product, advertisers still find a way to claim scientific validity. There's "Sinarest. Created by a research scientist who actually gets sinus headaches." Sounds nice, but what kind of research does this scientist do? How do you know if she is any kind of expert on sinus medicine? Besides, this ad doesn't tell you a thing about the medicine itself and what it does.

Advertising Doublespeak Quick Quiz

46 Now it's time to test your awareness of advertising doublespeak. (You didn't think I would just let you read this and forget it, did you?) The following is a list of statements from some recent ads. Your job is to figure out what each of these ads really says.

DOMINO'S PIZZA: "Because nobody delivers better."

SINUTAB: "It can stop the pain."

TUMS: "The stronger acid neutralizer."

MAXIMUM STRENGTH DRISTAN: "Strong medicine for tough sinus colds."

LISTERMINT: "Making your mouth a cleaner place."

CASCADE: "For virtually spotless dishes nothing beats Cascade."

NUPRIN: "Little. Yellow. Different. Better."

ANACIN: "Better relief."

SUDAFED: "Fast sinus relief that won't put you fast asleep."

ADVIL: "Better relief."

PONDS COLD CREAM: "Ponds cleans like no soap can."

MILLER LITE BEER: "Tastes great. Less filling."

PHILIPS MILK OF MAGNESIA: "Nobody treats you better than MOM (Philips Milk of Magnesia)."

BAYER: "The wonder drug that works wonders."

CRACKER BARREL: "Judged to be the best."

KNORR: "Where taste is everything."

ANUSOL: "Anusol is the word to remember for relief."

DIMETAPP: "It relieves kids as well as colds."

LIQUID DRÁNO: "The liquid strong enough to be called Dráno."

JOHNSON & JOHNSON BABY POWDER: "Like magic for your skin."

PURITAN: "Make it your oil for life."

PAM: "Pam, because how you cook is as important as what you cook."

IVORY SHAMPOO AND CONDITIONER: "Leave your hair feeling Ivory clean."

TYLENOL GEL-CAPS: "It's not a capsule. It's better."

ALKA-SELTZER PLUS: "Fast, effective relief for winter colds."

The World of Advertising

47 In the world of advertising, people wear "dentures," not false teeth; they suffer from "occasional irregularity," not constipation; they need deodorants for their "nervous wetness," not for sweat; they use "bathroom tissue," not toilet paper; and they don't dye their hair, they "tint" or "rinse" it. Advertisements offer "real counterfeit diamonds" without the slightest hint of embarrassment, or boast of goods made out of "genuine imitation leather" or "virgin vinyl."

48   In the world of advertising, the girdle becomes a "body shaper," "form persuader," "control garment," "controller," "outerwear enhancer," "body garment," or

"anti-gravity panties," and is sold with such trade names as "The Instead," "The Free Spirit," and "The Body Briefer."

49   A study some years ago found the following words to be among the most popu-lar used in U.S. television advertisements: "new," "improved," "better," "extra," "fresh," "clean," "beautiful," "free," "good," "great," and "light." At the same time, the following words were found to be among the most frequent on British television: "new," "good-better-best," "free," "fresh," "delicious," "full," "sure," "clean," "wonderful," and "special." While these words may occur most frequently in ads, and while ads may be filled with weasel words, you have to watch out for all the words used in advertising, not just the words mentioned here.

50   Every word in an ad is there for a reason; no word is wasted. Your job is to fig-ure out exactly what each word is doing in an ad—what each word really means, not what the advertiser wants you to think it means. Remember, the ad is trying to get you to buy a product, so it will put the product in the best possible light, using any device, trick, or means legally allowed. Your own defense against advertising (be-sides taking up permanent residence on the moon) is to develop and use a strong critical reading, listening, and looking ability. Always ask yourself what the ad is *re-ally* saying. When you see ads on television, don't be misled by the pictures, the vi-sual images. What does the ad say about the product? What does the ad *not* say? What information is missing from the ad? Only by becoming an active, critical con-sumer of the doublespeak of advertising will you ever be able to cut through the doublespeak and discover what the ad is really saying.

51   Professor Del Kehl of Arizona State University has updated the Twenty-third Psalm to reflect the power of advertising to meet our needs and solve our problems. It seems fitting that this chapter close with this new Psalm.

The Adman's 23rd
The Adman is my shepherd;
I shall ever want.
He maketh me to walk a mile for a Camel;
He leadeth me beside Crystal Waters
    In the High Country of Coors;
He restoreth my soul with Perrier.
He guideth me in Marlboro Country
For Mammon's sake.
Yea, though I walk through the Valley of the
    Jolly Green Giant,
In the shadow of B.O., halitosis, indigestion,
    headache pain, and hemorrhoidal tissue,
I will fear no evil,
For I am in Good Hands with Allstate;
Thy Arid, Scope, Tums, Tylenol, and Preparation H—
They comfort me.
Stouffer's preparest a table before the TV

In the presence of all my appetites;
Thou anointest my head with Brylcream;
My Decaffeinated Cup runneth over.
Surely surfeit and security shall follow me
All the days of Metropolitan Life,
And I shall dwell in a Continental Home
With a mortgage forever and ever.

Amen.

EXPLORING THE TEXT

1. How did weasel words get their name? Does it sound like an appropriate label? Why, according to Lutz, do advertisers use them?
2. What regulations restrict the use of the word *new*? How can these regulations be sidestepped? In your opinion, do these regulations serve the interests of the advertiser or the consumer?
3. Do you think that most people fail to comprehend how advertising works on them? When you read ads or watch commercials on television, do you see through the gimmicks and weasel words?
4. According to the author, how can consumers protect themselves against weasel words?
5. The author uses "you" throughout the article. Do you find the use of the second person stylistically satisfying?
6. What do you think of Lutz's writing style? Is it humorous, informal, academic? What difference strategies does he use to involve the reader in the piece?
7. What do you think about Lutz ending his article with a parody of the Twenty-third Psalm? Do you find it appropriate and funny? Does it suit the theme of the essay?

WRITING ASSIGNMENTS

1. The essays in this chapter deal with advertising and its effects on consumers and their value systems. Describe how understanding the linguistic strategies of advertisers—as exemplified by Lutz here—will or will not change your reaction to advertising.
2. As Lutz suggests, look at some ads in a magazine and newspaper (or television and radio commercials). Then make a list of all uses of one of the following weasel words you find over a 24-hour period: *help*, *new*, *improved*, and *introducing*. Examine the ads to determine exactly what is

said and what the unwary consumer thinks is being said. Write up your report.

3. Imagine that you are the customer relations director for a popular cosmetic product that promised it would "help stop the aging process." Write an answer to a letter from a disgruntled customer who bought your product and found it not satisfactory because it did not live up to the advertising claims.

GROUP ASSIGNMENTS

1. Working with a small group of classmates, rewrite five ads for the same type of heavily advertised product (e.g., beer, gasoline, aspirin, or sparkling water), "literally and exactly, according to the dictionary definition." Discuss the weasel words, unfinished words, and subjective words that you have replaced. Write up a report and pass it in with your ads.

2. Brainstorming with classmates, invent a product and have some fun writing an ad for it. Use as many weasel words as you can to make your product irresistible.

3. Working in a group, undertake a research project on theories of advertising: Find books by professional advertisers or texts for courses in advertising and marketing and then go through them trying to determine how they might view Lutz's interpretation of advertising techniques. How would the authors view Lutz's claim that advertising language is loaded with "weasel words"?

CON

The Language of Advertising
Charles A. O'Neill

Taking the minority opinion is a former advertising executive Charles A. O'Neill, who disputes the criticism of advertising language by William Lutz and other critics of advertising. While admitting to some of the craftiness of his profession, O'Neill defends the huckster's language—both verbal and visual—against claims that it debases reality and the values of the consumer. Examining some familiar television commercials and recent print ads, he explains why the language may be seductive but far from brainwashing.

This essay, originally written for *Exploring Language,* edited by Gary Goshgarian, has been updated for this text. O'Neill is an independent marketing consultant.

1 The figure on the billboard and in the magazine ads looked like a rock singer, perhaps photographed in the midst of a music video taping session. He was poised, con-

fident, shown leaning against a railing or playing pool with his friends. His personal geometry was always just right. He often wore a white suit, dark shirt, sunglasses. Cigarette in hand, wry smile on his lips, his attitude was distinctly confident, urbane.

2   He was so successful, this full-lipped, ubiquitous dromedary, that his success quite literally killed him. By mid-1997, with such people and agencies as President Clinton and the Federal Trade Commission harassing him at every turn, his masters had no choice. Camel market share reportedly climbed from 3.9 percent in 1989 to 4.4 percent by 1990. According to the FTC, six years after Joe was introduced, more than 13 percent of all smokers under the age of 18 chose Camels as their nicotine delivery system of choice. Finally, the president lent his weight to what had already become a raging debate. "Let's stop pretending that a cartoon camel in a funny costume is trying to sell to adults, not children." New rules, introduced largely as a result of the debate about Joe, prohibit the use of cartoon characters in advertisements.

3   The obvious topic of the debate that finally killed Joe is cigarette advertising, but beneath the surface it signals something more interesting and broad based: the rather uncomfortable, tentative acceptance of advertising in our society. We recognize the legitimacy—even the value—of advertising, but on some level we can't quite fully embrace it as a "normal" part of our experience. At best, we view it as distracting. At worst, we view it as dangerous to our health and a pernicious threat to our social values. Also lending moral support to the debate about advertising is no less an authority than the Vatican. In 1997, the Vatican issued a document prepared by the Pontifical Council, titled "Ethics in Advertising." Along with acknowledgment of the positive contribution of advertising (e.g., provides information, supports worthy causes, encourages competition and innovation), the report states, as reported by the *Boston Globe,* "In the competition to attract ever larger audiences . . . communicators can find themselves pressured . . . to set aside high artistic and moral standards and lapse into superficiality, tawdriness and moral squalor."

4   How does advertising work? Why is it so powerful? Why does it raise such concern? What case can be made for and against the advertising business? In order to understand advertising, you must accept that it is not about truth, virtue, love, or positive social values. It is about money. Ads play a role in moving customers through the sales process. This process begins with an effort to build awareness of a product, typically achieved by tactics designed to break through the clutter of competitive messages. By presenting a description of product benefits, ads convince the customer to buy the product. Once prospects have become purchasers, advertising is used to sustain brand loyalty, reminding customers of all the good reasons for their original decision to buy.

5   But this does not sufficiently explain the ultimate, unique power of advertising. Whatever the product or creative strategy, advertisements derive their power from a purposeful, directed combination of images. Images can take the form of words, sounds, or visuals, used individually or together. The combination of images is the language of advertising, a language unlike any other.

6   Everyone who grows up in the Western world soon learns that advertising language is different from other languages. Most children would be unable to explain how such lines as "With Nice 'n Easy, it's color so natural, the closer he gets the

better you look!" (the once-famous ad for Clairol's Nice 'n Easy hair coloring) differed from ordinary language, but they would say, "It sounds like an ad." Whether printed on a page, blended with music on the radio, or whispered on the sound track of a television commercial, advertising language is "different."

7   Over the years, the texture of advertising language has frequently changed. Styles and creative concepts come and go. But there are at least four distinct, general characteristics of the language of advertising that make it different from other languages. They lend advertising its persuasive power:

1. The language of advertising is edited and purposeful.
2. The language of advertising is rich and arresting; it is specifically intended to attract and hold our attention.
3. The language of advertising involves us; in effect, *we* complete the message.
4. The language of advertising is a simple language; it holds no secrets from us.

Edited and Purposeful

8   In his famous book *Future Shock,* Alvin Toffler describes various types of messages we receive from the world around us each day. As he sees it, there is a difference between normal "coded" messages and "engineered" messages. Much of normal, human experience is "uncoded"; it is merely sensory. For example, Toffler describes a man walking down a street. Toffler notes that the man's sensory perceptions of this experience may form a mental image, but the message is not "designed by anyone to communicate anything, and the man's understanding of it does not depend directly on a social code—a set of agreed-upon signs and definitions."[1] In contrast, Toffler describes a talk show conversation as "coded"; the speakers' ability to exchange information with their host, and our ability to understand it, depend upon social conventions.

9   The language of advertising is coded. It is also a language of carefully engineered, ruthlessly purposeful messages. When Toffler wrote *Future Shock,* he estimated that the average adult was exposed to 560 advertising messages each day. Now, with the advent of 200-channel, direct-broadcast satellite television, the Internet, and other new forms of mass media Toffler could not have contemplated, this figure is surely exponentially higher today. None of these messages would reach us, to attract and hold our attention, if it were completely unstructured. Advertising messages have a clear purpose; they are intended to trigger a specific response.

Rich and Arresting

10   Advertisements—no matter how carefully "engineered"—cannot succeed unless they capture our attention. Of the hundreds of advertising messages in store for us each day, very few will actually command our conscious attention. The rest are screened out. The people who design and write ads know about this screening process; they anticipate and accept it as a premise of their business.

11   The classic, all-time favorite device used to breach the barrier is sex. The desire to be sexually attractive to others is an ancient instinct, and few drives are more

powerful. A magazine ad for Ultima II, a line of cosmetics, invites readers to "find everything you need for the sexxxxiest look around. . . ." The ad goes on to offer other "Sexxxy goodies," including "Lipsexxxxy lip color, naked eye color . . . Sunsexxxy liquid bronzer." No one will accuse Ultima's marketing tacticians of subtlety. In fact, this ad is merely a current example of an approach that is as old as advertising. After countless years of using images of women in various stages of undress to sell products, ads are not displaying men's bodies as well. A magazine ad for Brut, a men's cologne, declares in bold letters, "MEN ARE BACK"; in the background, a photograph shows a muscular, shirtless young man preparing to enter the boxing ring—a 'manly' image indeed; an image of man as breeding stock.

12   Every successful advertisement uses a creative strategy based on an idea that will attract and hold the attention of the targeted consumer audience. The strategy may include strong creative execution or a straightforward presentation of product features and customer benefits.

- An ad for Clif Bars, an "energy bar," is clearly directed to people who want to snack but wouldn't be caught dead in a coffee house eating ginger spice cake with delicate frosting, much less ordinary energy bars—the kind often associated with the veggie and granola set: The central photograph shows a gristled cowboy-character, holding a Clif Bar, and asking, in the headline, "What 'n the hell's a carbohydrate?" Nosiree. This here energy bar is "bound to satisfy cantankerous folk like you."
- Recent cigar ads attract attention through the use of unexpected imagery. An ad for Don Diego cigars, for example, shows a bejeweled woman in an evening dress smoking a cigar, while through the half-open door her male companion asks, "Agnes, have you seen my Don Diegos?"
- A two-page ad for Diesel clothing includes a photo showing the principal participants in the famous Yalta conference in 1945 (Churchill, Roosevelt, and Stalin) with one important difference: Young models in Diesel clothing have been cleverly added and appear to be flirting with the dignitaries. The ad is presented as a "Diesel historical moment" and "the birth of the modern conference." This unexpected imagery is engaging and amusing, appealing to the product's youthful target audience.

Even if the text contains no incongruity and does not rely on a pun for its impact, ads typically use a creative strategy based on some striking concept or idea. In fact, the concept and execution are often so good that many successful ads entertain while they sell.

13   Consider, for example, the campaigns created for Federal Express. A campaign was developed to position Federal Express as the company that would deliver packages, not just "overnight," but "by 10:30 A.M." the next day. The plight of the junior executive in "Presentation," one TV ad in the campaign, is stretched for dramatic purposes, but it is, nonetheless, all too real: The young executive, who is presumably try to climb his way up the corporate ladder, is shown calling another parcel delivery service and all but begging for assurance that he will have his slides in hand by 10:30 the next morning. "No slides, no presentation," he pleads. Only a viewer with a heart of stone can watch without feeling sympathetic as the next morning our

junior executive struggles to make his presentation *sans* slides. He is so lost without them that he is reduced to using his hands to preform imitations of birds and animals in shadows on the movie screen. What does the junior executive *viewer* think when he or she sees the ad?

1. Federal Express guarantees to deliver packages "absolutely, positively overnight."
2. Federal Express packages arrive early in the day.
3. What happened to that fellow in the commercial will absolutely not happen to me, now that I know what package delivery service to call.

14   A sound, creative strategy supporting an innovative service idea sold Federal Express. But the quality and objective "value" of execution doesn't matter. A magazine ad for Merit Ultra Lights made use of one word in its headline: "Yo!" This was, one hopes, not the single most powerful idea generated by the agency's creative team that particular month—but it probably sold cigarettes.

15   Soft drink and fast-food companies often take another approach. "Slice of life" ads (so-called because they purport to show people in "real-life" situations) created to sell Coke or Pepsi have often placed their characters in Fourth of July parades or other family events. The archetypical version of this approach is filled-to-overflowing with babies frolicking with puppies in the sunlit foreground while their youthful parents play touch football. On the porch, Grandma and Pops are seen quietly smiling as they wait for all of this affection to transform itself in a climax of warmth, harmony, and joy. Beneath the veneer, these ads work through repetition: How-many-times-can-you-spot-the-logo-in-this-commercial?

16   More subtly, these ads seduce us into feeling that if we drink the right combination of sugar, preservatives, caramel coloring, and a few secrete ingredients, we'll fulfill our yearning for a world where young folks and old folks live together in perfect bliss.

17   If you don't buy this version of the American Dream, search long enough and you are sure to find an ad designed to sell you what it takes to gain prestige within whatever posse you do happen to run with. As reported by *The Boston Globe,* "the malt liquor industry relies heavily on rap stars in delivering its message to inner-city youths, while Black Death Vodka, which features a top-hatted skull and a coffin on its label, has been using Guns N' Roses guitarist Slash to endorse the product in magazine advertising." A malt liquor company reportedly promotes its 40-ounce size with rapper King T singing, "I usually drink it when I'm just out clowning, me and the home boys, you know, be like downing it . . . I grab me a 40 when I want to act a fool." A recent ad for Sasson jeans is a long way from Black Death in execution, but a second cousin in spirit. A photograph of a young, blonde (they do have more fun, right?) actress appears with this text: "Baywatch actress Gena Lee Nolin Puts On Sasson. OO-LA-LA. Sasson. Don't put it on unless it's Sasson."

18   Ads do not often emerge like Botticelli's Venus from the sea, flawless and fully grown. Most often, the creative strategy is developed only after extensive research. "Who will be interested in our product? How old are they? Where do they live?

How much money do they earn? What problem will our product solve?" Answers to these questions provide the foundation on which the creative strategy is built.

Involving

19 We have seen that the language of advertising is carefully engineered; we have discovered a few of the devices it uses to get our attention. R. J. Reynolds has us identifying with Joe in one of his many uptown poses. Coke and Pepsi have caught our eye with visions of peace and love. An actress offers a winsome smile. Now that they have our attention, advertisers present information intended to show us that their product fills a need and differs from the competition. It is the copywriter's responsibility to express, exploit, and intensify such product differences.

20 When product differences do not exist, the writer must glamorize the superficial differences—for example, differences in packaging. As long as the ad is trying to get our attention, the "action" is mostly in the ad itself, in the words and visual images. But as we read an ad or watch it on television, we become more deeply involved. The action starts to take place in us. Our imagination is set in motion, and our individual fears and aspirations, quirks, and insecurities, superimpose themselves on that tightly engineered, attractively packaged message.

21 Consider, once again, the running battle among the low-calorie soft drinks. The cola wars have spawned many "look-alike" advertisements, because the product features and consumer benefits are generic, applying to all products in the category. Substitute one cola brand name for another, and the messages are often identical, right down to the way the cans are photographed in the closing sequence. This strategy relies upon mass saturation and exposure for impact.

22 Some companies have set themselves apart from their competitors by making use of bold, even disturbing, themes and images. For example, it was not uncommon not long ago for advertisers in the fashion industry to make use of gaunt, languid models—models who, in the interpretation of some observers, displayed a certain form of "heroin chic." Something was most certainly unusual about the models appearing in ads for Prada and Calvin Klein products. A young woman in a Prada ad projects no emotion whatsoever; she is slightly hunched forward, her posture suggesting that she is in a trance or drug-induced stupor. In a Calvin Klein ad, a young man, like the woman in the Prada ad, is gaunt beyond reason. He is shirtless. As if to draw more attention to his peculiar posture and "zero body fat" status, he is shown pinching the skin next to his navel.

23 Just as he publicly attacked Joe Camel, President Clinton took an aggressive position against the depiction of heroin chic. In a speech in Washington, D.C., the president commented on the increasing use of heroin on college campuses, noting that "part of this has to do with the images that are finding their way to our young people." One industry observer agreed, asserting that "people got carried away by the glamour of decadence."

24 Do such advertisers as Prada and Calvin Klein bear responsibility—morally, if not legally—for the rise of heroin use on college campuses? Emergency room visits connected with heroin use reportedly grew from 63,200 in 1993 to 76,000 by 1995,

echoing a strong rise in heroin addiction. Is this a coincidence? Does heroin chic and its depiction of a decadent lifestyle exploit certain elements of our society—the young and uncertain, for example? Or did these ads, and others of their ilk, simply reflect profound bad taste? In fact, on one level, all advertising is about exploitation: the systematic, deliberate identification of our needs and wants, followed by the delivery of a carefully constructed promise that Brand X will satisfy them.

25   Symbols offer an important tool for involving consumers in advertisements. Symbols have become important elements in the language of advertising, not so much because they carry meanings of their own, but because we bring meaning to them. One example is provided by the campaign begun in 1978 by Somerset Importers for Johnnie Walker Red Scotch. Sales of Johnnie Walker Red had been trailing sales of Johnnie Walker Black, and Somerset Importers needed to position Red as a fine product in its own right. Their agency produced ads that made heavy use of the color red. One magazine ad, often printed as a two-page spread, is dominated by a close-up photo of red autumn leaves. At lower right, the copy reads, "When their work is done, even the leaves turn to Red." Another ad—also suitably dominated by a photograph in the appropriate color—reads: "When it's time to quiet down at the end of the day, even a fire turns to Red." Red. Warm. Experienced. Seductive.

26   As we have seen, advertisers make use of a great variety of techniques and devices to engage us in the delivery of their messages. Some are subtle, making use of warm, entertaining, or comforting images or symbols. Others, like Black Death Vodka and Ultima II, are about as subtle as MTV's "Beavis and Butt-head." Another common device used to engage our attention is old but still effective: the use of famous or notorious personalities as product spokespeople or models. Advertising writers did not invent the human tendency to admire or otherwise identify themselves with famous people. Once we have seen a famous person in an ad, we associate the product with the person: "Joe DiMaggio is a good guy. he likes Mr. Coffee. If I buy a Mr. Coffee coffee maker and I use it when I have the boss over for dinner, then maybe she'll think I'm a good guy, too." "Guns 'N Roses rule my world, so I will definitely make the scene with a bottle of Black Death stuck into the waistband of my sweat pants." "Gena Lee Nolin is totally sexy. She wears Sasson. If I wear Sasson, I'll be sexy, too." The logic is faulty, but we fall under the spell just the same. Advertising works, not because Joe DiMaggio is a coffee expert, Slash had discriminating taste, or Gena knows her jeans, but because we participate in it. In fact, we charge ads with most of their power.

A Simple Language

27 Advertising language differs from other types of language in another important respect; it is a simple language. To determine how the copy of a typical advertisement rates on a "simplicity index" in comparison with text in a magazine article, for example, try this exercise: Clip a typical story from the publication you read most frequently. Calculate the number of words in an average sentence. Count the number of words of three or more syllables in a typical 100-word passage, omitting words that are capitalized, com-

binations of two simple words, or verb forms made into three-syllable words by the addition of *-ed* or *-es.* Add the two figures (the average number of words per sentence and the number of three-syllable words per 100 words), then multiply the result by .4. According to Robert Gunning, if the resulting number is 7, there is a good chance that you are reading *True Confessions.*[2] He developed this formula, the "Fog Index," to determine the comparative ease with which any given piece of written communication can be read. Here is the complex text of a typical cigarette endorsement:

> I demand two things from my cigarette. I want a cigarette with low tar and nicotine. But I also want taste. That's why I smoke Winston Lights. I get a lighter cigarette, but I still get a real taste. And real pleasure. Only one cigarette gives me that: Winston Lights.

The average sentence in this ad runs 7 words. *Cigarette* and *nicotine* are three syllable words, with *cigarette* appearing four times; *nicotine,* once. Consider *that's* as two words, the ad is exactly 50 words long, so the average number of three-syllable words per 100 is ten.

$$
\begin{array}{ll}
7 & \text{words per sentence} \\
+\,10 & \text{three-syllable words/100} \\
\hline
17 & \\
\times\ .4 & \\
\hline
6.8 & \text{Fog Index}
\end{array}
$$

According to Gunning's scale, this ad—which has now been consigned to the dustbin of advertising history thanks to government regulations—is written at about the seventh-grade level, comparable to most of the ads found in mass-circulation magazines.

28   It's about as sophisticated as *True Confessions;* that is, harder to read than a comic book, but easier than *Ladies Home Journal.* Of course, the Fog Index cannot evaluate the visual aspect of an ad—another component of advertising language. The headline, "I demand two things from my cigarette," works with the picture (that of an attractive woman) to arouse consumer interest. The text reinforces the image. Old Joe's simple plea, "Try New Camel Lights," is too short to move the needle on the Fog Index meter, but in every respect it represents perhaps the simplest language possible, a not-distant cousin of Merit Ultra Lights' groundbreaking and succinct utterance, "Yo!"

29   Why do advertisers generally favor simple language? The answer lies with the consumer: Consider Toffler's speculation that the average American adult is subject to some 560 advertising or commercial messages each day. As a practical matter, we would not notice many of these messages if length or eloquence were counted among their virtues. Today's consumer cannot take the time to focus on anything for long, much less blatant advertising messages. In effect, Toffler's "future" is here now, and it is perhaps more "shocking" than he could have foreseen at the time. Every aspect of modern life runs at an accelerated pace. Overnight mail has moved

in less than ten years from a novelty to a common business necessity. Voice mail, pagers, cellular phones, e-mail, the Internet—the world is always awake, always switched on, and hungry for more information, now. Time generally, and TV-commercial time in particular, is now dissected into increasingly smaller segments. Fifteen-second commercials are no longer unusual.

30   Toffler views the evolution toward shorter language as a natural progression: three-syllable words are simply harder to read than one- or two-syllable words. Simple ideas are more readily transferred from one person to another than complex ideas. Therefore, advertising copy uses increasingly simple language, as does society at large. In *Future Shock,* Toffler speculates:

> If the [English] language had the same number of words in Shakespeare's time as it does today, at least 200,000 words—perhaps several times that many— have dropped out and been replaced in the intervening four centuries. The high turnover rate reflects changes in things, processes, and qualities in the environment from the world of consumer products and technology.

It is no accident that the first terms Toffler uses to illustrate his point ("fast-back," "wash-and-wear," and "flashcube") were invented not by engineers, or journalists, but by advertising copywriters.

31   Advertising language is simple language; in the ad's engineering process, difficult words or images—which in other forms of communication may be used to lend color or fine shades of meaning—are edited out and replaced by simple words or images not open to misinterpretation. You don't have to ask whether King T likes to "grab a 40" when he wants to "act a fool," or whether Gena wears her Sassons when she wants to do whatever it is she does.

Who Is Responsible?

32 Some critics view the advertising business as a cranky, unwelcomed child of the free enterprise system—a noisy, whining, brash kid who must somehow be kept in line, but can't just yet be thrown out of the house. In reality, advertising mirrors the fears, quirks, and aspirations of the society that creates it (and is, in turn, sold by it). This factor alone exposes advertising to parody and ridicule. The overall level of acceptance and respect for advertising is also influenced by the varied quality of the ads themselves. Some ads, including a few of the examples cited here, seem deliberately designed to provoke controversy. For example, it is easy—as President Clinton and others charged—to conclude that Joe Camel represented a deliberate, calculated effort by R. J. Reynolds to encourage children to smoke cigarettes. But this is only one of the many charges frequently levied against advertising:

1. Advertising encourages unhealthy habits.
2. Advertising feeds on human weaknesses and exaggerates the importance of material things, encouraging "impure" emotions and vanities.

3. Advertising sells daydreams—distracting, purposeless visions of lifestyles beyond the reach of the majority of the people who are most exposed to advertising.
4. Advertising warps our vision of reality, implanting in us groundless fears and insecurities.
5. Advertising downgrades the intelligence of the public.
6. Advertising debases English.
7. Advertising perpetuates racial and sexual stereotypes.

33 What can be said in advertising's defense? Advertising is only a reflection of society. A case can be made for the concept that advertising language is an acceptable stimulus for the natural evolution of language. Is "proper English" the language most Americans actually speak and write, or is it the language we are told we should speak and write?

34 What about the charge that advertising debases the intelligence of the public? Those who support this particular criticism would do well to ask themselves another question: Exactly how intelligent is the public? Sadly, evidence abounds that "the public" at large is not particularly intelligent, after all. Johnny can't read. Susie can't write. And the entire family spends the night in front of the television, channel surfing for the latest scandal—hopefully, one involving a sports hero or political figure said to be a killer or a frequent participant in perverse sexual acts.

35 Ads are effective because they sell products. They would not succeed if they did not reflect the values and motivations of the real world. Advertising both reflects and shapes our perception of reality. Consider several brand names and the impressions they create: Ivory Snow is pure. Federal Express won't let you down. Absolut is cool. Sasson is sexxy. Mercedes represents quality. Our sense of what these brand names stand for may have as much to do with advertising as with the objective "truth."

36 Advertising shapes our perception of the world as surely as architecture shapes our impression of a city. Good, responsible advertising can serve as a positive influence for change, while generating profits. Of course, the problem is that the obverse is also true: Advertising, like any form of mass communication, can be a force for both "good" and "bad." It can just as readily reinforce or encourage irresponsible behavior, ageism, sexism, ethnocentrism, racism, homophobia, heterophobia—you name it—as it can encourage support for diversity and social progress. People living in society create advertising. Society isn't perfect. In the end, advertising simply attempts to change behavior. Do advertisements sell distracting, purposeless visions? Occasionally. But perhaps such visions are necessary components of the process through which our society changes and improves.

37 Joe's days as Camel's spokesman are over. His very success in reaching new smokers was the source of his undoing. But standing nearby and waiting to take his place is another campaign; another character, real or imagined; another product for sale. Perhaps, by learning how advertising works, we can become better equipped to sort out content from hype, product values from emotions, and salesmanship from propaganda.

Notes

1. Alvin Toffler, *Future Shock* (New York: Random House, 1970), p. 146.
2. Curtis D. MacDougall, *Interpretive Reporting* (New York: Macmillan, 1968), p. 94.

EXPLORING THE TEXT

1. O'Neill opens his essay with a discussion of the one-time controversial figure of Joe Camel. If you recall the ads, where did you stand on the controversy? Did you think such ads targeted young people and, thus, deserved to be outlawed?
2. Do you think it is ethical for advertisers to create a sense of product difference when there really isn't any? Consider ads for gasoline, beer, and instant coffee.
3. Toward the end of the essay, O'Neill anticipates potential objections to his defense of advertising. What are some of these objections? What does he say in defense of advertising? Which set of arguments do you find stronger?
4. O'Neill describes several ways in which the language of advertising differs from other kinds of language. Briefly list the ways he mentions. Can you think of any other characteristics of advertising language that set it apart?
5. What is "proper English," as contrasted with colloquial or substandard English? Do you use proper English in your written course work and in your own correspondence? What do you think about using proper English in advertising?
6. O'Neill asserts that "symbols have become important elements in the language of advertising" (paragraph 25). Can you think of some specific symbols from the advertising world that you associate with your own life? Are they effective symbols for selling? Explain your answer.
7. In paragraph 26, O'Neill claims that celebrity endorsement of a product is "faulty" logic? Explain what he means? Why do people buy products sold by famous people?
8. William Lutz teaches English and writes books about the misuse of language. Charles O'Neill is a professional advertiser. How do their views about advertising reflect their occupations? Which side of the argument do you agree with?
9. Both Lutz and O'Neill consider advertising messages to be incomplete, but in different ways. How does each author deal with this incompleteness, according to his negative or positive view of advertising?
10. How effective do you think O'Neill's introduction paragraphs are? How well does he hook the reader? What particular audience might he be ap-

pealing to early on? What attitude toward advertising is established in the introduction?

11. What are the differences in tone between the paired articles? Notice the use of the first-person plural at times in O'Neill's article, compared with overall use of second person in Lutz's essay. Which technique do you prefer?

WRITING ASSIGNMENTS

1. Obtain a current issue of each of the following publications: the *New Yorker, Time, GQ, Vogue,* and *People.* Choose one article from each periodical and calculate its Fog Index according to the technique described in paragraphs 27 and 28. Choose one ad from each periodical and figure out its Fog Index. What different reading levels do you find among the publications? What do you know about the readers of these periodicals from your survey of the reading difficulty of the articles? Write up your findings in a paper.
2. Clip three ads for products that use sex as a selling device, yet have no sexual connotations whatsoever. Explain how sex helps sell the products. Would feminists consider these ads demeaning to women? (Or, you may refer to the 12 ads that follow.)
3. O'Neill believes that advertising language mirrors the fears, quirks, and aspirations of the society that creates it. Do you agree or disagree with this statement? Explain in a brief essay.
4. Choose a brand-name product you use regularly and one of its competitors—one whose differences are negligible, if they exist at all. Examine some advertisements for each brand. Write a short paper explaining what really makes you prefer your brand.
5. Write a paper on sexism or racism in advertising. Use specific examples from current print ads and television commercials.

GROUP PROJECTS

1. Working in a group, develop a slogan and advertising campaign for one of the following products: sneakers, soda, a candy bar, or jeans. How would you apply the principles of advertising, as outlined in O'Neill's article, to market your product? After completing your marketing strategy, "sell" your product to the class. If time permits, explain the reasoning behind your selling technique.
2. With classmates brainstorm a list of some commercials or advertisements that especially annoyed you. Why exactly did they bother you? Try to locate any cultural, social, or intellectual reasons behind your annoyance or distaste. How do these commercials compare to the marketing strategies explored by O'Neill's article? Share your findings with the class.

3. With your group, identify the slogans or advertising pitches for several products such as chips, soda, games, sport products, beer, and clothing. Discuss why you think the slogan works. Can you think of any slogans that still exist in our language even after the product is no longer popular or has embraced a new marketing strategy?

4. From the collection of ads that follows, select one without much copy. (Do not use milk, Diesel, or Clif Bar.) Write an endorsement blurb for the product. When the group is satisfied with the copy, apply the Fog Index to the blurb. How does your endorsement measure on the Gunning scale? Based on your results, would you make any changes to your blurb?

Sample Ads and Study Questions

The following section features ten recently published magazine advertisements for cars, liquor, bras, energy bars, designer clothing, cigars, sneakers, milk, phone services, and the U.S. Army. Diverse in content and style, some ads use words to promote their product, while others depend on emotion, visual appeal, and name recognition. They present a variety of sales pitches and marketing techniques.

Following each ad is a list of questions to help you analyze how the ads work their appeal to promote their products. When studying them, consider how they target our social perceptions and basic desires for happiness, beauty, and success. Approach each as a consumer, an artist, a social scientist, and a critic with an eye for detail.

Love

Mercedes-Benz

1. How does this photograph capture you attention? Can you tell at a glance what this ad is selling? Consider the lighting used in the ad. Where are your eyes directed? How long does it take one to figure out what the product is? Is this a positive or negative aspect of the ad?
2. Who do you think is the target audience for this ad? To whom does it have more appeal, men or women? Why? Which socioeconomic level? In your answers, consider the associations we have with chocolate. Also consider the quality of chocolates displayed. How do the chocolates contribute to the selling of automobiles?
3. This ad appeared in a February ad campaign by Mercedes-Benz. Could it be used at any time of year? Explain.
4. How much does this ad rely on symbol recognition? How many different symbols are depicted in the picture? What meanings are associated with them?
5. What is the message of this ad?

Smirnoff

1. If you were leafing through a magazine and came across this ad, would you stop and look at it for a moment? Why or why not?
2. How does the placement of the vodka bottle impact the viewer? Why do you think it is placed in this position? Why do you think the bottle is presented sideways instead of as a full-front label view? (The label, by the way, is red, white, and gold.)
3. What does the inside of the vodka bottle reveal? What does it imply about the perception of those who drink Smirnoff vodka? Why might this impression be ironic?
4. Consider the slogan for the product—"Pure Fantasy." How does the slogan apply to the product and to the advertisement?
5. What "old sayings" can you apply to the advertisement? How do such visual puns contribute to the sale of the product?
6. Imagine that you had no clue what Smirnoff was, and you saw this advertisement. What would you conclude about the product from this ad? What would you think it would do for you?

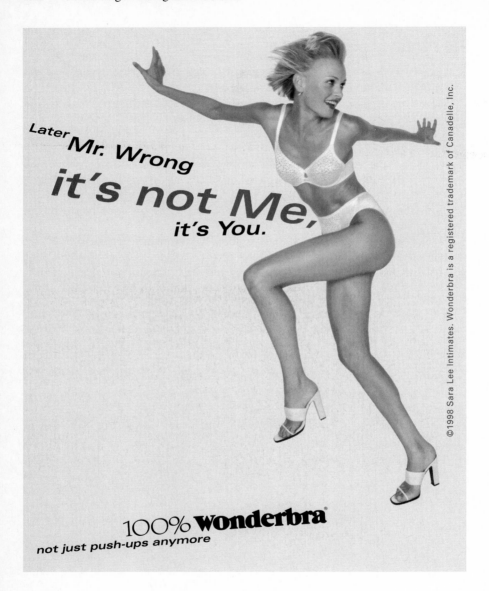

Wonderbra

1. If you were leafing through a magazine and came across this ad, would you stop and look at it? Why or why not? What are your first impressions of the model? Why do you think she is posed in this position? What images are projected by this action pose? Why is she wearing shoes?

2. Visually, this advertisement features the human body (in underwear) to help carry its message. What do you think this message is? Consider how the written copy works with the visual portion of the advertisement. How would your impression of the ad change were there no accompanying text?

3. What is the product in this ad specifically designed to do? Is the product's purpose demonstrated in the ad? What might be the "wonder" of the Wonderbra? How does the copy promote its special promise? Explain your answer.

4. Find some other print ads for women's underwear. How does the ad for Wonderbra differ from these other ads? What seems to be conventional—that is, what is shared—in the Wonderbra ad? Where does the Wonderbra ad deviate from the norm?

5. Who is the target audience for the Wonderbra ad? What social values are expressed in the ad? How are these values conveyed to the target audience?

6. Would your impression of Wonderbra change if the model were looking straight out of the picture? What if she were in a different position, such as standing on both feet with her hands on her hips or sitting in a lounge chair?

7. Consider the model's physique and features. Would this ad be effective if the model had a different body type—for instance, heavier or shorter-limbed? Would the ad be effective if the model had dark hair or if her hair were worn down? What if she were wearing black underwear?

What 'n the hell's a carbohydrate?

"Those other energy bars. . . ?
Tried 'em. Taste like wood chips. And all this talk about protein and carbohydrates. . .nothin' but jibberish to me.

Now I'm likin' these Clif Bars.™ Baked whole grains with some fruit mixed in. Looks like real food with heft to it. And talk about flavor. My granny would've been real proud to bake somethin' this good."

Whether you're heading up a herd of cattle or a 4,000 foot mountain pass, take a few Clif Bars along. You don't need a whole canteen of water to wash 'em down. And they won't get brittle in a blizzard.

Clif Bar—the natural energy bar™ that's bound to satisfy cantankerous folk like you.

REAL FOOD...REAL TASTE...REAL ENERGY.™ Clif Bars (2.4 oz.) contain 250 calories with 2-4 grams of fat, 43-53 grams of carbohydrates and 4-10 grams of protein. They're free of highly processed substances such as maltodextrin, high fructose syrups and glucose polymers. Clif Bars are also wheat-free and dairy free. **For more information about all seven Clif Bar flavors—including our new Crunchy Peanut Butter Clif Bar, call 1-800-884-KALI.**

Clif Bar

1. How is this ad different from others that promote energy bars? What type of person do we expect to promote energy bars?
2. What is the image projected by the man's outfit? In particular, the cowboy hat and denim vest? What associates do you have with this image? How does the man's image help promote Clif Bars?
3. How would this ad change if the man were dressed in business attire? If he were clean-shaven? How would this ad be affected if he were smiling? Does he look as if he's enjoying the Clif Bar? Explain the strategy in the choice of his expression.
4. Apply the Fog Index from "The Language of Advertising" by Charles O'Neill to the text at the bottom of the advertisement. At what level is the ad written. What happens if you separate the text on the bottom left from that on the right and apply the Fog Index? What do you think accounts for the difference in the results?
5. Consider the man's age. How would your reception of the ad change if he were a young man? Does age matter in advertising? Thumb through some popular magazines. How many older models do you find in ads? What products are they selling? Are these products age-specific or are they universally used? What conclusions can you reach about age and advertising?
6. In the article "The Language of Advertising," Charles O'Neill comments that advertising "uses a creative strategy based on an idea that will attract and hold the attention of the targeted consumer audience." Who is the target audience for this product? How can you tell? How does this ad apply O'Neill's principle of advertising?
7. Consider the line "What 'n the hell's a carbohydrate?" How does this line catch the reader's attention? Does it make you want to read the finer print that follows? Does the print match the picture? How?

Diesel

1. What product is being advertised here? How can you tell? Does the wording in the advertisement indicate what is being sold?
2. Yalta was an extremely important meeting of three of the most influential world leaders in 1945. What happened at Yalta? Locate a photograph of the real Yalta Conference. Who are the men in the picture? Why would Diesel want to use this picture in their ad?
3. Women were absent from the Yalta Conference because they had little political influence in 1945. While the images of women were electronically inserted into the ad, the spirit of the original picture—and the absence of women—is still felt. Why do you think that is? How does the clothing the women are wearing help maintain this feeling of political absence?
4. Do you think this picture is sexist? Why or why not?
5. Does the manipulation of the photograph affect your impression of the event? Why or why not?
6. How are the models positioned in the picture? Why do you think they are placed where they are and in such ways? What impact do they make on the overall effect of the photograph?
7. The Web site for Diesel is given in the ad (www.diesel.com). Did the ad entice you to access their Web site? Explain why or why not. Try looking up the Diesel Web site to see what you learn about their products.
8. Does this ad work to sell the product? Is its effectiveness influenced by gender or age? For example, how do you think a 60-year-old man would react to this ad? How about a 25-year-old woman?
9. How much does this ad rely on brand-name recognition? What does the Diesel name mean to you? Do you own any Diesel products or do you know of anyone who does?
10. What is your overall impression of this advertisement? Explain your feelings.
11. Consider the models' clothing and hair styles. Why are they portrayed as such? What effect does their attire have on the picture? On you?
12. Apply the Gunning Fog Index from "The Language of Advertising" by Charles O'Neill to the words at the bottom of the right-hand side of the page. Compare your results with the blurb in the "Milk" advertisement. Are they different? Why or why not?
13. How does the slogan "For Successful Living" apply to the product? How does it apply to the photograph? Finally, how does the photograph apply to the product?
14. The first line of the copy at the bottom right-hand side reads: "We are pleased to offer you the perfect environment for a modern and successful conference." What, according to Diesel, do you think makes for a successful conference?
15. Taking into consideration your analysis of the various aspects of this ad, are you motivated enough by it to go out and buy Diesel products? Explain your reasoning.

A word of warning. Don't let your Don Diegos out of your sight.
These hand-crafted, rich-flavored, premium cigars have been known to disappear into thin air.

Don Diegos

1. Cigar sales have enjoyed a recent resurgence in popularity. Once targeting only a male purchasing public, many cigar companies are inviting women to join their smoking ranks. Explain how this ad may appeal to males or females, or both. Take into account the slogan, "Agnes, have you seen my Don Diegos?"
2. What advertising slant is operating here? How does this slant help sell the product? How does sex appeal work to sell a product?
3. Consider how the woman in the ad smokes her cigar. Does she look like a real cigar smoker? Explain your answer taking into account the cigar, her expression, and the position of her body.
4. Many people like to "relax and enjoy a good cigar." Does this model look relaxed? Where is she sitting? How does her pose contribute to the message of the ad?
5. What does the attire of the man and woman in the ad say about the target audience of Don Diego Cigars? How would the ad be affected if the woman was wearing blue jeans?
6. Consider the lighting and setting of the picture. How might the ad change if the setting were outside in broad daylight?
7. Smoking has come under fierce debate in recent years. What image does the ad promote about smoking cigars? Would the ad have the same effect if the woman were smoking a cigarette?
8. How does the use of a female subject affect the overall message of the ad? What does the photograph imply about the type of women who smoke cigars?

Airwalk

1. What image is projected by the attire of the two people on the skateboard? How is their attire different? Why is their clothing important in promoting the product—sneakers?
2. How would the effect of the ad be different if the young man was featured alone on the skateboard? How about the young woman?
3. The title of this ad is "Action Sports Heroes." Who do we assume is the "hero" in the picture? Why is this person a hero? How do body position and eye direction contribute to our assumptions about who the hero is here?
4. Consider the angle shot of the photograph. How would its impact be changed if it were shot from above? From straight on instead of from below? Explain your answer.
5. Consider the setting of this ad. How does the particular setting help promote the product and the product's image? How would your image of Airwalks change if the background was in a mall? At a beach?
6. How do the microphones and cameras contribute to the ad? Whom are the microphones aimed at? Does anyone look as if they're ready to be interviewed? Why or why not? How would the picture change if we could see the faces of the people holding the microphones and cameras?
7. What would you say is the target audience for this ad? Consider age, gender, economic level, and lifestyle. Explain your responses.
8. How would the effect of this ad change if the young woman was not smiling? What message is this ad projecting to its viewing audience?

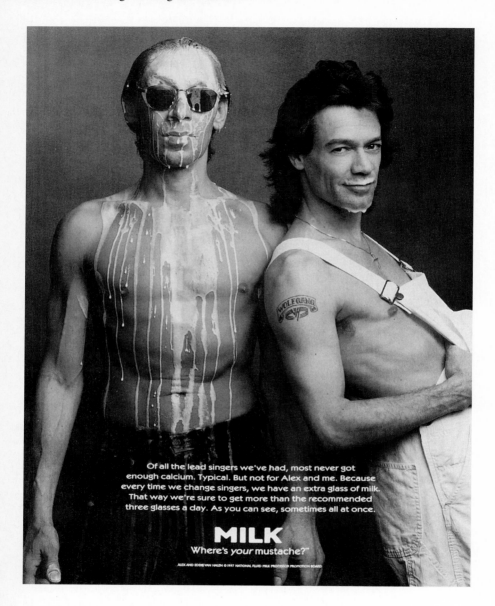

Milk

1. The National Fluid Milk Processor Promotion Board has featured many famous people, including athletes, supermodels, puppets, and actors in their campaign. Even if there were no words on the page, would you recognize the product of this particular ad? How does style repetition influence advertising?
2. Who are the people in the photograph? Would you recognize one without the other? How would your view of the ad change if only the man with the sunglasses were featured? How about the man with the coveralls?
3. The man on the left has apparently had milk dumped on his head. The other man sports only a milk mustache and a dribble on his chin. How does the ad invite you to explain what just happened? In fact, what do you think happened?
4. How does the ad copy contribute to the effect of the ad? What references do the men make to things other than milk?
5. At what audience do you think this ad is aimed? How do you think a 10-year old would react to this ad? A 25-year old? A 50-year old?
6. Do you think this ad effectively promotes the product? Explain.
7. Consider the clothing the two men are wearing. How does their attire influence the viewers' perception of the product?
8. What is the image of milk? Who drinks milk? How might this ad impact public perception of the product?
9. Apply the Fog Index from "The Language of Advertising" by Charles O'Neill to the blurb at the bottom of the page. What is the grade level of the language? Why do you think the writing is on this level?

(you always know how to get to me.)

©1997 AT&T

Plan all sorts of engagements with AT&T Long Distance. Why wait? Give her a ring.

It's all within your reach.

AT&T

1. At first glance, what catches your eye in this ad? Consider the layout, the photograph, the copy. What makes you stop and study the ad?
2. What different messages are relayed by the slogan "You always know how to get to me"? How does the woman's expression reinforce the slogan (presumably her words)? How does the accompanying text continue this theme of multiple messages?
3. Because of the nature of the product, this ad cannot visually depict what is being sold—that is, telephone long-distance service. Yet, how does AT&T relay its message? Consider for instance, how the emotions of the model and of the viewer help promote the product. How do the model's facial expression, her body position and even the object she holds motivate the viewer to choose AT&T?
4. Does the model's ethnicity narrow the target audience for this ad? Why or why not? Who do you think the target audience is?

Ready. Aim. Click.
www.goarmy.com
BE ALL YOU CAN BE.

1-800-USA-ARMY

U.S. Army

1. This ad features a computer mouse "wearing" fatigues. How does this image promote the U.S. Army?
2. Exactly what is being advertised here? What is the motivation behind it? What do the advertisers hope to achieve with this particular ad?
3. Consider the words at the bottom of the advertisement: "Ready. Aim. Click." How does this phrase surprise you? How might it affect your impression of the army? What's the effect of offering the army's Web site address? How does the familiar army slogan, "Be all you can be," take on a different meaning in this ad?
4. How does the photograph of the computer mouse influence your opinion of the army? What is the "traditional" view of the army? Does this ad reinforce or change this view?
5. Consider the simplicity of the advertisement. How does the minimalist touch help promote the "product"?
6. Do you consider this an effective way of advertising the army? Explain your view.
7. If the word *army* did not appear anywhere in the advertisement, would you know what this ad was "selling"? Why or why not?
8. To whom might this ad appeal? Why?

3
Television: Friend or Foe?

Television is the prime mover of American culture. In a mere five decades it has become the country's foremost source of entertainment and news. More than any other medium, television regulates commerce, lifestyles, and social values. But the medium is also the source of considerable scorn. Throughout the decades, television has been blamed for nearly all our social ills—the rise in crime, increased divorce rates, lower voter turnouts, racism, falling SAT scores, increased sexual promiscuity, dope addiction, and the collapse of the family. In short, it has been cited as the cause of the decline of Western civilization.

Certainly, television can be blamed for piping into America's living rooms hours of brain-numbing, excessively violent, exploitative trash. And given the fact that the average 20-year-old viewer will have spent nearly three years in front of the television set, it can be demonstrated that television has damaging effects on children and adults alike. But to categorically condemn the medium is to be blind to some of the quality shows television is capable of producing—and not just PBS or educational shows. In the latter half of the 1990s some prime-time shows have proven they are indeed very *prime.* The essays in this chapter will explore some of the various ways this extraordinary entity has become part of our lives—for better or worse—and will argue where television has failed and where it shines. At the end of the chapter, two opposing views of what to do about television's destructive powers will be presented.

The chapter opens with one major complaint: that television has become too sexual and sexy—that it has lost its innocence. As Nancy Hass explains in "Sex and Today's Single-Minded Sitcoms," sex was totally absent from television in the early days of the medium—no double entendres, no off-color jokes, virtually no kissing. In perhaps the most popular sitcom in television history, *I Love Lucy,* Lucille Ball and Desi Arnaz slept in separate beds. In the 1960s, sex came only in "veiled fantasies," as Hass observes, in such shows as *My Living Doll* and *I Dream of Jeannie.* But in the 1970s, taboos were broken, and by the 1980s sexuality settled in to television's lifestyle. Today sexual language and sex play fill the sitcoms, accounting for most of the gags and laughs. And Hass wonders just how much we've lost in this coming of age.

While some critics decry the junk that passes as sitcoms, others are disturbed by what they see as the dumbing down of nonfiction shows, including the news. This trend is no more apparent than on television talk shows. In the next essay, Charles Oliver examines daytime talk shows only to find himself appalled by the mindless sensationalism that passes as substance—sensationalism driven by a Darwinian scramble for viewership. As the title, "TV Talk Shoes: Freak Parades," suggests, he regards daytime talk shows as the electronic equivalent of carnival sideshows, designed to provide audiences with sordid, voyeuristic thrills.

The next piece examines broadcast news—not national network news shows, but those local broadcast packages you will find in almost every American city. In fact, that "cookie-cutter" formula is the focus of media critic Elayne Rapping's complaint in "Watching the Eyewitless News." In her analysis of the familiar and "comforting" appeal of community coverage, the author discovers some truths more disturbing than what is found in the usual junk television.

"If you want to know just how bad television can be, check out *Homeboys in Outer Space.*" With that statement, media critic Frederick L. McKissack Jr. launches an attack on the way television has depicted African Americans. It has been more than 30 years since the television industry took the chance of creating black shows and black characters. One would think that by now black Americans would be viewed in all their complexities. And, yet, as we see in "The Problem with Black T.V.," most black shows center on simple-minded, jive-talking clownish stereotypes. Because of marketing concerns, network television, with a few rare exceptions, is reluctant to take chances on serious black drama with higher artistic merit.

In the mid-1990s television experienced a trend toward growing acceptance of gays and lesbians by the mainstream media. Homosexual marriages figured prominently on a few top-rated shows including *Roseanne* and *Friends.* And one night in May 1997, Ellen DeGeneres came out of the closet and announced that she was a lesbian, marking hers as the first show featuring a lesbian as lead character. With so many gay characters in sitcoms, movies, soaps, and talk shows why, asks Barbara Raab, are there no openly gay and lesbian news reporters or anchors? That question is explored in the next piece, "Gays, Lesbians, and the Media: The Slow Road to Acceptance."

So far we've been looking at how bad television is—how it is guilty of stooping to the lowest common denominator with its slew of dumb, low-grade shows that stereotype, discriminate, and undermine social and family values. But not all media critics are so ready to damn television. Some, in fact, have made peace with the tube after taking a closer look at recent productions. In her essay "In Defense of Prime Time," Martha Bayles cites some of the "prime" of prime-time shows and explains why they are worth watching. Countering the scorn of detractors, she explains how television's best shows give us "morality plays" of everyday life.

One of the most original and popular shows of the late 1990s is *The X-Files.* What started out as an off-time, cult-like event for geeks and conspiracy hounds has become prime time's coolest series on television. For its high production values, eerie intelligence, clever wit, and talented cast the show has won several Golden Globe Awards, including best actor, best actress, and best series. In the next essay, "Into the Heart of Darkness," movie and television critic Terrence Rafferty takes an analytic look at this television phenomenon. Comparing it to its less successful spin-off *Millennium,* he explains how *The X-Files* taps into our collective unconscious, forcing us to confront our greatest fears.

This chapter closes with a pro/con debate on one of the most troubling controversies regarding television—its effects on children. Not only is there a lot of dumb, consumerist junk pouring out of the tube day and night, but, according to the National Coalition on Television Violence, the average American child will have seen 200,000 violent acts on television by the age of 18, including 16,000 murders. Critics complain that such heavy exposure to broadcast mayhem threatens to desensitize viewers, especially young ones, while prompting real violence. The debate is what to do about it. In one corner is David Nyhan who declares his stand in the title of his piece, "Turn off the TV Before It Ruins Us." In the other corner is media critic Susan Douglas whose essay "Remote Control: How to Raise a Media Skeptic" agrees that a lot of television, including children's shows "is, ideologically, a toxic waste dump." But instead of killing your television, Douglas recommends ways of teaching young people how to detect the poisons.

Sex and Today's Single-Minded Sitcoms
Nancy Hass

Why is there a lot more sex on television these days than there used to be? Are the shows better for it? Does all the "adult" humor make comedy shows better or funnier? These are some of the questions television critic Nancy Hass raises in the article below. While reviewing the loss of television's innocence over the decades, Hass wonders more about the quality of television's sexual humor than moral issues. Prime-time sex isn't the problem, she argues, it's the dumb, low-brow scripts.

Hass writes frequently about culture and the entertainment business. This piece originally appeared in the *New York Times* in 1997.

1   It's an early January evening in 1967, and with the dinner dishes cleared the nuclear family settles in around the Magnavox black-and-white. Samantha seethes at Endora for turning Darrin into a donkey on the night before an important presentation. Sister Bertrille, the Flying Nun, has got herself in trouble again, trying to raise money for the orphanage. The Riddler is leading Batman and Robin on a wild-goose chance—wham!—through the sewers of Gotham City.

2   Flash forward 30 years, to an early January evening in 1997. The Domino's pizza boxes are in the trash, and what's left of the nuclear family clicks on the 27-inch Sony and hunkers down for some prime-time tube. On "The Nanny," Fran, in a skintight mini, teases her handsome boss with not-so-veiled allusions to her sex life. On "Men Behaving Badly," Jamie runs out of coffee filters and uses his underwear to make coffee for a woman he is trying to pick up. On "The Jamie Foxx Show, the comedian jumps out of a cake half-nude, Chippendale's-style. A promo for "Spin City" promises that Michael J. Fox's character will be impotent with his live-in girlfriend.

3   By all measures, the television sitcom has changed radically in 30 years. Some people moan over the demise of the Golden Era, saying there's too little original humor. Others counter that series like "Seinfeld" and "The Larry Sanders Show" (and "Cheers" a few years back) represent a hybrid form that meshes intelligent comedy with keen social observation. But there's one thing that virtually anyone who watches television comedies these days will agree on: sex is everywhere.

4   A study released in December by Children Now and the Kaiser Family Foundation, two public-policy groups, found that three out of every four shows in the "family hour"—8 P.M. to 9 P.M.—now contain "sexually related talk or behavior," a fourfold increase since 1976. The study has given new ammunition to family-values

advocates across the political spectrum who have been trying for months to persuade the television industry to adopt a ratings system that would specifically flag sexual material rather than simply characterizing shows according to age appropriateness.

5   But for many people within the industry—and no doubt many viewers—there is a more important issue at stake than the moral one. "The biggest problem with how much sex there is on TV now isn't whether it's offensive," says Norman Lear, one of the people who broke television's sexual taboos in the 1970's to raise social consciousness. "It's that most of the sex on TV today just isn't funny. It's stupid and boring."

6   As network executives point out heatedly, most of television's sex play doesn't proceed to sexual intercourse. Generally it involves a lot of "physical flirting," some stroking and a steamy kiss of two. In fact, the Kaiser-Children Now study concedes that out of 451 depictions of "sexual behavior" in the family hour, only 15 involved sexual intercourse.

7   But television characters do, without question, *talk* inordinately about sex. The study reported that in each 8 to 9 P.M. viewing hour examined, there were an average of 3.1 instances of "comments about other's sexual activity" and "comments about own sexual activity." After 9, the average goes up significantly. From the so-called quality sitcoms, like "Mad About You" and "Third Rock From the Sun," to more downscale versions of the genre, like "Martin" and "Married . . . With Children," a majority of story lines in prime time revolve around the characters' sexual gratification—or lack of it.

8   Parents, politicians and religious leaders will continue to argue about whether all this sex affects the nation's moral fiber. But what about the nation's need for laughs? In the last several decades, television's depiction of life has taken a 180-degree turn toward the prurient, but virtually no one—including the writers and producers responsible for today's shows—says that all this sex makes sitcoms inherently funnier.

9   "I don't think you could ever argue that," says Larry Charles, a former "Seinfeld" writer who is executive producer of "Mad About You." "There are reasons to write about sex and there are times when it's very funny, but most of the time it's cheap, easy and moronic."

10   Like many sitcom writers, Mr. Charles makes a distinction between good sex and bad on television. The sex on NBC's "Seinfeld," for example, is handled with great sophistication, he says. Even the famous episode in which the four main characters compete to see who can refrain longest from masturbating—Mr. Charles didn't write it—was executed with remarkable subtlety. "Most important," he says, "it was very, very funny."

11   NBC's "Frasier," says Mr. Lear, is another example of a show that deals with sex in a grown-up yet lighthearted manner. The unrequited physical desire of Niles, Frasier's repressed brother, for Daphne, their pragmatic working-class housekeeper, is both poignant and absurd. "And it adds another dimension to the show," Mr. Lear says. "Because it's all about sexual confusion and class distinctions."

12   On "Mad About You," Paul and Jamie, who are married and, for a little while longer, childless, seem to have plenty of sex *and* seem to spend plenty of time arguing about the amount of sex they're having. Last season they almost broke up be-

cause Jamie was almost having an affair. "'Seinfeld' is about the hopelessness of intimacy," Mr. Charles says, "whereas 'Mad About You' is about the hopefulness of it. We try to create a relationship that includes sex, just like relationships do in real life. It's not done to titillate; it's done to make our characters multidimensional."

13   Not so on shows like Fox's "Married . . . With Children," which began as a cleverly bawdy parody of the saccharine family sitcoms of the 1950's but has become, in many critics' opinions, an over-the-top parody of itself. "We don't have any sort of deep philosophical reason for joking about sex," says Ron Leavitt, the creator of the show. "Our intention was just to subvert the genre of squeaky-clean family entertainment."

14   After 10 seasons—it's the longest-running sitcom on the air—even the characters' outrageousness has become predictable. The few jokes that don't refer to the sexual habits of the characters (a sexually frustrated mother, a prematurely ejaculating father, a slutty daughter, a sleazy son) revolve around their bad personal hygiene. "It's pretty much lowest common denominator with an edge," Mr. Leavitt admits.

15   (In at least one case, life has been said to imitate so-called art. Tisha Campbell, a star of Fox's "Martin," several weeks ago sued her co-star, Martin Lawrence, accusing him of "repeated and escalating" sexual harassment. Ms. Campbell contends that Mr. Lawrence groped her body and simulated intercourse in front of the cast and crew members during rehearsal. He denies the accusations.)

16   The highly sexualized approach of the tamer, more mainstream shows is harder to categorize. On a recent episode of "Friends," which occupies the controversial 8 P.M. spot in NBC's highly rated Thursday lineup, Chandler's plan to make money by donating sperm affects his performance in bed, forcing him to master the skills of oral sex. The central premise of "Third Rock From the Sun," also on NBC, is that aliens learn to be human by learning about sex. And on a recent episode of NBC's "Men Behaving Badly," a man who has been nursing his sick girlfriend asks eagerly if he can give her another sponge bath. "I don't think so," she answers. "My breasts are clean enough to eat off of."

17   Michael Weithorn, who created Fox's "Ned and Stacey," says it is business realities that force writers these days to mine the mother lode of sexual humor. "The networks are aiming their programming at people between the ages of 18 and 49, and sometimes 18 and 34," he says. "The style of humor is aimed at them. That's what it takes sometimes to make them laugh." Although he tries to put "Ned and Stacey" "a step above that," he concedes that "sex is an easy place to go for a cheap laugh."

18   Eric Tannenbaum, the president of Columbia Tri-Star, the studio that developed "Mad About You" for NBC and "The Nanny" for CBS, says that there simply aren't enough talented writers to insure that sex will be handled with aplomb. "With all the new outlets—the WB, UPN and cable—there are two many shows and not enough originality," he says.

19   Concern about expense also plays a role. Most sitcoms are shot with three cameras, to give the shows their stage-play feel. But three-camera comedy is expensive; it's difficult to shoot on location and in the studio. So unconventional plots that could unfold away from the central set—and presumably focus on topics other than sex—are often impractical.

20   A live audience, now de rigueur for most sitcoms, also limits plot possibilities, writers say. When actors have to wait for laughter to subside, the pacing changes, and all too often the actors play to the gallery. Writers say that because of this, they often choose plots that will evoke properly timed titters. "The network keeps telling you, 'Make it funnier, more laughs, more laughs,' " says Amy Sherman, who spent four years writing for "Roseanne."

21   When Jay Tarses, who created "The Bob Newhart Show" in the early 1970's, began work on "Buffalo Bill" in 1983, he insisted that there be no audience. That show, which treated sex with a hilarious sourness that has not been seen on television since, needed the closed set to "liberate" the actors. "We couldn't do that today," he says, referring to a particularly surreal episode in which the star, Dabney Coleman, played out an imaginary World Series game in his living room to decide whether to pay for his girlfriend's abortion or to simply turn his back on the woman. "We would never be able to create that level of anarchy."

22   As clinical as Mr. Tarses' explanation seems, treating sex as any sort of technical issue or plot device was inconceivable before the 1970's. Before then, sex simply did not exist on the small screen, save for veiled fantasies like "My Living Doll" and "I Dream of Jeannie."

23   In the 1950's, the Kramdens' bedroom was virtually off limits to the camera, and Donna Reed radiated no more than wholesomeness to her husband. Lucy and Ricky Ricardo slept in separate beds—as did Rob and Laura Petrie and every other married couple in a sitcom in the 50's and 60's. There was even public outcry over Mary Tyler Moore's shapely appearance in capri pants. The raciest it got was when Morticia's pidgin French moved Gomez Addams to run his oily lips up her shrouded arm.

24   Back then, says Mr. Tarses, writers had to get creative with characterizations because there were so many things they couldn't say. "You couldn't even get away with a subtle double-entendre," he says.

25   The sea change came in about 1970, largely prompted by two men: Mr. Lear and James L. Brooks. True products of their era's new cultural explicitness, they were the first to champion sitcoms as realistic, albeit deeply ironic, reflections of the human condition. In 1971, Mr. Lear created "All in the Family," which, in addition to attacking bigotry, limned topics like abortion, breast cancer and sexual fantasy. Although Mary Richards, the heroine Mr. Brooks created for "The Mary Tyler Moore Show," was never shown puffing on a post-coital cigarette, it was understood that she sometimes had sex with the men she dated.

26   It wasn't laughs Mr. Lear was after when he broke those taboos, he says; it was a taste of truth. "We were dealing with the problems of human sexuality and with the societal condemnation that surrounded those problems," he says. "We didn't have much forethought about it; we just thought it should be done."

27   Mr. Lear also broke another, more subtle television taboo: he refused to adhere to the tradition of providing a punch line every two minutes. "There were times," he recalls, "that Edith and Archie talked for four or five solid minutes without a big joke. They said amusing things that went to the heart of their characters, but we didn't feel like we needed a big payoff all the time."

28   For Larry Charles, who was a teen-ager at the time, it was a "breathtaking time, an inspiration." "For the first time in situation comedy," he says, "the characters could have a normal conversation."

29   But Mr. Lear acknowledges that he was only allowed to test the limits because his show was a hit. "The public was ready for that kind of honesty, and there was a lot of support," he says. "When you have good ratings, the networks suddenly think all that crazy stuff you wanted to do is all right."

30   With the taboos broken, the sexual content of television reached a new high— or low—in the mid–1970's. Amid the disillusion surrounding Watergate and the dissoluteness of the disco era, Fred Silverman, then the programming guru at ABC, ushered in such "jigglefests" as "Three's Company." That phenomenally successful show, which ran from 1977 to 1984, was essentially a reworking of classic bedroom farce; virtually every joke sprang from the theoretically comedic situation of two women sharing an apartment with a lusty male roommate who had convinced the landlord that he was gay.

31   Although the show was weakly written and the characters barely two-dimensional by any standard, "Three's Company" showcased the slapstick talents of the young John Ritter. And it tapped what might be a perpetual audience hunger for lowbrow sex farce, an appetite that has existed, as Mr. Tarses says, "in some form since Feydeau—which doesn't mean it wasn't dumb."

32   In the 1980's, in the atmosphere of wholesomeness typified by "The Cosby Show" and that of nostalgia cultivated by Garry Marshall, the creator of "Happy Days" and "Laverne and Shirley," sitcoms grew tame again. Many people in the television business agree that "Cheers" and "Roseanne" were among the only shows of that era that explored sexual themes in a manner that was both acute and fresh. "Cheers was about to go deep within the heart of a womanizer and make him funny, sad and sympathetic," says Ms. Sherman, the former "Roseanne" writer, "and we introduced the world to a couple that was big and fat and still wanted to have sex all the time."

33   By the early 1990's, sex had seeped back into sitcoms in a big, and often broad, way. Many shows trotted out gay characters, however marginal to the plot. Simultaneously, the smaller networks—Fox, WB and UPN—began to franchise leering sexual innuendo, especially after 9 P.M. With their biggest stations in large urban markets, the nascent networks began developing comedies they believed would appeal to young people living in the cities. So far that strategy has proved marginally successful; WB and UPN are gaining viewers, and Fox has created genuine hits like "The Simpsons."

34   What does the future hold? Will most sitcoms continue to recycle tired sexual themes of the wink-and-nudge variety? Probably, writers seem to concede. "I don't think audiences know how to be audiences anymore," says Mr. Lear. "They just want to hoot and make sounds."

35   But Mr. Charles says that some of the writers of his generation do see themselves as heirs to Mr. Lear and Mr. Brooks, and to Les and Glen Charles of "Cheers." The question of whether television sex is funny is ultimately a question of the quality of writing, he says. Mr. Weithorn of "Ned' and Stacey" agrees. "A show

that does clunky and gratuitous sexual humor is not likely to be well written in any way," he points out.

36   For Mr. Charles, the challenge is to resist the "urge to recycle" to fill the industry's insatiable hunger for product. "We need to step up to the next level," he says, "to include more dramatic elements and explore sexuality in greater depth. The sitcom has to break the boundaries again. Otherwise it will eat its young."

EXPLORING THE TEXT

1. How do Hass's opening scenarios suggest her ideas about the makeup of the American family in 1967 and in 1997? What are her assumptions about 1967? What are her assumptions about 1997?

2. How does Hass use the Kaiser-Children Now study to set up her argument about sexuality (paragraph 4)? How does her use of the study change in paragraph 6? Discuss the ways in which she uses the study to support her argument and whether or not you are comfortable with the various uses she makes of the same data.

3. What connection do politicians attempt to make between what's on television and "its effect on the nation's moral fiber" (paragraph 8). Does the example in paragraph 15 sufficiently address the complexity of the debate as Hass presents it?

4. What distinctions does Hass make between so-called quality sitcoms and "downscale versions" (paragraph 7). How is this distinction important to her argument?

5. Hass claims that live audiences have had an important effect on sitcoms. Why is this important to her argument?

6. Discuss the argument Hass makes about the Norman Lear and James L. Brooks sitcoms of the 1970s. What did she see as distinctive and valuable in those programs as opposed to so many others?

7. What evidence does the text provide of Hass's tone with regard to this topic? List several examples.

WRITING ASSIGNMENTS

1. Return to question 4 above, where Hass discusses quality sitcoms versus downscale versions. In what ways does she establish criteria for shows in each of these categories? Think of other examples from television and discuss which category they should be placed in and why. Hass suggests that the quality sitcoms are inherently funnier. Why? Do you agree with her assessment? Do you find the second category less funny? Are these categories too subjective? Write an essay in which you present your findings and explain your conclusions.

2. The focus of Hass's article is on sex as it is used in sitcoms, and yet the Kaiser-Children Now study doesn't draw a distinction between sitcoms

and other types of television shows—it merely measures sex on television. Write an essay in which you expand Hass's argument to include other types of television shows—that is, dramas, talk shows, children's programming, and so on.

GROUP PROJECTS

1. In small groups look at the television rating system recently established and consider the impact it would have on Hass's argument. What is its history? How does it operate? Who is responsible for the ratings? How effective are attempts to limit or control what children see on television? What about the technologies available to help parents monitor what children watch? Present a report on your findings.

2. Research the censorship debates that have been common throughout the twentieth century. Look at historical as well as current arguments. Begin with film, but also focus on television and radio. Divide the topic into parts and assign each member of the group to thoroughly research one part of the discussion. Present your findings to the class.

TV Talk Shows: Freak Parades
Charles Oliver

Whatever happened to carnival sideshows? According to Charles Oliver, they are alive and well and appearing daily on your nearest television screen. Oliver argues that ordinary people have a taste for voyeurism, for vicarious thrills, for fantasy. That's why, he believes, daytime talk shows are so heavily populated with extraordinary individuals: people with extreme physical conditions, exotic sex lives, or outrageous political views. And why are these shows so appealing? Oliver maintains that people, especially women at home, need reassurance that their own conventional—even boring—lives are superior. What do you think?

This article was first published in *Reason* in April 1995. Oliver is a contributing editor of that publication and also writes for *Investor's Business Daily.*

1   Bearded ladies. Siamese twins. Men and women who weigh more than 300 pounds each. Tattooed men. These are just a few of the guests to grace the stages of daytime talk shows in recent months. If those examples remind you of a carnival sideshow, there's a reason.

2   In the 19th century and for the first few decades of this century, carnivals crisscrossed the United States, providing entertainment to people in small towns. Carnivals catered to the dark side of man's need for spectacle by allowing people to escape temporarily from their dull everyday lives into a world that was dark, sleazy,

and seemly dangerous. Of course, the danger wasn't real, and the ultimate lure of the carnival was that you could safely return from its world to your everyday life.

3   Television and regional amusement parks took their toll on the carnival. Today, the few carnivals in existence are generally sad collections of rickety rides and rigged games. But man's need for dark spectacle hasn't gone away, and a new generation of entrepreneurs has found a way to allow people to experience the vicarious thrill of the dark, the sleazy, and the tawdry—all without leaving the safety of their homes.

4   The gateways to this dark world are daytime talk shows. Phil Donahue created the mold for this genre, and Oprah Winfrey carried it to perhaps its greatest success. Both their shows are essentially women's magazines on the air, alternating celebrity profiles, services-oriented features, discussion of political issues, and more exploitative episodes. Both mix the tawdry with the serious. Donahue was the man who gave us daytime debates between presidential candidates, and he was also the man who wore a skirt on a show devoted to cross dressing.

5   However, a new generation of hosts has emerged that trades almost exclusively in the sleaze their audiences demand: Geraldo, Montel, Ricki, Jerry. Their names may not be familiar to you, but they have millions of viewers. *Oprah* alone is watched by 7 million households each day. Each has managed to recreate the carnival in a contemporary setting.

6   One of the main attractions of the old carnivals were the "hoochie coochie" dancers. Men would eagerly wait in line, enticed by the talker's promise that these women would "take it off, roll it up, and throw it right at you." This was the origin of modern striptease. Today, the heirs of Little Egypt are a staple on daytime television. In fact, they are so common that producers really have to try to come up with new angles. Male strippers, female strippers, old strippers, grossly overweight strippers, amateur strippers—these are just a few of the variations that I saw on daytime talk shows in just one four-week period. Of course, these people didn't just talk about their profession; they inevitably demonstrated it. While the television viewer could see the naughty bits only in digitized distortions, the live audiences for these shows were treated to an eyeful.

7   However, most of the strippers on these shows are attractive young women. Given that the audience for daytime talk is also women, this seems like a strange choice of guests. I can only assume that at least some of the women who watch these shows are intrigued by the profession and wonder what it would be like to be a stripper. By presenting these women strippers—indeed, by actually taking their cameras into clubs for performances—talk shows give those women viewers the chance to live out their fantasies vicariously without risking any of the dangers involved. Based upon the comments offered, female audience members generally seem to sympathize with the strippers who appear on these shows, usually defending them against those brought on to attack the profession.

8   Of course, at times the subject of stripping is simply an excuse for these shows to engage in emotional voyeurism. A perfect example was an episode of *Jerry Springer* dealing with strippers and family members who disapproved of how they earned their money. Naturally, the strippers couldn't just talk to their parents and siblings: they had to demonstrate their art to them. So while the assembled families and the studio audience watched, the girls stripped naked.

9　　On one side of a split television screen, the home audience saw a lovely young girl strip down to her distorted birthday suit. On the other side, her family, some of them crying, averted their eyes and tried to ignore the hooting and catcalls of the audience.

10　　It was tacky; it was sleazy. It was the perfect daytime moment. Whoever thought of it is a veritable P. T. Barnum of the airwaves. At once, this sordid mess provides the viewer with the voyeuristic thrill of seeing a family conflict that one really shouldn't observe, the vicarious thrill of stripping before an audience, and, ultimately, the confirmation that a dull, "normal" lifestyle is superior to that of the women on the show.

11　　An important part of carnivals was the freak show, an assortment of real and contrived physical oddities: pinheads, fat people, bearded ladies. While the carnival talkers would try to entice people into the sideshow tents with come-ons about the scientific oddities inside, the real lure of these attractions wasn't intellectual curiosity. It was terror and pity. The customer could observe these people and think to himself that no matter how bad his life seemed at times, it could be much, much worse.

12　　Daytime talk shows have their own version of the freak show. Indeed, on her now-defunct show, Joan Rivers had actual sideshow freaks. These were politically correct "made" freaks (people who had purposefully altered their bodies), not natural ones. The guest who drew the biggest reaction from the audience was a man who lifted heavy weights attached to earrings that pierced various parts of his body. (I've actually seen this guy perform, and I can say that the audience didn't see his most impressive piece of lifting. But there was no way that it could have been shown on television, at least not without some serious digitizing of the screen.)

13　　More often, talk shows will feature people with physical conditions similar to those who were attractions in sideshows. I've seen various shows do episodes on women with facial hair, and the lives of the very large are always a popular topic. One episode of *Jerry Springer* featured greeting card models who weigh more than 300 pounds. In typical fashion these women were not dressed as they presumably would be in everyday life, but in revealing lingerie. So much the better for gawking, I guess.

14　　Again, the host will set up one of these shows with some remarks about understanding these people, and to their credit, many of the guests on these programs do try to maintain their dignity. The greeting card models seemed a happy, boisterous lot of people. But more often guests are asked to tell tales of discrimination and broken hearts. It's easy to conclude that they were invited on the show so that the audience could feel sorry for them and feel superior to them.

15　　And speaking of feeling superior, how could anyone help but laugh at and feel better than the endless parade of squabbling friends and relatives who pass through these shows? Judging from the looks of guests on some of these shows, you'd think that the producers comb every trailer park and housing project in the nation looking for them. In fact, most are solicited through telephone numbers given during the show: "Are you a white transsexual stripper whose family disapproves of your Latino boyfriend? Call 1–800-IMA FREK."

16　　The guests then are invited on the show, where they battle it out for the amusement of the audience. A typical example was a show hosted by Ricki Lake on the topic of promiscuity. Ricki began by introducing Shannon, a girl who claimed her best friend Keisha sleeps around too much. Amid much whooping from the audience, Shannon detailed her friend's rather colorful sex life: "It ain't like she getting paid."

17   Then Keisha came out and accused Shannon of being the one who sleeps around too much. They spent an entire segment arguing. After the break Ricki introduces a mutual friend of the two and asked the question everyone in the audience now wanted to know: "Which one is the real slut?" A dramatic pause. The emphatic answer: "Both of them." The audience erupts.

18   Conflict is a key element on the new breed of talk shows. Physical fights seem to break out on Ricki Lake's show more frequently than at hockey games. These conflicts are not always mere arguments between friends or family members. Often, there are clear-cut good guys whom the audience is supposed to cheer and bad guys whom the audience boos. These episodes resemble the low-brow morality plays of professional wrestling.

19   Pro wrestling, in fact, had its origins in the carnival. Sometimes the resemblance to pro wrestling is quite pronounced. Daytime talk shows have a fascination with the Ku Klux Klan. It seems a week doesn't go by without one show bringing on members of the Klan to discuss their views on race relations, welfare, abortion, or child rearing. Usually there'll be representatives from some civil rights organization present to offer an opposing view.

20   The Klansmen look every inch the pro wrestling "heel." They are invariably overweight and have poor skin and a bad haircut. Watching them sitting there in their Klan robes, shouting racial slurs at their opponents as the audience curses them, I always expect these people to pull out a set of brass knuckles and clobber the "babyface" while the host has his back turned.

21   More often, though, the villains on talk shows are a little more subtle. The audience seems to value family quite a bit because the most common types of villains on these shows are people who pose a threat to the family: child-deserting wives, cheating husbands, and abusive parents.

22   One typical show was an episode of *Jenny Jones* where women who date only married men faced off with women whose husbands had left them for other women. The women who dated married men certainly made no attempt to win the audience over. They came in dressed in short skirts or low-cut dresses. They preened; they strutted; they insulted the other guests and the audience members; they bragged about their sexual prowess. "Nature Boy" Buddy Rogers himself could not have worked the crowd better.

23   Why do such people even show up for these shows? It can't be for the money, since guests receive no more than a plane ticket and a night in a nice hotel. After watching countless shows, I've come to the conclusion that these people really think there is nothing wrong with what they do, and they usually seem quite surprised that the audience isn't on their side.

24   Is the public's appetite for this sleaze unlimited? Probably not. After all, the carnival came around but once a year. With close to two dozen daytime talk shows competing for viewers, people are bound to grow jaded. Last year, Oprah Winfrey, who already had one of the less sleazy shows, began a policy of toning down the tawdry elements. Even her sensational admission to using crack cocaine during the 1980s came in the middle of an "inspirational" program on recovering addicts. The

show, which was already the top-rated daytime program, saw its ratings climb. But for those with a taste for the dark side of life, there'll always be a Ricki Lake or a Gordon Elliott.

EXPLORING THE TEXT

1. According to Oliver what is the appeal of the carnival?
2. In paragraph 4, Oliver talks about some early talk shows and compares them to women's magazines. What characteristics do they have in common?
3. Why are strippers (and sexual deviants) so popular on these shows? Does Oliver's answer seem sufficient? What is the underlying assumption being made about female fantasies? Do you have a better answer?
4. Define what, for Oliver, constitute the three elements of sleaze. Explain the importance of these elements.
5. In what ways does Oliver include class as an issue in his discussion? Focus on particular examples.
6. What are the underlying family values as presented on the talk shows? What does Oliver understand as family?
7. List several elements in the text that reveal Oliver's tone and attitude with regard to this subject.

WRITING ASSIGNMENTS

1. Oliver's discussion, and the discussion of other authors in this chapter (Terrence Rafferty, for example), focus on the quality of television programming but also claim that programs are often designed to deliver what an audience wants to see. In a carefully written essay, discuss and describe your own wants. What do you watch on television? What would you like to see more of? What would you like to see less of? Is there a difference between what is desirable in daytime and evening? How do your desires relate to the ideas presented throughout this chapter?
2. If possible, watch the "Humbug" episode of *The X-Files,* the action of which revolves around a so-called "freak show." Compare speeches and dialogue in the episode that discuss the attraction and role of freaks to the claims Oliver makes throughout this essay. In what ways can we see this essay as a comment on freak shows? In what ways does it differ from the "Humbug" commentary?

GROUP PROJECTS

1. Make a semiotic analysis of a daytime talk show. That is, try to interpret the cultural and ideological "signs." Note the subject matter of the program, list the commercials aired during the show, describe in detail the way

in which various people are dressed (and how it relates to the subject matter), note the decor of the set. Compare these elements to the ideas and claims Oliver presents. Does your analysis support his claims or argue against them? Each group member could focus on one program so that you have a wide range of results. Combine your findings and prepare a report of your conclusions.

Watching the Eyewitless News
Elayne Rapping

What's new? What's news? Elayne Rapping asks us to consider what we know about our world and community, but more importantly to consider how we come to know it. Her focus in this discussion is the phenomenon of "local" news programming that, she argues, is actually anything but local. Rapping describes the conventions of local news and notes how universally— and successfully—they have been adopted in markets all over the country. She asks us to notice how similar it all is from town to town—the news readers, their dress and attitudes, the kinds of stories covered, the amount of information actually offered. What's new? What's news? How can you tell?

Rapping, the author of *Media-tions: Forays into the Culture and Gender Wars* (1994), wrote this essay for the March 1995 issue of the *Progressive.*

1 Jimmy Cagney, the ultimate street-smart wise guy, used to snap, "Whadya hear? Whadya know?" in the days of black-and-white movies and READ ALL ABOUT IT! headlines. But that was then and this is now. Today, when gangsta rap has replaced gangster movies, and television has replaced newsprint as the primary source of information (for two-thirds of us, the *only* source), Cagney's famous question is not only antiquated, it is beside the point. What we hear when we consume "the news" has only the most marginal relationship to what we *know* about anything.

2 I'm not referring here to CNN or the "evening news" on the national broadcast networks. I'm referring to what passes for news in the homes and minds of the vast majority of Americans today: the *Eyewitless, Happy Talk* local newscasts that run in many cities for as much as an hour and a half to two hours a day, on as many as seven or eight different channels.

3 The rise of local news, the infotainment monster that ate the news industry, is a long and painful story about a key battlefront in the endless media war between capitalism and democracy, between the drive for profits and the constitutional responsibility of those licensed to use the airwaves to serve the public interest. We know who's winning, of course. The game was rigged from the start.

4 To make sure it stays that way, most members of the Federal Communications Commission are appointed—no matter who's in the White House—from the ranks of the industry itself. Indeed, if there is any phenomenon that gives dramatic support

to Leonard Cohen's baleful lines, "Everybody knows the war is over/Everybody knows the good guys lost," it's the specter of local news, slouching roughly across a wider and wider stretch of airwave time, planting its brainless images as it goes.

5   Local news as we know it was invented in 1970, the brainchild of a marketing research whiz hired by the industry to raise ratings by finding out what audiences "wanted to see." The Jeffersonian notion that public media should cover what citizens "need to know" was not a big consideration. Nor was it a concern to respect the audience's intelligence or diversity.

6   The researchers offered a limited, embarrassingly vapid list of choices of formats and subjects, while ignoring the possibility that different groups might want different kinds of information and analysis. More annoying still, they ignored the possibility that individual views, of all kinds, might want and need different things at different times for different reasons. Nope, said the marketing whizzes, this master model of "The News" will buy us the most overall-ratings bang per buck. Wrap it up and send it out.

7   And it worked. Their invention has conquered the TV world. The sets, the news lineups, the anchors, the weather maps, the sports features—all developed for a New York City market—quickly became a universal formula, sent out to every network affiliate and independent station in America, complete with fill-in-the-blanks guidelines for adaptation to any community, no matter how large or small, urban or rural. Local news today is the single most profitable form of nonfiction television programming in the country and, for most stations, the only thing they actually produce. Everything else comes from the networks. As time went by, this tendency toward cookie-cutter formulas, exported far and wide from a central media source, reached ever more depressing depths. The trend has led to ever more nationally produced, generic features exported to local stations to be passed off as "local."

8   So today we have a phenomenon euphemistically called "local news," although it is anything but, filled with images of a pseudo-community called "America," which is actually closer to Disney World in its representation of American life. But why should that surprise us, in a national landscape now filled, from coast to coast, with identical, mass-produced shopping malls that pass for town marketplaces, and hotels and airports that pass for village inns? In postmodern America, after all, this kind of brand-name synthetic familiarity appears to be the only thing that holds us— a nation of endlessly uprooted and mobile strangers—together.

9   When you turn on the news, whether at home or in an airport or Holiday Inn in some totally strange locale, you see a predictable, comforting spectacle. The town or city in question, whether Manhattan or Moose Hill, Montana, is presided over by a group of attractive, charming, well-dressed performers—whose agents, salaries, and movements up and down the ladder of media success, gauged by the size of the "market" they infiltrate, are chronicled each week in *Variety*. They seem to care endlessly for each other and us. "Tsk, tsk," they cluck at news of yet another gang rampage or Congressional scandal. "Ooh," they sigh, at news of earthquakes and plane crashes, far and near.

10   If it bleeds, it leads is the motto of the commercial news industry and local news. Its endless series of fires, shootouts, collapsing buildings, and babies beaten

or abandoned or bitten by wild dogs is the state-of-the-art showcase for the industry. As Don Henley once put it, in a scathing song about the local-news phenomenon, "It's interesting when people die." And it's especially interesting when they die in bizarre or inhuman situations, when their loved ones are on camera to moan and wail, when a lot of them die at once. And since so much of our news is indeed personally terrifying and depressing, we need to have it delivered as cleverly and carefully as possible. And so we have the always smiling, always sympathetic, always confidently upbeat news teams to sugarcoat the bad news.

11   Not that local news ignores the politically important stories. Well, not entirely anyway. When wars are declared or covered, when elections are won or lost, when federal budgets and plant closings do away with jobs and services or threaten to put more and more of us in jail, for less and less cause, the local news teams are there to calm our jagged nerves and reassure us that we needn't worry.

12   This reassurance is sometimes subtle. National news items typically take up less than two minutes of a half-hour segment. And what's said and seen in that brief interlude is hardly enlightening. On the contrary, the hole for "hard news" is generally filled with sound bites and head shots, packaged and processed by the networks, from news conferences with the handful of movers and shakers considered "newsworthy"—the President and his key henchmen and adversaries, mostly.

13   But even local issues of serious import are given short shrift on these newscasts. Hard news affecting local communities takes up only a minute or two more airtime than national events. And local teams are obsessed with "man-on-the-street" spot interviews. Neighbors on local TV are forever gasping and wailing the most clichéd of reflex responses to actual local horrors, whether personal or social.

14   "It's so horrible," they say over and over again, like wind-up dolls with a limited repertoire of three-word phrases, when asked about a local disaster. And when the crisis affects them directly—a school budget cut or neighborhood hospital closing, for example—their on-air responses are equally vapid. "I don't know *what* we're going to do without any teachers or books," they say with puzzled, frenzied expressions as they try desperately to articulate some coherent reply to a complex issue they've just heard about.

15   I am not suggesting that the news should not feature community residents' views and experiences. Of course it should. But the local news teams' way of presenting such community responses is deliberately demeaning and fatuous. No one could say much worth saying in such a format. And if someone managed to come up with something serious and intelligent, rest assured it would be cut in favor of a more sensational, emotional response.

16   But real news, even about cats in trees or babies in wells, is hardly what takes up the most airtime. "Don't bother too much about that stuff," say the guys and gals in the anchor chairs. Here's Goofy Gil with the weather, or Snappy Sam with the sports—the two features which, on every local newscast, are given the longest time slots and the most elaborate and expensive props. The number and ornateness of the weather maps on local news, and the endlessly amazing developments in special-effects technology to observe climate changes and movements of impending "fronts" is truly mind-boggling.

17   Who needs this stuff? But we're not forgetting that this is not the question to ask. "Who wants it?" is the criterion for news producers, and it is, understandably, the weather and sports that most people, most of the time, are likely to sit still for. If local news is meant to be a facsimile of a sunny Disneyesque community of happy, cozy campers, in which the bothersome bad guys and events of the day are quickly dealt with so that community harmony may once more reign, at least for the moment—and that *is* the intended fantasy—then what better, safer, kind of information than weather reports. Historically, after all, the weather is the standard small-talk item for people wishing to be pleasant and make contact without getting into anything controversial or heavy. It is the only kind of news we can all share in—no matter what our face, class, gender, or political differences—as members of a common community.

18   The researchers are not entirely wrong, after all, about what people in this kind of society want. They do want comfort, reassurance, and a community where they belong and feel safe. And why shouldn't they? They find precious little of those things in the streets and buildings they traverse and inhabit in their daily lives. In my urban neighborhood, parents warn children never to make eye contract with anyone on the street or subway; never to speak to anyone, even in case of tragedy or emergency; never to look at or listen to the pathetic souls who regularly beg for money or ramble incoherently in the hope that someone, anyone, will take pity and respond.

19   Remember when California was God's country, the Promised Land of Milk and Honey, to which people migrated for clean air, good jobs, and single-dwelling homes? Try to find these things in overpopulated, polluted, socially vexed and violent LA today. Don Henley, again, said it best some twenty years ago: "Call some place paradise/Kiss it good-bye."

20   But if we can't all dream of moving to sunny California anymore, there's always TV, where something resembling that innocent dream still exists. Eyewitness News and its various clones allow us to believe, just for a moment, that there really is a Santa Claus, a Mary Poppins, a Good Samaritan giving away fortunes to the needy, a spirit of Christmas Past to convert the most cold-hearted of corporate Scrooges. Indeed, this kind of "good news" is another staple of the genre. Charities, celebrations, instances of extraordinary good luck or good works by or for local residents are ever-present on local newscasts. Every day, in the midst of even the most dreadful and depressing news, there are legions of friends and neighbors to mourn and console each other, offering aid, bringing soup and casseroles to the victims of natural and man-made disasters, stringing lights and hanging balloons for festive neighborhood gatherings.

21   The news teams themselves often play this role for us. They march at the head of holiday parades and shake hands and kiss babies at openings of malls and industrial parks. They are the neighbors—often thought of as friends by the loneliest among us—we wish we had in real life, there to do the right thing on every occasion. That is their primary function. They are not trained in journalism. They often cannot pronounce the local names and foreign words they read from teleprompters. But they sure can smile. And joke around. And let us in on the latest bargain to seek out or scam to avoid. In fact, the "Action Line" and "Shame on You" features, in

which reporters hang out at local shopping centers trying out new gadgets, testing fabrics, and trapping shady shopkeepers in their nefarious efforts to sell us junk, poison, and instant death, are among the most popular and cheery things on the air.

22　　The news teams also bring us gossip, at a time when more and more of us are lonely and scared of each other. The gossip is not about our actual neighbors of course, those suspicious, *different*-looking folks who just moved in. We don't open the door to them for fear they will shoot us or rape us. No, no.

23　　The news teams bring us word of our nice friends and neighbors, the celebrities we have come to know and love through their ever-present images on the TV screens that have become our virtual homes and communities. Marla and The Donald, Michael and Lisa Marie, Lyle and Julia, Richard and Cindy—we know and love these people and delight in sharing the latest bits of harmless scandals about them with co-workers and other semi-intimates.

24　　Sociologist Joshua Gamson has suggested, in an insightful essay, that there is a lesson to be learned from the enormous popularity of tabloid television—a category in which I would certainly include local news. The lesson is not that people are stupid, venal, "addicted," or otherwise blameworthy for their fascinated interest in junk TV. On the contrary, it is those responsible for the quality of our public life who are more deserving of such terms of contempt and opprobrium. For it is, says Gamson, "Only when people perceive public life as inconsequential, as not their own, [that] they readily accept the invitation to turn news into play." And people most certainly do perceive public life as inconsequential and worse these days, whether outside their doors or in Washington or on Wall Street.

25　　Only I don't think it is primarily the desire to "play" that drives people in droves to local newscasts, or even the trashier tabloid shows like *Hard Copy.* What people are getting from local newscasts—and here the researchers were right on the money, literally—is indeed *what they want,* in the most profound and sad sense of that phrase. They are getting what they always sought in fantasy and fiction, from *The Wizard of Oz* to *As the World Turns.* They are getting, for a brief moment, a utopian fantasy of a better, kinder, more decent and meaningful world than the one that entraps them.

26　　It is not only that public life is inconsequential, after all. It is, far more tragically, that public and private life today are increasingly unjust, inhumane, painful, even hopeless, materially and spiritually, for many of us. And there is no relief in sight except, ironically, on the local newscasts that are a respite from reality. Only, unlike the utopian villages of soap opera and fairy tale, these "imagined communities" are supposed to be, pretend to be, real and true. And for that reason they are more troubling than the trashiest or silliest of pop-culture fictions.

EXPLORING THE TEXT

1. How does Rapping define the sides of the debate? Where do you stand on the issue?
2. What is the formula that local network news follows? Why is it effective?

3. Why does Rapping call the representation of America on local news a "pseudo-community" (paragraph 8)? Explain your answer.
4. What problems does Rapping have with news features devoted to the views and experiences of community residents? Why does she find that segment of the local news lacking?
5. What is the relationship between the preestablished formula and content? Explain your answer.
6. How does Rapping characterize the weather segments of the news? What kinds of topics aren't so safe or polite? What, then, is the function of "safe" news?
7. How does Rapping define "good news"? What is it opposed to? What would she define as "politically important" news?

WRITING ASSIGNMENTS

1. In what ways can we compare tabloid news programs (such as *Hard Copy*), as described by Rapping, with the so-called news presented on certain talk shows, as Charles Oliver describes in "TV Talk Shows: Freak Parades"? What is tabloid news versus more credible, hard news? What are the boundaries between the two according to each author? Review examples of each by analyzing episodes over the course of a week. Write an essay in which you discuss your findings.
2. How do fictional accounts of the workings of a newsroom and the roles of reporters play into stereotypes that Rapping and Charles Oliver ("TV Talk Shows: Freak Parades") above describe? Write an essay in which you compare the critical comments made by Oliver and Rapping with fictional accounts. Choose a film (e.g., *To Die For, Network, Natural Born Killers*) or television program (*Murphy Brown, News Radio, Ink, Mary Tyler Moore*) or review some of the song lyrics Rapping refers to in making your comparison.

GROUP PROJECTS

1. Have members of your group observe different local newscasts and consider the ways in which they fit Rapping's model or ways in which they deviate from this model. What differences are notable between networks? What differences are notable between local and national news? What assumptions seem to be made about the audiences of the various newscasts? You might want to consider stories, and their order, for a number of news programs on the same date. Also consider how people are dressed, the set, the advertisements that air during the broadcast, and so on. Write an essay in which you describe what you discover and analyze its relevance.

2. Near the end of this essay, Rapping claims that people actually get what they want when they watch. Prepare a questionnaire that seeks to find out just what it is that people want to watch on television news. Consider your questions carefully to make sure that they will elicit specific and reliable information (you might do some research on the various ways to write a questionnaire or conduct a reliable survey). Then have each member of the group poll a number of people to get answers to these questions. As a group tabulate and prepare a report on the findings.

The Problem with Black T.V.

Frederick L. McKissack Jr.

One of the most popular prime-time television shows of the 1980s was *The Cosby Show*, a sitcom starring Bill Cosby and focusing on the Huxtable family. That this show was popular was especially significant because it presented a positive image of an attractive black family to all Americans. This was important because television historically has presented a range of unattractive black images to the American audience. In this essay, Frederick L. McKissack Jr. looks at "black television" in the years since *The Cosby Show* and evaluates its influence and its quality. Although African Americans comprise a significant portion of the viewing audience and although shows by and about blacks have proliferated, McKissack argues that the quality of such programming leaves much to be desired.

McKissack is editor of The Progressive Media Project. This article was first published in the *Progressive* in February 1997.

1 If you want to know just how bad television can be, check out *Homeboys in Outer Space.*

2 *Homeboys,* which is shown on UPN, is the kind of television situation comedy that makes you wonder what the pitch meeting was like: "Let's send two funny black guys into outer space. It'll be like *Star Trek* meets *Sanford and Son.*"

3 The show is more like *Star Trek* meets *Amos 'n' Andy.*

4 *Homeboys in Outer Space* stars Darryl Bell as Morris Clay and Flex as Ty Walker—a pair of ne'er-do-well, new-jack haulers of cargo in the twenty-third century. While Captains Kirk and Picard had the *Enterprise* and the Doctor had the *TARDIS,* our boys trek around the galaxy in the *Hoopty,* a twenty-third-century cross between low-rider and eighteen-wheeler.

5 Accompanying the homies in their wacky outer-space adventures is Loquatia (Rhonda Bennett), the ship's onboard computer. "This tart-tongued maven of the mainframe resents that she's confined to the console, shown only as a talking head on a monitor installed in the *Hoopty*'s instrument panel," says a synopsis I read on UPN's web site. "In perpetual overdrive, she enjoys tormenting Ty with her caustic remarks and teasing Morris with her cybernetic feminine wiles."

6   Of course Loquatia resents being confined to the console. Given the producers' limited imaginations, Loquatia should do a Hal and deep-six these knuckleheads, then head off to join the Federation. At least in Picard's interpretation of the twenty-third century, women can actually captain ships (see Janeway on the *Voyager*).

7   Loquatia almost escaped once, when she was offered a chance to become a music-video star. In her absence, Ty Walker and Morris Clay install a new computer, also with a female persona, which promptly accuses the two of sexual harassment. A computer lawyer, who looks and acts like Johnnie Cochran, files a lawsuit against the homies. Loquatia comes back and saves the day. All is well.

8   Another episode has Morris and Ty delivering human cargo—cryogenized bodies from the late 1990s—to a sinister scientist who wants to sell body parts. But Morris and Ty don't know this until Morris realizes that his great, great, great, great, great, grandmother is one of the frozen few and thaws her. Ty, who is a habitually horny but lovable firstmate, hits on Morris's newly young granny big-time. After some totally inane scenes that hark back to late 1970s television, Morris is able to send his grandmother back to the nineties.

9   The Hubbell telescope has led scientists to believe that the size of the known universe has been grossly underestimated. There are billions of stars in our galaxy alone, and millions of galaxies out there. Yet the best Hollywood can do for blacks is two 1990s b-boys in orbit. The writing lacks the depth of Sam Delaney and the wit of Douglas Adams. *Homeboys in Outer Space* is even more visually inept than a *Doctor Who* episode, although what it lacks in special effects *Doctor Who* makes up for in charm.

10   "When people look back at this decade, the 1990s, they will write that this was the decade of black mediocrity in the arts," says cultural critic and poet Kevin Powell. "Television, especially, but film and even literature, it's all pretty bad out there. *Homeboys in Outer Space* is just part of what's wrong."

11   "It's quite easy to see how it got on television," says Ken Perkins, television critic with the *Fort Worth Star-Telegram*. "The name itself is attractive to the demographic of the audience. But it's a very unfunny show."

12   Ironically, the nineties was supposed to showcase a renaissance in black entertainment. Networks and advertisers have realized that the black community is hungry for programming that reflects its image. But the shows they come up with are pathetic.

13   Many shows featuring black characters are not even creatively controlled by African Americans. Last season, *Cleghorne!* a canceled WB sitcom featuring comedian Ellen Cleghorne, had one black writer among eight. Often the producers of a Fox program called *The Show,* featuring a black star, would call over to *Cleghorne!* and ask for anecdotes. See, black people are often hired as writers just to make sure the jive is right.

14   The network executives are unwilling to push past common themes and characters when it comes to blacks and other ethnic minorities. "In the new offerings, so far, there's lot of head-twitching, whipping around of necks, high-pitched defiant tones," wrote A. J. Jacobs in *Entertainment Weekly* last June. "When the story line goes beyond dating, there is still a lot of bumbling about decision-making. And fre-

quently the targets of put-downs are the educated and seemingly middle-class characters, who use longer words and sentences and might hesitate a minute before rushing into a situation."

15   While *Fresh Prince of Bel Air*—a story about a Philly kid (Will Smith) who moves in with his rich uncle, aunt, and cousin in Bel-Air—was a truly funny comedy, all too often the butt of jokes was Carlton, a dweeby oreo who used big words. Carlton's lack of street smarts and street language made him ridiculous on the show. Big words and preppy clothing are not black, at least by television standards.

16   *Martin,* as well, seems to revel in the down-wit-it, anti-intelligent, self-absorbed street style of its main character, played by Martin Lawrence. He has range, but is rarely given the chance to do anything but be a clown. Martin shares the anti-feminism of Archie Bunker and is the antithesis of the funny but intelligent Heathcliff Huxtable.

17   Blacks are increasingly pigeonholed in simpleminded comedies. At a time when the big four—NBC, CBS, ABC, and Fox—have only a handful of shows centered around blacks, UPN and WB have anchored their programming with comedies featuring African Americans. Of the twenty-one shows the two networks pushed this past fall, eleven were comedies.

18   "We have to counterprogram, so we went after [black] talent in a big way," Mike Sullivan, UPN Entertainment's president, told *Entertainment Weekly* last summer. "Comedies have a great track record. Success dictates where you go."

19   Sullivan's boss, Lucie Salhany, UPN's president and chief executive officer, agreed.

20   "We wanted the funniest comedies we could get," she told the *Cincinnati Enquirer.* "Comedy is comedy. And people want to laugh."

21   Comedies are the engines that drive the network train. Dramas centered around black families fail, and usually fail quickly.

22   A recent example is *Under One Roof.* The show, featuring James Earl Jones and Joe Morton, lasted only a few weeks before it was unceremoniously canceled. The show was a critical success, but an embarrassing bust in the ratings.

23   Several factors killed it, including a horrible Saturday-evening time slot. The show's producer, Thomas Carter, recently said that networks bury the shows they feel won't go anywhere. This leads to a self-fulfilling prophecy.

24   "It's far more deep-seated than having a bad time slot," says Ken Perkins. "There is nothing more difficult than trying to get a serious black drama on television. There are some unwritten rules about doing it. First, whites will not watch shows on the black condition. Second, middle-class blacks are not interested in watching shows on the black condition."

25   Because *Under One Roof* appealed to neither of these groups, the network decided not to risk a long run. "*Under One Roof* wasn't on long enough to build an audience," says Perkins. "Hollywood likes shows that are safe and doesn't like concepts that haven't been proven."

26   But, as Perkins points out, Hollywood's preoccupation with safety leads audiences to expect limited kinds of T.V. "I really do believe that black audiences have

been conditioned," he says. "If you've been raised on comedies, you develop a taste only for comedies."

27   The networks have been less than eager to find new black dramas. Several attempts have been made lately, but none were successful. Spike Lee, the most successful black director in mainstream cinema history, had a development deal with CBS, but the show was not picked up.

28   UPN is apparently working on a black-oriented drama, although its premise is just as predictable as are UPN's comedies: It will center around high-school basketball.

29   The larger networks, when questioned, have been vague about getting more blacks on T.V. more often. Warren Littlefield, president of NBC Entertainment, has said that he is committed to diversity and is looking for ways to improve the color imbalance on the network.

30   Leslie Moonves, head of programming for CBS, which has the most prominent new black series on television in *Cosby,* told the *Miami Herald* that blacks are playing major roles on shows throughout the network.

31   "As opposed to going specifically for all-black shows, or all-white shows, we've mixed them up quite a bit," she said.

32   While African-Americans make up 12 percent of the total population, black viewers watch 50 percent more television than any other group.

33   And black viewers watch the shows that feature black characters. "People are just glad to see black people on television," says Pat Tobin, a public-relations executive in Los Angeles who has worked with a number of African-American entertainers. "You want to watch and see black people. I know a child who goes to a prestigious school where he is the only African American. He doesn't see his image anywhere. So, he watches the television shows."

34   When Fox started to challenge the big three networks in the 1980s and early 1990s, it was with shows that centered on African Americans (*Martin*), had African Americans in prominent roles (*21 Jump Street*), or appealed to black viewers (*Married with Children*). This strategy was a success for Fox, because at one time the network was attracting 38 percent of black viewers.

35   UPN and WB have borrowed that strategy, and it's beginning to pay off. WB's *The Wayans Brothers,* for example, has 11.7 percent of black households, although it only captures 2.7 percent of all households.

36   "This heavy solicitation of the African-American viewer is just one signal of the growing importance of the market, especially its younger adults," says Jacqueline Trescott of *The Washington Post,* in a review of blacks on television this season. "That is the good news—the recognition of the black consumer. Also, the series are showcases for talented performers who rarely have such consistent high-profile exposure."

37   While there is talk about the homogeneity of television casting, there is a serious difference between what white families will watch, and what black families view. This is the reason why color television looks black and white when it comes to casting.

38   The top shows at the end of the 1995 season in white households (in descending order) were *Frasier, Coach, Monday Night Football, NYPD Blue, The Single Guy, Caroline in the City, Friends, Seinfeld,* and *E.R.*

39   Among black households, the story was drastically different. *New York Undercover* was number one, followed by *Living Single, In the House* (dropped by NBC, and picked up by UPN), *The Crew* (canceled by Fox), *Fresh Prince of Bel Air* (canceled by NBC after several successful seasons), *Martin, Family Matters, Monday Night Football, NBC Monday Night at the Movies,* and *The Preston Episodes* (Fox canceled), which starred David Allen Greer as a journalist.

40   Two shows that do not show up in either list, but which are favorites for both black and white audiences are *Married with Children* and *The Simpsons,* both on Fox. One reason these shows are popular with black audiences may be that looking at white folks having a difficult time of it is funny—especially when Fox has so many rich, spoiled whiners from hell on such shows as *Beverly Hills 90210* and *Melrose Place.*

41   But some African Americans who watch both shows identify with the blue-collar, oppressed, repressed lives of Homer Simpson and Al Bundy. Homer has the loving respect of his family, which he needs in order to get through a day of working for the tyrant boss of a nuclear-power plant. Likewise, Al, although off-the-wall with his slobbishness and sexism, slaves away as a shoe salesman at a mall, lives in a small house, and suffers through his wife's and his children's insults.

42   For the black community, the lack of artistic merit on television is especially damaging because television shows such as *Homeboys in Outer Space, Martin* (a survivor on Fox), and *The Wayans Brothers* (a hit on WB) have become the iconography, at least for some whites, of the black community.

43   A survey published in *Journalism Quarterly* in the early 1980s found that in a test group of 316 white fourth, sixth, and eighth graders in California and Michigan, 60 percent believed that blacks on television talked like real black people, and 56 percent believed that black teenagers on television were realistic. Just under half of the test subjects believed that the portrayals of black men and women on television were accurate.

44   Most characters were in minor roles and less prestigious jobs (the kindly janitor, the nice school nurse, the friendly doorman), so these children believed in portrayals of African Americans as friendly but subservient.

45   "Although finding no direct stimulus-response relationship between the way television portrayed blacks and how real blacks were perceived by the children, the researchers found that the selective perception of the young viewers could interpret the television programming to reinforce existing racial attitudes," wrote Clint C. Wilson II and Felix Gutierrez in their 1995 book, *Race, Multiculturalism, and the Media.*

46   "There is just no balance, and as long as it is like that the shows Hollywood produces will be picked apart," says Perkins. "The shows will always have these broad, over-the-top characters. We need to be portrayed from A–Z. We need sophisticated sit-coms, like *Seinfeld* and *Frasier,* good dramas, and shows like *Martin,* as well."

47   One of the few shows that does a good job of portraying black life, albeit in a humorous light, is *The Parent 'Hood.* No wonder. Robert Townsend, the star, co-

creator, and co-executive producer of *The Parent 'Hood,* made his mark with his film *Hollywood Shuffle,* the best—and funniest—postmodern deconstruction of Hollywood and race ever produced.

48   Townsend plays Robert Patterson, a communications professor at NYU, who, along with his wife Jerri (Suzanne Douglas), a law student, raises a family of four kids in New York.

49   Townsend keeps up with his deconstruction of Hollywood and blacks in the episode, "I'm Otay, You're Otay." His youngest son, eight-year-old Nicholas, decides to be Buckwheat as his class project for Black History Month.

50   The family is miffed and embarrassed. Robert explains to his son—via a brief montage on a mythical black comedy from the 1930s called *Paintin' Fools,* featuring himself and his best friend Wendell (Faizon Love)—that characters like Buckwheat are looked at with disgust. Nicholas understands, but still decides to go to the school function as Buckwheat. After the other schoolchildren portray the usual heroes of the black community (including some white kids acting the roles of black heroes), Nicholas hits the stage as Buckwheat, bad grammar, bad hair, tragic fashion sense, and all. Shock, embarrassment, shame. But Nicholas takes off his wig and launches into a quick and meaningful discussion of who these early black film stars were and why they acted the way they did. Standing ovation, smiles, and even I was moved.

51   But the irony is that while Nicholas and Robert discussed how Hollywood has moved past the days of Steppin' Fetchit, I can think only that we have progressed to *Homeboys in Outer Space.*

EXPLORING THE TEXT

1. Note the strategies McKissack employs in the first four paragraphs of this text. How does his choice of language reveal his attitude? Locate other phrases throughout the text that are similarly revealing. What assumptions does he make about who his audience is and what they know?

2. What point does McKissack make about the gender roles presented in *Homeboys in Outer Space*? How does this concern fit into the context of his argument overall?

3. Race is obviously the central concern of this text, but discuss the ways in which McKissack incorporates ideas about class as an additional concern in his argument.

4. Why is comedy the format for most black television? Do you agree with this assessment?

5. Why, according to McKissack, do dramas about black families fail? Do you agree with his assessment?

6. In what ways are audiences "conditioned" to want and expect certain kinds of programs? In what ways is this conditioning desirable? Undesirable? Explain your answer.

7. Why does McKissack argue that "for the black community, the lack of artistic merit on television is especially damaging" (paragraph 42).

WRITING ASSIGNMENTS

1. McKissack says that demands centered around black families fail. Is this still true? What dramas are poplar today? Are any of them centered around families, black or white? Carefully consider the most popular drama today and write an essay in which you explore these questions and present your findings.
2. Look at other science fiction portrayals of race and racial tensions (the various versions of *Star Trek;* films, such as *Alien, Independence Day,* or *Men in Black;* and so on) and compare them to *Homeboys in Outer Space.* (If this program is not available on television, rely on McKissack's discussion.)

GROUP PROJECTS

1. Research *Amos 'n' Andy* and other early black television shows and compare them to current shows. Research books or articles that discuss these shows, and watch videos of the actual shows. Look for trends and patterns among and between various programs and present a group report on your findings.
2. Compare black television dramas with black film dramas. Are the same problems apparent? Are black film dramas more successful? Discuss the similarities and differences by focusing on several texts. Have each group member focus extensively on one text. The entire group should present a discussion of your conclusions.

Gays, Lesbians, and the Media: The Slow Road to Acceptance
Barbara Raab

In the spring of 1997, Ellen DeGeneres portrayed the first lead character in a television program to "come out" as lesbian. Many people hailed this as a cultural watershed, a milestone in the struggle for the acceptance of gays and lesbians by heterosexual American society. In this essay, Barbara Raab continues the critique of television newscasting that Elayne Rapping began earlier in this chapter. Like Rapping, Raab continues the influence of television news in establishing values and setting priorities. This recognition leads her to conclude that the absence of openly gay and lesbian newscasters perpetuates dangerous cultural blindness, at best, and indicates discrimination in more drastic scenarios.

Raab is a broadcast producer of *NBC Nightly News,* a member of the NBC News Diversity Advisory Council, and vice president of the New York Chapter of the National Lesbian and Gay Journalists Association. This piece was first published in *USA Today* magazine in July 1996.

1 In 1990, ABC lost half its advertisers and $1,000,000 for an episode of "thirtysome-thing" showing two men in bed. Just a few years ago, "Roseanne" was slammed for an on-screen lesbian kiss with Mariel Hemingway, and the Fox network got cold feet and cut a gay kiss from its ultra-hip "Melrose Place."

2 That was then. This is now: "Friends" celebrated a lesbian wedding in which Speaker of the House Newt Gingrich's real-life lesbian half-sister Candace offici-ated as minister. Transvestite RuPaul made a guest appearance as a flight attendant on "The Crew," a Fox comedy. On "Mad About You," the male lead's sister an-nounced she is a lesbian. A gay precinct receptionist is a regular character on "NYPD Blue" and there was an openly gay secretary on "High Society." The list goes on and on. According to *US* magazine, during the 1994–95 television season alone, there were more than 15 lesbian and gay recurring characters on regular primetime shows. In 1996, the gay and lesbian presence in prime-time television is unprecedented.

3 On cable, the Comedy Central network has presented several successful edi-tions of a program called "Out There," a showcase for gay comedians. MTV carried the story of the late Pedro Zamora, a young gay Cuban man with AIDS, on "The Real World." It also has announced that lesbians and gays will be included in at least one episode of the network's dating game show, "Singled Out." (Imagine the old "Dating Game" letting bachelorettes question bachelorettes.)

4 On public television, there's a long-running gay and lesbian program called "In the Life." Television talk shows, though often crass and tacky, constantly are giving gays and lesbians a forum for shattering the silence about their lives. "Oprah," for example, did a show on gay marriage.

5 Over on the news side of television, where I work, though stories about and im-ages of gays and lesbians have been slower in coming and less integrated into over-all coverage, there have been big changes in a relatively short time. Take, for in-stance, the way NBC News has covered one specific event that has taken place three times: the gay rights marches on Washington, first in 1979, then in 1987, and most recently in the spring of 1993.

6 In the 1979 broadcast, anchorwoman Jessica Savitch told the story of the march in approximately 25 seconds, in "voice-over" format, in which viewers see video-tape of the event, but do not hear from any participants. At one point, Savitch clearly was perplexed by the word "homophobia" in the script she was reading; she said the word as though she never had heard it before. Today, of course, "homophobia" is used widely.

7 Coverage of the 1987 march lasted approximately 35 seconds, again in voice-over format, although anchorman Garrick Uttley put the march in better perspective. He reported that the demonstrators came to Washington to demand more protection from discrimination, as well as more money for AIDS research. The report used the term "AIDS victim," which people with AIDS always have found offensive, and ended by noting that "police reported no arrests and no incidents," a rather odd thing to say given that the videotape showed a very peaceful and compliant crowd.

8 By 1993, the news media had a much better sense of what the gay rights march was all about and had elevated its importance in its coverage. On NBC, Uttley was broadcasting live from Moscow on the night of the march. Normally, when an an-

chorman is on location, he's there for a journalistic reason that almost always is the lead story. On this night, though, the top story was that hundreds of thousands of "men and women gathered in the nation's capital, raising their voices and demanding change." Rather than a short voice-over read by the anchorman, it was reported by a correspondent live on the scene, with a taped report in which many participants were interviewed. The reporter took notice of the fact that organizers disputed the Park Police's crowd estimates and explained that the event was meant to be "more than just a gay rights march. It was an attempt to demonstrate gay political power." In 1993, print coverage was far more extensive as well, both leading up to and after the march. Almost every daily newspaper in the U.S. featured a photograph of the march on its front page the following morning.

9   Coverage of the three marches is typical of the expansion and improvement of television news coverage of the "big ticket" stories involving gay issues. Topics such as homosexuals in the military, AIDS, and gay-bashing are too big for the news media to ignore.

10   There also has been some integration of lesbian and gay lives into over-all television news reporting. On Father's Day, 1995, for example, the "CBS Evening News" did a story about two men raising their two sons together. A broadcast of CNN's "Inside Business" series focused on marketing to the gay and lesbian consumer. On ABC, when Barbara Walters did a long profile of Hollywood billionaire David Geffen, they matter of factly discussed his homosexuality. The same thing occurred when Jane Pauley profiled breast cancer surgeon Susan Love on "Dateline NBC," as the doctor's lesbian partner was included in the story. In 1995, my show, "NBC Nightly News," won an award from the Gay and Lesbian Alliance Against Defamation media watchdog group for a three-part series called "Gay in America."

11   The print news media greatly have increased their reporting on gays and lesbians, and some newspapers, including *The New York Times,* have an official gay beat. Deb Price is a nationally syndicated lesbian columnist for the Gannett chain, and other newspapers around the country have openly gay columnists as well.

12   Magazines, too, are paying attention. A July, 1995, cover story in *Newsweek* was about bisexuals. In the August issue of *New Woman,* the mother of a gay son who just had come out of the closet asked the magazine's columnist whether she should send him to a psychiatrist. Dr. Harriet Lerner's advice was absolutely not; homosexuality, she said, is as normal as heterosexuality, and "the right to be who we are, is the most precious right we have." The executive editor of *Essence,* Linda Villarosa, is an African-American lesbian who came out of the closet in the pages of her own magazine and since has written another article on what it's like to live openly as a black Christian lesbian. *Advertising Age* assigns a reporter to the gay beat; *Entertainment Weekly* devoted an entire issue to "The Gay 90s"; and *People'*s coverage of rock star Melissa Ethridge's birthday celebration noted that "the party's crowning moment came when her live-in lover took off her blouse and danced topless."

13   On the silver screen, there has been an explosion of movies with gay themes and characters: "Philadelphia," "To Wong Foo, Thanks for Everything! Julie Newmar," "Four Weddings and a Funeral," and even "The Brady Bunch," to name just a few. More than a dozen gay and lesbian films debuted in 1996 at the prestigious Sundance Film Festival.

14   Let's not forget about the music industry, where k.d. lang, Boy George, Janis Ian, and other openly homosexual musicians are writing songs and making videos about same-sex love that are selling like hotcakes.

15   Gays and lesbians are moving from the media margins to the media mainstream at a fast and furious pace. That indeed is encouraging to those of us who believe that, no matter who you are, what you see and hear in our powerful popular culture should be a true, fair, and accurate picture of our world. It's not the entire story, though.

16   Despite all the mainstream media attention, gays and lesbians continue to struggle with the same basic issues we always have struggled with: coming out, overcoming shame and self-hatred, how to convey the reality of our lives, how to live free from violence, and how to live and raise families as openly gay people. Mainstream media visibility has not taken the sting out of the facts of gay life.

Double Standards

17 In many ways, the mainstream media continues to keep lesbian and gay people on the margins. There are the double standards; visible affection between gay people, for instance, remains taboo. A kiss is much more than a kiss when a gay or lesbian character is the kisser. The simplest same-sex kiss somehow is more controversial than the steamiest heterosexual one or a typical love scene in a typical daytime soap opera. The "Friends" wedding did not include a kiss. ABC rescheduled the "December Bride" episode of "Roseanne" about the wedding of two gay male characters so that it would be seen later in the evening than usual.

18   Advertisers sometimes exert a lot of pressure on the networks when they include gay and lesbian characters or story lines, and that may be one reason why gays and lesbians get portrayed in the most bland ways. Our individuality and our differences are minimized and erased so that we are acceptable to the mainstream.

19   The news media marginalizes gay men and lesbians by ghettoizing us and seldom integrating us into ordinary everyday news and feature coverage. When was the last time you saw a gay or lesbian couple in a news story about home-buying, tax-planning, or workplace issues? Gays and lesbians usually are covered in stories about being gay, and not about being homebuyers, taxpayers, or workers. Gay people thus are marginalized in supposedly fact-based coverage even though we are the readers' and viewers' family, friends, neighbors, and co-workers.

20   Here's a glaring example: in 1993, the Fourth International Gay Games competition in New York City drew more participants than the Olympics. Nevertheless, there was not one word about the Gay Games in *Sports Illustrated*. Despite the fact that some of the athletes set world records, the editors viewed the event as a gay story, not as a sports one. That is marginalizing.

21   Lesbians tend to be particularly marginalized in television news coverage, along with women in general. Most gay people who appear on news programs are white men, even though they represent only a portion of gay Americans. One of the interesting angles on the Million Man March, for example, was the dilemma facing gay black men who supported the goals of the march, but were offended deeply by what they saw as Nation of Islam leader Louis Farrakhan's blatant homophobia.

With the exception of an article in *The New York Times,* however, that part of an otherwise extensively covered story remained invisible, on the margins.

22   Another double standard that seems to be disappearing is the mandate that reporters "balance" their coverage of gay rights with opposing views. You don't see the mainstream media seeking out an opinion from white supremacists each time it presents a story about the NAACP, so why must there be an "anti-gay" spokesperson in all stories about gay rights?

23   There is the issue of invisibility in high-profile news media positions. How many openly gay newscasters can you name? Chances are, the answer is none.

24   Why, when there are gay characters in movies, sitcoms, talk shows, and soap operas, are there not openly gay and lesbian TV anchorpeople and news reporters? There *are* a few openly gay men on the air at various local news stations around the country—Los Angeles, San Francisco, Miami—but not in New York. Moreover, there are no openly gay men or women on any of the national newscasts.

25   It's not that there aren't any gay people working in these places—trust me, there are—but many of them earn a lot of money and are afraid that coming out could be a career killer. There is some evidence to support their fears. A few years ago, I coordinated a survey of news directors in local stations around the country for the National Lesbian and Gay Journalists Association (NLGJA). One of the questions was: "Would you be willing to put an openly gay reporter or anchor on the air, or to keep that person on the air if he or she came out?" The majority of the news directors in the survey said they weren't sure. No wonder nobody wants to take a chance.

Workplace Dilemmas

26   Gay and lesbian employees remain on the margins of their workplaces in some other very profound ways that are not visible to the viewer or the reader. Coming out and being out at work remains a complicated and stressful proposition for many lesbians and gay men who work in the media. NBC knew I was gay when I was hired, and I never have regretted the decision to be "out" from the start. Yet, it can be frightening to come out at work, so many gay people stay closeted, and that can feel very marginalizing because it means those employees hesitate to suggest stories about gay issues, never bring a same-sex partner to company functions, and never join gay and lesbian employee groups where they can get support and encouragement.

27   When gay employees in the newsroom do come out, they often face a new dilemma: the danger of being perceived as having "an agenda." We know that many of our co-workers suspect us of being gay activists just by virtue of being honest about who we are, so, to counter that, we may hesitate to bring up interesting and important news stories that we know about. We silence ourselves and bend over backwards to prove that we are generalists, rather than "special interest" journalists. That is marginalizing, and it diminishes the editorial product.

28   Then there's the flip side. When we do work on stories involving gay issues, we worry about the response we may get from our gay friends. Will they think it's good enough? Will they be angry that there are some characters in the story who don't

support their views? It's a constant mind game: worrying, on the one hand, that our mainstream media companies will marginalize us for being biased; worrying, on the other hand, that gay people will view us as "too mainstream."

29   Gay employees also can be marginalized when hemophobia in the workplace is accepted passively, or when heterosexual employees are permitted time off to care for an ailing spouse, but bereavement leave for a partner's death from AIDS is denied. Gay employees feel marginalized when it feels too awkward to bring a same-sex partner to office parties. We are marginalized when our health and other company benefits are not extended to our same-sex partners. We are marginalized when the newspapers we work for refuse to print same-sex wedding announcements or mention same-sex partners in obituaries. We are marginalized when there are no standards set for acceptable language in stores about homosexuality; thus, Reuters' use of the term "normal heterosexual sex" in a story about HIV transmission. (The error, once called to Reuters' attention, promptly was corrected.) We are marginalized when reporters are not expected to cultivate contacts in the local gay and lesbian community, the way they do in other communities. We are marginalized when workplace diversity seminars do not address sexual orientation. We are marginalized when editors practice a double-standard about revealing the sexual identities of public and political leaders.

30   The mainstream media can help bring gay and lesbian employees off the margins by making it clear that it is safe to come out; by explicitly including sexual orientation in company-wide non-discrimination policies and diversity training seminars; and by making it clear that "fag jokes" and other homophobic behavior are not acceptable, just as racist and sexist remarks and behavior are unacceptable. An increasing number of mainstream media companies are recognizing the relationships of their gay employees by extending so-called domestic partner benefits to their same-sex partners; it's a benefit that is both economic and psychological. When the mainstream media is willing to recognize same-sex relationships in obituaries and social announcements and to tell the truth about the relevant personal lives of public and political figures, gay people inside and outside the newsrooms will be far less marginalized.

31   Finally, gays and lesbians in the media are facing a backlash by radical right-wing forces determined to stop the momentum from margin to mainstream. Pat Robertson's "700 Club," for instance, ran a report on the NLGJA. The report, and an accompanying "fact sheet" available at no cost through an 800 number, asserted that today's mainstream media "overwhelmingly support the homosexual agenda"; that gay people are rising to newsroom management positions and are infecting news coverage with "pro-homosexual perspectives"; and that, according to Robertson, "the truth is that the so-called mainstream media are becoming more and more marginalized because they are so far outside the mainstream of America."

32   These kinds of allegations have a marginalizing effect. I have heard some openly gay journalists say their news outlets are pulling way back on gay coverage or are subjecting certain stories to a higher standard before they can get in the paper or on the air.

33   There are several organizations working hard to assure gays and lesbians are not marginalized in the media or in their workplaces. One is the National Lesbian and Gay Journalists Association, which has nearly 1,200 members in 18 chapters.

The organization's mission is to promote, from within the news industry, fair portrayal of gay and lesbian people, equal treatment of gay and lesbian journalists, and the elimination of gay bias in newsrooms. NLGJA has helped to move gay journalists and journalism on gay subjects toward the mainstream, in large part by giving many gay and lesbian journalists the courage to come out in their workplaces and take an active role in contributing to coverage.

34   The Gay and Lesbian Alliance Against Defamation's West Coast headquarters monitors the entertainment industry, while its East Coast office pays close attention to the news media. Hollywood Supports is a Los Angeles-based organization founded by leading figures in the entertainment industry to counter workplace fears and discrimination based on sexual orientation and HIV status. It successfully has lobbied for adoption of domestic partnership benefits at over 40 entertainment companies, including all but one of the major studios.

35   In the end, new technologies may marginalize the mainstream media itself. The Internet, for example, is allowing every single one of us to communicate with the entire world on whatever subject we want. Until that happens, the fact remains that being visible in the mainstream media is to achieve a certain measure of cultural legitimacy. That is why gays and lesbians want their stories, in their voices, told and why gay people who work in the media want to have the same freedom as their straight co-workers to be who they really are.

EXPLORING THE TEXT

1. Raab begins her essay by pointing to a number of examples of homosexuals depicted on television shows other than those on the "news side." On what other sides or types of television programming does she focus? How are these similar to or distinct from news coverage (in other words, what are the goals of the different types of programming)? How do the so-called soft news programs such as *Hard Copy, PrimeTime, Live* and *20/20* fit into this consideration?

2. In paragraph 6, Raab criticizes Jessica Savitch for apparently not being familiar (or comfortable) with the word *homophobia,* and goes on to suggest that the word is now used widely. What does this word mean? Why does Raab seem to think it is so important to know this word? What is the importance of the word (and concept) in the context of Raab's discussion?

3. Raab claims, "Topics such as homosexuals in the military, AIDS, and gay-bashing are too big for the news media to ignore" (paragraph 9). How does she develop support for this claim?

4. What, according to Raab, are the double standards? Make a list of as many as you can identify in her discussion.

5. In paragraph 22 Raab describes the news mandate for "balanced" coverage. Why does she see balance as a double standard? Is this truly "disappear-

ing" as she claims? Think of particular examples and discuss your answer in detail.

6. What, according to Raab, are the workplace dilemmas? Make a list of as many as you can identify from her discussion.

7. Raab's discussion, ultimately, suggests several solutions to the problem she describes in the mainstream media. What role does she believe new technologies will play in overcoming the marginalization of gays in the news media? Does her argument seem plausible?

WRITING ASSIGNMENTS

1. Who are the people presenting the news to us on television? Review a television news program and list the various qualities and characteristics of the newscasters. Consider gender, race, and age, but also look for particular qualities that make a newscaster "trustworthy." Write an essay in which you discuss a particular newscast and evaluate it with the criteria Raab establishes in her discussion.

2. Write an essay in which you analyze the adequacy of Raab's solutions to the problem she presents. Evaluate her solutions and present additional solutions of your own. Keep in mind that you may need to redefine the problem as you suggest alternative solutions.

GROUP PROJECTS

1. Raab primarily discusses the cultural influence of the television medium, but films are no less influential. Working as a group, brainstorm a list of films that address gay issues or that include openly homosexual characters. In what ways does Hollywood address (or readdress) the issue of gay visibility. As Raab did with television, try to chart a similar progression of visibility and acceptability of gays in films. Also, since popularity is an issue with television, consider the extent to which such films are (or are not) popular with mainstream audiences.

2. Raab begins her discussion by presenting a historical overview of the growing presence of gays on a variety of television programs. Divide your group so that different group members survey one week's worth of a particular kind of television programming, including talk shows, dramas, sitcoms, "hard" news, and "soft" news. Prepare a report that updates Raab's overview and considers whether there has been a "backlash," as she suggested, or a continuously expanding gay presence on television programs. Either way, discuss the current situation of gays and gay issues on television.

In Defense of Prime Time
Martha Bayles

People typically bemoan the poor quality of television programs—the excessive sex and violence, the cheesy excuses for comedy, the mindless blather that passes for in-depth news, the endless roar of commercials. But what we have below is a rare defense of television—a tribute, in fact, to the prime of prime time. To Martha Bayles, television drama constitutes an important popular art form with serious moral lessons apparent in particular shows. In her discussion, Bayles takes a jab at those who dismiss television as "low" art by reminding us that it is just such "art" that reveals the values of a society and that much of what we revere today was once considered "low" art.

Bayles is the literary editor of the *Wilson Quarterly* and the author of *Hole in Our Soul: The Loss of Beauty and Meaning in Popular American Music* (1996). This article was first published in the *Washington Post* on March 10, 1996.

1 The rain is cold, almost freezing. It floods the suburban road where young Dr. Ross's car stalls. There's a phone booth ahead, but instead of making a call, Dr. Ross sits watching the rain sluice down his windshield. He is in trouble at work and not eager to get to the party anyway. His car stalling is the perfect excuse. Brooding, he picks up a marijuana cigarette that a patient palmed off on him. He knows he shouldn't smoke it, but he is so depressed he feels tempted.

2 That's when he hears the voice crying for help. Hesitantly he gets out of the car and follows the sound. A young boy is trapped in a culvert, waist deep in icy, garbage-laden water, and clinging to an iron grate that blocks his escape. The water is rising, and the boy is succumbing to hypothermia. What does Dr. Ross do?

3 Well, folks, this is prime-time television. Indeed, it is the top-rated episode of the top-rated program, "ER." You can't get through a supermarket checkout line without learning that Dr. Ross (played by George Clooney) is America's heartthrob. Advertisers pay top dollar to place commercials next to this handsome devil with the eyes of an angel, who yearns for true love but ends up having casual affairs instead.

4 Occasionally we see Dr. Ross under the sheets with some woman he doesn't care about, and when such a scene is followed by the kind of commercial in which a sexy model confides that "getting close" requires only that her partner use the right deodorant, it's tempting to agree with Bill Bennett that the ruling philosophy of prime time is "self-indulgence, self-aggrandizement, instant gratification."

5 But what about the boy in the culvert? If Bennett is right, then Dr. Ross will bungle this situation as badly as bungles his love life. He'll promise to help the boy (self-aggrandizement) but then, after making sure no one has seen him, he'll turn tail and run (self-indulgence). But as 42 million viewers know, this is not what Dr. Ross does.

6 In an extraordinary hour of television, he rescues and resuscitates the boy. And he does so in a way that is dramatically consistent with his obviously flawed character—thereby putting a human face on at least six of the virtues celebrated in Ben-

nett's "Book of Virtues": self-discipline, compassion, responsibility, courage, perseverance and faith. Plus a couple that (for some reason) never made it into the book: modesty and humility.

7   Bennett has been an effective debunker of exploitative material such as gangsta rap and daytime talk shows. But his recent denunciations of television are too sweeping. He concedes that there are some "quality shows" on the air but fastidiously avoids naming any. Instead, he repeats the bromide that the medium is the message—not just "broadcast content" but "things endemic to the medium" are fomenting "the wreckage of civilization." In the same vein, James Bowman of the New Criterion recently called television an "airless medium" that "reduces everything to blandness." For Bowman, hearing someone praise TV is like "being told by a friend of his love affair with a tart."

8   A bland tart out to wreck civilization? This is not useful criticism. It doesn't even make the basic moral and aesthetic distinctions that countless Americans make when they argue about whether "NYPD Blue" is improved by Steven Bochco's puerile obsession with gratuitous profanity and nudity. Yes, there is a streak of perversity flowing through the culture. But it flows through every medium, not just television. Yes, there are sitcoms that specialize in nasty sexual humor that (among other things) isn't funny. But the better ones, such as "Frasier" and "Seinfeld," are witty comedies of manners that do not need perversity. Likewise, the better prime-time dramas, such as "ER." "Law & Order," "Homicide: Life on the Street" and even the unpredictable "NYPD Blue" are complex morality plays about imperfect human beings struggling to behave virtuously in spite of the evils that surround them.

9   At this point, the high-minded response is to invoke Great Art. Bowman writes: "I would like to hear some defense of the idea that these . . . shows are first-rate in any sense which doesn't involve comparison merely to other crummy TV shows." Well, the first step is to compare TV shows, not with novels (as Bowman does), but with their counterparts in the performing arts. "Frasier" may not be Moliere. But the best sitcoms have, over the years, qualified as a latter-day *commedia del'arte,* the form of popular theater that was one of Moliere's chief sources.

10   And, no, "ER" is not "Hamlet." But the spirit of tragedy breathes in the best prime-time dramas, precisely because they are not morally simplistic melodramas in the mode of old-fashioned cops-and-robbers entertainment. Consider, for example, the episode of "ER" in which Dr. Greene's informed by mistaken diagnoses cause the death of a pregnant woman. As for mixing the comic and the tragic, that is done very deftly by my favorite program, "Law & Order," which also offers a quite sophisticated critique of the criminal justice system.

11   Bowman in particular should recall T. S. Eliot's admonition that the cultural achievement of an entire society cannot, and should not, be judged according to the standard of the most cultivated individual. The topic on the table is popular art and its relationship to popular art and its relationship to popular morality. Bennett gets it right when, along with Shakespeare, his "Book of Virtues" quotes Hans Christian Anderson, P. T. Barnum, Edgar Guest and Babe Ruth. A couple million Americans paid $27.50 for that eclectic compendium of tales. Maybe it's possible that millions more are watching prime-time television, not because it reduces them to quivering

hedonism, but because it, too, tells tales about how ordinary people manage to hold onto decency when decency is under assault.

EXPLORING THE TEXT

1. Bayles opens her discussion with an extended summary of a scene from *ER*. Why does she do this? How does this strategy lead into the argument she presents? Does it work?
2. Who is Bill Bennett? How does Bayles use his book to set up her own argument? What are the "virtues" Bennett describes? To what extent does Bayles agree with him?
3. Who is James Bowman and what is the *New Criterion* for which he writes? What is Bayles's strategy in bringing his ideas into the discussion along with Bennett's? How does Bayles position these men in relation to other Americans?
4. Consider what Bayles says about "useful criticism" (paragraph 8). What is useful? What is not useful? Do you agree? Explain your answer.
5. In paragraph 9, Bayles quotes Bowman's desire for television to be "Great Art," but she argues that his definition of Great Art is insufficient. What problems does Bayles point out in Bowman's definition? What new definition does she offer?
6. What is Bayles's rhetorical strategy in quoting T. S. Eliot in the final paragraph? How does Eliot relate to the other people she mentions in the same paragraph? What then is Bayles saying about the relationship between high art and low art? Explain your answer.
7. What does Bayles's use of phrases such as "Bill" Bennett (in paragraph 4) or "quivering hedonism" (paragraph 11) reveal about her tone? List several other phrases from the text that are similarly revealing.

WRITING ASSIGNMENTS

1. Bayles refers to the *commedia del'larte* in paragraph 9. What is this? How does it relate to her argument overall? Do some research on this art form, define what it is, and compare its conventions to a television sitcom. Write an essay explaining what you discover.
2. Bayles's use of the Doug Ross anecdote is presented as a kind of "morality play." Earlier in this chapter, Charles Oliver argued that television talk shows present a kind of morality play, in the sense of a freak parade. Write an essay in which you discuss the idea of morality play as used by each author. Define what a morality play is and discuss its historical and cultural significance. Question whether the two authors mean the same thing when

they use the term. Discuss how the format of the programs influences the distinctions. You might want to look for other examples of morality plays in other television genres.

GROUP PROJECTS

1. Get Bennett's *Book of Virtues* from the library. Study the discussion of the virtues. Look at his examples. Consider how they measure against the examples Bayles uses. Divide the group into two and prepare your own debate of these issues. One side should defend Bennett from Bayles's criticism. The other side should be ready to expand Bayles's criticism. Focus on particular television programs as examples and evidence. Present your debate to the class.
2. Test Bayles's ideas by watching a series of television dramas and providing a similar, but more extensive, critique of Bennett's ideas. Each group member should focus on one or more programs, making extensive notes and looking for evidence of the virtues Bennett advocates. Your discussion might be aided by a careful review of ideas Bayles argues against in Bennett's book. Prepare a report of your findings.
3. Charles Oliver ("TV Talk Shows: Freak Parades") argues that television talk shows present a kind of morality play, in the sense of a freak parade. Martha Bayles uses a scene from *ER* to represent a kind of "morality play." Write an essay in which you discuss the idea of morality play as used by each author. Define what a morality play is and discuss its historical and cultural significance. Question whether the two authors mean the same thing when they use the term. Discuss how the format of the programs influences the distinctions. You might want to look for other examples of morality plays in other television genres.

Into the Heart of Darkness
Terrence Rafferty

Why do we love books and movies and television shows that scare us? Terrence Rafferty thinks he knows why. He says we want answers to things we don't understand or can't control. We want vicarious experiences that tap into our unconscious suspicions and fears. We want heroes and heroines who are bigger than life, who contend with dark and unknown forces and survive the experiences. According to Rafferty, these are some of the reasons why *The X-Files* and its spinoff, *Millennium,* have been so enormously popular. Unlike some of the other articles in this chapter, Rafferty's presents a strong defense of television—when it is good.

Rafferty is a film critic and the author of *The Thing Happens: Ten Years of Writing About the Movies* (1993). This article first appeared in the April 1997 issue of *GQ* where Rafferty is a staff writer.

1 "Terror," Stephen King once wrote, "often arises from a pervasive sense of disestab-lishment; that things are in the unmaking." That evocative statement, which appears in King's 1981 critical survey of the horror genre, *Danse Macabre,* might serve as the motto of Chris Carter, the creator of *The X-Files* and *Millennium.* Carter's TV shows, like King's novels and stories, rely on meticulous pulp-fiction craftsmanship to tap into an audience's collective fear of dissolution, of encroaching chaos. King—who also observed, accurately, in *Danse Macabre* that "the history of horror and fantasy on television is a short and tacky one"—clearly recognizes a kindred spirit: After volunteering himself for *Millennium,* he is now working on a script for *The X-Files.* "We do the same thing," Carter says. "We scare people."

2 What Carter has done in nearly four seasons of *The X-Files* is a little different from King-style horror, though. He supplies week-in-week-out terror with continu-ing characters—something that's virtually unprecedented, not only in the medium but in the venerable genre itself. Writers of detective stories, Westerns, spy thrillers, "hard" science fiction (like *Star Trek*) and heroic fantasy (like Robert E. Howard's Conan stories) often depend on series heroes, but horror writers—even virtuosos like King—usually don't, for the simple and very sound reason that any character who is *repeatedly* exposed to monsters and supernatural phenomena risks turning into a comic figure and thus blowing the genre's cover completely. That's what hap-pened to the small screen's most interesting previous attempt at a nonanthology hor-ror series, *Kolchak: The Night Stalker* (1974–75). Its hero, a newspaper reporter, made his first appearance in a genuinely frightening made-for-TV movie; but as Kolchak's encounters with the unearthly and the unseemly multiplied—one a week, regular as clockwork—the series' producers had no choice but to play his adven-tures for laughs. Although Carter acknowledges the program as an influence, *Kolchak* was, if anything, more a precursor of *Ghostbusters* than *The X-Files.* (And when he cites *Kolchak* scenes that impressed him in his youth, they're invariably from the original movie, not a series episode.) In the protagonists of *The X-Files,* FBI agents Fox Mulder (David Duchovny) and Dana Scully (Gillian Anderson), Chris Carter has given the horror genre its first archetypal heroes: the Holmes and Watson of the paranormal. And the appearance of those sorts of pop-mythological figures is a phenomenon as unforeseeable, and perhaps as inexplicable, as a UFO sighting. You can watch the cultural skies for a long, long time before spotting any-thing with the weird radiance of *The X-Files.*

3 The usual response to such manifestations is mass hysteria—which is a fair de-scription of the fan culture that the show has generated, especially on the Internet. One of the series' writers, Darin Morgen, was stunned to discover that a throwaway line he'd written about Mulder's neckties had sparked heated on-line discussions among the so-called X-Philes. "I had no idea I was tapping into the collective un-conscious," he said. The obsessiveness of the neckwear monitors may not be repre-sentative of the general audience's level of interest, but it *is* an indication that some-

thing unusual is going on here. Mulder and Scully aren't just the hero and the hero-ine of a weekly series anymore; they now star in novels and comic books, too, and a feature film is in the works. The fans' near delusional sense of the reality of the characters is a reaction that only the most powerful fictional creations induce. The X-Philes—whose berserk scholarship mirrors that of the dedicated Holmesians known as the Baker Street Irregulars—are proof that Mulder and Scully have achieved the kind of parafictional autonomy that is the pop-culture equivalent of the Holy Grail. *The X-Files* somehow excites the primitive, childlike curiosity that is one of the most important—and most elusive—goals of storytelling, and you don't have to be a conspiracy buff or a UFO fancier to succumb to it. Mulder and Scully work out of a basement office whose most prominent decoration is a poster with the legend I WANT TO BELIEVE. No wonder we identify with these characters. They want exactly what every viewer and every reader of fiction wants: a story that makes perfect sense of the dense and apparently insoluble mysteries that surround us.

4   It's almost impossible to invent a franchise myth of such magnitude deliber-ately, and in the case of *The X-Files,* the qualities that make Mulder and Scully so compelling have their origins not in some grand design to awaken the audience's collective unconscious but in practical, ingenious solutions to storytelling problems. Needing a hero who, unlike Kolchak, could plausibly become involved with the su-pernatural, the extraterrestrial or the merely uncanny on a regular basis, Carter dreamed up an investigator whose job it is to explain the unexplained and who, moreover, has access to a voluminous supply of mysteries to explore: hence, FBI agent Mulder and the X-Files, the bureau's secret repository of bizarre, unsolved cases. Mulder is a firm believer in the paranormal and in the existence of extrater-restrial life, and in order to acknowledge the ordinary viewer's rational objections to the hero's speculations, the show provides him with a skeptical partner—Scully, an agent with a medical degree and a no-nonsense scientific temperament. She's more than a sidekick: The *X-Files* pilot introduced her first, and in many episodes—par-ticularly in the first season—the final word is her official report. (Early in the series, the differences between the agents teased viewers with the possibility of romance; when Mulder and Scully disagreed, their exchanges often suggested the playful sparring of a screwball-comedy couple. Their relationship has since developed into a kind of absolute trust that seems to transcend physical attraction: It's parasexual.) The philosophical opposition is, of course, heavily weighted in Mulder's favor, but although Scully's scientific theories always prove inadequate, her outsider's per-spective is what makes the series' weekly terrors bearable. Seeing this strange world through only the hero's eyes would be exhausting—or deranging, like the fevered first-person narratives of Poe or Lovecraft.

5   And because it's important that Mulder not strike the viewer as a madman, Carter supplies him with an urgent personal motive for his preoccupation with the otherworldly and the occult. Early on—about halfway through the pilot—we learn that Mulder's younger sister, Samantha, disappeared when he was 12 years old and that later, under hypnosis, he remembered details suggesting that she had been ab-ducted by aliens. That experience, we're given to understand, is what drives the hero's obsession with proving the existence of extraterrestrial "visitors" and his de-

termination to expose the government's cover-up of alien activity on earth. In *The X-Files'* paranoid take on the Holmes-and-Watson formula, the role of Professor Moriarty, the evil genius, has been assumed by the government—or, rather, by a shadowy government-within-the-government, whose most prominent and sinister representative is a quiet character known as the Cigarette-Smoking Man (or sometimes as Cancer Man). Although the Samantha Mulder back story probably owes its existence to Carter's need to explain his hero's apparently irrational willingness to pit himself against a vast conspiracy, it has become increasingly clear that the emotional resonance of Mulder's search for his sister is stronger than anything a simple, functional narrative gambit could provide. Mulder's hopeful mantra, which is also the epigraph that appears in almost every episode's opening credits, is "The truth is out there," and what he means, really, is that *she* is out there somewhere—recoverable, not lost forever. The hero's quest for his sister, which initially lent urgency to his investigations, now inevitably has a different effect, because, after almost a hundred episodes, Samantha Mulder *still* has not been found, and her brother's mission is thus haunted by the possibility of failure. These days what *The X-Files* appears most interested in exposing is the heart of its own growing darkness. The luster of the supernatural has, in some episodes, dimmed almost to the point of invisibility; the aliens don't seem to drop in as frequently as they used to; and all the characters—even the Cigarette-Smoking Man—behave less like warriors in a cosmic battle than wanderers in a country graveyard. And the show is scarier than ever.

6   Over time *The X-Files* has evolved from a UFO-conspiracy show anchored by an *Avengers*-like platonic couple (who, perhaps in homage to John Steed and Emma Peel, address each other only by surnames) to a series that is, in effect, a sustained horror-fiction epic. Even in the program's alien-intensive first season, Carter and his writing staff took pains to vary the formula, with episodes whose story lines bypassed the larger conspiracy arc. The inclusion of these self-contained stories is, like everything else about the series' genesis, evidence of Carter's pragmatic intelligence. The independent episodes are an ideal way to keep the show fresh and unpredictable and to reduce the possibility that in the long run the continuing irresolution of the cover-up plot will bore his writers and annoy his viewers. (The conclusive proof of his wisdom is the inane knockoff called *Dark Skies,* a flying-saucer show that makes watching the skies seem duller than staring at a test pattern.) The standalone hours also demonstrated, right from the start, the unusual flexibility of the series' concept: The program ranged freely among the distinct genres of fantastic narrative, and Mulder and Scully didn't look out of place in any of them. One of that season's most memorable episodes, "Ice," was a gripping sci-fi biohazard thriller, set in a snowbound geological research station near the Arctic Circle and involving a parasitic worm that induces homicidal aggression in its host. Two episodes dealt with a self-reincarnating serial killer named Eugene Tooms. The conditions of his immortality are that he kill five people every thirty years and eat their livers; to carry out this ambiguous project, he makes use of an enviable ability to elongate his body and slither down chimneys and through barred windows.

7   In the first season, Carter and his writers (notably the team of Glen Morgan and James Wong, who wrote "Ice" and the Tooms episodes) established that all things strange and dangerous could find a home within the series' format and could be dra-

matized effectively by exploiting, in every X-Files investigation, the basic tension of the believer/skeptic dialectic. Among the show's fans, there are undoubtedly those who consider the self-contained episodes irritating digressions from the overall story line, but for many of us these shows are the standouts. It's easy to lose track of the baroque twists and turns of what Carter calls the "mythology" episodes; it's hard to forget the sight of the Arctic worm wriggling into a victim's ear, or of Eugene Tooms squirting through a heating vent into Scully's apartment.

8   The show's writers, directors and actors—and Carter himself—invariably cite nonmythology episodes as their favorites. The nearly unanimous in-house choice for the best episode of *The X-Files'* first season is Morgan and Wong's "Beyond the Sea," in which Luther Lee Boggs (Brad Dourif), a murderer on death row, offers to use his purported psychic abilities to help the bureau catch an at-large serial killer; in exchange, he wants his death sentence commuted to life imprisonment. "Beyond the Sea," which aired exactly halfway through the season, boldly flips the terms of the Mulder/Scully dialectic. Here, he's dubious and she's receptive—because she has just buried her father, and Boggs holds out to her the tantalizing prospect of channeling a final message from the dead man. It's an eerie, unsettling and tremendously moving hour of television, and it's also a crucial moment in the greater scheme of *The X-Files'* development, because we can't help seeing Scully's grief-fueled willingness to believe in Boggs's extrasensory powers as a poignant reflection of Mulder's tenacious belief in alien abduction. Scully's atypical credulity creates an unexpected emotional bond between the temperamentally opposed protagonists and, in doing so, raises the possibility that Mulder's faith is, like hers, largely wishful—that a belief in powers beyond earthly reality is, in essence, a stubborn refusal to believe in the reality of death.

9   In a way, Carter's new show, *Millennium,* forces the viewer to look at Mulder's terrifying world without the comfort of paranormal hypotheses. The genre here is the nonsupernatural horror fiction of serial-killer sagas like Thomas Harris's *Red Dragon* and *The Silence of the Lambs,* in which investigators chase down psychopaths with a kind of daredevil empathy: Harris's detectives plunge headlong into the murderers' grotesque thought processes and then have to extricate themselves from the mental swamp before they're pulled under. Carter's hero, Frank Black (Lance Henriksen), is a profiler employed by an organization called the Millennium Group, which police departments consult for expert advice on multiple-murder cases. Frank has some psychic ability, which means that he does literally what other profilers do metaphorically: He can see through the eyes of the killer. These insights tend to come in quick bursts—chaotic flashes of the awful moment of the victim's death. The protagonist's gift (the show's sole paranormal touch) is used sparingly—often just for an unnerving jolt of visual dissonance—and it isn't always important to the solution of the crimes. Its real function may simply be to streamline a genre that doesn't adapt easily to hourly television. Investigations of serial killers—who select their victims randomly (or, rather, according to patterns dictated by the tortured logic of their psychoses)—are by nature painstaking, incremental processes. The narrative fascination of novels like Harris's lies in the patient narrowing of possibilities, the slow zoom into a close-up of the killer. *Millennium* doesn't have the luxury of unfolding a story in that way, and Frank's psychic seizures give Carter the

means, when necessary, to substitute an intuitive leap for the halting pace of forensic procedure and thereby make a long story short—short enough, anyway, to be an episode of a television series.

10   *Millennium* isn't a bad show, but it hasn't hit the ground running, as *The X-Files* did. The laws of probability aren't in Carter's favor; pop archetypes, like lightning, hardly ever strike twice in the same place. A more fundamental reason for the show's frustrating inability to establish a distinctive identity is, I think, that it's genre is less pliable, more unforgiving than the imaginative spaces in which *The X-Files* roams so blithely. In attempting to speed up the police-procedural form, *Millennium* deprives itself of the primary source of the genre's power: the steady, cumulative intensity of its narrative momentum. You have to admire the audacity of Carter's reworking of the genre; it makes the series a lot more interesting than the conceptually similar *Profiler,* which plays as a standard cop show with creepier-than-average villains. But *Millennium* would probably be better if it were a little more conventional—if, that is to say, it at least met the demands of the procedural form halfway and allowed its stories to develop in multiepisode arcs (in the manner of *Wiseguy* or this season's much improved *Murder One*). *Millenium*'s swift, elliptical episodes generate quick, nasty shocks rather than unshakable horrors; everything comes at us in flashes.

11   The domestic, everyday paranoia of Carter's new show isn't yet as potent as the cosmic paranoia of his first. What's most intriguing about *Millennium* at this point is the light it sheds on the complex melancholia that has become the predominant tone of *The X-Files.* Imagine that Samantha Mulder had been abducted not by aliens but, like most little girls who disappear forever, by a twisted human being. To think that is to realize Frank Black's world is Fox Mulder's nightmare. Lance Henricksen's middle-aged weariness—which, week after week, supplies *Millennium*'s most suggestive effects—seems, at times, to represent Carter's image of what Mulder would be if he lost his peculiar capacity for belief. And as *The X-Files* proceeds, with the fierce survival instinct that long-running TV series need, the question of spiritual exhaustion inevitably takes on a certain urgency. Carter and his staff are probably resourceful enough to sustain the suspense of the mythology arc as long as they have to, but are Mulder and Scully resilient enough to keep chasing ETs and dodging the Cigarette-Smoking Man without sooner or later giving up hope? The heavy, doom-laden mood of *Millennium* is an oblique response to that question. It's like a scream of frustration, an extended panic attack.

12   Back on the franchise, however, the atmosphere is rueful and sort of antic. This season's varied array of episodes shows both a playful experimentation with different styles and a deepening commitment to exploring the core of the series' sense of horror. In "Home," which treated viewers to the grisly exploits of a family of inbred human monsters, the show presented the most frightening hour in the history of television and managed it with only the faintest trace of the paranormal—it's a black comedy about reproduction, evolution and the creatures lurking in our genetic pool. In another episode, Mulder sees his own death in a previous incarnation. In a third, Scully tracks down a Tooms-like autoregenerative serial killer; this one sustains himself by eating cancerous cells. When she comes face to face with him, he says what he says to all his victims: "You've got something I need." (Tests later confirm

that Scully does indeed have a malignant—probably inoperable—tumor.) The season's most daring and funniest episode, written by Glen Morgan, fills in some of the gaps in the biography of the Cigarette-Smoking Man. We're not entirely surprised to learn that he killed JFK *and* Martin Luther King Jr.; it is, however, startling to discover that he was also responsible for the U.S. hockey team's upset victory over the Soviet Union in the 1980 Olympics and for the Buffalo Bills' inability to win the Super Bowl. What's genuinely brilliant about "Musings of a Cigarette-Smoking Man," though, is that it unmasks the series' chief villain as a failed pulp writer, of the Tom Clancy macho-thriller school. He is, in turns out, a pathetic dreamer who manipulates reality much more adroitly than he manipulates the imaginative world of fiction, and the only market he can sell his lurid fantasies to is the secret government.

13   *The X-Files,* in its middle age as a television series, is trying on new attitudes and different tones and in the process seems to be groping its way toward an unusually mature approach to horror. It has gradually revealed that its true subject—which is the true subject of all horror fiction—is mortality. Carter is letting his characters face it squarely and watching them as they defend themselves with every weapon at their disposal—imagination, science, faith and humor. The generous form of *The X-Files* accommodates all those responses (the tighter form of *Millennium* doesn't), and because Carter makes use of every one of them, the series, despite its outré subject matter, feels unusually lifelike: It has the ring of an emotional truth that isn't as far out there as we might have thought. In the series' best single episode, a third-season Darin Morgan script called "Clyde Bruckman's Final Repose," the title character (played by Peter Boyle) is an insurance man who has the unwanted ability to foresee the manner and the exact date of people's deaths, including his own. As he helps Mulder and Scully in their search for yet another serial killer, he knows that his own end is approaching fast. His attitude throughout the hour is an oddly appealing mixture of resignation, irritability, self-deprecating irony and blunt gallows humor. The temperament of this lonely, reluctant clairvoyant is, in a way, the precise embodiment of the current spirit of *The X-Files* as it heads toward the terror of its ultimate unmaking. In the recent mythology episodes, the series seems to be turning further and further inward, using Scully's cancer as a controlling metaphor for everything that makes us feel helpless and isolated; she speaks of her illness as a kind of alien invasion of her body. Carter has turned *The X-Files* into a show about a pair of existential detectives, and in the process he has both expanded and slyly subverted its paranoid premise. Finally, it is not the presence of unidentified flying objects but our increasing identification with *The X-Files'* human protagonists that tells us, beyond dispute, that we are not alone.

EXPLORING THE TEXT

1. Rafferty begins his discussion with a quote from Stephen King about "disestablishment" and "things . . . in the unmaking" (paragraph 1). How does Rafferty apply these ideas to his discussion of *The X-Files?* Explain your answer.

2. In paragraph 2, Rafferty claims that the genre of horror writing has not depended on series heroes. In what ways are Mulder and Scully the exception to this rule?
3. According to Rafferty, what are the ways in which viewers identify with Mulder and Scully? Do you agree? Explain your answer.
4. What is the object of Mulder's (the hero's) quest? How has that changed over the course of the show?
5. How does Rafferty define "non-mythology episodes" (paragraph 8)? What is their function?
6. What are some of the philosophical differences between *Millennium* and *The X-Files?* How does Rafferty use these differences to argue why *The X-Files* is a better show?
7. What is the true subject of all horror fiction, according to Rafferty? How do the creators of *The X-Files* make use of that subject?

WRITING ASSIGNMENTS

1. During the first four years of production, episodes began with the epigraph, "The truth is out there," which is supported by the office poster stating "I want to believe." Rafferty relates these notions to the activity and attitude of viewers who want "a story that makes perfect sense of the dense and apparently insoluble mysteries that surround us" (paragraph 3). In later episodes, however, the epigraph was changed to "Believe the lie." Write an essay in which you discuss the differences (and similarities) between these three statements.
2. Rafferty calls Mulder and Scully the horror genre's first archetypal heroes (paragraph 2) and compares them to Sherlock Holmes and Watson. What heroic characteristics can be attributed to each character? How would you define their relationship? Is Rafferty's claim that it is "parasexual" adequate? Is Scully more than a sidekick?

GROUP PROJECTS

1. Have members of your group review other examples of the horror genre (books, films, other television shows) and describe the role of women as heroes and/or victims. (You might even consider the horror novels *Rough Beast* and *The Stone Circle,* written by the editor of this textbook.) In what ways does Scully fit or break the mold? Present a report of your findings and the conclusions you draw.
2. In *The X-Files,* viewers are presented with crime-fighting partners. Consider other examples of such partners—for example, Sherlock Holmes and Watson or television characters Cagney and Lacey. Make a comparison of the Scully/Mulder partnership with other partnerships and discuss what is similar or different (each group member should choose one part-

nership). Focus on issues of class, gender, authority, and so on in making this comparison. How do these influence or define the relationship between characters? Explain the significance of your findings in a report to the class.

Pro/Con: Kill Your Television

In the early 1990s, there was a popular bumper sticker that said, "Kill Your Television." Underlying that declaration was the message that television is bad for you—that it lacks artistic and social value, that it rots your brain, that it turns you into a zombie. While the next two pieces agree that television can be harmful to your health, the authors take contrary views on what to do about it.

PRO

Turn Off the TV Before It Ruins Us
David Nyhan

> Starting with the title, David Nyhan doesn't mince words in this essay. Television is bad for children and other living things, he maintains. It's "an open sewer." According to him, excessive viewing is a disease that threatens the future of American society and one that requires protection. He offers a long list of symptoms and side effects and a sure measure of prevention. While Nyhan raises many of the same issues that Susan Douglas does in the next essay, he makes his case in a voice ready for combat.
>
> Nyhan is a columnist for the *Boston Globe* where this selection originally appeared in September 1996.

1   I'm not a doctor, but I play one when I'm talking about TV.

2   And the American Medical Association and I agree: Television is bad for kids.

3   Young people not only would kill to watch TV; they do kill from staring goggle-eyed at the box, a truly infernal machine that delivers 200,000 acts of violence to the typical youngster's brain pan before he's old enough to drive.

4   Every kid in America, on average, witnesses 16,000 murders on TV before reaching the ripe old age of 18. And you wonder why they throw candy wrappers on the sidewalk or refuse to give an old lady a seat on a crowded bus? Geddoudda here, witch, or I'll blow you away!

5   Four hours a day is what the average kid watches. That 28 hours per week, over the year, is more time than he spends in school (less than one-fourth of the day for less than 180 days).

6   The AMA has studied the phenomena of self-hypnotic television consumption and concluded: Aaaaarrrrrgh!!!

7   Did you know that wherever television-watching is introduced, homicide rates double within a decade and a half? The babies born to households where TV was just coming in grow up (if they're lucky) to be 15 year olds in communities with twice as many homicides.

8   Little kids who OD on TV kick and punch and bite much more frequently than the little monsters who do not have their sensitivities dulled by the repetitive and mindless violence of the cathode ray projector.

9   How bad does it get for a teen-ager who watches a lot of TV? He or she is fatter, sicker, more likely to drink and smoke and drug and more likely to engage in premature sexual conduct that can be harmful to him or the kid he's messing with.

10   TV is an open sewer running into the minds of the impressionable, and progressively desensitized, young. It is a conveyor belt of cynicism, of self-gratification, of violence-inducing behavior, of role modeling gone wrong, of tasteless drivel. The more meretricious the content, the more successful the sale of same. TV is repackaged dross on video for the ages, syndication rights reserved.

11   It is ruining the country. Our society's rot owes more to television than any other single cause. As the dominant medium, it overwhelms the periodic, valiant and ultimately futile appeals to a higher morality and a more inspirational way of dealing with the rest of humanity.

12   Television makes everyone cynical, more convinced that no one is honest, no one pure, no one even admirable. All the politicians are crooks, the athletes crooks, the journalists cynics, the businessmen greedheads, the clergy corrupt, the movie stars perverse.

13   Six out of 10 family meals take place under the baleful glare of a working TV set. More than half of America's kids have TV sets in their bedrooms, where they can pig out on whatever vile fare is lowest common denominator of the day.

14   We already have 1.6 million Americans behind bars. That's almost 2 percent of our total employment rate. Most of them are young, most are uneducated, and most are coming out, eventually, to a community near you. They watched too much TV when they were kids, raised in single-parent, often violence-racked households where they got cuffed around when they weren't staring at some stupid television program.

15   Does it get any better if we shut off the tube and ask them to listen to music? Not much. Three out of four of the top-selling CDs of 1995 use cuss words and exalt guns, rape or murder, according to a *Providence Journal-Bulletin* report.

16   Between Grades 7 to 12, teen-agers drain in 10,500 hours of rock music—that's more hours than they spent in class in all the years between second grade and graduating from high school.

17   The impact on our kids of electronic media—ranging from the soporific to the truly horrific—is the single biggest problem our society faces. It's a much bigger deal than the deficit or taxes or "job-loss anxiety" labels tossed about in the election campaigns.

18   The degrading of our human capital by the corrosive moral erosion of television and the related video-audio industries is a challenge of immense significance. The politicians nibble around the edges for slivers of political advantage.

19   But the dumbing-down of a generation, the deadening of moral sensitivity in millions of youngsters, is a much greater threat than anything rumbling in the Mid-

dle East. Our real problem is the Middle West, and the rest of Middle America. Our kids are bathed in filth, in trivia, in meaningless violence, in false happy endings, in cynical nattering from false media gods.

20   It's a disease. It requires prevention. And vaccination. And, occasionally, something drastic, like amputation. In my family we still talk about one Super Bowl eve when my sister got so mad at the stupefied gazes on the faces of her four kids that she lugged the TV set into her car, drove to the reservoir and tossed it in, leaving it sitting cockeyed and unplugged on the ice she forgot to take into account.

21   The AMA is on the right side on this one. Our future is rotting, one channel at a time.

EXPLORING THE TEXT

1. Nyhan's opening reference is to an old television advertisement in which an actor who plays a doctor encourages people to buy a particular brand of aspirin. What does this opening sentence tell you about his position? What other evidence of his tone can you identify?

2. In making his argument, does Nyhan appeal to ethos (ethics), pathos (emotion), or logic (reason)? How might his argument be different if he had appealed to one or both of the other possibilities?

3. List the various metaphors Nyhan uses, noting especially how often he uses them and how many kinds he uses. Briefly discuss the extent to which they help clarify or support his argument.

4. Using paragraph 9 as a model, talk about the way in which gender pronouns are used in this argument. Does Nyhan seem to be giving equal weight to male and female experience? What can we determine about the author's attitude in light of this approach?

5. Though his discussion focuses primarily on television, what other media does Nyhan blame for negatively influencing young people? How influential are these media in the lives of typical young people?

6. In what ways does Nyhan define the political problem? How does he define the threat of television? Explain your answer.

7. Evaluate Nyhan's authority to speak on this issue. Consider the specific information he presents (and the manner in which he presents it). Is he reliable? Credible? Do you find his argument convincing, ultimately? Explain your answer.

WRITING ASSIGNMENTS

1. Write a thoughtful response to Nyhan's argument in which you carefully critique his logic and argue against his claims. Be sure to refer to specific evidence in your rebuttal.

2. Nyhan ends his argument by using the metaphor of disease (paragraph 20). He refers to prevention and vaccination and, yet, ultimately opts for the more drastic remedy of amputation. Susan Douglas also uses a medical metaphor in discussing the influence of television, but she opts for inoculation as the best remedy. Develop your own metaphor to describe the impact of television on American culture, especially young people. Write your own essay in which you argue for or against the power of television and carefully incorporate your metaphor into that discussion.

GROUP PROJECTS

1. As a group, prepare a questionnaire for young people that tests the claims Nyhan makes in this article. Carefully consider the questions you ask to make sure that you get reliable and exact information. Think in terms of who, what, where, when, why, how, and other particular questions. Distribute this questionnaire to other students in your school or neighborhood and prepare a report of your findings.
2. Nyhan argues that rock music has a powerful—and negative—impact on youth because of its bad language and exaltation of guns, rape, and murder. As a group, survey currently popular music. Have each group member choose a particular type of music and carefully analyze the lyrics, video, and packaging of that music and prepare a short report outlining whether the music reinforces Nyhan's position or argues against his claims. Combine the short reports and prepare a presentation for the class.

CON

Remote Control: How to Raise a Media Skeptic
Susan Douglas

In the previous essay, David Nyhan called television "an open sewer." In the piece below, media critic Susan Douglas calls television "a toxic waste dump." Like Nyhan, Douglas admits that television viewing can be like exposure to a disease. But unlike Nyhan, she does not advocate dumping our sets. Instead, she argues that kids should be inoculated, not quarantined. Children need to learn to evaluate what they see and hear on television, so she encourages parents to teach them how to see through the distorted images and values.

Douglas is a professor of media and American studies at the University of Michigan. She also serves as media critic for the *Progressive.* She has written articles for a wide variety of magazines and newspapers and is the author of *Inventing American Broadcasting,*

1899–1922 (1984), *Where the Girls Are* (1994), and *Radio* (1998) This article first appeared in the January/February 1997 issue of the *Utne Reader.*

1   Mommy, Mommy, come here now! Hurry, you're gonna miss it. It's Barbie's High-Steppin' Pony, and its legs really move! Hurreeeeey!"

2   "No!" I bark, as I'm wiping the dog barf up from the carpet, stirring the onions again so they don't burn, and slamming the phone down on a caller from Citibank who wants to know how I'm doin' today. It is 5:56 p.m., and I'm in no mood. "I don't come for commercials, and besides, the horse doesn't really move—they just make it look that way."

3   "Oh yeah?" demands my daughter, sounding like a federal prosecutor. "It can too. It's not like those old ones where you told me they faked it—this one really does move."

4   So now I have to go see and, indeed, the sucker takes batteries, and the stupid horse moves—sort of. "See, Mommy, the commercials don't always lie."

5   Moments like this prompt me to wonder whether I'm a weak-kneed, lazy slug or, dare I say it, a hypocrite. See, I teach media studies, and, even worse, I go around the country lecturing about the importance of media literacy. One of my talking points is how network children's programming is, ideologically, a toxic waste dump. Yet here I am, just like millions of parents during that portion of the day rightly known as hell hour—dinnertime—shoving my kid in front of Nickelodeon so my husband and I can get dinner on the table while we whisper sweet nothings like "It's your turn to take her to Brownies tomorrow" and "Oh, shit, I forgot to tell you that your mother called three days ago with an urgent message."

6   We let her watch Nickelodeon, but I still pop in to ridicule Kool-Aid commercials or to ask her why Clarissa's parents (on *Clarissa Explains It All*) are so dopey. I am trying to have it both ways: to let television distract her, which I desperately need, and to help her see through its lies and banalities. I am very good at rationalizing this approach, but I also think it isn't a bad compromise for overworked parents who believe Barbie is the anti-Christ yet still need to wash out grotty lunch boxes and zap leftovers at the end of the day.

7   It's best to be honest up front: My house is not media proofed. I am not one of those virtuous, haloed parents who has banished the box from the home. I actually believe that there are interesting, fun shows for my daughter to watch on TV. (And I'm not about to give up ER.)

8   But I'm also convinced that knowing about television, and growing up with it, provides my daughter with a form of cultural literacy that she will need, that will tie her to her friends and her generation and help her understand her place in the world. So instead of killing my TV, I've tried to show my daughter basic bullshit-detecting techniques. Don't think your choices are either no TV or a zombified kid. Studies show that the simple act of intervening—of talking to your child about what's on television and why it's on there—is one of the most important factors in helping children understand and distance themselves from some of the box's more repugnant imagery.

9   I recommend the quick surgical strike, between throwing the laundry in and picking up the Legos. Watch a few commercials with them and point out that com-

mercials lie about the toys they show, making them look much better than they are in real life. Count how many male and female characters there are in a particular show or commercial and talk about what we see boys doing and what we see girls doing. Why, you might ask, do we always see girls playing with makeup kits and boys playing with little Johnny Exocet missiles? Real life dads change diapers, push strollers, and feed kids, but you never see boys doing this with dolls on commercials. Ask where the Asian and African-American kids are. Point out how most of the parents in shows geared to kids are much more stupid than real-life parents. (By the way, children report that TV shows encourage them to talk back to their folks.) Tell them that all those cereals advertised with cartoon characters and rap music (like Cocoa Puffs and Trix) will put giant black holes in their teeth that only a dentist with a drill the size of the space shuttle can fix.

10   One of the best words to use when you're watching TV with your kids is *stupid,* as in "Aren't Barbie's feet—the way she's always forced to walk on her tiptoes—really stupid?" or "Isn't it stupid that Lassie is smarter than the mom on this show?" (My favorite Barbie exercise: Put your kitchen timer on for a minute and make your daughter walk around on her tiptoes just like Barbie; she'll get the point real fast.) *Cool*—a word that never seems to go out of style—is also helpful, as in "Isn't it cool that on *Legends of the Hidden Temple* (a game show on Nickelodeon) the girls are as strong and as fast as the boys?" Pointing out what's good on TV is important too.

11   See, I think complete media-proofing is impossible, because the shallow, consumerist, anti-intellectual values of the mass media permeate our culture. And we parents shouldn't beat ourselves up for failing to quarantine our kids. But we can inoculate them—which means exposing them to the virus and showing them how to build up a few antibodies. So don't feel so guilty about letting them watch TV. Instead, have fun teaching them how to talk back to it rather than to you.

EXPLORING THE TEXT

1. Douglas begins her discussion by telling an anecdote about her daughter and a Barbie advertisement; she refers to Barbie again in paragraph 10. Douglas suggests there is more at play here than a simple toy. What is the importance of Barbie in American culture?

2. How does Douglas define her role in the text? How does her career connect to her interaction with her daughter? Does she fit into any cultural stereotypes (mothers, working women)? How does her self-described role relate to the stereotypes presented in paragraph 9?

3. Douglas talks about "the importance of media literacy" (paragraph 5) and "cultural literacy" (paragraph 8). What does she mean by these terms? How are they relevant to her argument overall?

4. In paragraph 5, Douglas refers to children's programming as a "toxic waste dump," an idea that recalls David Nyhan's description of television as "an open sewer." In what ways do these metaphors present a similar image of the role of television in our society? Given this similar starting point, how

do the authors arrive at different solutions? Discuss the different ways in which the authors use this metaphor and how it relates to their arguments overall.

5. What is the role of humor in this essay? Does it add to or detract from the effectiveness of Douglas's argument?

6. Douglas's solution is inoculation, but what more exactly does she mean by this? What strategies does she suggest?

7. Evaluate Douglas's authority to speak on this issue. Consider the specific information she presents (and the manner in which she presents it). Is she reliable? Credible? Is she more (or less) credible than Nyhan? Do you find her argument convincing, ultimately? Explain your answer.

WRITING ASSIGNMENTS

1. In an effort to make her point, Douglas narrates part of her life and uses a personal anecdote to exemplify her views on the role television plays in the lives of many families, as well as its influence on children. In your essay, using Douglas as a model, create a narrative that is both reflective and critical of your own childhood experience with television and television commercials.

2. As one means of improving "cultural literacy," Douglas encourages parents to ask children to question "where the Asian and African-American kids are" (paragraph 9). How do her ideas relate to Frederick L. McKissack Jr.'s argument in "The Problem with Black T.V." earlier in this chapter? Write an essay in which you take on the racial issues raised in these essays. Consider a variety of television programs and critically evaluate their relevance.

GROUP PROJECTS

1. As a group, do research to test the ideas presented by Nyhan and Douglas in their essays. Conduct an interview with children and parents you know. How much television do kids watch? How involved are parents in what they watch? How influential is television, really? What are the best (and most viable) solutions to this problem?

2. In paragraph 5, Douglas claims that network children's programming is, ideologically, a toxic waste dump. Define this term and discuss just what she seems to mean. Then, test her ideas. Have different group members watch and critique a particular network children's program and determine whether it supports (or argues against) Douglas's claim.

4

Gender Battles on the Big Screen

From the small screen we move to the big screen and to what might be the most genuinely American art form: movies. Like any art form, movies are more than entertainment. In sight and sound, they tell us something about what it's like to be human. They are a constant source for our cultural heroes, icons, ideals, values, and the myths of our past and future. They reflect and project and help mold the patterns of our lives, and in particular how we relate to our age, our world, and each other. And because movies reach so many people, they have the potential to achieve what all great art does—binding diversified segments of our society together in a highly aesthetic experience.

This chapter explores how movies reflect and perpetuate the images of men and women and how they relate to each other. These essays will examine some expectations about gender—that is, what particular roles males and females play, what behavior norms are upheld. By looking at some recent movies, you will examine how three decades of modern feminism have helped moviemakers come a long way from tired old stereotypes of passive, adoring females and strong, active males. You will also see how some popular films widely praised for the abandonment of constricting gender stereotypes have actually repackaged them in subtle dress.

The chapter opens with "Women on the Big Screen" in which media critic Elayne Rapping praises some recent movies for their strong female roles. Yet even the best of women's roles, she argues, suffer from sentimentality rather than demonstrating inner female strength. And while she praises Hollywood's gritty realism, she is also critical of the way such powerful roles too often are limited by traditional Hollywood myths about female behavior.

One of the oldest stereotypes in movies—and world fiction, in fact—is the object of complaint in the next piece, "Hostages to Sexism," by newspaper columnist Leonard Pitts. In spite of the many tough female roles in some 1990s action blockbusters, Pitts argues that today's audiences still "like our damsels in distress." As he explains, this demand rises "not out of sweet chivalry" but some tired old conventions that keep the gender roles clear and distinct.

But not all action movie female roles yield to conventions. In fact, after decades of being damsels in distress, women in late 1990 flicks are bringing to the screen "unprecedented displays of female grit." Such is the argument of Margaret Talbot in the next piece, "Hasta la Vista, Arnold." Looking at movies from the late 1990s, the author examines a new breed of heroines—women capable of being Arnold Schwarzenegger tough and heroic without being glamorized or roboticized.

One name synonymous with the cinematic studly action hero is Sylvester Stallone. For audiences around the world he represents quintessential masculinity—the handsome, beefcake loner who wins impossible battles. But what about the man behind that strongman stereotype? Doesn't that role get tiresome from movie to movie? In a fascinating interview with feminist author Susan Faludi, Stallone speaks candidly about seeking liberation from the macho image that brought him to stardom. In "The Masculine Mystique—An Interview of Sylvester Stallone," the man who made Rocky and Rambo household names admits to suffering a gender crisis. Touching upon cultural views of masculinity, male body image, and self-pride, Stallone explains why he is tired of playing the testosterone hero.

The above pieces address the kind of thinking that goes on behind the making of movies—that is, the images and messages that the creators intend to project to their audiences. The next piece takes a close look at the kind of early planning that went into the making of the 1995 Disney blockbuster *Pocahontas*. As the authors describe in "Redesigning Pocahontas," Disney executives wanted to avoid at all costs the kind of heavy criticism the studio took from racial and ethnic groups over the stereotyping perceived in previous Disney films, *Aladdin* and *The Lion King*. In *Pocahontas*, the studio said it wanted to show greater sensitivity in portraying Native Americans by avoiding the "Hollywood Indian," while at the same time telling an engaging story of intolerance and racism and the need for mutual cultural respect. Such intentions were the theme behind the movie's huge advertising campaign. But as authors Gary Edgerton and Kathy Merlock Jackson explain in their analysis of *Pocahontas*, what Disney promised and what it projected onto the screens were, ideologically speaking, miles apart.

The next selection is a student's gender analysis of one of the most popular movies of this decade, *Silence of the Lambs*. The winner of four Academy Awards, the movie was praised for being a feminist narrative. With Jodie Foster playing a tough and self-sufficient FBI agent who proves victorious over a brutal psychopath, the movie seems to celebrate female heroism. But as Lynn Dornink demonstrates in a close analysis of the visual elements, that's simply the surface of things. In "Silencing of the Feminine," Dornink demonstrates that the film fails its alleged feminist aims by actually presenting the female as undesirable.

The chapter closes with two opposing views of a very popular movie from the mid-1990s, *Waiting to Exhale*. Based on the best-selling novel of the same name by Terry McMillan, the movie was a box office success and represented for many the first presentation of a black, female buddy movie that spoke to contemporary middle-class black female moviegoers. In "Breathing Easier with a Rare Film," Dorothy Gilliam praises the movie as "an allegory for the male-female conflicts" going on in black American women.

But not all black women celebrated that movie. In "Mock Feminism," author and cultural critic bell hooks passionately condemns *Waiting to Exhale* as not only an inauthentic representation of contemporary black relationships, but a movie whose perspective is distinctly "white" even though it was written and directed by African Americans. Worse still, she finds the film full of racist and sexist stereotypes.

Women on the Big Screen
Elayne Rapping

Quick, think of your favorite film characters. How many of these are females? According to Elayne Rapping, most female film roles represent little more than Hollywood "types" with little depth and limited interest. In the 1996 Oscar nominations, however, Rapping notes an unusual twist: Female roles for that year actually represented a number of "interesting and serious" female characters. A large number of movies focused on women, but most of them, she claims, were "candy-coated valentines." Yet in the midst of these offerings, Rapping finds a few bright spots and looks at Sharon Stone in *Casino,* Jennifer Jason Leigh in *Georgia,* and Elisabeth Shue in *Leaving Las Vegas* and argues that these films suggest an important improvement in the movie scene. Looking at films since 1996, do you think she is right?

Rapping is the author of *Media-tions: Forays into the Culture and Gender Wars* (1994) and *The Culture of Recovery: Making Sense of the Self-Help Movement in Women's Lives* (1996). This essay first appeared in her media column in the *Progressive* in the March 1996 issue.

1 Well, what do you know? As Oscar time approaches, I can actually name—for the first time in memory—more than ten actresses cast in meaty enough roles to make the Best Actress and Supporting Actress races interesting and serious this year.

2 And what unlikely actresses most of them were. When you get past the two predictably stunning performances in predictably "uplifting" roles—Meryl Streep in *The Bridges of Madison County* and Susan Sarandon in *Dead Man Walking*—what you have left is a list of highly unlikely actresses in far from uplifting, or even typically Hollywood, roles.

3 Jennifer Jason Leigh, brilliant once more in *Georgia,* is the only one of the bunch that one might have expected to be "Oscar-qualified." She is, after all, the designated "serious young actress" of the moment now that Jodie Foster has turned director.

4 But Sharon Stone? Nicole Kidman? Elisabeth (who?) Shue? Who would have guessed that any of them would have turned in hauntingly powerful, nuanced performances in such challenging, downbeat films as *Casino, To Die For,* and *Leaving Las Vegas?*

5 Nor were these the only remarkable and unexpected female performances. Mira Sorvino in *Mighty Aphrodite,* Linda Fiorentino in *Jade*—I could go on, and you probably could, too. There was, in truth, an embarrassment of riches this year for those of us who are perennially starved for the sight of powerful women on the big screen.

6 Of course, to feminists who insist on positive images, this list of portrayals must hardly seem heartening. Prostitutes, junkies, and cold-blooded killers are not exactly the role models we would choose for our daughters. But there was a surprisingly long list of "good-girl," "female-bonding" movies in which groups of mismatched friends saw each other through conflict and crisis, good men and bad, to a predictably soft-focus moment of sisterhood triumphant.

7 For a variety of reasons, we were offered an unprecedented number of well-meaning movies last year: more women in decision-making positions in studios and in the director's seat; more women seeing movies, and buying their own tickets; more female stars, desperate for decent scripts, producing their own movies; more money men willing to take risks on female-driven movies since *Thelma and Louise, Little Women, A League of Their Own,* and a few others hit pay dirt. Among the uplifting films were *How to Make an American Quilt, Moonlight and Valentino, Boys on the Side, Now and Then, The Baby-Sitters' Club* (a preteen version), and *Waiting to Exhale*—noteworthy for its presentation of African-American women as successful and upwardly mobile.

8   But as welcome as these candy-coated valentines to female audiences were, they amounted to pretty thin stuff. In fact, they all tend to merge into a single, soppy blur of sugary sentimentality, with only the barest hint of spice. Even *Waiting to Exhale*—the only one of the bunch with any spirit or passion at all—in the end was no more than a cartoon cutout version of the feisty novel upon which it was based.

9   For all the understandable clamor for "positive" roles and representations, the movies in which female virtue and talent were rewarded—whether with love or money, personal fulfillment or professional triumph—ran the gamut from forgettable to annoying to inane.

10   By contrast, the performances that have stuck in my mind have all been bad-girl/loser roles. For my money, the three most outstanding performances were the three that dug deepest into women's experiences in the dark side of American life. Two—Sharon Stone as a hustler and addict, and Elisabeth Shue as a street-walker—are set in the seediest of American landscapes: Las Vegas. And the third, Jennifer Jason Leigh as a failed bar singer, alcoholic, and junkie, is set fairly close to that spiritual vicinity.

11   If you want to say something socially and emotionally important about women in American life, you are obliged today to tackle the gloomier areas of our social and psychological landscape. Sadly, that's where the most serious truths about gender are still most likely to be found.

12   Ugly Truth Number One: many decent women do—indeed, often must—turn to prostitution when all else fails. Why? Not because they are "bad." Not even, in most cases, because they were "victims" of some sort of abuse (although that is a factor in too many cases). No, the primary reason is, and always has been, economic. In a market-driven, sexist society, the female body is the one economically "valuable" commodity a woman will always be able to sell. Spiritual desperation will often accompany this kind of economic despair. And so it is understandable that addiction itself often serves as cinematic metaphor for such spiritual desperation.

13   Hollywood has always loved its bad girls, especially its whores. Male directors have, in fact, been obsessed with the theme of the "fallen woman." But until now, they have chosen to give us only the most degraded or romantically absurd stereotypes of such women. Thus the endless list of "whore-with-a-heart-of-gold" fables—from the euphemistic "showgirls" in *Gentlemen Prefer Blondes* to Julia Roberts's star-making performance in *Pretty Woman.*

14   In these, and their many clones, prostitutes with virginal souls find Prince Charmings who recognize their essential goodness and carry them off into a diamond-strung sunset. Thus does Hollywood periodically wish away the sorry truth about female degradation and its true causes and cures, and send its male viewers home with clean consciences. (No surprise that Woody Allen, the man for whom the term "denial" was invented, has stuck with this hokey, "whore-with-a-heart-of-gold" image in *Mighty Aphrodite.*)

15   The uglier—and far more common—film version, the one in which the woman meets a tragic end in the gutter or morgue, is less likely to form the central storyline of any Hollywood movie. Rather, the standard role for female prostitutes (and junkies, for that matter) is not even supporting, but more often merely bit.

16   Usually we see a prostitute, cast as a woman of color, on screen briefly to be brutalized—a prop to illustrate the viciousness (or even worse, the macho bravado) of a male character. The current hit *Heat* is classic: virtually every female character is betrayed, humiliated, and exploited, but only the African-American woman, a prostitute, is brutally strangled and disposed of in a five-minute sequence.

17   We've seen this version of the Hollywood whore millions of times. It is truer to life, unfortunately, than the "prostitute as virginal princess-to-be." But the fact that it is presented so casually, so matter-of-factly, works as an endorsement of its legitimacy: she must have done something to deserve such a fate is the implicit assumption, since no other explanation is hinted at. (The parallel with the "black, single mother on welfare," so popular in political discourse, is obvious. In our world, the most unfortunate among us are also the most often stigmatized and blamed for their sorry fates.)

18   What makes the Stone, Leigh, and Shue vehicles so much more interesting than any of these earlier film versions is that they reverse the Hollywood tradition. In these films, the prostitutes and addicts are central characters, not bit players to be mutilated and discarded. And each—refreshingly and realistically—is closer to Divine Brown than Julia Roberts.

19   But while all three are worth seeing, only Mike Figgis's remarkable *Leaving Las Vegas* manages to allow its heroine to emerge from the squalor of her life with real dignity and self-respect.

20   *Casino,* despite its many, oft-noted flaws, would be well worth seeing even if it didn't offer so powerful a female character. That's because, like most Scorsese films, it delves deeply, relentlessly, and unsentimentally into the source of America's moral and spiritual decay: the driving lust for power and wealth as ends in themselves. It lays out the economic and political workings of Las Vegas—always a perfect metaphor for American capitalism at its rawest.

21   But what makes the film particularly interesting is that Martin Scorsese—the classic director of male-centered, tough-guy films in which women play the usual brutalized roles—sees fit this time to include a woman in his rogue's gallery of lost souls. Sharon Stone's Ginger McKenna is a player, a woman who uses her body and her seductiveness to elbow her way into the high-stakes male game on her own terms. She does well in this game, as long as she sticks to hustling. But when she agrees—because she is offered more money, gold, and jewels than she can refuse—to give up her role as a partner in crime to Robert De Niro's casino manager and become a wife and mother, she is doomed. The domestic-housewife role stifles and destroys her, and she ends up as a pathetic, grotesque junkie.

22   *Casino,* like all Scorsese's darker films, is a tragedy about people who are brought down by their own character flaws, and by the built-in booby traps of the system they choose to work within, and hope—desperately and foolishly—to beat. For Scorsese, human nature never rises above the level of the degraded world that spawns it. It is therefore inevitable that every one of them, including Ginger, will end in ignominy, and, more often than not, brutal death.

23   Nonetheless, the figure of Ginger McKenna, doomed and degraded as she is, is intriguing. And her tragedy reveals something about the sexism of the system that Scorsese hasn't previously tackled: the gendered playing field that puts women—

forced into traditionally stifling roles—at so great a disadvantage in the male world of power and money.

24   *Georgia* is another matter entirely. Jennifer Jason Leigh—as Sadie, the talent-less sister of a semi-big-time folk-rock singer (the Georgia of the title)—does not play a hooker and does not make it to the Las Vegas big-time of American, and fe-male, degradation. But that is only because the film is so much less honest than *Casino*. *Georgia* chooses to analyze its character's downfall—not surprisingly in these days of "recovery"—in terms of the dynamics of a (yawn) "dysfunctional" family. Sadie envies and tries to compete with her successful, much-loved sister. Her sister, although the film fails to develop this much, is (yawn again) a classic "passive-aggressive" type who "enables" her sister's addiction by constantly "rescu-ing" her from "hitting bottom" and "seeking help." When Sadie reaches the point where most such women begin turning tricks for drugs and booze, her sister wires her money to enter detox and nurses her back to health so she can return for yet an-other round of this childish routine.

25   As I watched this film, I was mesmerized and emotionally drained by the power of Leigh's performance as a self-destructive bar singer with no talent but lots of guts.

26   It was only later, when I had recovered from the emotional blows, that I began to realize that the film is hollow, the characters ultimately flat and unbelievable. And the reason is that there is absolutely no social—much less economic or politi-cal—context to its near hysteria over human suffering. Family dysfunction (and there the film parallels the thinking of the recovery movement itself) is seen as oper-ating in a social and economic vacuum. There is no acknowledgment of the larger context in which "dysfunctional" families are produced; no hint that—to use a cliché that is nonetheless true—"the personal is political"; that the pain and destruc-tion Sadie's family experiences are a direct reflection of the pain and destructive-ness of so much of American social and political life itself.

27   Sadie and Georgia are the perennial "bad girl" and "good girl" of American cul-ture. But the tragic dynamic they act out—in which love and success and approval are seen as scarce goods for which women must compete to the death—is rooted in social, economic, and historical conditions this film never dares to examine. And so, despite its often riveting scenes and characters, it remains an essentially disingenu-ous picture of white, middle-class, female degradation.

28   Mike Figgis's *Leaving Las Vegas* manages to avoid the failings of both *Georgia* and *Casino*. This remarkable low-budget film tells the story of an alcoholic screen-writer (Nicholas Cage) who comes to Vegas to drink himself to death, falls in love with a streetwalker named Sera (Elisabeth Shue), and spends his last dying weeks with her. *Leaving Las Vegas* doesn't hedge or skirt around the harsh truths of life on America's bottom rung. Nor does it cynically damn its characters along with their environment. By refusing to deal with any of the Hollywood clichés or stereotypes about addiction and prostitution, the film achieves something startlingly original.

29   It takes as given the corrupt, male-dominated, money-and-power-driven Las Vegas landscape, and then proceeds to ask a really interesting question: For those who find themselves in such a state of material and spiritual squalor, how might it be possible to live with a degree of dignity, self-respect, and even love?

30   The film's answers are not political. It offers no hope for those of us who would like to see the entire corrupt political and economic system revamped.

31   What this film does offer is, in its own way, precious. In the character of Sera, we have a woman who is beaten down, and beaten up, daily, by the world she lives in and the men who control it. And yet, in each of her encounters—with pimps, with johns, with landlords, with casino bouncers—she meets insult and assault with a dignity that seems to grow from her core. And when she meets a man who treats her with respect, she manages to offer him a caring, loving last few weeks.

32   Most critics have viewed this film as Cage's, but that must surely be because most critics see films from the male point of view and assume what film theorists call the "male gaze." In fact, this film is Sera's. It is narrated by her and seen from her perspective. And it is Sera, not the doomed Cage, who acts and grows and changes throughout.

33   There are no happy endings here, no family wiring funds for detox, no Prince Charming to wipe away the tears. But neither is there the cynical despair and hopelessness about the human condition that fuel most serious films about such people. The premise of this film—the notion that these few, often sordid and painful weeks might be the best that a woman like Sera could aspire to—is depressing. But *Leaving Las Vegas* was, for me, one of the most inspiring movies of the year. For it showed a woman trapped in the worst kind of social and spiritual degradation, yet managing to rise above the sordid conditions with her humanity and nobility intact.

EXPLORING THE TEXT

1. In paragraph 1, Rapping describes three female roles as "interesting and serious." Identify several places in the text where she provides specific examples of what she means by those words.

2. Why does Rapping reject what she calls the "well-meaning" female roles of earlier films? What does she like about the "bad-girl/loser" roles in the 1995 Oscar nominations? How does she make the argument that these roles are "strong" even though the characters are not necessarily "positive"?

3. How do the movies Rapping discusses counter her statement that "Hollywood has always loved its bad girls, especially its whores" (paragraph 13).

4. In the beginning paragraphs, Rapping repeatedly uses words such as *typical* and *unlikely,* suggesting that Hollywood works with certain set models. What are some of these models that she refers to? Can you think of any other models from movies you know?

5. In Rapping's review of *Casino,* she states, "the economic and political workings of Las Vegas [offer] . . . a perfect metaphor for American capitalism at its rawest" (paragraph 20). List several of the places in this essay where Rapping links capitalism to gender issues. How does this link relate to Rapping's positive reviews of each female character? Explain.

6. Consider the tone of this essay. What does the opening sentence reveal about Rapping's attitude? Note the parenthetical comments scattered

throughout (e.g., paragraphs 14–17 and 24), the statements set off by dashes, the questions asked. What is the effect of these interjections? Explain your answer.

7. Look carefully at the way Rapping has structured her argument and outline its major and minor points. Do her choices as a writer make it easy for a reader to follow her argument? Discuss other ways that she might have organized her material and whether they might have been more effective.

WRITING ASSIGNMENTS

1. In this essay, Rapping talks about prostitutes as Hollywood types. Consider movies you have seen in the past (and other movies discussed in this chapter) and list examples of other Hollywood types (e.g., action heroes, Indians, etc.). Consider several movies in which you have seen one type and list the characteristics that help us to recognize the type as opposed to the individual. Discuss the role and importance of this type in the various movies you discuss. What is gained by use of a type character? What is lost?

2. Choose any one of the films that Rapping discusses and watch it at least once making careful notes about the leading female role. What are we told about her? How is she dressed? How does she interact with other characters? Then, evaluate whether these details support Rapping's evaluation of this female character. If they do, explain how. If they don't, explain what they show instead.

3. Find a female character in another movie that you can argue is "strong" as opposed to "positive" as Rapping defines those words. Describe the desirable (and undesirable) qualities the film attaches to this character. Would Rapping find the role "interesting and serious"? Do you? Explain.

GROUP PROJECTS

1. Other selections in this chapter focus on the female characters in *Waiting to Exhale, Silence of the Lambs,* and *Pocahontas.* Arrange to view one of these movies as a group and take careful notes on the female characters. Consider the characteristics attached to female characters. Which characteristics are praiseworthy? What shortcomings do the characters show? Have a group discussion comparing your observations and perhaps look again at provocative scenes. Then write a collaborative review of the film that discusses how it defines feminine roles. Are the women what Rapping would consider "interesting and serious"?

2. Working in small groups, list and describe several of the female roles nominated for an Academy Award since Rapping's essay. Which roles represent what Rapping calls traditional or "typical" (paragraph 2) female roles?

Which might she call "interesting and serious" (paragraph 1)? Think of characters in other recent movies that more or less fit the same type and make a list of the characteristics they share—the things that make them types rather than unique individuals. Is there any evidence of a change occurring in female hero types? Explain your answer.

Hostages to Sexism
Leonard Pitts

Like other authors in this chapter, Leonard Pitts looks at female "types" commonly depicted in Hollywood films and considers whether they have kept pace with the changing role of women in American society. More particularly, he looks at the action adventure stories and compares films to comic strips. Pitts argues that in the comics we actually see strong women as heroic characters while in the movies women are still "damsels in distress" waiting to be saved by powerful male heroes. Underlying Pitts's discussion is his belief that the movies have a powerful influence on how we see and interpret our world, and he is worried about the way in which we have been (and continue to be) socialized to believe that women are "helpless" and men are inherently "capable."

This article was published in the *Atlanta Journal/Atlanta Constitution* in September 1995. Pitts is a columnist for the *Miami Herald*.

1   A woman's place is in the chains.

2   That thought struck me the other day as I sat enduring "Mortal Kombat" in a multiplex full of boys—two of them mine. One of the combatants in the action flick is a woman who, we are led to believe, is as tough as any of the guys. Yet when the script calls for a character to be kidnapped and held hostage, guess who gets the nod?

3   It's a woman thing. From "Beverly Hills Cop" to "True Lies," the woman in peril is as pervasive an action cliché as the gun that never runs out of bullets.

4   I tried to explain to my boys why this was sexist. They didn't get it. I wouldn't have understood when I was their age, either. As a boy, I absorbed the same message, largely from the pages of Marvel comics: A woman's place is in the chains. Or behind the force field, as the case may be. Held hostage.

5   Take Sue Storm, the Invisible Girl. Dr. Doom often did. The Sub-Mariner, too. Her primary contribution to Fantastic Four plots was to be captured by would-be rulers of the world. Her doting male partners would rush to the rescue. And on those occasions when she actually had to fight, the strain was inevitably too much and she'd collapse into her husband's arms.

6   The woman was so useless that fans once mounted a "Dump Sue" letter-writing campaign.

7   Of course, uselessness is as distinctly feminine as eye shadow in the world of action and adventure—a "truth" we learn early and at a fundamental level. But you know what? Most of the women I met in comics 30 years ago have become tougher,

smarter, more sure of themselves—mirroring, perhaps, two decades of painful debates (about the glass ceiling, abortion, child care, sexual harassment) that have forced us to re-evaluate basic assumptions about the role and rights of women. Our attitudes and expectations have changed.

8   But go see any action film, where everyone knows from the first frame that the female lead will be the designated hostage, and it still seems as natural as tax cheats in the spring.

9   We like our damsels in distress. Not out of sweet chivalry so much as out of habit, a crusty holdover from less politically correct times. But even a P.C.-hater ought to be troubled at the idea that is being perpetuated here: Women are helpless without men. And those who *seem* capable really aren't.

10   The distressed damsel is one of the oldest conventions in fiction—the plot device that allows the hero to prove his mettle and reinforce his masculinity. But flip the script. Try to envision Halle Berry rushing to save a terrorized Bruce Willis or Sarah Jessica Parker fighting to rescue a fearful Sylvester Stallone.

11   You can't imagine it. Because we have been socialized to accept the essential helplessness of women and the inherent capability of men.

12   Do that many of us—men and women—still want it this way?

13   I can say only this: Last time I saw Sue Storm, she was kicking backside and taking names, having been transformed by writers—male writers, by the way—into a capable, driven woman who rescues as often as she is rescued. In that, she is part of a growing movement of able, tough-minded women that includes Rogue, Storm and Martha Washington. If there's been a corresponding loss of interest among the male readers who dominate the comics audience; I haven't seen it.

14   There's a message in this, one I wish the makers of action-adventure movies understood. Even within the confines of that macho medium, it ill serves us all to relegate women to the role of de facto hostage.

15   Surely by the mid–1990s, we should be able to agree that strength, decisiveness and courage are not, by definition, male.

16   Take Sue Storm. I dare you.

EXPLORING THE TEXT

1. How does Pitts define the role women play in comic books today? How has this role changed in the past 30 years? Does Pitts credit movies with having made the same advance?

2. What does Pitts mean by the phrase "damsels in distress" (paragraph 9)? Why does he say, "We like our damsels in distress"? Who is the "we" he refers to? Do you agree?

3. What happens when we "flip the script" as Pitts describes it (paragraph 10). Describe in your own words what happens when men rescue women—what are they reinforcing? If women rescue, what would they be reinforcing?

4. Consider the tone of this essay. What is the effect of the first sentence? The two final sentences? His rhetorical questions (paragraphs 2 and 12)? How

does Pitts's statement about political correctness (paragraph 9) reveal his point of view? What about his statement, "You can't imagine it" (paragraph 11)? Discuss the cumulative effect of these strategies (and any others you identify).

5. One of the organizational choices Pitts has made in this essay is to move back and forth between discussion of comic books and action films. Evaluate this choice. Do you have any difficulty as a reader following his ideas? How would the discussion be different if he had made all his points about comics and then gone on to make his points about film?

6. This is a brief discussion that assumes we (the audience) already know much about the various topics discussed. Pitts doesn't offer much evidence. Does this brevity make it hard to follow his ideas? What other kinds of information would you like to have in order to more fully appreciate Pitts's argument? He doesn't consider any examples that might run counter to his point overall. Can you think of counterexamples?

WRITING ASSIGNMENTS

1. Since Pitts recalls his childhood experiences, and those of his sons, think back on your own early experiences with comics and film. List some of the characters you enjoyed reading about or watching—list both male and female characters. Focus on particular films or episodes of favorite series. How do the characters resemble those Pitts discusses? How are they different? What kinds of situations do they get themselves into (and out of)? How are conflicts resolved? Based on your experience, discuss whether or not you find Pitts's argument convincing.

2. There are movies in which females are the action heroes (*Terminator, Alien* and its sequels, *La Femme Nikita,* etc.). Consider one or more of these films and discuss whether the female character acts in the way that Pitts argues is most desirable.

GROUP PROJECTS

1. In your group brainstorm a list of as many action heroes as you can. Then, divided the list and log on to the Internet individually to search for material on these heroes or action heroes more generally. Take notes on the different sites and entries you encounter (and download especially interesting information). Who is represented? What kind of information is offered in conjunction with certain characters? What visual and sound elements are included? Who does the information seem to be aimed toward? What conclusion can you draw from this information? Compare your findings with other group members, and write a report of your collective findings.

2. Have group members watch different cartoon shows, making careful notes about the traits and activities associated with male or female characters. Organize and present your findings to the class.

3. Write your own comic book, either by hand or on a computer, in which you create a story line that includes the reversals Pitts advocates. Assign some group members to write the script and others to create the graphics.

Hasta la Vista, Arnold
Margaret Talbot

Arnold Schwarzenegger. Sylvester Stallone. Bruce Willis. Harrison Ford. Mira Sorvino? Winona Ryder? The title of this essay assumes we are all familiar with the names and faces (and one-liners) of Hollywood action heroes and the men who portray them. The title also suggests, however, that recent summer movies have signaled a shift toward female action heroes. This trend, suggests Margaret Talbot below, *might* reveal changing cultural attitudes; however, she worries that this trend might also reinforce stereotypes. Focusing much attention on Sigourney Weaver's *Alien* film series, Talbot suggests that in many ways these films offer the best model for what female action heroes should be.

This piece was originally published in *Vogue* magazine in the May 1997 issue.

1 When I was eight or nine, I'd sometimes fantasize about single-handedly saving my classmates—all 32 of them—from some impending doom. Say we had a fire drill or a bomb scare at school, but this time the fire or the bomb was real. And only I knew about it.

2 Unlike my other girlhood fantasies of omnicompetence, though, this one was always a little fuzzy at the center, where the various feats of physical prowess should have been. How, exactly, was I to save them? I'd seen a few action-hero movies, but they never had women or girls in the action-hero roles. Could a woman wield fists of fury if she had to? Or bolt through a wall of flame, grateful classmates in tow? What if she were wearing platform shoes? I wanted to be brave—spiritually, I was pretty sure I could be—but the physicality of bravery eluded me.

3 That was 1970 or so, and not even Charlie's ultra-coiffed Angels had been set in motion yet. Whatever the song said, not everybody was kung-fu fighting. Maybe now it's easier for girls to imagine themselves in postures of defiance. Maybe their fantasies of derring-do aren't quite so likely to sputter out. They've seen movies like *Terminator 2* and *Speed* and the *Alien* series in which women—tough, buff, inexhaustibly resourceful women—play the central roles. They've seen *Xena: Warrior Princess,* the syndicated TV show that brings the Amazon virtues to *Baywatch* territory. ("In a time of ancient gods, warlords, and kings," the voice-over intones each week, "a land in turmoil cried out for a hero. She was Xena, a mighty princess forged in the heat of battle.") If they're nerdy-cool types, they may have seen some

Hong Kong action movies—dizzy, kinetic kick-fests that have long made room for actresses trained in the martial arts to give as good as they get.

4   And as it happens, they are about to see many more female icons like these. For this, you might say, is the year of the action heroine, the year when women steer the blockbusters—the blow-hard, die-hard behemoths, the intergalactic star vehicles, the box-office bonanzas. This summer's *Speed 2: Cruise Control* has Sandra Bullock, as the plucky-by-nature Annie, fending off terrorists who have hijacked a cruise ship. The fourth *Alien* movie, due this fall, has Sigourney Weaver and Winona Ryder in the starring roles. The new *Batman* movie features Alicia Silverstone as (the perhaps inevitable) Batgirl. Actresses who seem to have been genetically engineered to play grimly determined action leads are playing them (Demi Moore as a Navy SEAL), and so are actresses who don't (Mira Sorvino in *Replacement Killers,* Minnie Driver in *The Flood*). There's even a spoofy send-up of the action genre, *Austin Powers: International Man of Mystery,* that costars Elizabeth Hurley as a trained fighter in Emma Peel rig-out.

5   Among other things, the new gender-bent action movie will bring us unprecedented displays of female grit. The wondrous Michelle Yeoh, a veteran of Hong Kong movies who upends her opponents with the tensile grace of the dancer she once was, will be starring as "a good guy" (her words) in the next James Bond movie. And though she's small (five feet four inches and 103 pounds) and beautiful (she's a former Miss Malaysia), Yeoh has a wicked roundhouse kick and a charming "Oh, do I have to save his sorry ass again?" expression. (See the Jackie Chan vehicle *Police Story III: Supercop,* in which she hops around like a Mexican jumping bean, hurling grenades and sucker-punching various mainland Chinese baddies—all the while trussed up in a bulletproof vest strapped with explosives.) Yeoh describes herself, simply, as "an actress who likes to do her own stunts. I like to be challenged. What can I say? I like strong women. I don't like wimps—of either sex."

6   Several of the actresses starring in upcoming action movies said they relished the chance to show their stamina. "You really have to be in pretty great shape to do this part," says Sigourney Weaver, whose latest incarnation of Ripley has her swimming out of the flooded kitchen of a spaceship while battling ever-rapacious aliens. By all accounts, Weaver, at 47, *is* in great shape and does most of her own stunts.

7   Not so long ago, women hovered at the edges of action movies. They were the sacrificial lambs whose rapes or murders set our hero on his quest. Or they were the decorative gewgaws who offered proof of his heterosexuality. If they had power, it was the nefarious power of the spider woman, the vagina dentata, the comically wicked Bond villainess. (My favorite sub-B-grade version of this is the fifties sci-fi classic *Attack of the 50-Ft. Woman,* in which a neurotic housewife gets irradiated, grows to colossal proportions, and handily pulverizes the puny blond who stole her husband. "No, no, Mrs. Archer!" the sheriff keeps shouting into the wind created by her Brobdingnagian crop top.)

8   Good women in action movies were never powerful, and powerful women were never good enough. Now, though, all that has begun to shift. Women are occupying the center of the story, almost as likely to play the avengers as the avenged. If an actress is strong—physically strong, especially—it's likely to be a

sign of her character's integrity. Or as Iris Grossman, senior vice president of talent and casting at Turner Broadcasting, puts it, "The studios have finally woken up to the fact that women are as capable of running and jumping and slamming cars around as anyone else."

9   Not that this is exactly a feminist awakening. Conscience is nice, but money comes through a lot clearer on a cell phone. And the fact is that women have more power to make or break a film than ever before—or at least that's how the studios see it these days. Like soccer moms in last year's political campaigns, women moviegoers, especially those over 25, are the new swing constituency, sought after, fought over, and patronized. Women have been going to movies somewhat more often recently, according to figures from the Motion Picture Association of America. Female audiences were crucial to the success of several of this past year's most profitable films—including *The First Wives Club* and *Jerry Maguire.*

10   Besides, in this era of girl power and "work-life issues" and fashionable breast cancer fund-raisers, there is a kind of ineffable sense that catering to women, or being seen to do so, will earn you a mantle of virtue. Women are a "minority," but they are the biggest minority around; speaking feelingly of their special needs can be an easy way for politicians or companies or moviemakers to broadcast their compassion and rack up cultural brownie points for what George Bush memorably called "the vision thing."

11   When it comes to the new crop of action movies, the thinking goes something like this. On the one hand, big, loud blockbusters with lots of things exploding in them are what Hollywood mostly does these days; the studios are in thrall to their money-making potential. On the other hand, women seem to like more character-driven movies and have turned some of those into big hits. So why not glom the two together? Put women in action movies, rejigger the genre slightly to accommodate the tastes of female audiences, and voilà—you've got what you hope is a new sure-fire formula. "The aim is to do action films that are more women-friendly; that is, having strong women in top roles and taking out a lot of the violence," William Mechanic, chairman and CEO of Fox Filmed Entertainment, told *The New York Times* recently. "Women are not only driving the box office but also video-cassette rentals and sales and TV watching. Not respecting their taste level is silly." (And probably a lot harder to do now that so many more women executives are making green-light decisions at the major studios. At Paramount Pictures for example, close to half the top creative executives are women; at 20th Century Fox, about a third are, and many more women are making production deals.)

12   Maybe, too, we're at a cultural moment when we're willing, even eager to see women in strong roles—but we'd just as soon they be strong in space, or the future, or at least some pretty outlandish, exceptional circumstances in the here and now. Let them be queens for a day, just not every day. "I know that Ripley has become a feminist icon," says Sigourney Weaver when I ask her if she conceives of her *Alien* character that way. "But I've always thought that was kind of strange because everywhere I go, I see women doing everything, all kinds of physically demanding jobs. The fact that in general movies don't reflect that day-to-day reality is a measure of how out of it Hollywood is."

13 For actresses, the new availability of action roles is a boon, but not an unmitigated one. Action movies propel a few of them into the salary stratosphere as nothing else can. They still don't occupy the same gilded bracket as, say, Schwarzenegger, Stallone, or—God help us—Jim Carrey, all of whom make $20 million a film. But Sandra Bullock did take home $12.5 million for *Speed 2: Cruise Control,* and Sigourney Weaver got $11 million for *Alien Resurrection.* On the other hand, the roles can be, well, a bit robotic. Elizabeth Hurley had fun playing a jokey action heroine in silver lamé boots but says she's not especially eager to sign up for a lot of rock-'em-sock-'em blockbusters. "I really prefer to do a scene that you can get your teeth into, rather than just waiting around for things to blow up. Action films can be a little tedious." Minnie Driver agrees. In *The Flood,* she plays, of all things, a church restorer who manages to save her work and her town from rising waters and marauding robbers. She says she liked playing a character who was "definitely not a damsel in distress," and she's encouraged by the prospect of more parts for "women who can be strong across the board without being bitches." Still, Driver says she "wouldn't necessarily do another action thriller," because she's "interested in movies that are more about character. Though I have to say that if it involved somebody more like Sigourney Weaver's character in the *Alien* movies, I'd make an exception. That role, and Sigourney in it, has such grace and passion. It's never cheesy." Weaver herself worries that action movies may not embrace women who, like Ripley, project a sinewy tenacity rather than something more traditionally feminine. "The important thing in introducing new female action heroes," Weaver says, "is that they don't try to make us too glamorous, put us all in see-through uniforms or something."

14 The great strength of the *Alien* movies is their relative psychological complexity—above all, their ability to evoke a Freudian sense of the uncanny. All three of the previous *Alien* movies, with their dominant metaphor of violent birth, muck about in that mire. The next one, directed by Jean-Pierre Jeunet (*Delicatessen, City of Lost Children*), takes cloning as its dominant metaphor. The plot has Ripley, who plunged to a self-sacrificing death in the last installment, brought to life by the usual nefarious military-industrial complexers, who aim only to get at the alien inside her and to clone it for their own uses. That notion, too, has a primal pull. "I found the idea of being brought back to life against your will quite seductive," Weaver says. (The producers and publicists on *Alien Resurrection* may be among the few people who are positively cheerful about the recent cloning of a sheep and its implications for human experimentation. Everybody on the set is talking about it. Morally troubling, sure, but good box office.) Still, none of this would move us or scare us if we didn't have a central character—a woman pressing hard against her bodily limitations, not escaping her femaleness but letting her heroism transcend it—whose fate we cared about and whose strength we trusted.

15 On a recent visit to the *Alien Resurrection* set, I thumbed through a stack of stills from the movie. There she was again, the nearly six-foot-tall Weaver as the larger-than-life Ripley. In the last movie, *Alien 3,* the bleakest and least successful of the series, poor Ripley was more beaten down than she'd been before. Still, even with her head shaved and her options spooled out, she at least had the charisma of

her exhaustion—hollowed-eyed, sallow, a bruise blooming like a rose tattoo at her temple. She won't rest until It is vanquished. This time Ripley has hair, and her costume for most of the movie, a tunic and pants of dark, glistening leather, hugs her like a second skin. (Winona Ryder as a mechanic on a ragtag spaceship gets the somewhat humbler outfit—a blue-gray jumpsuit.) But even slightly glamorized, Weaver manages to look austere and haunted, her face an irreducible sliver of recognizable emotion in a technoslimed wasteland.

16   How important is it, I asked Bill Badalato, the producer of *Alien Resurrection,* to have a woman in the central role? Does it ensure greater audience appeal, bigger box office? Badalato, who produced *Broken Arrow,* among other noisy action films, steepled his fingers and thought for a bit. "Well, the *right* woman in the role is very appealing to an audience," he said at last. "Sigourney manages to convey this steely persona that is feminine at the same time. It's a delicate balance: If a women acts too tough and macho, an audience isn't going to buy it. If she acts too girly and gushy, they aren't going to buy it."

17   He's right, too. The best women action heroes aren't doing comic-book turns as girls with brawn *and* breasts. And they aren't doing Steven Seagal in drag, either. What you like about them is the sense that they are playing women, just women who might be a little—OK, a lot—stronger than you and me. Or, as Badalato put it of the ideal women's action role, "If men admire it and don't giggle at it and women admire it and aspire to it, then you've got it right." That's all I wanted when I was eight, after all. Is it so much to ask?

EXPLORING THE TEXT

1. Talbot begins her discussion with a personal reminiscence about her own childhood. What is the effect of this beginning? How does it relate to the title of the piece? How does her anecdote draw us in to the issues of this discussion? Explain your answer.

2. Talbot suggests that there have recently been women characters who are "tough, buff, inexhaustibly resourceful" (paragraph 3). She seems to suggest that women aren't typically depicted this way, but that men (at least male action heroes) were. Is she correct? List the characteristics of one male action hero and one female action hero you've seen in a film. Briefly describe the extent to which each does (or does not) meet these criteria.

3. What does Talbot argue are the more traditional roles of women in action movies? Why does she see these roles as undesirable? Explain your answer in detail.

4. In paragraph 9, Talbot says that "this is [not] exactly a feminist awakening." What does she mean? What evidence does she offer in support of this claim?

5. Though Talbot speaks of the "cultural moment" (paragraph 12) and the changing attitudes toward women in certain roles, she is not completely

satisfied with the images Hollywood is producing. Why is this? What support does she offer for her position?

6. In paragraph 13, Talbot notes Sigourney Weaver's worry that Hollywood will not "embrace women who . . . project a sinewy tenacity rather than something more traditionally feminine." What is Weaver worried about? What exactly is being contrasted here? How does this concern fit into Talbot's discussion overall?

7. How does the discussion of the *Alien* movies help to clarify the issues and also establish a standard to which other movies can aspire? How does Talbot's choice to quote Weaver at such length establish this series as the best option?

WRITING ASSIGNMENTS

1. Compare this discussion with Elayne Rapping's essay in this chapter ("Women on the Big Screen"). Rapping presents an argument in favor of some recent movies that present more desirable (and less traditional) female "types." How do her claims of what is desirable compare to Talbot's claims? How does her discussion of female characters compare to Talbot's discussion of Ripley in the *Alien* series? What exactly is the need that each author identifies? What kinds of movies have been produced since these two articles were written? Do these movies seem, indeed, to address this need? Write an essay in which you explain your answers to these questions.

2. In the final paragraph of this essay Talbot states, "The best women action heroes aren't doing comic-book turns as girls with brawn *and* breasts. And they aren't doing Steven Seagal in drag, either." How does this idea relate to other discussions in this chapter? Would Talbot and Pitts agree? What do you think Stallone would say about Talbot's definitions of femininity (see the Faludi interview)? Write an essay in which you compare—and perhaps debate—the positions argued by these authors.

GROUP PROJECTS

1. Talbot describes Ripley in the *Alien* movies as a "steely persona that is feminine" and who is "not escaping her femaleness but letting her heroism transcend it" (paragraph 14). Think about the issues and attitudes underlying these statements. Review several action films with females and male heroes by assigning one group member to watch and carefully note the details in a particular film. Focus on questions such as the following: How do these movies define masculine and feminine? What are the traits that lead to success? What traits have to be overcome? What, then, do action movies say about traditional gender divisions of characteristics? (You might also

consult Sylvester Stallone's ideas in the Susan Faludi interview below.) Prepare a report that details your findings.

2. In paragraph 3, Talbot wonders if little girls growing up more recently have a different idea of what it is to be heroic. She says, "Maybe now it's easier for girls to imagine themselves in postures of defiance. Maybe their fantasies of derring-do aren't quite so likely to sputter out." Work to define what is heroic from a variety of perspectives. As a group prepare a survey. Work to create questions that will elicit very particular information on characteristics of heroes, good and bad, as well as examples of real and fictional characters people see as heroic. Question both males and females as well as people from a range of ages and backgrounds. Are there different definitions? What is the source of people's definitions (Hollywood or other entertainment? Church? Politics? Family?)? Do the definitions indeed change? Do little girls have a different definition from little boys? From older women? Prepare a report in which you evaluate Talbot's claims (or answer her questions) in light of your group's findings.

The Masculine Mystique—An Interview of Sylvester Stallone

Susan Faludi

Sylvester Stallone has been one of Hollywood's biggest action heroes since his Academy Award–winning performance in *Rocky* two decades ago. In this interview with Susan Faludi, the superstar offers unusual insight into how he defines his action hero image—and the limitations of such roles. Of special interest are Stallone's comments on his body image. For Rocky and Rambo, Stallone's densely wadded macho physique was an essential element of the characters. Yet he also acknowledges that the exaggerated attention to physical appearance is something more typically defined as "feminine." His insights on how Americans define masculine and feminine, and the judgments we attach to such definitions, are fascinating—especially in light of several other articles in this chapter that focus on female roles and heroes.

This interview appeared in the December 1996 issue of *Esquire* magazine. Faludi is noted for her work on male-female relations in American society and is the author of *Backlash: The Undeclared War Against American Women* (1991).

1 One night not long ago, Sylvester Stallone made an appearance at the Planet Hollywood on Fifty-seventh Street in Manhattan. The occasion was a charity fundraiser, and Stallone gamely stood in the pit before the sea of gawkers and hawked the restaurant's latest Celebrity Limited Edition collectible: a black cotton T-shirt

streaked with a skeleton-and-sinew torso bursting from claylike globs of red and yellow paint. It was a reproduction of a Stallone painting entitled *Hercules O'Clock,* from his Man and Superman series. Hercules, back to the viewer, raises his rippling arms as if for crucifixion and turns his skull sideways to reveal a single bullet hole. The wound gushes bright blood. By his side rests a large clock, its pink hands paused at seven o'clock. Stallone described to me later what he was trying to evoke with the painting: the fleeting quality of modern-day fame, the way celebrity has corrupted, and caused the death of, the classical hero. "It's Hercules assassinated," he said.

2   Knowing what I know about Stallone's current struggle with celebrity, I wondered whether Hercules' wound was self-inflicted. Stallone is in the process of trying to shatter the carapace of his own cinematic image, which, along with the musculature accompanying it, has begun to feel, he says, less like a showcase and more like a full-body cast. This shelf self was born when *Rocky* became an instant hit two decades ago, and it was only fortified by Rambo. As Stallone put it to me, "Lightning hit twice." In the years since, Stallone has tried repeatedly to shuck off the shell, only to be met with discouragement from the studios, dismay from his fans, and ridicule from the media.

3   The problem with becoming a superhero is that it is a miracle, and miracles are not easily undone. As a child, Stallone, like postwar boys all over America inspired by George Reeves's characterization of Superman, dressed up as the caped hero and, hoping he could fly, leaped off his family's roof and broke his collarbone. But in adulthood, the cape worked. And now he can't seem to get it off his back—or find his way back to the phone booth.

4   Stallone's latest movie, *Daylight,* in which he and a band of survivors flee a burning and flooding replica of the Holland Tunnel, is an escape film. But it's part of a greater personal escape—a subtle first step toward breaking the mold by portraying a doubting, stumbling hero. At the time of his visit to Planet Hollywood, Stallone was in New York for the second step, the filming of *Copland,* a serious, low-budget drama featuring Robert De Niro and Harvey Keitel and directed by award-winning independent filmmaker James Mangold. Stallone plays a diffident and partially deaf sheriff named Freddy Heflin—a "noble turtle," as Stallone puts it. That Freddy is a sad sack may be the less notable reason the film signals a break from Stallone's celluloid past. After all, the original Rocky was a loser, too. The key difference is that this time the noble turtle has no protective, confining shell. Freddy is . . . fat.

5   During the filming of *Copland,* I met Stallone at the bar of the Four Seasons Hotel for the first of a series of conversations about his efforts to change his image. He made his way across the room with that resigned, rolling shamble that is particular to heavier men, with his eyes slightly downcast, his lack of form concealed in an oversize Hawaiian shirt.

6   His new appearance has caused some alarm among the hotel's denizens. "I was having breakfast here the other day," he tells me, "and the guy sitting next to me was doing this—" Stallone flexes and assumes a bodybuilder's post. "I guess the other two guys were trying to pitch him on exercise equipment or something. So I walked

in, he was like"—Stallone goes into a deep, Rockyish voice—" 'How ya doin',
Sly!' and gave me one of these——" He shows a thumbs-up. "So now the whole
meal, he's in this state of complete rigidity. And I sit down, and what do I order?
Pancakes, french fries, and an omelette, and more french fries. The whole meal, he's
looking over at me like this——" Stallone feigns a look of horror. "The whole meal,
he's talking to them, 'Uh-huh, mm-hmm,' and looking at me like 'Oh, my God!' He
was probably thinking, 'Well, if it's good enough for him, maybe I should just blow
up!' He's thinking, 'So Rambo is a walking greasy french fry?' "

7   **Faludi:** Why did you want to play this flabby, bumbling guy in *Copland?*

8   **Stallone:** I knew I couldn't continue to do the same thing anymore. And when I
say I don't want to do action anymore, well, that was my foundation. It's like
John Wayne saying, "I don't want to do any westerns." Uh, so what are we going to put you in, Noël Coward? But I had to do it. And I knew I had to do something that was physically just so different that it would affect the acting. If you
were to put on thirty pounds, you're going to talk differently, you're going to
walk differently, you're going to think differently about yourself. You're not
going to be walking into a room with your chest held up. You're going to be
like—— [*Hunches over with a mortified expression on his face, then tugs on the
collar of his baggy shirt.*] That's why I'm wearing these Tom Selleck shirts!

9   You've got to mess up your body mechanics if you're going to be something different. De Niro understood that very early on, in *Taxi Driver,* when he
cut his hair like that, which was pretty radical back then. He had to be so oblivious to what people thought of him that he was in his own frequency now. . . .
If you really want to *act*—not perform, *act*—then you have to do something
different with yourself.

10   **Faludi:** To a lot of people, you *are* your body.

11   **Stallone:** That's the greatest barrier for me to override, the mere fact that
there's an expectancy of torqued musculature, pulsating veins. In *Daylight,* the
shirt never comes off. That's a first for me in quite a while.

12   **Faludi:** You didn't consider just using special effects to look fat, as Eddie
Murphy did in *The Nutty Professor?*

13   **Stallone:** Oh, no. I have to be *him.* [*Points to one of several out-of-shape bald
men slouched over their drinks at the bar.*] See these guys? Sitting there, just
sitting there, waiting for a miracle. And they know no great-looking woman's
going to come over there. . . . For me to show up with a thirty-one-inch waist
and eighteen-inch arms, looking like a lifeguard, going, "I'm fat and lonely.
Whaddya think?" No.

14   **Faludi:** I gather than *Copland*'s crew was worried you wouldn't get fat enough?

15   **Stallone:** Yeah. He [director Mangold] would call up on the phone: "Have you
gained weight?" I said, "I'm up to 185 . . . 191. Good enough?" "No. You've
got to gain a little more." I said, "Please, I can't." So he comes to check me out.

And I'm sticking my stomach out. He goes, "Well, it's kind of impressive, but it's kind of a Chicken Little thing."

16 **Faludi:** How do you stay heavy? Do you have a fat diet?

17 **Stallone:** Every day for breakfast, I eat five or six hotcakes, an order of French toast, a bowl of oatmeal, two bagels with peanut butter, and ten eggs, two yolks.

18 **Faludi:** So you don't go to the gym anymore?

19 **Stallone:** No. And it's very hard. I can feel my waist. It's like a thirty-nine. It was thirty on *Daylight.* But that's the—I was going to say that's the easy part, but it's not. But the other part is, to get where I wanted to get mentally, I had to divest myself of pride, of *any* self-image. I swear to you, I rarely look and go— [*Makes a motion of primping and fixing his hair in the mirror.*] I show up at the set just like this. Because you know you're not going to impress anyone anymore. You are just trying to *be.* It is sort of a relief. It's like "Who are you making fun of, fatso? Look at you, you're no day in the park! No one's hanging you in the Louvre."

20 **Faludi:** Sam Fussell wrote in *Muscle: Confessions of an Unlikely Bodybuilder* that gussying up his body like that was "a principally feminine exercise." So maybe by getting out of shape, you are going back to a more traditionally masculine state?

21 **Stallone:** Very much so. Even having a conversation when you are in shape is—[*Affects a Mr. Universe-like pose, arms raised overhead, biceps flexed.*] I'm telling you, *everything* is a display. It has a paralyzing effect on character. You take a serious gym rat, a man who lives in a gym, it's like, what do you *do* with it? You've got it, but it comes out in this vanity thing which borders on the world of exotic dancing with women. . . .

22 The guy with the eighteen-inch arms, the thirty-one-inch waist, the male-model, chiseled, Calvin Klein-ad type of person, he is, for the nineties, the woman with the triple E. He's taking the place of the blond bombshell of the fifties. The woman on the street doesn't want to be Jayne Mansfield. But if I see another guy walking through Central Park in a tank top and bicycle shorts, it's like, why don't you just get a billboard that says, "Look at me! Don't take me seriously!" It's sad, because there's no sense of self-worth, and your own entrée into people's line of consciousness for a synaptic millisecond is your body, so that they go, "Oh, look at that idiot!"

23 **Faludi:** But weren't you one of the big models of that pumped-up ideal?

24 **Stallone:** Yes, oh, sure. And I don't judge them, because I did that. And I know, to a point, what they are thinking. And it's fool's gold. It's appalling to me that I don't know what cries out in myself or certain people, that this is our calling card to the world.

25 **Faludi:** Were you embarrassed about appearing in public? I mean, no one knows you gained the weight for a movie.

26   **Stallone:** Oh, cut down to the ground. Terrible! Still am. I knew I was on the road to recovery when I wasn't issuing disclaimers. "This isn't me! I'm doing this for a *film*!" I should've gotten a little sign. I started doing it with *strangers.* "Hi, how ya doing? This isn't me." It's been good for me, movie aside, because now I don't present that. No one's intimidated by me, not even close. Everyone goes, "I'm built much better than him," so that's out of the way.

27   **Faludi:** You used to want to intimidate them, though.

28   **Stallone:** I grew up with a pretty profound complex of inadequacy. And I thought the only way to override that was through creating an imposing exterior. But as I grew older, I became unaware that I was doing it. Yet I was wondering why people were not finding me accessible. And then taking this part, I didn't realize how extremely difficult it would be to change my shape and to let it go. Then I realized I had been using it as a psychological tool for a very long time.

29   **Faludi:** Rocky and Rambo both seem to me to be all about that American male compulsion to prove yourself by going up against these incredible odds.

30   **Stallone:** Men require a challenge. They just have to have it. Whether it's eyeing each other over the seat of a bus or cutting in on somebody who's dancing. They'll go out of their way sometimes to create catastrophe just to prove their mettle. Men have to validate themselves. And when they don't, they live in a netherworld of fertility frustration.

31   **Faludi:** But the hoops that American men go through now to prove themselves seem so extreme, almost ludicrous, both on- and offscreen.

32   **Stallone:** Life is becoming very stationary for a lot of men. The options are few and far between. That's why all these drugs and alcohol are on the rise. It's not by accident. And then you get these ghoulish individuals who go into a post office and take out ten people. That's their validation. The opportunities for men to validate themselves are diminishing. The frontiers are diminishing. So they seek these extreme outlets. The bungee cord—let's talk about that, please! Car surfing. Sixty miles per hour on the subway roof! Hanging on to the sides of buses!

33   **Faludi:** So you're through with these extreme forms of validation?

34   **Stallone:** Maybe it's age, but when I was doing the last scene in *Daylight,* where I'm trying to claw my way through this clay wall, I was struck with the realization that this is the experience of someone who wants to be hurt. Because I was truly hurt a great deal [in filming action movies]. I have a lot of debilitating injuries now—arthritis and bones that have been broken. But I'm happier now in my life. I no longer need to go into that dark neighborhood anymore and stand there, exposed, praying for someone to try and kill me.

35   **Faludi:** Do your fans accept that?

36   **Stallone:** The bright side is, I realize that I don't need to vindicate myself or vilify myself or celebrate myself anymore. But the bad part is, the audience doesn't realize this! They could care less! The fact that you've come around

and you've kind of transcended it, that you've gone to a higher plane, they don't want to know about that. They are like "We want what we want! We want what we expect when we plunk down eight bucks!" So it's "Yes, Sly, you can be free, but not from *us*."

37   The next morning, Stallone headed out to the set of *Copland,* in Cliffside Park, New Jersey, to be mobbed, as he is every day, by fans. They weren't there, however, to see the new Sly. As his limousine passed, a teenage boy reached through the window to thrust into Stallone's arms a large portrait he had etched and elaborately framed: It was of Rocky in the ring, muscles taut, face bloodied.

38   "I know your name," a little boy declared as Stallone walked from his trailer to the set.

39   "No you don't," Stallone said.

40   "Yes I do!" the boy said, adamant. "It's Rocky!"

41   Pat Bertelli, a forty-year-old single mother whose son had recently become a devotee of working out, insisted that Stallone autograph her bare back. He signed his real name. "I keep calling him Rocky," she told me. "Oh, God, Rocky! That chest!" she said, oblivious to the fact that the chest was no more.

42   **Faludi:** You picked *Copland* to escape the superhero mold. Were the film's makers dubious that you could?

43   **Stallone:** When I met the director, well, I don't want to put words in his mouth, but I think there was a skepticism on his part because, you know, for a fellow that's packing this much baggage [*points to himself*], this is the complete antithesis of what I do. My character can't beat anybody up. So we talked, and we hit it off very well, and I said, "There's nothing more pleasurable to me than to go into, like, thespetic bondage, where the actor just turns himself over and goes with it." He said, "No!" And I said, "Absolutely!"

44   **Faludi:** You've said that one of your great frustrations was that you haven't been able to attract strong directors. Are they scared of Rocky?

45   **Stallone:** I think they worry, am I going to bring a certain amount of telltale taste from another genre? It's like all of a sudden, you have a predominant red or a glaring yellow that's throwing the whole canvas off. It's like that story of Rodin. One of the earlier versions of *The Three Shades.* People keep commenting on the sculpture's extraordinary hand, the hand, the hand, just the hand. Finally, he took a hammer and smashed the hand off. He said, "Now what do you think of the sculpture?"

46   **Faludi:** Is that what you are trying to do to your own body by gaining weight?

47   **Stallone:** Yes. I'm smashing the hand.

48   **Faludi:** Are you having to unlearn a lot of superhero habits, a lot of action tics?

49   **Stallone:** Very much so. Like, everyone has a better side. A speech rhythm that has delivered the desired effect quite a few times—you can't do it. This is more halting and higher, much higher. And there's an awkwardness. Whereas in the

other films, there's this smoothness—[*Flexes a bicep and poses.*] I normally make eye contact. With this character, he just—[*looks down*], because he doesn't have any confidence in what he says. No signs of strength. Any kind of indication of strength is wrong. Any gesture with the hands. Any encroachment on that three-foot territory around people.

50   **Faludi:** So in a way, you have to think of everything that's seen as traditionally manly and then work against it?

51   **Stallone:** Yes, which in a sense turns out to be very manly. Because I'm dealing with the courage of the heart, the courage of the mind. The body has none. He physically poses no threat.

52   **Faludi:** If you can break out of the mold, what would you want to break *into?*

53   **Stallone:** I'd like to go head-to-head with the opposite gender. . . . I'd like to make a movie that's about the shifting balance of power between the sexes, the trials of trying to make a relationship work. I'm not talking about a self-serving love story. I'd want it to be something that was caustic and funny and sparring, verbally.

54   **Faludi:** Why do you want to struggle with women, not men?

55   **Stallone:** How can you really delve into your own psyche, and really spread yourself across the cinema canvas, if you haven't really taken on the most crucial of all relationships, which is between man and woman? Man against man, man against evil empire, and so forth, what is that really? Why are you trying to save the empire? Why are you trying to pursue the killer? To make the world a better place for more men? No. It's all to impress the fairer sex.

56   **Faludi:** What sort of masculine hero would you prefer to portray?

57   **Stallone:** I want to be the man who is the instigator, the catalyst. I'm always reacting. I'm trying to get away from that image of being victimized. It's always been for me redemption or resurrection or modern-day Lazarus.

58   **Faludi:** Why have you always played the victim?

59   **Stallone:** I think that's because of the primary impression derived by the success of *Rocky.* He basically was fate's child. He really wasn't responsible for any of his success. Only through a fluke, through someone else's disdain for the plight of the poor man, does he get a break. And the perception of the kind of heroes I play became men that are driven along by the whims of others.

60   **Faludi:** In that regard, Freddy isn't that far from the original Rocky.

61   **Stallone:** *Copland* is very *Rocky*ish. The irony is, I've just never been involved in a dramatic vehicle in the past twenty years that was not prone toward overt physicality to get to its end result, the showdown. This one is a man who eventually has the same showdown, but he's not dependent on physical superiority; it's actually physical inferiority—his inability to hear, his inability to retreat.

   Faludi: But Freddy in *Copland* is another victim. So you're still having the problem you talked about in an interview in 1978, when you said you wanted "to play a leader of men instead of a man who is led," but couldn't seem to find such a role.

62 **Stallone:** I said that in 1978? So nothing's changed. How depressing!

63 **Faludi:** So maybe you're never going to play the leader of men.

64 **Stallone:** Am I an alpha man?

65 **Faludi:** I'll let you answer that one!

66 **Stallone:** Well, now, an alpha man is—like John Wayne would be an alpha man. The guy who goes to the door, jumps first, and it's "Everyone follow me! I'll save Masada" kind of thing. Hits the beach first and not prone to revealing his innermost pain and that kind of thing . . . So, no, I guess I'm not.

67 **Faludi:** What sort of maleness do you represent, then, if it's not alphaness?

68 **Stallone:** I rise to the occasion. That's what I'm all about. But to go in there and play King Arthur or whatever, the leader of men and constantly stoic, Sean Connery, I don't think that's what I'm about. So I tend to rely upon, for lack of a better description, feminine instincts, the rather exposed, unabashed emotional outpouring. I think, by and large, and I hope this doesn't sound wrong, acting is a feminine profession, in the sense that it is an emotional profession. Women will show a great deal more of their soul. And I would aspire toward that aspect of the feminine.

69 **Faludi:** Well, if that's feminine, what's manliness?

70 **Stallone:** Manliness is . . . [*Long pause.*] It's someone who doesn't reveal their strengths; he knows they are there. He's very aware of who he is. He doesn't have to blow a bugle in your face to let you know he's going to charge. I think you can be very boisterous, almost boorish, but you can still be a man. A man can be a drunkard, a womanizer. Because that has nothing to do with being a *man.* That's just personality traits. The *man* is one who's willing to sacrifice, pure and simple. And that's the difference. That's honor. That's what I look for in a man. The protector.

71 **Faludi:** In many movies today, the hero is the victim, not the protector.

72 **Stallone:** It seems like it's much more heroic now to be on the defensive and coming to the rescue. So the degree to which one is a hero is only weighed against the power and charisma of the villain. So the villain is more important than the hero. The villain is more ingenious, more intelligent, more facile. And our hero is basically inept and stumbles his way into a victory. He sometimes even baffles the villain by his simplicity and absurdness. Like *Die Hard:* multi geniuses versus a cop with broken glass in his feet.

73 **Faludi:** Well, why?

74 **Stallone:** For each generation of men, things get further and further beyond their reach. Like every team in the next ten years will be owned by a corporation. Every stadium will be Coca-Cola Stadium, Pepsi University, Coors Hospital. It's gotten beyond the reach of mortal man, so these villains are basically thinly disguised metaphors for the technological bludgeoning we're getting every day.

75   And in the end, the hope is that righteousness will eventually dominate. I think we're still holding to a thinly disguised Christian doctrine of Daniel before the lions—the hope of martyrdom, that the martyr will eventually succeed because he has God on his side.

76   **Faludi:** So the male heroes are victims because the only kind of heroism they can hope for is to be martyred?

77   **Stallone:** To know that the odds are so high that only through the perishing of your life will the minions survive, that's love. That's heroism. But in very few films today, much to my chagrin, do the heroes die. The heroes don't perish, which I think diminishes any chance for becoming legend. It's just: Oh, another superhero. Who will it be tomorrow?

78   **Faludi:** Now it's another day, another hero.

79   **Stallone:** The media has diluted the male heroes. Make them causes célèbres for fifteen minutes. One hundred years ago, a feat of daring would go into lore. They'd write songs about it. It'd be passed down. It would be like the James brothers or the Man on the Flying Trapeze. Today, a man can go in and save fifteen children out of a burning building, and the next week he can't get a job. He'll say, "Remember me?" Nope. The ink's dried, pal. It's over. That's the difference.

80   When I painted a few years ago, I did these "media heroes." I put a clock on all these paintings, and each was to see people in their prime—six o'clock is their prime; by twelve o'clock it's over. Because as time moves on, if our heroes don't die, they somehow become obsolete or discredited, especially in films.

81   Take the Lone Ranger. The ideal man. And they wanted to take his mask away. So he had to walk around with wraparound sunglasses! The actor who played him on TV makes a living showing up now and then at supermarkets. And they [the corporate holders of the Lone Ranger trademark] said, "Hey, pal, the mask is *ours*." And he knows that the only thing he has left is his friggin' mask. He doesn't come in with the hat. He doesn't come in with the horse. The mask, that's *all he's got.*

82   **Faludi:** So the fame clock is kind of racing these days?

83   **Stallone:** Because the heroics of the movie hero are now reliant upon one-upmanship. . . . You have to constantly make your feats of daring so extraordinary. You can't save one person anymore. You have to save a nation. You have to save armies and legions of people. And then it gets to the point where you've done these extraordinary feats, and where does it go now? All right, we've tapped him out!

84   **Faludi:** But the clock seems frozen, too. The male "heroes" onscreen today more often than not are playing these sort of petulant boys.

85   **Stallone:** I think *they* think that's sexy. And endearing. And also they are afraid of moving on to that middle-age thing. The actors, you know, they choose the material.

86   **Faludi:** But movie actors a generation ago, as they aged, didn't play little boys.

87 **Stallone:** Men like John Wayne or Kirk Douglas and Burt Lancaster and Joel McCrea, they came from immigrants, hardworking people. And I think it was drilled into a man's head very early that he must be a *man.* He may be taking over the family at fourteen years old. He may be working six hours a day after school when he's twelve years old. So it was an ethic.

88   So I think the actors are "grown," but they're grown up to the standards that have been presented to them. There's no deficiency in the men today; they are merely reacting to the stimulus around them. They turn on the TV, and it's all about: Tear it down! Destroy this! Be your own person! . . . You didn't have that kind of confusion before.

89 **Faludi:** So where is this confusion leading? If not fatherly protectors, what will they be?

90 **Stallone:** I think the leading man of the future will be one who is beleaguered by the need to constantly define on film the male-female relationship. Where do men stand? Are we equals, or do you not need me anymore? Is the man's parenting role diminishing? Is the man even necessary? I think the love affairs will be much more contrite. I think we'll see women in these big role reversals, being quite dominant.

91 **Faludi** Well, *is* the male necessary?

92 **Stallone:** The male is necessary in the actual—well, in technological procreation, no, he's not. It can be mechanically induced. But the man, I think, is something very comforting in having . . . well, a different smell, a different body type, a different voice, the illusion of the protector and guardian.

93 **Faludi:** The illusion? You mean, as opposed to really being the protector?

94 **Stallone:** Well, exactly. Because in this day and age, there is no security he can offer. Nothing is really protected. We think it is. We hope it is. But in reality, there is no security.

95 **Faludi:** So a lot of what being a man is about now is about creating illusions?

96 **Stallone:** The definition of a masculine man is one who is defending himself by the way he performs against these imagined dragons. It's like in *A Tree Grows in Brooklyn,* where the father was deluding the daughter into thinking these magical, wonderful things about how he's out there conquering the world when basically he was sitting on the steps somewhere, getting drunk. But he would never let her see that side. A man wants for you to believe that he's riding into the Valley of Death but he's going to conquer all. I think we all harbor a kind of dwindling hero complex.

97 **Faludi:** So what happened to proving manhood in the real world?

98 **Stallone:** The idea of confrontation is very suppressed in the culture. It's not acceptable by today's standards. It's like to be a man is to be nonconfrontational. People are afraid to lose everything, so the less confrontational they are, the more likely they are to be around. The day of the rebellion is history. . . . The Black Panther movement, the Chicago Seven, that doesn't seem to be in

vogue. It's almost as if to be aggressive for *any* reason is to be violent. A hero can be violent only after he's been pushed to the wall and it's a matter of defense, not offense. That's why the hero's a victim. People want to nurture the underdog. The day of the strongman is over.

99   **Faludi:** Are you saying masculinity has been lost from our culture?

100   **Stallone:** It's not lost. It's just, we've lost what it *means* to be masculine. It's not anyone's fault. It's just the masculine endeavors—the jobs, the positions, the challenges—are diminishing. It's like some great nomadic tribe that's slowly being fenced in. And as they fail to wander, they no longer seem to exist.

101   **Faludi:** The "masculine endeavor" of playing the action hero no longer feels like a challenge?

102   **Stallone:** I know a few performers who thought action was a sure thing, dramatic actors, and they wouldn't get near it again. It's a painful kind of empty experience that is totally reliant on the effects around you. Basically, all the actor does is he lights the fuse and survives the explosion. The big bang has nothing to do with you. You are a piece of celebrity machinery that performs a function that requires very little in the way of explanation. But it does require a great deal in physical demonstration. So you are this machine that goes up and down and around, but no one every really cracks the exterior. You are looked at as just a piece of machinery.

103   **Faludi:** And you're a machine that does the same thing every time?

104   **Stallone:** Everything is derivative. It's four guys arriving in a limousine and they all put on Nixon masks and they rob the bank. And then, sure enough, next movie, they arrive and they rob the yacht. And then they rob the train. But it's the *same thing.* And everybody wants to drop a virus. I mean, well, who cares? Everybody wants to blow up New York. Let 'em! I'd help them walk the bomb through the door! And everybody wants a billion dollars to do it. It's so dumb. If you are really going to blow it up, blow it up for an ideology. But don't ask for money.

105   **Faludi:** The hero of these new action films, is his role then just to be along for the ride?

106   **Stallone:** The action film is no longer the action film. It's the ultraviolence film, which has nothing to do with why the actor ever entered this business. So now you're kind of giving yourself up. It's more like what a farmer must've felt like, you know, a strong-backed real son of the earth looking at the Industrial Age, saying, "Jesus, they don't need me anymore. I'm just there to start the machine." But the machine is the thing. Well, in these films today, the actor is standing there looking at a big blue screen, seeing things that don't exist, and being made to fly through areas that he's not flying in.

107   **Faludi:** Have you done one of those films against a blue screen?

108   **Stallone:** Yes, *Judge Dredd* was quite like that. You are on a cable, on a flying motorcycle that leans left and leans right, and then they'll say, "React to this. Above you, there's three soldiers coming at you, and they're shooting. Duck!"

And then you go back and you do it again. And it's weeks on end, weeks on end. It's unbearable.

109 **Faludi:** It sounds like an actor playing these "powerful" heroes would feel pretty unpowerful. The way you describe it, the action genre seems to—

110 **Stallone:** To castrate you? Yeah.

111 **Faludi:** The way you're just an ornamental addition to the special effects seems like the opposite of macho.

112 **Stallone:** It is the opposite. And therein lies the depressing dichotomy. Because if you are so macho like your screen image, why don't you do something that's really macho and go against the tide, buck the system, face the firing squad of your own insecurities?

113 **Faludi:** You are trying to buck the Hollywood system now by departing from the action role. What's been the reaction? [Stallone still has big-picture studio commitments pending, most notably a $60 million deal with Universal to make three movies.]

114 **Stallone:** Well, it wasn't like "Bon voyage, babe! Great, we'll see you soon!" It was more like "Okay, let him get this out of his system. And then we get back to business." And from a business point of view, they are absolutely right, and I support them 100 percent. But when do you say, "Okay, let me fail for all the right reasons rather than succeed for all the wrong ones?"

115 **Faludi:** And so what happened after you let it be known you wanted non-action material?

116 **Stallone:** What happened was everything came to a standstill. In other words, *no* scripts were forthcoming. It was like on a will-notify basis. Now good things are percolating, but it hasn't been a bombardment of material. What has happened is, thanks to being involved with these other world-class performers [in *Copland*], it has subdued the majority of the skepticism and has alleviated a great deal of the pressure of having to perform as a one-man band.

117 **Faludi:** A few years ago, you were quoted in *The New York Times* as saying, "I'm a stereotype. I can't break away from that." Now that you're making *Copland* and all, are you feeling more hopeful about breaking out?

118 **Stallone:** [*Laughs.*] No, I'm still a stereotype. I always will be. But at least I'd like to be a versatile stereotype. . . . If I can't break out, then . . . all I'm asking for is a stay of execution, a weekend pass!

119 **Faludi:** Why doesn't your audience want you to break out?

120 **Stallone:** Let me ask you something. Do you think holding me in a certain kind of film is the same perhaps as not wanting the hero to disappear? Do you think that's possible? That it's "Oh, my God. He's the last dinosaur. And now the last dinosaur has decided he wants to change? Forget it!"

121 What is really the greatest departure of *Copland* for Stallone is not that he is playing a character who is fat or is timid or doesn't make eye contact. It's that he's playing a character who, in the course of the movie, actually changes.

122   And it may be that the "dinosaur" action hero, like the average man facing the diminishing frontier, will have to do something even more difficult than shedding his armored musculature if he wants to discover a new identity. He'll also have to tune out all the clamoring voices, from the fans and the studios and the media, telling him he can't, and shouldn't, change.

123   **Faludi:** Is there any personal lesson you can draw from Freddy's transformation?

124   **Stallone:** Something happens that's symbolic in the movie. They shoot out his other eardrum. [Freddy is already deaf in one ear.] He no longer can hear ridicule. He can no longer hear scorn, jokes at his expense. He can no longer hear danger. And the only thing that he can hear—it's not the bullets. Finally, he's listening to his own voices.

125   **Faludi:** Is that what you are trying to do in a way—make yourself deaf to all those who want you to stay the muscleman?

126   **Stallone:** It is like a weird experiment with myself. But I think it's healthy, because it's frightening.

127   **Faludi:** Frightening?

128   **Stallone:** It's one thing to live in an illusion. It's another thing to act out an illusion and find out that you are not anywhere near the neighborhood you thought you'd be in. Living an illusion is, you sit there with a drink in your hand and say, "Oh, I could do that. Gimme a break—anybody could do that! You know why he's there? He has the material! Gimme the material, I would've been there." Okay, well, here's the material. Go.

129   **Faludi:** So this is a showdown with yourself, in a way.

130   **Stallone:** And I don't want anything that's beyond the realm of deservedness. I just want to be able to test myself, really. I don't have any delusions about having this giant revelation. The, oh, it's a New Man. But I think it's extremely important to try to change, and this isn't just true for me, it's true for every man, every waiter here [at the bar]. It's every man who has hit the wall, the "'Okay, is this it from now on? Is this my MO until my demise? Is this it?'" That's what's terrible. So whether it be on any scale, no matter how minute, I think you have to take a chance and put it all on one roll of the dice.

131   And maybe my doing it will be beneficial, in a way, to other men. I don't know, maybe that sounds ridiculous. But in that, if *I* can change, then . . .

132   **Faludi:** Anyone can change?

133   **Stallone:** And I could be delusional. I could. But I want to find that out. That's all.

134   **Faludi:** Delusional?

135   **Stallone:** Well, maybe things won't change. Maybe I'm not as versatile as I'd like to be, you know? But at least I'll know. I'll know. I think it's very important to look in the mirror and actually see the person that's staring back at you.

EXPLORING THE TEXT

1. Consider Sylvester Stallone's discussion of how the body affects the mind, especially his comments about public image, shame, and embarrassment. What are his attitudes? Is he always consistent?

2. How does Stallone define "masculine"? What does he mean when he discusses "alpha maleness"? List some of his film heroes and describe what it is that makes them particularly masculine by this definition.

3. What role does Stallone suggest he would now prefer to play. Why? What does he see as more desirable in this role? How does it compare to other roles he has played previously?

4. How does Stallone define "feminine"? What is the relationship between Stallone's ideas of masculine and feminine? How do these ideas relate to his description of acting as a feminine profession? How about his statements regarding personal image and vanity?

5. How does Stallone define the role of the hero? What relation does he see between hero and victim? In what way do his movie heroes fit or defy these distinctions?

6. Consider the interview format in this article. What would you say are some of the advantages and disadvantages to this kind of a format. What is the role of the interviewer? List the different kinds of questions Faludi asks in order to elicit certain responses from Stallone. What evidence is there in this text of Faludi's preparation for this interview? Discuss, then, what helps to make a good interview.

7. Though this is an interview, Faludi chooses to begin her discussion with a long prose passage written by her that includes her own observations; she repeats this strategy at two other points in the article. What is the effect of these interjected passages? What, specifically, does Faludi accomplish that she could not have accomplished had she stuck with the interview format? How do her comments influence how we read the interview passages?

WRITING ASSIGNMENTS

1. Early in the article, Faludi uses the word *carapace*. Look this word up in a good dictionary. Pointing to specific passages from throughout the text, discuss how carapace can be seen as a controlling metaphor for this article.

2. Susan Faludi interviews Sylvester Stallone about, among other things, his role as an action hero. Especially interesting in relation to Leonard Pitts's essay ("Hostages to Sexism") are Stallone's statements about men as "protectors." Find these statements and compare Stallone's ideas to Pitts's. You might even interject information from particular scenes in Stallone's action films. In what ways do these men agree? How do they disagree?

1. Stallone speaks of the importance of the images we construct and relates that idea to his action hero roles. Working with a small group of other students, test his definitions of masculine and feminine, of heroes as protectors, of victims. Choose one (or perhaps two) scenes from a Stallone movie and revise his character so that he conforms to one of the alternative models Stallone describes—change the clothes, the dialogue, various character details, the setting, the choreography, the music, etc. Present your revised movie role to the class, first offering a videotape of the scene being revised, then acting out the revised version.

2. Consider Stallone's ideas in the context of the broader culture. Do you agree that the day of the masculine hero is over? Where would one look to find an answer to this question? Where can you find the masculine as Stallone defines it? Working in a group, list places to look (publications, events, television, stores, entertainment spots, etc.) and things to look for (images, actions, speech, dress, etc.). Write a report on what you find and whether this supports Stallone's claim.

Redesigning Pocahontas
Gary Edgerton and Kathy Merlock Jackson

Disney. Childhood. America. These ideas are culturally bound together in most people's minds. For more than half a century, American kids have grown up on Walt Disney movies. A visit to one of the Disney theme parks constitutes an American family obligation for most people. Mickey Mouse is an ageless icon recognized in remote parts of the world. Disney is everywhere. In the essay below, Gary Edgerton and Kathy Merlock Jackson ask us to consider what happens when the Disney Studios decide to retell an important piece of American history—the story of Pocahontas and Captain John Smith. What kinds of images do they create? How do they define gender relationships? How do they present complex issues so that children can understand them? According to the authors, Disney seems less concerned with history than with entertainment and profit. As a result, a piece of America's past has been repackaged to fit preconceived notions and cultural stereotypes. And the impact, especially on children, is powerful.

Edgerton is a professor and chair of the Communications and Theatre Arts Department at Old Dominion University; Jackson is a professor and coordinator of communications at Virginia Wesleyan College. This article was first published in the *Journal of Popular Film and Television* in the summer of 1996.

It is a story that is fundamentally about racism and intolerance and we hope that people will gain a greater understanding of themselves and of the world around them. It's also about having respect for each other's cultures.

—Thomas Schumacher, senior vice president of Disney Feature Animation
(*Pocahontas* 35)

The challenge was how to do a movie with such themes and make it interesting, romantic, fun. —Peter Schneider, president of Disney Feature Animation (*Pocahontas* 37)

1   Thomas Schumacher and Peter Schneider are two of the key executives who have
re-established the Walt Disney Company as the premier animation studio in Hollywood. Schneider, in particular, became president of Disney Feature Animation in
1985, and since that time has assembled a coterie of first-rate talent and guided the
division to a level of unprecedented success, boasting a lineup of recent productions
that now includes *The Little Mermaid* (1989), *Beauty and the Beast* (1991), *Aladdin*
(1992), *The Lion King* (1994), and *Pocahontas* (1995). Disney is the film industry's
exemplar for creating blockbuster motion pictures, fueling the releases with highly
sophisticated advertising and marketing campaigns, and then maximizing profit by
licensing literally hundreds of ancillary products. For example, the film *The Lion
King* and its merchandise have already grossed an estimated $2 billion worldwide
(Biskind 81). With each subsequent feature, Disney executives try to equal or top
their last success.

2   Disney executives and animators had a related, though secondary, goal with
Pocahontas, however. They wanted to address the rise in public criticism from various ethnic groups over racial stereotyping in their most recent productions. Arab
American groups, for instance, protested against certain imagery and lyrics in
Aladdin (Kim 24; Sharkey 22). African American critics similarly pointed out that
the three hooligan hyenas in *The Lion King* were thinly disguised black and Hispanic characters who seemed to be living in a jungle equivalent of an inner-city
ghetto (Sharkey 22). Disney executives understood from the outset that *Pocahontas*
could be similarly problematic for the studio and planned to be more careful and
sensitive in designing the film's portrayal of Native Americans.

3   The genesis of *Pocahontas* actually came from the eventual co-director, Mike
Gabriel, who was trying to initiate a new project after finishing *The Rescuers Down
Under* in 1990. He wanted to do a western, "a big scale epic that would lend itself to
the kind of Broadway-oriented animated musicals that Disney had recently reinvigorated" (*Pocahontas* 36). Peter Schneider, for his part, had been considering an animated version of *Romeo and Juliet* for several years. The two seemingly disparate
ideas merged for Gabriel when "somehow the name Pocahontas came into my mind
. . . everyone knew the tale about her saving John Smith's life and it seemed like a
natural for telling a story about two separate clashing worlds trying to understand
each other" (*Pocahontas* 36). The Pocahontas narrative also furnished source material that could easily conform to the coming-of-age and romantic dictates of the Disney formula, as well as provide a spunky heroine as protagonist in the mold of Ariel
in *The Little Mermaid,* Belle in *Beauty and the Beast,* and Jasmine in *Aladdin.*

4   Within this conventional framework, then, the talent at Disney Feature Animation began shaping its portrayals. Writers Carl Binder, Susannah Grant, and Philip
LaZebnik drafted a script, while 12 interrelated teams of animators started experi-

mental sketches of the characters and setting. Supervising animator Glen Keane journeyed to Tidewater, Virginia, hiring a number of local Native American consultants to advise his production team. Native American performers, moreover, were cast to provide the voices and characterizations for the main American Indian roles, including former American Indian Movement activist-turned-actor Russell Means, who would play Chief Powhatan, Pocahontas's father. The Walt Disney Company was apparently making all the appropriate and necessary preparations for an elaborate update of the Native American on film.

The "Hollywood Indian"

5 The "Hollywood Indian" is a well-established image that has appeared on movie screens around the world for nearly a century. The parameters of the stereotype are already outlined in a handful of useful studies (Bataille and Silet; Friar and Friar; Marsden and Nachbar; O'Connor). These analyses focus on representative types and traits, furnishing us with a composite that is deeply conflicted and contradictory, as is the case of most racial, ethnic, and gender stereotypes. In the essay "The Indians in the Movies" in *Handbook of North American Indians,* Michael T. Marsden and Jack Nachbar described the cultural context of captivity narratives, dime novels, stage melodramas, and Wild West shows, all of which contributed to the film industry's rendition of the Native American. They also offer a three-part model of American Indian characterizations on film, in which men compose the first two stereotypes, as either "noble anachronisms" or "savage reactionaries," and women are presented as "Indian princesses" in the third, if they are presented on-screen at all.[1]

6 In this respect, Disney's *Pocahontas* (dir. Mike Gabriel and Eric Goldberg) promised to be an intriguing departure from the usual, male-centered storyline, as well as the general portrayal of American Indians. As the epigraphs suggest, the company's executives stressed a seriousness of purpose not usually connected with one of their animated pictures. For Roy Disney, Walt Disney's nephew and the board member who supervises the Feature Animation Division, "*Pocahontas* is a story that appealed to us because it was basically a story about people getting along together . . . which is particularly applicable to lots of places in the world today" (*Pocahontas* 33). Schneider confirmed, "It is an important message to a generation to stop fighting, stop killing each other because of the color of your skin" (*Pocahontas* 37).

7 Disney publicists asserted that "in every aspect of the storytelling, the filmmakers tried to treat Pocahontas with the respect she deserved and present a balanced and informed view of the Native American culture" (*Pocahontas* 34). Producer James Pentecost added, "We also tried to tap into [Pocahontas's] spirituality and the spirituality of the Native Americans, especially in the way they relate to nature" (*Pocahontas* 33). Finally, Russell Means conferred a much-welcomed imprimatur:

> When I first read the script, I was impressed with the beginning of the film. In fact, I was overwhelmed by it. It tells the truth about the motives for Europeans initially coming to the so-called New World. I find it astounding that Americans and the Disney Studios are willing to tell the truth. (*Pocahontas* 34)

8   Given the intentions voiced by the makers of *Pocahontas,* we intend in this article to examine the representation of Native Americans in the film, analyzing selected images, words, and sounds for their ideological content, particularly as they
reflect points of view on race, gender, and social position. We assume that this
newest version of the Pocahontas story resides in the fusion of movie and merchandise, generating a kind of cultural supertext that clearly has been a huge financial
success for the Walt Disney Company on a global scale. We will next survey critical
and corporate responses to the film, reflecting on those reactions as telling indicators of mainstream and alternative viewpoints toward Native Americans today, and
we will conclude with suggestions on how to use *Pocahontas* as a teaching tool in
our homes and classrooms.

The Disney Version

> You have to approach it carefully. The Disney version becomes the definitive
> version. —Glen Keane (qtd. in Gleiberman 42)
>   Three things are inevitable in 1995: death, taxes, and Disney's *Pocahon-
> tas.* —Pat H. Broeske (8)

9   When Disney began marketing *Pocahontas* nearly five months before the film's
eventual release, conventional wisdom in Hollywood alleged that the film could
never approach the money-making performance of *The Lion King.* Insiders carped
about the historical nature of the subject matter, and, more disturbingly, the so-
called "girl factor." "Boys won't want to go to a girl picture" (Shapiro and Chang
57). What the rumor mill in the film industry underscored, of course, is how out-of-
proportion Hollywood expectations are in the 1990s. To date, *Pocahontas*'s box-
office and merchandising proceeds are still described as modest when compared to
those of *The Lion King,* which with *E.T.* (1982) and *Jurassic Park* (1993) is one of
the three most-profitable films of all time. On the other hand, *Pocahontas* has already generated over $1 billion in revenues on an $80 million investment (a $55
million production budget and $25 million for advertising and marketing), and its
total earnings just keep on mounting (Walt Disney Company Annual Report, 1995:
13, 31, 50).

10   Disney's campaign to sell *Pocahontas* began on 3 February 1995 with a 24-city
mall display, complete with an animation kiosk where shoppers could electronically
paint a cel from the film and view a 26-foot model of John Smith's ship. The promotional juggernaut continued that spring with dozens of tie-ins; for example,
Burger King distributed 55 million toy replicas of the film's characters with kids'
meals, Payless Shoes featured a line of moccasins, and Mattel peddled a Barbie-like
Pocahontas doll (Broeske 8). No doubt the most effective technique was attaching a
Pocahontas trailer to the March release of *The Lion King* on home video, one which
retailed 20 million units in just six days and ended by shattering all existing records,
with more than 50 million tapes sold by year's end (Walt Disney Company Annual
Report, 1995: 19).

11   Disney's marketing of *Pocahontas* peaked with a highly publicized 10 June premiere in New York's Central Park on four, eight-story-high screens, before 110,000 spectators. This extravaganza was not only covered amply by the print and electronic news media, but it was also telecast live as programming on the newly launched United Paramount Network. *Pocahontas* eventually earned $91 million in its first four weeks of domestic release and became a certifiable blockbuster by reaping more than $300 million at film theaters worldwide during the remainder of 1995 (Kilday and Thompson 28–29).

12   All told, *Pocahontas* entered the American mainstream during the spring and summer of 1995 to share space with O. J. Simpson, *Batman Forever,* Hootie and the Blowfish, and a handful of other high-profile popular cultural phenomena. Fashioned within the no-holds-barred commercial milieu of the Walt Disney Company, this animated feature erupted into the public sphere as the focal point of a massively successful advertising and marketing offensive. The film's storyline and characters were soon adapted into other media and provided the basis for an assortment of other widely retailed products, generating additional sales and promotions. Pocahontas, the 400-year-old legend, was expertly redesigned to Disney's usual specifications—meaning a full-length animated feature with a host of commodity tie-ins—thus becoming the version of the Pocahontas story that most people recognize today.

Don't Know Much About History

> Moviemakers shouldn't be handcuffed when using real stories as jumping-off places for works of entertainment. —James Pentecost (Kim 24)
>   We never wanted to do a docu-drama, but something that was inspired by legend. —Peter Schneider (*Pocahontas* 37)

13   Representatives of the Walt Disney Company inadvertently alienated their chief Native American consultant, Shirley "Little Dove" Custalow McGowan, by sending her mixed signals about the kind of guidance they were seeking from her. Co-director Eric Goldberg, for example, remembers how "we met with surviving members of the Algonquin nation in Virginia and realized that it would be fascinating to show their culture in our film. We wanted to be as faithful as possible" (*Pocahontas* 34). In response, Custalow McGovern recalls

> I was honored to be asked by them . . . but I wasn't at the studio two hours before I began to make clear my objections to what they were doing . . . they had said that the film would be historically accurate. I soon found that it wasn't to be. . . . I wish my name wasn't on it. I wish Pocahontas' name wasn't on it. (Vincent, Disney E5)

14   The filmmakers at Disney never really intended *Pocahontas* to be historically accurate, despite all the sentimental rhetoric; they were producing yet another animated feature after all. Native American advisors were hired to secure a more positive, even hagiographic, portrayal of Native American characters within an earnestly sympathetic narrative. Studio executives were, therefore, banking on the likelihood that a postmodern restyling of Pocahontas and her legend would also be an im-

mensely popular and profitable version for audiences in the mid-1990s. They were, moreover, attempting to favorably affect public opinion regarding "Disney's America," a historical theme park planned for Northern Virginia, which was subsequently abandoned.

15   Artists and authors have actually been reshaping Pocahontas and her history for nearly four centuries. In *Pocahontas: Her Life and Legend,* William M. S. Rasmussen and Robert S. Tilton surveyed literally dozens of depictions, beginning during Pocahontas's lifetime, when she was "living proof that American natives could be Christianized and civilized" (7). Fact and fiction were blended at the outset into this legendary personality who symbolized friendly and advantageous relations between American Indians and English settlers from a distinctly Anglo-American point of view. Disney's animators are merely part of that longer tradition, the latest in a series of storytellers, painters, poets, sculptors, and commercial artists who have taken liberties with Pocahontas's historical record for their own purposes (Rasmussen and Tilton).

16   Disney's *Pocahontas* is, once again, a parable of assimilation, although this time the filmmakers hinted at a change in outlook. Producer James Pentecost for instance reported that

> "Colors of the Wind" perhaps best sums up the entire spirit and essence of the film . . . this song was written before anything else. It set the tone of the movie and defined the character of Pocahontas. Once Alan [Menken] and Stephen [Schwartz] wrote that song, we knew what the film was about. (*Pocahontas* 51–52)

Schwartz agreed with Pentecost, adding that his lyrics were inspired by Chief Seattle's famous speech to the United States Congress that challenged white ascendancy in America and the appropriation of American Indian lands (*Pocahontas* 52).

17   "Colors of the Wind" functions as a rousing anthem for *Pocahontas,* extolling the virtues of tolerance, cross-cultural sensitivity, and respect for others and the natural environment:

> You think you own whatever land you land on
> The earth is just a dead thing you can claim
> But I know ev'ry rock and tree and creature
> Has a life, has a spirit, has a name
> You think the only people who are people
> Are the people who think and look like you
> But if you walk the footsteps of a stranger
> You'll learn things you never knew
> You never knew.

These lofty sentiments, however, are down-played by the film's overriding commitment to romantic fantasy. Pocahontas, for example, sings "Colors of the Wind" in response to John Smith's remark that her people are "savages," but the rest of the technically stirring sequence plays more like an adolescent seduction than a lesson teaching Smith those "things [he] never knew [he] never knew."

18   Pocahontas's search for her "dream," a classic Disney plot device, is a case in point. A great deal of dramatic energy is spent on Pocahontas's finding her "true path." She is sprightly, though troubled, in her conversations with Grandmother Willow. She is struggling with her own youthful uncertainties as well as her father's very definite plans for her:

> Should I choose the smoothest course
> Steady as a beating drum
> Should I marry Kocoum
> Is all my dreaming at an end?
> Or do you still wait for me, dreamgiver
> Just around the river bend?

Unsure of Kocoum, but regarding love and marriage as her own options, Pocahontas finally finds her answer in John Smith.

19   What this development discloses, of course, is the conventional viewpoint of the filmmakers: Pocahontas essentially falls in love with the first white man she sees. The film's scriptwriters chose certain episodes from her life, invented others, and in the process shaped a narrative that highlights some events, ideas, and values, while suppressing others. The historical Pocahontas and John Smith were never lovers; she was 12 and he was 27 when they met in 1607. In relying so completely on their romantic coupling, however, Disney's animators minimize the many challenging issues that they raise—racism, colonialism, environmentalism, and spiritual alienation.

20   The entire plot structure is similarly calculated to support the Disney game plan. The film begins in London in 1607 with John Smith and the Virginia Company crew setting out for the New World, and it concludes with Smith's return trip to England in 1609, although the duration of the movie seems to span weeks rather than years. The scriptwriters, nevertheless, terminate the narrative at the most expedient juncture, avoiding the more tragic business of Pocahontas's kidnapping by the English; her isolation from her people for a year; her ensuing conversion to Christianity; her marriage and name change to Lady Rebecca Rolfe; and her untimely death from tuberculosis at age 21 in England (Barbour; Fritz; Mossiker; Woodward). Disney's filmmakers did, in fact, research those details of Pocahontas's life before starting production, but obviously their aim was to keep audiences as comfortable as possible by providing a predictable product.

21   Co-director Eric Goldberg later claimed that "it's important for us as filmmakers to be able to say not everything was entirely hunky-dory by the end . . . which it usually is in a traditionally Disneyesque movie" (Mallory 24). Given the eventual fate of Pocahontas and the Algonquins, though, Disney's animators could hardly have opted for the usual "happily ever after" finale. The filmmakers, after all, were genuinely trying to offend no one, including the Native American community and their consultants.

22   *Pocahantas*'s climactic sequence further establishes the film's dominant, love-story narrative, albeit with some variations of the classic Disney formula. After En-

glish settler Thomas shoots and kills Kocoum, tensions between the American Indians and the British mount. John Smith is captured by Kocoum's companions, blamed for his death, and immediately slated for execution. In a replay of the legendary rescue scene, Pocahontas risks her life to save John Smith, catalyzing peace between the English and the American Indians. In the process, the film's animators and scriptwriters complete their upgrade of the Indian princess characterization by making Pocahontas more assertive, determined to realize her "dream," and according to her father, "wis[e] beyond her years."

23   The film, moreover, concludes with Pocahontas standing alone on a rocky summit, watching the ship carrying a wounded John Smith sail for England. She has presumably resolved to stay behind in Virginia and take her rightful place alongside her father as a peacemaker, even though her actions in the previous 80 minutes of the film suggest that her "path" lies elsewhere. *Pocahontas* thus reinforces another resilient stereotype that the main purpose of a Disney heroine is to further the interests of love, notwithstanding the bittersweet coda. Pocahontas's newfound ambition to become a mediator, then, is a workable if somewhat disingenuous solution, especially considering the latent historical realities percolating beneath this romantic plotline.

24   The questions then arise: Can a Disney animated feature be substantive as well as entertaining? Can race, gender, and the rest of *Pocahontas*'s postmodernist agenda be presented in a thought-provoking way that still works for the animation audience, especially children? We believe the answer is yes, but we also believe the studio has an obligation to create a more forward-looking alternative to existing stereotypes and to deal more fully and maturely with the serious issues and charged imagery that it addresses.

25   Consider the redesigning of the character of Pocahontas. Supervising animator Glen Keane remembered how former studio chairman Jeffrey Katzenberg charged him with reshaping Pocahontas as "the finest creature the human race has to offer" (Kim 24). He also admitted, "I don't want to say a rut, but we've been doing mainly Caucasian faces" (Cochran 24). Keane, in turn, drew on four successive women for inspiration, beginning with paintings of Pocahontas herself; then Native American consultant Shirley "Little Dove" Custalow McGowan; then 21-year-old Filipino model Dyna Taylor; and finally white supermodel Christy Turlington (Cochran 24). After studio animators spent months sketching her, their Pocahontas emerged as a multicultural pastiche. They started with Native American faces but eventually gravitated to the more familiar and Anglicized looks of the statuesque Turlington. Not surprisingly, all the key decision makers and supervising artists on *Pocahontas* were white males. Disney and Keane's "finest creature" clearly is the result of very conventional viewpoint.

26   Accordingly, what of avoiding old stereotypes? Native American actors were cast in all the native roles in the film; still, Pocahontas's screen image is less American Indian than fashionably exotic. Many critics, for example *Newsweek*'s Laura Shapiro, refer to the makeover as "Native American Barbie" (Shapiro and Chang 77)—in other words, Indian features, such as Pocahontas's eyes, skin color, and wardrobe, only provide a kind of Native American styling to an old stereotype.

The British colonists also replace the Indians as stock villains in *Pocahontas,* with Governor Ratcliffe, in particular, singing about gold, riches, and power in the appropriately titled song "Mine, Mine, Mine." The film's final impression, therefore, is that, with Ratcliffe bound, gagged, and headed back to England, American Indians and Europeans are now free to coexist peacefully. Race is a dramatic or stylistic device, but the more profound consequences of institutional racism are never allowed even momentarily to invade the audience's comfort zone.

27   Perhaps the Disney studio should trust its patrons more. Fairy tales and fantasies have traditionally challenged children (and adults) with the unpleasant realities lurking just beneath their placid exteriors. Audiences are likely to enjoy added depth and suggestiveness enough to buy plenty of tickets and merchandise. Disney's *Pocahontas* raises important issues but does not fully address them; it succeeds as a king-sized commercial vehicle, but fails as a half-hearted revision.

> The meaning of a text is always the site of a struggle. —Lawrence Grossberg (86)
>
> History is always interpreted. I'm not saying this film is accurate, but it is a start. I grew up being called Pocahontas as a derogatory term. They hissed that name at me, as if it was something dirty. Now, with this film, Pocahontas can reach a larger culture as a heroine. No, it doesn't make up for 500 years of genocide, but it is a reminder that we will have to start telling our own stories. —Irene Bedard (qtd. in Vincent E5)

28   The comments of Irene Bedard, the Native American actress who plays the voice of Pocahontas, augment many of the critical responses that surfaced after the release of *Pocahontas* in the summer of 1995. She offers audiences some valuable insights into the Native American perspective, especially with her painful recollection of being ridiculed with the surprising taunt, "Pocahontas." As she says, this film signals a welcomed counterbalance to such insults; most significantly, she calls for the emergence and development of a truly American Indian cinema that is the next needed step for fundamentally improving depictions of Native Americans on film.

29   Until that time, however, we can extend our understanding of *Pocahontas,* in particular, and established and alternative views toward Indian people in general, by examining the spectrum of critical reactions that the animated film engendered. The most striking aspect of *Pocahontas*'s critical reception is the contradictory nature of the responses: the film is alternately described as progressive or escapist, enlightened or racist, feminist or retrograde—depending on the critic. Inherently fraught with contradictions, Disney's *Pocahontas* sends an abundance of mixed messages, which probably underscores the limits of reconstructing the Native American image at Disney or, perhaps, any other major Hollywood studio that operates first and foremost as a marketer of conventional dreams and a seller of related consumer products.

30   As teachers, critics, parents, or students of popular culture, we can usefully extend the scope of our examinations of *Pocahontas* by studying the various critical communities that have engaged the Disney version with their own unique perspectives. These additional points of view help to illuminate not only what *Pocahontas* presented directly—such as mainstream representations of race and gender—but also what it underplayed or ignored—such as peripheral outlooks on those issues or the historical reality underlying the legend.

31   The Native Americans who worked on the film—such as Russell Means, the voice of Powhatan, and Irene Bedard—generally commended it. Means specifically called it "the single finest work ever done on American Indians by Hollywood" (*Pocahontas* 34). His comments especially drew fire from the Native American press, where a number of both columnists and readers who sent letters to the editor wondered if the former head of the American Indian Movement had "sold out to the white man and his money" (Rattler D1). Means's pronouncements evidently became a source of controversy in the debate that highlights the competing conceptions of American "Indian-ness" that co-exist in contemporary America.

32   A valuable place to start the discussion on *Pocahontas* is Robert Berkhofer Jr.'s seminal work *The White Man's Indian: Images of the American Indian from Columbus to the Present*. This insightful analysis underscores that the dominant view of Native Americans has always originated with Euro-American culture, reflecting Anglicized attitudes and preferences and ultimately pushing native perspectives to the margins of society, if not entirely out of view. Disney's *Pocahontas* is thus another example of the "white man's Indian," mostly because the studio was only willing to partially incorporate its consultants' advice. Berkhofer's book can also be supplemented with Daniel Francis's *The Imaginary Indian: The Image of the Indian in Canadian Culture,* which again emphasizes how most popular representations of Native Americans are the products of white needs, intentions, and purposes.

33   *Pocahontas* is, moreover, a text in which the issues of race and gender intersect. Bedard found herself at odds with several Native American women writers when she remarked, "When I was growing up, I wanted so much to be Barbie. Now, some little girl might want to be Pocahontas. That's a step in the right direction" (Vincent E5). Martina Whelsula and Faith Spotted Eagle countered Bedard's sentiment in their review of the film in the Spokane *Review-Perspective,* reprinted in *Indian Country Today*. They stated that Disney's *Pocahontas* is "part of Barbie culture. A culture that relies on sexism, capitalism and lookism . . . where a woman is elevated only on her appearance . . . where a heroine lives only for approval from men" (D1).

34   This flashpoint again supplies a productive basis on which to encourage discussion on the social construction of beauty standards and race. From it can be gained a sense of the profound distress that is still elicited in the native community by the longstanding traditions of the "Hollywood Indian." Even Disney's relatively benign portrayal prompted consultant Shirley "Little Dove" Custalow McGowan to say her "heart sorrowed" upon first seeing the film (Silver 61). Two letters to the editor of *Indian Country Today* likewise expressed dismay and anger, especially about Disney's use of the song "Savages," which the authors found highly offensive (Letters D2). University of Texas anthropologist Pauline Turner Strong aptly explains the reasons behind such a reaction when she writes that

> for many Native Americans "savage" is the "S" word, as potent and degrading as the word "nigger." I cannot imagine the latter epithet repeated so often, and set to music in a G-rated film and its soundtrack. It is even more shocking to write it in a review. Is "savage" more acceptable because it is used reciprocally? But then does this not downplay the role the colonial ideology of savagism played in the extermination and dispossession of indigenous people? (Strong, H-Net)

35   The portrayal of the English in *Pocahontas* similarly triggered outrage in the British press. The 30 July 1995 *Times,* for instance, referred to Pocahontas as

> history's most famous squaw. . . . The English are thugs, all greed, gold, and guns, and they treat natives like savages. The Indians, by contrast, are civilized, peace-loving and eco-conscious. The animators have significantly made the Redskins look pretty much like modern paleface Americans, and speak like them, too. . . . Disney's fable of an arcadian American history wrecked by incursions from the Old World is obviously a means of allaying a bad conscience, while voicing xenophobic resentments about corrupt Europeans. (Adair 9)

Evidently the shoe is now on the other foot, and this symbolic inversion can lead to a fruitful exchange about multiculturalism and the function of stock villainy in popular film. As Betsy Sharkey writes in the *New York Times,* "British males seem to be one of the few safe villains in these politically correct times" (22). Paying attention to such cues can produce striking illustrations of intercultural differences in perspective, allowing us all to "learn [some] things [we] never knew [we] never knew."

36   The majority of America's mainstream press coverage also concentrated on *Pocahontas*'s racial and gender depictions, along with instances in which the film differed from the historical record. On one hand, Caryn James of the *New York Times* called *Pocahontas* "a sharp revision of the classic Disney fairy tale formula . . . [and] a model of how smartly those elements can be reinvigorated." She, moreover, viewed Pocahontas as "the most subversive heroine in the Disney canon" (F1). In contrast, Owen Gleiberman of *Entertainment Weekly* provided a more scathing, albeit glib, description:

> Pocahontas herself has been conceived as a strapping, high-cheek-boned update of the usual Disney Princess—she's an aerobicized Native American superbabe, with long, muscular brown legs, regal shoulder blades, and silky black hair flowing down to her waist. With her vacuous Asian doll eyes, she looks ready to host *Pocahontas' House of Style.* (42)

37   Mal Vincent of the *Virginian-Pilot* and *Ledger-Star* (of Norfolk) concurred with James that " 'Pocahontas' is a signal that Disney animators are willing to take new, and daring, risks" (Vincent, Pocahontas E2). David Sterritt of the *Christian Science Monitor* disagreed, saying that Disney is

> clinging to formulas that refuse to grow in any but superficial ways. True enough, "Pocahontas" tips its hat to such trendy (and worthy) causes as conservation and environmentalism, and even delivers a hearty endorsement of interracial dating. Yet the studio can hardly be congratulated for "taking a stand" on socially relevant issues, since it's careful to wrap its ideas in an aura of nostalgic fantasy that neutralizes their ability to challenge or stimulate us. (13)

Whether "subversive" or sexist, "daring" or reactionary, *Pocahontas* is a deeply conflicted text.

38   Finally, *Pocahontas*'s widespread popularity has produced a corresponding upsurge in interest in the historical Pocahontas and in Native Americans. After the release of *Pocahontas* in June 1995, admissions to the Jamestown Settlement rose 60

percent over those of July 1994 (Holland), eventually reaching 38 percent more than the average for the previous five summers (Renewed 3). Although other factors contributed to Jamestown's increased tourism, such as various marketing strategies and the 400th anniversary celebration of the birth of Pocahontas, the Disney film contributed greatly to the upturn.

39   In the words of one Jamestown historical interpreter, tourists are "coming here to learn. I've been pleasantly surprised at how much parental concern there is for children getting more than was shown in the movie" (Renewed 3). *Pocahontas* can be used as a springboard to encourage our students and children to look beyond the movie and the merchandise. Jean Fritz's young adult history, *The Double Life of Pocahontas,* is a wonderful place to start for adolescents. The informative books Philip Barbour's *Pocahontas and Her World,* William Rasmussen and Robert Tilton's *Pocahontas: Her Life and Legend,* and Robert Tilton's *Pocahontas: The Evolution of an American Narrative* and the 1995 half-hour documentary *Pocahontas: Ambassador of the New World* (A Perpetual Motions Production for the A&E Television Network) are other rewarding alternatives to the ubiquitous Disney version.

Notes

1. In the first category, a "noble anachronism" embodies Rousseau's notion of "natural man and his inherent goodness," who is ultimately doomed by the onslaught of Euro-American culture. Second, a "savage reactionary" confronts white manifest destiny with violent defiance but is also annihilated for the overall good of advancing civilization. Lastly, an "Indian princess" is rooted in the legend of Pocahontas. She is typically maidenly, demure, and deeply committed to some white man—for example, John Smith in the case of *Pocahontas.*
2. Keane was the animation supervisor for *Pocahontas.*

Works Cited

Adair, Gilbert. "Animating History." (London) *Sunday Times* 30 July 1995: 10.

Barbour, Philip L. *Pocahontas and Her World.* Boston: Houghton Mifflin, 1970.

Bataille, G., and C. Silet, eds. *The Pretend Indians: Images of Native Americans in the Movies.* Ames: Iowa State UP, 1980.

Berkhofer, Robert, Jr. *The White Man's Indian: Images of the American Indian from Columbus to the Present.* New York: Vintage, 1979.

Biskind, Peter. "Win, Lose—But Draw." *Premiere* July 1995: 81+.

Broeske, Pat H. "The Pocamotion: Promotion of Walt Disney's 'Pocahontas.' " *Entertainment Weekly* 5 Feb. 1995: 8.

Cochran, Jason. "What Becomes a Legend Most?" *Entertainment Weekly* 16 June 1995: 42.

Francis, Daniel. *The Imaginary Indian: The Image of the Indian in Canadian Culture.* Vancouver: Arsenal Pulp, 1992.

Friar, R., and N. Friar. *The Only Good Indian . . . The Hollywood Gospel.* New York: Drama Book Specialists, 1972.

Fritz, Jean. *The Double Life of Pocahontas.* New York: Puffin, 1983.

Gleiberman, Owen. "Disney's Indian Corn." *Entertainment Weekly* 16 June 1995: 42.

Grossberg, Lawrence. "Reply to the Critics." *Critical Studies in Mass Communication* 3 (1983): 86–95.

Holland, Erik. Telephone interview. Jamestown Settlement Interpreter Program Manager and Supervisor, Powhatan Village. 2 Oct. 1995.

James, Caryn. "Belle and Ariel Never Chose Duty Over Love." *New York Times* 18 June 1995: F1.

Kilday, Gregg, and Anne Thompson. "To Infinity and Beyond." *Entertainment Weekly* 2 Feb. 1996: 27–32.

Kim, Albert. "Whole New World?" *Entertainment Weekly* 23 June 1995: 22–25.

"Letters to the Entertainment Editor." *Indian Country Today* 6 July 1995: D2.

Mallory, Michael. "American History Makes Animation History." *The Disney Magazine* Spring 1995: 22–24.

Marsden, Michael T., and Jack Nachbar. "The Indians in the Movies." *Handbook of North American Indians.* Washington, D.C.: Smithsonian Institution, 1988.

Mossiker, Frances. *Pocahontas.* New York: Knopf, 1976.

O'Connor, J. *The Hollywood Indian: Stereotypes of Native Americans in Films.* Trenton: New Jersey State Museum, 1980.

"*Pocahontas:* Press Kit." Burbank: Walt Disney Pictures, 1995.

Rasmussen, William M. S., and Robert S. Tilton. *Pocahontas: Her Life and Legend.* Richmond: Virginia Historical Society, 1994.

Rattler, Terri. "Letters to the Entertainment Editor: Do We Teach History or Fiction to our Children?" *Indian Country Today* 6 July 1995: D1.

"Renewed National Interest in Pocahontas Has Impact at Jamestown Settlement." *Jamestown-Yorktown Foundation Dispatch* Fall 1995: 3.

Shapiro, Laura, and Yahlin Chang. "The Girls of Summer." *Newsweek* 22 May 1995: 56–57.

Sharkey, Betsy. "Beyond Teepees and Totem Poles." *New York Times* 11 June 1995: 2:1, 22.

Silver, Mark. "*Pocahontas* for Real." *U.S. News & World Report* 19 June 1995: 61.

Sterritt, David. "'Pocahontas' Doesn't Stray Far From Disney Game Plan." *The Christian Science Monitor* 23 June 1995: 13.

Strong, Pauline Turner. Rev. of *Pocahontas.* Online posting. Popular Culture and American Culture Associations/H-Net Discussion List. 30 June 1995. Availability: [H-PCAACA@msu.edu].

Tilton, Robert S. *Pocahontas: The Evolution of an American Narrative.* Cambridge: Cambridge UP, 1994.

Vincent, Mal. "Disney vs. History . . . Again." *Virginia-Pilot* and *Ledger-Star* 20 June 1995: E1, E5.

———. "'Pocahontas': Discarding the History, It's still a Terrific Show." *Virginian-Pilot* and *Ledger-Star* 24 June 1995: E1–E2.

Whelshula, Martina, and Faith Spotted Eagle. "Pocahontas Rates an 'F' in Indian Country." *Indian Country Today* 6 July 1995: D1–2.

Woodward, Grace Steele. *Pocahontas.* Norman: U of Oklahoma P, 1969.

EXPLORING THE TEXT

1. Consider the epigraph placed at the beginning of this article. Have the goals been met? Does the statement provide an accurate description of the movie?

2. Edgerton and Jackson call *Pocahontas* a "parable of assimilation" (paragraph 16). What do the authors mean by this? In what ways does *Pocahontas* fit that model?

3. Edgerton and Jackson raise central questions: "Can a Disney animated feature be substantive as well as entertaining? Can race, gender, and the rest of

Pocahontas's postmodernist agenda be presented in a thought-provoking way that still works for the animation audience, especially children? (paragraph 24)" What do they mean by "postmodernist agenda"? What are the issues these questions raise? What are the arguments on each side of the debate? What social positions do the different sides represent (progressive, racist) according to the authros?

4. Discuss the historical realities the authors describe and the changes incorporated into the film. How does the Disney version change the historically verifiable story? What are the effects of these changes on the audience?

5. Describe the elements of romantic fantasy incorporated into the Disney story. How do they help to define Pocahontas as a female character? What role does race play in this romance? Do these romantic fantasy elements work against her being defined as a strong female? Explain your answer.

6. Consider the politics of language as revealed in this essay: Edgerton and Jackson use the term *Native American* instead of *Indian*. What does it mean that this choice was made? What are the issues surrounding such a choice?

7. Look at the title and discuss its influence on how we read this essay. How do the epigraphs that begin each section influence how we interpret the information that follows? Look at particular examples and discuss in detail.

WRITING ASSIGNMENTS

1. Consider the information here about how one might construct an idea of how a person should look. Consider Katzenberg's request (paragraph 25) that Pocahontas be "the finest creature the human race has to offer" in light of the "exotic" image the Disney people created. What is the relationship between exotic and normal? Do the authors use *exotic* in the same way you would use the word? What does it mean that this choice was made? Given the choice, create an argument of what the film is actually saying about image.

2. Research the history of Pocahontas and other contacts between colonials and Native Americans. Compare (and contrast) the information you uncover with the "history" presented in the movie. Based on the changes incorporated, what can you conclude are the film's primary concerns? How do they differ from the concerns of historians?

3. This movie tells the story of an interracial love affair. Consider another film with a similar focus (e.g., *Jungle Fever* or *West Side Story*). What do different characters in each film have to say about the issues of race and romance? How might different audiences be said to influence each film's ultimate statement on this issue?

4. Sylvester Stallone's ideas about heroes and body image ("The Masculine Mystique: An Interview of Sylvester Stallone"), as well as his discussion about the hero as "protector," relate to ideas raised in the Leonard Pitts article on female action heroes and Gary Edgerton and Kathy Merlock Jack-

son's discussion of Pocahontas as female hero. Identify the various points at which these discussions overlap and write a comparison of the various points of view offered.

GROUP PROJECTS

1. This essay refers to the "Hollywood Indian" as a recognizable type. Working in small groups, brainstorm a list of Indians from as many movies as you can recall (don't forget other Disney movies). Recalling specific scenes, images, and language, compile a list of traits we might identify as belonging to this Hollywood type. Make another list of Native American characters who do not fit into this type and some of their characteristics. What conclusions can you draw about Hollywood attitudes toward Native Americans? Can you identify any trends or changes in attitude? What factors, including those outside of Hollywood, might be influencing such trends or changes?

2. Working with others who have seen Disney films, see if you can create a definition of the Disney heroine as a "type" (or, in the alternative, argue that there is no such thing as a typical Disney heroine). To do this, your group should work together to list as many Disney heroines as you can recall—animated and live action—and make a list of how they look (especially purely constructed animated images), what they say, how they interact with other characters, and other film elements that help to define these heroines. What similarities do you see between these female characters? What differences? How important are these elements in defining each heroine?

Silencing of the Feminine
Lynn Dornink

Throughout this chapter you can read how professional authors, scholars, and critics have responded to a variety of films. But how should you, as a student, respond to a film? Like other authors in this chapter, Lynn Dornink has chosen to look at a film with a central female character and to critically evaluate how this character has been created—by her actions, her words, and how other characters respond to her. Like the professional authors, Dornink makes her argument by focusing on the details of the film itself and relying on her own knowledge of people to create her argument. And Dornink takes a powerful stand. She argues against the common view that Clarice Starling, protagonist of the highly popular Academy Award–winning film, *Silence of the Lambs,* represents a positive and powerful female image—the kind of image other authors advocate. Rather, on close analysis Dornink finds a strong antifemale slant to the film's details—and she offers compelling evidence for her interpretation.

Dornink wrote this paper for a film course while a student at Northeastern University. It has been revised for this text.

1   In her acceptance speech for best actress for her role in *Silence of the Lambs* (1991), Jodie Foster thanked the academy and the public for embracing Clarice Starling, the strong feminist heroine she played. With its triumphant and self-sufficient female FBI agent, the film was widely seen as offering a much-needed revision of the terrorized woman saved by the strong male formula. Yet a close examination of the film's visual elements reveals some disturbing gender constructions, particularly in its glorification of the "masculinized" female and its demonization of the "feminized" male.

2   The film celebrates Clarice's rite of passage into the "masculine" world of the FBI In her journey through this violent, frightening world, it is clear that Clarice is at a disadvantage because she is female. In order to make her way, she needs the guidance of two father figures—her boss Jack Crawford and the evil genius, Hannibal Lecter. Both of these men are connected to the idealized memory of her late father who was a sheriff—the first flashback of her father occurs after Clarice has visited Lecter, and the second one occurs in the funeral home after she has flown to West Virginia with Jack Crawford. Lecter pumps Clarice for feelings about her father, and Crawford tells her that her "father would have been proud" of her at her graduation from the academy. Clarice is eager to please these father figures and to take her place "among the men."

3   Clarice's growing ability to live in the "masculine" world of violence can be traced by looking at the key initiation scenes where Clarice must prove her ability to control her emotions and to look upon horrific sights; she must assume the role of the male spectator. In her first interview with Lecter, Clarice enters a dungeon full of psychopathic maniacs. She must look at men who are called monsters. Typical of a fledgling, "a little starling" as Lecter calls her, Clarice is not in a position of control. Lecter toys with her, and although she is able to keep up a facade of control, she is clearly no match for him. Several shots toward the end of this scene emphasize Clarice's inability, at this point, to function in this world. As the block erupts with the wild cries of the inmates, Clarice begs Lecter for one more clue; he shouts at her to go. The camera then "chases" Clarice as she runs down the hall in a near panic. The next shot shows Clarice outside the prison trying to catch her breath. Two guards holding a prisoner pass behind her. Their stoic faces and physical massiveness draw attention to Clarice's smallness and the tears standing in her eyes. The scene ends with a long shot of a tiny Clarice sobbing against her car, the huge red brick prison looming in the background.

4   Significantly, the next shot is an extreme close-up of Clarice blazing away with her gun on the practice range. The look of stern concentration on her face seems to suggest her need to confirm her power through violence and her determination to carry out violence efficiently and without emotion. This scene foreshadows Clarice's final initiation test—her showdown with Jame Gumb, the feminized male who must be destroyed.

5   Jame Gumb is a serial killer of frightening pathology. Like Clarice, he is evolving, but as his name suggests, his evolution is confused. Jame sounds like an ugly

hybrid of James and Jane. Jame's greatest desire is to become a woman, a true Jane, and in an effort to achieve this he is sewing a "woman suit" from the skins of his victims. Because he is said to "skin his humps," the police nickname Jame Buffalo Bill. Jame's/Buffalo Bill's otherness is communicated in several ways by the film. The character is often shot from low angles that create a sense of ominousness. For instance, in the scene where he commands Catherine to rub the lotion on herself, he is shot entirely from below, distorting his features and making it difficult to see what he really looks like. These low shots of him cuddling his white poodle Precious are intercut with shots that look down on Catherine as she huddles in the pit, emphasizing her helplessness and fear and his indifference to her. What he wants is her "product": her smooth, soft skin.

6   Buffalo Bill is characterized as seeing Catherine as an object. "It rubs the lotion on its skin, or it gets the hose," he remarks in his strange, strangled voice. This ability to objectify humans is commented upon in the film as part of Jame's pathology. Clarice remarks as Catherine's mother pleads with her captor to let her daughter go: "If he sees her as a human being, it will be harder for him to cut her up." Yet the film objectifies Jame again and again, most tellingly in the "photo shoot" scene.

7   In this scene, the alternating cuts between Jame and Catherine again equate the characters, just as the similarity of the close-up shots of Clarice and Lecter during their "sessions" equate them. But the Clarice/Lecter cuts emphasize her growing ability to enter into the masculine world—a place of privilege and power and also a place where one has the power to look, rather than to be looked at. In this scene both Jame and Catherine are feminized and objectified as the camera gazes upon them.

8   Jame is further objectified by a series of shots that show him as a series of parts, rather than as a whole person. As Catherine attempts to lure Precious into the pit, we see a hand with the word "love" tattooed across the knuckles swirling a brush in a pot of eye shadow. The next shot pans down from Jame's hair to his left eye as he carefully brushes on the makeup. Looking closely, the viewer realizes that he is wearing one of his "scalps" on his head. The camera then pans up his chest showing another crude tattoo that looks like a knife dripping blood. The sense of this "creature's" perversion is increased as the camera focuses on his pierced nipple, which he tugs, suggesting that he is a masochist as well as a sadist.

9   Several more shots focus on his chin and chest as he adorns himself with necklaces. Then there are four shots of his mouth. In the first, he is applying pink lip gloss with a brush. In the next three, the brush plays around his lips as he croaks, "Would you fuck me?" "I'd fuck me," "I'd fuck me so hard." Throughout this scene the sordidness of Jame's attempts to feminize himself are underscored by the juxtaposition of the desperate Catherine (the "real" woman whose full face is shown) in her pit, with Jame's tacky "disco," complete with pounding music, glittering silver ball, and flashing lights.

10   Mannequins arranged carefully in the background further point to Jame's nonhumanness and artificiality. As he leans into both the film camera and his own still camera, preening like the beautiful female model he sees himself becoming, his face is grotesquely distorted. His need to expose himself to the camera is revealed as "sick," not only because his makeup job is so poorly done, but because of his des-

perate and pathetic need to be seen as a desirable sexual object—that is, a woman, when he is so clearly a man. The scene climaxes with Jame finally shown in his entirety as he backs up from the fixed gaze of the camera. The viewer sees this "freak" with his horrific teased hair and thigh-high blue stockings. We also see his horrible "lack" of genitalia as he spreads his kimono "wings" like the death's-head moth with which he is equated throughout the film.

11   In the climactic showdown between Clarice and Jame, Clarice kills the covetous Jame. This scene is Clarice's final test in her rite of passage into the masculine world. Clarice's entry into Jame's lair follows the pattern of the classical hero's journey—she must descend and she must do it alone. Common sense might suggest going for help, or waiting outside for an escape attempt, but Clarice pulls out her gun and, like the macho lone hero, goes to the rescue of the damsel in distress.

12   Catherine's hysterical screaming in the pit is in contrast to Clarice's methodical, by-the-book attempt to search the basement. Although Clarice is clearly frightened, she continues to crash through doors, "checking the corners" as she has been taught. Each room seems to contain a worse horror than the last, but still Clarice pushes on. Finally, Jame plunges the last room into complete darkness and begins to stalk Clarice with his night goggles. He is now in the typical masculine role—he looks—and she is in the typical feminine role—she is looked at. Yet Jame still covets those womanly assets and cannot help but reach out to touch Clarice's hair when he should be shooting her. In the test of quicker reflexes, Clarice triumphs, blasting Jame several times in the chest. In the process, she breaks the blackened window and light floods in, illuminating the dark secrets of Jame Gumb's basement (his unconscious). Here agent Starling clearly aligns herself with patriarchy in her willingness to act as a policing superego that attempts to "clean up" and order the "feminine," chaotic unconscious through violent means.

13   Clarice has passed her final test—she has killed. She can now graduate in triumph from school (as we see in the next scene) and can reach out and shake Jack Crawford's hand as a peer. Clarice has fully entered the violent "male" world by bonding with her powerful father figures, and through their tutoring, learned how to look upon and destroy the "feminized" male.

EXPLORING THE TEXT

1. Dornink begins her discussion by making reference to Clarice Starling as a "feminist heroine" (paragraph 1). Explore what Dornink (and others) mean by this phrase. What are the basic ideas we associate with heroes? How might a feminist heroine be different from a male hero? How might she be different from other kinds of heroines?

2. How does Dornink define the " 'masculine' world" (paragraph 3)? What traits are associated with masculine and what with feminine in the world of this film?

3. What does Dornink mean when she refers to "the role of the male spectator" in paragraph 3? What effects can we anticipate if a viewer is male

rather than female? List examples of information you receive that come from a distinctly male or female point of view (think of the masculine and feminine divisions discussed in question 2).

4. What evidence has Dornink offered to support her claim that Clarice and Jame are both "evolving" characters (paragraph 5)? How is this similarity between these two character an important element of the hero story?

5. The division between masculine and feminine is exemplified, in Dornink's discussion and in the movie itself, by various references to sexuality and sexual desirability. Locate the places where Dornink incorporates evidence of sexuality and discuss its importance in supporting her thesis.

6. Consider Dornink's strategy in beginning her discussion with a paraphrase of Jodie Foster's quote. How would you define "feminist"? What expectation does its use establish? Why would it be important that Foster (and others) see the film as feminist when, according to Dornink, it isn't feminist at all? Explain your answer.

7. List the places throughout this essay where Dornink describes a conflation between feminine and masculine characteristics in both Clarice and Jame. Do you think that the way she has labeled certain traits as masculine or feminine is typical of how people label such traits generally? Discuss how important these divisions are to Dornink's argument overall.

WRITING ASSIGNMENTS

1. Dornink's essay takes on the issue of the "feminist hero." Other authors in this chapter also focus on the idea of heroes, male and female, especially Leonard Pitts and Susan Faludi. Should a feminist hero be similar to any kind of a hero as described in these other texts? Should she be different? Write a paper in which you discuss the concept of hero, generally, and discuss whether or not you agree that a hero is bound to act in certain ways depending on her or his gender.

2. Other authors in this chapter (Elayne Rapping, Gary Edgerton and Kathy Merlock Jackson, Dorothy Gilliam and bell hooks) focus on female characters and present arguments about what makes some characters strong and positive and what makes others typical and traditional. Write an essay in which you discuss how Clarice Starling compares to one or more female characters discussed by these other authors. Is she a hero? Is she a desirable female character? Is she just another example of a common "type"?

GROUP PROJECTS

1. Have your group use the Internet, newspaper and periodical indexes, and other databases to find other discussions of this movie. Look for film reviews, articles focused around the 1992 Academy Awards show, and inter-

views with Jodie Foster, Anthony Hopkins, Johanthan Demme (the director), and/or Thomas Harris (the author of the original novel). Compare findings and prepare a report on the various interpretations offered about the character of Clarice, especially those defending her status as a "feminist hero." Discuss the extent to which people agree or disagree with Dornink's argument and what you learned by comparing the different discussions.

2. Define the feminine hero. Make a list of other "thriller" films that present a strong female as the main character (this will require research). Each group member should select one film and watch it, taking careful note of the masculine or feminine traits ascribed to the heroine. Compare your results with Dornink's essay and with each other. Prepare a group report that proposes a precise definition of the female hero based on what these films present and considering the extent to which she is similar to or different from male heroes.

Pro/Con: Reviews of *Waiting to Exhale*

The 1996 film *Waiting to Exhale,* based on Terry McMillan's best-selling novel, was an instant success—and an instant controversy. To many African American women, the movie was hailed as a cinematic breakthrough in its celebration of the sisterhood of real black middle-class women as they relate to good and not-so-good black men. To others, the film was two hours of anti-feminist male-bashing. Below are two very contrary reviews of that important film.

PRO

Breathing Easier with a Rare Film
Dorothy Gilliam

As Dorothy Gilliam explains, she was thrilled by *Waiting to Exhale* because, finally, here was a film that offered American audiences a view of "contemporary black women, in their limitless variety"—a film she and her friends could relate to. Though bell hooks argues directly against Gilliam's stand in the next piece, it might prove interesting to consider Gilliam's celebration of the "reality" of these characters in light of other observations on Hollywood female "types" in this chapter, especially those of Elayne Rapping and Margaret Talbot.

Gilliam is a columnist for the *Washington Post* where this article first appeared in January 1996.

1   Ahaaaaaaaaaaaaaa.

2   Ahaaaaaaaaaaaaaa.

3   Have you exhaled yet? I have. Twice.

4   Exhaling has come to mean, for some of my friends, "Have you seen 'Waiting to Exhale' yet, girl?" When Helen exited the theater with a joyful group of female pals, they stood outside, grinned and hugged each other, and together, they said, "Ahaaaaaaaaaaaaaa."

5   Still others are living in a constant state of exhalation because there is a rare black female buddy movie on the screen. They can relate to the strong sisterhood, discuss the bad choices, cheer for the good ones, revel in its sharp-looking images and support the movie.

6   From it, they are extracting lessons, messages, healing, cleansing, affirmation, empowerment and meditations on rejecting victimization.

7   "Waiting to Exhale" is about totally contemporary black women, in their limit-less variety, and the choices they make. It is an allegory for the male-female con-flicts and problems that are going on in every American city and suburb and inside the heart of every black woman who has ever loved a man or wanted a man to love.

8   "It was a film about me—a black woman," said my friend Joyce, a highly placed corporate supervisor. "When I went to see it, I wanted to feel good about something. I'll see it again." Leonade, a corporate financial officer, asked rhetori-cally: "How often do we get to relate to a film? The transition from the book to the screen was authentic, and I could relate to the women and the men."

9   It was a recent Saturday. We had gathered for coffee after an early show. "The way Gloria gets the guy in the end," said another bubbly pal ironically also named Gloria, "I could have been her. . . . Black women will write this movie across their chests."

10   One reason is that black women are starved to see themselves portrayed in mo-tion pictures as real people, with the whole range of human emotions. "It made us relate to our own lives," said Candy, another corporate executive. "I liked the way the relationships between the women grew in honesty."

11   Friendships between women are older than the biblical Ruth and Naomi. This movie is also about sisterhood, the permission some women give themselves to be increasingly open, honest and loving. "You knew from the start that these women were going to handle those men," Helen said. "It just had to do with the sisterhood."

12   Other friends of mine agreed that the four female characters' strong sisterhood made them real and wonderful. When Robin's need for a man pushed her to pursue Russell "even though in my heart I know he's a dog," her friends counseled her in vain and finally pronounced her "pitiful." At the movie's end, as Robin decided to keep Russell's baby, whom she had foolishly conceived, the circle closed around her, vowing to support her in that big decision.

13   Despite the prevalence of men like Russell, black male friends with whom I have talked and others I've heard about don't seem to view this film with the venom they brought to "The Color Purple." Even though the film exposed the myth of uni-versal black male sexual prowess, my black male friends seemed to handle more of the negative images without taking them personally. Maybe it is a sign of their growing inner strength.

14   From New Age vegetarians to macho carnivores, from blue collar to white col-lar, many black men think the movie reflected "real life" and was not out only to

bash them. Black director Forrest Whitaker had two good guys—the Wesley Snipes and Gregory Hines characters—bring balance.

15   Although some women in our *kaffeeklatsch* wished they'd seen more good brothers in the movie, none agreed with the man on the Oprah Winfrey show who urged a boycott of the film because it "scapegoated" black men. Women have in fact done the opposite—seen it two or three times because Hollywood finally has made a film we want to see.

16   But in presenting women with warts as well as beauty marks, the onus was left on us to accept responsibility for our choices. If we choose to love married men, drug abusers and those with flash over substance, we have to accept the consequences.

17   Black men more often than black women choose a partner of a different race—one of the relationships in the book and movie. When Bernadine rails at her husband for walking out on their 11-year marriage and two children for a white woman, he asks, "Would it be better if she was black?" The depth of her anger is revealed when she shoots back: "No, it would be better if you were."

18   Although the movie is about black women, white women have been thronging to it with equal ebullience. They, too, make lousy choices, and women of all races relate to the film's experiences and lessons. "The movie allows people to heal," said my friend Anne. "Been there, done that, made those mistakes. Now I can move on."

19   Toni thought the women in the movie take the first step when they get honest about the men they choose and the behavior they will or will not accept. "Hopefully," she continued, "we will be able to take the next step, which is not about the men at all. It is about women and what we are not expressing—our inhibitions and fears about valuing our sexuality and our feminine power—and expressing it."

20   With the exception of a few pioneers, only with women of recent generations is there the possibility of defining themselves outside their relationships with men. Only when a woman defines herself is she whole enough to sustain a healthy relationship with a man.

21   Whether the movie will change our choices is up for grabs, but even the fleeting thought that it will is exhilarating. It sort of makes one want to go "Ahaaaaaaaaaaaaaa."

EXPLORING THE TEXT

1. After viewing *Waiting to Exhale,* make a list of the various "types" of women presented. List all significant female characters, even those other than the four featured friends, and then list the various characteristics attached to each woman. What is the significance of these types being presented? To what extent are these common types of all women? To what extent are the types unique to black women? Discuss the relevance of your findings.

2. Make a list of the various "types" of men presented. List all significant male characters and then list the various characteristics attached to each male. What is significant about these types? To what extent are these com-

mon types of all men? To what extent are the types unique to black men? Discuss the relevance of your findings.

3. Gilliam suggests that the film is "a rare black female buddy movie" (paragraph 5). To what extent do you agree that *Waiting to Exhale* is indeed rare? Would it be considered rare because of gender, race, or a combination of these two elements? List other movies you know that incorporate one or more of these elements: a focus on blacks as main characters, a focus on females as main characters, a story about buddies. Which of these incorporate more than one of these characteristics.

4. Consider the elements of this film and the ways in which this film is "typical" as much as "rare." List other films with characters similar to one or more of the characters in this film. List several other movies that deal similarly with themes of love, family, and friendship. Can you find anything unusual or surprising about the development of the plot or the end of this film? Explain your answer.

5. The positive reception of this film seems based on its treatment of the friendship among four women, but is it only a movie about friendship? Or is it a film about women finding men, or something else? Consider the other themes apparent in this film and discuss the ways in which they relate to the primary focus on friendship.

6. How is the audience an integral part of the discussion? How does Gilliam use audience input to make her point? Why does she clearly identify each speaker by job status, etc.? How persuasive is this strategy? Discuss your answer.

7. What do you make of the way Gilliam plays with film's title throughout her discussion, particularly at the beginning and end? What does exhaling suggest in the movie? How does Gilliam make it an effective metaphor for her discussion? As a reader, do you think it's an effective rhetorical strategy? Explain your answer.

WRITING ASSIGNMENTS

1. As with *Pocahontas,* discussed earlier in this chapter, this film takes on the touchy issues of race and sex, though each film is focused on different audiences and addresses these issues in different ways. Prepare a discussion of specific scenes in each film that touch on these issues and compare the different ways in which each film presents (and resolves) these issues.

2. Consider other female buddy movies (e.g., *Thelma and Louise, Men on the Side, The Truth About Cats and Dogs, Fried Green Tomatoes, Passion Fish,* or something more recent). What are the elements that make these films buddy movies? What kinds of relationships do the women share? What are the similarities in plot line? To what extent do the characters contend with similar issues? Now apply your findings to *Waiting to Exhale.*

Does it work along the same lines? To what extent does it work, also, as a romance? Do the other movies work as romances? Explain the significance of your findings.

GROUP PROJECTS

1. Be reporters at large. As a group attend a film that focuses on issues of race, female friendship, or other themes in *Waiting to Exhale.* Prepare a brief set of questions (no more than three) that ask audience members to react to the film in the way that Gilliam sought reaction on *Waiting to Exhale.* Make sure your questions are not offensive or intrusive. Poll several audience members about their reactions and write out your interpretation of their reactions as Gilliam has done.
2. Since this film was based on a popular novel, consider just how well the filmmakers translated the written version to the screen. Have each group member choose one character. Compare the depiction of that character in the book with the depiction in the film. Make note of physical characteristics and particular scenes, as well as the overall story line. Bring your results to the larger group and compile everyone's findings into a report. Does your group agree with Leonade (paragraph 8) who claims that the "transition from the book to the screen was authentic"?

CON

Mock Feminism
bell hooks

Unlike Dorothy Gilliam, bell hooks (who doesn't use upper case letters in her name) most definitely does not applaud the film *Waiting to Exhale.* She thinks the film is "lightweight" at best, and, more importantly, that it is a "white supremacist capitalist patriarchal cultural appropriation." Strong words that reflect a strong opinion. hooks objects to several opinions typically offered about the film: that it is a "black film," that it represents a "feminist narrative," that the characters depicted are realistic—or desirable—that it is "ethnographic cinema." Much like other authors in this chapter, she condemns the roles, male and female, as "types" rather than fully developed characters, and she is concerned about the ideas these "types" perpetuate in American society. hooks is even more concerned about the black women who celebrate this movie, believing they have been duped by marketing ploys and have failed to treat the film critically.

This essay is from bell hooks's book, *reel to real: race, sex, and class at the movies* (1996). bell hooks is a noted author and cultural critic.

1   In the past a black film was usually seen as a film by a black filmmaker focusing on some aspect of black life. More recently the "idea" of a "black film" has been appropriated as a way to market films that are basically written and produced by white people as though they in fact represent and offer us—"authentic" blackness. It does not matter that progressive black filmmakers and critics challenge essentialist notions of black authenticity, even going so far as to rethink and interrogate the notion of black film. These groups do not have access to the levels of marketing and publicity that can repackage authentic blackness commodified and sell it as the "real" thing. That was certainly the case with the marketing and publicity for the film *Waiting to Exhale.*

2   When Kevin Costner produced and starred in the film *The Bodyguard* with Whitney Houston as co-star, the film focused on a black family. No one ever thought to market it as a black film. Indeed, many black people refused to see the film because they were so disgusted by this portrayal of interracial love. No one showed much curiosity about the racial identify of the screenwriters or for that matter, anybody behind the scenes of this film. It was not seen as having an importance, for black women by the white-dominated mass media. Yet *Waiting to Exhale*'s claim to blackness, and black authenticity, is almost as dubious as any such claim being made about *The Bodyguard.* However, that claim could be easily made because a black woman writer wrote the book on which the movie was based. The hiring of a fledgling black director received no critical comment. Everyone behaved as though it was just normal Hollywood practice to offer the directorship of a major big-budget Hollywood film to someone who might not know what they are doing.

3   The screenplay was written by a white man, but if we are to believe everything we read in newspapers and popular magazines, Terry McMillan assisted with the writing. Of course, having her name tacked onto the writing process was a great way to protect the film from the critique that its "authentic blackness" was somehow undermined by white-male interpretation. Alice Walker had no such luck when her book *The Color Purple* was made into a movie by Steven Spielberg. No one thought this was a black film. And very few viewers were surprised that what we saw on the screen had little relationship to Alice Walker's novel.

4   Careful publicity and marketing ensured that *Waiting to Exhale* would not be subjected to these critiques; all acts of appropriation were carefully hidden behind the labeling of this film as authentically a black woman's story. Before anyone could become upset that a black woman was not hired to direct the film, McMillan told the world in *Movieland* magazine that those experienced black women directors in Hollywood just were not capable of doing the job. She made the same critique of the black woman writer who was initially hired to write the screenplay. From all accounts (most of them given by the diva herself) it appears that Terry McMillan is the only competent black woman on the Hollywood scene and she just recently arrived.

5   It's difficult to know what is more disturbing: McMillan's complicity with the various acts of white supremacist capitalist patriarchal cultural appropriation that resulted in a film as lightweight and basically bad as *Waiting to Exhale,* or the public's passive celebratory consumption of this trash as giving the real scoop about black women's lives. Some bad films are at least entertaining. This was just an utterly bor-

ing show. That masses of black women could be cajoled by mass media coverage and successful seductive marketing (the primary ploy being that this is the first film ever that four black women have been the major stars of a Hollywood film) to embrace this cultural product was a primary indication that this is not a society where moviegoers are encouraged to think critically about what they see on the screen.

6   When a film that's basically about the trials and tribulations of four professional heterosexual black women who are willing to do anything to get and keep a man is offered as a "feminist" narrative, it's truly a testament to the power of the mainstream to co-opt progressive social movements and strip them of all political meaning through a series of contemptuous ridiculous representations. Terry McMillan's novel *Waiting to Exhale* was not a feminist book and it was not transformed into a feminist film. It did not even become a film that made use of any of the progressive politics around race and gender that was evoked however casually in the novel itself.

7   The film *Waiting to Exhale* took the novelistic images of professional black women concerned with issues of racial uplift and gender equality and turned them into a progression of racist, sexist stereotypes that features happy darkies who are all singing, dancing, fucking, and having a merry old time even in the midst of sad times and tragic moments. What we saw on the screen was not black women talking about love or the meaning of partnership and marriage in their lives. We saw four incredibly glamorous women obsessed with getting a man, with status, material success and petty competition with other women (especially white women). In the book one of the women, Gloria, owns a beauty parlor; she is always, always working, which is what happens when you run a small business. In the movie, girlfriend hardly ever works because she is too busy cooking tantalizing meals for the neighbor next door. In this movie food is on her mind and she forgets all about work, except for an occasional phone call to see how everything is going. Let's not forget the truly fictive utopian moment in this film that occurs when Bernie goes to court divorcing her husband and wins tons of money. This is so in the book as well. Funny though, the novel ends with her giving the money away, highlighting her generosity and her politics. McMillan writes: "She also wouldn't have to worry about selling the house now. But Bernadine wasn't taking that fucker off the market. She'd drop the price. And she'd send a nice check to the United Negro College Fund, something she'd always wanted to do. She'd help feed some of those kids in Africa she'd seen on TV at night . . . Maybe she'd send some change to the Urban league and the NAACP and she'd definitely help out some of those programs that BWOTM [Black Women on the MOVE] had been trying to get off the ground for the last hundred years. At the rate she was going, Bernadine had already given away over a million dollars." Definitely not a "material girl." It would have taken only one less scene of pleasure fucking for audiences to have witnessed Bernie writing these checks with a nice voice-over. But, alas, such an image might have ruined the racist, sexist stereotype of black women being hard, angry, and just plain greedy. No doubt the writers of the screenplay felt these "familiar" stereotypes would guarantee the movie its crossover appeal.

8   Concurrently, no doubt it helps that crossover appeal to set up stereotypically racist, sexist conflicts between white women and black women (where if we are to

believe the logic of the film, the white woman gets "her" black man in the end). Let's remember. In the novel the book is based on, only one black man declares his love for a white woman. The man Bernie meets, the lawyer James, is thinking of divorcing his white wife, who is dying of cancer, but he loyally stays with her until her death, even though he makes it very clear that the love has long since left their marriage. Declaring his undying love for Bernie, James moves across the country to join her, sets up a law practice, and gets involved with "a coalition to stop the liquor board from allowing so many liquor stores in the black community." Well, not in this movie! The screen character James declares undying love for his sick white wife. Check out the difference between the letter he writes in the novel. Here is an excerpt: "I know you probably thought that night was just something frivolous but like I told you before I left, it meant more to me than that. Much more. I buried my wife back in August, and for her sake, I'm glad she's not suffering anymore . . . I want to see you again, Bernadine, and not for another one-nighter, either. If there's any truth to what's known as a 'soul mate,' then you're as close to it as I've ever come . . . I'm not interested in playing games, or starting something I can't finish. I play for keeps, and I'm not some dude just out to have a good time . . . I knew I was in love with you long before we ever turned the key to that hotel room." The image of black masculinity that comes through in this letter is that of a man of integrity who is compassionate, in touch with his feelings, and able to take responsibility for his actions.

9   In the movie version of *Waiting to Exhale,* no black man involved with a black woman possesses these qualities. In contrast to what happens in the book, in the film, James does not have a one-nighter with Bernie, because he is depicted as utterly devoted to his white wife. Here are relevant passages from the letter he writes to Bernie that audiences hear at the movie: "What I feel for you has never undercut the love I have for my wife. How is that possible? I watch her everyday. So beautiful and brave. I just want to give her everything I've got in me. Every moment. She's hanging on, fighting to be here for me. And when she sleeps, I cry. Over how amazing she is, and how lucky I've been to have her in my life." There may not have been any white women as central characters in this film, but this letter certainly places the dying white wife at the center of things. Completely rewriting the letter that appears in the novel, which only concerns James's love and devotion to Bernie, so that the white wife (dead in the book but brought back to life on-screen) is the recipient of James's love was no doubt another ploy to reach the crossover audience: the masses of white women consumers that might not have been interested in this film if it had really been about black women.

10   Ultimately, only white women have committed relationships with black men in the film. Not only do these screen images reinforce stereotypes, the screenplay was written in such a way as to actively perpetuate them. Catfights between women, both real and symbolic, were clearly seen by the screenwriters as likely to be more entertaining to moviegoing audiences than the portrayal of a divorced black woman unexpectedly meeting her true love—an honest, caring, responsible, mature, tender, and loving black man who delivers the goods. Black women are portrayed as so shrewish in this film that Lionel's betrayal of Bernie appears to be no more than an act of self-

defense. The film suggests that Lionel is merely trying to get away from the black bitch who barges in on him at work and physically attacks his meek and loving white wife. To think that Terry McMillan was one of the screenwriters makes it all the more disheartening. Did she forget that she had written a far more emotionally complex and progressive vision of black female-male relationships in her novel?

11   While we may all know some over-thirty black women who are desperate to get a man by any means necessary and plenty of young black females who fear that they may never find a man and are willing to be downright foolish in their pursuit of one, the film was so simplistic and denigrating in its characterization of black womanhood that everyone should be outraged to be told that it is "for us." Or worse yet, as a reporter wrote in *Newsweek*, "This is our million man march." Whether you supported the march or not (and I did not, for many of the same reasons I find this film appalling), let's get this straight: We are being told, and are telling ourselves that black men need a political march and black women need a movie. Mind you—not a political film but one where the black female "stars" spend most of their time chainsmoking themselves to death (let's not forget that Gloria did not have enough breath to blow out her birthday candle) and drowning their sorrows in alcohol. No doubt McMillan's knowledge of how many black people die from lung cancer and alcoholism influenced her decision to write useful, unpreachy critiques of these addictions in her novel. In the novel the characters who smoke are trying to stop and Black Women on the Move are fighting to close down liquor stores. None of these actions fulfill racist fantasies. It's no accident that just the opposite images appear on the screen. Smoking is so omnipresent in every scene that many of us were waiting to see a promotional credit for the tobacco industry.

12   Perhaps the most twisted and perverse aspect of this film is the way it was marketed as being about girlfriend bonding. How about that scene where Robin shares her real-life trauma with Savannah, who is busy looking the other way and simply does not respond. Meaningful girlfriend bonding is not about the codependency that is imaged in this film. At its best *Waiting to Exhale* is a film about black women helping each other to stay stuck. Do we really believe that moment when Savannah rudely disses Kenneth (even though the film has in no way constructed him as a lying cheating dog) to be a moment of profound "feminist" awakening. Suddenly audiences are encouraged to believe that she realizes the dilemma of being involved with a married man, even one who has filed for a divorce. Why not depict a little mature communication between a black man and a black woman. No doubt that too would not have been entertaining to crossover audiences. Better to give them what they are used to, stereotypical representations of black males as always and only lying, cheating dogs (that is, when they are involved with black women) and professional black women as wild, irrational, castrating bitch goddesses.

13   Nothing was more depressing than hearing individual black women offering personal testimony that these shallow screen images are "realistic portrayals" of their experience. If this is the world of black gender relations as they know it, no wonder black men and women are in serious crisis. Obviously, it is difficult for many straight black women to find black male partners and/or husbands. Though it is hard to believe that black women as conventionally feminine, beautiful, glam-

orous, and just plain dumb as the girlfriends in this film can't get men (Bernie has an MBA, helped start the business, but is clueless about everything that concerns money; Robin is willing to have unsafe sex and celebrate an unplanned pregnancy with a partner who may be a drug addict; Gloria, who would rather cook food for her man any day than go to work; Savannah has sex at the drop of a hat, even when she does not want to get involved). In the real world these are the women who have men standing in line.

14   However, if they and other black women internalize the messages in *Waiting to Exhale* they will come to their senses and see that, according to the film, black men are really undesirable mates for black women. Actually, lots of younger black women, and their over-thirty counterparts, go to see *Waiting to Exhale* to have their worst fears affirmed: that black men are irresponsible and uncaring; that black women, no matter how attractive, will still be hurt and abandoned, and that ultimately they will probably be alone and unloved. Perhaps it feels less like cultural genocide to have these messages of self-loathing and disempowerment brought to them by four beautiful black female "stars."

15   Black woman seeking to learn anything about gender relationships from this film will be more empowered if we identify with the one black female character who rarely speaks. She is the graceful, attractive, brown-skinned lawyer with naturally braided hair who is a professional who knows her job and is also able to bond emotionally with her clients. Not only does she stand for gender justice (the one glimpse of empowering feminist womanhood we see in this film), she achieves that end without ever putting men down or competing with any woman. While we never see her with a male partner, she acts with confident self-esteem and shows fulfillment in a job well done.

16   The monetary success of a trashy film like *Waiting to Exhale,* with its heavy sentimentality and predictable melodrama shows that Hollywood recognizes that blackness as a commodity can be exploited to bring in the bucks. Dangerously, it also shows that the same old racist/sexist stereotyeps can be appropriated and served up to the public in a new and more fashionable disguise. While it serves the financial interests of Hollywood and McMillan's own bank account for her to deflect away from critiques that examine the politics underlying these representations and their behind-the-scenes modes of production by ways of witty assertions that the novel and the film are "forms of entertainment, not anthropological studies," in actuality the creators of this film are as accountable for their work as their predecessors. Significantly, contemporary critiques of racial essentialism completely disrupt the notion that anything a black artist creates is inherently radical, progressive, or more likely to reflect a break with white supremacist representations. It has become most evident that as black artists seek a "crossover" success, the representations they create usually mirror dominant stereotypes. After a barrage of publicity and marketing that encouraged black people, and black women in particular, to see *Waiting to Exhale* as fictive ethnography, McMillan is being more than a bit disingenuous when she suggests that the film should not be seen this way. In her essay, "Who's Doin' the Twist: Notes Toward a Politics of Appropriation," cultural critic Coco Fusco reminds us that we must continually critique this genre in both its pure

and impure forms. "Ethnographic cinema, in light of its historical connection to colonialist adventurism, and decades of debate about the ethics of representing documentary subjects, is a genre that demands a special degree of scrutiny." Just because writers and directors are black does not exempt them from scrutiny. The black female who wrote a letter to the *New York Times* calling attention to the way this film impedes the struggle to create new images of blackness on the screen was surely right when she insisted that had everyone involved in the production of this film been white and male, its blatantly racist and sexist standpoints would not have gone unchallenged.

EXPLORING THE TEXT

1. How does hooks define authentic blackness? How does she relate her idea of authenticity to the marketplace (or to how a movie is marketed)?

2. In paragraph 5, hooks refers to the "white supremacist capitalist patriarchal cultural appropriation." What does she mean by this phrase? Define the words and discuss their importance in the context of this essay.

3. Consider the language of this essay, as well as the knowledge one needs to understand it. Based on these, who seems to be hooks's target audience? In what ways is this audience different from Gilliam's? Refer to specific points of comparison between the two articles.

4. hooks argues against this film's being a " 'feminist' narrative" (paragraph 6), although that's one way it was marketed. What are some of her complaints? How would a feminist narrative be different?

5. In her final paragraph, hooks presents her conclusion that this film incorporates "heavy sentimentality and predictable melodrama" (paragraph 16). What evidence has she offered throughout her discussion that supports this claim? What other evidence does the film offer to support this charge? Is there any evidence that argues against hooks's conclusion?

6. hooks begins her discussion by offering a contrast: The studio that marketed the film *The Bodyguard* didn't think to suggest that it is a black film, although the central character and her family are black. Why not? What elements in *Waiting to Exhale* relate directly to issues of race? What issues stand outside of race?

7. hooks and Gilliam opt for different persuasive strategies in presenting their arguments. Consider the strengths and weaknesses of each strategy. Gilliam used testimonial evidence (see her paragraph 10) to add the credibility of firsthand accounts of the movie experience. hooks opted for a different style. In paragraph 9, she looks at a particular scene in the film and presents her own analysis of its relevance. In paragraph 7, she relies on the authority of the original novel to support her analysis. Do you find one way of arguing more credible than the other? Discuss the pros and cons of each style.

WRITING ASSIGNMENTS

1. In her conclusion, hooks claims that *Waiting to Exhale* is "fictive ethnography" (paragraph 16). What does she mean by this term? What support has she offered for this claim? How does the idea of ethnography relate to other claims she makes throughout the essay, especially those with regard to appropriation and authenticity? Develop your response with specific textual references and discussion.

2. Write an essay that carefully analyzes differences in tone between hooks's and Gilliam's texts. Tone includes each author's attitude and emotional relationship to the material she discusses—it becomes evident in the particular words she chooses and her underlying assumptions. Make a list of words or phrases from each piece that provide insight into the author's tone and discuss what these choices reveal about her attitude, her intention, and her purpose. To what extent is either author objective or emotional in her discussion? What emotions are revealed, specifically? Does the presence of emotion add to or detract from the effectiveness of each argument? In what ways are these authors similar to each other? How are they different? What is the ultimate effect of these similarities (or differences) on readers?

3. Use Sylvester Stallone's descriptions of various male and female "types" and compare them to the types described in the articles on *Waiting to Exhale* (Dorothy Gilliam and bell hooks). In what ways do his definitions offer insight into how we might see these characters and interpret their actions in the film?

GROUP PROJECTS

1. Begin with hooks's references to categories of film (some are romances, some are stories of males protecting female victims, some present the viewpoint of a particular race) as well as her discussion of *The Bodyguard* in particular. Divide your group into three subgroups, assign each group one of the above categories, and watch *The Bodyguard* carefully. Have each subgroup identify the elements of their assigned category and construct an argument that says this movie *best* fits their category. The subgroup will need to discover just what makes a film fit into any of the three areas of classification. Have subgroups debate their positions in front of the class, relying on specific scenes from the film as well as a more general knowledge of the elements of each film category. After the debate, encourage the class to discuss the effect of insisting the film fits into the mold of only one category and how this might be seen to relate to the arguments for and against *Waiting to Exhale*.

2. Working in a group, brainstorm a list of as many black women characters in films as you can. Define the characteristics of these characters; consider their importance and activities in the context of the overall story. Then di-

vide the list to distinguish black females appearing in films made by black people from black females appearing in films made by whites. (You might need a good guidebook on films and filmmakers, or you might look for reviews of particular films.) Look for patterns within each list. Compare the patterns between lists. Are there differences in how black women characters are presented in films by black directors, etc., and in those made by whites? What are the differences? How are the differences significant? Discuss your findings in detail and apply your insights to hooks's claims that *Waiting to Exhale* has been profoundly influenced by the whites involved with its production, that it might have been very different if blacks had had more direct influence on it. Is her position consistent with your research or do your findings disagree with her? Explain your answer.

If you were asked to list ten American heroes and heroines, you would probably name some or all of the following: George Washington, Abraham Lincoln, Daniel Boone, Martin Luther King Jr., Amelia Earhart, Susan B. Anthony, Jacqueline Kennedy Onassis, Helen Keller, Elizabeth Cady Stanton, and Rosa Parks. If next you were asked to list people who are generally admired by society, who somehow seem bigger than life, you might come up with an entirely different list. You might, in fact, name people who are celebrated for their wealth and glamour rather than their achievements and moral strength of character. And you would not be alone, because pollsters have found that people today do not choose political leaders who shape history for their "Most Admired" list, but rather movie and television celebrities, fashion models, professional athletes, and even comic book and cartoon characters. In short, media icons.

By definition, heroes and heroines are men and women distinguished by uncommon courage, achievements, and self-sacrifice made most often for the benefit of others—they are people against whom we measure others. They are men and women recognized for shaping our nation's consciousness and development as well as the lives of those who admire them. Yet, some people say that ours is an age where true heroes and heroines are hard to come by, where the very ideal of heroism is something beyond us—an artifact of the past. Some maintain that because the Cold War is over and because America is at peace our age is essentially an unheroic one. Furthermore, the overall crime rate is down, poverty has been eased by a strong and growing economy, and advances continue to be made in medical science. Consequently, bereft of cultural heroes, we have latched onto cultural icons—media superstars such as actors, actresses, sports celebrities, television personalities, and people who are simply famous for being famous.

Cultural icons are harder to define, but we know them when we see them. They are people who manage to transcend celebrity, who are legendary, who somehow manage to become mythic. But what makes some figures icons and others mere celebrities? That's hard to answer. In part, their lives have the quality of a story. For instance, the beautiful young Diana Spencer who at 19 married a prince, bore a king, renounced marriage and the throne, and died at the moment she found true love. Or Elvis Presley—shy, good-looking kid whose music could drive females crazy and whose sexiness was the envy of every young male. Good looks certainly help. So does a special indefinable charisma, with the help of the media. John Wayne hated horses and never served in the military, but he has become an icon of the Wild West and a warrior hero. But nothing becomes an icon more than a tragic and early death—such as, Martin Luther King Jr., John F. Kennedy, Marilyn Monroe, John Lennon, Tupac Shakur, Selena, James Dean, and Princess Diana.

The essays in this chapter will consider the difference between heroes and icons and will at the same time take a look at some of the more poplar figures who have left their mark on our age—people whose elevated stature says something about us and our system of values.

In the first piece, "Where Are the Heroes?" media critic Ed Siegel laments that our one-time ideals of heroism have passed from public life—that myths of strength, courage, and achievement have all but disappeared from politics, religion, and the art world where once upon a time they dominated. But as Siegel points out, our age is not completely devoid of heroics, for our cultural idols can still be found on the playing fields.

The next four pieces shift the focus of adoration to women. In the first, "Heroine Worship: The Age of the Female Icon," Holly Brubach argues how the celebrity-driven media has latched onto particular women, packaging and elevating them to a goddesslike status for an easily bored yet star-hungry public—in particular, a female public, women caught up in a culture that convinces them that they need to be remade in the images of others.

The three pieces that follow look at women whose deaths have elevated them beyond role models to iconic status. Perhaps no other figure in recent history better exemplifies the elevation of a woman to icon and our culture's obsession with celebrity than Princess Diana. In life, hers was the most recognized face in the world. In death, hers was the funeral witnessed by more than a third of the world's population. In "Princess Diana: Her True Face," biographer Andrew Morton explains how Diana Spencer in her 36 short years broke out on her own—and why she will remain an iconic image of fascination.

Tragically murdered at the age of 23, Selena has become an icon for millions of Hispanic Americans. Born Selena Quintanilla Perez, the young queen of *tejano* music was rapidly preparing herself to cross over into the American mainstream market when a bullet put an end to her dream in 1995. And, yet, as Larry Rohter explains in "Selena: A Legend Grows, and So Does an Industry" the young singer who had been called a Latina Madonna has in death become the object of adoration and adulation to her fans as Marilyn Monroe and Elvis Presley have to theirs.

Amelia Earhart, the first woman to cross the Atlantic in a solo airplane, also died a tragic death. It has been over 60 years since Earhart mysteriously disappeared in the Pacific in an attempt to fly around the world. Until her death, as pointed out in the next selection, Earhart was perhaps the most celebrated woman in the world. While her flight has since been duplicated, Earhart today is still held in high esteem, as evidenced by the next essay, "Amelia Earhart: The Lady Vanishes," in which social critic and author Camille Paglia celebrates Earhart as a personal heroine and an icon of female determination and daring.

The next two pieces look at two men—one living, one dead—who have captured the popular cultural consciousness in ways nearly unmatched by any others. It might be said that Michael Jordan is *the* most celebrated icon of our popular media culture. He is a man for whom respect seems to transcend gender, race, class, and even professional basketball. In "Rare Jordan," Nelson George explains how this NBA superstar, sex symbol, and living commodity is so many things to so many people, but especially is a role model for African American males.

John Wayne has been dead nearly 20 years, but he, too, is still many things to many people. And according to a recent poll, he is still America's number-one movie star. In "John Wayne: America's Favorite Icon," biographer and social critic

Garry Wills offers some illuminating insights as to what defining images John Wayne projected from the movie screen, what needs he fulfilled in his audience, and why he is still a vital presence in America's cultural psyche.

As Wills points out, part of John Wayne's bigger-than-life appeal was fashioned in part by the directors who created his movies. That is, they took the raw material of Wayne's mystique and manufactured a viable cultural archetype. To an extent that is the iconic intention behind television's *Xena: Warrior Princess.* Since 1995, the superheroine played by Lucy Lawless has evolved into a feminist icon, a role model for girls, and a fighter who uses her considerable powers to defend the weak. And as Donna Minkowitz explains in "Xena: She's Big, Tall, Strong—and Popular," Xena is long overdue, for no other female television character has ever rivaled heroic male archetypes as Xena has.

We close this chapter with a poem, "Barbie Doll," about a figure that has been an icon for American girls for 40 years. For millions of women, the Barbie had been more than a little-girl toy, more than an ageless, unchanging piece of plastic to dress up. As we see in Marge Piercy's powerful poem, Barbie is a reminder of the seemingly innocent yet potentially insidious social forces that mold one's self-image and behavior.

Where Are the Heroes?
Ed Siegel

> Would a composer of classical music be your first choice for a hero? How about a painter or playwright? If you're like most people, the answer to both questions is "no." More likely, a sports figure would be your heroic first choice—or so argues Ed Siegel. In "Where Are the Heroes?" Siegel laments that the world of contemporary art has become so antiheroic in nature that few people can relate to it. But there is one last place we can find true heroic behavior—on the athletic field.
>
> Siegel is a critic-at-large covering the arts for the *Boston Globe* where this piece first appeared on the morning of January 26, 1997, when the New England Patriots met the Green Bay Packers for Super Bowl XXXI. Green Bay won the laurels.

1   Toward the end of his first "Young People's Concert" telecast in 1958, Leonard Bernstein played an excerpt from the finale of Tchaikovsky's Fifth Symphony, turned to a national audience and described the music this way: "The whole orchestra sounds joyful and triumphant, like someone who has just made a touchdown and is the hero of the football game."

2   As virtually the entire region, if not the nation, settles in front of their television sets at about 6 o'clock tonight for Super Bowl XXXI between the New England Patriots and the Green Bay Packers, hoping that Drew Bledsoe or Curtis Martin or

Terry Glenn becomes the hero of this larger-than-life event, the last thing on any-one's mind will be Tchaikovsky's Fifth, or classical music—or any work of art.

3   That's a shame. That the world of professional sports and the world of contem-porary art exist in separate orbits may seem like the natural state of affairs, but as Bernstein suggested, it wasn't always so. Arts organizations and their audiences may sneer at the amount of money and attention devoted to what is only, after all, a game. And they are right to lament how art of all kinds has been taken out of the schools, as well as bemoaning the media's continuing drift toward popular culture, the Republican sacking of national endowments and all the other reasons for their troubles.

4   It may be, though, that the art world sealed its own diminished fate when, not long after Tchaikovsky's Fifth was first performed in 1888, modernists began to re-ject the heroic ideal as a primary topic for artistic consideration. If, as mythologist and folklorist Joseph Campbell suggested, we are all drawn to the hero's adventure as a universal myth, is it any wonder that we turn to sports and turn away from con-temporary art to see those myths played out? Particularly when the idea of heroism has also been erased from public life, be it politics, religion or the media?

5   Sports is one of the last places where those myths can be experienced. One of the reasons the Patriots are in the Super Bowl, for example, is because they won their final regular-season game, which led to a first-round bye and home-field ad-vantage in the playoffs. Few fans at halftime of that game thought the Patriots had a chance. They were losing, 22–0, to the New York Giants, and the mood was akin to the beginning of that Tchaikovsky symphony—"sad and gloomy and depressed" in Bernstein's words.

6   In order to win, the Patriots had to summon up every ounce of heroism as indi-viduals and as a collective. The punt-return team had to block impeccably to free Dave Meggett for a stunning touchdown return. Bledsoe had to be fearless against Giants trying to crush him, and he had to throw perfect passes, including the win-ning one to Ben Coates, who may have surprised even himself by getting into the end zone with three tacklers hanging onto him. And the defense had to play as if di-vinely possessed.

7   There was, in that second half, almost everything that we get from myth—selflessness, determination, ingenuity, courage, nobility. Even if those myths are played out in terms of brute strength and athletic achievement, they are still metaphors for the human struggle, just as are those in "Ulysses," either the Homer or James Joyce version.

8   Can those myths be found today in the music of Pierre Boulez? The plays of David Mamet? The paintings of Willem De Kooning? This isn't to say that these artists don't have other things to offer or that it was undesirable to undermine the bombast of Wagnerian opera and romantic literature.

9   The question is whether too much of contemporary art has gone too far in di-vorcing itself from mythic and heroic concerns. In a 1995 lecture at Massachusetts Institute of Technology, in acceptance of the Killian Faculty Achievement Award, Pulitzer Prize-winning composer John Harbison welcomed "the end of a historical

period, an interesting one but not always the best one for the production of works of music, a sort of heroic age, which I call the 'Masterpiece Age.' "

10   Granted, not every piece of music has to be a soundtrack for a Patriots' victory, and not every novel and play has to touch on universal myth. But Harbison, who has written distinguished music, speaks to the problems that the arts face today. If the arts are alienated from striving toward some ideal, then doesn't it stand to reason that potential patrons will be alienated from the arts?

11   When Eugene O'Neill, in "Long Day's Journey Into Night," changed Shakespeare's quote from "We are such stuff as dreams are made on" to "We are such stuff as manure is made on," he was shouldering a banner for a tough and bold standard of how art would measure human life. O'Neill's is quite likely the best play written in this country, but its call to anti-heroic arms speaks volumes about why people shrink from contemporary art.

12   The concept of heroism hasn't exactly disappeared and has even gone through some fascinating permutations in Joyce and elsewhere. There is May Sarton's great quote, "One must think like a hero to behave like a merely decent human being." John le Carré used that in his epigraph to "The Russia House" and Tom Stoppard incorporated it in his screenplay of the novel.

13   Another Pulitzer Prize-winning composer, the late Stephen Albert, believed that we have lost the narrative thread to our lives and that abstraction in 20th-century art was part of the problem. Albert and Yo-Yo Ma both won Grammys for one of his final compositions, the Cello Concerto, which reconnected the thread. As Ma says in the liner notes, "It is like one of the old romantic concertos—an autobiography of the wounded hero. This music is in the strongest sense personal and soulful, and it takes us through the same emotional journey Stephen was going through when he composed it."

14   You can find similar hero's journeys in John Corigliano's Symphony No. 1, the plays of Athol Fugard, the jazz of Wynton Marsalis or Abdullah Ibrahim. But by and large, the idea of art as heroic seems to be acceptable only in pursuit of a political issue.

15   One of the few other places besides sports we can regularly turn to for heroes is pop culture—rock music and film in particular. The divide between so-called high and pop art was symbolized a few weeks ago in a New York Times classical-music column. Bernard Holland announced he had little desire to see the movie "Shine" because of the triviality of the music it showcased, Rachmaninoff's Third Piano Concerto.

16   He has a point, in that the piece does symbolize the dull excesses of romanticism, but the reason the movie is such a huge arthouse hit is because both David Helfgott's life and the music are mythic in nature. Helfgott, of course, had to fight back from mental illness. And imagine if he had been rehearsing something like Anton Webern's "Variations for Piano." Audiences would have said that's why he flipped out, as they were leaving the theater halfway through the movie.

17   There are variations of heroism everywhere you look in movies, ranging from the light entertainment of "Jerry Maguire" to "Hamlet" to "Secrets and Lies."

Movies go too far in the other direction, making something heroic out of everything, even such questionable figures as Eva Peron and such unquestionably unheroic figures as Larry Flynt.

18   Rock music has its share of unsavory "heroes" as well, particularly gangsta rappers. But Bruce Springsteen, Beck and the ex-Prince all give their fans a heroic pose along with relatively sophisticated content. And it's not an all-boys' myth-making club anymore, either, as Madonna, Queen Latifah, Alanis Morissette and Joan Osborne can attest to. Whatever you think of their music, all four of these women speak to taking charge of their lives, and it's easy to see why they are heroes to their fans.

19   But sports still seems to be the pop-culture form that possesses many of the noblest attributes we used to look to high art to illuminate, despite the increasing thuggery professional sports tolerates and the free agency that makes a joke out of the idea of loyalty.

20   Still, only on rare occasions like the tearing down of the Berlin Wall, has a performance of Beethoven's Ninth so captured the ideals of that music, as well as the aftermath of the Celtics beating the Philadelphia 76ers in the seventh game of their semifinal series in 1981 by one point. Perfect strangers were hugging each other on Causeway Street in celebration.

21   The world doesn't offer us many heroes anymore, so Mayor Thomas M. Menino had better beware, even if the Patriots don't win today. If the team leaves the city, it won't matter how many good things he does in office. If the Cleveland Patriots are in some future Super Bowl, Menino will always be remembered as the villain who forced the heroes out of the city.

22   Win or lose, the Patriots have already spoken to us about what most of us strive for—working well with other people, interracial harmony, determination, fortitude, and, most of all, a sense that we can all share in something larger than ourselves. The art world should take note:

23   Look down your nose if you want. If the Patriots win today, I'll be celebrating with a fifth of Tchaikovsky.

EXPLORING THE TEXT

1. Summarize Siegel's thesis.
2. What makes the Patriots' victory in the playoff game against the Giants particularly heroic? For Siegel, how does this game represent many of the qualities found in myth?
3. Discuss the difference between Shakespeare's line, "We are such stuff as dreams are made on," and O'Neill's reinterpretation, "We are such stuff as manure is made on" (paragraph 11). What do each of these lines suggest about the nature of humanity? How do they support Siegel's point?
4. Do you agree with Siegel that movies have gone too far in making heroes of such "questionable figures as Eva Peron and . . . Larry Flynt" (paragraph 17)? Who else would you add to the list of people who have been unjustifiably glamorized by the movies?

5. Siegel argues that sports allow us to "share in something larger than ourselves." Do you agree with this? Are there other things that allow for this?

WRITING ASSIGNMENTS

1. Siegel feels that sports offer the public an arena to see heroes and heroic behavior. However, many stories about sports figures focus on their misdeeds—drug abuse, gambling debts, sexual escapades, and egotistical temper tantrums. Write an essay discussing whether you think the media's reporting of athletes' foibles has gone too far or if this scrutiny is necessary to avoid blind hero worship.
2. Write an narrative about a sporting event—either one you watched, or one you participated in—where you feel the athletes demonstrated heroic behavior. What qualities did the team players display that made for an uplifting experience? How did the crowd react?

GROUP PROJECT

1. Throughout his essay, Siegel argues that the modern arts—particularly drama, art, and music—have failed to offer audiences works that celebrate human achievement and possibility, thus audiences are alienated. Because of this alienation, audiences turn to sports and popular culture for their role models. Do some research to see if you find Siegel's theory to be valid. Arrange for your group to visit a local museum or attend a performance of a modern play or piece of music. Discuss your reactions. Did your experiences validate Siegel's argument, or do you feel that there is another side? Did different group members feel differently? After you have talked amongst yourselves, have each group member write a brief essay about how they felt about their cultural experience. (Be sure to refer to Siegel's essay in your discussion.)

Heroine Worship: The Age of the Female Icon
Holly Brubach

Madonna, Oprah Winfrey, Cindy Crawford, Hillary Rodham Clinton . . . women who enjoy a fame and visibility today that could not have been imagined 100 years ago. In this essay, Holly Brubach examines the rise of women as icons and role models in our starstruck culture. She concludes that girls and women today have more choices of whom to emulate than ever be-fore—so many, in fact, that modeling themselves on just one individual seems "arbitrary and limiting." Do you agree?

This article first appeared on November 24, 1996 in the *New York Times Sunday Maga-zine* of which Brubach is the style editor.

1   It's the 90's, and the pantheon we've built to house the women in our minds is get-ting crowded. Elizabeth Taylor, Eleanor Roosevelt, Oprah Winfrey, Alanis Moris-sette, Indira Gandhi, Claudia Schiffer, Coco Chanel, Doris Day, Aretha Franklin, Jackie Onassis, Rosa Parks—they're all there, the dead and the living side by side, contemporaneous in our imaginations. On television and in the movies, in advertis-ing and magazines, their images are scattered across the landscape of our everyday lives. Their presence is sometimes decorative, sometimes uplifting, occasionally in-furiating. The criteria for appointment to this ad hoc hall of fame that takes up so much space in our thoughts and in our culture may at first glance appear to be utterly random. In fact, irrespective of their achievements, most of these women have been apotheosized primarily on the basis of their ability to appeal to our fantasies.

2   An icon is a human sound bite, an individual reduced to a name, a face and an idea: Dale Evans, the compassionate cowgirl. In some cases, just the name and an idea suffice. Few people would recognize Helen Keller in a photograph, but her name has become synonymous with being blind and deaf to such an extent that she has inspired an entire category of jokes. Greta Garbo has gone down in collective memory as an exalted enigma with a slogan about being alone. Asking a man if that's a gun in his pocket is all it takes to invoke Mae West. Catherine Deneuve's face, pictured on a stamp, is the emblem of France. Virginia Woolf has her own T-shirt. Naomi Campbell has her own doll. Celebrity being the engine that drives our culture, these women have been taken up by the media and made famous, pack-aged as commodities and marketed to a public eager for novelty and easily bored. . . .

3   Our icons are by no means exclusively female, but the male ones are perhaps less ubiquitous and more accessible. The pedestals we put them on are lower; the service they are called on to perform is somewhat different.

4   Like women, men presumably look to icons for tips that they can take away and apply to their lives. The men who are elevated to the status of icons are the ones who are eminently cool, whose moves the average guy can steal. They do not prompt a fit of introspection (much less of self-recrimination), as female icons often do in women. What a male icon inspires in other men is not so much the desire to *be* him as the desire to be accepted by him—to be buddies, to shoot pool together, to go drinking. I have all this on good authority from a man of my acquaintance who in-sists that, though regular guys may envy, say, Robert Redford for his ability to knock women dead, what they're thinking as they watch him in a movie is not "Hey, I wonder if I have what it takes to do that, too," but "I wonder if Redford would like to hang out with me."

5   Whereas women may look at an icon like Raquel Welch, whose appeal is clearly to the male half of humanity, and ask themselves, "If that's what's required to appeal to a man, have I got it, or can I get it?" (The thought of hanging out with

Welch—going shopping together or talking about boyfriends—would, I think it's safe to say, never cross most women's minds.)

6   An entire industry, called fashion, has grown up around the business of convincing women that they need to remake themselves in someone else's image: makeup and clothes and other products are presented not as alterations but as improvements. The notion of appearance and personality as a project to be undertaken is inculcated early on. A man may choose to ignore certain male icons; a woman has no such luxury where the great majority of female icons are concerned. She must come to terms with them, defining herself in relation to them—emulating some, rejecting others. In certain cases, a single icon may exist for her as both an example and a reproach.

7   Our male icons are simply the latest entries in a tradition of long standing, broad enough in any given era to encompass any number of prominent men. But the current array of female icons is a rare phenomenon, the outgrowth of aspirations many of which date back no more than 100 years.

8   What were the images of women that informed the life of a girl growing up 200 years ago? It's hard for us to imagine the world before it was wallpapered with ads, before it was inundated with all the visual "information" that comes our way in the course of an average day and competes with real people and events for our attention. There were no magazines, no photographs. In church, a girl would have seen renderings of the Virgin Mary and the saints. She may have encountered portraits of royalty, whose station, unless she'd been born an aristocrat, must have seemed even more unattainable than that of the saints. There were picturesque genre paintings depicting peasants and chambermaids, to be seen at the public salons, if anyone thought to bring a girl to them. But the most ambitious artists concentrated on pagan goddesses and mythological women, who, being Olympian, inhabited a plane so lofty that they were presumably immune to quotidian concerns. History and fiction, for the girl who had access to them, contained tales of women whose lives had been somewhat more enterprising and action-packed than those of the women she saw around her, but her knowledge of most women's exploits in her own time would have been limited to hearsay: a woman had written a novel, a woman had played hostess to one of the greatest philosophers of the age and discussed ideas with him, a woman had disguised herself as a man and gone to war. Most likely, a girl would have modeled herself on a female relative, or on a woman in her community. The great beauty who set the standard by which others were measured would have been the one in their midst—the prettiest girl in town, whose fame was local.

9   Nineteenth-century icons like Sarah Bernhardt and George Sand would have imparted no more in the way of inspiration; their careers were predicated on their talents, which had been bestowed by God. It was Florence Nightingale who finally provided an example that was practicable, one to which well-born girls could aspire, and hundreds of women followed her into nursing.

10 Today, the images of women confronting a girl growing up in our culture are far more diverse, though not all of them can be interpreted as signs of progress. A woman who in former times might have served as the model for some painter's rendering of one or another pagan goddess is now deployed to sell us cars and soap.

The great beauty has been chosen from an international field of contenders. At the movies, we see the stories of fictional women brought to life by real actresses whose own lives have become the stuff of fiction. In the news, we read about women running countries, directing corporations and venturing into outer space.

11   The conditions that in our century have made possible this proliferation of female icons were of course brought on by the convergence of advances in women's rights and the growth of the media into an industry. As women accomplished the unprecedented, the press took them up and made them famous, trafficking in their accomplishments, their opinions, their fates. If, compared with the male icons of our time, our female icons seem to loom larger in our culture and to cast a longer shadow, perhaps it's because in so many cases their stories have had the urgency of history in the making.

12   When it comes to looking at women, we're all voyeurs, men and women alike. Does our urge to study the contours of their flesh and the changes in their faces stem from some primal longing to be reunited with the body that gave us life? Women have been the immemorial repository of male fantasies—a lonesome role that many are nonetheless loath to relinquish, given the power it confers and the oblique satisfaction it brings. The curiosity and desire inherent in the so-called male gaze, deplored for the way it has objectified women in art and in films, are matched on women's part by the need to assess our own potential to be found beautiful and by the pleasure in putting ourselves in the position of the woman being admired.

13   Our contemporary images of women are descended from a centuries-old tradition and, inevitably, they are seen in its light. Women have often been universalized, made allegorical. The figure who represents Liberty, or Justice, to say nothing of Lust or Wrath, is a woman, not a man—a tradition that persists: there is no Mr. America. The unidentified woman in innumerable paintings—landscapes, genre scenes, mythological scenes—transcends her circumstances and becomes Woman. It's the particular that is customarily celebrated in men, and the general in woman. Even our collective notions of beauty reflect this: a man's idiosyncrasies enhance his looks; a woman's detract from hers.

14   "I'm every woman, it's all in me," Chaka Khan signs, and the chords in the bass modulate optimistically upward, in a surge of possibility. Not all that long ago, the notion that any woman could be every women would have been dismissed as blatantly absurd, but to our minds it makes evident sense, in keeping with the logic that we can be anything we want to be—the cardinal rule of the human-potential movement and an assumption that in America today is so widely accepted and dearly held that it might as well be written into the Constitution. Our icons are at this point sufficiently plentiful that to model ourselves on only one of them would seem arbitrary and limiting, when in fact we can take charge in the manner of Katherine Hepburn, strut in the way we learned by watching Tina Turner, flirt in the tradition of Rita Hayworth, grow old with dignity in the style of Georgia O'Keeffe. In the spirit of post-modernism, we piece our selves together, assembling the examples of several women in a single personality—a process that makes for some unprecedented combinations, like Madonna: the siren who lifts weights and becomes a mother. We contemplate the women who have been singled out in our culture and the permutations

of femininity they represent. About to move on to the next century, we call on various aspects of them as we reconfigure our lives, deciding which aspects of our selves we want to take with us and which aspects we want to leave behind.

EXPLORING THE TEXT

1. Brubach argues that "what a male icon inspires in other men is not so much the desire to be him as the desire to be accepted by him" (paragraph 4), while for women, female icons tend to produce the response, "If that's what's required to appeal to a man, have I got it, or can I get it?" (paragraph 5) How does this affect how men and women relate to their respective icons?

2. According to Brubach, a girl 200 years ago would most likely have modeled herself on "a female relative, or on a woman in her community" (paragraph 8). What differences do you see between these local role models and today's internationally famous role models? How does the relationship between a girl and her role model differ today from in the past?

3. Explain why Florence Nightingale is called the first role model who "provided an example that was practicable" (paragraph 10).

4. Do you agree with Brubach that female icons "seem to loom larger in our culture and to cast a longer shadow" (paragraph 11)? Who are currently the biggest male and female box office draws? Most popular musicians? Most influential political figures? Do your examples refute or support Brubach's statement?

5. Discuss what the author means by the "male gaze" (paragraph 12). How has this way of looking at women proven to be a double-edged sword for women?

6. Discuss Brubach's closing paragraph where she argues that girls/women today have the opportunity to draw from various female role models—that they can "piece" themselves together. What advantages and/or disadvantages might these choices about who they want to model themselves after offer women?

WRITING ASSIGNMENTS

1. Throughout the 1980s and early 1990s, Madonna ruled the media as one of the most talked-about and well-known female icons ever. Write a brief essay discussing what qualities you think made Madonna so popular and famous. Has anyone been able to duplicate Madonna's fame? If so, who? What qualities does this new "it girl" possess?

2. Brubach begins her article with a list of women who she considers icons. Brubach says, "these women have been apostheosized primarily on the basis of their ability to appeal to our fantasies." Write a sentence or two by each woman's name, describing her major claim to fame. (If you're not

sure about some of them, ask others for help or do some quick research.) Then consider what fantasies each woman appeals to and add that to your previous information. Do you see any patterns among these women in terms of the qualities that they possess?

3. Write an essay about your personal heroine. Explain why you like and admire this person. What qualities of your heroine would you most like to have yourself?

GROUP PROJECTS

1. Brubach talks about images of women in art (painting, sculpture, photos) in several places in the essay. Arrange for your group to visit a local art museum. (If this is impossible, you could check art books out of the library as an alternative.) Examine and analyze the representations of women. Look for images from several different centuries. Do you see any similarities in the presentation of the women? What type of women are most often represented in art? Certainly you'll find a number of Madonnas, saints, and goddesses. What else did you see? Present your findings to the class. (Be sure to bring postcards, photos, or reproductions of some representative figures so that the class can see the images for themselves.)

2. Take a poll on who the female icons of the moment are by surveying students on your campus. (If you would like to broaden your investigation, examine Web home pages as well.) Try for a mix of respondents in terms of gender, race, and age. To focus responses you may simply want to ask: "Who do you consider the three most influential women today?" Tabulate your results in a list and distribute to the class. Have the class discuss whether they agree with the results and what they think the results say about the way we currently evaluate women and women's roles.

3. Using Brubach's idea that women today are free to mix and match characteristics from various heroines, see if your group can create a composite woman who would make the ideal female icon. Feel free to draw on any woman, living or dead, for characteristics, but be sure to explain why you have chosen her. To make things more interesting, make groups same sex only. Have all the groups present their "superwoman." Were there any notable differences between the male and female groups' creations?

Princess Diana: Her True Face
Andrew Morton

Princess Diana's death on August 31, 1997, shocked the entire world. The murky and violent circumstances surrounding the Paris car crash that claimed her life and that of her two companions only added to the media frenzy that ensued following the accident. Her funeral a week later was watched by an estimated two billion people around the world. But such an extraordinary outpouring of grief and affection far exceeded any contributions that she was able to make in her 36 years. For more than any other person in recent times, Diana had both in life and in death achieved the status of icon—a status created by an age obsessed with celebrity. In his essay below, Andrew Morton looks at the changing image of the princess—from the shy child bride of her wedding day, to the outspoken and socially conscious woman she became in the years before her tragic death.

Morton is the author of *Diana: Her True Story* (1993) in which he talks candidly about Diana's struggle with her eating disorders, depression, and unhappy marriage, all of which helped make Diana a sympathetic figure in her attempts to break free of the royal family's control over her. This article first appeared in the September 15, 1997, issue of *Newsweek*.

1 Perhaps it was those penetrating cornflower blue eyes that could seduce at a glance. Or maybe it was her nose, slightly too prominent, her strong jaw line and high, arrogant cheekbones that gave her the appearance of determination bordering on willfulness. Then again there was the look, that characteristic droop of the shoulders and swoop of the head, which could inspire instant devotion or pity.

2 What elevated Diana from the simply glamorous to the iconographic, however, was not just her many faces: it was her endless enigmatic personality. There have been other modern legends, of course—Marilyn Monroe, Princess Grace, Jacqueline Onassis. But no other woman so captured the Zeitgeist of this particular age than Diana. She began as "Dynasty Di" in the go-go '80s but ultimately became a very '90s kind of figure—a serious-minded single mother struggling to recover from a broken marriage. Hers was not an easy journey: she was, at different times, sex symbol, virgin mother, grieving wife, avenging saint and, finally, liberated woman.

3 I would not have thought that she would have come so far, so quickly, when she walked into a meet-the-press party in the unlikely setting of a casino hotel in Alice Springs, Australia, in 1983. It was the first day of her first overseas visit of her blossoming royal career, and it was my first proper examination of the woman who would touch all our lives. She was jet-lagged, red-faced from sunbathing—and very nervous about meeting the media.

4 Way back then she was happy to play the role of dutiful child bride, anxiously following in the footsteps of her articulate husband. In those far-off days, royal men were judged by what they said and royal women by what they wore. Diana was more than happy to conform. In her first TV interview she admitted: "I feel my role is supporting my husband whenever I can, and always being behind him, encouraging him. And also, most important, being a mother and a wife. And that's what I try to achieve." Feminists groaned, but those inside the palace redoubt were quietly satisfied. This marriage was conforming exactly to script.

5 Then the royal couple started to forget their lines. In the mid-1980s, Diana, wife and mother, turned into a fashion queen while her husband devolved into a figure of fun, a man who talked to plants when he wasn't delivering woolly, indecipherable speeches. Meanwhile, there were even deeper tensions developing in the royal fairy tale. The princess has been clinically depressed after the birth of Prince William; she suffered from the eating disorder bulimia nervosa, and was perennially jealous of

her husband's relationship with Camilla Parker Bowles. By the early 1990s, the princess had entered what she was to call the "dark ages" of her royal career. She felt powerless and frustrated. In any earlier era, she would have had no way out of her unhappy marriage—and no way to alter her image of superficial glamour. She would have been a latter-day Queen Alexandra, the betrayed wife of Edward VII: celebrated for beauty, refinement and grace but trapped with an unfaithful husband.

6   But the times, and Diana, were different. As her private life disintegrated, she gained strength—and public support, a useful weapon in her war against the Windsors—from comforting the sick. She was surprised to find that when she embraced emotions and causes which others, particularly the royal family, shied away from, it gave her the will to carry on.

7   Confined as much by her image as her royal position, her marriage effectively over, Diana's tacit cooperation for my book, "Diana: Her True Story," broke the cycle of defeat and sacrifice. For the first time it told the unvarnished truth about the hostile palace establishment and her distant husband. Her ensuring transformation from silent victim to eloquent ambassador was probably the defining moment of her life. She was finally able to shape her own agenda and style. It was an achievement not lost on ordinary people, especially women. I received many, many letters, mainly from American women, who sensed in Diana echoes of their own lives and their own struggles.

8   "I see myself as a princess for the world, not the Princess of Wales," she once said. Her sentiments may have been grandiose, but they were not arrogant. In the three years or so before her death she was learning her true power to move people and to draw them into the causes she espoused. Her decision to auction her gowns in New York for AIDS charities symbolized a deliberate shedding of the past: the royal clotheshorse had become a workhorse. Perhaps the crowning achievement of her career was her campaign against land mines, a concern that symbolized how Diana's appeal now had a truly global resonance.

9   As she stood on the brink of a new life, her past, a universe she could never escape, caught up with her in the shape of the trailing *paparazzi.* She may have flown the cage of Buckingham Palace and liberated herself as a woman in her own right, but the world would never let her break out from her abiding image as a glamorous and rather frivolous woman. Her life came a tragic full circle: the camera loved her to death.

EXPLORING THE TEXT

1. Discuss the title of the essay. Does Morton seem to imply that he shows us Diana's "true face"? Does the title contradict his statement in paragraph 2 that Diana's personality was "endlessly enigmatic"? What does Morton seem to conclude was Diana's "true face" at the time of her death?

2. How does Morton characterize Diana in the early 1980s? What were her main concerns as a new royal wife? Discuss the use of the word *admitted* in paragraph 4. How does this shape our view of Diana's words?

3. Morton's article chronicles the changing faces of Diana over the course of nearly two decades. What does he see happening to her image in the mid-1980s? Discuss how this affected her marriage.

4. How did Diana's problems (and her willingness to speak about them) add to her popularity with the public, while alienating her from the royal family? Do you feel Diana was justified in talking openly about her eating disorders, her depression, and Charles's infidelity to the press?

5. Morton states in paragraph 7, "Her ensuing transformation from silent victim to eloquent ambassador was probably the defining moment of her life." What "face" does he create for Princess Diana in this paragraph? What do you make of this "defining moment" occurring at the same time Diana co-operated with Morton on his biography of her?

6. Do you agree that Diana became a "princess for the world, not the Princess of Wales" (paragraph 8)? Does Morton offer evidence to support this notion? If so, what?

7. What final conclusions does Morton come to about Princess Diana's image? Do you agree with his final statement that "her life came a tragic full circle"? Why or why not? What part does he seem to feel the media played in this tragedy?

WRITING ASSIGNMENTS

1. Princess Diana's death and funeral were the major media events of the 1990s. While the paparazzi were vilified as causing her death, some critics point out that the "legitimate press" also contributed to the media "feeding frenzy" that haunted her in life and death. Write an essay discussing the differences and/or similarities you see between "tabloid" journalism and "legitimate" journalism. You may want to start by brainstorming a list of media you consider to be either one or the other. You may also want to look at the overlap between the two. For instance, are there any tabloid elements to the nightly national news? Give examples in your essay.

2. Pick three readings in this chapter and write an essay discussing each subject's role as icon. For instance, can you find any common ground between Michael Jordan, Princess Diana, and Selena? What, to you, makes someone move beyond the arena of celebrity and into the arena of an icon? In your essay, draw on your own opinion, but also use quotes and/or examples from the texts where appropriate.

3. Many people were especially moved at Princess Diana's funeral by Elton John's song "Candle in the Wind 1997." This song was originally written as a tribute to Marilyn Monroe (another icon who also died at the age of 36); new words were written in honor of Diana a few days before her funeral. Do you feel this song was an appropriate tribute? What other songs can you think of that commemorate someone's death (e.g., Eric Clapton's "Tears from Heaven," various tributes to Tupac Shakur and the Notorious

B.I.G.)? Write an essay discussing how you see these songs playing a role in the process of grieving, both for the individual artist and for the public at large.

GROUP PROJECTS

1. Mother Theresa died about a week after Princess Diana, and her funeral also received a good deal of coverage. Many in the media tried to make a connection between these two deaths—there were numerous pictures of the tall, glamorous Diana holding the hand of the tiny, simply clad old woman. Using the library and/or the Internet, find several articles about the funerals of each woman. As a group, read the articles and see what conclusions you can draw about how each of these women was painted at the end of her life. Pay particular attention to the idea of sainthood. Present your analysis to the class.

2. Princess Diana was one of the most photographed women of the century. As a group, collect as many photos of Diana from as many different sources as you can. (Don't tear pictures out of library newspapers or magazines; a photocopy will do.) Together, create a collage of these images. (Your collage could be arranged along a rough time line or you could organize it by different roles—Diana as mother, social activist and glamour queen—or it may simply be a random collection of images.) After creating your collage, write an analysis of what you feel made Diana such a compelling subject for photographers. What, besides her beauty, made her so photogenic?

Selena: A Legend Grows, and So Does an Industry
Larry Rohter

Many people were shocked and horrified when Selena Quintanilla Perez, the rising young Mexican American music star, was gunned down in a motel lobby by one of her employees in 1995. Since her death, however, Selena's legend has grown, and her fans remain steadfastly loyal. Her records continue to sell in the millions, and her life has become the subject of movies, books, and memorabilia. In this piece, Larry Rohter examines Selena's role as a groundbreaking Latina icon and discusses why she is as popular today—maybe even more popular—than she was before her tragic death.

Rohter writes about jazz and popular music for the *New York Times,* where this article first appeared on January 12, 1997.

1   Long before the murder that belatedly brought her to the attention of the English-speaking world, Selena had earned the title Queen of Tejano Music and the affection of Mexican-Americans in small towns like this one, the self-styled strawberry capital of Texas. So it was only fitting that when a Hollywood production company decided to transform the martyred singer's short life into a movie and to film some of its concert scenes at the county fairgrounds here, the crowd of extras that assembled was full of people who had seen the real Selena perform and adored her.

2   Deep into the night on a warm autumn Saturday, grandmothers with babies in tow, entire families and knots of teen-agers stood transfixed as Jennifer Lopez, the actress playing their idol, lip-synched Selena's greatest hits. "For me, it has always been Selena and always will be," Roxane Avila, a 16-year-old fan, said between takes. "I went to see her twice and always told my mom that I wanted to be like her. Now I can't bring myself to play her records because it's just too painful. So is this. But even so, I couldn't miss it."

3   Less than two years after being shot to death by a disgruntled employee of hers in a Corpus Christi motel room, Selena is well on her way to becoming as much an icon for Latin Americans and Spanish speakers in the United States as Elvis Presley is for rock-and-roll fans, Marilyn Monroe for film buffs or Jerry Garcia for one-time hippies. "The torchbearer for a new generation of Latinos" is how the movie's Mexican-American director and screenwriter, Gregory Nava, describes Selena.

4   That passion has also fed a flood of posthumous books, records and memorabilia, making Selena better known today than at the peak of her career. Or as Sue D'Agostino, a publicist at EMI Records, the company that groomed Selena for stardom, puts it, "She has had a life of her own after her death."

5   To Mr. Nava, whose previous movies include "El Norte" and "My Family: Mi Familia," there is an especially mythic quality to the story of a singer who rose from humble beginnings through hard work and talent, overcoming barriers of language and culture, only to die violently at the age of 23, just as her career was taking wing. "Look at Elvis, James Dean and Marilyn," he said. "They were all brought down by their self-destructive natures. But for Selena to have been brought down this way is more tragic than the others because she really was living the American Dream."

6   In Selena's case, everything started with the music and her capacity to produce on cue the sob in the voice that is common both to the blues and to Mexican music. "That teardrop she had in her vocal cords gave her an ability to interpret and communicate in her songs as if she had lived far beyond her years," said Jose Behar, president of EMI Latin Records, who in 1989 signed the band then known as Selena y los Dinos to a recording contract and nurtured her career through the recording of "Dreaming of You," the posthumous release that sold three million copies in the United States.

7   With that came a sharply-defined, even defiant, sense of style and self that has proved just as important to her growing band of admirers. Last year, a casting call in four cities to young Hispanic women to audition for the part of Selena as a child drew more than 20,000 applicants, all of them made up to look just like Selena, whose features "were definitely more indigenous than royal Spanish," as the actor Edward James Olmos, who plays her father in the movie, pointed out. In death, as in

life, in other words, Selena Quintanilla Perez has come to represent a new standard of Latin beauty and self-confidence.

8   Jennifer Lopez, the actress who plays the adult Selena, is from the Castle Hill section of the Bronx, not South Texas, and is of Puerto Rican descent, not Mexican. "But Selena was dark, like me, and had a Latin body, like mine, and didn't try to hide that," Ms. Lopez said. "She went up there on stage and said: This is who I am, and I like it. Why should I aspire to be blond and thin?" Yet there is more to Selena's continued appeal than just her appearance, as Ms. Lopez and others are quick to acknowledge.

9   Christy Haubegger, a Mexican-American from Houston who is publisher of *Latina,* a New York-based magazine for Hispanic women, said: "Selena is an icon to us because she is both culturally and physically like we are, someone born here in the United States and definitely an American, but also a Latina, proud of who she is and able to say she didn't have to lose her culture to be successful. She not only embodied ideals of Latina beauty but the struggle we live with every day, between two cultures, two languages, and two sets of values."

10   Even before Selena was born, of course, Latinas like Rita Hayworth and Raquel Welch had built large followings. But they gained their fame only by changing their names, trying to discard their identities as Hispanic women and projecting an exotic image that was sexy and submissive. That formula reinforced "a stereotype of us being the oppressed half of a patriarchy, which we certainly aren't," as Ms. Haubegger put it.

11   "Latinas have been accessories for many years," she added. "Selena was the main act," leading a band that was full of men.

12   The emergence of Selena, who spoke Spanish with a Texas accent and made a point of favoring the English pronunciation of her name (suh-LEE-na) over its Spanish version (say-LAY-na), also played with the ambiguity Mexican-Americans feel toward the cultures on both sides of that hyphen. "To this day, Mexican-Americans are not viewed as kindred souls" on either side of the border, Mr. Olmos said. "We're always right next door. You're not fully accepted by the country you live in, and in the country you're from, you're left out to hang."

13   For example, Mr. Nava said that when he had first pitched his Selena proposal to Hollywood executives, they thought she was Mexican, not American. "She could no more have come out of Mexico than Frank Sinatra out of Italy," he said.

14   South of the border, too, there was resistance at first to what Selena represented. In the upper-class neighborhoods of Mexico City, she was at first derided as "naco," an ethnic and class slur meaning coarse or vulgar, because of her mestizo, or mixed European and Indian, features, which were in marked contrast to those of the typically fair-skinned and light-haired soap opera stars, and also because of her fondness for tight bustiers and even tighter pants.

15   Selena flaunted all of that, perhaps to offend the stuffier elements of the Mexican upper class but certainly to delight her fellow Mexican-Americans. "She was so tacky, but she knew it and she loved it," said Karina Duran, a makeup artist working on the film.

16   The movie being made here is only one manifestation of Selena's continued pull on the imagination of fellow Americans and Latin Americans. Eight unautho-

rized biographies of her brief life have already been published, including a bilingual paperback, with one cover in English and the other in Spanish. Televisa, Mexico's leading television network, having already produced a soap opera in which a main character is obsessed with Selena, is considering making another, only this one based on her life. Last month the E! cable network broadcast a docudrama telling her story. Home pages dedicated to Selena have sprung up on the Internet.

17   Posters of the singer can now be found in peasant huts throughout Central America and the Caribbean, and several "corridos," a type of topical ballad popular in Mexico and the Southwest, have been written about her life and death. Tribute issues of magazines are also circulating with titles like "Selena—A Latin Goddess: An Angel Whom Heaven Reclaimed. Her Image and Fragrance Are Still Present."

18   "This was something Shakespearean in its sweep, with people crying in the streets and wandering around trying to touch this tragedy," said Joe Nick Patoski, author of "Selena: Como la Flor," explaining what compelled him to write his book. "I know a lot of people put their hopes and dreams on Elvis, but I believe this runs even deeper. So much of Mexican society has been built on suffering and sadness since the time of the conquistadors, so this event was really made for this culture."

19   The books, the T-shirts and the rest are a mere prelude, however, to the onslaught that will come when Warner Brothers releases its film in March. A CD called "Siempre Selena," a selection of 10 songs in Spanish and English, some new, some remixed, is already out. But the opening of the movie will be accompanied by a soundtrack record and promotional campaigns with the likes of Coca-Cola and Wendy's.

20   "The movie is a big bus, and the soundtrack is the wheels on that bus," said Mr. Behar, the record company president. "The more resources that EMI and Warners can combine for marketing purposes, the better; whether it is through your eating a hamburger or buying a cassette or whatever. We want to leave no stone unturned here."

21   Even without that big push, the sites associated with Selena in her hometown, Corpus Christi, are now tourist attractions. The municipal auditorium has been renamed in her honor, but the principal draws are the places where she worked and lived: the boutique where the clothes she designed are on sale, the house where she lived with her parents, brother and sister, and the one just down the block where she moved after she married Chris Perez, the lead guitarist in her band. At the management office still run by Abraham Quintanilla, her father, the staff is deluged with "boxes and boxes of letters," he said. They're also mounting a display of her trophies, the costumes in which she performed and her car.

22   Ginger Routh, a volunteer at the Corpus Christi Visitors Center, said: "We actually used to give out a map where you could drive by her parents' house, but we had to quit that because the neighbors were going mad from the streets being full all the time. But we still get people from all over, not just the United States, coming in here on a daily basis."

23   Much to the distress of her father, Selena's grave site, at Seaside Memorial Park, has also become a place of pilgrimage, engulfed in memorials and flowers, much like Presley's grave at Graceland. "People take their kids and ask her to heal them, or they pray to Selena," said Mr. Quintanilla, who is a follower of the Jehovah's Witnesses group. "I don't want to promote that because it is idolatry, and I believe adoration and worship should only be to the Creator."

24   But Mr. Patoski, her biographer, noted that images of Selena had also begun appearing at religious festivals in Texas and northern Mexico. He doubts that the devotion to her will diminish anytime soon. "The person we are talking about may have been shot and killed, but the phenomenon continues," he said. "As a symbol of good and suffering, she is now right up there with the Virgin of Guadalupe."

EXPLORING THE TEXT

1. What, according to Rohter, accounts for Selena's amazing popularity, particularly among Latina girls and women?
2. Discuss in what ways Selena embodies the American Dream.
3. What qualities made Selena's singing particularly noteworthy? How might this quality contribute to her legend?
4. What point does the author make about Selena's looks? Why was Selena at first mocked by upper-class Mexicans? What does "naco" mean?
5. What difficulties do Mexican Americans face according to actor Edward James Olmos? What difficulties as a Mexican American woman did Selena face?
6. What do you think accounts for the worship of Selena that Rohter describes at the end of the article? What qualities do people see in Selena that make her appear "saintly"?
7. Discuss the title of the piece: "A Legend Grows, and So Does an Industry." Does the article suggest to you that Selena is being exploited in death? Why or why not?

WRITING ASSIGNMENTS

1. Rent the video *Selena* and review it. Did you feel the movie captured Selena's essence? How was Jennifer Lopez in the title role? Would you recommend this movie to others? Why or why not?
2. Rohter points out that Selena had come to "represent a new standard of Latin beauty and self-confidence" (paragraph 7) for Latinas, particularly because she did not make herself over as other Hispanic stars such as Rita Hayworth and Raquel Welch had. Write an essay discussing the issues that minority women face when they attempt to break into mainstream popularity. Do you see evidence of minority women still having to conform to a "white" standard of beauty, or are many, like Selena, bucking this tradition? Use specific examples to support your point of view.
3. As the article points out, our culture seems to have a fascination with celebrities who die young (think of James Dean, Jim Morrison, Kurt Cobain, Tupac Shakur, and Selena). Write a brief essay exploring what you believe lies behind this fascination. Why do you think these stars are "worshiped" years after their deaths?

GROUP PROJECTS

1. Break up into a small group and do some research on Selena's continuing popularity by investigating her on-line fan clubs. How many Web sites dedicated to Selena did your group find? What are fans talking about? Chat with a few fans, ask some questions, download some images if possible. Collate your data and write up your findings and report back to the class.

2. Have your group do a report on *tejano* music for your class. Try to determine what *tejano* means? What is the history of the music? Have group members bring in some examples of *tejano* music (including some of Selena's records, if possible) for the class to hear.

3. As a group determine how the movie *Selena* was received by the critics and the public. Have members gather reviews from five or six sources. Were critics generally favorable? Are there plans for more movies dealing with Selena? Collate your findings and prepare a report to be presented to the class.

Amelia Earhart: The Lady Vanishes
Camille Paglia

Camille Paglia, a professor at the University of the Arts in Philadelphia, came to fame with the publication of her 1990 book, *Sexual Personae,* and has since become known as a provocative writer unafraid to weigh in with unpopular opinions. In the article below, she discusses how Amelia Earhart, the first woman to cross the Atlantic by air, helped define a new kind of modern woman, and, in so doing, became an important role model to her as both a teenager and as an adult woman.

Paglia is the author of several books including collections of her essays, *Sex, Art, and American Culture* (1992) and *Vamps and Tramps* (1994). This article first appeared in the *New York Times* in November 1996.

1 Amelia Earhart symbolizes modern woman's invasion of the male world of daring adventure. As an aviator, she broke barriers and made the machine age her own. As a recreational athlete and automobile driver, she embodied fitness, energy and breezy mobility.

2 The tall, shy, boyish Earhart was dubbed "Lady Lindy" after a 1928 flight that made her the first women to cross the Atlantic by air, although she was little more than a passenger. Four years later, determined to prove her mettle, Earhart became the first woman to fly the Atlantic solo, overcoming near-fatal weather hazards and equipment failure. Until her strange disappearance in the Pacific after a trouble-plagued around-the-world flight in 1937, Earhart was probably the most famous woman in the world and a constant presence in the media. Dashing in man-tailored shirts, jackets and slacks, Earhart epitomized the rapidly evolving new woman who

sought self-definition and fulfillment outside the home. Her ability to open her mysterious, poetic inner self to the camera lens was as advanced as any movie star's.

3   In 1961, at age 14, I saw an article about Earhart in a Syracuse newspaper and had a stunning conversion experience. Marooned in a desert of perky blondes (Doris Day, Debbie Reynolds, Sandra Dee), I was in wild adolescent revolt against American sex roles. Earhart's life was a revelation. Through her and Katharine Hepburn, I discovered the achievements of women of the 1920's and 30's, who swept into amazing visibility after the passage of suffrage. I embarked on an obsessive three-year research project on Earhart with the aim of producing a book that would celebrate her as a model of the liberated woman. I ransacked libraries, wrote hundreds of letters and met Earhart's sister near Boston. A curator of the National Air and Space Museum opened a safe to show me Earhart's medals and other personal effects. At Movietonews in New York, I was given a private showing of Earhart newsreels. On family car trips, I visited Earhart's birthplace in Kansas and the obscure field near Miami where she began her last flight. At Purdue University, I tried on her battered leather jacket.

4   By vanishing into thin air, Amelia Earhart seemed to merge with the elements of nature, which she had so often challenged and conquered. She became the archetype of the androgynous winged seraph who escapes the bondage of reproduction and biology. For me, she represented high aspiration and freedom of thought. Hers was a mature, enlightened feminism that never indulged in shallow male-bashing. She enjoyed an easy companionship with men, from mechanics to Presidents. She respected the greatness of what men had achieved and simply desired to show that women could perform just as well or better. And she believed that leading by example would systematically transform society.

EXPLORING THE TEXT

1. Why was Earhart called "Lady Lindy"?
2. For the teenage Paglia, what did Amelia Earhart embody?
3. Earhart came to fame in the late twenties and thirties. How does Earhart's persona contrast with the popular icons of the fifties?
4. Discuss how the details of Paglia's search for Earhart memorabilia add to the article. How do they illustrate what Paglia was searching for beyond the physical objects?
5. How does Paglia define Earhart's feminism?

WRITING ASSIGNMENTS

1. Both Paglia and Larry Rohter in "Selena: A Legend Grows" write about heroines who broke barriers and died young. Write an essay discussing parallels between Amelia Earhart and Selena focusing on their roles as pioneers.

2. Many adolescents have the same experience Paglia did—that is, they discover someone who serves as a role model and source of fascination for them. Write a narrative about a time you discovered a celebrity whom you greatly admired and emulated.

GROUP PROJECTS

1. A recent book by Jane Mendelsohn, *I Was Amelia Earhart* (1966), imagines what happened to Earhart after she mysteriously disappeared. As a group do some research about the various theories of what happened to Earhart. After you've gathered your information, write up a report about what seems the most plausible explanation to you. Present your theory to the class.
2. There have been many films and documentaries made about Earhart's life. Arrange to show one of these to the class. As a group, lead the discussion after the viewing.

Rare Jordan
Nelson George

A 1997 *Sports Illustrated* poll picked Michael Jordan as the greatest basketball player of all time. Jordan has led the Chicago Bulls to numerous championships and, in so doing, has earned tremendous wealth and fame for himself. However, Nelson George feels there's more to Jordan than flashy basketball moves and lucrative product endorsements. George sees Jordan as "rare" in his ability to appeal to both blacks and whites in equal measure and in his ability to move seamlessly between the basketball court and the corporate world, but especially in his ability to remain true to himself, despite the tremendous pressure and scrutiny he endures as America's most famous athlete.

This essay first appeared in the November 1996 issue of *Essence* magazine.

1 A few seasons ago, in the now-defunct Chicago Stadium, Michael Jordan was being guarded by the eager but overmatched John Starks. I sat 15 rows behind them, wearing my Knicks cap amid a sea of Bulls red and black. I'd flown in the day before and scalped tickets, determined to see Starks and the rest of my beloved New York team finally dethrone the Bulls.

2   What a joke.

3   Sometime during the second half, Jordan rises, the No. 23 on his chest suspended in air as Starks elevates. The Knick, who earlier in the series jammed in Jordan's face, has hops, but no one is Jordan. Starks begins his journey back to earth, but Jordan continues to hang, defying gravity. He releases the ball and, like a bird of

prey, the potential three-pointer soars toward the hoop. The shot is good. The crowd explodes. I cringe and of course the Knicks lose. Of the 54 points Jordan scores that night, it is this single shot that lingers in my mind.

4   This is my Jordan moment. You probably have your own. Built one by one, they have lifted him to the enviable, extraordinary and undoubtedly taxing position of African-American hero—with equal emphasis placed on the African and the American. His achievement comes in an era when unqualified Black male heroism is rare and thus particularly precious. While White-chosen heroes (Christopher Darden, Clarence Thomas), flawed icons (Tupac Shakur, Mike Tyson) and polarizing forces (Marion Barry, Louis Farrakhan) proliferate, Jordan has universal respect from women and men, Blacks and Whites and children of all ages.

5   That's not to say the ride has always been smooth. There have been failures, eccentric choices and profound tragedies in his otherwise charmed life. These trials, along with the triumphs, have shaped him into something of a living, breathing Rorschach test. When this country looks at Jordan, it sees its dreams, obsessions—even its fears.

6   After all, there are many Michael Jordans. There is Jordan the star. Jordan the athlete. Jordan the family man. Jordan the sex symbol. Jordan the commodity. Jordan the role model. And Jordan the personification of Black masculinity. By that I mean that Michael embodies some of the deepest fantasies Black men have of themselves. Like those of Jack Johnson, Joe Louis, "Sugar" Ray Robinson, Jackie Robinson, Willie Mays, Muhammad Ali, Julius Erving and a handful of others. Michael Jordan's movements, boldness and skill allow African-American men to see the best of themselves projected in the symbolic war of sports.

7   In every culture the warrior plays the role of elemental icon of a community's spirit. In America our history of enslavement sometimes makes us nervous about how much emotion we should invest in these athletes. Are they not just well-paid studs? Do they not entertain at the whim of wealthy White men? No doubt both observations have some merit.

8   But to negate the individual will of these men, to ignore the power and glory of their prowess, is to deny ourselves access to the purity and strength they display. There is a thrill, a kinetic quality of life that a Louis, a Mays, a Jordan taps into that we need. Now African-Americans need other things too. (An emphasis on literacy would be a great start.) Yet Michael's brand of Black masculinity—explosive, graceful, yet grounded in work and morality—is quite simply beautiful and essential.

9   Jordan, of course, consistently transcends his role as mere player. Through a series of megabuck endorsement deals, he hovers above the game as a commercial staple, a Black face with the mass appeal to sell goods (and himself), rivaled only by prime time's favorite sepia pitchman, Bill Cosby. Plying the media with his cool southern charm, while playing the game spectacularly, Jordan defies the stereotypes of the street-hardened, inner-city athlete. He grew up in the Sunbelt state of North Carolina in a solid nuclear family.

10   Religious, well-spoken and with none of the wariness of Whites that hampers many African-American men, Michael Jordan represents the flip side of the crack dealers who populate the local news broadcasts of big cities. With the exception of Julius Erving, no previous African-American basketball hero has had the same bal-

ance of tremendous talent, public poise and personal charisma. But it's the late tennis great Arthur Ashe whom, because of his southern background, charm and crossover appeal, Jordan calls to mind. While Ashe was the real-life Sidney Poitier amid the country-club set, Jordan, with his clean-cut, starched shirt on Sunday morning, epitomizes Black masculinity—without the rough edges of so many Generation X players.

11   More than any other contemporary African-American athlete, he thrives in the pressure cooker of corporate commitments—appearances at charitable events, golf tournaments and commercial shoots—while never making any embarrassing "I'm not Black, I'm universal" comments and without selling his soul. He works in the system while retaining his Black identity, and he has arrived without a nose job or a White wife.

12   Just as he succeeded Erving on the court, Jordan followed the elegant Dr. J as the preeminent Black athletic sex symbol. And Jordan's smooth, chocolate handsomeness has made it easier for brothers to get dates when the Bulls come to town. His wagging tongue, baggy (now standard issue) shorts and 800-watt smile reflect a stylish, idiosyncratic and confident man. By coolly accepting his baldness, he made his glistening Black dome the defining African-American hairstyle of the era, chasing out the seemingly entrenched high-top fade. At the same time Jordan's public-speaking style grew increasingly polished, a welcome alternative to the you-know-what-I'm-sayin' syndrome that too many other brothers display.

13   When I ask women what they like about Jordan, the answer is often, "He married the mother of his children," which they felt spoke to his morality and class. Unlike many other Black sports superstars of this era, Michael never let himself be perceived as a dog. He married Juanita Vanoy in September 1989, within a year of the birth of their first child, Jeffrey Michael. Two more children, Marcus and Jasmine, followed. Though Jordan wisely guards his home life with his wife and children, it's clear that his professional accomplishments are made possible by the solid foundation he and Juanita have created at home.

14   The credit for Jordan's character goes back to the steadying influence of his parents. During his childhood, they set the kind of hardworking example so many Black men lack. His late father, James, a smallish, relaxed southern man, worked his way up from forklift operator to a supervisor at Wilmington's General Electric plant. His mother, Deloris, who recently authored a book on child rearing and was the stern disciplinarian, worked as a clerical supervisor at United Carolina Bank. On occasions when Michael had misbehaved, she wasn't averse to taking him along to sit beside her and do his homework.

15   But Jordan's loving childhood and his astute decision making haven't immunized him against the violence that rocks our community. Which brings me to my next Jordan moment, one that is sure to linger in my mind long after he retires. In fact, for anyone who saw it, it helped redefine the man. The moment came right after the Bulls knocked out the Seattle Supersonics in game six last June, when Jordan snatched the game ball and fell to the floor, clutching it as teammates and fans began celebrating around him.

16   Then, seeking privacy, he sprinted to the locker room, where despite all the frivolity, he sought a moment of solitude. Of course he didn't get it. Cameras, a constant in his life, dogged his steps, and with them came the eyes of the whole world.

We watched as he lay on the floor, crying for the man who could not be there. It was Father's Day, and the basketball great grieved anew for his father, who had been murdered three years before.

17   Unlike so many contemporary public figures, Michael never used his tragedy to gain sympathy for himself. No cheap sentimentality. No playing the victim. No sobbing on *Oprah*. He has handled the entire matter with a dignity as heroic as any jump shot. And yet, in a moment of profound public triumph, he gave in to private pain. The journey Jordan has taken in recent years—retirement, baseball career, the difficult comeback—arguably has as its catalyst his father's death. So it was only fitting that James Jordan's presence loom large in that championship locker room.

18   Over time, the lesson of Michael's career may be to illustrate how even the great can be humbled. Steeled by fire, he returned to basketball with heightened appreciation for the game and his role within it. Moreover he has made peace with aging. These days, his atmospheric forays to the hoop are far less frequent. Instead he attacks with a pump fake, turning a defender's legs into jelly and then burying a jump shot. No more a sprinter, he, like a canny distance runner, paces himself until the crucial third and fourth quarters.

19   Ultimately, history will not judge Jordan's greatness by his vicious slam dunks or clever ad campaigns. Rather it will judge him as a father and a son, and as a man, a Black man—one of the best we've ever had.

EXPLORING THE TEXT

1. How does the opening anecdote establish the qualities that first brought Michael Jordan fame? Underline the verbs George uses to create the image of Jordan's ability to "fly" and to outdo even the most tenacious opponent with ease.

2. What makes Jordan especially rare as an African American hero?

3. Explain what George means when he refers to Jordan as a "warrior." Identify the other "warriors" George lists in paragraph 6. What qualities do these men share with Jordan?

4. Discuss George's comment that Jordan "has arrived without a nose job or a White wife" (paragraph 11). What is he suggesting about Jordan here?

5. What qualities does George see as distinguishing Michael Jordan from many of his fellow players?

6. According to George, what was Jordan's family life like? How has this influenced who he is today?

7. Discuss the significance of the title.

WRITING ASSIGNMENTS

1. George describes his "Jordan moment" and says "you probably have your own" (paragraph 4). Write a descriptive paragraph about a time you saw an amazing athletic performance—whether it was baseball, basketball,

gymnastics, boxing, hockey, etc. The performance could be one you saw in person or on television. Try to make your description as vivid as possible (concentrating especially on lively verbs), so that the reader can see the action.

2. Using George's essay as a model, write a tribute to an athlete of your choice.

GROUP PROJECTS

1. Have your group look into Jordan's role as an advertising pitchman. What are the various products Jordan endorses? Has he been more successful with some products than others? Find out how advertisers and marketers view Jordan's ability to sell products.
2. Many athletes have tried to make the transition form sports to movies. Jordan appeared in the 1996 film *Space Jam.* As a group investigate how Jordan was received in this film. Arrange for a clip to be shown to the class. Afterward, ask the class to discuss what they think Jordan may do after he retires from basketball.

John Wayne: America's Favorite Icon
Garry Wills

Who do you consider to be America's favorite star? According to a 1995 Harris poll, John Wayne was number one, earning twice as many votes as the third most popular choice, Mel Gibson. Surprised? In this essay, Garry Wills examines the power and longevity of Wayne's movie legend and considers why Wayne is "America's Favorite Icon."

Wills is a highly respected writer and is the author of 20 books on a wide range of subjects. His works include *Under God: Religion and American Politics* (1990), *Lincoln at Gettysburg: The Words That Remade America* (1992), and *Witches and Jesuits: Shakespeare's Macbeth* (1995). This piece was excerpted from Wills's *John Wayne's America: The Politics of Celebrity* (1997).

1 In 1993, pollsters asked a representative sample of more than a thousand Americans, "Who is your favorite star?" John Wayne came in second, though he had been dead for fourteen years. He was second again in 1994. Then, in 1995, he was number one, getting more than twice the number of votes that put Mel Gibson in the third spot and nearly six times the number of Paul Newman's votes.[1] Reversing the laws of optics, Wayne seems to become larger the farther off he goes. In the 1995 list, only one other dead actor was included. Here is the list:

1. John Wayne
2. Clint Eastwood

3. Mel Gibson
4. Denzel Washington
5. Kevin Costner
6. Tom Hanks
7. Sylvester Stallone
8. Steven Seagal
9. Arnold Schwarzenegger
10. Robert De Niro
10. Robert Redford
11. Harrison Ford
11. Clark Gable
11. Paul Newman
11. Brad Pitt

2   The choice for number one in 1993 and 1994 was Clint Eastwood, and he is the star who has ranked second to Wayne in box-office appeal over the years. For twenty-five out of twenty-six years—from 1949 to 1974—Wayne made the top ten in distributors' lists of stars with commercial appeal, and was in the top four nineteen times. Eastwood has been in the top ten on the same lists twenty-one times, and in the top ten on the same lists twenty-one times, and in the top four fifteen times.[2] No other actor approaches these two. But does anyone expect Eastwood to be America's favorite star a decade and half after his death? Wayne's durability is astonishing, though it does not impress our society's elite.

3   Intellectuals have other tastes in cult objects. Their pop icons are figures enlarged by special dooms. These idols tend to die young or violently—Rudolph Valentino, Jean Harlow, James Dean, John Lennon. They fascinate by their vulnerabilities (Elvis, Marilyn) or their defiance of social norms (Madonna, Michael Jackson). They are murkily erotic objects to their devotees—Marilyn Monroe to Norman Mailer, Elizabeth Taylor to Camille Paglia, Jacqueline Onassis to Wayne Kostenbaum. Cult figures who live on into old age become caricatures of their rebellious selves—the immured Garbo, Dietrich trickily lit like youth's ghost, Bette Davis imitating her imitators. Or they *become* the things that symbolized them—Charlie swallowed up in the Tramp, Groucho in perpetual ambush behind his eyebrows, Barrymore's profile lingering in the air like the grin of an alcoholic Cheshire cat.

4   John Wayne never won that kind of cult attention. Yet Wayne-olatry is a larger phenomenon—more consequential (for good or ill)—than any of those specialized legends. Marilyn Monroe was one of the top ten moneymakers in Hollywood only three times—and never one of the top four. Elvis started no wars. Masses of American men did not grow up imitating Valentino.

5   Though Wayne never served in the military, General Douglas MacArthur thought he was the model of an American soldier, the Veterans of Foreign Wars gave him their gold medal, and the Marines gave him their "Iron Mike" award.[3] The critic Eric Bentley thought he helped start the Vietnam War—which made him "the most important man in America."[4] Two boys who adored him in *Sands of Iwo Jima* grew up to become, respectively, the Speaker of the House of Representatives, and a

Vietnam paraplegic. Newt Gingrich's stepfather said the young Newt always tried to walk like Wayne—his way of being a man. But Ron Kovic was unmanned by his devotion: "I gave my dead dick for John Wayne."[5]

6   Both friends and critics of American foreign policy in the 1960s and 1970s said it was afflicted with a "John Wayne syndrome." President Nixon thought that domestic affairs, symbolically represented for him by the Charles Manson cult-murder case, could be straightened out by taking Wayne's performance in *Chisum* as a model.[6] Ronald Reagan tried to imitate Wayne, on and off the screen.[7] Congress struck a special gold medal in his honor. The way to be an American was to be Wayne—a claim given eerie confirmation by the fact that the 1990s Chairman of the Joint Chiefs of Staff, John Shalikashvili, taught himself English, as an immigrant, by watching Wayne movies.[8] When another immigrant, Henry Kissinger, attributed his diplomatic success to Americans' admiration for cowboys who come into town alone, he was drawing on the Wayne legacy.[9]

7   For decades John Wayne haunted the dreams of Americans—making his face, said Joan Didion, more familiar to her than her husband's.[10] The protagonist in Walker Percy's novel *The Moviegoer* remembers Wayne's shoot-out in *Stagecoach* more vividly than the events in his own life.

8   Other pop icons tend to be young, rebellious, or deviant. Cult loves shadow, and theirs is a mysticism of the dark, of troubled youth and neuroses. Wayne's legend was of a rarer sort—a cult of daylight reality (or what passes for that). The legend came upon him in his maturity. He did not become a top star until he was forty; but he remained one till his death at seventy-two. He was a figure of authority, of the normative if not the normal. Yet what kind of country accepts as its norm an old man whose principal screen activity was shooting other people, or punching them out?

9   If one looks to other authority figures in the movies, they tend to be creaky with wisdom like Judge Hardy. Spencer Tracy stood more for integrity than authority. Robert Young had to leave the movies to become an image of stability on television (in *Father Knows Best* and *Marcus Welby, M.D.*). Most movie stars are glamorously pitted against authority—Clark Gable, Humphrey Bogart, James Cagney, Marlon Brando, Paul Newman. But Wayne, even when not playing an officer in the Seventh Cavalry, was usually on the sheriff's side.

10   What can explain this cult so at odds with the general run of cults? Why was Wayne's popularity mainstream and long-lived, not fleeting and marginal? Why does he still fill the channels on late-night TV? His fans remain loyal, with their own magazine (*The Big Trail*) and seasonal Western celebrations. He has more monuments than do real war heroes—an equestrian statue on a high podium in Los Angeles (before the Great Western Bank), a colossal striding statue at the airport named for him in Orange County, an eight-foot bronze statue in front of an Irish pub in San Diego. A foundry in Oregon makes a variety of statues for private devotions in the home.

11   Wayne's innate qualities are not enough to explain so large a social fact. He had to fill some need in his audience. He was the conduit they used to communicate with their own desired selves or their own imagined past. When he was called *the* American, it was a statement of what his fans wanted America to be. For them, Wayne always struck an elegiac note. He stood for an America people felt was disappearing or

had disappeared, for a time "when men were men." Though some critics agreed with Eric Bentley that he got us into Vietnam, Wayne-olators thought we lost in Vietnam because not enough John Waynes were left to do what was necessary for winning.

12   The disappearing frontier is the most powerful and persistent myth in American history. It is not a sectional myth but a national one. We do not have "Easterns" or "Southerns"—which *would* be sectional. We have Westerns—since America was, at the outset, *all* frontier.[11] America is the place where European settlers met an alien natural environment and social system. As the frontier moved from the Eastern seaboard west, Americans experienced, over and over again, the excitement of the "birth moment" when the new world was broken into, tamed, absorbed. James Fenimore Cooper created the archetypal figure for this movement when he sent his "Hawkeye," in chronologically ordered novels, from the forests of New York to the Great Lakes and then to the western prairies where he died.

13   After Hawkeye, other figures stood for the whole frontier experience—Daniel Boone, Kit Carson, Davy Crockett, Buffalo Bill. These men began in reality, but ended in myth. Wayne reverses the process. Beginning in myth, he entered the company of those who actually lived on the frontier. As a figure in the American imagination, he is closer to Kit Carson than to his fellow actors. He became so identified with the West that he looked out of place in other kinds of movies—even his war movies. Gary Cooper was "the Virginian" for a while, or "the Plainsman." But he was also Sergeant York, or Mr. Deeds. Wayne was never quite at ease off the range. His large rolling walk was baffled by four walls. He was clearly on leave when doing screen duty as a modern soldier—Kit Carson holidaying with the Seabees.[12] In his own clumsy productions, the elephantine *Alamo* was at least more convincing than the hippopotamian *Green Berets.*

14   Some think Wayne's frequent confinement to Westerns is a sign of his narrow range as an actor. That may be true. But some very good actors have been limited by their success in one kind of role. James Cagney's stuttery urban rhythms made him a misfit in his Western *The Oklahoma Kid* (1939). Humphrey Bogart, in that same misbegotten film, had to wait for the roles that finally defined *him.* He had been out of place in most of his thirties films, with their jumpy pace and crackling dialogue. It took postwar "existentialism" to give his lassitudinous slump its mythic eloquence. A powerful image that defines a star can haunt all his or her later roles. People kept looking for Brando's blue jeans and torn T-shirt under the toga of Mark Antony or the Godfather's business suit. Other actors expressed fleeting moods in the nations—Astaire the sophistication people yearned for in the thirties, Bogart the romantic cynicism of the fifties. But Wayne was saddled up to ride across the decades.

15   It may be true that the greatest actors escape such restriction of their image, though even great Shakespearean players like John Gielgud, Ralph Richardson, and Alex Guinness were at times not convincing in heroic roles—just as Olivier could not equal them in comedy. The greatest screen actor, so far as range is concerned, may have been Spencer Tracy; but his very escape from any large type meant that he left few searing images on the imagination. Judith Anderson was a far greater actress than Marilyn Monroe; but she took up little psychic space in the movie audience's dreamworld. . . .

16   [An] air of invincibility gave Wayne his special status in Westerns. Richard Widmark, a personal and political adversary, admits, "He was the definitive Western star."[13] Howard Hawks said that he and John Ford "used to discuss how tough it was to make a good Western without Wayne."[14] One can imagine other actors replacing even very good performers in famous Westerns. Henry Fonda could have played Gary Cooper's role in *High Noon.* Jimmy Stewart could have taken Fonda's role in *The Oxbow Incident.* Several actors could have equaled Alan Ladd in *Shane.* Sergio Leone proved in *Once Upon a Time in the West* that he could make close-ups of hard eyes work as well with Fonda as with Eastwood. But no one else could be as convincingly unswerving as Wayne in *Red River, The Searchers,* or *Big Jake.* Even the jokey *True Grit* worked because, underneath all the slapstick, it was finally believable that *this* fat old drunk could face down an entire gang. . . .

17   Wayne's control of his body was economical, with no motions wasted. This gave a sense of *purpose* to everything he did. He worked out characteristic stances, gestures, ways of sitting his horse. He learned to choreograph his fight moves with the creative stuntman, Yakima Canutt. In stills from his early pictures, even when the face is fuzzy, one can identify Wayne by his pose or gait, the tilt of his shoulders, the contrapposto lean of his hips. Classical sculptors worked out the counterpoised position to get the maximum of both tension and relaxation, both motion and stillness, in the human body: the taut line of the body is maintained through the hip above the straight leg, while the torso relaxes, it deviates from rigid lines, on the other side, where the leg is bent. Wayne constantly strikes the pose of Michelangelo's *David.* Sometimes, with a wider throw of hip, he becomes Donatello's *David.* He was very conscious of his effects. Richard Widmark used to laugh when Wayne, directing *The Alamo,* shouted at his actors: "Goddamnit, be *graceful*—like me!"[15] . . .

18   Wayne created an entire Western language of body signals. The most explicit of these were the Indian signs he often used—paradoxically dainty and slow arcs and swoops made by his large hands ("big as hams," Widmark said) and thick wrists (emphasized with a gold bracelet). His physical autonomy and self-command, the ease and authority of his carriage, made each motion a statement of individualism, a balletic Declaration of Independence.

19   The whole language cohered—as did the vocal aspect of his performance. Wayne's calculated and measured phrasing gave his delivery the same air of control, of inevitability, that his motions conveyed. He dealt out phrases like dooms: "Touch that gun and I'll kill ya." The stop-and-go phrasing is what all his imitators get; but few capture the melodic intervals of his cadenced speech. As a cavalry office, he directs his troops with two notes more stirring than the trumpet's: *"Yoh-*oh" (a two-and-a-half-tone drop). Joan Didion's girlhood memory of him was an acoustical one, of the *commands* he gave.[16] His throwaway comments, quietly delivered, were just as effective: *"He'll* do" (two-tone drop). I have watched Wayne's films dubbed in Italy, and been impressed with how much of his performance depends on the timbre, the melodic and rhythmic turns, of his voice on the soundtrack.

20   The most obvious element in Wayne's physical performance is his walk—the manly stride Newt Gingrich tried to imitate as an adolescent. The walk became so famous that various people took credit for inventing it and drilling Wayne on how to

do it. Paul Fix, the Western star who worked often with Wayne, claimed he showed Wayne how to walk in the dramatic scene of *Red River,* but Hawks scoffed at the idea: "You don't have to tell Wayne anything about walking through cattle. Wayne knew."[17] . . .

21   Wayne's time of maximum popularity coincided with . . . immense societal effort, and he internalized its demands in his own life as well as in his films. He joined the hunt for sympathizers with the foe, and helped expel them from Hollywood. He tied his own greatest financial project, the making of *The Alamo,* to the electoral struggle of 1960, in which he felt that *real* patriots should support Richard Nixon. He defended the war in Vietnam, and made *The Green Berets* as a personal statement on that conflict. Though the mystique of some Westerns has been one of freedom and individualism, of a creative anarchy, Ford's movies stressed the need for *regimentation* as necessary to survival under threat. Ironically, this reflected conditions in the real West of the 1860s–1890s more accurately than did the myth of emancipated spirits on the frontier.

22   Wayne-olatry grew in such a climate. It is the greatest popular expression of the tensions in that half-century of muted struggle (1945–1985). What followed, in terms of Hollywood symbols, was a reversion to radical individualism. The end of the Cold War should have been a comforting development but it was also seen as the end of empire. America *lost* Vietnam, with a corresponding breakdown in its internal imperial discipline, leading to a sense of drift, a new awareness of crime as raveling out the social fabric. It is significant that gender studies of movie masculinity have added a third item to their treatment of naked gods and troubled boys—the "hard bodies" of the Vietnam era, men engaged in revenge fantasies. Rambo goes after the abandoned relics of empire in Vietnam ("Do we get to win this time?"). "Rocky Balboa" beats the Russian giant when Rocky's government has to confine itself to nuclear standoff. Dirty Harry goes after the punks who have made the city a jungle, using tactics forbidden to the ineffective police force. Citizens must take up arms, alone or in private militias, since the government has failed its subjects, abroad and at home. Conan the Barbarian, created by John Milius (the same man who developed the Dirty Harry character), becomes an avenger after his whole village is wiped out. In Milius's *Red Dawn,* teenagers must fight for a government that adults have surrendered.[18]

23   The sense of opposing tremendous odds, of standing against the whole of established society, calls for a hypertrophy of the individual's musculature and weaponry. Stallone and Schwarzenegger are fitted out with bodies that are nothing but body *armor.* Stripped naked, they carry huge cannon and automatic firing systems. Dirty Harry's gun gets longer and longer, blowing away whole phantom structures of evil, not just single bad guys. The note of these films is rage. Wayne did not normally have the contempt for his opponent that Dirty Harry does. The Wayne hero could be calm, in a time of the empire's dominance. His self-discipline was counted on to awe or attract others. The mature Wayne was lightly weaponed—a rifle, or one pistol, and he often did not have to use that. He faced down foes. The villain in the "shoot-out" is undone by Wayne's stride as he comes down the street.

24   The individualism of the Rambos is conveyed by their naked bodies. They wear no uniform, not even that of normal civil society. Bruce Willis's *Die Hard* police

hero ends up shorn of civilized symbols (including shoes and shirt)—though large firing systems are magically available. The Seventh Cavalry is not going to ride to the rescue—why put on its epaulets? There is no one or nothing to turn to but one's gun. As the father tells Conan in Milius's film: "No one in this world can you trust—not men, not women, not beasts. This [steel] you can trust."

25   Though some critics found homoeroticism in the classic Westerns, more have explored its presence in the narcissism of the bodybuilders, Stallone and Schwarzenegger, or the phallic prolongations of Dirty Harry's gun.[19] (Anticipating such a reaction, the Dirty Harry films plant homosexuals for Harry to mock, dissociating himself from them.) The rage of these avenger movies—or the nihilism and apocalyptic violence of Sergio Leone's and Sam Peckinpah's Westerns—may make Wayne and Ford look moderate in retrospect. In Peckinpah's *The Wild Bunch,* lives previously meaningless acquire validity in the apocalyptic ending that brings down "the system." Conan tells his "sidekick" that winning is less important than the fact "that two stood against many."

26   Wayne helped articulate the system that could not sustain its mission of a *pax Americana.* The imperial reach led to the postimperial letdown. In that sense, we owe Rambo to Wayne, even though Rambo seems to reject what Wayne stood for. The strength of Wayne was that he embodied our deepest myth—that of the frontier. His weakness is that it was only a myth. Behind the fantasies of frontier liberation, as historian Patricia Limerick reminds us, was a reality of conquest. And conquest has a way of undoing the conquerors. . . .

Notes

1. Louis Harris & Associates polls.
2. The Quigley poll of film distributors has been the accepted measure of box-office moneymakers since 1931. The top stars for the first fifty years of the poll were Wayne, Eastwood, and Gary Cooper. Eastwood was in the top ten nineteen times (the top four fourteen times). Cooper was in the top ten eighteen times (the top four seven times). See *International Motion Picture Almanac* 1992 (Quigley Publications), pp. 50–51. Distributors' rating of stars was important because it affected contracts for the stars and the distribution prices of their pictures. See Tino Balio, *Grand Design: Hollywood as a Modern Business Enterprise, 1930–1939* (Charles Scribner's Sons, 1993), p. 145.
3. John Wayne, *Playboy* Interview, May, 1971, reprinted in Judith M. Riggin, *John Wayne: A Bio-Bibliography* (Greenwood Press, 1992), p. 40. Charles John Kieskalt, *The Official John Wayne Reference Book* (Citadel Press, 1993), p. 176.
4. Eric Bentley, "The Political Theatre of John Wayne." Bentley (and his editors) thought enough of this essay to publish it in three places—*Performance* (December, 1971), *Film Society Review* (March–May, 1972), and *Theatre of War* (Viking Press, 1972).
5. Dale Russakoff, "He Knew What He Wanted," Washington *Post,* December 8, 1994, p. A28. Gingrich told the reporter, "I went over and over [to Wayne movies] and saw *The Sands of Iwo Jima* four times in one day." Ron Kovic, *Born on the Fourth of July* (McGraw-Hill, 1976), p. 98. See also pp. 43, 72 for Kovic's fascination with Wayne.
6. "Nixon Press Statement," New York *Times,* August 4, 1970. Nixon, who had just seen *Chisum,* said that it represented the coming of law into American society.

7. Reagan became an independent agent in Hollywood in order to make Westerns after "John Wayne, saber in hand, rode right into the number one box-office spot." Reagan, *Where's the Rest of Me?* (Hawthorn Books, 1965), p. 233.

8. Claudia Dreifus, article on General John Shalikashvili, New York *Times Sunday Magazine,* May 21, 1995: "I must have gone to all kinds of movies. But I remember most the John Wayne movies"—each of which Shalikashvili watched "at least twice" to improve his English.

9. Oriana Fallaci, *Intervista con la storia* (Rizzoli, 1974), p. 29. Kissinger was still at it in 1995, when he wrote "Superstars Strive for Approbation, Heroes Walk Alone" in the New York *Times Book Review,* July 16, 1995, p. 7. A right-wing leader in Italy was "radicalized" when Communist demonstrators prevented him from getting to a Wayne movie—see New York *Times Sunday Magazine,* April 21, 1996, p. 43, on Gianfranco Fini.

10. Joan Didion, "John Wayne, A Love Song," in *Slouching Towards Bethlehem* (Touchstone, 1968), p. 41.

11. G. Edward White makes the point that Westerns are a national myth, not a sectional one, in *The Eastern Establishment and the Western Experience* (Yale University Press, 1968), p. 1.

12. One way to overcome this was to equate his war films with Westerns. In *Sands of Iwo Jima,* Wayne's rallying call as Sergeant Stryker of the infantry is "Saddle up!" In *Green Berets,* the Special Forces camp is called, on a timber sign with rough lettering, "Dodge City."

13. Author's interview with Richard Widmark, January, 1995.

14. McBride, op. cit., p. 114.

15. Author's interview with Richard Widmark, January, 1995.

16. Didion, op. cit., p. 30.

17. Joseph McBride, *Hawks on Hawks* (University of California Press, 1982), p. 120.

18. For these citizen-revenge movies, see Susan Jeffords, *Hard Bodies: Hollywood Masculinity in the Reagan Era* (Rutgers University Press, 1994). For the connection of such films (especially those of John Milius) with the end (and the betrayal) of empire, see James William Gibson, *Warrior Dreams: Paramilitary Culture in Post-Vietnam America* (Hill and Wang, 1994).

19. Stephen Neale argued that all Westerns are implicitly homoerotic in *Genre* (British Film Institute, 1980), p. 59, and some work was done on Anthony Mann's and Howard Hawks's films (rarely John Ford's—though we shall see that his own actors found some gay themes there). The Stallone-Schwarzenegger films (pecs against tanks) are partly a throwback to Steve Reeves "classical" epics and Victor Mature Bible stories—films where, as Groucho Marx put it, the man's chest is bigger than the woman's. For Dirty Harry's phallic firearms, see Peter Lehman, "Penis-Size Jokes and Their Relation to Hollywood's Unconscious," in *Running Scared* (Temple University Press, 1993), pp. 105–9.

EXPLORING THE TEXT

1. What support does Wills offer in the opening paragraphs for John Wayne being "America's favorite icon"? What do Wills's findings suggest about Wayne's popularity?

2. How is Wayne's legend different from cult stars such as Marilyn Monroe, James Dean, and Elvis Presley?

3. Discuss how Wills connects Wayne to the myth of the frontier. What fictional or historical figures set the pattern for the character that people associate with Wayne?

4. Explain why Wills feels that "the Western deals with the 'taming' of the West. Wayne was uniquely convincing at this task." Discuss, particularly, how Wayne's physical persona came across on the screen as "undeterrable as fate."

5. How did Wayne's delivery of dialogue add to the power and balletic quality of his movements? How conscious was Wayne of these things?

6. How did Wayne's personal politics serve to reinforce his movie image? Why do so many politicians (Reagan, Gingrich, Kissinger, Buchanan) seem to admire Wayne?

7. Comment on Wills's writing style, paying special attention to his use of description. Even if you know very little about John Wayne, did the article make him "come alive"? Pick out three or four descriptive passages that you find effective.

WRITING ASSIGNMENTS

1. Do a ten-minute freewrite on John Wayne. Let your mind (and pen) go where they want to. Don't worry if you don't know much about Wayne (though you probably know more than you think), just keep your pen moving. Read freewrites aloud. Did similar images occur in many people's freewrites? Discuss what Wayne seems to represent for the class as a whole.

2. Write an essay comparing and contrasting Wayne's popularity with the popularity of Selena (see Larry Rohter's essay, "Selena: A Legend Grows," above). Do you see any similarities between these seeming opposites? Or compare and contrast Wayne and Michael Jordan (see Nelson George's essay, "Rare Jordan," above). How do both men seem to embody the fantasies of millions of Americans?

3. Watch a John Wayne movie. You may want to choose one of the films Wills mentions—they should be available on video. After the viewing, write an essay discussing whether you feel Wayne still holds a great deal of power over our imagination, or do you feel that Wills has overstated his significance? Be sure to use examples from the film to support your argument.

GROUP PROJECTS

1. In small groups, take your own poll about who the most popular stars are. Ask your subjects to name their top three favorite stars. Try to get a variety

of people to respond (don't forget to ask those over 30). Compile your list and present it to the class. How different were your results from the Harris poll? If your list was almost entirely different, what does this lead you to believe about polls?

2. The question the Harris pollsters asked, "Who is your favorite star?" appears to be gender neutral, yet everyone on the list that Wills presents is male. Do some research about how male and female stars compare in terms of salary, box office draw, and Hollywood clout. The Internet or magazines such as *Variety, Entertainment Weekly, Premier,* or *People* will probably be the best sources of information. After you have gathered information, discuss your findings in your group and prepare a report on gender equity (or inequity) in current Hollywood.

Xena: She's Big, Tall, Strong—and Popular
Donna Minkowitz

Most of us are familiar with mythic male warriors such as Hercules, Ulysses, or Achilles—men of densely wadded muscles who run around in leather shorts, grabbing flying arrows out of the air and slashing their way through hordes of demon meanies in defense of the good and the powerless. But, as many a prime-time viewer knows, there's a new name to add to the list— Xena. In the piece below, Donna Minkowitz looks at this star of the popular syndicated series *Xena: Warrior Princess* as a much-needed feminist icon who embodies the strength and courage of the traditional warrior, but with an interesting postmodern twist.

Minkowitz is a freelance writer. Her article first appeared in the July/August 1996 issue of *Ms.* magazine.

1   A six-foot-tall woman dressed like a warrior walks into an ancient "bar" filled with men. When one pats her ass, she knocks him across the room. After that, every man in the bar is polite to her and her woman companion.

2   Three children stare gratefully at the fighter who has saved their village from an invading army. "Did you see the way she finished off those guys?" one boy chirps. "Zing! Pow!"

3   In successive weeks, a mortal woman rescues Prometheus, defeats the war god Ares, enters the underworld, and returns from it. In between, she saves poor farmers from enslavement and defends women from a roving band of rapists. "You like shoving women around so much?" she says to one. "Try me!"

4   Many feminists have been dreaming of mass-culture moments like this since feminism came into being. But we've almost never seen these fantasies realized. The Bionic Woman smiled too much. Even Cagney and Lacey worried about looking

"overmasculine." No woman television character has exhibited the confidence and strength of the male heroes of archetype and fantasy—or if she did, she was a one-episode fluke, and her anomalous presence could reassure viewers that next week all the regular women characters would be back, nervous and self-questioning as ever.

5   Until now. Each week since September 1995, *Xena: Warrior Princess* has begun with these words: "In a time of ancient gods, warlords, and kings, a land in turmoil cried out for a hero. She was Xena, a mighty princess forged in the heat of battle." The grim warrior, played by Lucy Lawless, wanders through the ancient world, protecting the powerless—chiefly women, children, and poor people. Xena, an "ancient Greek" hero invented out of whole cloth by the series' producers, doesn't apologize for being a better fighter than almost every man on earth. And she doesn't smile at men unless she really, really likes them—which is seldom.

6   *Xena* is a spin-off of the popular *Hercules: The Legendary Journeys,* itself a feminist and progressive retelling of Greek myth. But its female protagonist was initially conceived as an evil figure. Executive producer Rob Tapert says he based Xena on the "evil warrior princesses" portrayed by Hong Kong cult film star Lin Ching Hsia in movies like *The Bride with White Hair* and *The Swordsman II* and *III.*

7   When Xena first appeared as a guest character on *Hercules,* she pillaged the countryside at the head of a rapacious army and murdered thousands. She delighted only in profit and cruelty. Xena, who came from a family of farmers like the ones whose homes she burned, was eventually called "princess" because she was such a powerful warlord.

8   MCA TV, the studio to which Tapert proposed the spin-off, and which now syndicates the show, was not pleased with the character's image. "The studio said, 'Can you get her turned around so that she's good?' " Tapert remembers. "I said, 'I guess, but it won't be as much fun.' " After initial misgivings, I, for one, am glad about the change. *Xena*'s writers have used their hero's evolution as the backdrop for a sophisticated discussion of morality. Xena isn't good because of innate virtue. She has genuinely struggled with questions of ethics, and has finally chosen to act on her moral impulses. In fact, the show's greatest innovation may not be the toughness of its female lead, but her deep awareness of her own desire to exploit and intimidate others.

9   Xena continually confronts the parts of herself that are least likable. She keeps meeting people who are terrified of her because of the atrocities they've seen her commit. And though she's reformed, Xena is one hero whose ethical struggles are never over. In one episode, after a prolonged period of imprisonment and beatings, Xena slugs her best friend, Gabrielle. The punch is presented as stemming from the imperfections that are a part of us all—even feminist superheroes.

10   In just one season, *Xena* has become the most successful new action series in syndication and has ranked as high as number 11 overall, beating out *Baywatch* and *Star Trek: Deep Space Nine.* Many local stationmasters initially refused to air the show because "they thought no one would want to see a woman hitting men," says executive producer Tapert, "but they were wrong." Tapert and coexecutive producer Sam Raimi had built their careers with male fantasy thrillers and cult movies like

Darkman, but Tapert was eager to try his hand at a fantasy story with a female hero. "I believe, in the basest and crassest of ways, that there's a formula to stories about heroes," Tapert says, "and no one had ever tried to do it before with a woman hero. Or if they did, they made excuses for her being a woman."

11   Fighting men and refusing to smile aren't the only ways that Xena breaks the rules. There's also sex:

- The warrior princess doesn't have a boyfriend. Xena has taken a number of male lovers, including, on occasion, Hercules, but never settled down with any of them. "That will never happen," promises Tapert.
- Xena is one of the first white women in TV history to passionately kiss a black man onscreen. Several times, in fact. She was in love with this character, a warrior named Marcus, who reappeared in several episodes.
- In our interview, Tapert spontaneously brings up the possibility that Xena also has love relationships with women. "People ask me frequently about Xena's sexual orientation," he informs me, "especially about her relationship with Gabrielle. I tell them that she has had a string of lovers in her life and that now she is trying to get control of her emotions." It's hard to imagine a more ambiguous statement, but it's certainly not an utter denial. Indeed, Tapert proudly tells me that the show "has become a favorite with gay women" and that some lesbian bars have special *Xena*-viewing nights. (So do a number of women's prisons.) "Early on, the studio came down on me, because they wanted to make sure no one perceived Xena and Gabrielle as lesbians," the producer says. He doesn't seem to be trying very hard to accede to their demands.

12   On the show's Web site, male and female viewers allude supportively to Xena's perceived sexual relationship with Gabrielle, whom Xena rescued from a forced marriage in the opening episode. Ever since then, the pair have been inseparable. Gabrielle, a girlish storyteller with lots of pluck but not much combat skill, functions as a feminine foil for her kick-boxing friend. (As the season has progressed, Gabrielle has gradually learned how to defend herself under Xena's tutelage. In the season's final episode, Gabrielle led the people of her home village in a successful stand against an imperialist army.)

13   The Xena-Gabrielle friendship is a deeply committed one. The women risk their lives for each other, refuse to leave each other for men, even work on "issues" in their relationship, such as Xena's reluctance to include Gabrielle in situations that might become dangerous. Despite the innuendo, the two women are never overtly sexual with each other, as they are with men (although Gabrielle, fascinatingly, is a virgin, a status depicted as neither superior nor inferior to Xena's status as sexually active). If they are lovers, it is mostly in the covert Batman and Robin way.

14   Whether Xena is gay or straight is ultimately beside the point—but it is disturbing that in a show set in ancient Greece, not one of the characters has an identifiable gay or lesbian relationship. "I've proposed that to the writing staff, but I have to tread very carefully," Tapert says. "We don't want to alienate people. We don't want to alienate kids."

15   While *Xena* is breaking new ground in its treatment of sex, it doesn't ignore the old standby of adventure films—violence. But even here, there's a progressive gloss on the mayhem. Unlike some feminist fantasy figures—say, Hothead Paisan—the warrior princess and her sometime costar Hercules never attack out of vengeance. They nurse their enemies' wounds after a battle. And they kill only to defend themselves.

16   Still, *Xena* isn't primarily a political vehicle, but a delightfully cheesy schlock drama that often looks like *Spartacus, American Gladiators,* and *Mad Max* rolled into one. It wouldn't be entirely truthful to say that the show doesn't romanticize violence. Half its thrill comes from the blows our hero administers to exploiters and rapists. So much time and love are devoted to the combat scenes that we might as well see the ecstatic Pow! and Zap! titles they used on the sixties *Batman* TV series. It's probably impossible to completely separate fantasies of ethical resistance from fantasies of breaking heads and making people crawl. But for what it's worth, Xena and her creators try hard to do just that.

17   All these surprises, plus the campy story lines, add up to a program that is extremely popular with young adults of both sexes. According to Tapert, *Xena*'s most faithful viewers are women and men ages 18 to 34. That's almost identical to *Hercules*' demographics, except the strongman pulls in more kids. "*Hercules* has a much bigger audience among girls and boys ages four to six, the toy-buying demographic," Tapert says. "*Xena*'s audience is older and probably a little hipper." Tapert will not speculate as to why this is. Are little boys unwilling to watch a woman warrior? The conventional wisdom among producers of children's television is that boys won't watch shows with female leads, but girls will watch shows with female or male leads. If that's right, why aren't girls watching *Xena* by themselves? Is it possible that parents object to *Xena*'s feminist content?

18   Though they apparently aren't watching the show enough to make a dent in the demographics, young girls do write fan letters by the hundreds to Lucy Lawless. "I'm thrilled," she tells me in a phone interview from her native Auckland, New Zealand. "They write about how encouraging it is to see someone who's so strong. Mostly very young girls. I have all these photos of little girls with Xena costumes on." Tapert says Lawless got a letter from a pair of five- and six-year-old sisters who refused to use their proper names. "They just wanted to be called Xena."

19   But Lawless seems defensive when asked if she thinks *Xena* is a feminist show. "No, I don't! Well . . . yes, it is. But it is not anti-men! I suppose it could be called feminist in that it's about women who do not see themselves as at all limited by their femininity. Personally, I never believed in glass ceilings or in being handicapped because of being a woman, but if women draw strength from the show, that could be called feminism. Though we're not male-bashing in any way!"

20   Lawless says she is not a feminist, though she does allow that "feminists might identify with me because I'm unapologetic in what they think is a male-dominated world . . . no, I guess, what *is* a male-dominated world, but in my microcosm [New Zealand], women are not disadvantaged, except by their own fear." Lawless says that as a child she never longed to see a woman superhero like Xena, because "I never saw it lacking from my life." Good thing she's a good actor.

21   Lawless also differs from Xena in her approach to athletics: she's not in the least delighted with the physical training she's had to endure for the role. "I've been trained and bullied into some level of proficiency. When I started, my coordination was hopeless." In fact, her grueling schedule of weight training gave her a back injury, Lawless says. As for her costume, a sort of sleeveless leather-breastplated jumpsuit that, nicely enough, doesn't emphasize her breasts, Lawless describes it as "hellish to wear." In Auckland, where the series is filmed, "in winter it's utter cold, and you're running along some cliff with the wind whipping at you, in this costume that leaves your lungs bare, and it's tight. Being in constant discomfort can make you cry, especially if you're doing bloody kung fu."

22   I suppose a worker-friendly environment and a politicized star would be too much to ask from a show that has already favorably portrayed the Amazons (Gabrielle became an honorary Amazon after a mysterious bonding ceremony with the Amazon Queen) and created a feminist ending for *The Iliad* (Xena to Helen of Troy: "What do you want to do?" Helen: "No one's ever asked me that before!").

23   Sex appeal is surely another reason that people watch the show. "Everything about the show is sexy," Lawless offers, "because it has this energy—charisma, self-confidence. We want to take people out of the humdrum." But a friend of mine took one look at Xena's long legs and tight leather breastplate and decided that the warrior princess was just another R. Crumb drawing in the guise of a feminist hero.

24   Is Xena sexually objectified by the show? If so, does it matter? The answer probably depends on your definition of objectification. On the Internet, Tapert says, there are arguments between men and women as to whose hero Xena is: "whether she's a hero for women, or a hero *and* a sex symbol for men."

25   Although having men treat a feminist hero as a sex object might make many of us uncomfortable, I can remember only one occasion on which Xena's sex appeal was depicted offensively—a commercial for the show in which a male character stared up at the warrior and sighed, "Those boots! That leather! Those legs!" It's worth noting that *Hercules'* star, Kevin Sorbo, displays his body just as much as Lawless does. "We've gotten a lot of feedback, from both straights and gays, that people really like it when Kevin takes his shirt off," Tapert says. It's important to consider, too, that men who are Xena fans may be motivated by factors other than sex appeal. Many women fans somehow manage to bring together an appreciation for Xena's feminism with an appreciation for her body. Why is it so difficult to imagine men doing the same?

26   Finally, if straight men find Xena erotic, it may be a sign that their eroticism is changing. Both *Hercules* and *Xena* make occasional, coded references to women dominating men sexually ("You're cute when you're nervous," Atalanta, Greek mythology's powerful runner, told Hercules in one episode, lifting the blushing hero high in the air). Then again, some men who watch the show may simply be excited by a woman who refuses to be subservient. Or by a woman of tremendous physical strength and courage. "She doesn't fall into this svelte, silicone image," Tapert says. "She's a big woman with big shoulders, big hipbones, and big thighs."

27   And a bloodcurdling battle cry.

EXPLORING THE TEXT

1. What qualities does Xena possess that make her stand out from other television heroines?
2. Why does the fact that Xena was originally evil make her particularly interesting to the author?
3. Describe Xena and Gabrielle's relationship. In what ways is it unusual? What does Minkowitz mean when she calls Gabrielle a "feminine foil for her kick-boxing friend" (paragraph 12)?
4. According to the author, how does the show's treatment of sex and sexual roles break the typical television "rules"?
5. How does Minkowitz feel about the show's treatment of violence?
6. What theories does the article offer for why *Xena* is not as popular as *Hercules* among children ages 4 to 6?
7. How does the author seem to feel about actress Lucy Lawless's take on the show?
8. How does Minkowitz respond to the charge that *Xena* objectifies its main character?

WRITING ASSIGNMENTS

1. This assignment calls for some television watching. Do a comparison/contrast of *Xena* and any other female star on television (a major character on any soap opera, nighttime comedy, or drama). How do the characters compare? Do you see the kind of feminism in Xena that Minkowitz does? How does your other character stand up in terms of being a feminist role model?
2. Lucy Lawless talks in the article about little girls writing her fan letters. Write an essay discussing what messages popular culture sends young girls through its heroines. For instance, what do you make of female characters in such Disney films as *Beauty and the Beast, Pocahontas, The Lion King,* or *Hercules*? Do you think these characters offer positive depictions of females? Why or why not?

GROUP PROJECTS

1. Minkowitz argues that *Xena* offers a progressive and feminist retelling of Greek myths and legends. Try your hand at creating a feminist revision of a classic Greek myth or story such as Pandora's Box, Helen of Troy, Demeter and Persephone, the voyages of Ulysses, etc. Find a traditional telling, then have your group write a revision in the form of script (using dialogue) that you can perform for the class.

2. Visit *Xena*'s Web site. What do people seem to be particularly interested in discussing? Has the show's popularity continued since the publication of this article in the summer of 1996? As a group formulate a few questions and/or comments and take part in the discussion. Report to the class what you have learned.

Barbie Doll
Marge Piercy

The Barbie doll, first introduced in America in 1959, has proven to be one of the best selling and most influential toys of all time. With her long legs, tiny waist, and silky hair, Barbie represents, for some, the "ideal woman." In her poem below, Marge Piercy uses Barbie as the central metaphor to illustrate how women are socialized by society into particular gender roles that may be dangerous to their health.

Piercy is the author of several books of poetry including *Mars and Her Children* (1992) and several novels including *He, She, and It* (1991) and *City of Darkness, City of Light* (1996).

1 This girlchild was born as usual
and presented dolls that did pee-pee
and miniature GE stoves and irons
and wee lipsticks the color of cherry candy.
5 Then in the magic of puberty, a classmate said:
You have a great big nose and fat legs.

She was healthy, tested intelligent,
possessed strong arms and back,
abundant sexual drive and manual dexterity.
10 She went to and fro apologizing.
Everyone saw a fat nose on thick legs.

She was advised to play coy,
exhorted to come on hearty,
exercise, diet, smile and wheedle.
15 Her good nature wore out
like a fan belt.

So she cut off her nose and her legs
and offered them up.
In the casket displayed on satin she lay
20 with the undertaker's cosmetics painted on,
a turned-up putty nose,

dressed in a pink and white nightie.
Doesn't she look pretty? everyone said.
Consummation at last.
25 To every woman a happy ending.

EXPLORING THE TEXT

1. Why is the poem called "Barbie Doll"? Do you think the title is appropriate?
2. The poem follows a woman's life from birth to death. What do you think the poem is saying about the persona's life?
3. How do the images of "fat legs" and "a great big nose" play against the description of the persona's other characteristics in stanza two?
4. What was the tone of the last two lines?
5. Explain how the poem is a satire.

WRITING ASSIGNMENTS

1. Write a paraphrase of the poem—that is, retell the story in your own words, avoiding using Piercy's language as much as possible. After you've paraphrased the poem, write a paragraph or two about what shades of meaning became clear through this exercise. Plan to read your paraphrase in class.
2. Since Barbie's introduction in 1959, she has been one of the most popular toys ever created. Write an essay analyzing Barbie's mass appeal. Does the doll appeal only to girls? How have the makers of Barbie attempted to have the doll evolve over the decades? Can you think of any other toy that rivals Barbie for longevity and fame?
3. Write a narrative about a toy that you especially loved as a child. What do you think the significance of this toy was for you? Do you "read" (interpret) the toy differently as an adult?
4. Discuss the difference between the image of woman as presented by Xena (see "Xena: She's Big, Tall, Strong—and Popular") and the image presented by Barbie. Do these characters have anything in common? Do they represent mutually exclusive role models, or as Holly Brubach suggests in her essay "Heroine Worship: The Age of the Female Icon," do they simply offer more heroines to mix and match in creating a new "hybrid" icon?

GROUP PROJECTS

1. Some social critics have complained that Barbie dolls present an extremely limited image of female beauty—that is, few women have Barbie's per-

fectly even features, silky hair, long legs, and tiny hips and waist. As a group, do some research on Barbie's influence on our culture's view of female beauty. Group members may want to start by finding out some history about Barbie. Several books have been written about her that should be available in your school's library. You may also want to do research on the Web. Has Barbie changed in any significant way since her introduction in 1959? What do you make of such phenomena as the Barbie Twins, sisters who have had extensive plastic surgery in order to look more like Barbie? Create a report to present to the class.

2. Your group's job is to create a doll who will be the "anti-Barbie." Have some members of the group design the doll (give her a name, describe her "characteristics" and the accessories that accompany her, make a sketch of her). Have other members be the marketing/advertising team who sells her (come up with a campaign, complete with visual if possible). Present your campaign to the class and let them decide if "anti-Barbie" has an audience.

The United States is a union predicated on like-minded moral values, political and economic self-interest, and a common language. But lest we forget, America is also a nation of immigrants—people of different races, ethnic identities, religions, and languages. It is a nation whose motto, *e pluribus unum* ("one out of many"), bespeaks the pride in its multicultural heritage. It is also a nation whose complexion is rapidly changing, whose racial and ethnic minorities are growing in number.

By early in the next century, one-third of our nation will be made up of people of color. In many states, African Americans, Hispanic Americans, Asian Americans, and Native Americans will comprise the majority of the population. Likewise, with growing immigration and more mixed marriages, we are becoming a nation of sweeping racial and ethnic diversity—people with some black, white, yellow, and red bloodlines. And the divisions are beginning to blur.

Although America has been a multiethnic and multiracial society since its founding, it was not until the last three decades that different groups of Americans began to reassert their ethnic and racial identity. In their search for roots, African Americans and Native Americans, Latinos and Latvians alike have looked with pride to their heritage to distinguish themselves from the mainstream. In the name of multiculturalism they have challenged the traditional educational system, arguing that the curricula in literature, American history, government, and social sciences are slanted toward white Europeans, that they neither reflect the contributions to American culture by minorities nor the growing cultural diversity of American society. In short, once marginalized racial and ethnic groups demanded inclusion.

But can people be both separate yet included? Can we be many and still part of a whole? Can the barricades of intolerance and prejudice at last come down? These are some of the questions we will address in this chapter as we examine the experiences of people whose identity is torn between different cultures—their traditional ethnic/racial roots and the large homogeneous entity of America.

Although written from different ethnic slants, each of the first four essays in this chapter argues that the world would be a better place if people were more tolerant of those who are culturally different. Drawing from personal experiences, the authors demonstrate that tolerance is the first step to eliminating the most ugly signs of prejudice—ethnic and racial stereotypes.

In the first essay, "The Revolt of the Black Bourgeoisie," Leonce Gaiter addresses stereotypical expectations thrust upon African Americans. The author, an accomplished black professional raised in a middle-class home, must often confront the befuddled reaction of colleagues who assume that he couldn't *really* be black if he doesn't talk jive, have a prison record, and play basketball. The next essay, "Crimes Against Humanity," focuses on a debate over some seemingly innocuous symbols and caricatures. To Ward Churchill, a Native American, naming football teams the Washington Redskins and the Atlanta Braves is not just an insult to his people, but just one of the many denigrations his race has suffered in movies, television, and books. In "Getting to Know About You and Me," Chana Schoenberger clearly illustrates the dangerous kind of ignorance that many people suffer when it comes to other people's religious identities. Although she was with 20 other scholarship students representing eight different religions, Schoenberger was astounded to learn that the only Jews some people knew were those from the Bible. The next piece moves the discussion of stereotyping and presumptions to a white man whose surname and dark complexion have led to a wide span of mistaken identities. As John Yemma amusingly explains in "Innocent and Presumed Ethnic," his Italian, German, and French blood make him something of a mongrel. Yet, wherever he goes—in this country and abroad—he experiences the universal compulsion of people to fit others into ethnic pigeonholes.

As more people migrate to the United States, major questions regarding assimilation arise: Can individuals from a traditional ethnic background maintain their defining heritage—language, customs, dress, cultural identities—and still be American? Can they maintain double identities? Should they? To some people, cultural assimilation is a desired achievement, for it means becoming part of the American Dream. To others, it is selling out, relinquishing a cherished heritage. Some even regard the process as a form of oppression—a yielding to majority culture perhaps out of fear of being just another marginalized group. The next two pieces take a look at the uneasy attempts of some to blend into the greater American culture. They also consider the problems through the added complication of generational conflicts. In "A Puerto Rican Stew," Esmeralda Santiago explains that in order to escape the poverty and lack of options in her homeland, her mother moved her and her family to the United States to pursue the American Dream of making a good life. But like so many children of immigrants, the author grew up "American" only to confront a crisis of cultural identity—and one that put distance between her and her family. "Secrets and Anger" reverses the point of view by pondering assimilation from the parent's perspective. In that essay, David Mura, a Japanese American married to a white woman, speculates on just what identity his daughter will adopt when she grows up, living in a society where Asian Americans traditionally were marginalized.

In spite of the heightened multicultural consciousness of the last several years, not all people have rushed to proclaim their ethnic heritage. In "Cultural Baggage," Barbara Ehrenreich explains that coming from a long line of white, Anglo-Irish atheists, she felt culturally nondistinct—like a woman from "a race of none." But instead of feeling deprived or un-American, she learned to enjoy her cultural nullity. In fact, she argues that the world would be a better place were people not caught up in the different ethnic and religious rituals of their heritage.

The Revolt of the Black Bourgeoisie
Leonce Gaiter

To create and shape one's identity is a difficult task, made more so when battling negative stereotypes. Leonce Gaiter, a middle-class, educated, and professionally accomplished black man, found himself constantly fighting the expectations that a *real* black person was a "semiliterate, hoop-shooting former prison inmate." In this essay, the author examines why one segment of the black community—namely the underclass—has been selected to represent the whole. He exhorts African Americans not to "perpetuate the notion that African Americans are invariably doomed to the lower class."

    Gaiter lives in Los Angeles and frequently writes about social issues. This article originally appeared in the *New York Times Sunday Magazine* in 1994.

1   At a television network where I once worked, one of my bosses told me I almost didn't get hired because his superior had "reservations" about me. The job had been offered under the network's Minority Advancement Program. I applied for the position because I knew I was exceptionally qualified. I would have applied for the position regardless of how it was advertised.

2   After my interview, the head of the department told my boss I wasn't really what he had in mind for a Minority Advancement Program job. To the department head, hiring a minority applicant meant hiring someone unqualified. He wanted to hire some semiliterate, hoop-shooting former prison inmate. That, in his view, was a "real" black person. That was someone worthy of the program.

3   I had previously been confronted by questions of black authenticity. At Harvard, where I graduated in 1980, a white classmate once said to me, "Oh, you're not really a black person." I asked her to explain. She could not. She had known few black people before college, but a lifetime of seeing black people depicted in the American media had taught her that real black people talked a certain way and were raised in certain places. In her world, black people did not attend elite colleges. They could not stand as her intellectual equals or superiors. Any African-American who shared her knowledge of Austen and Balzac—while having to explain to her who Douglass and DuBois were—had to be *willed* away for her to salvage her sense of superiority as a white person. Hence the accusation that I was "not really black."

4   But worse than the white majority harboring a one-dimensional vision of blackness are the many blacks who embrace this stereotype as our true nature. At the junior high school I attended in the mostly white Washington suburb of Silver Spring, Md., a black girl once stopped me in the hallway and asked belligerently, "How come you talk so proper?" Astonished, I could only reply, "It's proper*ly*," and walk on. This girl was asking why I spoke without the so-called black accent pervasive in the lower socioeconomic strata of black society, where exposure to mainstream society is limited. This girl was asking, Why wasn't I impoverished and alienated? In her world view, a black male like me couldn't exist.

5   Within the past year, however, there have been signs that blacks are openly beginning to acknowledge the complex nature of our culture. Cornel West, a professor of religion and the director of Afro-American Studies at Harvard University, discusses the growing gulf between the black underclass and the rest of black society in his book "Race Matters"; black voices have finally been raised against the violence, misogyny and vulgarity marketed to black youth in the form of gangsta rap; Ellis Cose's book "The Rage of a Privileged Class," which concentrates on the problems of middle- and upper-income blacks, was excerpted as part of a Newsweek maga-

zine cover story; Bill Cosby has become a vocal crusader against the insulting depiction of African-Americans in "hip-hop generation" TV shows.

6　　Yes, there are the beginnings of a new candor about our culture, but the question remains, How did one segment of the African-American community come to represent the whole? First, black society itself placed emphasis on that lower caste. This made sense because historically that's where the vast majority of us were placed; it's where American society and its laws were designed to keep us. Yet although doors have opened to us over the past 20 years, it is still commonplace for black leaders to insist on our community's uniform need for social welfare programs, inner-city services, job skills training, etc. Through such calls, what has passed for a black political agenda has been furthered only superficially; while affirmative action measures have forced an otherwise unwilling majority to open some doors for the black middle class, social welfare and Great Society-style programs aimed at the black lower class have shown few positive results.

7　　According to 1990 census figures, between 1970 and 1990 the number of black families with incomes under $15,000 rose from 34.6 percent of the black population to 37 percent, while the number of black families with incomes of $35,000 to $50,000 rose from 13.9 percent to 15 percent of the population, and those with incomes of more than $50,000 rose from 9.9 percent to 14.5 percent of the black population.

8　　Another reason the myth of an all-encompassing black underclass survives—despite the higher number of upper-income black families—is that it fits with a prevalent form of white liberalism, which is just as informed by racism as white conservatism. Since the early 70's, good guilt-liberal journalists and others warmed to the picture of black downtrodden masses in need of their help. Through the agency of good white people, blacks would rise. This image of African-Americans maintained the lifeline of white superiority that whites in this culture cling to, and therefore this image of blacks stuck. A strange tango was begun. Blacks seeking advancement opportunities allied themselves with whites eager to "help" them. However, those whites continued to see blacks as inferiors, victims, cases, and not as equals, individuals or, heaven forbid, competitors.

9　　It was hammered into the African-American psyche by media-appointed black leaders and the white media that it was essential to our political progress to stay economically and socially deprived. To be recognized and recognize oneself as middle or upper class was to threaten the political progress of black people. That girl who asked why I spoke so "proper" was accusing me of political sins—of thwarting the progress of our race.

10　　Despite progress toward a more balanced picture of black America, the image of black society as an underclass remains strong. Look at local news coverage of the trial of Damian Williams and Henry Watson, charged with beating the white truck driver Reginald Denny during the 1992 South-Central L.A. riots. The press showed us an African-print-wearing cadre of Williams and Watson supporters trailing Edi M. O. Faal, William's defense attorney, like a Greek chorus. This chorus made a point of standing in the camera's range. They presented themselves as the voice of South-Central L.A., the voice of the oppressed, the voice of the downtrodden, the voice of the city's black people.

11   To anyone watching TV coverage of the trial, all blacks agreed with Faal's contention that his clients were prosecuted so aggressively because they are black. Period. Reporters made no effort to show opposing black viewpoints. (In fact, the media portrait of the Los Angeles riot as blacks vs. whites and Koreans was a misrepresentation. According to the Rand Corporation, a research institute in Santa Monica, blacks made up 36 percent of those arrested during the riot; Latinos made up 51 percent). The black bourgeoisie and intelligentsia remained largely silent. We had too long believed that to express disagreement with the "official line" was to be a traitor.

12   TV networks and cable companies gain media raves for programs like "Laurel Avenue," an HBO melodrama about a working-class black family lauded for its realism, a real black family complete with drug dealers, drug users, gun toters and basketball players. It is akin to the media presenting "Valley of the Dolls" as a realistic portrayal of the ways of white women.

13   The Fox network offers a differing but equally misleading portrait of black Americans, with "Martin." While blue humor has long been a staple of black audiences, it was relegated to clubs and records for *mature* black audiences. It was not peddled to kids or to the masses.

14   Now the blue humor tradition is piped to principally white audiences. If TV was as black as it is white—if there was a fair share of black love stories, black dramas, black detective heroes—these blue humor images would not be a problem. Right now, however, they stand as images to which whites can condescend.

15   Imagine being told by your peers, the records you hear, the programs you watch, the "leaders" you see on TV, classmates, prospective employers—imagine being told by virtually everyone that in order to be your true self you must be ignorant and poor, or at least seem so.

16   Blacks must now see to it that our children face no such burden. We must see to it that the white majority, along with vocal minorities within the black community (generally those with a self-serving political agenda), do not perpetuate the notion that African-Americans are invariably doomed to the underclass.

17   African-Americans are moving toward seeing ourselves—and demanding that others see us—as individuals, not as shards of a degraded monolith. The American ideal places primacy on the rights of the individual, yet historically African-Americans have been denied those rights. We blacks can effectively demand those rights, effectively demand justice only when each of us sees him or herself as an individual with the right to any of the opinions, idiosyncrasies and talents accorded any other American.

EXPLORING THE TEXT

1. Analyze the story Gaiter tells in the first two paragraphs about his experience applying for a job in a television network. How does this anecdote introduce the major themes of Gaiter's argument? Explain how the hiring program's title—the Minority Advancement Program—contributes to the expectations of Gaiter's department head.

2. Consider the other two anecdotes with which Gaiter opens his essay: the conversations with a white female student at Harvard (paragraph 3) and a black female student in junior high (paragraph 4). Why does Gaiter describe his college experience first? How do the settings for each anecdote add to the persuasiveness of this portion of his argument? How do all three anecdotes raise what Gaiter calls "questions of black authenticity" (paragraph 3)?

3. Analyze Gaiter's attitude toward the "black political agenda" described in paragraph 6. Who precisely in the black community was that agenda designed to serve? How successful has it been, according to Gaiter?

4. How, according to Gaiter, have white liberals helped to sustain the "myth of an all-encompassing black underclass" (paragraph 8). What is Gaiter's personal opinion of these liberals? How can you tell? Explain how the perpetuation of this myth caused Gaiter and other middle-class blacks to be accused of "thwarting the progress of our race" (paragraph 9).

5. In paragraphs 10–15, Gaiter gives examples of the way television portrays African Americans. Is there a particular logic behind Gaiter's move from news coverage to the blue humor of *Martin?* What is the relationship Gaiter implies here between fact and fiction?

6. Consider Gaiter's choice of the term *bourgeoisie* instead of *middle class* to define his constituency. What are the usual connotations of this word? How does Gaiter's use of it indicate his political bias?

7. Consider the effect of Gaiter's second reference to the junior high school student's question about his speech in paragraph 9. What purpose does it serve to allude to this incident a second time? In what ways does altering the context for the student's words contribute to Gaiter's point?

8. Notice that in paragraph 5 Gaiter shifts from anecdotes related to anonymous black and white women to a list of prominent black males. What is the effect of this shift? What does it tell us about the way Gaiter views these men and their influence on the future of black America?

9. Consider paragraph 7, a portion of the essay dedicated exclusively to the citation of statistics. What do these statistics show? How effective is their use at this particular moment in the essay? What is the significance of the fact that Gaiter allows the numbers to speak for themselves, with relatively little interpretation?

10. In paragraphs 16 and 17, Gaiter addresses black readers directly, using words like "we," "our children," and "ourselves." To what extent does this language represent a shift in Gaiter's sense of audience? What is the rhetorical effect of using this particular language at this point in his essay?

WRITING ASSIGNMENTS

1. Write an essay analyzing Gaiter's political bias. Use your discussion to consider the value of openly acknowledging one's political assumptions in argument.

2. Should soap operas and sitcoms be treated as serious registers of America's racial consciousness? Write an essay arguing for or against Gaiter's conclusions about the influence such programs have on public opinion, supporting your argument with secondary articles as well as primary observations.

3. Write an essay exploring Gaiter's claim that most white liberals conceal racism beneath their dedication to achieving racial equality. Your research should include interviews with faculty and staff who have been hired to perform affirmative action or equal opportunity initiatives. Also, determine to what extent programs designed to "advance" minorities are doomed to failure because, by definition, they reinforce the stereotype of racial inferiority.

GROUP PROJECTS

1. To what extent do African Americans subscribe to the view of " 'real' black people" described in paragraph 3? Research this question with other students in your class. Based on personal observation, discussions with friends and acquaintances, and secondary research, analyze and critique Gaiter's assumption that most African Americans subscribe to the vision of " 'real' black people described in paragraph 2. Try to locate opinions from social groups not represented by Gaiter, including low-income African Americans. Write either one group essay or several individual essays on this topic, in either case supporting your argument with the group's research.

2. Working with a few classmates, write up a report on the image of middle-class and upper-middle-class black Americans as portrayed in recent movies or on television shows. Begin by brainstorming a list of screen characters. To what extent do these portraits seem derived from traditional underclass stereotypes and myths? Write up your report to be presented to the class.

Crimes Against Humanity
Ward Churchill

As Leonce Gaiter has demonstrated, racial stereotypes are unfortunately built into American popular culture. To Ward Churchill, a man of Creek and Cherokee blood, none has been so damning as those regarding Native Americans. In this essay, Churchill argues that professional sports teams that take Indian names or use Indian cultural images and symbols as mascots and logos and for advertising ultimately defame Native Americans. In fact, he argues that such seemingly innocent practices perpetuate the crimes against Native Americans.

Churchill is the coordinator of the American Indian Movement for the state of Colorado. He is the author of several books on Native Americans including *Fantasies of the Master Race: Literature, Cinema, and the Colonization of American Indians* (1992), *Indians Are Us* (1993), and most recently *From a Native Son: Selected Essays on Indigenism, 1985–1995* (1996). He teaches in the Center for Studies of Ethnicity and Race in America at the University of Colorado, Boulder. This essay originally appeared in *Z Magazine* in March 1993.

1 During the past couple of seasons, there has been an increasing wave of controversy regarding the names of professional sports teams like the Atlanta "Braves," Cleveland "Indians," Washington "Redskins," and Kansas City "Chiefs." The issue extends to the names of college teams like Florida State University "Seminoles," University of Illinois "Fighting Illini," and so on, right on down to high school outfits like the Lamar (Colorado) "Savages." Also involved have been team adoption of "mascots," replete with feathers, buckskins, beads, spears and "warpaint" (some fans have opted to adorn themselves in the same fashion), and nifty little "pep" gestures like the "Indian Chant" and "Tomahawk Chop."

2 A substantial number of American Indians have protested that use of native names, images and symbols as sports team mascots and the like is, by definition, a virulently racist practice. Given the historical relationship between Indians and non-Indians during what has been called the "Conquest of America," American Indian Movement leader (and American Indian Anti-Defamation Council founder) Russell Means has compared the practice to contemporary Germans naming their soccer teams the "Jews," "Hebrews," and "Yids," while adorning their uniforms with grotesque caricatures of Jewish faces taken from the Nazis' anti-Semitic propaganda of the 1930s. Numerous demonstrations have occurred in conjunction with games— most notably during the November 15, 1992 match-up between the Chiefs and Redskins in Kansas City—by angry Indians and their supporters.

3 In response, a number of players—especially African Americans and other minority athletes—have been trotted out by professional team owners like Ted Turner, as well as university and public school officials, to announce that they mean not to insult but to honor native people. They have been joined by the television networks and most major newspapers, all of which have editorialized that Indian discomfort with the situation is "no big deal," insisting that the whole thing is just "good, clean fun." The country needs more such fun, they've argued, and "a few disgruntled Native Americans" have no right to undermine the nation's enjoyment of its leisure time by complaining. This is especially the case, some have argued, "in hard times like these." It has even been contended that Indian outrage at being systematically degraded—rather than the degradation itself—creates "a serious barrier to the sort of intergroup communication so necessary in a multicultural society such as ours."

4 Okay, let's communicate. We are frankly dubious that those advancing such positions really believe their own rhetoric, but, just for the sake of argument, let's accept the premise that they are sincere. If what they say is true, then isn't it time we spread such "inoffensiveness" and "good cheer" around among *all* groups so that *everybody* can participate *equally* in fostering the round of national laughs they call for? Sure it is—the country can't have too much fun or "intergroup involvement"— so the more, the merrier. Simple consistency demands that anyone who thinks the Tomahawk Chop is a swell pastime must be just as hearty in his or her endorsement of the following ideas. The same logic used to defend the defamation of American Indians should help us all start yukking it up.

5   First, as a counterpart to the Redskins, we need an NFL team called "Niggers" to honor Afro-Americans. Half-time festivities for fans might include a simulated stewing of the opposing coach in a large pot while players and cheerleaders dance around it, garbed in leopard skins and wearing fake bones in their noses. This concept obviously goes along with the kind of gaiety attending the Chop, but also with the actions of the Kansas City Chiefs, whose team members—prominently including black team members—lately appeared on a poster looking "fierce" and "savage" by way of wearing Indian regalia. Just a bit of harmless "morale boosting," says the Chiefs' front office. You bet.

6   So that the newly-formed Niggers sports club won't end up too out of sync while expressing the "spirit" and "identity" of Afro-Americans in the above fashion, a baseball franchise—let's call this one the "Sambos"—should be formed. How about a basketball team called the "Spearchuckers"? A hockey team called the "Jungle Bunnies"? Maybe the "essence" of these teams could be depicted by images of tiny black faces adorned with huge pairs of lips. The players could appear on TV every week or so gnawing on chicken legs and spitting watermelon seeds at one another. Catchy, eh? Well, there's "nothing to be upset about," according to those who love wearing "war bonnets" to the Super Bowl or having "Chief Illiniwik" dance around the sports arenas of Urbana, Illinois.

7   And why stop there? There are plenty of other groups to include. Hispanics? They can be "represented" by the Galveston "Greasers" and San Diego "Spics," at least until the Wisconsin "Wetbacks" and Baltimore "Beaners" get off the ground. Asian Americans? How about the "Slopes," "Dinks," "Gooks," and "Zipperheads"? Owners of the latter teams might get their logo ideas from editorial page cartoons printed in the nation's newspapers during World War II: slant-eyes, buck teeth, big glasses, but nothing racially insulting or derogatory, according to the editors and artists involved at the time. Indeed, this Second World War–vintage stuff can be seen as just another barrel of laughs, at least by what current editors say are their "local standards" concerning American Indians.

8   Let's see. Who's been left out? Teams like the Kansas City "Kikes," Hanover "Honkies," San Leandro "Shylocks," Daytona "Dagos," and Pittsburgh "Polacks" will fill a certain social void among white folk. Have a religious belief? Let's all go for the gusto and gear up the Milwaukee "Mackerel Snappers" and Hollywood "Holy Rollers." The Fighting Irish of Notre Dame can be rechristened the "Drunken Irish" or "Papist Pigs." Issues of gender and sexual preference can be addressed through creation of teams like the St. Louis "Sluts," Boston "Bimbos," Detroit "Dykes," and the Fresno "Fags." How about the Gainesville "Gimps" and Richmond "Retards," so the physically and mentally impaired won't be excluded from our fun and games?

9   Now, don't go getting "overly sensitive" out there. None of this is demeaning or insulting, at least not when it's being done to Indians. Just ask the folks who are doing it, or their apologists like Andy Rooney in the national media. They'll tell you—as in fact they *have* been telling you—that there's been no harm done, regardless of what their victims think, feel, or say. The situation is exactly the same as when those with precisely the same mentality used to insist that Step 'n' Fetchit was

okay, or Rochester on the Jack Benny Show, or Amos and Andy, Charlie Chan, the Frito Bandito, or any of the other cutesy symbols making up the lexicon of American racism. Have we communicated yet?

10   Let's get just a little bit real here. The notion of "fun" embodied in rituals like the Tomahawk Chop must be understood for what it is. There's not a single non-Indian example used above which can be considered socially acceptable in even the most marginal sense. The reasons are obvious enough. So why is it different where American Indians are concerned? One can only conclude that, in contrast to the other groups at issue, Indians are (falsely) perceived as being too few, and therefore too weak, to defend themselves effectively against racist and otherwise offensive behavior.

11   Fortunately, there are some glimmers of hope. A few teams and their fans have gotten the message and have responded appropriately. Stanford University, which opted to drop the name "Indians" from Stanford, has experienced no resulting drop-off in attendance. Meanwhile, the local newspaper in Portland, Oregon recently decided its long-standing editorial policy prohibiting use of racial epithets should include derogatory team names. The Redskins, for instance, are now referred to as "the Washington team," and will continue to be described in this way until the franchise adopts an inoffensive moniker (newspaper sales in Portland have suffered no decline as a result).

12   Such examples are to be applauded and encouraged. They stand as figurative beacons in the night, proving beyond all doubt that it is quite possible to indulge in the pleasure of athletics without accepting blatant racism into the bargain.

13   On October 16, 1946, a man named Julius Streicher mounted the steps of a gallows. Moments later he was dead, the sentence of an international tribunal composed of representatives of the United States, France, Great Britain, and the Soviet Union having been imposed. Streicher's body was then cremated, and—so horrendous were his crimes thought to have been—his ashes dumped into an unspecified German river so that "no one should ever know a particular place to go for reasons of mourning his memory."

14   Julius Streicher had been convicted at Nuremberg, Germany of what were termed "Crimes Against Humanity." The lead prosecutor in his case—Justice Robert Jackson of the United States Supreme Court—had not argued that the defendant had killed anyone, nor that he had personally committed any especially violent act. Nor was it contended that Streicher had held any particularly important position in the German government during the period in which the so-called Third Reich had exterminated some 6,000,000 Jews, as well as several million Gypsies, Poles, Slavs, homosexuals, and other untermenschen (subhumans).

15   The sole offense for which the accused was ordered put to death was in having served as publisher/editor of a Bavarian tabloid entitled *Der Sturmer* during the early-to-mid 1930s, years before the Nazi genocide actually began. In this capacity, he had penned a long series of virulently anti-Semitic editorials and "news" stories, usually accompanied by cartoons and other images graphically depicting

Jews in extraordinarily derogatory fashion. This, the prosecution asserted, had done much to "dehumanize" the targets of his distortion in the mind of the German public. In turn, such dehumanization had made it possible—or at least easier—for average Germans to later indulge in the outright liquidation of Jewish "vermin." The tribunal agreed, holding that Streicher was therefore complicit in genocide and deserving of death by hanging.

16   During his remarks to the Nuremberg tribunal, Justice Jackson observed that, in implementing its sentences, the participating powers were morally and legally binding themselves to adhere forever after to the same standards of conduct that were being applied to Streicher and the other Nazi leaders. In the alternative, he said, the victorious allies would have committed "pure murder" at Nuremberg—no different in substance from that carried out by those they presumed to judge—rather than establishing the "permanent bench-mark for justice" which was intended.

17   Yet in the United States of Robert Jackson, the indigenous American Indian population had already been reduced, in a process which is ongoing to this day, from perhaps 12.5 million in the year 1500 to fewer than 250,000 by the beginning of the 20th century. This was accomplished, according to official sources, "largely through the cruelty of [Euro-American] settlers," and an informal but clear governmental policy which had made it an articulated goal to "exterminate these red vermin," or at least whole segments of them.

18   Bounties had been placed on the scalps of Indians—any Indians—in places as diverse as Georgia, Kentucky, Texas, the Dakotas, Oregon, and California, and had been maintained until resident Indian populations were decimated or disappeared altogether. Entire peoples such as the Cherokee had been reduced to half their size through a policy of forced removal from their homelands east of the Mississippi River to what were then considered less preferable areas in the West.

19   Others, such as the Navajo, suffered the same fate while under military guard for years on end. The United States Army had also perpetrated a long series of wholesale massacres of Indians at places like Horseshoe Bend, Bear River, Sand Creek, the Washita River, the Marias River, Camp Robinson, and Wounded Knee.

20   Through it all, hundreds of popular novels—each competing with the next to make Indians appear more grotesque, menacing, and inhuman—were sold in the tens of millions of copies in the U.S. Plainly, the Euro-American public was being conditioned to see Indians in such a way as to allow their eradication to continue. And continue it did until the Manifest Destiny of the U.S.—a direct precursor to what Hitler would subsequently call Lebensraumpolitik (the politics of living space)—was consummated.

21   By 1900, the national project of "clearing" Native Americans from their land and replacing them with "superior" Anglo-American settlers was complete; the indigenous population had been reduced by as much as 98 percent while approximately 97.5 percent of their original territory had "passed" to the invaders. The survivors had been concentrated, out of sight and mind of the public, on scattered "reservations," all of them under the self-assigned "plenary" (full) power of the federal government. There was, of course, no Nuremberg-style tribunal passing judgment on those who had fostered such circumstances in North America. No U.S. offi-

cial or private citizen was ever imprisoned—never mind hanged—for implementing or propagandizing what had been done. Nor had the process of genocide afflicting Indians been completed. Instead, it merely changed form.

22   Between the 1880s and the 1980s, nearly half of all Native American children were coercively transferred from their own families, communities, and cultures to those of the conquering society. This was done through compulsory attendance at remote boarding schools, often hundreds of miles from their homes, where native children were kept for years on end while being systematically "deculturated" (indoctrinated to think and act in the manner of Euro-Americans rather than as Indians). It was also accomplished through a pervasive foster home and adoption program—including "blind" adoptions, where children would be permanently denied information as to who they were/are and where they'd come from—placing native youths in non-Indian homes.

23   The express purpose of all this was to facilitate a U.S. governmental policy to bring about the "assimilation" (dissolution) of indigenous societies. In other words, Indian cultures as such were to be caused to disappear. Such policy objectives are directly contrary to the United Nations 1948 Convention on Punishment and Prevention of the Crime of Genocide, an element of international law arising from the Nuremberg proceedings. The forced "transfer of the children" of a targeted "racial, ethnical, or religious group" is explicitly prohibited as a genocidal activity under the Convention's second article.

24   Article II of the Genocide Convention also expressly prohibits involuntary sterilization as a means of "preventing births among" a targeted population. Yet, in 1975, it was conceded by the U.S. government that its Indian Health Service (IHS), then a subpart of the Bureau of Indian Affairs (BIA), was even then conducting a secret program of involuntary sterilization that had affected approximately 40 percent of all Indian women. The program was allegedly discontinued, and the IHS was transferred to the Public Health Service, but no one was punished. In 1990, it came out that the IHS was inoculating Inuit children in Alaska with Hepatitis-B vaccine. The vaccine had already been banned by the World Health Organization as having a demonstrated correlation with the HIV-Syndrome which is itself correlated to AIDS. As this is written, a "field test" of Hepatitis-A vaccine, also HIV-correlated, is being conducted on Indian reservations in the northern plains region.

25   The Genocide Convention makes it a "crime against humanity" to create conditions leading to the destruction of an identifiable human group, as such. Yet the BIA has utilized the government's plenary prerogatives to negotiate mineral leases "on behalf of" Indian peoples paying a fraction of standard royalty rates. The result has been "super profits" for a number of preferred U.S. corporations. Meanwhile, Indians, whose reservations ironically turned out to be in some of the most mineral-rich areas of North America, which makes us, the nominally wealthiest segment of the continent's population, live in dire poverty.

26   By the government's own data in the mid-1980s, Indians received the lowest annual and lifetime per capita incomes of any aggregate population group in the United States. Concomitantly, we suffer the highest rate of infant mortality, death by exposure and malnutrition, disease, and the like. Under such circumstances, alco-

holism and other escapist forms of substance abuse are endemic in the Indian community, a situation which leads both to a general physical debilitation of the population and a catastrophic accident rate. Teen suicide among Indians is several times the national average.

27 The average life expectancy of a reservation-based Native American man is barely 45 years; women can expect to live less than three years longer.

28 Such itemizations could be continued at great length, including matters like the radioactive contamination of large portions of contemporary Indian Country, the forced relocation of traditional Navajos, and so on. But the point should be made: Genocide, as defined in international law, is a continuing fact of day-to-day life (and death) for North America's native peoples. Yet there has been—and is—only the barest flicker of public concern about, or even consciousness of, this reality. Absent any serious expression of public outrage, no one is punished and the process continues.

29 A salient reason for public acquiescence before the ongoing holocaust in Native North America has been a continuation of the popular legacy, often through more effective media. Since 1925, Hollywood has released more than 2,000 films, many of them rerun frequently on television, portraying Indians as strange, perverted, ridiculous, and often dangerous things of the past. Moreover, we are habitually presented to mass audiences one-dimensionally, devoid of recognizable human motivations and emotions; Indians thus serve as props, little more. We have thus been thoroughly and systematically dehumanized.

30 Nor is this the extent of it. Everywhere, we are used as logos, as mascots, as jokes: "Big Chief" writing tablets, "Red Man" chewing tobacco, "Winnebago" campers, "Navajo" and "Cherokee" and "Pontiac" and "Cadillac" pickups and automobiles. There are the Cleveland "Indians," the Kansas City "Chiefs," the Atlanta "Braves" and the Washington "Redskins" professional sports teams—not to mention those in thousands of colleges, high schools, and elementary schools across the country—each with their own degrading caricatures and parodies of Indians and/or things Indian. Pop fiction continues in the same vein, including an unending stream of New Age manuals purporting to expose the inner works of indigenous spirituality in everything from pseudo-philosophical to do-it-yourself styles. Blond yuppies from Beverly Hills amble about the country claiming to be reincarnated 17th century Cheyenne Ushamans ready to perform previously secret ceremonies.

31 In effect, a concerted, sustained, and in some ways accelerating effort has gone into making Indians unreal. It is thus of obvious importance that the American public begin to think about the implications of such things the next time they witness a gaggle of face-painted and war-bonneted buffoons doing the "Tomahawk Chop" at a baseball or football game. It is necessary that they think about the implications of the grade-school teacher adorning their child in turkey feathers to commemorate Thanksgiving. Think about the significance of John Wayne or Charleton Heston killing a dozen "savages" with a single bullet the next time a western comes on TV. Think about why Land-o-Lakes finds it appropriate to market its butter with the stereotyped image of an "Indian princess" on the wrapper. Think about what it means when non-Indian academics profess—as they often do—to "know more about Indians than Indians do themselves." Think about the significance of charla-

tans like Carlos Castaneda and Jamake Highwater and Mary Summer Rain and Lynn Andrews churning out "Indian" bestsellers, one after the other, while Indians typically can't get into print.

32   Think about the real situation of American Indians. Think about Julius Streicher. Remember Justice Jackson's admonition. Understand that the treatment of Indians in American popular culture is not "cute" or "amusing" or just "good, clean fun."

33   Know that it causes real pain and real suffering to real people. Know that it threatens our very survival. And know that this is just as much a crime against humanity as anything the Nazis ever did. It is likely that the indigenous people of the United States will never demand that those guilty of such criminal activity be punished for their deeds. But the least we have the right to expect—indeed, to demand—is that such practices finally be brought to a halt.

EXPLORING THE TEXT

1. Before you read this essay, did you feel that the use of Native American names, mascots, and symbols by sports teams and car manufacturers was denigrating and insulting to Native Americans? Did this essay change your way of thinking? Explain your answer.

2. How did the press react to the protests by Native Americans of their degradation by professional sports teams? How might the media's reaction have been more appropriate? Does Churchill supply any examples of suitable responses?

3. To make his point, Churchill suggests other racial and ethnic groups for sports teams' names and halftime activities. What specific racial stereotypes does he offer for different groups? What is the tone of his suggestions? Would you say his analogies are an effective part of his argument? Explain.

4. In paragraph 13, Churchill mentions Julius Streicher. Who was Streicher? How did Streicher's trial and execution serve as a "'permanent benchmark for justice'" (paragraph 16)? What point does Churchill make by placing this historical information immediately after his satire of team names?

5. According to Churchill, why has society gotten away with offensive stereotypes of Native Americans but not with stereotypes of other groups?

6. Now that you have read Churchill's essay, do you agree that it is time for a change, that the use of Native American names, images, caricatures, symbols, and so on for sports teams perpetuates crimes against this segment of humanity? Explain.

7. How well does the title of this essay fit the discussion? Explain, citing details from the text.

8. Beginning in paragraph 17, Churchill offers a brief historical survey of the crimes against Native Americans. Did you find this too much of a digression from the rest of his argument? Or do you think it was necessary for

Churchill to bolster his argument regarding the cultural denigration of Native Americans by names for teams and products? Explain.

WRITING ASSIGNMENTS

1. Compose a letter to Churchill, explaining how and why you agree or disagree with his position in this essay. If you disagree with only some of his ideas here, make sure you explain which parts you agree with, so that your letter will offer persuasive evidence that you have read and thought about all that he has said.
2. Churchill complains in paragraph 31 about traditional movie images of Native Americans as "'savages,'" as well as seemingly positive images like the "'Indian princess'" in the butter packaging. How do positive as well as negative images contribute to harmful cultural stereotyping? Answer this question in a paper, referring to at least three different cultures (examples of groups that have been stereotyped: Asian Americans, people with disabilities, religious groups, gays and lesbians, southerners, the middle class, and athletes). You need not limit the idea of culture to race and ethnicity.
3. Churchill reports that Native Americans have the lowest income of any cultural group in America. Using your library, create a profile of the socioeconomic status (income level, unemployment statistics, schooling, governmental participation, etc.) of a particular Native American group. (Depending on your sources, you may wish to limit yourself to a tribe or to the native peoples living in a particular state, city, or region.) As best you can, analyze the causes and effects of this group's condition and its success in improving its status.

GROUP PROJECTS

1. Try to analyze the beliefs, attitudes, and values held by the media, professional sports teams, and non-Native American fans regarding Native Americans. Working in small groups, try to determine what stereotypes of Native Americans are maintained by professional sports teams that make use of Native American names and symbols. Write a paper on your exploration of the questions to be presented in class.
2. Churchill argues that Hollywood has portrayed Native Americans in the most derogatory manner. Working in small groups, brainstorm the kinds of negative stereotypes found in movies and television. What about more recent films by major studios, such as *Pocahontas, Squanto,* and *Dances with Wolves*—do these films stereotype? Research the reviews each movie received. Have Native Americans been marginalized "as props" (paragraph 29) or stereotyped? Report your findings to the class.

Getting to Know About You and Me
Chana Schoenberger

By definition, stereotypes are erroneous assumptions about individuals based on their race, ethnic descent, religion, social class, gender, physical appearance, and so forth. Forged by ignorance and fear, stereotypes damningly reduce whole groups of people to certain ascribed characteristics so as to justify their presumed faults. Jews are materialistic, blacks are lazy, Latins are hot-tempered, Asians are mysterious, Native Americans are stoical, French are oversexed, Irish are drunks. Not only are such caricatures simplistic impositions on others, they restrict and distort our expectations of the victims. This essay is a young woman's account of religious ignorance in action. As Chana Schoenberger explains, even the smartest students in a summer scholarship program thought Jews still practiced animal sacrifice.

This essay first appeared in *Newsweek* in September 1993 when Schoenberger was a high school student in Bethesda, Maryland.

1   As a religious holiday approaches, students at my high school who will be celebrating the holiday prepare a presentation on it for an assembly. The Diversity Committee, which sponsors the assemblies to increase religious awareness, asked me last spring if I would help with the presentation on Passover, the Jewish holiday that commemorates the Exodus from Egypt. I was too busy with other things, and I never got around to helping. I didn't realize then how important those presentations really are, or I definitely would have done something.

2   This summer I was one of 20 teens who spent five weeks at the University of Wisconsin at Superior studying acid rain with a National Science Foundation Young Scholars program. With such a small group in such a small town, we soon became close friends and had a good deal of fun together. We learned about the science of acid rain, went on field trips, found the best and cheapest restaurants in Superior and ate in them frequently to escape the lousy cafeteria food. We were a happy, bonded group.

3   Represented among us were eight religions: Jewish, Roman Catholic, Muslim, Hindu, Methodist, Mormon, Jehovah's Witness and Lutheran. It was amazing, given the variety of backgrounds, to see the ignorance of some of the smartest young scholars on the subject of other religions.

4   On the first day, one girl mentioned that she had nine brothers and sisters. "Oh, are you Mormon?" asked another girl, who I knew was a Mormon herself. The first girl, shocked, replied, "No, I dress normal!" She thought Mormon was the same as Mennonite, and the only thing she knew about either religion was that Mennonites don't, in her opinion, "dress normal."

5   My friends, ever curious about Judaism, asked me about everything from our basic theology to food preferences. "How come, if Jesus was a Jew, Jews aren't Christian?" my Catholic roommate asked me in all seriousness. Brought up in a small Wisconsin town, she had never met a Jew before, nor had she met people from most of the other "strange" religions (anything but Catholic or mainstream Protestant). Many of the other kids were the same way.

6   "Do you all still practice animal sacrifices?" a girl from a small town in Minnesota asked me once. I said no, laughed, and pointed out that this was the 20th century, but she had been absolutely serious. The only Jews she knew were the ones
from the Bible.

7   Nobody was deliberately rude or anti-Semitic, but I got the feeling that I was
representing the entire Jewish people through my actions. I realized that many of my
friends would go back to their small towns thinking that all Jews liked Dairy Queen
Blizzards and grilled cheese sandwiches. After all, that was true of all the Jews they
knew (in most cases, me and the only other Jewish young scholar, period).

8   The most awful thing for me, however, was not the benign ignorance of my
friends. Our biology professor had taken us on a field trip to the EPA field site
where he worked, and he was telling us about the project he was working on. He
said that they had to make sure the EPA got its money's worth from the study—he
"wouldn't want them to get Jewed."

9   I was astounded. The professor had a doctorate, various other degrees and
seemed to be a very intelligent man. He apparently had no idea that he had just made
an anti-Semitic remark. The other Jewish girl in the group and I debated whether or
not to say something to him about it, and although we agreed we would, neither of
us ever did. Personally, it made me feel uncomfortable. For a high-school student to
tell a professor who taught her class that he was a bigot seemed out of place to me,
even if he was one.

10   What scares me about that experience, in fact about my whole visit to Wisconsin, was that I never met a really vicious anti-Semite or a malignantly prejudiced
person. Many of the people I met had been brought up to think that Jews (or Mor-
mons or any other religion that's not mainstream Christian) were different and that
difference was not good.

11   Difference, in America, is supposed to be good. We are expected—at least, I always thought we were expected—to respect each other's traditions. Respect requires some knowledge about people's backgrounds. Singing Christmas carols as a
kid in school did not make me Christian, but it taught me to appreciate beautiful music and someone else's holiday. It's not necessary or desirable for all ethnic groups
in America to assimilate into one traditionless mass. Rather, we all need to learn
about other cultures so that we can understand one another and not feel threatened
by others.

12   In the little multicultural universe that I live in, it's safe not to worry about explaining the story of Passover because if people don't hear it from me, they'll hear it
some other way. Now I realize that's not true everywhere.

13   Ignorance was the problem I faced this summer. By itself, ignorance is not always a problem, but it leads to misunderstandings, prejudice and hatred. Many of
today's problems involve hatred. If there weren't so much ignorance about other
people's backgrounds, would people still hate each other as badly as they do now?
Maybe so, but at least that hatred would be based on facts and not flawed beliefs.

14   I'm now back at school, and I plan to apply for the Diversity Committee. I'm
going to get up and tell the whole school about my religion and the tradition I'm
proud of. I see now how important it is to celebrate your heritage and to educate oth-

ers about it. I can no longer take for granted that everyone knows about my religion, or that I know about theirs. People who are suspicious when they find out I'm Jewish usually don't know much about Judaism. I would much prefer them to hate or distrust me because of something I've done, instead of them hating me on the basis of prejudice.

EXPLORING THE TEXT

1. What kinds of misconceptions did Schoenberger's friends at the National Science Foundation Young Scholars Program have about people of different religions? Did you find yourself laughing at any of the mistakes they made? Do the questions they ask seem to be determined by the religion of the person asking the question?

2. How did members of the eight religious groups respond to each other's questions? That is, were they tolerant, intolerant, sarcastic, belligerent, or other? Have you ever asked, or responded to, a question about religion (or race, ethnicity, or nationality)? If so, what kinds of feelings did you have about the question or the response?

3. Why is Schoenberger so shocked at her professor's statement that he didn't want the EPA "to get Jewed" (paragraph 8)? How is this statement different from the kinds of discussions she has had with other young scholars?

4. Do all Jews like Dairy Queen Blizzards and grilled cheese sandwiches? If not, why does Schoenberger seem concerned that her friends from the program will believe this statement? Is she worried about something more than food here? Have you ever been in a situation where your own unique qualities have been taken to mean something about a group of people?

5. Where does Schoenberger finally explain the issue she raised in paragraph 1 about the importance of her high school's Passover celebration? Why does she say it is important? What good does she think it will do?

6. Why does Schoenberger move from innocuous, silly comments at the beginning of her article to more serious problems? How does this strategy shape her characterizations of her friends and her biology professor? How does this strategy affect the way audiences are likely to respond to the article?

7. Why does Schoenberger spend so much time emphasizing the intelligence of her friends in the Young Scholars Program? How would this article have been different if she had been describing a group of young people on parole for minor offenses, students in a remedial class, or honor roll nerds?

8. Do you think Schoenberger's article has a thesis? Or is it a personal experience narrative without a thesis? What do you think the thesis, or the purpose for this narrative, is? Why do you think Schoenberger does not state it forthrightly?

WRITING ASSIGNMENTS

1. Like Leonce Gaiter ("The Revolt of the Black Bourgeoisie"), Schoenberger describes a situation where people had distorted expectations of her because of her ethnic cultural identity. Have you ever been in a situation where out of ignorance people demonstrated preconceived notions about you based on your race or ethnic culture? Or where your own unique qualities were construed to designate something about your particular cultural group? If so, write a paper that captures that experience. How did you react? What might have been the basis for such attitudes?

2. Using your telephone directory and your school's resources (such as spiritual counseling, worship or support groups for students of a specific religion, chaplaincy, a religious studies faculty member) identify a local meeting or worship service of a group to which you do not belong, but at which you would be welcome. This might be a mass, a Passover seder, or a study group. Write a report on your visit. What did you find familiar? What was new and different to you?

3. Choose a religion about which you know very little. Before you begin the assignment, write a list of things you know about people who practice this religion and about the beliefs they hold. Then, using your school's library resources, find as complete a description as possible about practices and beliefs. If possible, try to find members of the religious group you can interview. Compare your findings to your original list. What were you able to confirm? What turned out to be false or incomplete?

GROUP PROJECTS

1. Try to imagine that someone from an entirely different country (or even a different planet) has come to your classroom to study Americans. This visitor will base his or her entire set of impressions on the information and observations possible in only one class session. Brainstorming with other classmates, try to come up with different kinds of ideas the visitor would have of Americans. For instance, what misimpressions would your visitor get from just one visit? After pooling your group's ideas, try to capture this visitor's impressions in a report.

2. Working in small groups, consult your library's resources to locate some contemporary discussions of how and why study of the Holocaust—the extermination of six million Jews under Nazi rule in Germany during World War II—must be continued. You may wish to focus on historical scholarship, on the creation of museums and monuments, or even on allegations that the Holocaust never really happened. You might even contact members of local Jewish organizations and synagogues. What role does anti-Semitism play in contemporary discussions?

Innocent and Presumed Ethnic

John Yemma

Today a new level of ethnic awareness enhances the American cultural experience for all. Like so many of us, the author of this piece, John Yemma, loves ethnic foods and music and "generally enjoy[s] splashing around in the full, glorious pool of pluralism." Yet he has profited in an additional and unique way. Because of the spelling of his last name he has, over the years, been taken for a member of a variety of ethnic groups, often in welcome but sometimes with suspicion. Whether or not you can identify with Yemma, however, his own experience reflects society's compulsion to reduce people to presumptions about race and ethnicity.

Yemma is a professional journalist who writes for the *Boston Globe* where this piece originally appeared in August 1994.

1 Ethnic awareness is a great thing. It has enhanced the self-esteem of millions of Americans and rescued our nation from slow death by Cheez Whiz and wingtips. It has put color in our workplace, salsa in our diet, soul in our music and has made America a warmer, healthier, vastly more interesting place than the white-bread Levittown it might otherwise have become.

2 Personally and professionally, I'm an ethnophile. I appreciate Afropop, Los Lobos and ZZ Top. I put Vietnamese hot sauce on burritos, adore sushi, love falafel and generally enjoy splashing around in the full, glorious pool of pluralism.

3 I am not, however, from a major, what's-happening-now ethnic group. I know no folk dances, have never tricked out my car with purple running lights and don't sport a culturally significant hairstyle. When I was a kid, our family spoke English, drove a Ford, played touch football and never experienced discrimination that I've been told about.

4 Which is why I'm a little amused to have spent much of my adult life PE—Presumed Ethnic.

5 My first brush with PE status came when I was in high school in Texas. Late in my senior year a guidance counselor summoned me to her office with good news: I had been awarded a scholarship from the LULAC organization.

6 This was wonderful, I said, but isn't LULAC a Latin-American group?

7 "Yes, it is," said the counselor.

8 "I don't know if I can take it," I said. "I'm not Latin American."

9 The counselor leaned over and lowered her voice. Clearly, she had seen this sort of thing before: an earnest young man trying to pass as an Anglo.

10 "John," she said, "don't be afraid to acknowledge your heritage."

11 I wanted the scholarship money, but I really didn't qualify. My dark complexion and vowel-ending name made me seem like the promising young Latino I wasn't. (I finally convinced the counselor and she found me a Rotary Club scholarship instead.)

12   Over the years, I have inadvertently, or very nearly, benefited from being PE any number of times. For one thing, I know I have been thought of as an ethnic by companies and organizations that enjoy the idea of diversity but are too polite to ask. For another, I have developed great sympathy for the challenges faced by legitimately ethnic colleagues.

13   A career in journalism, mostly in the field of foreign news, has helped familiarize me with most ethnic issues and understand the need for self-affirmation that comes from hanging with a group. While I accept that for others, however, I myself believe that the group isn't as important as the individual. OK, I know that is passe and I'm not here to try to sell you on the idea, but I'm hard-wired to believe this and can't change.

14   For most people, it's not enough that I feel like I'm just me. It doesn't explain things or allow for easy assumptions about my putative beliefs and prejudices. I must be covering up or trying to pass. Or—greatest of all sins—deeply in denial.

15   As a foreign editor, I've received a number of complaints from readers who have decided that my name betrays vicious biases and secret sympathies. This is especially true when it comes to the Middle East. Lately, though, fresh groups of ready-to-be-offended people have emerged from the Balkans and Central Asia, areas that enjoy histories of intolerance and suspicion every bit as rich as the Middle East. On a number of occasions I've been told that some innocent error or omission in a news story clearly reflects my Armenian, Turkish, Serb, Croat, Polish, Arab and/or Jewish biases.

16   But I'm not complaining. I have the kind of coloration that probably prevented me from becoming a kidnap victim in Beirut and has minimized the kind of casual anti-Americanism that one runs into in places like Mexico City or Paris. Also, you get to meet nice people when you're PE.

17   The hotel clerks in Cairo became fast friends after telling me my name sounded like the Arabic word for mother.

18   After I'd written some articles from Tokyo, a kindly Japanese reader phoned to ask if I was Japanese-American. My wife thought this, too, when she first heard my name, before we met face to face.

19   I have gotten hearty *shaloms* in West Jerusalem and *salaam-aleikums* in East Jerusalem.

20   And not long ago I got a call from the Kenyan embassy in Washington. A diplomat was on his way to Boston and said he very much wanted to come see me. He would be most welcome, I said.

21   "Ah, my friend," he responded in a rich, resonant East African voice. "It will be *my* pleasure to meet a Yemma."

22   When he walked in my office a few days later, I immediately sensed his disappointment. Until that moment, he confessed, he thought I might have had roots in his country. It turns out there is a tribe in northern Kenya with the name Yemma.

23   I intend to find them one day.

24   For the record, I was born in the United States. My father's parents were born in Italy; my mother is of German-French descent. The family name was modestly changed at Ellis Island: Y instead of I. Go figure.

25   So, the only Yemmas that exist are in the United States. This makes my name exclusively and precisely American. And that's what I am.

26   I wonder if that will ever be enough.

EXPLORING THE TEXT

1. In paragraphs 1–3, how does Yemma say he feels about American ethnic diversity?

2. In paragraphs 4–11, why does Yemma say he rejected a college scholarship? How would you have responded to such a mistaken offer? Would you have taken the scholarship? Why or why not—justify your response.

3. In paragraphs 12–13 and 16, how does Yemma say he has benefited from mistakes about his ethnic identity? In paragraphs 14–15, how does Yemma say he has been harmed by the same mistakes?

4. A diplomat tells Yemma of a tribe bearing his last name in Kenya, yet Yemma says that "the only Yemmas that exist are in the United States" (paragraph 25). Why does he make this claim? How does his explanation show that his name is "exclusively and precisely American"?

5. The author is a staff writer for the *Boston Globe;* he says he grew up in Texas and that he is not from a "major, what's-happening-now ethnic group" (paragraph 3). Would his Italian-German-French ancestry be considered "ethnic" in other regions of America? Why or why not?

6. What kinds of cultural contrasts does Yemma list to "Cheez Whiz and wingtips" and "white-bread Levittown" (paragraph 1)? What kinds of metaphors does he use for people and their attitudes? How effective do you think these contrasts are?

7. What are the connotations of Yemma's title "Innocent and Presumed Ethnic" and his abbreviation "PE"? What other phrases do these terms remind you of? How do they help create a specific tone for this article?

8. In paragraphs 14 and 26, Yemma expresses doubt that his own individual talents are not "enough." What does he mean by this? Why doesn't he explain what "enough" means? Do you think this helps or harms his efforts to gain reader sympathy for his case?

9. This article is written as a series of personal anecdotes, rather than as an analytic or philosophical piece. If it were not an anecdotal piece, what would a good thesis sentence be? How would the effect and tone of the article be different?

10. Yemma has been mistaken for Latino, Armenian, Turkish, Serb, Croat, Polish, Arab, Jewish, Japanese, and Kenyan. Why do you think he lists such an extensive catalog of mistaken identities? How would his article have been different if this laundry list of ethnicities had been omitted?

11. Why do you think Yemma waits so long to reveal the truth about his own ethnicity? What effect would it have had on the article if he had begun with the statement, "I am of Italian-German-French descent"? What did you

imagine Yemma looked like as you read through the article? Why did you imagine him the way you did?

WRITING ASSIGNMENTS

1. Make a list of your classmates' first and last names. Then, try to match ethnicities with the names. How many times were your guesses accurate? Did your opinion of the individuals change once you found out something about their ethnicity that the name did not reveal? If so, why?
2. If Yemma were equal parts Italian, German, French, and Latino, would he be entitled to take the LULAC scholarship that his guidance counselor initially offered him? In your opinion, why or why not? Justify your answer. If your instructor directs, set up a pair of teams to debate the issue.

GROUP PROJECTS ────────────────────────────

1. With two or three classmates, consult your library's resources to research the history of name changes at Ellis Island in New York City or at other entry points into the United States. Why were these changes made? Do you think these changes were appropriate? Justify your answer. As best you can, try to determine how people whose names were changed felt about their new names. Can any of your group's family members recall name changes?
2. Working in small groups, try to determine which of you are "ethnic" and which of you are members of a "major, what's-happening-now ethnic group." Explain your answers. Try to determine what particular ethnic/racial/cultural features or qualities determined the answers to these questions. Write up your findings in a report to present to the class.

──

A Puerto Rican Stew
Esmeralda Santiago

When she was 13 years old, Esmeralda Santiago moved to the United States with her mother and family to escape a life of poverty in Puerto Rico, to seek out options not available in their homeland. Over the next 15 years Santiago learned English, went to American schools, and became assimilated into American society. The process was successful, but her family wanted the American Dream success without Americanization—an impossibility for the author. When after many years she returned to her native Puerto Rico, her closest relatives considered her a "turncoat" for having abandoned her culture—an experience shared by many immigrants. And, yet, as Santiago explains, she found her own recipe for identity that did not exclude her heritage.

Santiago is the author of *When I Was Puerto Rican* (1993), a memoir. Her essay first appeared in the *New York Times Sunday Magazine* in December 1994.

1   I'm in my kitchen, browsing through Puerto Rican cookbooks, when it hits me. These books are in English, written for people who don't know a *sofrito* from a *sombrero*. Then I remember the afternoon I returned to Puerto Rico for the summer after 15 years of living in the United States. The family gathered for dinner in my mother's house. The men settled in a corner of the living room, while Mami and my sisters chopped, washed, seasoned. I stood on the other side of the kitchen island, enjoying their Dance of the Stove with Pots and Pans—the flat metal sounds, the thud of the refrigerator door opening and closing, the swish of running water—a percussive accompaniment enhancing the fragrant sizzle of garlic and onions in hot oil.

2   "Do you cook Puerto Rican?" Norma asked as she cored a red pepper.

3   "No," I answered, "I never got the hang of it."

4   "How can you be Puerto Rican without your rice and beans?" joked Alicia.

5   "Easy," said Mami. "She's no longer Puerto Rican."

6   If she had stabbed me with the chicken-gutting knife in her hand it would have hurt less. I swallowed the pain. "Si, Mami," I said, "I have become *Americana*."

7   "I knew it the minute you stepped off the plane."

8   I parried with "Wasn't that what you wanted when you first brought us to New York?"

9   As Mami split the chicken, her voice rose, indignant: "I only wanted the best for you."

10   The dance was over, a knife suspended above tomato halves, rinse water running through rice clear as sunshine. I walked away, pushed by their silence—my mother, my sisters, my brothers-in-law. No one followed me, or challenged her assessment of me as a turncoat who had abandoned her culture. I stood in the gravelly yard, the soles of my sandals separating me from the ground as if I were on stilts, unable to touch my native soil, unable to feel a connection. I wanted to cry, but would not give them nor myself the satisfaction of tears. Instead, I leaned against a fence and wondered if her words hurt so much because they were true.

11   Whatever I was, Puerto Rican or not, had been orchestrated by Mami. When I was 13, she moved us from rural Puerto Rico to Brooklyn. We were to learn English, to graduate from high school, to find jobs in clean offices, not factories. We were to assimilate into American society, to put an end to the poverty she was forced to endure for lack of an education.

12   I, the oldest, took up the challenge. I learned English so well that people told me I didn't "speak like a Puerto Rican." I gave up the bright, form-fitting clothes of my friends and relatives for drab, loose garments that would not brand me as a "hot tomato." I developed a formal, evasive manner when asked about my background. I would not admit to being poor, to living with my mother and 10 sisters and brothers

in a three-room apartment. I would tremble with shame if newspapers identified a criminal as Puerto Rican.

13   Mami beamed when I got a job as a typist in Manhattan. She reminded me that I was to show my sisters and brothers the path to success without becoming "Americanized," a status that was never clearly defined but to be avoided at all costs.

14   That afternoon in her kitchen was the first time we had spoken in seven years. The grudge we held was so deep, neither could bridge it without losing *dignidad,* an imperative of Puerto Rican self-esteem. The break had come when I stopped being a "good" Puerto Rican girl and behaved like an American one.

15   At 21, I assumed I was old enough to live my life as I pleased. And what I pleased was a man a year older than Mami. I ran away with him, leaving a letter telling Mami I wouldn't be home after work because I was eloping. "Don't worry," I signed off, "I still love you."

16   She tracked me down to an apartment in Fort Lauderdale more luxurious than any we'd ever lived in, to say that if I returned home all would be forgiven. I refused. During those seven years, the man for whom I'd left my mother turned out to be as old-fashioned, possessive and domineering as she had seemed. From him, too, I ran away.

17   To question my Puerto Rican identity that afternoon in her kitchen was Mami's perfect comeback to what had surely been seven years of worry. It was also her way of recognizing her own folly. She had expected me to thrive in American culture, but I was to remain 100 percent Puerto Rican.

18   Mami came to realize the impossibility of such a demand, how difficult it is for someone from a "traditional" culture to achieve success in the United States without becoming something other than the person she set out to be. My one act of rebellion forced her to face what she had never expected. In the United States, her children would challenge her authority based on different rules of conduct. Within a year of my leaving home, she packed up the family and returned to Puerto Rico, where, she hoped, her children would be what they couldn't be in the United States: real Puerto Ricans.

19   I stayed behind, immersed in the American culture she feared. But I never considered myself any less Puerto Rican. I was born there, spoke its language, identified with its culture. But to Puerto Ricans on the island during my summer there, I was a different creature altogether. Employers complained that I was too assertive, men said I was too feminist, my cousin suggested I had no manners, and everyone accused me of being too independent. Those, I was made to understand, were Americanisms.

20   Back in the United States, I was constantly asked where I was from, and the comments about my not looking, behaving or talking like a Puerto Rican followed me into the era of political correctness, when it's no longer polite to say things like that.

21   I've learned to insist on my peculiar brand of Puerto Rican identity. One not bound by geographical, linguistic or behavioral boundaries, but rather, by a deep identification with a place, a people and a culture which, in spite of appearances, define my behavior and determine the rhythms of my days. An identity in which I've forgiven myself for having to look up a recipe for *arroz con pollo* in a Puerto Rican cookbook meant for people who don't know a *sombrero* from a *sofrito.*

EXPLORING THE TEXT

1. What explains the estrangement of the author from her mother? Does that explanation surprise you? Can you identify with it? Do you know of people who have become estranged from family because they became Americanized?

2. Santiago writes that *"dignidad* [(dignity) was] an imperative of Puerto Rican self-esteem" (paragraph 14). At what different points in the essay does Santiago demonstrate this trait? How do these examples illustrate what she concludes about identity at the end of the essay?

3. What reasons does Santiago offer for leaving the man with whom she had eloped? How does she demonstrate the similarities between this man and her own mother? Cite specific examples and explain why you think she may have been attracted to the man in the first place.

4. In paragraph 18, the author says that her mother had returned to Puerto Rico so that her other children would grow up "real Puerto Ricans," not Americans. Look over the essay again and try to determine what cultural traits—superficial and otherwise—distinguish Santiago from her relatives back home. Why do you think she does not list these traits clearly and explicitly?

5. At the end of the essay Santiago says that she has forgiven herself for her ignorance of certain aspects of Puerto Rican identity. She seems at peace with her status. Do you suppose that her mother could ever forgive her, too? Is there anything in the essay that indicates that she would accept her daughter fully? Explain your answer.

6. How appropriate is the title of this essay for its contents? How well does it fit Santiago's discussion? In your answer, consider references to cooking throughout the essay.

7. How would you describe the tone of this essay? Is it reasonable? Emotional? Cool and detached? Balanced? Or some combination of these qualities or others. Explain your answer by citing specific statements from the text.

WRITING ASSIGNMENTS

1. Write an essay discussing your own family's sense of ethnic or racial identity. Did your parents, their parents, or anyone in your immediate family come from another country or culture? If so, interview these family member, trying to determine how they dealt with their immigration and with the vast diversity of America. What new cultural attitudes did they encounter? What customs and values? What prejudices? Do you wish you knew more about their original culture? When you have completed your interviews, compare findings with classmates, then write a report on the similarities of experiences and differences.

2. Santiago confesses that in becoming American, she distanced herself from her Puerto Rican culture. If you and/or your parents were born in a foreign

country, write a paper on how distant from your home culture you have become since entering America. You might consider the changes brought on since entering grade school or college. Has assimilation created any tensions among family members? Have you come to terms with those tensions and your own identity?

GROUP PROJECTS

1. In paragraph 20, Santiago remarks that people comment on her "not looking, behaving or talking like a Puerto Rican." Working in small groups, try to determine what ethnic and cultural beliefs are associated with Puerto Ricans. Consider the kinds of stereotypes about Puerto Ricans projected by movies and films. Write up your findings in a report.
2. Working with other members of your class, research the issues of Puerto Rican immigration in the United States, focusing on patterns of immigration, settlement, cultural events, community organizations, churches, and so on. For your research consult your library and conduct interviews with members of your community, as well as with leaders from any local Puerto Rican community organizations. Write up your findings in a well-documented research paper.

Secrets and Anger
David Mura

The author is Japanese; his wife is white. Their daughter looks Asian, but her name is not. In the piece below, the author wonders what his daughter will face growing up a Japanese American in a dominant white culture. While we like to believe in the melting pot ideal and that in America racial differences blur, the author is realistic in his expectations that his daughter will face prejudice, that she will see how Asian men and women have been marginalized and reduced to cultural stereotypes. But he wonders how she will identify herself—as white, Japanese American, or neither? The more Mura ponders what identity his daughter will assume, the more he struggles with his own identity.

Mura is the author of several books including a collection of poems, *After We Lost Our Way* (1989), and *Turning Japanese* (1991). This article was originally published in *Mother Jones* in 1992.

1   On the day our daughter was born, as my wife, Susie, and I waited for the doctor to do a cesarean section, we talked about names. Standing at the window, I looked out and said, "Samantha, the day you were born was a gray and blustery day." We decided on Samantha Lyn, after my sisters, Susan Lynn and Lynda. I felt to give the

baby a Japanese name might mark her as too different, especially since we live in St. Paul, where Asian Americans are a small minority. I had insisted that her last name be hyphenated, Sencer-Mura. My wife had argued that such a name was unwieldy. "What happens when Samantha Sencer-Mura marries Bob Rodriquez-Stein?" she asked. "That's her generation's problem," I said, laughing.

2   I sometimes wish now we'd given her a Japanese middle name, as Susie had wanted. Perhaps it's because I sense that the world Samantha's inheriting won't be dominated by the melting-pot model, that multiculturalism is not a project but a reality, that in the next century there will no longer be a white majority in this country. Or perhaps I simply feel guilty about having given in to the dominant culture once again.

3   I am working on a poem about my daughter, about trying to take in her presence, her life, about trying to link her with my sense of the past—my father and mother, the internment camps, my grandparents. I picture myself serving her sukiyaki, a dish I shunned as a child, and her shouting for more rice, brandishing her *hashi* (a word for chopsticks, which I never used as a child and only began to use after my trip to Japan). As I describe Samantha running through the garden, scattering petals, squashing tomatoes, I suddenly think of how someone someday will call her a "gook," that I know this with more certainty than I know she'll find happiness in love.

4   I speak to my wife about moving out to the West Coast or to Hawaii, where there would be more Asian Americans. In Hawaii, more than a third of the children are *happa* (mixed race); Samantha would be the norm, not the minority. I need to spend more time living in an Asian-American community: I can't tell its stories if I'm not a part of it. As I talk about moving one evening, Susie starts to feel uneasy. "I'm afraid you'll cross this bridge and take Sam with you, and leave me here," she says.

5   "But I've lived all my life on your side of the bridge. At most social gatherings, I'm the only person of color in the room. What's wrong with living awhile on my side of the bridge? What keeps you from crossing?"

6   Susie, a pediatric oncologist, works with families of all colors. Still, having a hybrid daughter is changing her experience. Often when she's in the grocery with Sam, someone will come up to her and say: "Oh, she's such a beautiful little girl. Where did you get her?" This has happened so often Susie swears she's going to teach Sam to say: "Fuck you. My genes came all the way over on the *Mayflower*, thank you."

7   These incidents mark ways Susie has experienced something negative over race that I have not. No one asks me where Sam came from: they assume I'm her father. For Susie, the encounters are a challenge to her position as Samantha's biological mother, the negation of an arduous pregnancy and the physical work of birth and motherhood. For me, they stir an old wound. The people who mistake Sam for an adopted child can't picture a white woman married to an Asian man.

8   Six ways of viewing identity: Identity is a social and historical construction. Identity is formed by political and economic and cultural exigencies. Identity is a

fiction. Identity is a choice. Identity may appear unitary but is always fragmentary. Identity is deciding to acknowledge or not acknowledge political and economic and cultural exigencies.

9   When I address the question of raising my daughter, I address the question of her identity, which means I address the question of my identity, her mother's, our parents', and so on. But this multiplication of the self takes place along many lines. Who knows where it stops? At my grandparents? At the woman in the grocery store? At you, the imagined reader of this piece?

10   In the matrix of race and color in our society, there is the binary opposition of black and white. And then there are the various Others, determined by race or culture or gender or sexual preference—Native Americans, Hispanic Americans, Asian Americans, Japanese Americans, women, men, heterosexuals, homosexuals. None of these definitions stands alone; together they form an intricate, mazelike weave that's impossible to disentangle.

11   I wrote my memoir, *Turning Japanese,* to explore the cultural amnesia of Japanese Americans, particularly those of the third generation, like myself, who speak little or no Japanese. When I give readings, people often ask if I'm going to raise Samantha with a greater awareness of Japanese culture than I received as a child. The obvious answer is yes. I also acknowledge that the prospects of teaching her about Japanese culture feel to me rather daunting, and I now have more sympathy for my nisei parents, whom I used to criticize for forgetting the past.

12   And yet, near the end of my stay in Japan, I decided that I was not Japanese, that I was never going to be Japanese, and that I was not even going to be an expert on Japanese culture. My identity was as a Japanese American. That meant claiming the particularities of Japanese-American history; it meant coming to terms with how the dominant culture had formed me; it meant realizing my identity would always be partially occluded. Finally, it meant that the issues of race were central to me, that I would see myself as a person of color.

13   Can I teach these things to my daughter? My Japanese-American identity comes from my own experience. But I am still trying to understand that experience and still struggling to find language to talk about the issues of race. My failures are caused by more than a lack of knowledge; there's the powerful wish not to know. How, for instance, can I talk to my daughter about sexuality and race? My own life is so filled with shame and regret, so filled with experiences I would rather not discuss, that it seems much easier to opt for silence. It's simpler to pretend multiculturalism means teaching her *kanji* and how to conjugate Japanese verbs.

14   I know that every day Samantha will be exposed to images telling her that Asian bodies are marginalized, that the women are exotic or sensual or submissive, that the men are houseboys or Chinatown punks, kung fu warriors or Japanese businessmen—robotlike and powerful or robotlike and comic. I know that she will face constant pressure to forget that she is part Japanese American, to assume a basically white middle-class identity. When she reaches adolescence, there will be strong messages for her to dissociate herself from other people of color, perhaps from the children of recent Asian immigrants. She may find herself wanting to assume a privilege and status that come from not calling attention to her identity or from playing

into the stereotype that makes Asian women seem so desirable to certain white men. And I know I will have no power over these forces.

15   Should I tell her of how, when I look at her mother, I know my desire for her cannot be separated from the way the culture has inculcated me with standards of white beauty? Should I tell her of my own desire for a "hallucinatory whiteness," of how in my twenties such a desire fueled a rampant promiscuity and addiction to pornography, to the "beautiful" bodies of white women? It's all too much to expect Samantha to take in. It should not even be written down. It should be kept hidden, unspoken. These forces should not exist.

16   Samantha's presence has made me more willing to speak out on issues of race, to challenge the status quo. I suppose I want her to inherit a different world than the one I grew up in.

17   One day last year, I was talking with two white friends about the landmark controversy over the Broadway production of *Miss Saigon*. Like many Asian Americans, I agreed with the protest by Actor's Equity against the producer's casting. I felt disturbed that again a white actor, the British Jonathan Pryce, was playing a Eurasian and that no Asian-American actor had been given a chance to audition for that role. Beyond that, I was upset by the Madame Butterfly plot of *Miss Saigon*, where an Asian woman pines for her white male lover.

18   Both my friends—Paula, a painter, and Mark, a writer—consider themselves liberals; Mark was active in the antiwar movement during the sixties. He was part of my wedding and, at the time, perhaps my closest male friend. But neither agreed with me about *Miss Saigon*. They argued that art represented freedom of the imagination, that it meant trying to get inside other people's skin. Isn't color-blind casting what we're striving for? they said.

19   "Why is it everyone gets so upset when a white actor may be denied a role?" I asked. "What about every time an Asian-American actor tries out for a part that says 'lawyer' or 'doctor' and is turned down?"

20   But reverse discrimination isn't the answer, they replied.

21   I don't recall exactly what happened after this. I think the argument trailed off into some safer topic, as such arguments often do. But afterward, I felt angrier and angrier and, at the same time, more despairing. I realized that for me the fact that Warner Oland, a Swede, played Charlie Chan was humiliating. It did not show me that art was a democracy of the imagination. But for Paula and Mark, my sense of shame was secondary to their belief in "freedom" in the arts.

22   When I talked to my wife about my anger and despair, she felt uncomfortable. These were her friends, too. She said I'd argued before with them about the role of politics in art. Mark had always looked ruefully at his political involvement in the sixties, when he felt he had gone overboard with his zealous self-righteousness. "He's threatened by your increasing political involvement," Susie said. She felt I should take our disagreement as just another incident in a long friendly dialogue.

23   But when I talked with a black friend, Garth, who's a writer, he replied: "Yeah, I was surprised too at the reaction of some of my white artist friends to *Miss Saigon*. It really told me where they were. It marked a dividing line."

24   For a while, I avoided talking about my feelings when Paula and Mark came by. Susie urged me to talk to them, to work it out. "You're trying to get me to have sympathy with how difficult this is for them or for you, how this creates tensions between you and them," I said. "But I have to have this conversation about *Miss Saigon* with every white friend I have. Each of you only has to have it with me." My wife said that I was taking my anger out on her—which, in part, I was.

25   Finally, in a series of telephone calls, I told Paula and Mark I not only felt that their views about *Miss Saigon* were wrong but that they were racially based. In the emotionally charged conversations, I don't think I used the word "racist," but I know my friends objected to my lumping them together with other whites. Paula said I was stereotyping them, that she wasn't like other whites. She told me of her friendships with a few blacks when she lived back East, of the history of her mother's involvement in supporting civil rights. "It's not like I don't know what discrimination is," she said. "Women get discriminated against, so do artists." Her tone moved back and forth between self-righteousness and resentment to distress and tears about losing our friendship.

26   Mark talked of his shame about being a WASP. "Do you know that I don't have a single male friend who is a WASP?" he said. I decided not to point out that, within the context of color, the difference between a WASP male and, say, an Irish Catholic, isn't much of a difference. And I also didn't remark that he had no friends of color, other than myself. I suppose I felt such remarks would hurt him too much. I also didn't feel it was safe to say them.

27   A few months later, I had calmer talks with Mark, but they always ended with this distance between us. I needed some acknowledgment from him that, when we began talking about race, I knew more about it than he did, that our arguing about race was not the same as our arguing about free verse versus formal verse. That my experience gave me insights he didn't have.

28   "Of course, that's true," he said. "I know you've had different experiences." But for him, we had to meet on an equal basis, where his views on race were considered at the start as just as valid as mine. Otherwise, he felt he was compromising himself, giving away his soul. He likened it to the way he gave away his self in his alcoholic family, where he denied his own feelings. He would be making himself a "victim" again.

29   At one point, I suggested we do some sessions with a therapist who was counseling him and whom I had also gone to. "No," said Mark. "I can't do that now. I need him on my side."

30   I can still see us sitting there on my front steps, on a warm early-spring day. I looked at this man with whom I'd shared my writing and my most intimate secrets, with whom I'd shared the process of undergoing therapy and recovery, and I realized we were now no longer intimates. I felt that I had embarked on a journey to discover myself as a person of color, to discover the rage and pain that had formed my Japanese-American identity, and that he would deny me this journey. He saw me as someone who would make him a victim, whose feelings on race were charged with arrogance and self-righteousness. And yet, on some level, I know he saw that my journey was good for me. I felt I was asking him to come on that journey with me.

31   Inevitably I wonder if my daughter will understand my perspective as a person of color. Will she identify with white friends, and be fearful and suspicious of my anger and frustration? Or will she be working from some viewpoint I can't quite conceive, some line that marks her as a person of color and white and neither, all at the same time, as some new being whose experiences I will have to listen to and learn from? How can I prepare her for that new identity?

32   Will it be fair or accurate or helpful for me to tell her, "Unless the world is radically different, on some level, you will still have to choose: Are you a person of color or not?"

33   It took me many months to figure out what had gone down with Paula and Mark. Part of me wanted to let things go, but part of me knew that someday I'd have to talk to Samantha about race. If I avoided what was difficult in my own life, what would I be able to say to her? My black friend Alexs and I talked about how whites desperately want to do "the victim limbo," as he called it. Offered by many as a token of solidarity—"I'm just the same as you"—it's really a way of depoliticizing the racial question; it ignores the differences in power in this country that result from race.

34   When white people engage in conversation about racism, the first thing they often do, as Paula did with me, is the victim limbo: "I'm a woman, I know what prejudice is, I've experienced it." "I'm Jewish/working class/Italian in a WASP neighborhood, I know what prejudice is." The purpose of this is to show the person of color that he or she doesn't really experience anything the white person hasn't experienced, that the white person is a victim too. But Alexs and I both knew that the positions of a person of color and a white person in American society are not the same. "Whites don't want to give up their privilege and psychic comforts," said Alexs. "That's really why they're so angry. They have to choose whether they're going to give up power or fight for it."

35   Thinking this through, though, does not assuage the pain and bitterness I feel about losing white friendships over race, or the distance I have seen open up between me and my white friends. Nor does it help me explain to my daughter why we no longer see Paula or Mark. The compensation has been the numerous friendships that I've begun to have with people of color. My daughter will grow up in a household where the people who visit will be from a wider spectrum than were those Japanese Americans and whites who visited my parents' house in the suburbs of Chicago.

36   Not that teaching her about her Asian-American self has become any easier. My wife has been more conscious than I've been about telling Sam that she's Japanese. After playing with blond Shannon, the girl from next door, Sam said: "She's not Japanese, Mom. We're Japanese." "No," said Susie. "Daddy's Japanese, and you're part Japanese, but I'm not Japanese." Sam refused to believe this: "No, you're Japanese." After a few minutes, Susie finally sorted out the confusion. Sam thought being Japanese meant you had black hair.

37   For many liberal whites, what seems most important in any discussion of race is the need for hope, the need to find some link with people of color. They do not see how much that need serves as a tool of denial, how their claims of solidarity not only ignore real differences but also blot out the reality of people of color. How can we

move forward, they ask, with all this rage you seem to feel? How can you stereotype me or group me in this category of whiteness?

38   I tell them they are still unwilling to examine what being white has meant to their existence. They think their rage at being classified as a white person is the same rage that people of color feel when they are being stereotyped. It is not. When whites feel anger about race, almost always they are feeling a threat to their comfort or power.

39   In the end, whites must exchange a hope based on naiveté and ignorance for one based on knowledge. For this naive hope denies connections, complexities. It is the drug of amnesia. It says there is no thread from one moment to the next, no cause and effect. It denies consequence and responsibility.

40   For my wife, this journey has been a difficult one. The arguments we have over race mirror our other arguments; at the same time, they exist in another realm, where I am a person of color and Susie is white. "I realize that in a way I've been passing too," she said a few months ago. "There's this comfort I've got to give up, this ease." At her clinic, she challenges the mainly white children's books in the waiting room, or a colleague's unconscious assumptions about Hmong families. More and more, she finds herself at gatherings where she as a white person is in the minority.

41   Breaking through denial, seeing how much needs to be changed, does not have to blunt the capacity for hope. For both of us, our daughter is proof of that capacity. And if I know that someday someone will call Samantha a gook, I know today she's a happy child. The love her mother and I share, the love we bear for her, cannot spare her from pain over race, and yet it can make her stronger. Sam will go further than we will, she will know more. She will be like nothing I can imagine, as I am like nothing my parents imagined.

42   Today my daughter told me she will grow up and work with her mother at the hospital. I'll be a grandpa and stay home and write poems and be with her children. Neither race nor ethnicity enters into her vision of the future. And yet they are already there, with our hopes, gathering shape.

EXPLORING THE TEXT

1. In paragraph 4, Mura suggests to his wife that they move to an area where there are more Asian Americans. What are his fears? Can you identify with them? Looking back over the essay, do they seem justified?

2. How does Mura's wife respond to the suggestion that they move? Do her concerns seem justified or is she being selfish? How does this anecdote capture the fears and concerns of interracial families? Have you ever dated someone of another race or culture—and, if so, did you experience any similar concerns?

3. Beginning in paragraph 17, Mura brings up the protest over casting Jonathan Pryce as a Eurasian in *Miss Saigon*. What is the basis of his protest here? What is the view of his white liberal friends? How does Mura

view his friends on the issue of racism? How, according to Mura, do his friends view Mura on the issue?

4. Why does Mura ask his friend Garth how he feels about the issue? What does Garth say? How does Mura feel about Garth's response?

5. From Mura's description of his daughter, how old do you think Samantha is? What does race mean to her at this age? What does Mura think it will mean to her in the future?

6. Did this essay change your view of the struggle for identity experienced by members of interracial families? Explain your answer, drawing from personal experience and observations.

7. How well does the title of this essay fit the contents? What are some of the specific secrets and angers that Mura describes? If you were to rewrite the title to make it more descriptive, what would you write?

8. Try to determine the tone of this essay and any shifts in it. Does Mura's tone at any point evoke sympathy from his audience or does it magnify the conflict implicit in the different views of racism held by minorities and whites?

9. What is Mura's main purpose in writing this essay? Can you identify a thesis sentence or does his thesis seem to be implicit, unwritten? In your opinion, does he keep to his topic, supporting it throughout his discussion? Or does he seem to digress and thereby lose focus?

WRITING ASSIGNMENTS

1. Mura wonders whether his daughter will eventually identify with whites or will see herself as "a person of color and white and neither, all at the same time" (paragraph 31). If you are a person of mixed races, write a paper that focuses on the conflicting pressures to assimilate the dominant American culture while respecting all cultural backgrounds that are a part of your heritage. You might also write about someone you know who is of mixed races.

2. In paragraph 6, Mura touches upon the notion of interracial adoption. If you are somebody from one race who was adopted by parents of another race, or if you know somebody who is, write a report on how you handled the problems of identity. What efforts did your parents make to help you understand that your race was different from theirs? What shifts (if any) did you experience from early ages to later ones? What conflicts did you experience or do you continue to experience? You might also write about someone you know who was adopted by parents of another race.

3. Research what various groups of people have to say about mixed-race adoption, using your library's news sources, professional social sciences journals, and Internet resources. What are the benefits or reasons for allowing transracial adoption? What are the drawbacks or arguments against them?

4. Using your school's library, research the debates about casting decisions in *Miss Saigon*. You may want to examine theater trade journals, scholarly journals, or newspaper reporting. What arguments does Mura use here? What other objections were raised that Mura does not discuss? Once you have read a good sampling of editorials, decide what you think: Was the casting decision appropriate or not?

GROUP PROJECTS

1. In paragraph 14, Mura says that Samantha will be exposed to cultural images and stereotypes that marginalize Asians in America. Working with other students from class, consider what particular images and stereotypes you have seen of Asians in movies, on television, and in advertising. Make a list of characteristic images. Do any overlap with Mura's catalog? Write a paper in which you explore the various ways Asians are depicted in our culture—for better or worse.

2. In paragraph 2, Mura makes the claim that "multiculturalism is not a project but a reality, that in the next century there will no longer be a white majority in this country." Working in small groups, try to decide what the effect will be on each of you if, in fact, Mura is correct. Speculate on the way society and American culture will be affected. Discuss your conclusions in a paper.

Cultural Baggage

Barbara Ehrenreich

A society celebrating diversity encourages people to research their ethnic and racial roots and to revive family and cultural traditions practiced so ardently in the past. But when Barbara Ehrenreich is asked by a friend about her ethnic background, Ehrenreich is surprised to hear herself reply, "None." In her life ethnicity, religion, and family traditions had been eclipsed by "skepticism, curiosity and wide-eyed ecumenical tolerance"—attitudes that she feels may serve humanity well. This piece, which first appeared in the *New York Times Sunday Magazine* in April 1992, argues that going on to find new identities may be more important than resurrecting the old.

Ehrenreich is a widely respected author who writes witty analyses of social and feminist issues. She has worked as a contributing editor at *Ms.* magazine and also writes a column for *Time.* Her essays have appeared in such magazines as *Mother Jones, Nation,* and the *New York Times Sunday Magazine.* Ehrenreich is the author of *Fear of Falling: The Inner Life of the Middle Class* (1989), *The Worst Years of Our Lives: Irreverent Notes from a Decade of Greed*

(1990), and *Kipper's Game* (1994), her first novel. Her most recent book is *Blood Rites* (1997), an investigation into the origins of war.

1 An acquaintance was telling me about the joys of rediscovering her ethnic and religious heritage. "I know exactly what my ancestors were doing 2,000 years ago," she said, eyes gleaming with enthusiasm, "and *I can do the same things now.*" Then she leaned forward and inquired politely, "And what is your ethnic background, if I may ask?"

2 "None," I said, that being the first word in line to get out of my mouth. Well, not "none," I backtracked. Scottish, English, Irish—that was something, I supposed. Too much Irish to qualify as a WASP; too much of the hated English to warrant a "Kiss Me, I'm Irish" button; plus there are a number of dead ends in the family tree due to adoptions, missing records, failing memories and the like. I was blushing by this time. Did "none" mean I was rejecting my heritage out of Anglo-Celtic self-hate? Or was I revealing a hidden ethnic chauvinism in which the Britannically derived serve as a kind of neutral standard compared with the ethnic "others"?

3 Throughout the 60's and 70's, I watched one group after another—African Americans, Latinos, Native Americans—stand up and proudly reclaim their roots while I just sank back ever deeper into my seat. All this excitement over ethnicity stemmed, I uneasily sensed, from a past in which *their* ancestors had been trampled upon by *my* ancestors, or at least by people who looked very much like them. In addition, it had begun to seem almost un-American not to have some sort of hyphen at hand, linking one to more venerable times and locales.

4 But the truth is, I was raised with none. We'd eaten ethnic foods in my childhood home, but these were all borrowed, like the pasties, or Cornish meat pies, my father had picked up from his fellow miners in Butte, Mont. If my mother had one rule, it was militant ecumenism in all matters of food and experience. "Try new things," she would say, meaning anything from sweetbreads to clams, with an emphasis on the "new."

5 As a child, I briefly nourished a craving for tradition and roots. I immersed myself in the works of Sir Walter Scott. I pretended to believe that the bagpipe was a musical instrument. I was fascinated to learn from a grandmother that we were descended from certain Highland clans and longed for a pleated skirt in one of their distinctive tartans.

6 But in "Ivanhoe," it was the dark-eyed "Jewess" Rebecca I identified with, not the flaxen-haired bimbo Rowena. As for clans: Why not call them "tribes," those bands of half-clad peasants and warriors whose idea of cuisine was stuffed sheep gut washed down with whisky? And then there was the sting of Disraeli's remark—which I came across in my early teens—to the effect that his ancestors had been leading orderly, literate lives when my ancestors were still rampaging through the Highlands daubing themselves with blue paint.

7 Motherhood put the screws on me, ethnicitywise. I had hoped that by marrying a man of Eastern European-Jewish ancestry I would acquire for my descendants the ethnic genes that my own forebears so sadly lacked. At one point, I even subjected the children to a seder of my own design, including a little talk about the flight from

Egypt and its relevance to modern social issues. But the kids insisted on buttering their matzohs and snickering through my talk. "Give me a break, Mom," the older one said. "You don't even believe in God."

8   After the tiny pagans had been put to bed, I sat down to brood over Elijah's wine. What had I been thinking? The kids knew that their Jewish grandparents were secular folks who didn't hold seders themselves. And if ethnicity eluded me, how could I expect it to take root in my children, who are not only Scottish-English-Irish, but Hungarian-Polish-Russian to boot?

9   But, then, on the fumes of Manischewitz, a great insight took form in my mind. It was true, as the kids said, that I didn't "believe in God." But this could be taken as something very different from an accusation—a reminder of a genuine heritage. My parents had not believed in God either, nor had my grandparents or any other progenitors going back to the great-great level. They had become disillusioned with Christianity generations ago—just as, on the in-law side, my children's other ancestors had shaken off their Orthodox Judaism. This insight did not exactly furnish me with an "identity," but it was at least something to work with: we are the kind of people, I realized—whatever our distant ancestors' religion—who do *not* believe, who do not carry on traditions, who do not do things just because someone has done them before.

10   The epiphany went on: I recalled that my mother never introduced a procedure for cooking or cleaning by telling me, "Grandma did it this way." What did Grandma know, living in the days before vacuum cleaners and disposable toilet mops? In my parents' general view, new things were better than old, and the very fact that some ritual had been performed in the past was a good reason for abandoning it now. Because what was the past, as our forebears knew it? Nothing but poverty, superstition and grief. "Think for yourself," Dad used to say. "Always ask why."

11   In fact, this may have been the ideal cultural heritage for my particular ethnic strain—bounced as it was from the Highlands of Scotland across the sea, out to the Rockies, down into the mines and finally spewed out into high-tech, suburban America. What better philosophy, for a race of migrants, than "Think for yourself"? What better maxim, for a people whose whole world was rudely inverted every 30 years or so, than "Try new things"?

12   The more tradition-minded, the newly enthusiastic celebrants of Purim and Kwanzaa and Solstice, may see little point to survival if the survivors carry no cultural freight—religion, for example, or ethnic tradition. To which I would say that skepticism, curiosity and wide-eyed ecumenical tolerance are also worthy elements of the human tradition and are at least as old as such notions as "Serbian" or "Croatian," "Scottish" or "Jewish." I make no claims for my personal line of progenitors except that they remained loyal to the values that may have induced all of our ancestors, long, long ago, to climb down from the trees and make their way into the open plains.

13   A few weeks ago, I cleared my throat and asked the children, now mostly grown and fearsomely smart, whether they felt any stirrings of ethnic or religious identity, etc., which might have been, ahem, insufficiently nourished at home. "None," they said, adding firmly, "and the world would be a better place if nobody else did, either." My chest swelled with pride, as would my mother's, to know that the race of "none" marches on.

EXPLORING THE TEXT

1. How does the author attempt to be ethnic by embracing her husband's Jewish heritage? What are the consequences of those attempts? Might her treatment of Judaism be offensive to people of that culture?
2. What does Ehrenreich mean by the term *ethnic chauvinism* in the question posed in paragraph 2: "Or was I revealing a hidden ethnic chauvinism in which the Britannically derived serve as a kind of neutral standard compared with the ethnic 'others'"?
3. How has "Cultural Baggage" influenced your thinking regarding your own cultural heritage? What points do you find insightful? What points do you take exception to?
4. Briefly summarize Ehrenreich's argument. How does her ultimate endorsement of the "race of none" shape her argument?
5. How does the essay's title, "Cultural Baggage," foreshadow the tone of the essay? Do you feel that the traditions of your heritage are like "baggage" or a burden?
6. Where in this essay can you find examples that support the premise that Ehrenreich is addressing an audience like herself—people of white-Anglo descent?
7. Consider paragraphs 3, 11, and 12. Using evidence from these paragraphs, show how Ehrenreich deduces the belief that her "race of none" is more progressive than other cultures.

WRITING ASSIGNMENTS

1. Write a paper in which you support or defend the following statement: "In present-day American society, only a white person can shed his or her cultural baggage." Use examples from Ehrenreich and your own personal experiences as support for your position.
2. Consider the essay's title, "Cultural Baggage." Interview people in your dormitory or community who have strong roots in a foreign culture. Do these people feel that their native culture is "baggage" to be shed as they acclimate to American life? Or do they successfully maintain distinctions of their culture? Write a paper documenting your findings.

GROUP PROJECTS

1. Ehrenreich writes that "in 'Ivanhoe' it was the dark-eyed 'Jewess' I identified with, not the flaxen-haired bimbo Rowena" (paragraph 6). Working with other members of the class, try to come up with a list of childhood heroes and heroines. Did they always physically resemble you and members of your research group? If not, what qualities attracted you to them. How has your view of these heroes changed with the rise of cultural and multi-

cultural awareness? Write up your findings in a report to be presented to the class.

2. Working in small groups, research the kind of facilities and support networks that are available for immigrants moving into your community. To help, you might consider calling the Bureau of Immigration and local government offices. You can also research recent and pending legislation that would affect new citizens. If possible, try to locate and interview newcomers from foreign countries. When you have gathered sufficient data, write up your findings in a report to be shared with your class.

3. Working in small groups, consider how aspects of other cultures have influenced your daily life. Cite examples such as food, vocabulary, style of dress, music, movies, television, and advertising. After you have recorded your findings, write up your findings in a report to be delivered to the class, addressing the question of how people can adopt multicultural traits without losing their own particular cultural identity.

It might come as a surprise to some that English is not the official language of America. Nowhere in the Constitution is there such a provision. The Founders were apparently more concerned with establishing a common political philosophy than a common tongue. For the next 200 years, the new republic swelled with immigrants from every country on earth to become the "great melting pot" of cultures. But, of late, the melting pot has overheated with controversy. A growing number of Americans feel that the common tongue needs protection from non-English speakers.

The traditional assumption that English was *the* language of America first came into question in the 1960s with bilingual education programs in certain communities with large non-English-speaking members. Then in 1975 federal laws mandated bilingual ballots in such places. Soon a growing number of Americans began to feel that the common tongue needed protection. In 1981, a constitutional amendment proposed to make English the official language of the nation. Although it never passed, the proposal formed the basis of resolutions adopted by more than two dozen states limiting government documents and public discourse to English. Another 20 states are considering similar measures. Then in August 1996 the U.S. House of Representatives approved a bill that would make English the official language of the nation. Neither the Senate nor the president has yet decided on the bill.

At stake in the controversy are competing American traditions of multicultural tolerance and a quest for unity through a common language. Proponents of the English-only movement argue that bilingualism creates cultural division and hinders new immigrants' abilities to assimilate. They fear that bilingual education could turn the country into another Yugoslavia, where different cultures never find common ground and dissolve into warring factions. Opponents contend that such legislation is nationalistic, racist, and xenophobic. They argue that legislation will not only inflame prejudice against immigrants but will violate their civil rights.

This chapter will examine some of the arguments hovering around the English-only debate. You will examine arguments on both sides of the issue, moving from the more abstract and theoretical to those emanating from personal experience. The debate opens with John Silber, former president of Boston University and chairman of the Massachusetts State Board of Education. Clearly declaring his stand in its title, "One Nation, One Language, One Ballot," Silber argues that the Voting Rights Act amendment requiring bilingual ballots only degrades the very concept of naturalized citizenship by maintaining linguistic barriers. In direct opposition to Silber is "What's So American About English?" by Andrew Ward who contends that the English-only fears are founded on wrong assumptions about language and American identity. He argues that instead of moving toward social unity, the English-only movement threatens to further fractionalize the nation.

The debate over official English is not just about language, of course, but national and cultural identity. The next essay, "Seeking Unity in Diversity," examines the claims that the English Empowerment Act, which would require the federal government to conduct its business in English, is racist and xenophobic. Arguing that Spanish speakers the world over should safeguard their own language, Rolando Flores Acosta, a journalist on Hispanic issues, argues that it is wrongheaded to see the English Empowerment Act as xenophobic or anti-Spanish. On the contrary, he argues that politically correct bilingual policies are not only confusing and costly, but they ultimately disempower non-English-speaking Hispanics when it comes to voicing their legal rights.

The next piece looks at bilingualism in a city with the highest growth rate of non-English-speaking children in the nation—Los Angeles. As Carol Jago points out in "English Only—for the Kids' Sake," nearly 42 percent of children in California elementary schools are nonnative speakers, and most are Hispanic. Whatever the policy for educating so large a multi-lingual community, the prime goal, Jago argues, should be to provide all children the opportunity to become part of mainstream society.

"Mute in an English-Only World," was an outgrowth of recent protests over the proliferation of Korean signs along the streets in Palisades Park, New Jersey. In it, Chang-rae Lee offers a poignant personal recollection of his mother whose experience in a butcher shop years ago captures something of what it's like to be an outsider to the common tongue. The final piece in this chapter, "English Plus, Not English Only," by bilingual Canadian-born Michael E. Dickstein takes a look at how language issues threaten to tear apart Canada and offers a compromise solution to the growing language crisis in America.

One Nation, One Language, One Ballot
John Silber

John Silber, former president of Boston University and chairman of the Massachusetts State Board of Education, presents an argument in favor of English as the official language of the United States and opposes the multilingual ballots mandated by the 1975 Voting Rights Act. Like so many Americans, including authors in this chapter, he relies on memories of an immigrant parent and believes that immigrants need to learn English. Unlike some, however, he insists that English is a necessary component of our national identity. He calls ethnicity a "private matter" and argues that multilingual ballots are a "dangerous experiment."

This piece was originally published in 1996 in the *Wall Street Journal.*

1   English has never been declared our official language for the simple reason that, until recently, no one doubted that it already was. The country was established by English speakers, its founding documents and laws are written in English and its legislatures transact their affairs in English.

2   This is a lesson my father learned soon after he came to this country from Germany in 1903 to work on the German pavilion at the St. Louis World's Fair. When the fair closed he went to look for work. Walking down the street, he saw a sign saying, "Undertaker." Supposing this to be a literal translation of the German word "unternehmer," meaning "contractor," he went inside and was surprised to find himself in a room full of coffins. Embarrassed, he concluded that it was time to learn English.

3   Like all immigrants seeking naturalization, he had to demonstrate proficiency in English. It would never have occurred to him or to any of the millions of other

immigrants speaking many different languages to seek accommodations such as ballots in their native tongue. He, like them, had freely chosen to live in a country where the language was English.

4   This is our historic tradition. But in 1975 Congress amended the Voting Rights Act to require bilingual ballots. Thus the lawmakers abandoned tradition, making a change of Constitutional consequence, amending in effect the very concept of U.S. citizenship. The naturalization statutes presume that English is the language of U.S. citizens. Why else is English required for naturalization? The only exception, enacted in 1990, exempts applicants over 55 years of age who have lived in the U.S. for at least 15 years.

5   Citizens who are not proficient in English cannot, in most cases, follow a political campaign, talk with candidates, or petition their representatives. They are citizens in name only and are unable to exercise their rights. Providing them with bilingual ballots does not enable them to exercise those rights in any meaningful sense.

6   Moreover, even though access to bilingual ballots is mandated in the Voting Rights Act, this access is not a right. If it were, it would be possessed by all citizens. But in a 1992 amendment, Congress required bilingual ballots only in elections where there are 10,000 voters not proficient in English, or where five or more of the eligible voters are not proficient in English.

7   The thousands of citizens in smaller linguistic minorities are not denied a right, but only an accommodation. If there were a right to bilingual ballots, it would be protected by the 14th Amendment, and voting in the U.S. would become impossibly expensive and chaotic, as officials attempted to provide ballots and instructions in hundreds of different languages, some of them not yet written down. That is what a right to bilingual ballots would require.

8   In truth, such ballots may be an undesirable accommodation. Though their dollar cost is relatively unimportant, they impose an intolerable cost by degrading the very concept of the citizen to that of someone lost in a country whose public discourse is incomprehensible to him.

9   Much worse, bilingual ballots, by helping to sunder our linguistic unity, move us toward a multicultural society. With the exception of Switzerland, nations with multilingual societies are being torn apart. Canada is riven by linguistic differences; Belgium has seen bloody rioting between French-speaking and Flemish-speaking citizens; India has suffered from even more serious rioting over language; and in Sri Lanka a murderous insurgency is driven largely by language differences.

10   The U.S. has been unique in that nowhere else in the world do so many people living in so large an area speak the same language. Our common language provides the unity that, paradoxically, enables us to understand and cherish our cultural diversity. As Nathan Glazer has pointed out, "The United States is perhaps unique in the states of the world in using the term 'nation' to refer not to an ethnic group but to all who choose to become Americans."

11   In the last weeks of the Soviet Union, I visited Moscow. I was struck, reading my visa application, to see that the Soviet government wanted to know both my citizenship and my nationality. I found this incomprehensible, for as an American, my citizenship and my nationality are one and the same. America is a nation based on a set of ideals and allegiance to those ideals—it's not based on ethnicity or national origin.

12   The success of America has depended upon making ethnicity a private matter. And our ethnic groups voluntarily celebrate their ethnicity with joyous passion. Irish-Americans honor St. Patrick's Day with a commitment unknown in Dublin; Italian-Americans celebrate the festivals of their saints; Polish-Americans commemorate their weddings with festivities that are a byword for communal rejoicing; Mexican-Americans celebrate the Cinco de Mayo with music and dance.

13   But these remain private undertakings. The government, until recently, has recognized no ethnic groups but only Americans. The federal mandate for bilingual ballots represents a dangerous experiment in deconstructing our American identity. Congress is now debating whether to repeal this mandate. To do so will be a clear and effective way to terminate this experiment before we lose our identity as Americans.

EXPLORING THE TEXT

1. In his early paragraphs, Silber describes the experiences of his immigrant father coming to the United States. Discuss what you think he intends to communicate with this example. Does it seem to be a fair use of his father's history? Can you argue against the claims he makes here?

2. In what sense does Silber argue that the Voting Rights Act, requiring bilingual ballots, is meaningless? What criteria does he insist on to count a vote as meaningful?

3. What distinction does Silber draw between "right" and "accommodation" as he uses the terms in paragraph 7?

4. How does Silber measure the "cost" of the accommodation? In what way might that word ("cost") have multiple meanings?

5. In paragraph 4, Silber refers to "our historic tradition," an idea he returns to at the end of the essay ("our common language" in paragraph 10, "our American identity" and "our identity" in paragraph 13). What does he mean by "our"? What is his rhetorical strategy here? How does this term help his argument? What criticisms can you suggest about this usage?

6. In paragraph 9, Silber refers to multilingual conflicts in several other nations. Describe the circumstances in each of the nations he lists. Briefly research the situations in each country to make sure that you understand the author's point. Do his comparisons hold up? What differences can you find between those countries and the United States?

7. How does Silber define "public"? How does he define "private"? What examples does he cite? Do you find them valid?

WRITING ASSIGNMENTS

1. In paragraph 10, Silber says that "our common language provides the unity that, paradoxically, enables us to understand and cherish our cultural diversity." Discuss his notion of "common language." What does he mean by

this? Is this more wishful thinking than fact? Brainstorm a list of current issues that surround language in American culture. Look for examples of language issues in the news and television media. Write an essay in which you discuss this and relate it to Silber's claim about unity. Does it inhibit diversity or encourage it?

2. What is the promise of America? Freedom? Justice? Opportunity? What are the responsibilities of citizens? Using the U.S. Constitution as your guide, write an essay that discusses the role that language plays in those rights and responsibilities.

GROUP PROJECTS

1. Silber argues from the assumption that a lack of "proficiency" in English necessarily means a lack of important information. Is this true? Have your group research the various ways in which information is disseminated to people in your community who are proficient in languages other than English. Look at newspapers, television and and radio stations, government agencies, and so on. Evaluate the quantity and variety of information available and present a report in which you test Silber's claim in light of the information you collect.

2. Have group members research government documents on the Voting Rights Act. Find the exact wording of the law. Locate the congressional testimony presented as the act was being considered. Look for statistics on who has voted as a result of the act and what impact those votes have (or have not) had on final election outcomes. After collating your findings, prepare an argument against Silber's claims and report it to the class.

What's So American About English?
Andrew Ward

Like John Silber, Andrew Ward suggests that language has much to do with identity, but he also describes some of the negative aspects of that identity based solely on how well one speaks English. Ward claims that what is most important to Americans is "the promise of freedom and justice and opportunity." In contrast to Silber, the danger that he sees is Americans becoming too intent on separating themselves from other Americans by language.

Ward is a writer who has contributed articles to a wide variety of magazines and newspapers. His most recent books is *Our Bones Are Scattered: The Cawnpore Massacres and the Indian Mutiny of 1857* (1996). This article was first published in the *Washington Post* in 1995.

1   A few years ago Donald Trump's octogenarian mother was mugged in a New York shopping mall and rushed to the hospital. Struggling to treat her injuries, her doctors

were dismayed by the delirious gibberish she was spouting and feared she might have suffered some permanent damage to the speech center of her brain.

2   As her son tried to come to terms with this possibility, an Irish nurse appeared on the ward, listened a moment to Mrs. Trump's ravings and announced that there was nothing whatever wrong with the old lady's brain. In her shock and rage, the former Mary Macleod of the Scottish Isle of Lewis had simply reverted to her girlhood Gaelic.

3   I've been struggling to figure out what it is that disturbs me about the campaign to make English our national language. I think there are some serious arguments in favor of it, some of them advanced by successful first- and second-generation immigrants who believe, with pride, that only by entirely discarding their native language and mastering English could they have partaken of the American dream.

4   But the most voluble proponents, some of them legislators, are another matter. Just as the Nazis, the Klan, skinheads and other boosters of the master race tend to be some of the planet's lease prepossessing Caucasians, so the most ardent champions of English as the national tongue tend to mangle what's left of the language.

5   They dangle their participles and misplace their modifiers and follow the local anchorperson's principle that the most awkward sounding disposition of pronouns—"Neither him nor here were available for comment"—must be correct. Perhaps once you make language official, it inevitably begins to sound like the language of officials.

6   Though my own education in the English language has been a slapdash do-it-yourself project, I bow to no one—not Edwin Newman, not William Safire—in my protective love of the mother tongue, and will face down any deranged and idle reader who may now choose to pore over my every published utterance for egregious grammatical mistakes.

7   I once considered founding an organization each of whose members would be assigned a particular common error—the pernicious use of "different than," for example—and provided with a stack of postcards courteously instructing malefactors in the proper construction—in this case, "different from," of course—which members could then send on to newscasters, politicians, talk show hosts and the like. How gratefully they would be received, and what a service we would provide to a language that seems always about to lose another of its splendid specificities.

8   But even I think it odd and perhaps even a little dangerous to wrap such pedantry in the Star-Spangled Banner. It is hard enough to be an American without adding another obstacle to the course.

9   When we talk about language we are really talking about identity, and making English our national language suggests that we are Americans only to the extent to which we know English. But what we should cherish most about America—the promise of freedom and justice and opportunity—is cherished most, I think, by our most recent immigrants: the Korean grocer, the Cambodian cook, the Iranian sales clerk down the street. What does their clumsiness with this complex and unfamiliar language have to do with their being Americans, with their wholehearted embrace of American principles, with their braving so much more to come to this country than the rest of us can even imagine?

10   And if we do require that in exercising certain rights, immigrants must entirely discard their own language, how exactly will America be the richer for it?

Won't it only serve to further isolate us, the least multilingual of peoples, from the rest of the world?

11   I do worry that Americans are becoming too fractionalized. Sometimes it seems that just as America once said no to its minorities, its minorities are now, in a sense, saying no to America, and each seems to be striving for a dangerous degree of separation from the rest.

12   But I can't help thinking that the English-as-a-national-language movement is a symptom of the same impulse. It tells immigrants they are not welcome here until they have ceased to discomfit the rest of us with their strangeness, as if the burden of our cohesion as a nation rests not with those of us who have been here long enough to do something about it, but with those of us who have just arrived.

EXPLORING THE TEXT

1. How does Ward define the American Dream? How does the anecdote about Donald Trump's mother offer clues?
2. In paragraph 5, Ward says, "Once you make language official, it inevitably begins to sound like the language of officials." What does he mean by "the language of officials"? Does he offer examples? If so, where?
3. Why according to Ward is a national language important? What arguments does he acknowledge for the opposition? How does his focus on grammar work to establish his argument?
4. If language is an insufficient indicator of "Americanness," what other qualities are necessary, vital? What example does Ward use to make his case?
5. The author seems to indicate that language has the potential both to connect and divide. Point to and discuss examples in the text that portray this dualism.
6. In paragraph 11, Ward states, "just as America once said no to its minorities, its minorities are now, in a sense, saying no to America." What is he referring to? Has America said no to its immigrants? Explain your answer.
7. What rhetorical strategy does the author rely on to make his argument? What kind of support does he offer for his point of view? Statistics? Anecdotes? Do you find this author convincing? Why or why not? Explain.

WRITING ASSIGNMENTS

1. Think about the way in which grammar is—or is not—an important part of how you think about language. How does it define groups or members within groups? What roles does language play in your schooling? In your writing? Does a knowledge of grammar necessarily suggest a command of the language? What other language issues are important in your life? Write an essay in which you explore and discuss these issues in relation to your personal experience.

2. Consider the rhetorical implications of Ward's comparison of language proponents with "Nazis, the Klan, skinheads and other boosters of the master race" (paragraph 4) and with Flores Acosta's reference to "fascists" and "politically correct bureaucrats." What ideas do we associate with such groups of people? What is their status in the culture? What kind of power do their ideas have? What, then, do the authors hope to achieve by comparing them to English-language proponents? Write an essay in which you discuss this rhetorical strategy and the power of association that it relies on.

GROUP PROJECTS

1. Research the legislation in your state and community that deals with English as an official language. Have your group members determine what kinds of laws are on the books (or research recent attempts to create such laws). Find out if there are any organizations in your community actively working on these issues. Are there any current news stories focused on English-only issues? Identify particular people or groups involved with these concerns and have each group member interview one such person. Compile your findings and write a group report on the status of this issue in your community.
2. Ward claims that when we talk about language we talk about identity. To what extent is language synonymous with identity? Are such divisions relevant only among languages? Can you think of different English-language communities: baseball players typically speak and write differently from lawyers (the language of the field, the vocabulary of the profession), but the differences in their language go beyond a simple difference in specialized vocabulary. For example, consider the different ways in which each profession uses the word *strike*. Brainstorm a list of different "discourse" communities. Divide the list between group members and have each member research the literary conventions and vocabulary of a different language or discourse community.

Seeking Unity in Diversity
Rolando Flores Acosta

Do we need to pass a law to make English the official language of the United States? Rolando Flores Acosta thinks so. While advocating the study and appreciation of native languages, he contends that immigrants must learn English in order to fully participate in American society. Although fluent in Spanish, he explains why he is in favor of the English Empowerment Act, which would require the government to conduct its business only in English.

Flores Acosta is an editorial writer for the Madrid daily *ABC*. This piece was published in the *Wall Street Journal* in August 1996.

1 After House approval this month, the English Empowerment Act of 1996 awaits a Senate vote on a similar measure in September. The bill, which would require the federal government to conduct most of its business only in English, has been consistently rejected by the civil rights lobby and openly criticized by academics and supporters of Spanish. Yet its provisions have already been adopted separately by 23 states, and seven other states are in the final stages of legislative debate on the subject.

2 Mr. Clinton supported a similar measure back in 1987 as governor of Arkansas, but if one passes Congress this fall he will most likely decide to veto it. He fears not that it would divide the nation, but that immigrants and Spanish culture supporters would respond negatively ahead of the coming elections.

3 Yet to reject this bill before weighing its advantages, as the Mexican writer Carlos Fuentes has also done, is quite wrong. Mr. Fuentes has erred seriously, I believe, in describing it as racist, xenophobic and fascist. Spanish speakers should disregard such paternalism and the instinct to overprotect our language. In the end, such attitudes can only harm those Hispanics they ostensibly seek to defend.

4 Of course, Spanish speakers all over the world should join constructive campaigns to promote our language. However, we cannot—and should not—see the English Empowerment Act as an anti-Spanish measure that seeks to discriminate against Hispanics or the Spanish language. Rather, this legislation would only help the Hispanic minority, and others, to integrate into American society.

5 To see why opposition to efforts like the English Empowerment Act leads to unworkable and ultimately discriminatory policies, consider the U.S. Supreme Court decision *Lau v. Nichols*. Ever since 1974, it has required that each educational district offer classes and special programs for non-English-speaking students. Tiny schools all over America have therefore been forced to take on the enormous financial burden of hiring Spanish-speaking instructors, and of modifying their school programs to facilitate an easy transition for non-English speakers to the Anglo system. Similarly, in states with large numbers of Hispanics, unemployment offices and other public offices must follow strict quotas mandating Spanish-speaking staff to allow everyone access to government services, as well as to prevent any imaginable discrimination. Every form, document and item of official information must be available in Spanish as well as in English.

6 But can we ignore the fact that more than 300 languages are spoken today in the U.S.? In Los Angeles, for example, there are more Mexicans than in any city other than Mexico City, and more Koreans than any place in the world but Seoul. In one L.A. school district alone, teachers have to gather and instruct students from 80 different nationalities, just 13% of whom speak English as their first language.

7 The inescapable questions, then, are these: In how many different languages should classes be offered? And public services? Would we not be discriminating against other minorities if only one or two languages were on offer? Should government adapt to the multitude of new languages and ethnic groups? Or should the new generations of minorities and immigrants learn English in order to integrate fully into American society?

8   Before answering these questions, supporters of official bilingualism need to consider their past failures. Arthur M. Schlesinger Jr. explained in "The Disuniting of America" how bilingual education at schools has retarded, rather than expedited, the movement of Hispanics into the English-speaking world. Placing students in transitional bilingual classes, ostensibly to move them as quickly as possible into mainstream English classes, has instead promoted segregation. This de facto apartheid generates antagonism and separatism, which only serves to emphasize racial differences and animosity among different groups—including, all too frequently, deadly gang violence.

9   Misplaced concern with identity politics has also corrupted university campuses, so much so that now Hispanic and black professors have laid claim to the teaching of Hispanic or black history, respectively. It's easy to imagine how this will inevitably lead to the absurd conclusion that only Hispanics can teach Hispanic history, only blacks African-American history, and only women women's history. No longer would students in America learn a sense of nation, of community, of *e pluribus unum.*

10   Wouldn't it be more advisable to seek unity in diversity, without dispersal, segregation or discrimination? Unity should not be seen as tantamount to rigid uniformity—which is rightly feared and rejected—but rather as an innate feature of America life, one that should exist in any pluralist society without the assistance of social engineers.

11   According to a document signed by the attorney general and the Treasury, education and health secretaries recommending the presidential veto, the English Empowerment Act will not only be discriminatory but difficult to implement in those states where many immigrants cannot read English. That can only be seen as self-discrimination. The federal government would not be leaving out non-English speakers by not using their languages. Immigrants, on the contrary, would be the ones discriminating against themselves by not speaking English.

12   The only reasonable way to achieve the necessary compromise is to implement a unifying linguistic policy similar to that which has inspired the English Empowerment Act. This would be a law that would enable minorities to protect their political and legal rights and represent their freedoms, as well as their social and labor rights.

13   America's long-standing multilingual tradition is a natural, spontaneous phenomenon, a private practice encouraged by the state and exercised freely by society, not an artificial creation imposed on citizens by politically correct bureaucrats. The study of our language, and of Hispanic culture generally, can and should be encouraged in a number of other ways. Yet to claim that every citizen has a right to communicate with the institutions of the state in his native language would only lead us back to the Tower of Babel.

EXPLORING THE TEXT

1. The focus of Flores Acosta's argument is the English Empowerment Act of 1996. How does the author define the act? Who is in favor of the act? Who are notable detractors?

2. In paragraph 3, Flores Acosta addresses the Spanish-speaking response to the act. Whose views does he criticize? Why? In doing so, how does the author define his own viewpoint?

3. What lessons does Flores Acosta want the reader to note with the example of *Lau v. Nichols?*

4. In paragraph 6, the author points to Los Angeles as an example of ethnic diversity. How does he use statistics? What point does the author want to to make in using these numbers?

5. In paragraph 7, Flores Acosta asks, "In how many different languages should classes be offered?" To answer this question, he asks the reader to consider the track record of bilingualism. Has that system been successful? Has it failed? Where? Why?

6. How, according to the author has the university been corrupted? What are the present and potential problems? What lessons should be learned?

7. As the title suggests, the author aims for the ideal of *e pluribus unum*. He is attempting to find "unity in diversity." What compromise does he offer to achieve that end? Is it adequate?

WRITING ASSIGNMENTS

1. In paragraph 9, Flores Acosta raises a concern about who should be allowed to teach information in certain disciplines and from certain perspectives. Research this problem as a current issue in American education today and write an essay that discusses the issues being raised and the arguments being made.

2. Flores Acosta talks about the motto *e pluribus unum* and the principles of being American (freedom, justice, and opportunity). Do these concepts represent reality or useful fiction? Do people have equal access to freedom, justice, and opportunity? Are these goals dependent solely on language fluency and literacy? What other characteristics play into this? Write an essay in which you attempt to answer some of these questions. You might want to interview one or more immigrants you know and use their stories as evidence in your discussion.

GROUP PROJECTS

1. Have your group look up the English Empowerment Act legislation and also the Supreme Court case of *Lau v. Nichols*. Though Flores Acosta refers only briefly to each, consider how he defines each document in terms of his own argument. Evaluate his summary of each. Does he fairly represent the facts and mandates in each text? Does he overlook any important elements? Can you find additional support for his arguments in these texts? Can you find information that would help to argue against him? Write a report of your findings.

2. Many films tell the story of the integration and education of immigrants in various American communities; see, for example, *Dangerous Minds, Lone Star,* and *Stand and Deliver.* As a group, consider two such films and note how the film defines or debates the issues, how the characters resolve the issues, and whether the presentation is realistic and convincing. Present your findings to the class and show clips of particularly relevant scenes if possible.

English Only—For the Kids' Sake
Carol Jago

How can the school system best serve the needs of the growing numbers of students who speak languages other than English? Carol Jago suggests that what is most important for her own state of California, and by extension the nation, is for all children to learn English. To ensure students' ability to compete in the marketplace, Jago proposes establishing minimum standards that students must meet in order to graduate from high school.

Jago teaches at Santa Monica High School and directs the California Reading and Literature Project at UCLA. She also edits the quarterly journal of the California Association of Teachers of English, *California English,* and writes a weekly education column for the *Outlook.* She is a regular contributor to the *Los Angeles Times* op-ed page where this essay first appeared in December 1996.

1   We used to call them ESL students to indicate that English was their second language. Then it was LEP for Limited English Proficient. The current term of choice is ELL, English Language Learners. Whatever the label, this growing body of students is challenging educators in innumerable ways. According to new data from the California Department of Education, there are 1.3 million such students in our public schools.

2   To give you some idea of the growth rate of this population, there has been a 141 percent increase since 1985. And to bring this statistic even closer to home, almost 42 percent of the statewide total in kindergarten through sixth grade were in Los Angeles County. Eighty percent of these children's first language is Spanish.

3   That the primary goal for these children is to learn English is not in question. How to make it happen often is. Bilingual programs, immersion programs, transition programs, sheltered programs and specially designed instruction all have their advocates. Properly executed, any of these methods can work.

4   What doesn't work, and unfortunately what all too many children experience in their first six years of school, is a helter-skelter approach to learning English. One year they have a bilingual teacher; the next year their teacher speaks only English. One year their content subjects are taught in their primary language; the next year no Spanish-speaking teacher can be found and they are learning math in English. One year the language on the playground is Spanish; the next year they have moved to a

campus with 60 languages spoken. Student mobility is a separate issue but not unrelated to English language instruction. Given that in many of our urban schools up to 30 percent of the student body is new in any school year, it seems to me that California needs a coherent, systematic method for teaching children to speak English.

5   I can hear the sighs already. A mandated curriculum? A one-size-fits-all program for children? What about local control? What about our child-centered curriculum and the belief that teachers teach children, not subjects? In answer, I can only say that the most important thing that we can do for our children, all our children, is to make them literate in English. Without this, they will forever play catch-up, both in school and in the job market.

6   Since California does not have and cannot quickly train one biliterate teacher for every 20 Spanish-speaking children, the language of instruction will have to be English. Russian-, Farsi- and Japanese-speaking students already go to school this way.

7   What I want for English language learners is exactly the same thing I want for my own child: a fair chance to compete in the marketplace. The California Education Round Table has sponsored a task force to write content standards in English and mathematics for high school graduates. When asked if nonnative speakers of English will be expected to meet the same standards to receive a high school diploma, the group has stated: "Yes, nonnative speakers of English who graduate from high school in California should be able to read, write, speak and listen at the level called for. . . . Lesser standards would be a disservice." The challenge is to make sure that these standards do not keep English language learners from receiving high school diplomas. To do that, we must start in kindergarten. The time for posturing is over. We need a K-12 curriculum that ensures that every California child learns English.

EXPLORING THE TEXT

1. Jago begins her discussion by saying, "We used to call them . . ." followed by a list of names. Who is "we"? Who is "them"? What is the effect of this listing? What issues does it raise? Are you comfortable with this tone? Discuss your answers in detail.

2. Note the way in which Jago uses statistics in paragraph 2. What is the effect of this presentation of numbers? Where else does she employ numbers to help support her points? Where does she decline to use specific numbers? Explain why these choices might be important.

3. In paragraph 3 Jago says, "That the primary goal for these children is to learn English is not in question." Is this true? Can you think of any other goals that might be seen to compete with this one as primary in a child's education?

4. Jago lists several kinds of programs intended to help ELL students succeed in their schoolwork (see paragraph 3). What do you know of these programs? What do they do? How are they different from each other? How ef-

fective are they? Rely on your own experience and provide a detailed answer that you can share with classmates who don't recognize what these programs entail.

5. How important is poverty in the issue that Jago discusses? Given that, how well do her proposed solutions address that part of the issue?

6. In paragraph 5 Jago says, "I can hear the sighs already." What does this phrase suggest about her sense of her audience and how people will react to what she says? Who is the primary audience intended for this piece? Where else can you find indications of her awareness of her audience's concerns and likely attitudes? What strategies does she employ to address their concerns and to try to change their attitudes? Explain your answer.

7. Jago suggests that the only way for young people to have "a fair chance to compete in the marketplace" (paragraph 7) is for them to be fluent in English. Is this a fact or an opinion? Can you think of any exceptions? Do they make her point any less compelling? Explain your answer.

WRITING ASSIGNMENTS

1. Compare this essay with John Silber's editorial earlier in this chapter. Evaluate and compare the tone each author chooses to employ. Who is the audience each seems to be addressing? What is her or his attitude toward that audience? How does he or she try to establish his or her authority? What does each author do to encourage audience members to agree with him or her? Do you prefer one author over the other? Is one more persuasive? Why or why not? In an essay, discuss the elements of each essay in detail and present your own description of how an effective editorial might be prepared.

GROUP PROJECTS

1. Do research into the different kinds of programs listed in paragraph 3. What does each offer? How effective is it? What are its advantages and disadvantages? Have group members interview people involved in each kind of program, including teachers, administrators, or students. Prepare a group report in which you evaluate Jago's claim that any program will work if "properly executed." Is she right? Are some programs better than others at teaching English (and other disciplines)? Are some more economical or otherwise easier to administer?

2. Interview a number of people who had to learn English as a second (or third, fourth, etc.) language. How did they do it? What difficulties did they encounter? What assistance were they given? What suggestions do they have for how the school system should address this problem? Encourage each in-

terviewee to share stories of success as well as failure. Compare your findings with your fellow group members and compile them into a report.

Mute in an English-Only World
Chang-rae Lee

Chang-rae Lee shares memories of his immigrant mother and her difficulty functioning in the United States before she became proficient in English. Like Rolando Flores Acosta above, Lee questions whether public information—here, road signs—should be presented in languages other than English. He concludes that immigrants should become proficient in English, but he also condemns intolerant Americans who fail to understand how difficult this can be.

Lee is the author of the novel *Native Speaker*. This Op-Ed essay originally appeared in the *New York Times* in April 1996.

1   When I read of the troubles in Palisades Park, N.J., over the proliferation of Korean-language signs along its main commercial strip, I unexpectedly sympathized with the frustrations, resentments and fears of the longtime residents. They clearly felt alienated and even unwelcome in a vital part of their community. The town, like seven others in New Jersey, has passed laws requiring that half of any commercial sign in a foreign language be in English.

2   Now I certainly would never tolerate any exclusionary ideas about who could rightfully settle and belong in the town. But having been raised in a Korean immigrant family, I saw every day the exacting price and power of language, especially with my mother, who was an outsider in an English-only world.

3   In the first years we lived in America, my mother could speak only the most basic English, and she often encountered great difficulty whenever she went out.

4   We lived in New Rochelle, N.Y., in the early 70's, and most of the local businesses were run by the descendants of immigrants who, generations ago, had come to the suburbs from New York City. Proudly dotting Main Street and North Avenue were Italian pastry and cheese shops, Jewish tailors and cleaners and Polish and German butchers and bakers. If my mother's marketing couldn't wait until the weekend, when my father had free time, she would often hold off until I came home from school to buy the groceries.

5   Though I was only 6 or 7 years old, she insisted that I go out shopping with her and my younger sister. I mostly loathed the task, partly because it meant I couldn't spend the afternoon playing catch with my friends but also because I knew our errands would inevitably lead to an awkward scene, and that I would have to speak up to help my mother.

6   I was just learning the language myself, but I was a quick study, as children are with new tongues. I had spent kindergarten in almost complete silence, hearing only the high nasality of my teacher and comprehending little but the cranky wails and

cries of my classmates. But soon, seemingly mere months later, I had already become a terrible ham and mimic, and I would crack up my father with impressions of teachers, his friends and even himself. My mother scolded me for aping his speech, and the one time I attempted to make light of hers I rated a roundhouse smack on my bottom.

7   For her, the English language was not very funny. It usually meant trouble and a good dose of shame, and sometimes real hurt. Although she had a good reading knowledge of the language from university classes in South Korea, she had never practiced actual conversation. So in America, she used English flashcards and phrase books and watched television with us kids. And she faithfully carried a pocket workbook illustrated with stick-figure people and compound sentences to be filled in.

8   But none of it seemed to do her much good. Staying mostly at home to care for us, she didn't have many chances to try out sundry words and phrases. When she did, say, at the window of the post office, her readied speech would stall, freeze, sometimes altogether collapse.

9   One day was unusually harrowing. We ventured downtown in the new Ford Country Squire my father had bought her, an enormous station wagon that seemed as long—and deft—as an ocean liner. We were shopping for a special meal for guests visiting that weekend, and my mother had heard that a particular butcher carried fresh oxtails, which she needed for a traditional soup.

10   We'd never been inside the shop, but my mother would pause before its window, which was always lined with whole hams, crown roasts and ropes of plump handmade sausages. She greatly esteemed the bounty with her eyes, and my sister and I did also, but despite our desirous cries she'd turn us away and instead buy the packaged links at the Finast supermarket, where she felt comfortable looking them over and could easily spot the price. And, of course, not have to talk.

11   But that day she was resolved. The butcher store was crowded, and as we stepped inside the door jingled a welcome. No one seemed to notice. We waited for some time, and people who entered after us were now being served. Finally, an old woman nudged my mother and waved a little ticket, which we hadn't taken. We patiently waited again, until one of the beefy men behind the glass display hollered our number.

12   My mother pulled us forward and began searching the cases, but the oxtails were nowhere to be found. The man, his big arms crossed, sharply said, "Come on, lady, whaddya want?" This unnerved her, and she somehow blurted the Korean word for oxtail, soggori.

13   The butcher looked as if my mother had put something sour in his mouth, and he glanced back at the lighted board and called the next number.

14   Before I knew it, she had rushed us outside and back in the wagon, which she had double-parked because of the crowd. She was furious, almost vibrating with fear and grief, and I could see she was about to cry.

15   She wanted to go back inside, but now the driver of the car we were blocking wanted to pull out. She was shooing us away. My mother, who had just earned her driver's license, started furiously working the pedals. But in her haste she must have flooded the engine, for it wouldn't turn over. The driver started honking and then

another car began honking as well, and soon it seemed the entire street was shrieking at us.

16   In the following years, my mother grew steadily more comfortable with English. In Korean, she could be fiery, stern, deeply funny and ironic; in English, just slightly less so. If she was never quite fluent, she gained enough confidence to make herself clearly known to anyone, and particularly to me.

17   Five years ago, she died of cancer, and some months after we buried her I found myself in the driveway of my father's house, washing her sedan. I liked taking care of her things; it made me feel close to her. While I was cleaning out the glove compartment, I found her pocket English workbook, the one with the silly illustrations. I hadn't seen it in nearly 20 years. The yellowed pages were brittle and dog-eared. She had fashioned a plain-paper wrapping for it, and I wondered whether she meant to protect the book or hide it.

18   I don't doubt that she would have appreciated doing the family shopping on the new Broad Avenue of Palisades Park. But I like to think, too, that she would have understood those who now complain about the Korean-only signs.

19   I wonder what these same people would have done if they had seen my mother studying her English workbook—or lost in a store. Would they have nodded gently at her? Would they have lent a kind word?

EXPLORING THE TEXT

1. What is the problem that Lee is confronted with in paragraph 1 of this essay.
2. Where do Lee's sympathies lie, initially? Given the rest of the article, why is this position surprising?
3. There are three ways to argue in traditional rhetoric: appeals to logos (reason), pathos (emotion), and ethos (ethics). What appeal does Lee make here?
4. Why does Lee keep returning to his mother's workbook? What effect does the workbook have as a recurrent image in this essay. How does it work as a symbol, especially as it progresses from its newness to its later status, wrapped and tattered?
5. How does Lee characterize immigrants regarding American culture and their own?
6. Is language the only communication at issue here? What other kinds of communication are evident? What differences can you locate in how proficiency is judged with regard to these other proficiencies? Explain your answer.
7. This essay is definitely a form of personal narrative, but what is its purpose? Does Lee want us simply to enjoy the story? Does he raise attitudinal issues or policy questions? Is this really a story about an important clash between different cultures or is it a story denouncing people who are impa-

tient and demanding of others within our culture? Point to particular passages from the text and discuss your answer in detail.

WRITING ASSIGNMENTS

1. In his article earlier in this chapter, John Silber attempts to separate public from private. Lee's approach emphasizes the personal over the political. Do you agree that the English-only debate is so neatly separated? Write an essay discussing how the terms *public* and *private* are defined by each author. In what ways are these distinctions important to the English-only debate? Are the boundaries between the two clearly maintained or are they shifting? Why might this be important?
2. Reread paragraph 19. What do you think? Provide your own anecdotal response to these ideas. Rely on memories of your past and your own experience as a foreigner, a novice mispronouncing a word, a country person in a city, and so on.
3. Write an essay in which you compare the process of language acquisition here (what is and what ought to be) with those processes described in the essays by Rolando Flores Acosta, Andrew Ward, and Chang-rae Lee in this chapter. What is similar among these process descriptions? What is different? Who, ultimately, is held responsible? What do you think would make the best possible system?

GROUP PROJECTS

1. Working in groups of two, identify a foreign market in some part of your own. At the library, do some research on the country or culture represented by this market. Get a dictionary of the language spoken there. Take a notebook and a pen. What things in the market would you classify as distinctly American? What things are foreign? Consider how it is that you can make such distinctions. What differences seem important? What seem relatively unimportant? Imagine shopping in this market for a typical American meal and being able to use only the native language of the market's owner. Try to communicate with the market's owners. Write a report on what you discover and tie your own insights into the argument Lee presents.
2. What happens to adults in your community who are trying to learn English. What kinds of adult language education programs are available? Have members of your group look for programs and schools in your community that focus on the needs of immigrants and other non-English-speaking adults. To what extend does the community help them to learn English? Does the help come from government? From churches? From other com-

munity groups? To what extent is the responsibility (and burden) on the nonnative speaker? How does the situation in your community relate to the requirements of *Lau v. Nichols,* the court case that Rolando Flores Acosta discusses elsewhere in this chapter?

English Plus, Not English Only
Michael E. Dickstein

So many of us Americans think of Canada as a friendly suburb to our north that we may not realize how that country is being torn apart. And at the center of the crisis is language. Residents of Quebec (the Quebecois) insist on French-only as their language, whereas most of the rest of Canada conducts itself in English. Citing some of the problems between Anglo and French Canadians, Michael E. Dickstein compares the situation to the English-only movement in the United States. He worries that a failure to clearly say what it means to be American could result in similar divisiveness and hostilities. His suggested solution is "English Plus," a compromise that stands in interesting contrast to the views of other authors in this chapter. Whose argument do you find most persuasive?

Dickstein grew up in Quebec and is bilingual. He is a Canadian citizen who practices law in San Francisco. This essay first appeared in the *Chicago Tribune* on May 13, 1997.

1 Imagine a country torn by language, not race. In that country, it is not unusual for power and wealth to be distributed based on mother tongue, not merit. Frictions evolve into an endless series of confrontations. Soon the vitality and vision of the country are entirely diverted by its obsession with the politics of language.

2 Imagine a country in which language police do their best to eradicate all signs not written in their mother tongue, in which the government legislates the language of private businesses and in which a leader calls for "revenge" against the "ethnics" who interfered with his plans for a purely unilingual nation.

3 Imagine a country in which terrorists explode bombs, kidnap a foreign diplomat and murder a cabinet-member, all in support of the creation of a new country that will speak their language. In response, martial law is declared. Battle-armed soldiers roam the streets, hundreds of people are arrested in the middle of the night and civil rights are suspended.

4 Imagining such a country is hard for most Americans. Imagining such a country existing in the heart of North America is even harder. But all of those events have happened in Canada, and if the United States is not careful they could happen here too.

5 Canada has supported the use of French by its minority but has failed to offer a compelling and unifying vision of what it means to be Canadian. This has left Canada on the verge of being torn into two lesser countries. In 1995, Canada barely survived the province of Quebec's referendum to separate (the margin of victory was just over 1 percent).

6   In contrast, Quebec has offered a compelling and unifying vision of what it means to be Quebecois, but that narrow vision has been found at the expense of free speech, cultural openness and societal harmony. In Quebec, language laws have been passed that severely limit the right of Quebec's citizens to communicate in the language of their choice, and non-French communities have been isolated, alienated and scapegoated.

7   The United States is now facing the beginnings of language problems like those in Canada. In 1996, in response to growing American fears that today's immigrants are not learning English and are not assimilating into mainstream culture, the House of Representatives passed the English Language Empowerment Act of 1996. The act emphasized that the "official language of the Federal Government is English" and mandated that "Representatives of the Federal Government shall conduct its official business in English."

8   This year similar legislation was introduced in the Senate. Thus, Congress joined the tide of over 20 states that had already taken steps towards passing "English-only" legislation.

9   Opponents of English-only laws have challenged the laws in court, asserting that they violate the right to free speech. On March 3, the U.S. Supreme Court guaranteed that the controversy over language issues would continue when it sidestepped ruling on one of those challenges.

10   The Canadian experience teaches that English-only is not the right solution to America's growing problem. Instead, the United States should strive for "English Plus." English Plus, like English-only, demands that everything feasible be done to encourage all Americans to achieve a minimum level of competence in English and to share a vision of what it means to be American. Without that, America, like Canada, could lose its coherence.

11   But where English-only prohibits the use of languages other than English, English Plus recognizes that English should be a floor, not a ceiling. While Americans must be taught English, they must then be allowed to express themselves as they choose.

12   The need for a shared language should not be confused with a need to impose uniformity or to interfere with free and effective communication. To do so could lead to the infringements on freedom and cultural openness experienced in Quebec. In an English-only world, the government would not communicate in any language but English. Communications to foreigners would be written only in English, even if the foreigners didn't speak English well. Bilingual government employees would be required to speak only in English, even if the person served would better understand another language. Ballots would be written only in English, even if that led to an increase in uniformed voting.

13   English-only advocates argue that these restrictions are necessary if non-Anglophones are ever to learn English. But if immersion in America's overwhelmingly English culture does not teach English, neither will brief encounters with unilingual bureaucrats.

14   Quebec's French-only world provides many tangible examples of the problems that would exist with English-only. For instance, the Quebec government raised a

large sign at the United States border warning Americans that speed limits are posted in kilometers per hour. The sign was written in French only. Most of the tourists spoke English only. Not surprisingly, baffled American tourists could be found careening around corners at 100 mph instead of 62 mph (100 kmh).

15   No one learned French speeding recklessly around Quebec's corners, and no one will learn English by being confronted with English-only ballots. English Plus recognizes this simple fact. In an English-Plus world, English would be taught in classes by teachers, not in lines by postal clerks.

16   English Plus insists upon the benefits of English-only while avoiding its detriments. In an English-Plus world, laws that support the ability to communicate in English would be encouraged (for example, laws that provide for English education for immigrants, require mandatory English testing to graduate from high school or require that all interaction with the government be possible in English). Laws that squelch free expression or interfere with effective communication would be rejected (for example, laws that require private signs to be written in English only or require all private and government business to be conducted in English).

17   English Plus recognizes that sometimes English-only is just not enough.

EXPLORING THE TEXT

1. What does the author assume about the connection between language and identity?
2. What does Dickstein mean by "English-only"? What does he mean by "English Plus"? What are the ramifications of each position?
3. In paragraph 10, Dickstein expresses his concern that America, like Canada, "could lose its coherence." What does he mean by "coherence"? Is America coherent? Can you argue against this claim?
4. Look at the various "needs" that Dickstein identifies in paragraph 12: "the need for a shared language" is set against "a need to impose uniformity or to interfere with free and effective communication." Are these truly needs? Consider how Dickstein supports this idea, but also consider the extent to which you can agree or disagree with him.
5. In presenting his argument, has Dickstein clearly presented the concerns of both sides of the Canadian issue? Does the information he presents, and the way in which he argues his points, reveal any kind of bias? Can you think of arguments that others might raise against his claims?
6. Dickstein opens this essay with a series of "Imagine . . . " statements that invite American readers to consider how their own world might be different and that claim to present a picture of how things are in Canada at present. Does this opening strategy seem to have worked? Do the pictures he asks you to imagine jibe with your own knowledge of Canada?
7. Consider the tone and word choice Dickstein employs throughout this essay, but especially in paragraphs 15 and 16. What is the effect of words like

recklessly, squelched, or *interfere?* How should they affect how you read this argument?

WRITING ASSIGNMENTS

1. Consider the other readings in this chapter. Which authors, like Dickstein, suggest that the problem of language is actually a problem of identity? Carefully consider the arguments presented by at least three authors and write a paper in which you discuss the extent to which they agree or disagree with each other. In preparing the essay, identify specific issues and points of view, then carefully consider what the various authors include in their discussions, what they leave out, and what ultimately this all seems to mean to us.

2. Dickstein argues for "English Plus" rather than "English-only." Consider the arguments presented by other authors in this chapter. Which authors would agree with Dickstein? Which would disagree with him? Write an essay in which you evaluate Dickstein's argument by using the ideas and insights of these other authors, as well as your own analysis and experience.

GROUP PROJECTS

1. Have your group research the 1995 Quebec referendum and the issues it raised. As there were many issues raised by the referendum, first identify several that seem relevant to the language and were raised by this article, then assign different group members to research the pros and cons of each. Have group members try to interview Canadians—Anglo and Quebecois—to discover the views; the Internet should offer an opportunity to question a number of Canadians. Prepare a report of your findings.

2. This essay and others in this chapter discuss the various laws and programs intended to help people learn English. As a group make a list of the various laws discussed in these readings and investigate their status in your community. (Be sure to distinguish between local, state, and federal laws.) What laws have passed? What programs are in effect? How effective are they? Who is helped? Who is left out? Your research should include written materials, but you will also want to interview people who are involved in such programs and in enforcing English-only laws to discover their opinions on these issues. Prepare a report of your findings.

Before 1990, very few people had ever heard of the Internet. And fewer still could have guessed its impact on American culture, education, and business. The Internet is used as a research tool, a social hangout, a shopping mall, an advertising marketplace, a political forum, and an information resource. We use the Internet to keep in touch with friends, family, and business contacts; share ideas in newsgroups; get information; even keep apprised of the latest sports scores. Experts estimated that two-thirds of American households will be on-line by the year 2000.

Originally designed by computer scientists for scientists and engineers, the Internet has expanded beyond information technology. By some estimates, the Internet is currently doubling in size each year, with over two million new users a month worldwide! For most people, the social and political issues that face the Internet directly relate to the increasing popularity of the World Wide Web—a graphically based, visually rich application providing user-friendly access to the Internet. However, the Web's decentralized structure makes it difficult to quantify. It has no hard boundaries, with many types of connections and servers in hundreds of countries. As the Web becomes more accessible, it also becomes more controversial.

The Internet has a unique culture all its own. Newsgroups provide support networks for people with diverse interests and a variety of social backgrounds. You can log on to a newsgroup any time of the day or night and connect with others, a concept explored by Howard Rheingold in his essay "The Virtual Community." For business, the Web means increased exposure of products and services. On the Web, companies are equalized, because advertising there is free. In his article "The Web: Infotopia or Marketplace?" Peter McGrath explores the changing face of the Internet as the Web is increasingly used for marketing agendas.

The issue of protecting children from offensive material or contact with individuals who mean them harm has motivated some parent groups to push for legislation to control Web content. Other groups fear that such control violates First Amendment rights of freedom of speech and threatens the inclusive quality of the Internet—a point Esther Dyson makes in her article "Cyberspace: If You Don't Love It, Leave It." Dyson notes that the Internet is a powerful communication tool with merits that far exceed occasional abuse. But just who has access to this powerful tool? LynNell Hancock's article "The Haves and the Have-Nots" discusses how some schools have Internet access while others leave students behind in the electronic age. This difference, claims Hancock, can only serve to prevent urban children from successfully competing in the future workforce.

Returning to the theme of Web marketing, Kathryn C. Montgomery's article "Children in the Digital Age" addresses the targeting of children by advertisers. Montgomery asserts that pornography isn't what threatens children on the Web—it's the advertisers parents must protect their children from. As the Web increases its influence in advertising and communication world, television has attempted to get in on the act. Bill Machrone, in his editorial "The Digital Scapegoat," explores how television has supported groups that push for content control of the Internet. Machrone conjectures that this support stems from television's fear that it is losing its power of influence over the general public. This fear may be founded. After all, as Howard Rheingold notes, "the Web might create a power shift that changes everything."

The Virtual Community

Howard Rheingold

It is midnight and you are listening to the steady beep of your child's respirator as she sleeps in the next room. You feel alone and restless. Where do you turn? The Internet, according to Howard Rheingold. The Internet provides instant and immediate access to people around the world. On the Internet, there is always someone willing to listen to you and keep you company. Within the unique "virtual community" there is companionship.

Rheingold explores the role of the Internet in a world that seems to become more lonely every day. Rather than view cyberspace as a cold, computerized environment, Rheingold claims that the Internet can bring a sense of community back to our isolated lives. In a world where few people know even their neighbors, we can forge our own virtual communities on the Internet. The following essay is an excerpt from Rheingold's book *The Virtual Community* (1993).

1 In the summer of 1986, my then-2-year-old daughter picked up a tick. There was this blood-bloated *thing* sucking on our baby's scalp, and we weren't quite sure how to go about getting it off. My wife, Judy, called the pediatrician. It was 11 o'clock in the evening. I logged onto the WELL, the big Bay Area infonet, and contacted the Parenting conference (a conference is an on-line conversation about a specific subject). I got my answer on-line within minutes from a fellow with the improbable but genuine name of Flash Gordon, M.D. I had removed the tick by the time Judy got the callback from the pediatrician's office.

2 What amazed me wasn't just the speed with which we obtained precisely the information we needed to know, right when we needed to know it. It was also the immense inner sense of security that comes with discovering that real people—most of them parents, some of them nurses, doctors, and midwives—are available, around the clock, if you need them. There is a magic protective circle around the atmosphere of the Parenting conference. We're talking about our sons and daughters in this forum, not about our computers or our opinions about philosophy, and many of us feel that this tacit understanding sanctifies the virtual space.

3 The atmosphere of this particular conference—the attitudes people exhibit to each other in the tone of what they say in public—is part of what continues to attract me. People who never have much to contribute in political debate, technical argument, or intellectual gamesmanship turn out to have a lot to say about raising children. People you knew as fierce, even nasty, intellectual opponents in other contexts give you emotional support on a deeper level, parent to parent, within the boundaries of this small but warmly human corner of cyberspace.

4 In most cases, people who talk about a shared interest don't disclose enough about themselves as whole individuals on-line to inspire real trust in others. But in the case of the subcommunity called the Parenting conference, a few dozen of us, scattered across the country, few of whom rarely if ever saw the others face to face, have a few years of minor crises to knit us together and prepare us for serious busi-

ness when it comes our way. Another several dozen read the conference regularly but contribute only when they have something important to add. Hundreds more read the conference every week without comment, except when something extraordinary happens.

5   Jay Allison and his family live in Massachusetts. He and his wife are public-radio producers. I've never met them face to face, although I feel I know something powerful and intimate about the Allisons and have strong emotional ties to them. What follows are some of Jay's postings on the WELL:

6   Woods Hole. Midnight. I am sitting in the dark of my daughter's room. Her monitor lights blink at me. The lights used to blink too brightly so I covered them with bits of bandage adhesive and now they flash faintly underneath, a persistent red and green, Lillie's heart and lungs.

7   Above the monitor is her portable suction unit. In the glow of the flashlight I'm writing by, it looks like the plastic guts of a science-class human model, the tubes coiled around the power supply, the reservoir, the pump.

8   Tina is upstairs trying to get some sleep. A baby monitor links our bedroom to Lillie's. It links our sleep to Lillie's too, and because our souls are linked to hers, we do not sleep well.

9   I am naked. My stomach is full of beer. The flashlight rests on it, and the beam rises and falls with my breath. My daughter breathes through a white plastic tube inserted into a hole in her throat. She's 14 months old.

10   Sitting in front of our computers with our hearts racing and tears in our eyes, in Tokyo and Sacramento and Austin, we read about Lillie's croup, her tracheostomy, the days and nights at Massachusetts General Hospital, and now the vigil over Lillie's breathing and the watchful attention to the mechanical apparatus that kept her alive. It went on for days. Weeks. Lillie recovered, and relieved our anxieties about her vocal capabilities after all that time with a hole in her throat by saying the most extraordinary things, duly reported on-line by Jay.

11   Later, writing in *Whole Earth Review,* Jay described the experience:

12   Before this time, my computer screen had never been a place to go for solace. Far from it. But there it was. Those nights sitting up late with my daughter, I'd go to my computer, dial up the WELL, and ramble. I wrote about what was happening that night or that year. I didn't know anyone I was "talking" to. I had never laid eyes on them. At 3:00 a.m. my "real" friends were asleep, so I turned to this foreign, invisible community for support. The WELL was always awake.

13   Any difficulty is harder to bear in isolation. There is nothing to measure against, to lean against. Typing out my journal entires into the computer and over the phone lines, I found fellowship and comfort in this unlikely medium.

14   Many people are alarmed by the very idea of a virtual community, fearing that it is another step in the wrong direction, substituting more technological ersatz for yet another natural resource or human freedom. These critics often voice their sadness at what people have been reduced to doing in a civilization that worships technology, decrying the circumstances that lead some people into such pathetically dis-

connected lives that they prefer to find their companions on the other side of a computer screen. There is a seed of truth in this fear, for communities at some point require more than words on a screen if they are to be other than ersatz.

15   Yet some people—many people—who don't do well in spontaneous spoken interaction turn out to have valuable contributions to make in a conversation in which they have time to think about what to say. These people, who might constitute a significant proportion of the population, can find written communication more authentic than the face-to-face kind. Who is to say that this preference for informal written text is somehow less authentically human than opting for audible speech? Those who critique computer-mediated communication because some people use it obsessively hit an important target, but miss a great deal more when they don't take into consideration people who use the medium for genuine human interaction. Those who find virtual communities cold places point at the limits of the technology, its most dangerous pitfalls, and we need to pay attention to those boundaries. But these critiques don't tell us how the Allisons, my own family, and many others could have found the community of support and information we found in the WELL when we needed it. And those of us who do find communion in cyberspace might do well to pay attention to the way the medium we love can be abused.

16   Although dramatic incidents are what bring people together and stick in their memories, most of what goes on in the Parenting conference and most virtual communities is informal conversation and downright chitchat. The model of the WELL and other social clusters in cyberspace as "places" emerges naturally whenever people who use this medium discuss its nature. In 1987, Stewart Brand quoted me in his book *The Media Lab* about what tempted me to log onto the WELL as often as I did: "There's always another mind there. It's like having the corner bar, complete with old buddies and delightful newcomers and new tools waiting to take home and fresh graffiti and letters, except instead of putting on my coat, shutting down the computer, and walking down to the corner, I just invoke my telecom program and there they are. It's a place."

17   I've changed my mind about a lot of aspects of the WELL over the years, but the sense of place is still as strong as ever. As Ray Oldenburg proposes in his 1989 book *The Great Good Place,* there are three essential places in people's lives: the place we live, the place we work, and the place we gather for conviviality. Although the casual conversation that takes place in cafés, beauty shops, pubs, and town squares is universally considered to be trivial, idle talk, Oldenburg makes the case that such places are where communities can come into being and continue to hold together. These are the unacknowledged agoras of modern life. When the automobilecentric, suburban, fast-food, shopping-mall way of life eliminated many of these "third places" from traditional towns and cities around the world, the social fabric of existing communities started shredding.

18   Oldenburg puts a name and a conceptual framework on a phenomenon that every virtual community member knows instinctively, the power of informal public life:

19   Third places exist on neutral ground and serve to level their guests to a condition of social equality. Within these places, conversation is the primary activity

and the major vehicle for the display and appreciation of human personality and individuality. Third places are taken for granted and most have a low profile. Since the formal institutions of society make stronger claims on the individual, third places are normally open in the off hours, as well as at other times. The character of a third place is determined most of all by its regular clientele and is marked by a playful mood, which contrasts with people's more serious involvement in other spheres. Though a radically different kind of setting for a home, the third place is remarkably similar to a good home in the psychological comfort and support that it extends.

20   Such are the characteristics of third places that appear to be universal and essential to a vital informal public life. . . .

21   The problem of place in America manifests itself in a sorely deficient informal public life. The structure of shared experience beyond that offered by family, job, and passive consumerism is small and dwindling. The essential group experience is being replaced by the exaggerated self-consciousness of individuals. American lifestyles, for all the material acquisition and the seeking after comforts and pleasures, are plagued by boredom, loneliness, alienation, and a high price tag. . . .

22   Unlike many frontiers, that of the informal public life does not remain benign as it awaits development. It does not become easier to tame as technology evolves, as governmental bureaus and agencies multiply, or as population grows. It does not yield to the mere passage of time and a policy of letting the chips fall where they may as development proceeds in other areas of urban life. To the contrary, neglect of the informal public life can make a jungle of what had been a garden while, at the same time, diminishing the ability of people to cultivate it.

23   It might not be the same kind of place that Oldenburg had in mind, but many of his descriptions of third places could also describe the WELL. Perhaps cyberspace is one of the informal public places where people can rebuild the aspects of community that were lost when the malt shop became a mall. Or perhaps cyberspace is precisely the *wrong* place to look for the rebirth of community, offering not a tool for conviviality but a life-denying simulacrum of real passion and true commitment to one another. In either case, we need to find out soon.

24   Because we cannot see one another in cyberspace, gender, age, national origin, and physical appearance are not apparent unless a person wants to make such characteristics public. People whose physical handicaps make it difficult to form new friendships find that virtual communities treat them as they always wanted to be treated—as thinkers and transmitters of ideas and feeling beings, not carnal vessels with a certain appearance and way of walking and talking (or not walking and not talking).

25   One of the few things that enthusiastic members of virtual communities in places like Japan, England, France, and the United States all agree on is that expanding their circle of friends is one of the most important advantages of computer conferencing. It is a way to *meet* people, whether or not you feel the need to affiliate with them on a community level. It's a way of both making contact with and main-

taining a distance from others. The way you meet people in cyberspace puts a different spin on affiliation: In traditional kinds of communities, we are accustomed to meeting people, then getting to know them; in virtual communities, you can get to know people and *then* choose to meet them. Affiliation also can be far more ephemeral in cyberspace because you can get to know people you might never meet on the physical plane.

26   How does anybody find friends? In the traditional community, we search through our pool of neighbors and professional colleagues, of acquaintances and acquaintances of acquaintances, in order to find people who share our values and interests. We then exchange information about one another, disclose and discuss our mutual interests, and sometimes we become friends. In a virtual community we can go directly to the place where our favorite subjects are being discussed, then get acquainted with people who share our passions or who use words in a way we find attractive. In this sense, the topic is the address: You can't simply pick up a phone and ask to be connected with someone who wants to talk about Islamic art or California wine, or someone with a 3-year-old daughter or a 40-year-old Hudson; you can, however, join a computer conference on any of those topics, then open a public or private correspondence with the previously unknown people you find there. Your chances of making friends are increased by several orders of magnitude over the old methods of finding a peer group.

27   You can be fooled about people in cyberspace, behind the cloak of words. But that can be said about telephones or face-to-face communication as well; computer-mediated communications provide new ways to fool people, and the most obvious identity swindles will die out only when enough people learn to use the medium critically. In some ways, the medium will, by its nature, be forever biased toward certain kinds of obfuscation. It will also be a place where people often end up revealing themselves far more intimately than they would be inclined to do without the intermediation of screens and pseudonyms.

28   Point of view, along with identity, is one of the great variables in cyberspace. Different people in cyberspace look at their virtual communities through differently shaped keyholes. In traditional communities, people have a strongly shared mental model of the sense of place—the room or village or city where their interactions occur. In virtual communities, the sense of place requires an individual act of imagination. The different mental models people have of the electronic agora complicate the question of why people seem to want to build societies mediated by computer screens. A question like that leads inexorably to the old fundamental questions of what forces hold any society together. The roots of these questions extend farther than the social upheavals triggered by modern communications technologies.

29   When we say "society," we usually mean citizens of cities in entities known as nations. We take those categories for granted. But the mass-psychological transition we made to thinking of ourselves as part of modern society and nation-states is historically recent. Could people make the transition from the close collective social groups, the villages and small towns of premodern and precapitalist Europe, to a new form of social solidarity known as society that transcended and encompassed all previous kinds of human association? Ferdinand Tönnies, one of the founders of

sociology, called the premodern kind of social group *gemeinschaft,* which is closer to the English word *community,* and the new kind of social group he called *gesellschaft,* which can be translated roughly as *society.* All the questions about community in cyberspace point to a similar kind of transition, for which we have no technical names, that might be taking place now.

30   Sociology student Marc Smith, who has been using the WELL and the Net as the laboratory for his fieldwork, pointed me to Benedict Anderson's *Imagined Communities,* a study of nation-building that focuses on the ideological labor involved. Anderson points out that nations and, by extension, communities are imagined in the sense that a given nation exists by virtue of a common acceptance in the minds of the population that it exists. Nations must exist in the minds of their citizens in order to exist at all. "Virtual communities require an act of imagination," Smith points out, extending Anderson's line of thinking to cyberspace, "and what must be imagined is the idea of the community itself."

EXPLORING THE TEXT

1. What is a virtual community? What is its appeal? Why do virtual communities "require an act of imagination"?
2. Why do some people, as Rheingold suggests in paragraph 24, feel alarmed by the idea of a virtual community?
3. What are the limitations of virtual communities? How can this medium be abused?
4. Consider how Rheingold begins his essay. How does his story affect the audience and the overall theme of his article?
5. Rheingold quotes Ray Oldenburg's claim that there are three essential places in our lives "the place we live, the place we work, and the place we gather" (paragraph 17). Apply this statement to when the place we gather is in cyberspace.
6. How does the excerpt of Jay Allison's posting support Rheingold's argument? How does this excerpt impact the reader?
7. Rheingold contrasts the differences between how we meet people in a traditional community and how we meet them in a virtual one. What are the similarities and differences between the two? Can one be better than another? Explain your perspective.
8. What impact does anonymity have on relationships in cyberspace?

WRITING ASSIGNMENTS

1. Write an essay examining our concept of community. What is a community? What holds it together? Consider the leap of imagination we must make when rethinking our concept of community as it applies to cyberspace. Or do we have to rethink it at all?

2. Pretend you have unlimited access to the Internet. What newsgroups (discussion groups) do you join? Discuss the role of newsgroups in our lives. What does a newsgroup offer that we cannot find anywhere else?

3. Discuss the role of conversation in our lives. How do we communicate? What are the different ways we communicate? (Remember we can communicate without words!) Evaluate the possibilities and limitations of cybertalk. What impact do you think the Internet will have on this "major vehicle for the human personality"?

4. If you could design your own discussion group, what topic would you choose and why? What issues might you face as moderator for the group? Would you restrict discussions and if so, how? Explain your reasoning?

GROUP PROJECTS

1. Locate a discussion group (or groups) on-line that your group finds interesting. Evaluate the styles of communication you read there. Print out several discussions and analyze them for form, style, and content. What patterns emerge? What conclusions can you draw regarding on-line communication?

2. Form an electronic newsgroup in class to discuss this course. Everyone must post on the group at least three times over the course of the week. Did you notice any difference in your communication style over the Internet from how you communicate in person or on paper? What did you discover about Internet communication?

3. Discuss with your group what a virtual community means. If you were to form relationships with people on the Internet, what would you want to know about your Internet friends? What do you think you would have a right to know? How would you go about finding out the personal information you wanted to know? Or would it matter?

The Web: Infotopia or Marketplace?
Peter McGrath

The World Wide Web, or simply "the Web," was developed by scientists who wanted to exchange information, for free, across the world. The Web "began" in March at Conseil Europeen pour la Recherche Nucleaire (CERN) in Switzerland. With the World Wide Web, scientists could share large quantities of graphically based data and information in seconds across oceans and continents. Thus, we often call the Web the "information superhighway."

However, many other uses for the Web soon emerged. Companies saw the Web as fertile ground for advertising products and services. Individuals running small businesses, with little money for advertising, could advertise in this new medium for free. In the following article, Peter McGrath addresses how the Web has become an advertiser's dream. Companies, both legitimate and disreputable, can advertise and sell merchandise over the Internet. What does this trend mean for the future of the Web and marketing and for consumers as we enter the next millennium? This article appeared in the January 21, 1997, issue of *Newsweek,* where McGrath is the editor of new media.

1 A current conceit says that Internet time must be reckoned in dog years. The pace of change is so fast that one year on the Internet is like seven years in any other medium. By this scheme, it has been nearly a century since the Internet was born. It has been 14 years since the emergence of the World Wide Web as an electronic-publishing vehicle. And by the year 2000, the Internet will have undergone another two decades' worth of growth and development.

2 Every step has aroused great expectations. Some thought it would usher in an era of cooperation, as both work and play became digitalized. Others saw the "citizen-controlled" Internet as a radical challenge to establishment control of information outlets, or as a civic marketplace. In his book "Life After Television," supply-side theorist George Gilder says the networked personal computer will transform capitalism into "a healing force in the present crisis of home and family, culture and community."

3 But today the Internet itself is being transformed—into something closer to a marketplace. Advertisements and sales brochures are proliferating among the Webzines and newsgroups and bulletin boards. "Cyberstores" offer everything from music CDs to certificates of deposit. The most interesting new technologies are those that foster transactions. As the vendors and the marketers crowd their way into the bitstream, is the Internet on the verge of becoming just one more mass commercial medium? Does anything remain of the original Infotopia?

4 It is almost a truism that no new communications medium turns out the way its inventors imagined. The developers of the Bell System conceived of the telephone as a business tool; they were both surprised and appalled when their customers diverted it to the "trivial" purpose of social conversation. The radio was meant to be a wireless telegraph, a medium of two-way messaging; none of its creators anticipated broadcasting and mass programming. Television began as radio with pictures; early programs were actually simulcasts, video transmissions of a radio program on a radio set with a radio audience. It took years for broadcasters to discover television as a medium with its own unique properties and powers.

5 So it is with the Internet. The original goal, in the 1960s, was a sharing of resources. The founders of network computing wanted researchers at Stanford to be able to use software on a machine at MIT, even where the two computers had incompatible operating systems. From there it was a short step to exchanges of messages and documents—the origin of e-mail. Soon the Internet became a reference medium, where research papers could be read by anyone on the network. It was the World Wide Web that brought the Internet into the consumer marketplace. Developed in 1990 as a system for delivering a graphics-rich, pagelike file over conventional telephone lines using Internet technology, the Web lured traditional news and

entertainment companies into electronic-publishing ventures. The potential audience was vast: by the end of 1996, according to Jupiter Communications, a New York-based research-and-consulting firm, more than 15 million North American households had some form of online access. In the year 2000, the projection is that North America will have 38* million online households—more than one third of all households, most of them affluent.

6   But a funny thing happened on the way to Infotopia. The costs of electronic publication proved higher than expected, and the receipts turned out to be negligible. The Web is awash in information, much of it created by small start-up companies, and the competition has made it difficult for traditional media companies to charge for access to their Web sites. Besides, many of the early Internet users were devout believers in the proposition that all information should be free, and that attitude still lingers. The result is that the Web is a marketplace of fierce price resistance. Last September The Wall Street Journal, for example, began charging a subscription fee of $49 a year for its online edition ($29 for subscribers to the printed newspaper) and saw a dramatic decline in its Web readership. Even Slate, Microsoft's political Webzine, abandoned its plans to sell subscriptions.

7   At the same time, advertising has failed to take up the slack. Despite the attractive demographics of online households, the Web is not yet a mass medium. Advertisers are suspicious of the Web, too, because its interactive qualities make it easy for consumers simply to bypass an ad. They are also uncomfortable with audience measurements in the new medium; the industry has yet no standard comparable to those used in print, radio and television. As reality sets in, many Web-site operators are scaling back expectations. Microsoft officials admitted recently that they expect to lose millions of dollars a year on MSNBC for at least the next four years.

8   But on another front, Web technology fosters commerce. The same interactive function that makes advertisers nervous leads to a new kind of marketing—the transactional advertisement. An example of this is a Web-based service called Auto-By-Tel, which allows prospective buyers to search for information about car models that match their preferences, then sends their names to the appropriate dealers near them. The dealers pay for the service and in return get qualified leads that would cost them far more to acquire through conventional means. In the case of small consumer goods that customers don't feel they need to inspect before purchase, the software can actually complete the sale for home delivery. The amazon.com Web site has created a successful market niche by selling books. The model is essentially mail-order retailing.

9   With the development of secure transmissions of credit information—Visa and MasterCard are jointly testing a system scheduled for introduction by early 1998—transactions will play an increasingly large part in Internet activity. The Web is particularly effective at selling services backed by research, such as discount stock trading, an area with several successful sites already, including e.Schwab and a Web-only company called E*Trade. Financial services generally lend themselves to Web marketing, as do travel services, because the transactions can be supported by extensive computer databases of useful information. And every month sees the introduction of new software to automate transactions.

10 The latest adaptation of Web technology is for business-to-business marketing. This is done through "extranets," extensions of a company's private, internal network (or intranet) to corporate customers and suppliers. Extranets are a hot subject for companies like Netscape, the creator of the most widely used Web browser, and America Online, the country's largest commercial online service. An example of an apparently successful extranet is the one built by General Electric to sell machine and appliance parts to its customers; GE was expecting 1996 online sales of about $1 billion.

11 With such a flurry of activity, it's easy to imagine that commerce will soon drown information on the Internet. That won't necessarily happen, but almost certainly the Web will contain a rising tide of information subsidized in some way by commercial activity. Advertising has always underwritten the largest share of most media companies' costs. The question is whether Web advertising will ever reach a volume that can support large investments in reporting news, building deep information databases and creating new entertainment. Many analysts believe the critical mass to be about 30 million households, which suggests that the Web will become a true mass medium about the year 2000. Nicholas Negroponte, founder of the cutting-edge MIT Media Lab and author of "Being Digital," argues that the Web by its very nature may be too personalized ever to be a mass medium, but he believes that commerce may flourish there anyway, with advertising targeted to small market niches or even individual customers.

12 This blurring of the line between "editorial" content and advertising is precisely what worries most traditional publishers. The Web is already flooded with "information" sites that are centers of partisan pleading and crackpot theories masquerading as facts. In an environment without many of the traditional markers of high-quality content, how is the hapless consumer to tell the difference? The answer is, once again, a commercial one: brand names. As the Web expands and the number of "publishers" grows, brand names that are known and trusted will become progressively more important. Everything on the Web is ultimately about trust, says Negroponte. "We trust brands, rightly or wrongly. We trust friends . . . And we trust our own experience, which may be the most faulty of the lot. I have these same three choices in cyberspace."

13 In the dog years to come, cyberspace will continue its transformations. We can expect a rash of new "non-PC devices," such as Internet TVs and Internet telephones. The Internet TV in particular is a promising device, if only because it would benefit from the growing market in Web-based videogames—likely to be a hot area itself by the year 2000, as new video-compression techniques increase the realism of on-line game-playing. Commerce, too, will continue to thrive, especially in the area of consumer purchases, which will benefit from the development of electronic cash and "smart" cards that allow for "micropayments" of as little as 25 cents. We can also expect that commercial activities will enable further inroads into personal privacy, as customers willingly put more and more of their spending and consumption patterns into databases. Is that a troubling prospect? It depends on our confidence in new encryption techniques, and on Web sites' sincerity about deploying them. As Negroponte says, everything on the Web is ultimately about trust.

EXPLORING THE TEXT

1. McGrath states that the Internet "is being transformed . . . into something closer to a marketplace" (paragraph 3). From your own experience with the World Wide Web, do you agree or disagree with this statement?

2. What are the implications of McGrath's statement that many Web sites cannot compete with their paper counterparts? Why not? Do you agree with his assessment?

3. Evaluate McGrath's writing style in this article. Can you tell his position from his writing?

4. McGrath draws parallels between the "inventors" of the Internet and the inventors of the telephone and radio. He specifically notes that all three were ultimately used for things other than their original purpose. How does this parallel support his argument?

5. According to McGrath, the Web "fosters commerce." Would you buy something from a Web site? Why or why not? Consider what issues consumers face when purchasing something from the Web.

6. Consider the original reason why the World Wide Web was designed. How do you think its "inventors" feel about how the role of the Web has changed in the last decade? What does this tell us about inventing new products?

7. McGrath notes that by the year 2000, "North America will have 38 million online households . . . most of them affluent" (paragraph 5). What implications does this fact have for those households that do not fall under the "affluent" category? How might this influence commerce on the Web?

8. Many advocates of Web marketing point out that every business, from small T-shirt silk-screening operations to large corporations such as Kelloggs, can advertise there. The Web makes advertising affordable to everyone. In effect, it serves as an advertising equalizer. But is this true? Discuss the difference between the sites of big corporations and those of small businesses.

WRITING ASSIGNMENTS

1. One important point of McGrath's essay is that consumers are vulnerable to the Web sites of disreputable companies because it is so easy to masquerade as a legitimate site on the Web. Why is this so? Drawing from your own experiences with printed and electronic media, write an essay on the assumptions we have regarding technology. How does print impact our expectations and assumptions about a product? What assumptions might we make when viewing a technically impressive Web site?

2. McGrath points out that the Web primarily is accessed by "affluent" households. Is the Web elitist? Write an essay examining the implications of a medium accessible to only a portion of society.

3. Who are the target audiences of the Web? Consider what type of product is best sold on the Web and who would want to buy something from a Web site. How do audience and product impact the marketplace of the Web?
4. What role, if any, do you think commerce plays in the promotion of inventions? How have advertising and marketing influenced radio, telephone, and the Internet? Can such inventions survive without the support of advertising?
5. Write an essay on how you feel the Web should be used and why.

GROUP PROJECTS ───────────────────────────────

1. With your group, create a product or service you would like to promote. If you were to design your own Web page for marketing purposes, what would you include? Consider what makes one Web site more marketable than another. How would you make yours stand out? Drawing from Mc-Grath's article, what factors do you think you should consider when developing a Web page?
2. Locate some business Web sites on the Internet and print out their Web pages. Discuss with your group what elements you believe work well in a marketing-oriented Web page and what don't work. Compile a list of do's and don'ts and share it with the class.
3. As a group identify several advertisements from a magazine that you feel work especially well from a marketing standpoint. Try to find their electronic equivalents on the Web. How do the two compare? Do you think one medium has an advantage over the other? If you cannot find an equivalent, discuss why not. Present your conclusions to the class.

Cyberspace: If You Don't Love It, Leave It
Esther Dyson

The debate over governmental regulation of the Internet remains unsolved. The dazzling appeal of the World Wide Web can mask the more sordid realities of child pornography and racial propaganda. The question at hand is who ultimately decides what can appear on the Internet. While some people push for government legislation, others fervently defend the Internet's right of free speech. In the following piece, Esther Dyson defends the autonomy of cyberspace, maintaining that the Internet allows everyone, no matter what their social, economic, ethnic, or sexual background, a place where they can find a supportive network of people with common interests. Cyberspace, she contends, has room for everyone.

Dyson is chairwoman of the Electronic Frontier Foundation, which has challenged the federal Communications Decency Act, a law that would hold Internet providers liable if customers gain access to indecent material. Dyson has written on Internet issues for *New York Times* and the computer magazine *Wired*. The following essay first appeared in the *New York Times* in 1995.

1 Something in the American psyche loves new frontiers. We hanker after wide-open spaces; we like to explore; we like to make rules instead of follow them. But in this age of political correctness and other intrusions on our national cult of independence, it's hard to find a place where you can go and be yourself without worrying about the neighbors.

2 There is such a place: cyberspace. Lost in the furor over porn on the Net is the exhilarating sense of freedom that this new frontier once promised—and still does in some quarters. Formerly a playground for computer nerds and techies, cyberspace now embraces every conceivable constituency: schoolchildren, flirtatious singles, Hungarian-Americans, accountants—along with pederasts and porn fans. Can they all get along? Or will our fear of kids surfing for cyberporn behind their bedroom doors provoke a crackdown?

3 The first order of business is to grasp what cyberspace *is*. It might help to leave behind metaphors of highways and frontiers and to think instead of real estate. Real estate, remember, is an intellectual, legal, artificial environment constructed *on top of* land. Real estate recognizes the difference between parkland and shopping mall, between red-light zone and school district, between church, state and drugstore.

4 In the same way, you could think of cyberspace as a giant and unbounded world of virtual real estate. Some property is privately owned and rented out; other property is common land; some places are suitable for children, and others are best avoided by all but the kinkiest citizens. Unfortunately, it's those places that are now capturing the popular imagination: places that offer bomb-making instructions, pornography, advice on how to procure stolen credit cards. They make cyberspace sound like a nasty place. Good citizens jump to a conclusion: better regulate it. . . .

5 Regardless of how many laws or lawsuits are launched, regulation won't work.

6 Aside from being unconstitutional, using censorship to counter indecency and other troubling "speech" fundamentally misinterprets the nature of cyberspace. Cyberspace isn't a frontier where wicked people can grab unsuspecting children, nor is it a giant television system that can beam offensive messages at unwilling viewers. In this kind of real estate, users have to *choose* where they visit, what they see, what they do. It's optional, and it's much easier to bypass a place on the Net than it is to avoid walking past an unsavory block of stores on the way to your local 7-11.

7 Put plainly, cyberspace is a voluntary destination—in reality, many destinations. You don't just get "onto the Net"; you have to go someplace in particular. That means that people can choose where to go and what to see. Yes, community standards should be enforced, but those standards should be set by cyberspace communities themselves, not by the courts or by politicians in Washington. What we need isn't Government control over all these electronic communities: We need self-rule.

8 What makes cyberspace so alluring is precisely the way in which it's *different* from shopping malls, television, highways and other terrestrial jurisdictions. But let's define the territory:

9   First, there are private e-mail conversations, akin to the conversations you have over the telephone or voice mail. These are private and consensual and require no regulation at all.

10   Second, there are information and entertainment services, where people can download anything from legal texts and lists of "great new restaurants" to game software or dirty pictures. These places are like bookstores, malls and movie houses—places where you go to buy something. The customer needs to request an item or sign up for a subscription; stuff (especially pornography) is not sent out to people who don't ask for it. Some of these services are free or included as part of a broad service like Compuserve or America Online; others charge and may bill their customers directly.

11   Third, there are "real" communities—groups of people who communicate among themselves. In real-estate terms, they're like bars or restaurants or bath-houses. Each active participant contributes to a general conversation, generally through posted messages. Other participants may simply listen or watch. Some are supervised by a moderator; others are more like bulletin boards—anyone is free to post anything. Many of these services started out unmoderated but are now impos-ing rules to keep out unwanted advertising, extraneous discussions or increasingly rude participants. Without a moderator, the decibel level often gets too high.

12   Ultimately, it's the rules that determine the success of such places. Some of the rules are determined by the supplier of content; some of the rules concern prices and membership fees. The rules may be simple: "Only high-quality content about oil-industry liability and pollution legislation: $120 an hour." Or: "This forum is un-moderated, and restricted to information about copyright issues. People who insist on posting advertising or unrelated material will be asked to desist (and may eventu-ally be barred)." Or: "Only children 8 to 12, on school-related topics and only clean words. The moderator will decide what's acceptable."

13   Cyberspace communities evolve just the way terrestrial communities do: Peo-ple with like-minded interests band together. Every cyberspace community has its own character. Overall, the communities on Compuserve tend to be more techy or professional; those on America Online, affluent young singles; Prodigy, family ori-ented. Then there are independents like Echo, a hip, downtown New York service, or Women's Wire, targeted to women who want to avoid the male culture prevalent elsewhere on the Net. There's SurfWatch, a new program allowing access only to locations deemed suitable for children. On the Internet itself, there are lots of pas-sionate noncommercial discussion groups on topics ranging from Hungarian politics (Hungary-Online) to copyright law.

14   And yes, there are also porn-oriented services, where people share dirty pictures and communicate with one another about all kinds of practices, often anonymously. Whether these services encourage the fantasies they depict is subject to debate—the same debate that has raged about pornography in other media. But the point is that no one is forcing this stuff on anybody.

15   What's unique about cyberspace is that it liberates us from the tyranny of gov-ernment, where everyone lives by the rule of the majority. In a democracy, minority groups and minority preferences tend to get squeezed out, whether they are minori-

ties of race and culture or minorities of individual taste. Cyberspace allows communities of any size and kind to flourish; in cyberspace, communities are chosen by the users, not forced on them by accidents of geography. This freedom gives the rules that preside in cyberspace a moral authority that rules in terrestrial environments don't have. Most people are stuck in the country of their birth, but if you don't like the rules of a cyberspace community, you can just sign off. Love it or leave it. Likewise, if parents don't like the rules of a given cyberspace community, they can restrict their children's access to it.

16 What's likely to happen in cyberspace is the formation of new communities, free of the constraints that cause conflict on earth. Instead of a global village, which is a nice dream but impossible to manage, we'll have invented another world of self-contained communities that cater to their own members' inclinations without interfering with anyone else's. The possibility of a real market-style evolution of governance is at hand. In cyberspace, we'll be able to test and evolve rules governing what needs to be governed—intellectual property, content and access control, rules about privacy and free speech. Some communities will allow anyone in; others will restrict access to members who qualify on one basis or another. Those communities that prove self-sustaining will prosper (and perhaps grow and split into subsets with ever-more-particular interests and identities). Those that can't survive—either because people lose interest or get scared off—will simply wither away.

17 In the near future, explorers in cyberspace will need to get better at defining and identifying their communities. They will need to put in place—and accept—their own local governments, just as the owners of expensive real estate often prefer to have their own security guards rather than call in the police. But they will rarely need help from any terrestrial government.

18 Of course, terrestrial governments may not agree. What to do, for instance, about pornography? The answer is labeling—not banning—questionable material. In order to avoid censorship and lower the political temperature, it makes sense for cyberspace participants themselves to agree on a scheme for questionable items, so that people or automatic filters can avoid them. In other words, posting pornography in "alt.sex.bestiality" would be O.K.; it's easy enough for software manufacturers to build an automatic filter that would prevent you—or your child—from ever seeing that item on a menu. (It's as if all the items were wrapped, with labels on the wrapper.) Someone who posted the same material under the title "Kid-Fun" could be sued for mislabeling.

19 Without a lot of fanfare, private enterprises and local groups are already producing a variety of labeling and ranking services, along with kid-oriented sites like Kidlink, EdWeb and Kids' Space. People differ in their tastes and values and can find services or reviewers on the Net that suit them in the same way they select books and magazines. Or they can wander freely if they prefer, making up their own itinerary.

20 In the end, our society needs to grow up. Growing up means understanding that there are no perfect answers, no all-purpose solutions, no government-sanctioned safe havens. We haven't created a perfect society on earth and we won't

have one in cyberspace either. But at least we can have individual choice—and individual responsibility.

EXPLORING THE TEXT

1. How does Dyson compare American ideals of frontiers and freedom to the Internet? What appeal does she feel the Internet holds for Americans? Do you agree?
2. Instead of using the traditional analogy of the Internet as a "superhighway," Dyson compares it to real estate. How does this analogy help support her argument?
3. Dyson states that "regardless of how many laws or lawsuits are launched, regulation won't work" (paragraph 5). On what does she base this determination? Do you agree or disagree with her assessment?
4. In paragraph 18, Dyson states that proper labeling of Internet sites would prevent inadvertent access to certain Internet locations. She notes that the deliberate mislabeling of a site should be punishable. Do you agree with her solution? How does this solution connect with the rest of her argument?
5. Dyson asserts that cyberspace is a place that people choose to visit and that accessing Web sites is a voluntary and conscious action. Discuss the implications of this statement while considering the recent appeals of some groups for governmental regulation of the Internet.
6. Review Dyson's last paragraph. How do her closing statements affect her essay? Do you feel that her conclusion works with the overall theme of her essay?

WRITING ASSIGNMENTS

1. Dyson argues that parents should be responsible for what their children access on the Internet. As we have seen in previous chapters, this argument has been used for other forms of media, such as television programming and music. Write an essay on the role and responsibilities of parents for what their children see and hear.
2. Write an essay on how you feel about legislation controlling the content of the Internet. What are the pros and cons of legislative control? What impact would governmental restriction have on the Internet? Conversely, what impact might the lack of restriction have on the Internet and its users?
3. Several years ago, America Online attempted to protect its customers from "offensive" Internet sites by restricting access to sites with words the company deemed inappropriate. They included the word *breast* in their list of offensive words. They soon received hundreds of angry letters and calls

from women unable to access sites related to breast cancer, examinations, and feeding. Relate this incident to Dyson's concern with legislation. How do we balance issues of protection with issues of access?

GROUP PROJECTS

1. In the essay, Dyson parallels the cybersapce community to a real terrestrial community. With your group, outline the issues a terrestrial community faces. Are they the same issues that exist in a cybercommunity? Discuss their similarities and differences. What issues are unique to each?
2. Split your group in half. Choose half of the group to argue in favor of regulation and the other half to support free speech on the Internet. Each side should discuss their position amongst themselves, identifying issues and information to support their side of the argument. Then, discuss "your side" with the rest of the group. Remember that your goal is to try to persuade the other side by highlighting issues they might not have considered before.
3. Dyson mentions that parents must be responsible for their children's access to the Internet. Can you really control what children do all of the time? How would you prevent your children from accessing things you didn't want them to access on the Internet? Do you think it is an issue at all?

The Haves and the Have-Nots
LynNell Hancock

As we approach the year 2000, we move as a world firmly grounded in electronic communication. Everything from banking to pumping gas to grocery check out is computerized, and computer knowledge and skill are critical if students hope to successfully compete in the job market of the next century. While many schools are hooked up to the Internet, many still are not. In the following piece, LynNell Hancock points out that this discrepancy only serves to further widen the divide between those who have and those who have not. As suburban schools advance into the computerized world of the future, many urban schools will be left behind.

Hancock is an assistant professor of journalism at Columbia University who specializes in issues facing public education. This article first appeared in the February 1995 issue of *Newsweek.*

1   Aaron Smith is a teenager on the techno track. In America's breathless race to achieve information nirvana, the senior from Issaqua, a middle-class district east of Seattle, has the hardware and hookups to run the route. Aaron and 600 of his fellow students at Liberty High School have their own electronic-mail address. They can

log on to the Internet every day, joining only about 15 percent of America's school-children who can now forage on their own for documents in European libraries or chat with experts around the world. At home, the 18-year-old e-mails his teachers, when he is not prowling the World Wide Web to track down snowboarding conditions on his favorite Cascade mountain passes. "We have the newest, greatest thing," Aaron says.

2   On the opposite coast, in Boston's South End, Marilee Colon scoots a mouse along a grimy Apple pad, playing a Kid Pix game on an old black-and-white terminal. It's Wednesday at a neighborhood center, Marilee's only chance to poke around on a computer. Her mom, a secretary at the center, can't afford one in their home. Marilee's public-school classroom doesn't have any either. The 10-year-old from Roxbury depends on the United South End Settlement Center and its less than state-of-the-art Macs and IBMs perched on mismatched desks. Marilee has never heard of the Internet. She is thrilled to double-click on the stick of dynamite and watch her teddy-bear creation fly off the screen. "It's fun blowing it up," says the delicate fifth grader, twisting a brown ponytail around her finger.

3   Certainly Aaron was born with a stack of statistical advantages over Marilee. He is white and middle class and lives with two working parents who both have higher degrees. Economists say the swift pace of high-tech advances will only drive a further wedge between these youngsters. To have an edge in America's job search, it used to be enough to be well educated. Now, say the experts, it's critical to be digital. Employees who are adept at technology "earn roughly 10 to 15 percent higher pay," according to Alan Krueger, chief economist for the U.S. Labor Department. Some argue that this pay gap has less to do with technology than with industries' efforts to streamline their work forces during the recession. . . . Still, nearly every American business from Wall Street to McDonald's requires some computer knowledge. Taco Bell is modeling its cash registers after Nintendo controls, according to Rosabeth Moss Kanter. The "haves," says the Harvard Business School professor, will be able to communicate around the globe. The "have-nots" will be consigned to the "rural backwater of the information society."

4   Like it or not, America is a land of inequities. And technology, despite its potential to level the social landscape, is not yet blind to race, wealth and age. The richer the family, the more likely it is to own and use a computer, according to 1993 census data. White families are three times as likely as blacks or Hispanics to have computers at home. Seventy-four percent of Americans making more than $75,000 own at least one terminal, but not even one third of all Americans own computers. A small fraction—only about 7 percent—of students' families subscribe to online services that transform the plastic terminal into a telecommunications port.

5   At least in public schools, the computer gap is closing. More than half the students have some kind of computer, even if it's obsolete. But schools with the biggest concentration of poor children have the least equipment, according to Jeanne Hayes of Quality Education Data. Ten years ago schools had one computer for every 125 children, according to Hayes. Today that figure is one for 12.

6   Though the gap is slowly closing, technology is advancing so fast, and at such huge costs, that it's nearly impossible for cash-strapped municipalities to catch up.

Seattle is taking bids for one company to wire each ZIP code with fiber optics, so everyone—rich or poor—can hook up to video, audio and other multimedia services. Estimated cost: $500 million. Prosperous Montgomery County, Md., has an $81 million plan to put every classroom online. Next door, the District of Columbia public schools have the same ambitious plan but less than $1 million in the budget to accomplish it.

7   New ideas—and demands—for the schools are announced every week. The '90s populist slogan is no longer "A chicken in every pot" but "A computer on every desk." Vice President Al Gore has appealed to the telecommunications industry to cut costs and wire all schools, a task Education Secretary Richard Riley estimates will cost $10 billion. House Speaker Newt Gingrich stumbled into the discussion with a suggestion that every poor family get a laptop from Uncle Sam. Rep. Ed Markey wants a computer sitting on every school desk within 10 years. "The opportunities are enormous," Markey says.

8   Enormous, yes, but who is going to pay for them? Some successful school projects have relied heavily on the kindness of strangers. In Union City, N. J., school officials renovated the guts of a 100-year-old building five years ago, overhauling the curriculum and wiring every classroom in Christopher Columbus Middle School for high tech. Bell Atlantic provided wiring free and agreed to give each student in last year's seventh-grade class a computer to take home. Even parents, most of whom are South American immigrants, can use their children's computers to e-mail the principal in Spanish. He uses translation software and answers them electronically. The results have shown up in test scores. In a school where 80 percent of the children are poor, reading, math, attendance and writing scores are now the best in the district. "We believe that technology will improve our everyday life," says principal Bob Fazio. "And that other schools will piggyback and learn from us."

9   Still, for every Christopher Columbus, there are far more schools like Jordan High School in South-Central Los Angeles. Only 30 computers in the school's lab, most of them 12 to 15 years old, are available for Jordan's 2,000 students, many of whom live in the nearby Jordan Downs housing project. "I am teaching these kids on a system that will do them no good in the real world when they get out there," says Robert Doornbos, Jordan's computer-science instructor. "The school system has not made these kids' getting on the Information Highway a priority."

10   **Donkey Kong:** Having enough terminals to go around is one problem. But another important question is what the equipment is used for. Not much beyond rote drills and word processing, according to Linda Roberts, a technology consultant for the U.S. Department of Education. A 1992 National Assessment of Educational Progress survey found that most fourth-grade math students were using computers to play games, "like Donkey Kong." By the eighth grade, most math students weren't using them at all.

11   Many school officials think that access to the Internet could become the most effective equalizer in the educational lives of students. With a modem attached, even most ancient terminals can connect children in rural Mississippi to universities in Asia. A Department of Education report last week found that 35 percent of schools have at least one computer with a modem. But only half the schools let stu-

dents use it. Apparently administrators and teachers are hogging the Info Highway for themselves.

12   There is another gap to be considered. Not just between rich and poor, but between the young and the used-to-be-young. Of the 100 million Americans who use computers at home, school or work, nearly 60 percent are 17 or younger, according to the census. Children, for the most part, rule cyberspace, leaving the over-40 set to browse through the almanac.

13   The gap between the generations may be the most important, says MIT guru Nicholas Negroponte, author of the new book "Being Digital." Adults are the true "digitally homeless, the needy," he says. In other words, adults like Debbie Needleman, 43, an office manager at Wallpaper Warehouse in Natick, Mass., are wary of the digital age. "I really don't mind that the rest of the world passes me by as long as I can still earn a living," she says.

14   These aging choose-nots become a more serious issue when they are teachers in schools. Even if schools manage to acquire state-of-the-art equipment, there is no guarantee that trained adults will be available to understand them. This is something that tries Aaron Smith's patience. "A lot of my teachers are quite illiterate," says Aaron, the fully equipped Issaqua teenager. "You have to explain it to them real slow to make sure they understand everything." Fast or slow, Marilee Colon, Roxbury's fifth-grade computer lover, would like her chance to understand everything too.

EXPLORING THE TEXT

1. Consider the two students Hancock compares in her first two paragraphs. Are the examples parallel? How might her choice of these two students help or hinder her argument?

2. Hancock notes that according to the experts "it's critical to be digital" (paragraph 3). What does this statement mean, and is it true?

3. What impact does computer access have on the "haves" and the "have-nots"? Who are the haves and the have-nots and why is computer access so important to both groups?

4. What do you make of Negroponte's statement in paragraph 13 about the computer generation gap? Will you be able to earn a living in an office without computer knowledge?

5. Only ten years ago, if students wanted to learn about computers, they took a special computer class, taught by a computer science teacher. Now computers are popping up in classrooms of every subject, in every grade. What role should teachers play in computer education? What issues do both students and teachers face in computer education?

6. Consider the different levels of meaning of "have" and "have-not" in Hancock's essay. What does it really mean to be a have or a have-not?

7. Many advocates of the Internet maintain that it knows no race, color, creed, religion, or age. However, Hancock states that "technology . . . is not yet

blind to race, wealth and age" (paragraph 4). Why does she take this view? Do you agree with her position?

8. In paragraph 11, Hancock comments that with a modem, even old computers can link schools in areas such as rural Mississippi to universities in Asia. Why do you think she chose these two locations? How do they contribute to her argument?

WRITING ASSIGNMENTS

1. Describe the ideal computer classroom. What resources would you need to support it? What factors would you need to consider when going on-line in a classroom environment?
2. Consider your high school education. Are you a "have" or a "have-not"? What are the long-term ramifications of your "status"? Explain your answer.
3. Have you ever accessed a European library on the Internet? Would you? To what uses, if any, have you put the Internet, and what contributions do you feel it has made toward your overall education?
4. Hancock mentions several computer initiatives in her essay, but notes that few have actually been implemented. How would you propose to solve the computer inequalities between the "haves" and the "have-nots"?

GROUP PROJECTS

1. As a group, design a learning program for children on Internet basics. Identify your audience when designing your program. What should you tell them? What do you feel they need to know? How would you make your learning program interesting?
2. As a group, design a learning program for adults who are suspicious of computers. As in question 1, identify your audience when designing your program. What should you tell them? What do you feel they need to know? How would you make your learning program apply to their circumstances?
3. Your group is living and attending school in 1957. You are suddenly transported into the future and find yourselves in front of computers in the computer lab. How do you think you would react to computers and their role in the present decade? Relate your "reactions" to Hancock's point that many older adults are wary of the computers and the Internet.
4. Reminisce with your group on what it was like to be 10 years old, like Marilee Colon in the essay. If you were 10 years old again, to what use would you put computers if you had access to them? How would parents and teachers influence that use? Apply your conclusions to Hancock's essay.

Children in the Digital Age
Kathryn C. Montgomery

Few people will argue that the Internet and the World Wide Web allow students to access resources never before available in ordinary classrooms. The nature of the Web makes it an increasingly powerful tool for research and communication. Its visual appeal makes it an ideal learning device for children, encouraging them to learn and explore. On the other hand, manipulative forms of advertising targeting children on the Web may jeopardize its potential as a learning tool. Moreover, major advertising coalitions are currently lobbying Congress to ensure that advertising becomes the dominant mode of funding for on-line access and content.

In the following article, Kathryn C. Montgomery, president of the Center for Media Education, discusses the influence of the Web on children and what it may mean if advertisers assume control of online content. The key decisions made today, explains Montgomery, will determine the future of the Web and its role in American classrooms. This article appeared in the educational journal The *American Prospect.*

1   After 50 years of controversy over the impact of television on children, a new world of online media is emerging that may have even greater impact on them. Almost one million children in the United States are now using the World Wide Web, according to a research and consulting firm specializing in interactive technology, and 3.8 million have Web access—a figure that will grow rapidly in coming years. Like adults, children will increasingly be connected to a vast digital universe that transcends the family, the local community, and even the nation. Education will expand beyond the classroom and other traditional settings, as more interactive "edutainment" becomes available. New personal and portable technologies will enable children to inhabit their own separate electronic worlds.

2   The dazzling graphics and engaging interactivity of the new multimedia technologies will make them potent forces in the lives of children. If harnessed properly, the new media could enhance their drive to learn, provide them with access to a rich diversity of information and ideas, and enable them to reach across community and national borders. But there is also peril: Video game channels, virtual shopping malls, and manipulative forms of advertising targeted at children could further compound the problems in the existing media that have troubled parents, educators, and child advocates for decades.

3   We are in the mist of the formative stage of this new digital age. Government policies are being debated and enacted, marketing and programming strategies are being developed, and services for children are being designed. If we are to believe some hyperbolic visions of cyberspace, the information superhighway will be a great equalizing force that will bring unprecedented opportunity for all. Improvements in education and other benefits for children are often at the center of these visions. But history offers us cautionary lessons. In this century enthusiasts have hailed every new medium—from radio to FM to television to cable to satellites—

with claims that it would reinvigorate our culture, expand educational opportunities, and enhance the democratic process. None has lived up to these claims. In each case, powerful commercial forces have used civic values to gain support for the new medium—and then squelched the very policies necessary to serve the public good.

4   In this recent phase, powerful media companies have already poured vast amounts of money into lobbying to shape the 1996 Telecommunications Act. From the beginning, corporations were able to frame the debate. While some political leaders, such as Al Gore as a senator, compared the new information superhighway to the interstate highway system, the Clinton administration's vision quickly became a privately built and operated national information infrastructure (NII). The Telecommunications Act is designed to encourage competition by deregulating the telecommunications market. Public interest advocates, though pitifully underfinanced, were able to win only a few positive provisions for consumers. The interests of children were not central to the legislative debate, and the little attention paid to children was misdirected at indecent content on the Internet. As a result, the law ignores or inadequately addresses critical issues that will have a significant long-term effect. In the wake of the legislation, we need a new strategic understanding of what needs to be done to make the best of the new media—and to avoid the worst.

Electronic Inclusion

5 While traditional media are sometimes viewed as unnecessary diversions, digital media will soon become an integral part of daily life. Those without access to the communications system are likely to fall behind in education and be unable to compete in a highly selective job market. Yet just as access is becoming imperative, the number of children living in poverty, with little or no access to technology, is growing at an alarming rate. According to a 1994 survey, 11 percent of families with incomes of less than $20,000 have a computer, compared to 56 percent of families with incomes above $50,000. One out of ten children under the age of six lives in a home without a telephone.

6   To its credit, the Clinton administration has raised the issue of disparities between the information rich and information poor. In its 1993 Agenda for Action, the White House called for all schools, libraries, and hospitals to be connected to the national information infrastructure by the year 2000. The idea was to provide equitable access through these institutions, even if it couldn't be assured for all homes. At present, there are a handful of government programs intended to encourage innovation and pay for pilot projects, but the administration has mostly relied on private, voluntary efforts to meet this goal.

7   Some promising projects have emerged, such as California's NetDay, a one-day effort in March 1996, spearheaded by Sun Microsystems, in which volunteers across the state strung miles of wire to connect elementary and secondary schools to the Internet. Relying heavily on such voluntary efforts, however, will likely leave many communities and schools unconnected. The vast majority of public schools, particu-

larly for minority and low-income children, lack the basic technology and training to provide students access to computer networks.

8   Even if more children are able to use the new media through schools and libraries, they will still be at a disadvantage relative to children with access at home. An hour or two of computer laboratory time in school is not enough to acquire the technological competence that colleges and many jobs will require. Some argue that the costs of the equipment will go down dramatically in the next few years, making computer communications as affordable as televisions and VCRs. But monthly service charges are another barrier, and communications services that are now free or very inexpensive may become unaffordable. While some form of over-the-air television is likely to remain free, most other video services will require payment. For families in poverty, either the upfront cost of equipment or service charges may be insurmountable barriers.

9   The Telecommunications Act could have created comprehensive policies for ensuring equitable access to the national information infrastructure. But because of the conservative political climate, the federal deficit, and unprecedented lobbying expenditures and campaign contributions by the telecommunications industries, the legislation dealt very narrowly with the issue. The education and library communities were able to win a provision that requires telecommunications companies to offer less expensive connection and service charges to schools and libraries than to homes and businesses. But the Federal Communications Commission (FCC) must define what "affordable" means. In consultation with the states, the FCC is now supposed to develop a universal service policy for the new digital era that includes the provisions for schools and libraries.

A New Media Environment

10   Access isn't the only challenge; the quality of the new media culture for children also raises concern. Unlike TV, online media are dynamic and two-way. This participatory quality makes them particularly compelling to children. Such technological breakthroughs as real-time audio, real-time video, and virtual reality modeling language (which allows programmers to turn Web sites into three-dimensional environments) are transforming online media. Eventually, this interactive online world could supplant traditional television as the most powerful and influential medium in children's lives.

11   Many online services are now available that seek to challenge children by exposing them to places, people, and ideas far outside their everyday experiences. For example, Plugged In, a Web site created by a community computing center in Palo Alto, California, allows poor children to explore the Internet, produce their own art, and display it to other children around the world. . . . Another Web site, CyberKids, enables children to write and share their own stories in an online magazine. Special networks have been established to foster online communities for children. With help from a federal grant from the National Telecommunications and Information

Agency, the National Youth Center Network is addressing such problems as violent crime and unemployment by electronically linking youth centers in low-income neighborhoods.

12   These educational and civic services, however, are in danger of being overshadowed by a powerful interactive commercial culture with an unprecedented ability to capture children's attention. Marketing to children has become a multibillion dollar business. The direct spending power of children, almost all of it discretionary, has risen rapidly in recent years. In 1995, according to *Interactive Marketing News* and *Youth Markets Alert,* children under 12 spent $14 billion, teenagers another $67 billion, and together they influenced $160 billion of their parents' annual spending. As an executive for Turner Home Entertainment recently explained: "Probably for the first time in the consumer business, kids are now being recognized as a truly gigantic part of the consumer purchasing block." In the last decade, these trends triggered a proliferation of new TV networks aimed at capturing a segment of the hot children's market, including the controversial classroom news service Channel One, the highly profitable Nickelodeon cable channel, CNN's Cartoon Channel, and the Fox Children's Network.

13   With the FCC's deregulation of children's television in the mid-1980s, toy manufacturers began the wholesale creation of "kidvid" series that served as half-hour commercials for a line of licensed products—from He-Man to the Care Bears to the Transformers. Character licensing has become the driving force not only in children's television, but also in much of the rest of children's culture. Cross-promotion of licensed products through TV, movies, magazines, discount stores, and fast food restaurants has produced a proliferation of licensed characters that permeate every facet of a child's life.

14   The new online services for children are being developed in the context of this highly commercialized children's media culture. Children are a disproportionately important market for the new interactive media because they are early adopters of high-tech products. Marketers who view children as the "lucrative cyber-tot category" see the emerging media as a fertile new frontier for targeting children. As an executive from Saatchi and Saatchi, a leader in the online kids' marketing field, recently proclaimed, "There is nothing else that exists like it for advertisers to build relationships with kids."

15   Advertisers are already aggressively moving into cyberspace. A new Coalition for Advertising Supported Information and Entertainment (CASIE), led jointly by the American Association of Advertising Agencies and the Association of National Advertisers, is spearheading lobbying efforts to ensure that advertising becomes the dominant mode for funding online content and to ward off government restrictions. The coalition claims that advertiser support for online services is the only way to make information services affordable to all.

16   But the consequences of making advertising the key to universal access for children are troubling. Advertisers are not just supporting online content; they are shaping much of the virtual landscape for children. At Saatchi and Saatchi, psychologists and cultural anthropologists have perfected a variety of techniques—including play groups, art, and games—to probe children's feelings and behavior when they go on-

line. They are also studying the nature of "kids' culture" as a separate set of experiences and values from that of adults. Knowing that children often use computers alone, marketers are carefully cultivating this separateness in the design of online services that circumvent parental authority. One online children's service recently published results from a survey that asked children whom they trusted more—their parents or their computers. The majority of respondents said they put more trust in their computers.

17 According to advertising researchers, going online quickly puts children into a "flow state," that "highly pleasurable experience of total absorption in a challenging activity." This is an optimal condition for advertisers to reach children. Traditional commercials will not work online. "Anything that is perceived as an interruption of the flow state," explained a Saatchi and Saatchi executive, "whether it's artwork being downloaded as an ad that is obtrusively splattered on a screen, is going to get a negative reaction." So the solution is the seamless integration of content and advertising in "branded environments." The goal of these environments is to "get kids involved with brands"—including "brand characters, brand logos, brand jingles, and brand video."

18 Major children's advertisers have Web sites where children are encouraged to come and play for extended periods of time with such product "spokescharacters" as Ronald McDonald, Kellogg's Snap, Crackle, and Pop, and Chester Cheetah. The aim is to encourage children to develop ongoing relationships with the characters—and the products. Within days of visiting the Kellogg's Web site recently, for example, one child received unsolicited e-mail from Snap, Crackle, and Pop, urging her to return for more fun.

19 The new interactive media are being designed to compile personal profiles on each child to help in developing individually tailored advertising known as "microtargeting" or "one-to-one marketing." The sites get children to volunteer such personal data as e-mail address, street address, the identity of other family members, and purchasing behavior and preferences. Sophisticated computer software can track every move a child makes online and give marketers "clickstream data" or, in the vernacular of the business, "mouse droppings."

20 Federal regulations limit TV advertising to children, but no such rules exist in cyberspace. Marketers can pursue children with few restraints. Nothing prevents them from collecting personal information from children and selling it to third parties. The lines among advertising, entertainment, and information—already dangerously blurred in television and other media—are likely to disappear entirely in the new online environment. "What is really happening [on the Web]," explains one industry expert, "is what will ultimately happen on interactive television: the infomercialization of all programming." Adds another: "The blending of entertainment with advertising will work if packaged correctly: just look at how the toy industry has taken over production of Saturday morning cartoons."

21 Even traditionally noncommercial services are likely to be shaped by the norms of this new unregulated media environment. While PBS is prohibited from most forms of advertising on television, there are no restrictions on its use of advertising online. Children's Television Workshop, producer of such highly acclaimed non-

commercial programs as *Sesame Street* and *Ghostwriter,* has recently begun developing advertiser-supported cable and online services for children.

An Agenda for Reform

22 Although the 1996 Telecommunications Act established a broad framework for federal policy, there are still opportunities to influence the shape of the new electronic media. Three key goals should guide public and private voluntary efforts.

Ensuring Universal Access

23 Every child, regardless of income, should have access to the advanced communications technologies and services necessary for their education and full participation in society. Providing access to telecommunications can in no way be a technological quick fix for more complex social and political problems. But those problems will only intensify unless we adopt policies—and invest significant resources—to ensure access for all segments of society.

24 Political participation needs to be expanded beyond those groups that have traditionally been involved in telecommunications policy. Child advocacy, parent, health, and other constituencies need to understand what may seem to be a highly technical subject. Targeted strategic interventions at the state level could have a positive influence on local communications services. In such states as Ohio, coalitions of education, consumer, and low-income advocates have succeeded in obtaining substantial resources for community computing centers, educational technology, and training. Public interest groups need to monitor the plans of telecommunications companies to prevent "electronic redlining"—omitting low-income neighborhoods from new initiatives. Public hearings can help raise the level of the debate and create a forum for articulating a public vision for how the new telecommunications can serve children. Such organizing efforts could lay the groundwork for a national movement on behalf of children's interests in the national information infrastructure.

Developing Safeguards

25 Preventing the commercialization of online media for children may be impossible, but there is an important opportunity to influence the design of new interactive services. A report issued in late March by the Center for Media Education, the organization of which I am president, documented the emerging patterns of online advertising and marketing to children. In response, a few companies have stopped some of the most egregious practices, and industry trade associations have promised to adopt guidelines to regulate their own conduct. As past experience has shown, however, self-regulation is likely to have little impact unless there is effective government oversight and enforcement. New screening software programs, such as Net Nanny, Cyber Patrol, and SafeSurf, may enable parents to screen out certain content areas or restrict the information that children can give out, but these tools are unlikely to be sufficient. Because children are a particularly vulnerable audience, ef-

fective legal safeguards will be necessary to prevent manipulation by advertisers and to protect children and their families from invasions of privacy.

26   The Center for Media Education and Consumer Federation of America have jointly urged the Federal Trade Commission to develop guidelines for advertising to children in cyberspace. These rules would restrict the collection of personally identifiable information from children and require disclosures of data collection practices on all Web sites and online content areas directed at children. In addition, we are calling on the FTC to require clear separation between content and advertising in online services targeted at children. These rules should also apply to the interactive television services under development. Although the U.S. district court decision on June 12 restricts government regulation of indecent content on the Internet, it does not prohibit either regulation of commercial speech or government safeguards to protect online privacy.

27   The global nature of the Internet also calls for international efforts to develop standards for new media programs and services targeted at children. Since many countries already have stricter policies for protecting children than we do, international guidelines could raise the standards for children's interactive media in the United States.

Creating a Noncommercial Children's Civic Sector

28   The emerging media environment should serve children not only as consumers, but also as citizens. While a number of exciting services for children are available on the Internet, they may disappear or be overshadowed by an all-pervasive commercial culture that will capture and dominate children's attention. If, as current trends suggest, the dominant method of financing the new media is likely to be advertising, we need to assure the availability of noncommercial educational and informational services for children. Just as we have public spaces, playgrounds, and parks in our natural environment, so we should have public spaces in the electronic environment, where children will be able to play and learn without being subject to advertising, manipulation, or exploitation.

29   New models for producing and distributing noncommercial services need to be explored. For example, an alliance of nonprofits, artists, film makers, and educators might create a new children's service that combined the traditions of public television with the innovative potential of the Internet. Public and private funds might help launch a children's version of C-SPAN—"Kidspan." A consortium of government and private program suppliers from various countries might create an international children's programming service.

30   To ensure long-term survival, noncommercial programs and services need a dependable source of funds. One untapped revenue source could be the sale of broadcast spectrum, valued at as much as $70 billion. Other possibilities include the creation of a trust fund exclusively for children's services, using a combination of public and private money.

31   There is also a need for more civic-minded research to think through these issues. The telecommunications industries have enormous resources for sophisticated

economic analysis, but the public interest community has been ill-equipped to compete. New models for financing universal access and achieving other reform objectives need to be explored.

32 This is the ideal time for efforts to insure this new media system serves the needs of children. Once the new media institutions are firmly entrenched, it will be almost impossible to change them. The system is still fluid enough for those who care about the character of our culture and our children to create a rich electronic legacy for future generations.

EXPLORING THE TEXT

1. Montgomery notes that when the Telecommunications Act was shaped, little attention was given to the true interests of children. Instead, "the little attention paid to children was misdirected" (paragraph 4). Explain how she feels this attention was misdirected. On what should the law have focused?
2. Bill Clinton's 1993 "Agenda for Action" called for all schools, libraries, and hospitals to be connected to the Internet in order "to provide equitable access through these institutions" (paragraph 6). However, Montgomery asserts that institutionalized access is not enough. "Even if more children are able to use the media through schools and libraries, they will still be at a disadvantage relative to children with access at home" (paragraph 8). Is her argument valid? Do you agree or disagree with her view?
3. What is the appeal of the Internet to children?
4. Why are children an ideal target for Internet marketing schemes? What risks do children face on the Internet at the hands of advertisers and marketers?
5. Montgomery asserts that "every child, regardless of income, should have access to the advanced communications technologies" (paragraph 23). Is her expectation realistic? How can we realize such a difficult goal?
6. Why does Montgomery feel it is important to prevent the commercialization of on-line media for children?
7. Major advertising coalitions claim that the only way to make information services available to everyone is to allow for advertiser support for online services. If the coalitions are successful, what impact could such support have on the future of the Web?
8. Evaluate Montgomery's tone in the essay. How well does her tone support what is she trying to accomplish in this article?

WRITING ASSIGNMENTS

1. Whenever a new medium is introduced, "enthusiasts" promote it as a revolutionizing force in our culture. In paragraph 3 of her essay, Montgomery notes that "history offers us cautionary lessons" in regard to the revitalizing effect of new technologies. She also states that "none has lived up to these

claims." Write an essay exploring the influence of new technologies on education. What technology was available to you during your secondary education? Do you agree with Montgomery's position? Explain your view.

2. Montgomery compares the marketing agendas of children's programming on television to the emerging marketing agendas for children online. "Character licensing has become the driving force not only in children's television, but also in much of the rest of children's culture" (paragraph 13). Drawing from personal experience, discuss Montgomery's statement. How does character licensing impact children's "culture"? Try locating some children's sites on the Web. How do they apply to Montgomery's claim?

3. In paragraph 25, Montgomery notes that "past experience has shown [that] self-regulation is likely to have little impact unless there is effective government oversight and enforcement." Compare this statement to Esther Dyson's call for self-rule in her essay "Cyberspace: If You Don't Love It, Leave It."

4. In a thoughtful and well-considered essay, discuss what role you feel the Internet should play in education and why.

GROUP PROJECTS

1. Discuss ways that the marketing media targets children. In a group, make a list of the ways children can be influenced by marketing schemes. What impact do you think marketing agendas have on the self-image, psyche, and education of children?

2. With your group, brainstorm the elements that an educational Web site for children should contain. Then "design" one. Explain to the class why you chose your topic and the reasoning behind your design.

3. Based on personal experiences of group members and information from Montgomery's article, what role do you think the web will have in our lives in the year 2000 and beyond? Have your group present a report of its predictions.

4. With your group, access some children's Web sites with a marketing agenda. You can try popular cartoons, children's cereals, and trendy toys. What marketing techniques did you discover at your sites? How do you feel the sites you located would influence children?

The Digital Scapegoat
Bill Machrone

As the Internet mainstreams into American culture it seems we hear more and more about the dangers lurking there. Most people agree that our nation should ensure Internet access to all schools and libraries, a fact backed by Clinton's computer initiative. The ability to communicate around the world and gather information is a vital component of education. However, television coverage increasingly reports stories of how the Internet is a source of danger and iniquity. We hear very little coverage of the positive aspects of the Internet anymore. Why the discrepancy? Bill Machrone, an editor of *PC Magazine,* conjectures that the negative coverage stems from television's fear that the Internet is muscling in on its territory. This editorial appeared in the April 1997 issue of *PC Magazine.*

1   I'm not a big TV watcher, but I do keep an eye on the evening news programs and CNN Headline News, just so I know what's going on in the world. Sometimes I like the coverage even less than what's being covered. Within the last couple of weeks, I've watched at least half a dozen stories or special reports that focused on the Internet. Each began with a reporter at a crime scene or other telegenic locale. Jane Perky or Harry Hairslick would intone the reports, warning viewers of the evil influences lurking just beyond their keyboards.

2   The following excerpts aren't verbatim, but they're pretty darn close:

3   *Pornography is on the rise, much to the consternation of public officials. They cite the Internet as a major source and distribution medium. . . .*

4   *The FBI recorded nearly 2,000 bombings in 1995, which injured or killed 594 people. Bombing is on the rise, as more people vent their frustrations and express extremist points of view through violent means. It's easier than ever to learn how to make a bomb. On the Internet you can find. . . .*

5   *Jane Doe was the victim of a stalker. It started innocently enough, with an exchange of e-mail and visits to a chat room in cyberspace. Then, through the Internet, the man who called himself Loki. . . .*

6   *Runaway children know no social or economic level. And their numbers are rising rapidly. In case after case, children cite someone they met in a chat room on the Internet as an influence. . . .*

7   I really don't have much of a temper, but stories like these put me over the top. The last one caused me to start yelling at the TV., "The Internet! The Internet! The Internet!" My kids backed slowly out of the room with that worried/amused expression that meant old Dad had finally lost it, but they half feared I was going to start shooting at the set.

8   Stalkers, pedophiles, bombers, and pornographers are real. But when's the last time you saw a TV crew reporting from the parking lot of the adult bookstore? Or excoriating a newspaper for those transparent classified ads for "young models"? My buddies and I made some nasty, noisy concoctions from the classic guerrilla chemistry book, *Fortunes in Formulas.* Where was the anchorperson warning the public that this tome was a threat to society?

9   I don't see scare stories like the above in any other medium. Newspapers and general-interest magazines give the Web balanced coverage. Common sense tells us that if there's a medium, some people will figure out a way to exploit it or the people who use it. The public needs to know as much about the dangers of singles bars, classified ads, confidence games, and pyramid schemes as they hear about the Web's supposed dangers. Instead, we get this incredibly lopsided coverage. Here are a few theories on why this may be so.

10   1. TV can't cover the Internet. Web sites look dumb and static on television. On-line chatting looks moronic. So the only way to build in some excitement is to focus on negative stories.

11   2. TV subconsciously fears the Internet as a rival medium and tries to inculcate a sense in its audience that TV is the watchdog medium, there to protect an unsuspecting public. "Count on us to keep you informed," they're implying, "of the goings-on in this unruly, threatening new medium." Several recent surveys confirm that Web surfing time is coming out of TV's hide, so their fears are genuine.

12   3. Television excels at making people feel that the stars of its shows, especially the sitcoms and late-night shows, are your friends and peers. It also presents lowlifes extraordinarily well. Any time you're feeling bad about yourself, take a gander at the creeps on the afternoon talk shows or the manufactured meanies in the soap operas. Once you've tired of making your audience feel superior to people meaner and dumber than themselves, the only frontier left is to make them fearful of people smarter than themselves. You must be some kind of smart guy to use a computer and all that Internet stuff, and the leap from there to evil genius is a short one.

13   4. TV will always seek the man-bites-dog story, and there are more interesting and offbeat things going on at the forefront of technology than in the usual haunts. A "dark side" hook makes the story all the more interesting.

14   Perhaps I'm hard on television, but such a ubiquitous, influential medium must adhere to the highest standards. It must go beyond sensationalism and the story of the moment into balanced, informed reporting. We're not there yet.

EXPLORING THE TEXT

1. Consider Machrone's tone in this essay. How does he use humor to express his point? After completing the essay what message is left with his readers.

2. Machrone asserts that newspapers and magazines generally give more balanced coverage, while television zeroes in on only negative aspects of the Internet. What real stories have you heard recently that dealt with the Internet? Where did you hear them and how were they covered?

3. Review Machrone's theories as to why television provides such "lopsided coverage" of the Internet. Do his theories make sense?

4. Machrone makes some serious allegations against television and its viewers in his third "theory" in paragraph 12. Do you think he is right?

5. If, as Machrone claims, television's duty is to report balanced and unbiased information, is it living up to the job? Why or why not? What factors control television content? What other agendas must television deal with?

6. Machrone points out that television "will always seek the man-bites-dog story" (paragraph 13). What does he mean by this statement? How does it apply to television's coverage of the Internet?

WRITING ASSIGNMENTS

1. Select a negative story about the Internet that was covered on television. Locate reports on the story in newspapers, journals, and magazines. Was the story covered differently in the other mediums?
2. Machrone uses humor and well-considered logic to present his ideas. Identify something that upset you. In a short editorial, apply the elements of humor and logic to present your feelings on that subject.
3. Consider the ways the Internet has influenced your life. Write an essay on the positive and negative aspects of the Internet as it applies to your own personal experience.

GROUP PROJECTS

1. Locate some controversial Web sites. Discuss with your group how easy or difficult it was to locate your controversial site, and why you found it offensive. With your group, compile a list of subjects that may be considered offensive when viewed on the Web. Remember to identify the audiences who may find the site offensive and explain why.
2. Pretend your group operates a network television news program. Your job is to balance the negative coverage of the Internet with positive stories. What stories would you report? Write a three- to four-sentence blurb about each story and then "broadcast" to the class.

The American family is always in a state of change. How we perceive the very concept of *family* is based largely on where we come from and what values we share. We have a tendency to base our views on traditional constructs—models that are generations old. As a result, sociologists tell us, our vision of family is not based on realistic examples but on media archetypes and political ideals.

Yet the traditional family is obviously changing. Stepfamilies, same-sex relationships, single-parent households, and extended families with several generations living in one home—these all force us to redefine or at least reexamine our traditional definition of family. For example, divorce is a widely accepted reality of life and is no longer viewed a deviation from the norm. Nearly half of all marriages end in divorce court. Times have changed, and so have our attitudes. And as attitudes change, so do our expectations and perceptions.

In the first essay, "Oh, Those Family Values," Barbara Ehrenreich presents a rather nontraditional attitude concerning family life. In fact, she questions our widely held belief that the traditional family is the ideal living arrangement. She notes that women and children are more likely to suffer from violence in their own homes at the hands of a family member than out on the streets. Despite various campaigns for "family values," she argues that the family is a dangerous placed to be!

Yet we still desire a stable home life. For many parents and children, this stability is found the second time around—after divorce and remarriage. New families form, complete with stepsiblings and several sets of grandparents. In the article "Relatively Speaking," Jan Borst discusses our need to redefine our concept of family to accommodate these "grafted family tree[s]." We must work with new definitions, because divorced relationships will continue to be a reality for many families.

"Close to half of all children in the United States will experience divorce before they reach age 18." So says Barbara Dafoe Whitehead in her essay "Rethinking Divorce," where she reviews our changing attitudes. She argues that we have moved from a society that encouraged couples to stay together, putting children's needs first, to a society that views parental happiness as the priority. Adults keep trying for that ideal relationship, regardless of how divorce may impact children.

Perhaps we keep striving for an ideal that we cannot possibly achieve—when we base our expectations of family on old television models such as *Ozzie and Harriet* and *Leave It to Beaver,* we struggle toward a largely impossible goal. Rosalind C. Barnett and Caryl Rivers discuss the "Nostalgia Trap" and the toll it is taking on the current generation. Barnett and Rivers note that not only is this nostalgia obsolete, it can also be dangerous. Instead of pointing fingers, Barnett and Rivers urge society to change their attitudes to keep up with our changing times.

The practice of placing blame is further examined by Stephanie Coontz in "Single Mothers: A Menace to Society?" Single mothers, notes Coontz, have become a scapegoat for our social problems. Unfortunately, women have had to bear much of the brunt of this finger pointing. Coontz, like Barnett and Rivers, comments that we must stop looking to a lost, irretrievable, and largely media-constructed past if we are to succeed in the future.

Just as single mothers face social scrutiny, so does the "institution" of black fatherhood. Harvard Professor Cornel West addresses the difficulties faced in black paternity, as black fathers deal with inequality, racism, and social pressure. Facing down the stereotypes accompanying black fatherhood takes a certain courage as fathers try to balance injustice and instill a sense of pride in their children as they develop their social identity.

The two oppositional pieces that close this chapter focus on another challenge to the traditional model of family: gay marriage. The issue has been hotly argued for the last few years, resulting in many states banning same-sex marriages. A few states have since moved to veto the bans as discriminatory and divisive. However, the majority of American states maintain the ban arguing that it has nothing to do with discrimination, that it's simply about protection of a tradition. The debate opens with the defense presented by Andrew Sullivan. In "Let Gays Marry," Sullivan says that marriage should be a bond between two loving adults, regardless of gender. Taking the opposing view is William Bennett who in "Leave Marriage Alone" defends the sanctity of marriage as an expression of love and commitment between a man and a woman—the foundation of traditional family.

Oh, Those Family Values
Barbara Ehrenreich

In the essay below, social critic Barbara Ehrenreich examines the split personality that the ideal "family" has developed during the last decade of the twentieth century, especially in public discourse. On the one hand, politicians, news media, and public spokespeople use the term to invoke a complex of warm, fuzzy, sacred cow feelings about the institution of family. On the other hand, a number of high-profile news stories—perhaps reflecting a more accurate picture of how families really behave—show that the first image might be a dangerous illusion.

Ehrenreich is a widely respected author who writes witty analyses of social and feminist issues. She has worked as a contributing editor at *Ms.* magazine and also writes a column for *Time.* Her essays have appeared in such magazines as *Mother Jones, Nation,* and the *New York Times Sunday Magazine.* Ehrenreich is the author of *Fear of Falling: The Inner Life of the Middle Class* (1989), *The Worst Years of Our Lives: Irreverent Notes from a Decade of Greed* (1990), and *Kipper's Game* (1994), her first novel. Her most recent book is *Blood Rites* (1997), an investigation into the origins of war. The following article appeared in *Time* magazine in 1994.

1   A disturbing subtext runs through our recent media fixations. Parents abuse sons—allegedly at least, in the Menendez case—who in turn rise up and kill them. A husband torments a wife, who retaliates with a kitchen knife. Love turns into obsession,

between the Simpsons anyway, and then perhaps into murderous rage: the family, in other words, becomes personal hell.

2   This accounts for at least part of our fascination with the Bobbitts and the Simpsons and the rest of them. We live in a culture that fetishizes the family as the ideal unit of human community, the perfect container for our lusts and loves. Politicians of both parties are aggressively "pro-family," even abortion-rights bumper stickers proudly link "pro-family" and "pro-choice." Only with the occasional celebrity crime do we allow ourselves to think the nearly unthinkable: that the family may not be the ideal and perfect living arrangement after all—that it can be a nest of pathology and a cradle of gruesome violence.

3   It's a scary thought, because the family is at the same time our "haven in a heartless world." Theoretically, and sometimes actually, the family nurtures warm, loving feelings, uncontaminated by greed or power hunger. Within the family, and often only within the family, individuals are loved "for themselves," whether or not they are infirm, incontinent, infantile or eccentric. The strong (adults and especially males) lie down peaceably with the small and weak.

4   But consider the matter of wife battery. We managed to dodge it in the Bobbitt case and downplay it as a force in Tonya Harding's life. Thanks to O. J., though, we're caught up now in a mass consciousness-raising session, grimly absorbing the fact that in some areas domestic violence sends as many women to emergency rooms as any other form of illness, injury or assault.

5   Still, we shrink from the obvious inference: for a woman, home is, statistically speaking, the most dangerous place to be. Her worst enemies and potential killers are not strangers but lovers, husbands and those who claimed to love her once. Similarly, for every child like Polly Klaas who is killed by a deranged criminal on parole, dozens are abused and murdered by their own relatives. Home is all too often where the small and weak fear to lie down and shut their eyes.

6   At some deep, queasy, Freudian level, we all know this. Even in the ostensibly "functional," nonviolent family, where no one is killed or maimed, feelings are routinely bruised and often twisted out of shape. There is the slap or put-down that violates a child's shaky sense of self, the cold, distracted stare that drives a spouse to tears, the little digs and rivalries. At best, the family teaches the finest things human beings can learn from one another—generosity and love. But it is also, all too often, where we learn nasty things like hate and rage and shame.

7   Americans act out their ambivalence about the family without ever owning up to it. Millions adhere to creeds that are militantly "pro-family." But at the same time millions flock to therapy groups that offer to heal the "inner child" from damage inflicted by family life. Legions of women band together to revive the self-esteem they lost in supposedly loving relationships and to learn to love a little less. We are all, it is often said, "in recovery." And from what? Our families, in most cases.

8   There is a long and honorable tradition of "anti-family" thought. The French philosopher Charles Fourier taught that the family was a barrier to human progress; early feminists saw a degrading parallel between marriage and prostitution. More recently, the renowned British anthropologist Edmund Leach stated that "far from be-

ing the basis of the good society, the family, with its narrow privacy and tawdry secrets, is the course of all discontents."

9   Communes proved harder to sustain than plain old couples, and the conservatism of the '80s crushed the last vestiges of life-style experimentation. Today even gays and lesbians are eager to get married and take up family life. Feminists have learned to couch their concerns as "family issues," and public figures would sooner advocate free cocaine on demand than criticize the family. Hence our unseemly interest in O.J. and Erik, Lyle and Lorena: they allow us, however gingerly, to break the silence on the hellish side of family life.

10   But the discussion needs to become a lot more open and forthright. We may be stuck with the family—at least until someone invents a sustainable alternative—but the family, with its deep, impacted tensions and longings, can hardly be expected to be the moral foundation of everything else. In fact, many families could use a lot more outside interference in the form of counseling and policing, and some are so dangerously dysfunctional that they ought to be encouraged to disband right away. Even healthy families need outside sources of moral guidance to keep the internal tensions from imploding—and this means, at the very least, a public philosophy of gender equality and concern for child welfare. When, instead, the larger culture aggrandizes wife beaters, degrades women or nods approvingly at child slappers, the family gets a little more dangerous for everyone, and so, inevitably, does the larger world.

EXPLORING THE TEXT

1. The thesis sentence for Ehrenreich's article is the second half of her last sentence in paragraph 2. In this sentence, she uses a vivid phrase: "a nest of pathology and a cradle of gruesome violence." How many literary devices can you identify in this phrase?

2. What effect do the literary devices you were able to find in the thesis have on Ehrenreich's article? What tone do they establish at the beginning of the work? How else does Ehrenreich reinforce this tone throughout the article?

3. What examples of high-profile cases does the author use to support her thesis that family is less than an ideal, nurturing place? What do you recall of these cases?

4. Does Ehrenreich's argument rely more on statistical information and fact to support her thesis or is it an emotional appeal? In your opinion, is her approach successful?

5. Are there any local or national cases you can name that have helped to undermine a cherished image or institution? Since such nationally reported cases are by definition unusual, how does one case have the power to create such powerful doubts?

6. Before you read this article, what connotations came to your mind when the word *family* was used? Did you think of family as a good thing? Or were you more likely to think of family as sometimes flawed or even hurtful?

7. What recommendations does Ehrenreich make to improve families in her final paragraph? In your opinion, are these recommendations justifiable in a country that tries to allow its individual citizens to have as much control as possible over their personal lives and problems?

WRITING ASSIGNMENTS

1. In a letter to the politician or public figure of your choice, call for an end to the use of empty rhetoric such as "family values" and "profamily." Use Ehrenreich's observations about the problems using those terms; use any other arguments you have considered from this section of your textbook on families. Make sure you explain why this terminology is inaccurate and is simply a case of jumping on the bandwagon rather than clear thinking or reasoning.

2. If you are a practicing member of an organized religious faith, research your religion's beliefs on family, domestic violence, gender equality, and child-rearing. If you are not a member of an organized religion, select one faith's ideas to research. Be sure that you include materials from journals or news sources, from theologians, and, if possible, from interviews with religious leaders.

3. How serious is domestic violence and child abuse in your community, either where you attend college or the community you consider your home? Using newspapers, editorials, and information from agencies such as rape crisis centers and social outreach clearing houses, compile a report on your community's experience of the various kinds of family problems Ehrenreich describes. Are you surprised by any of your findings? Is the problem greater or lesser than you expected?

4. Using your library's news resources, look up information on the well-publicized cases of family violence that Ehrenreich cites. Choose any one of the following: Lorena and John Wayne Bobbitt (1993), Tonya Harding (1994), O. J. Simpson (1994), and Erik and Lyle Menendez (1989). (In each case, the year following the name indicates when you will find the first news coverage for the case.) Briefly examine the facts of the case. Then, examine opinions and editorials written in these news journals. What connection did commentators make between these cases and family values?

GROUP PROJECTS

1. Working in small groups, compare the perceptions of domestic violence among different groups of people. Drawing on your own experience, dis-

cuss with other class members your beliefs about the prevalence and seriousness that the following sorts of groups (or others) attach to family violence. Use the following list to help you compare ideas: ethnicity; region; size of town or community; able-bodied or disabled; gay, bisexual, or heterosexual; social or economic class status; religion; and educational level.

2. Once you and other class members have researched the ideas of various religions (see question 2, "Writing Assignments"), compare your findings with each other. Depending on how many class members have chosen a single religion, you may wish to set up small groups on a single religion and then make a group presentation to other class members. What differences do you find between religions? What similarities?

3. Working in separate small groups, try to come up with a serious, working definition for the term *profamily*. Take creative liberties if you feel the term is not adequately defined in public discussion or elsewhere. Then, compare notes with other groups' work. Did you come up with roughly similar ideas? Different ones? Important omissions or additions that aren't necessary? Can you come to a consensus as a class about the way the term ought to be defined?

Relatively Speaking
Jan Borst

With so many divorces and remarriages, the very definition of family is undergoing fundamental changes. In this article, Jan Borst uses the occasion of a family member's upcoming marriage to rethink the concept of family. In particular, she ponders the lack of names, conventions, and guidelines for blended families—that is, newlywed adults assuming parenting responsibilities for children of previous marriages. Although her thoughts, seasoned with dashes of humor and compassion, are drawn from her own personal experiences, Borst raises some serious issues that such families confront including what to call people and what their responsibilities are in the new "unconventional" families.

Borst is an instructor in family sociology at Emporia State University in Kansas. This essay first appeared in *Newsweek* magazine in July 1996.

1 Our daughter will be getting married soon. My husband and I recently met our future son-in-law, Ed, who seems to be a great guy. He has a good job providing a comfortable income. He's a spiritual man, with many talents, well thought of in the community, and more important, he's head over heels in love with our daughter—as she is with him.

2 We especially pay for their happiness because they're not your average twentysomething couple starting their marital journey with all the idealism of youth. They're in their late 30s, each bringing to this union the baggage of failed prior mar-

riages. They wish to recommit—to try again, in Samuel Johnson's words, "the triumph of hope over experience." As all parents do, we want this marriage not only to succeed but to flourish.

3   Like many other couples starting over, they have children—his daughter, her two girls. Their honeymoon will be brief. Then it's instant family. Mothering and fathering children they've known a short time. Two last names on the mailbox. Two girls in the house, a third there every other weekend. Child-support payments going out and coming in. One child's mother across town, a father a state away. Children confused over loyalties to the parents they live with and those they visit. The couple pulled in opposite directions by the wants and needs of their kids and their own need to form a successful, intimate marital relationship.

4   Their situation is pretty complex, but, these days, quite common. Some "step" families are more complicated than the word implies. Ours is one such family. I began by saying that our daughter will be getting married. Technically this is not true. My husband and I are in a second marriage ourselves, and the bride is my husband's child.

5   He was a widowed father of nine and I the divorced mother of four when we met at Parents Without Partners 16 years ago. Of the 13 children between us, only his four oldest were out of the house and on their own. The other nine children ranged in age from 4 to 19. Even though he and I were crazy about each other, we knew that combining our two households was not a good idea. Too many kids reared with different parenting styles. Two religions. Two income levels. Too much age difference (he is nearly a generation older than I). Yet we loved each other, so we become a weekend family of sorts, courting one another while surrounded by kids. Eventually the kids grew up, and six years ago we married. Our long courtship helped solidify the mutual affection all of us now enjoy. We are a family. But still the bonds are fragile.

6   Questions arise as to who is family. Will our daughter's new family be a family of four, made up of those who live in the house? Or a family of five—the four plus the child who visits on weekends? In their home, who is the real parent? Who sets the rules? When does the mother relinquish some of her parenting role to her husband? When does the stepparent step in; when does he or she back off? How much time should the visiting child spend alone with her father and how much time with her new family?

7   Then there's the question of what they call one another. If a child calls her stepfather "Dad," does this take something away from her real father? When children speak about their parents, whom are they referring to? When parents say "our children," should they explain the relationship?

8   In divorce, some words have taken on new meaning in our vernacular. Most states don't call it "divorce," but rather "dissolution of marriage," as if the process were some chemical reaction. A former spouse is an "ex"—it implies a prior position that no longer exists, but also suggests the unknown in math. Do our former in-laws become "ex-laws"? Or "out-laws"?

9   Whether "joint," "shared," "residential," "sole" or "split," parents either have, lose or give up "custody" of their offspring—custody being a term applied to criminals. "Visitation" used to mean making a call to someone hospitalized or going to a

funeral home; now it means seeing your own children via some prearranged schedule, possibly devised with the assistance of a family mediator, perhaps by court order.

10   Our language is even more heavily laden with family terms beginning with "step." Ed will be my stepson-in-law, but there's no simple way to state the relationship between his daughter, Amy, and me. She and I will be related only by the slender threads of two remarriages: her father's to my husband's daughter and mine to my husband. Amy becomes my husband's stepgranddaughter, his daughter's stepdaughter, his granddaughters' stepsister or his son-in-law's daughter. But to me, the linguistic link is truly unwieldy: my husband's stepgranddaughter, my stepdaughter's stepdaughter, my stepgrandchildren's stepsister!

11   Yet whatever we choose to call this relationship created through two remarriages, Amy will be part of our family. She will likely spend some Christmases at our home. She may join our granddaughters when they come to Kansas for their vacation. We've already begun sending her birthday cards and the same holiday treats and trinkets grandmothers (even stepgrandmothers) send grandchildren throughout the year. We will remember her in our thoughts and prayers as we do the other kids in the family.

12   All this has not escaped Amy, 11 years old going on 35. At our last meeting she asked me, "What shall I call you? You're like a grandmother, but not really my grandmother. I have two grandmothers already, you know." (What she didn't say was that should her mother remarry, she will have one more.)

13   "I know," I said with a sigh, "it is pretty complicated." We talked a bit, trying to make sense of this convoluted, many-branched, pruned and grafted family tree. We discussed some of the choices, tried out some of the step-this, step-that options, even suggested a step/step or double-step something or other. Each sounded more ridiculous than the last. Finally we decided it would be "Amy and Jan, Jan and Amy." That would have to do.

EXPLORING THE TEXT

1. Borst wishes her daughter well in the opening sentence of this article. What information does she reveal about the special needs and problems her daughter will face? Why is she especially concerned about the success of this marriage?

2. Why do you think that Borst doesn't reveal all of the special details about her daughter's upcoming marriage at once? Why does she set up information so readers realize gradually how unlike the stereotypical marriages this arrangement will be? What is the effect of delaying the details?

3. What practical problems about family membership will face the newly married adults and their children? What problems will they have in deciding how to name or identify their relationships?

4. What kinds of tensions do you think will arise as these five people settle into their first year as a new family? What kinds of problems does Borst

imply they will have? Are you in a similar situation? What kinds of problems did you have adjusting?

5. In paragraphs 8–10, how does Borst poke fun at the connotations of language surrounding divorce? What terms does she say have silly implications if taken logically? Why do you think she places this humorous material in a serious article? What is its effect?

6. Who is Amy, first mentioned in paragraph 10, in relation to Borst? How does Borst feel about Amy? Why do you two finally decide to call themselves "Amy and Jan, Jan and Amy"?

7. What rules of courtesy based on age does this set of names for each other violate? Why do you think that Jan and Amy choose to address each other by their first names, despite their age difference?

WRITING ASSIGNMENTS

1. In her article, Borst mentions that the new family will have three children, including one who stays with the family on alternate weekends. Make a list of some of the practical problems that will face other family members as they try to find ways to include this girl as a full-fledged member of the family. Be sure to try to suggest some solutions that you think will satisfy all family members.

2. In her article "Rethinking Divorce," Barbara Dafoe Whitehead claims that adults more often think of themselves than their children when making decisions about their marriages. In your opinion, is the situation that Borst has described in her article the result of selfish thinking? Why or why not?

3. Using your school's library, examine literature from the disciplines of psychology, social work, sociology, and other social sciences. What kinds of problems and challenges do specialists in these fields see adults and children facing in stepfamilies like the one Borst describes? What recommendations do these specialists offer for personal or social adjustment to these challenges. Does professional literature raise any kinds of problems that Borst does not mention in her article?

4. If gays and lesbians were to be allowed to marry, what would they call each other and their children? What kinds of issues similar to those Borst describes in her article do gays and lesbians who have children face now? What issues are different for gays and lesbians? As you examine responses to these questions, use gay and lesbian news publications, books, and journal literature to help document your ideas.

GROUP PROJECTS

1. As a class, see if you can map out the family tree for Borst's extended family. Include information about her second husband, the children she and her

second husband had by earlier marriages, the daughter's impending marriage, and Amy's potential fourth grandmother.

2. Using the family tree you have created in the previous exercise, try to invent creative, affectionate terms for as many of the nontraditional relationships as you can. For instance, can you come up with a good term to describe Amy's relationship to Jan?

3. Using wedding guides and etiquette manuals, plan a ceremony and reception for the newly formed family of Borst's stepdaughter. Make sure that you include a role for each of the family members, including the parents, former in-laws, and former spouses of both adult partners (assume that all are friendly and will want to attend), as well as a role for each of the three children. What advice were you able about to find about wedding planning? What did you have to make up or improvise?

Rethinking Divorce
Barbara Dafoe Whitehead

Divorce has become an American way of life. Nearly half of all children will see their parents' marriage terminate by the time they turn 18. What does that say about trends and attitudes regarding marriage? And what about the effects of divorce on children and on society itself? In the article below, Barbara Dafoe Whitehead examines our society's shifting views of marriage. She is especially concerned about the social attitudes our "divorce culture" is creating—attitudes that encourage selfishness, emotional isolation, and pessimism.

Whitehead is a sociologist and the author of the widely selling and controversial book, *Divorce Culture: How Divorce Became an Entitlement and How It Is Blighting the Lives of Our Children* (1997). This article was first published as an editorial in the *Boston Globe* in 1997.

1 During the past 30 years, divorce has moved from the margin of society into the mainstream. It is now an American way of life and a commonplace childhood event. Close to half of all children in the United States will experience divorce before they reach age 18. Half of those are also likely to go through a second divorce. This alone is cause for concern, since a mounting body of evidence shows that divorce creates hardship, loss, and disadvantage for many of the roughly 1 million children each year who experience it firsthand.

2 But the harmful impact of divorce goes far beyond just those lives. Widespread divorce has also given rise to a set of ideas and values that are antithetical to the interests of all the nation's children and destructive of the social commitments that promote their well-being. It is no coincidence that the cruel loss of the welfare entitlement for children has come on the heels of the divorce revolution. For the current rationale for divorce also undermines the case for public support for the next generation as a whole.

3   This rationale has emerged as the result of a historic change in the way Americans think about divorce and its consequences.

4   Divorce has been a feature of Western social life for 300 years, and, until recently, most Americans believed that divorce caused such severe and sometimes lasting damage to children that it should be avoided, except in cases where marriages were torn apart by violence or other severe abuse. Consequently, parents were enjoined to work out their marital problems (or at least conceal them), so that they could preserve the marriage, as the popular saying had it, "for the sake of the children."

5   This social injunction was not designed to ruin the lives of parents. Rather, its main purpose was to acknowledge that children are stakeholders in the parents' marriage, and so deserve to have their interests represented. According to this way of thinking, marriage was children's most basic form of social insurance. It tied both parents to the child's household and also brought together two families whose help and support might be turned to the child's advantage. Marriage also attached fathers to their biological children and promoted steady, ongoing paternal support and sponsorship. The legal dissolution of a marriage weakened the child's claim on these resources and thus was not to be entered into lightly.

6   Underlying this injunction against parental divorce was a child-centered ethic. It assumed that parents, as independent adults, had an obligation to represent and serve the interests of their dependent children. It viewed parents as emotionally resilient and able to withstand adversity, whereas children were emotionally vulnerable and should be protected from it.

7   After the mid-1960s, this injunction lost support and credibility, both as a statement about the sources of security for children and as a statement about the obligations of parents to their children. In 1972, advice columnist Ann Landers announced that she also no longer believed in staying together for the children. Academics, therapists, even clergy counseled against it. Women increasingly rejected the idea that parents should remain in unhappy marriages. In 1962, women were evenly divided over this question. Fifteen years later, 80 percent of women said parents should not stay together.

8   A new rationale emerged that justified divorce. It argued that a child's happiness depended on the happiness of the individual parent, especially the mother, rather than on the marriage itself. Thus, parents should look out for their own well-being first, and the children would benefit as well—a view one scholar has called "psychological trickledown."

9   This reversed the ethic. It was no longer child-centered. Now it was adults who were the emotionally fragile ones and thus had to be protected against adversity while children were the resilient ones and could take it. Not surprisingly, as this new ethic gained broad acceptance in the culture, the percentage of divorces involving children increased. Today, 6 out of 10 divorces occur in families with children.

10   As a consequence of this cultural shift, middle-class Americans today see divorce as an individual entitlement that must be protected against challenge, criticism or infringement. They reject the idea that children have an independent stake in the marriage partnership, and thus reject any social norm that affirms the child's stake.

Indeed, so thoroughly does this sense of individual entitlement shape public thinking that any expression of concern for the children of divorce is interpreted as an unfeeling attack on the divorced themselves.

11   For this reason, politicians of every stripe duck the issue of middle-class divorce. Democrats avoid it, too, because they do not want to anger their large constituency of women who see divorce as a hard-won freedom and prerogative, nor do they want to seem unsympathetic to divorced mothers. Republicans do not want to antagonize their wealthy constituents or the party's libertarian wing, both of whom favor easy divorce. Nor does either party wish to call attention to divorce among its own leadership.

12   This bipartisan consensus has been politically expedient, but it has taken an enormous toll on our public commitment to children.

13   For one thing, it allows the middle class to define family breakup as a "them" problem—concentrated among the poor and underclass—rather than a problem that also implicates "us": the divorcing middle class. Mainstream America clings to the comfortable illusion that the declining well-being of children has to do almost solely with the behavior of unwed teenage mothers or poor women on welfare rather than with the instability of marriage and the fragility of parental commitment within its own ranks.

14   This isolates poor children and weakens our sense of shared obligation to improve their lot. It leads to the scapegoating of the nation's most vulnerable families. Policymakers focus on the eclipse of marriage among the most economically stressed members of the society as the root cause of family decline in the nation today. Welfare legislation urges poor parents to get married and stay married. But no one is sending this marriage to the country club crowd.

15   Moreover, and even more troublingly, today's divorce ethic undermines the social foundation for our public commitment to children. A society cannot sustain a public ethic of obligation to children if it also embraces a private ethic that devalues and disenfranchises children. If parents are entitled to put their needs and interests before those of their own children, why should they or any other adults feel an obligation to help somebody else's children?

16   Despite marches on Washington, D.C., and media campaigns, children's advocates are having trouble gaining support for their cause. Their struggles remind us that altruism cannot be generated by exhortation alone. For the foundation of altruism lies chiefly in family life, where it must be cultivated and practiced. A sense of obligation to others grows out of a sense of binding obligation to kith and kin. Durable social bonds depend heavily on the existence of lasting and dependable family bonds.

17   Yet today's children are coming of age at a time when bonds are increasingly fragile and commitments notably weak. According to survey research, high school students say that they aspire to long-lasting, mutually satisfying relationships, but despair that they will be able to achieve them. Theirs is not the angst of adolescence but realistic expectation based on life experience. Children whose parents are divorced are two to three times more likely to get divorced themselves. So the breaking of the bonds is gaining cultural and generational momentum.

18   Unfortunately, the weakening of commitment to children could not have come at a worse time. Today's children need higher levels of both public and parental investment if they are to succeed in a demanding global economy. The characteristics that are most essential to making one's way in a dynamic world—initiative, resourcefulness, independence, risk-taking—are the very characteristics that children are less likely to acquire if they lose permanence and security in their primary family bonds. At the very time the world is asking more of today's children, we are giving them less and less.

19   Consequently, there is an urgent need to begin a conversation about divorce. Its purpose should not be to second-guess or criticize divorced adults. Divorce is a necessary institution. Instead, the conversation should help us reconsider our current philosophy of divorce. What's at stake is the ability of children and young adults to fulfill their desires for durable bonds and lasting commitments.

EXPLORING THE TEXT

1. According to Whitehead, who is most affected by divorce? How widespread is the problem? Are the people affected only those who have experienced divorce firsthand or are other people affected too?
2. What does Whitehead say happens to children whose parents divorce? What are the economic consequences of divorce for children? What are the emotional consequences?
3. Whitehead says that middle-class Americans, Democrats, and Republicans all avoid focusing on divorce as a problem to be resolved. What are their reasons for refusing to see a problem? How does Whitehead feel about this refusal? What words, phrases, or evidence does she supply that help you pinpoint her attitude?
4. Who do middle- and upper-class Americans erroneously blame for the growing number of children living in poverty? How are the blamed harmed by this scapegoating?
5. In paragraph 5, why does Whitehead call a family's home "the child's household"? What is the difference between a marriage that is child-centered and one that is adult-centered? Which does the author think is better—and how can you tell what she thinks?
6. Do you think divorces should be more difficult to obtain? If you could rewrite divorce laws, what provisions would you make for people who had no children? For victims of domestic violence? For other special circumstances?
7. What is "altruism"? How do Whitehead's conclusions about the decline of altruism describe a vicious cycle? That is, how does the cause of the problem create a still more serious version of the same problem?
8. What is wrong with today's average young people, according to Whitehead? Who is to blame for their character deficits? Why do you think

Whitehead does not more directly identify and chastise those she believes caused such problems?

9. What solutions does Whitehead provide to the problem she describes? Do you think the solutions are well developed? Sufficient to resolve the problem? If not, what does she imply she would like to see happen? Where do you find evidence for your response?

WRITING ASSIGNMENTS

1. Draft a letter to a pair of married friends with several children. They have become dissatisfied with each other and are thinking about divorcing. Assume that both parents are working and that they are considering a friendly, amicable divorce in which they continue their relationship with the children. Use Whitehead's arguments to try to persuade them not to divorce.

2. Using newspapers and news magazines, research a topic related to parents' financial support of their children. You might examine deadbeat dads, mothers paying child support, or the rates of child support payments actually made within your state or local area. You might also investigate controversial issues such as tying visitation rights to payment or efforts to coerce parents who fall behind in payments by publishing their names or confiscating their tax return money. Write an essay summarizing the results of your search.

3. Using your school library, trace the pattern of divorce trends over the last 30 years. Whitehead mentions this pattern briefly in her first paragraph; do you find any additional information that helps you to explain the problems divorce creates? Were you surprised at any of the information based on race, class, or part of the country? How might Whitehead use this additional information to support a longer, extended article on divorce?

4. Review news sources, Op-Ed columns, handbooks advising parents how to handle divorce, and similar sources of popular advice and information. Do they agree, either explicitly or implicitly, with Whitehead's observations in paragraph 9 that we wrongfully believe children to be "resilient"?

5. Using news sources and government reports, examine issues involved in restructuring welfare programs, especially Aid to Families with Dependent Children (AFDC). What evidence do you see to support Whitehead's claim that middle-class Americans and politicians are scapegoating poor families? Are any provisions especially punitive or harmful to children?

GROUP PROJECTS

1. As a group design and administer a poll for your classmates to answer anonymously, asking questions about family status (divorces, remarriage,

single parenthood, father's contributions). Then, administer the same poll to a group of people a generation older than you (perhaps your professors or college staff members). Do the results bear out Whitehead's observations that more families today are unstable?

2. In your group discuss and elaborate on the effects of divorce on children. Add to and flesh out Whitehead's list of both economic and emotional problems divorce causes children. Then compare notes with classmates to assemble a complete list. Based on this list, decide whether or not you agree that divorce should be more difficult to obtain.

3. More and more gay men and lesbians are becoming parents, through biological parenting, adoption, or partnership with a biological parent. Do Whitehead's arguments support the idea of extending marriage to gay men and lesbians or not? As a group brainstorm a list of ways that Whitehead might justify or refute such a change in the idea of marriage. Present your findings to classmates, either in arguments for or against gay and lesbian marriage or in a debate format if you can't agree.

The New Nostalgia
Rosalind C. Barnett and Caryl Rivers

In the last essay, Barbara Dafoe Whitehead lamented that the American divorce rate has created not just a social problem but a cultural one. She argues that the values of obligation and commitment, one time sacred foundations of marriages, are being lost to an ethic of personal growth and self-fulfillment. Underlying her words is a familiar complaint: that the decay of the family is linked to the loss of values held in the 1950s. But in the article below, Rosalind C. Barnett and Caryl Rivers tell us that we're really in much better shape than we think we are, if only we would stop apologizing for the state of our families and start recognizing adaptability as a strength. We haven't declined since the golden age of families, presented to us in 1950s sitcom returns. In fact, the very "problems" that critics of our new family structures want to fix may actually be creating longer-lasting, healthier marriages.

Barnett is a clinical psychologist and Rivers is a professor of journalism at Boston University and the author of several books, including most recently *Slick Spins and Fractured Facts: How Cultural Myths Distort the News* (1996). This piece has been excerpted from the authors' book, *He Works/She Works* (1996).

1 As he drops his daughter off at a very good day-care center staffed with well-trained, caring professionals, a father worries whether he's doing the right thing. Should he or his wife stay home with their daughter, even though they can't afford to? Will day care cause some problems for his child that he can't foresee? Is he do-

ing something dreadfully wrong because his life is so different from that of his parents back in the 1960s?

2 Guilt is the universal malady of working parents today, and one to which parents in past generations were seemingly immune. Did the woman setting out in the covered wagon for a prairie homestead worry about whether her children would be well-adjusted out there on the plains? Did the women in colonial times, whose days were filled with manufacturing the clothing and food that would keep the family alive, brood about whether she and her children were "relating" well enough? Did Victorian men worry that their children were spending too much time with nannies?

3 It's safe to say that no modern working parent has completely escaped those sudden, painful stabs of guilt. It might help to understand its roots, and we will examine them in this essay. But first, it's important to realize how this guilt feeds into the mistaken conviction that today's parents can't quite measure up to those of the past.

4 It is imperative, we believe, to understand that those of us in the two-earner lifestyle have been as good or *better* parents—not worse ones—than the Ozzie and Harriet model. The two-earner lifestyle that has emerged in the past two decades of American life has been a positive development, fitting well with current economic realities. While it has not been easy, men and women have connected to the world of work and its demands while expending considerable energies on nurturing their children. If this meant that at times they felt they had to juggle too much, that there were times they wondered if they were going to be able to do it all, they lived with that problem—and, most often, survived it in good health and good humor.

5 We are already raising a generation of children in two-earner families; if we really want them to be stressed, let's tell them that what we are doing is all wrong, that what we *should* be doing was what their grandparents did in the 1950s, and that that's the ideal they, too, should aspire to.

6 In fact, we must prepare our children for the world they will really be facing—not some rosy image of a past that never was all that wonderful, and which is not going to return. With a global economy on the horizon and with the United States continually having to compete with the Pacific Rim and Europe, we will probably continue to see a pattern of downsizing of U.S. companies as high productivity becomes the watchword of industry. Men's real wages have been declining since 1960: The median income of employed white men in 1967 was about $19,800; by 1987 it was $19,008, adjusted for changes in earning power—roughly $750 less than it had been twenty years before.[1]

7 More and more, women's wages will become essential to a family's economic survival—as they are today in so many families. The days when women worked for "extras" are long gone and are not likely to return. More and more, in such an unstable work world, men will turn to their families as a way of finding self-esteem. And women, like men, will prepare early for careers or jobs in which they will be involved for most of their lives. Economists who predict the shape of the early twenty-first century say that no longer will people remain in one job for a lifetime; the successful worker of the future will be one who is flexible, learns quickly, and can transfer skills from one work setting to another. Women may have to retool as the

economy twists and turns, but few will have the chance to be full-time, lifelong homemakers.

8   Not until we accept the working woman as the norm can we adequately prepare our sons and daughters for the lives they will really be leading. Our study conclusively proves that holding up the rigid and outdated lifestyle of the 1950s as a sacred icon will only add stress to their busy and often difficult lives. Perhaps the most important finding of the study on which the book is based is the fact that for working couples, a gap in gender-role ideology is a major and consistent source of stress. It is not merely annoying when your image of the ideal family does not jibe with that of your spouse; it can be an important source of stress in your life.

9   On the whole, we do not help young women prepare for the flexible jobs that will protect their economic futures and that of their families if we plant in their heads the idea that what they really *ought* to be doing is staying home. We don't prepare young men for the deep involvement they are going to have with their families if we create in them the idea that the *real man* doesn't change a diaper or drive the kids to nursery school.

10   But the actual facts about what is good for real American couples and their families today may well be drowned out by the clamor of what we call the "new nostalgia," a combination of longing for the past and a fear of change. It not only feeds the guilt that can tie individuals in knots, but can be major stumbling block to the creation of corporate and government policies that will help, not hinder, working families. The new nostalgia has already calcified in politics, in the media, in a spate of books that tell us we must retreat to the past to find solutions for the future. The messages of a reinvigorated right wing in politics pushes a brand of family values with which Ozzie and Harriet would have felt quite at home.

11   One steady, unblinking beacon of a message has been flashed to men and women over the past few years: Change is dangerous, change is abnormal, change is unhealthy. This message permeates our mass media, the books we read, the newscasts to which we listen, the advice from pop psychologists, the covers of news magazines. Men and women must stay in their traditional places, or there will be hell to pay.

12   The message comes in many guises. It comes from warnings that women are working themselves into sickness on the so-called second shift—the housework women do *after* they come home from work—doing so much that their health is in peril. It may be national magazines trumpeting the mommy track, concluding that women *must* seek achievement on a lower and slower track than men. It nests in headlines that claim women are simply unable to juggle the demands of work and home and are going to start having heart attacks just like men. It may be warnings that day care interferes with the mother-child bond—despite solid evidence to the contrary. It can be found in publications concluding that if people would just stay married or kids would stop having sex, all our social problems would disappear. It may be Robert Bly warning in *Iron John* that men have become weak, thanks to women, and they must find their warrior within.[2]

13   It is more than a backlash against the women's movement. Indeed, many of the warnings insist that men had better stay in the straitjacket of traditional masculinity.

These warnings are implicit in the spate of action-adventure movies aimed at young men, in which manhood is defined as domination and mayhem, with no ongoing relationships with women or children. They are implicit also in the ease with which the word "wimp" is hurled at any political candidate who does not employ slash-and-burn macho tactics.

14   The flashing message is only intensified by widely held but outdated ideas from the behavioral sciences proclaiming that a man's emotional health is primarily based on his life at work, while a woman can only find her identity through being a wife and mother. So intense has this bias been that, until recently, social scientists rarely examined men's lives at home or women's at home.

15   The new nostalgia fuels the guilt that many working parents feel. The flames are fanned by forces that many working parents don't understand—and the media play a large role in keeping the bonfire going.

16   Never in the past were parents confronted with constant and ongoing images of how their grandparents raised children. Old folk remedies may have been passed down, mothers and grandmothers gave advice, but times changed and people changed with them. It was the natural order of things. But parents today see Ozzie and Harriet and Donna Reed and all their ilk as wonderful, ideal parents night after night on the tube. (Even the President and the First Lady, whose lives resemble most working families' more than those of the old sitcoms, admitted that one of their favorite TV shows was reruns of *The Donna Reed Show*.)

17   The power those TV parents still exercise has more to do with the durability of images than it does with today's reality. As *Newsweek* magazine points out, "The television programs of the fifties and sixties validated a family style during a period in which today's leaders—congressmen, corporate executives, university professors, magazine editors—were growing up or beginning to establish their own families. (The impact of the idealized family was magnified by the very size of the post-war generation.)"[3]

18   It can be somewhat frightening to think that the legislators who are voting on family leave plans, the aides who create policies for presidential candidates, the chairs of university departments who decide what courses should be staffed—all have inside their heads the very same model of the way our families *ought* to be.

19   Yale historian John Demos points out that "the traditional model reaches back as far as personal memory goes for most of us who currently teach and write and philosophize."[4] And in a time when parents seem to feel a great deal of change, "that image is comfortingly solid and secure, counterpoint to what we think is threatening to the future." In other words, an unreal past seems so much more soothing than a bumpy present.

20   In the manufacture of guilt, add another potent factor: the nature of the news media. The news media don't hold a mirror up to the world, despite what news executives like to say. The media not only select which facts and images will be churned out as news, but they determine the frame in which those images will be presented. This frame is most often one of conflict, tension, and bad news. It's no wonder everyone assumes that the American family is falling apart. That's all we read or hear about.

21   Of course, what the TV news anchor *doesn't* tell you is that in the past, "family" issues were rarely part of the news. Domestic violence and child abuse were shameful secrets, rarely written about. Dramatic images of violent crime were less a part of daily life. In Washington, D.C., where Caryl Rivers grew up in the 1950s, some 90 percent of crimes by young men were committed by juveniles who were graduates of one city reform school. But you never saw their victims on the evening news—because there were no minicams to capture the mayhem on video and the kids didn't spray the streets with automatic weapons fire. Americans now consume many hours of television each day—and research shows that people who watch a lot of TV see the world as a much more frightening place than it really is.

22   One of the bad-news frames of which the media is most fond today is the decline of the family. A Nexis search of the past five years reveals 15,164 references in the press to either the breakup or the decline of the American Family, a chorus that is relentless. Do you believe that the decline of the family is absolute fact? Many Americans do. However, most media coverage of the alleged decline of the family does not answer a key question: What position of lofty perfection is the family declining *from?* There must have been a golden age of family, since the words *decline* and *breakdown* imply that very notion. But when was it? And do we really want to go back there? . . . Many Americans believe that past family life was always—and should always be—like *Leave It to Beaver, Father Knows Best,* and *Ozzie and Harriet.*

23   In fact, the 1950s *were* a golden age—economically. Never before had Americans enjoyed a period of such affluence. Women reversed a long-standing trend of moving into the workforce, and went home. One would have thought that with women in such a traditional role, social critics would have approved. Mom was by the hearth with her kiddies nestled about her. But what happened? In perhaps no decade were women savaged as thoroughly as they were in the 1950s. Sweet Mom, baking cookies and smiling, was destroying her kids—the boys, anyway. While nostalgic articles in today's media hark back to the happy 1950s, the critics of the time had no such beatific vision.

24   Social critic Philip Wylie, in his best-seller *Generation of Vipers,* coined the term "Momism." Momism, Wylie decreed, had turned modern men into flaccid and weak creatures and was destroying the moral fiber of America.[5] When American soldiers sometimes failed to resist "brainwashing" when they were captured by the Communist Chinese in Korea, it was said that their overprotective mothers had made them weak and traitorous. Children often got too much Mom and not enough Dad. The memoirs of men who grew up in the 1950s reveal that their fathers were often distant and overly involved in work.

25   It's not surprising that depression was the malady that most affected women in those years. What Betty Friedan termed "the feminine mystique" came smack up against the lengthening life span. At a time when society was telling women that home and children must be their whole lives, technology and medicine were making those lives last longer than ever before in history. Women would outlive, by many years, the childhood of their last-born, and the notion that they could spend all their time in mothering was absurd. The cultural messages and the reality of the modern

world were at odds. Kept out of the world of work in the suburban cocoons, physically healthier and longer-lived than their sisters in the past, women were far more prone than men to depression, and in fact the mental health of married women had reached crisis proportions by the end of the 1960s. Statistics rolling in from all across the developed world were so grim that the noted sociologist Jessie Bernard called marriage a "health hazard" for women.[6] . . .

26   One reason we hear so much today about how wonderful the 1950s were is that the voices of male cultural critics are those most often heard. Men and women, it seems, remember that era differently. In many ways, the 1950s were good for men. It was the first era in history in which the average middle-class man could, on his salary alone, support a lifestyle that was available only to the upper classes in the past. The mental health of men was vastly superior to that of women. The daughters of 1950s homemakers rejected en masse a lifestyle that created so much depression and anxiety, and few women today would trade their lives for that of their mothers. But many men today would gladly opt for the financial security and economic opportunities their fathers had.

27   Because the 1950s live on endlessly in rerun land, it is hard for us to accept that the decade was such an atypical time. Stephanie Coontz warns that "the first thing to understand about the Fifties family is that it was a fluke, it was a seven-year aberration in contradiction to a hundred years of other trends."[7] And Arlene Skolnick notes that "far from being the last era of family normality from which current trends are a deviation, it is the family patterns of the 1950s that are deviant."

28   Deviant? Ozzie and Harriet? Indeed they were, from the point of view of history. Theirs was an atypical era, in which trends that had been firmly established since early in the century briefly reversed themselves in the aftermath of World War II. For years, women had been moving into the workforce in increasing numbers. The high point was epitomized by Rosie the Riveter, the symbol of the women who went to work in the factories to produce the tanks and the guns and the planes needed to win the war. After the war, during the brief period of unprecedented affluence when America's economic engine was unchallenged throughout the world, women went home, and the American birthrate suddenly jumped to approach that of India. A huge baby-boom generation grew up in middle-class affluence that no other generation had known. . . .

29   By the late 1970s, the 1950s were only a distant echo. The women's movement unleashed women's untapped brainpower and economic potential, and millions of women flooded into the marketplace. This movement of women into the workforce in the late twentieth century is one of the great mass migrations of history, comparable to the push westward and the move from the farms to the cities. And just as those mass movements changed not only the face of American society but the lives of individual citizens, so too did this new movement rearrange our social geography.

30   Despite the media drumbeat about the decline of the family, despite those thousands of references to its decay in the media, the American family is a thriving institution. We are both more centered on the family and more frantic about its problems than our European counterparts. Arlene Skolnick writes, "Paradoxically, Americans have a stronger sense of both familistic values and family crisis than do other ad-

vanced countries. We have higher marriages rates, a more home-centered way of life, and greater public devotion to family values."[8]

31   The notion that we can return to some mythic past for solutions to today's problems is tempting, but it is a will-o'-the-wisp that should not engage our attention. The idea that we can find in Ozzie and Harriet and their lives workable solutions for today's rapidly changing economic and social patterns is a dream. Unfortunately, when we combine the new nostalgia with the old images, it's like taking a trip with only a 1955 road map to guide us. The old landmarks are gone, little backroads have become interstates, and the rules of the road have changed beyond recognition. Absurd as this image is, it is often precisely what we do when we think about the American family. Women who hurry out to work every morning can be trapped into thinking that *this* isn't what they are supposed to be doing; men with their hands in soapsuds after dinner can remember their fathers sitting and reading the newspaper while mom did the dishes. It's easy to feel resentful.

32   But the new nostalgia is more than harmless basking in the trivia of the past—it is, in fact, a major toxin affecting the health of today's men and women.

33   The "family values" crusade of the right wing, to the degree that it succeeds in invading people's thoughts, will only add to the stress of working couples by insisting on a model from the past that is increasingly impossible to achieve in the present. One newspaper poll showed that the proportion of adults who agreed with the statement "A preschool child is likely to suffer if his or her mother works" went up between 1989 and 1991.

34   As science, that statement is nonsense. There is plenty of evidence that no child is "likely to suffer" if his or her mother goes to work. But those adults agreeing with that statement—who are likely to be working parents—will get a huge dose of unnecessary stress. The family values crusade, to the extent that it glorifies homemakers and demonizes working mothers, will succeed only in making the lives of twenty-first-century Americans harder. The clock will not be turned back to the 1950s; that's as impossible as holding back the tide. If Americans feel guilty because they can't live up to some impossible, vanished ideal, their health will suffer.

35   The era of the two-earner couple may in fact create more closeness in families, not less. As the fast track becomes less available, men and women alike will turn to family for a strong sense of self-esteem and happiness. Divorces may decline as marriages become once again economic partnerships more like the ones they were before the industrial revolution. Today, of course, marriages will be overlaid with the demands for intimacy and closeness that have become a permanent part of modern marriage, but fewer people will be able to waltz easily out of marriage, as they might have in the days when a thriving economy made good jobs easy to come by. Middle-class couples are marrying later and many women are getting established in a career before having children. This pattern may promote more responsibility and happier marriages than those in the 1950s, when many young people felt they had to get married to have sex and discovered their emotional incompatibility only after they had children.

36   Negotiation and juggling, not the established gender roles of yesterday's marriages, are the features of modern coupledom. Who will stay home when a child is

sick? Who will take over what jobs when one partner has to travel for an important meeting? Whose career will take first place? Who has to sacrifice what—and when? Such issues, ones that June and Ward and Ozzie and Harriet never had to confront, are the day-to-day problems that today's partners have to wrestle with.

37   Today's couples are facing the demands of very busy lives at home and at work. If you listen to the media tell their story, they are constantly stressed, the women are disenchanted with trying to have it all, and the men are bitter about having to do work their fathers never had to do. Some of this is true—no lifestyle offers nirvana. On the other hand, today's couples have a better chance at achieving full, rich lives than did the men and women of the sitcom generation. While it may be no picnic to juggle the demands of work and family, research shows that working women are less depressed, less anxious, and more zestful about their lives than are homemakers. Today's man may have the stress of caring for children, but his relationship with his children may be warmer and more satisfying than was his own with his father. Most men who grew up in the 1950s don't tell stories about the warm, available dads we see in the sitcoms. More often, they speak of fathers who were distant, preoccupied, and unable to communicate with their sons on more than a superficial level. Many modern fathers, in fact, set out purposely to design lives that will be the exact opposite of their distant fathers'.

38   In their lifestyle, the men and women in our study are at the opposite end of the spectrum from Ozzie and Harriet. Both are breadwinners; and if they have children, both share the nitty-gritty everyday chores of parenting. They are true partners in supporting and nurturing their children and each other. They represent the new face of the American family, and the world they live in is not very much like the America of the 1950s.

39   Despite the ersatz glow of the new nostalgia, not much would be gained by a trip back in time—even if it were possible. How many women would want to return to the widespread depression and mental health problems of the 1950s? Catherine E. Ross, an Illinois University sociologist, says, "Any plea to return to the 'traditional' family of the 1950s is a plea to return wives and mothers to a psychologically disadvantaged position, in which husbands have much better health than wives."[9] And since research shows that the emotional health of the mother has a strong impact on her children, that's one bit of time travel we don't especially want to take.

Notes

1. Janet Riblett Wilkie, "The Decline in Men's Labor Force Participation and Income and the Changing Structure of Family Economic Support," *Journal of Marriage and the Family* 53 (February 1991).
2. Robert Bly, *Iron John* (New York: Holiday House, 1994).
3. "What Happened to the Family?" *Newsweek* Special Issue (Winter 1990/Spring 1991).
4. "What Happened to the Family?" (Winter 1990/Spring 1991).
5. Philip Wylie, *Generation of Vipers* (New York: Holt, Rinehart & Winston, 1955).
6. Jessie Bernard, *The Future of Marriage* (New York: World-Times, 1972).
7. Stephanie Coontz, *The Way We Never Were: American Families and the Nostalgia Trap* (New York: Basic Books, 1992).

8. Cited in Arlene Skolnick, *Embattled Paradise: The American Family in an Age of Uncertainty* (New York: Basic Books, 1991).
9. Quoted in Betsy A. Lehman, "Parenting Pain—But Also Joy," *Boston Globe,* (February 15, 1993).

EXPLORING THE TEXT

1. Are you familiar with the shows *Leave It to Beaver, Father Knows Best, Ozzie and Harriet,* and *The Donna Reed Show?* If so, what kinds of families were portrayed on each? How would you characterize them?
2. What is a modern, two-earner family? What assumptions do the authors make about the class and social status of this family? Why do parents in such a family feel guilty? What specifically are they worried will happen to their children? What should they really be worried about, according to Barnett and Rivers?
3. What is "gender-role ideology" in paragraph 8? In paragraphs 8–14, how are traditional men's roles described as harmful to men? How do the authors feel about the current men's movement urging men to "find their warrior within"? How can you tell what they feel about this movement?
4. What are the authors' attitudes toward change—specifically toward change in family roles and responsibilities? What phrases, images, and metaphors help you to identify their attitude in paragraphs 11–22?
5. The authors describe what the 1950s were really like for families in paragraphs 23–28. What were some of the problems families had? What were some of the problems people had fitting into these families? Why do the authors say we have adopted that decade's model of the ideal family?
6. Based on their response to the poll question in paragraphs 33 and 34, what do you think Barnett and Rivers would say to Barbara Dafoe Whitehead about the need to change divorce rates and policies? Do you think these authors would agree that marriages should be child-centered? Explain.
7. What improvements do the authors see in today's families? Why do they believe that such families are becoming stronger, rather than falling apart? Do you agree with their conclusions? Do you agree with their reasoning? Must you agree with their reasoning to accept their conclusions? Explain.
8. What are the authors' attitudes toward the media? (See paragraphs 20 and 21, also paragraph 13.) How important to their argument is the media's role in shaping Americans' perceptions about the state of the family?

WRITING ASSIGNMENTS

1. If you are a parent, or if you are thinking about marriage and children in your future, do you feel the kind of guilt that Barnett and Rivers describe in this article? If so, what do you think would help you feel less guilt—sup-

port from family and friends? Different government policies? Media messages? More and better child-care facilities? Other factors? Write up your thoughts in a paper.

2. Compare and contrast the tone of this article with that of Barbara Ehrenreich in "Oh, Those Family Values." How hopeful for the future do both articles seem to be? How do they regard the shams and illusions they expose? How well do they think the current family structure works for women, and how hopeful are they that whatever is wrong with it will change?

GROUP PROJECTS

1. Working in small groups, discuss and compare the structures of families within your own experiences. Think about the family you grew up in, the families you know well, and the families you have started. Tally up the kinds of families you find. These may include two-earner families, traditional families in which the father works and the mother stays home, families with no children, those in which the mother works and the father is primary caretaker of children, or other groupings. Compare notes with your classmates. How well do your findings match the description offered by Barnett and Rivers?

2. Working in small groups, research criticism and scholarly discussion of the four television shows the authors mention in this article; try to watch a few episodes of each show. (Or, if these shows aren't available, select comparable shows that are still running or are still in syndication—like *The Cosby Show, Married With Children,* or *Promised Land.*) What comments do reviewers make about the shows? How do these shows reflect something about our expectations for family roles and values?

3. Design and administer a poll to people outside your class. In it include questions that ask for opinions on the health of the American family versus its decline, the ideal roles that men and women should play in family structure, the desirability of day care, and so on. Also ask for anonymous information about your participants' age, class, and race. After you have assembled the data you collect as a class, analyze the results. Do any groups seem more or less optimistic or traditional about the American family?

Single Mothers: A Menace to Society?
Stephanie Coontz

As we have seen so far, there is no single definition of a "family unit." While some decry the loss of a former ideal—mother, father, and children—others have come to accept a variety of configurations, including single parenthood. In the essay below, Stephanie Coontz objects to the stigmatization of single mothers. Writing from the point of view of a single mother herself as well as a professional family historian, Coontz points out that the castigation of welfare mothers provides a scapegoat for society's problems. She also argues that the attack on single mother-hood is an attack on career mothers, divorced mothers, and women's independence itself.

Coontz is a professor of history and family studies at The Evergreen State College in Olympia, Washington, and author of *The Way We Never Were: American Families and the Nos-talgia Trap* (1992). This article first appeared in *Vogue* in December 1994.

1   Every time I open the paper or turn on the news, it seems as if some politician or pundit is going on about the dire consequences of single parenthood. And it's not just conservatives who are leading the way. Today, politicians and columnists of every stripe are proudly trumpeting a new "bipartisan consensus"—single mothers are a menace, both to society and to their children. After a brief period when people stopped calling babies illegitimate simply because the father was not married to the mother, the term has come back in favor, often attached to invective so mean-spir-ited and cynical that it takes my breath away.

2   A *Newsweek* column called illegitimacy "the smoking gun in a sickening array of pathologies—crime, drug abuse, physical and mental illness, welfare depen-dency." The children of unwed mothers have been labeled a "social scourge," a "catastrophe," and a "plague." Senator Daniel Patrick Moynihan, a Democrat, be-lieves that women who have children out of wedlock are engaging in "speciation." *Washington Post* columnist David Broder describes kids of single mothers as a whole new "breed" of human, a fearsome "species of fatherless children." Even President Clinton, himself the son of a single mother, now declares that single par-enthood "is simply not right. . . . You shouldn't have a baby when you're not mar-ried. You just have to stop it."

3   Well, it's a little too late for me to just stop it. I am a never-married mother with a thirteen-year-old son. That's my boy—wrestling with all the dilemmas adolescents face in contemporary America—they're talking about: Kristopher, the social scourge. The catastrophe. The plague.

4   "You obviously didn't inherit a normal set of eardrums," I tease him, over the blare of his electric guitar, "but I don't really think you're a new species." He grins when I joke about it like this, but he reads the papers, and I can tell it hurts. Teenagers take labels very seriously. All too often they try to live up to them. Or down, as the case may be.

5   Actually, I'm luckier than most unwed mothers. Because I'm white, middle class, and an older, well-established professional, my son is sometimes afforded a sort of honorary "legitimacy." Last year, for instance, when Kris objected to a par-ticularly cruel remark a health teacher made about single mothers, the teacher has-tened to explain that she knew his mom was educated, financially secure, and clearly loving. "I'm sure your mom had good reasons for what she did."

6   In other words, I could tell Kris not to worry; he's different from those other bastards. For most of the attacks are directed at the unwed welfare mom, the

teenager supposedly popping out new babies each year to get a hike of about $65 in her monthly check. These are the families that former secretary of education Bill Bennett is referring to when he proposes cutting off economic assistance to single mothers and sending their children to orphanages. That's not me and my son. If I sit back and keep my mouth shut, no one would guess that my creative, compassionate youngster is one of "those" kids. Why, then, does this rhetoric make me so angry?

7   For one thing, as a family historian I know that unwed motherhood is not the major cause of our society's problems, and eliminating one-parent families won't fix our inner cities or end the need for welfare. In fact, a recent study shows that even if we reunited every single child in America with his or her biological father, two-thirds of the children who are poor today would still be poor.

8   For another, while most of the cant about the dangers of illegitimacy is aimed at welfare mothers, I am struck by how quickly the rhetoric broadens into a more general attack on women's independence, sexual or otherwise. On television talk shows, the new family-values crusaders usually begin by castigating welfare mothers but move easily to "careerist" mothers who supposedly "rationalize material benefits in the name of children"; divorced women who put "individual self-actualization" before their kids' needs; women who remarry and expose their daughters to the "severe risk" of sexual abuse by men who lack a biological "investment" in the child. One *Fortune* magazine writer even blames our social ills on modern women's rejection of "the idea that women must be 'cared for' by men." It's time, they agree, to "restigmatize" both divorced and unwed mothers.

9   Yet I know from personal experience as well as sociological research that there are hundreds of paths leading to single motherhood. Some of the stories I hear would seem irresponsible to even the most ardent proponent of women's rights; others stem from complicated accidents or miscalculations that even the most radical right-winger would probably forgive.

10   At one recent workshop that I taught on family history, I met three other never-married mothers. One was a young girl who had gotten pregnant "by accident/on purpose" in the hope that her unfaithful boyfriend would marry her. It hadn't worked, and in the ensuing year she had sometimes left her baby unattended when she went out on dates. Jarred into self-examination after being reported for neglect, she realized that going back to school and developing job skills was a more promising way of escaping her abusive parents than chasing boys. Another, now 25, had been 15 when she became pregnant. She considered abortion, but she would have had to drive 600 miles, by herself, to the nearest provider, and she didn't even have the money for a hotel room. Both these mothers had relied on welfare assistance to get by in their early days, and one was still on food stamps as she attended school. The third was an older, well-paid professional woman who had had three wedding plans fall through. She attributed her failures with men to being caught between two value systems: She was old-fashioned enough in her romantic fantasies to be attracted to powerful, take-charge men, but modern enough in her accomplishments that such men generally found her threatening. Her last fiancé had left her pregnant at age 35. With her biological clock ticking "now or never" in her ear, she decided to have the child.

11   What government agency or morals committee should decide which of us single mothers to stigmatize and which to excuse, or which of our children should be
packed off to orphanages? And what about the harmful effects of such pronouncements and penalties on the children of all single parents?

12   Most single parents don't need politicians to heap more guilt and self-doubt on
our heads. We're doing that just fine on our own. Everywhere we turn we see the
statistics: Children of single-parent families are more likely to drop out of school,
exhibit emotional distress, get in trouble with the law, and abuse drugs or alcohol
than children who grow up with two biological parents. Most single parents I talk to
are consumed with guilt and fear. What they really need to hear is that single parenthood is not an inevitable sentence of doom for their children.

13   And that is just what the latest research confirms. Yes, there are disadvantages
for kids of single parents, but they are often exaggerated: Most kids, from every
kind of family, turn out fine, so long as their mothers are not overly stressed by
poverty, ongoing conflict with the child's father, or the very stigmatization that the
family-values crusaders want to magnify.

14   Of course there are significant hardships in raising a child alone, but even a
"traditional" family structure does not guarantee that the two parents are responsible, involved, or stable. Every family configuration offers certain challenges and
benefits. My son, for example, has always been more candid with me about what's
happening at school than most of his friends from two-parents families are with their
parents. But I have more trouble than those parents finding opportunities to meet
with Kris's teachers or scheduling a consistent time each day to be around while he
does his homework. This turns out to be a common theme for most single parents.
We typically spend less time supervising our child's schoolwork or taking to teachers than do adults in two-parent families, drawbacks that may lead to lower grades
for our children. But we also spend more time talking with our kids, which might
explain why children from one-parent households are often more articulate and experience themselves as more effective in the world than their two-parent peers. Single parents tend to praise good grades more than adults in two-parent families, providing an impetus for their children to do well in school. But single parents also tend
to get angrier when grades fall, a reaction that may lead the child to be defiant—often lowering grades even more.

15   There are other trade-offs as well. While children of single mothers often grow
up to be closer to their mothers and have more respect for working women than do
kids from two-parent homes, the adolescent years can be particularly trying. When a
teenager begins to demand more freedom, a single mother has no ally to take over
the nay-saying when her voice gives out or to help her withstand a youth's insis-
tence that "everybody else's parents let them. . . . " Like many single parents who
have close relationships with their children, I sometimes have trouble setting firm
limits, even though I've studied the problems that result when adults allow their
youngsters too much say in decision-making. I worry that my son's self-confidence,
and his sense that he is entitled to negotiate limits with others the way he has always
negotiated them with me, might lead him to do risky things or to question authority
once too often.

16   Surely it's more helpful for single parents to learn how to build on their strengths and compensate for their weaknesses than to be demonized by politicians and pundits. But taking a stand against "immoral" mothers is easier and less politically risky than tackling the problems of our inner cities or addressing middle-class concerns. Our government will spend $25 billion on Aid to Families with Dependent Children this year, compared with roughly $51 billion in direct giveaways to business and another $53 billion in corporate tax breaks. But debates over subsidies only get posed in moral terms when women's sexuality is involved. After savings-and-loan corporations failed to "just say no" to risky loans and promiscuous spending on salaries, Uncle Sam handed them $150 billion of the taxpayers' money. "Underwriting tragedy is one thing," *Washington Post* columnist Charles Krauthammer has explained. "Underwriting wantonness is quite another."

17   The new family-values crusade also appeals to those uncomfortable with the changing role of women by emphatically reestablishing men as the "heads of the household." Consult your dictionary to discover the distinction between a legitimate and an illegitimate child. According to the traditional definition, any child brought into the world without a man's name on the birth certificate is not real, not authentic, not genuine, not rightful. No matter how much love, care, and effort a woman devotes to raising her children, she can never make them legitimate. But no matter how little effort a man puts into child rearing, his name on a piece of paper makes all the difference in the world to the status of his child.

18   The ancient Greeks believed that a woman contributed nothing to the production of a child except nine months' storage. In English common law, a child born out of wedlock was a *filius nullius*—the child of no one. We haven't come very far when President Clinton remarks that unwed mothers are "raising a whole generation of children who aren't sure they're the most important person in the world to anybody."

19   I don't want to use my personal and professional advantages to wheedle special dispensation for my son to be treated as a legitimate person. Legitimacy and respect should be the birthright of every child. Anyone needing appeal to tradition to stand up for that principle can look back more than 300 years, to the response of the Native Americans when the first family-values crusaders arrived on the shores of this continent. The Jesuit missionaries told the Montagnais-Naskapi Indians that men should take control of women's sexuality and parents should discipline their children more harshly. Otherwise, the good fathers warned, your wives and daughters may give birth to babies that do not belong to you. The Native Americans were not persuaded. "You French people love only your own children," they replied, "but we love all the children of the tribe." Wouldn't it be nice if America's politicians quit beating up on single parents and started operating from that set of family values?

EXPLORING THE TEXT

1. What recently expressed attitudes about single motherhood provoked Coontz to write this essay?

2. Explain how Coontz supports her claim that "there are hundreds of paths leading to single motherhood" (paragraph 9). Does Coontz persuade you of this point? Why is it an important one for her argument?

3. Describe the impression you received from this essay of Coontz's 13-year-old son, Kristopher. Which details about Kristopher did you find most memorable? Why do you think Coontz included descriptions of her son? How does the portrait add to the effectiveness of her argument?

4. Analyze Coontz's skills as a mother. What are her strengths? What are her weaknesses? From reading this essay, how would you rate her parenting abilities, on a scale of one to ten?

5. Explain what Coontz means when she says that anti-illegitimacy rhetoric often "broadens into a more general attack on women's independence, sexual or otherwise" (paragraph 8). Does Coontz convince you of this point? Why or why not?

6. Explain how the word choice in the essay's first paragraph conveys Coontz's attitude toward her opposition.

7. How does Coontz establish credibility in this essay?

8. Analyze the end of the essay. Why do you think Coontz includes the anecdote about Native Americans and European Jesuits? What makes this ending particularly powerful and appropriate to Coontz's article?

WRITING ASSIGNMENTS

1. Write an essay attacking or defending Coontz's claim that "debates over subsidies only get posed in moral terms when women's sexuality is involved" (paragraph 16). To support your position, research public response to the savings and loan bailout mentioned by Coontz, as well as congressional and public debate on social welfare programs.

2. Imagining you are Kristopher Coontz, write a letter to the health teacher described in paragraph 5 encouraging her to rethink her attitude toward single mothers.

GROUP PROJECTS

1. Using free associations (anything that comes to mind), brainstorm a list of terms associated with the phrase *single mother* in a small group. How many associations are positive? How many are negative? Once you have come up with a list, see if you can identify the sources of your associations, such as television programs, news media, political campaign speeches, opinions you have heard from others, and so on. Which sources are grounded in fact? Which are not?

2. What images come to mind when you hear the term *single father*? List as many qualities and ideas as you can, working in small groups. Then, compare them to the ideas you have of single mothers—either the ones Coontz describes or those you listed in the previous exercise. How are they different? How much of the difference do you think has to do with different expectations of men's and women's roles as parents?

3. At the end of her article, Coontz refers to historical contact between two very different cultures: the French and the Montagnais-Naskapi Native Americans. The Native American rebuttal, that the people love all their children, seems like an ideal that many writers in this chapter would endorse. Working in small groups, describe the beliefs and institutions you would create if you could wave a magic wand over today's America. Compare notes with other groups. How similar are all of your utopias? How are they different?

On Black Fathering
Cornel West

In the personal essay below, Cornel West offers some general comments on the problems that black American men face as they try to fulfill their roles as fathers. His thoughts then lead to a moving eulogy for his father, Clifton Lincoln West Jr., who passed away in 1994. As the author praises his father's special gifts of love, remembering small but powerfully enriching moments he shared with his dad, he clearly presents his father as a role model for contemporary fathers—a man who is a shining example of triumph over the problems we all face.

West is a professor of Afro-American studies and religion at Harvard University. He is the author of the best-selling book *Race Matters,* as well as *Keeping Faith* and *Prophesy Deliverance*! He lectures widely on topics ranging from philosophy to democracy and contemporary race issues. This article appeared in a collection of essays *Faith of Our Fathers: African-American Men Reflect on Fatherhood* (1996) edited by Andre C. Willis.

1 One of the most difficult tasks to accomplish in American society is to be a solid, caring, and loving black father. To be a good black father, first you have to negotiate all of the absurd attacks and assaults on your humanity and on your capacity and status as a human being. Second, you have to provide materially and economically, as well as nurture psychologically, personally, and existentially. All of this requires a deep level of maturity. By maturity I mean a solid understanding of who one is as a person, and a sense of sacrifice and courage. For black men to reach that level of maturity and understanding is almost miraculous given the dehumanizing context for black men, and yet millions and millions have done it. It is a tribute to fulfill the highest standards of fatherhood. When I think of my own particular case, I think of

my father, my grandfather, and his father, because what they were able to do was to sustain some sense of dignity and sacrifice even as they dealt with all the arrows that were coming at them on every level in American society.

2   Let's consider the economic level. In America, generally speaking, patriarchal definitions of men in relation to the economic front means you have a job and provide for your family. Many black men did not (and do not) make enough money to provide for their families adequately because of their exclusion from jobs with a living wage. They then oftentimes tended, and tend, to accent certain patriarchal identities (e.g., predatory or abusive behavior) in lieu of the fact that they could not perform the traditional patriarchal roles in American society.

3   Then on the home front, where black men had and have, oftentimes, wives who were and are subject to such white supremacist abuse, either at the white home where these sisters work(ed) or as a service worker in other parts of white society, most black men had to deal with the kinds of scars and bruises that come from knowing that you were supposed to protect your woman, as it were, which is also part of the patriarchal identity in America—a man ought to be able to protect his woman but could not protect her from the vicious abuse. Many black men also recognized that there was a relation between their not being able to get a job given the discrimination and segregation on the one hand and the tremendous power wielded by those white men who were often condoning the abuse of their own wives.

4   How children perceive their father is another interesting component of the dynamic that black fathers have to negotiate. How are black fathers able to convey to their children some affirmative sense of self, some sense of reality—given what is happening to these men on the economic front, given what many of them know is happening to their lives outside of the house, and given the perception by their own children that they are unable to fulfill the expected patriarchal role? In the tradition of the black father, the best ones—I think my grandfather and dad are good examples—came up with ways of negotiating a balance so that they would recognize that exclusion from the economic sphere was real, and recognize that possible abuse of their wives was real, and also recognize that they had to sustain a connection with their kids in which their kids could see the best in them despite the limited and dehumanizing circumstances under which they functioned.

5   My mother happened to be a woman who was not abused in the fashion described above. I remember one incident when a white policeman disrespected my mother. Dad went at him verbally and, in the eyes of the police, ended up violating the law. At that point he just drew a line in the sand that said, "You're going too far." I thank God that a number of incidents like that didn't happen, or he would have ended up in jail forever—like so many other brothers who just do not allow certain levels of disrespect of their mother, wife, sister, or daughter. As a man, what I was able to see in Dad was his ability to transform his own pain with a sense of laughter, and a sense of empathy, and a sense of compassion for others. This was a real act of moral genius Dad accomplished, and I think that it is part of the best of a tradition of moral genius. Unfortunately, large numbers of black men do not reach that level because the rage and the anger is just too deep; it just burns them out and

consumes their soul. Fortunately, on the other hand, you do have many black men that achieve this level and some that go beyond it.

6   In my own case as a father, I certainly tried to emulate and imitate Dad's very ingenious ways of negotiating the balances between what was happening on these different fronts, but because of the sacrifices he and Mom made, I had access to opportunities that he did not. When my son Cliff was born, I was convinced that I wanted to try to do for him what Dad had done for me. But it was not to be—there was no way that I could be the father to my son that my dad was to me. Part of it was that my circumstances were very different. Another part was simply that I was not the man that my father was. My brother is actually the shining example of building on the rich legacy of my dad as a father much more than I am, because he gives everything—right across the board. He is there—whatever the circumstance—has spent time with the kids; he is always there in the same way that Dad was there for us. I'll always try to be a rich footnote to my brother, yet as a father I have certainly not been the person that he was. The effort has been there, the endeavor too, but the circumstances (as well as my not being as deep a person as he or my father), have not enabled me to measure up. On the other hand, my son Cliff turned out to be a decent and fascinating person—and he is still in process, of course.

7   The bottom line for my dad was always love, and he was a deeply Christian man—his favorite song was "I Will Trust in the Lord." He had a profound trust. His trust was much more profound than mine in some ways, even though I work at it. He had a deep love, and that's the thing I've tried to build on with Cliff. My hope and my inclination is that Cliff feels this love, but certainly it takes more than love to nurture and father a son or a daughter.

8   The most important things for black fathers to try to do is to give of themselves, to try to exemplify in their own behavior what they want to see in their sons and daughters, and, most important, to spend time with and give attention to their children. This is a big challenge, yet it is critical as we move into the twenty-first century.

The most difficult task of my life was to give the eulogy for my father. Everything else pales in the face of this challenge. Hence what Dad means to me—like my family, Cliff and Elleni—constitutes who and what I am and will be.

Eulogy

9   Clifton Lincoln West, Jr. What a man. What an individual. What a person. What a servant. We gather here this afternoon in this sacred place and this consecrated space to say good-bye. To bid farewell to a good man, a great Christian who lived a grand and loving life. When I think of my father, I cannot but think of what he said to that reporter from the *Sacramento Bee* when they asked him, "What is it about you and what is it about your family—do you have a secret?" Dad said, "No, we live by Grace—in addition to that, me and his mother, we try to *be there.*" I shall never forget that my father was not simply a man of quiet dignity, steadfast integrity, and high intelligence, but fundamentally and quintessentially he was a man of love, and love means being there for others. That's why when I think of Dad I recall that precious moment in the

fifteenth chapter of John in the eleventh and twelfth verse: "These things have I given unto you that my joy might remain in you, and that your joy might be full. This is my commandment that ye love one another as I have loved you."

10   In the midst of Dad's sophistication and refinement he was always for real. He was someone who was down-to-earth because he took this commandment seriously, and it meant he had to cut against the grain in a world in which he was going to endure lovingly and with compassion. Isn't that what the very core of the gospel is about? The thirteenth chapter of I Corinthians—that great litany of love that Dr. King talked about—deals with it. Dad used to read it all the time. I will never forget when he took me to college in Cambridge, the first time I ever flew on an airplane (it cost about ninety-five dollars then). Dad told me, "Corn, we're praying for you, and always remember: 'Though I speak with the tongues of men and of angels and have not love, I become as a sounding brass or a tinkling cymbal. And though I have the gift of prophecy, and understand all mysteries, and all knowledge; and though I have all faith, so that I could remove mountains, and have not love, I am nothing.'"

11   As we stand here on these stormy banks of Jordan and watch Dad's ship go by, may I remind each and everyone of you that we come from a loving family, a courageous people of African descent, and a rich Christian tradition. We have seen situations in which history has pushed our backs against the wall, and life has knocked us to our knees. In the face of despair and degradation sometimes we know that all we can do is sing a song, or crack a smile, or say a prayer. Yet we refuse to allow grief and misery to have the last word.

12   Dad was a man of love, and if I was to adopt his perspective at this very moment, he would say "Corn, don't push me in the limelight, keep your mother in mind, don't focus on me, keep the family in mind—I'm just a servant passing through." That's the kind of father I had.

13   But he didn't come to it by himself, you see. He was part of a family, he was part of a people, he was part of a tradition that went all the way back to gut-bucket Jim Crow Louisiana, September 7, 1928. He was not supposed to make it, you see. Nobody would have believed that Clifton Lincoln West, Jr., the third child of C. L. West and Lovey West, would have been able to aspire to the heights that he did. No one would have predicted or projected that he would make it through the first three months in Louisiana—Cliff was not supposed to make that trip, you know. He was born the year before the stock market crashed. His family stayed three months in Louisiana, and Grandfather and Grandmother, with three young children in a snowstorm, journeyed on a train to Tulsa, Oklahoma. You all know what Tulsa, Oklahoma, was like. It was seven years after the major riot in this country in which over three hundred folks—black folks—were killed and Greenwood, Archer and Pine—that GAP corner—the Wall Street of black America was all burned out. But Grandmama had something else in mind, and the Lord did too.

14   Dad went on to Paul Laurence Dunbar Elementary School—to give you an idea of what side of town they were living on—and George Washington Carver Junior High School, and Booker T. Washington High School. It was there that he got to

choose the idea of pulling from the best of the world but remaining not of the world. I like that about Dad. He wasn't so excessively pious or so excessively rigid that he became naive and got caught up in narrow doctrines and creeds and thought he was better than anybody else. That's not the kind of man he was. No. His faith was grounded in a love because he knew that he had fallen short of the glory of God. He knew he had inadequacies and shortcomings, but he was going to struggle anyhow; he was going to keep keeping on anyway.

15   After high school he went on to the military for three years. He could have easily given his life for this country. When he returned to Tulsa, Oklahoma, he was refused admission at the University of Tulsa, and then went on to that grand institution, Fisk University, where he met that indescribably wonderful, beautiful, lovable honor student from Orange, Texas—Irene Bias. I'll never forget when we were at Fisk together, he described the place right outside Jubilee Hall where they met. I said, "Dad, that's a special place," and he said, "Yes, that meeting was the beginning of the peak of my life." As their love began to grow and multiply, the army grabbed him back again for eighteen months, but in the years to come they had young Clifton, my brother, to whom I'm just a footnote; myself, of course; and Cynthia and Cheryl. We moved from Oklahoma through Topeka, Kansas, on our way to 8008 48th Avenue, Glen Elder. Yes, how proud we were driving up in that bright orange Mercury. We were at the cutting edge of residential breakdown in Sacramento, but along the way, for almost a decade, Dad, and the men of Glen Elder—Mr. Peters, Mr. Pool, Mr. Powell, Mr. Reed—these were black men who cared and who worked together. These overworked yet noble men built the little league diamond themselves,and then they organized the league into ten teams—minor and major leagues for the neighborhood. They provided a means by which character and integrity could be shaped among the young brothers. Then every Sunday, onto Shiloh—"can't wait for the next sermon of Reverend Willie P. Cooke, just hope that he didn't go too long"—but we knew that the Lord was working in him. Dad would always tell us, "You know how blessed I am, how blessed we are. Never think that we've come as far as we have on our own."

16   When we were in trouble, there was Mr. Fields, Mrs. Ray, and Mrs. Harris—there were hundreds of folks who made a difference. You all remember when Dad went to the hospital when he was thirty-one years old and the doctors had given up on him. There was a great sadness on Forty-eighth Avenue because he had left Mom with four little children. Granddad—the Reverend C. L. West, left his church for months to come and be with Mom—Grandmom came as well—and Dad was in the hospital in Oakland. They had given up on him; the medical profession had reached its conclusion and said they could do nothing. And we said, "We know the power. Let Him step in." We knew that Reverend Cook hadn't been preaching that "Jesus is a rock in a weary land, and water in dry places, and food when you are hungry, and a mind regulator and a heart fixer" for nothing. And we came to Calvary in prayer.

17   Can you imagine how different our lives would have been if we had lost Dad then, in 1961, rather than 1994? Even in the midst of our fear we rejoice. It would

have been a different world for each and every one of us, especially the children. Dad kept going after his recovery. He worked at McClellan Air Force Base— steadily missed some of those promotions he should have got, but he stayed convinced that he was going to teach people right no matter what, even given his own situation.

18   That's another thing I loved about him. People always ask me, "West, why do you still talk about love? It's played out. Why when you talk about blackness is it always linked to white brothers and sisters and yellow brothers and sisters and red brothers and sisters and brown brothers and sisters?" And I tell them about John 15:11–12. I tell them that I dedicated my life a long time ago to the same Jesus that Dad dedicated his life to, to the same Jesus that Reverend C. L. West dedicated his life, to the same Jesus that my grandfather on my mother's side and my grandmother on my mother's side dedicated their lives to, but, more important, I saw in the concrete, with Dad and Mom, a love that transcends skin pigmentation. I saw it on the ground. Dad taught us that even as you keep track of the injustice, you don't lose track of the humanity. That's what love and being there is all about. Dad made it a priority and preference to be there for us. He made a choice. It meant that he would have a life of interruptions because those who are fundamentally committed to being there are going to be continually interrupted—your own agenda, your own project, is going to be interfered with. Dad was always open to that kind of interruption. He was able to translate a kind of unpredictable interruption into a supportive intervention in somebody else's life. More important, Dad realized that a being-there kind of love meant that you had to have follow up and follow through. One could not just show up—one has to follow up and follow through. This is the most difficult aspect of it. Love is inseparable from pain and hurt and sadness and sorrow and disappointment, but Dad knew that you had to have follow up and follow through. He knew that you had to struggle in the midst of that pain that that hurt—you had to have just not simply the high moments of love, but the funk of love, the stink and the stench of love. In all of his relationships Dad embodied precisely that struggle with the high moments of love and the low moments of love. He knew that the cross was not just about love and that it was not just about celebration—it was about sadness, stench, and funk. That is what the blood was about, not Kool-aid but blood. That's how inseparable scars, bruises, and wounds are from joy, affirmation, and wholeness. If you were serious about love, if you were serious about being there for people you were going to be there in the midst of any situation, any circumstances, any condition. Dad realized that God being there for us in any situation and circumstance meant that if he was going to be Godlike, he had to be there in any situation for us. I've been alive now for forty years, and on Thursday I'll be forty-one years old, and *not once has my mother or father disappointed me.* They have always been there. That is a blessing, and I do not deserve it. It's a blessing, and I am thankful for it.

19   So as we bid farewell to Dad, I want you all to know that I am looking forward to a family reunion. I am looking forward to union together on the other side of the Jordan. I am looking forward to seeing Dad in a place where the wicked will cease

their troubling and the weary shall be at rest. I tell you when I get there, I'm going down Revelation Boulevard to the corner of John Street, right around the corner from Mark's place. But I want to go to Nahum's place. I don't want to be in Jeremiah's house, it would be too crowded. I don't even want to be down on Peter Street, too many people there—I want some quiet time. I want to sit down with C. L. West, I want to sit down with Nick Bias, and I want to sit down with Aunt Juanita, and I want to sit down with Aunt Tiny. And I want to sit down with Dad! I want to let them know that we did the best that we could to keep alive the best of the legacy of love that they left to us. And when we come together, we will come together in a way in which there will be no more tears, no more heartache, no more heartbreak, no more sadness and sorrow, no more agony and anguish. We shall sit at the feet of the Lord and be blessed, and our souls will look back and wonder how we got over, how we got over.

EXPLORING THE TEXT

1. According to West's description in the first three paragraphs, what problems and forces do black men have to overcome to be good fathers? What obstacles do they face?

2. West describes what a black father must do. From comments in this essay, and by reading between the lines, can you extrapolate his views on what black mothering might mean? Do you agree that fathering and mothering do (or should) differ?

3. What is the patriarchal role or patriarchal identity to which West refers? Does he find it completely good or completely evil? Refer to specific passages in the text to support your response.

4. How does West perceive his own abilities to fulfill the ideal of fathering? How does he say he measures up to his father's and his brother's examples? If you are a parent, how do you measure up to your own ideal of what a good parent should be? If you are not a parent, how do your parents measure up to their own ideals?

5. This article is made up of two separate parts: a set of comments on black fathering and a eulogy for Cornel West's father, Clifton Lincoln West Jr. How specific are the examples and statements in the first part, the general comments? How specific are the examples and statements in the second part? Why do you think West paired these two different pieces in one article?

6. West mentions a number of people and institutions his father was able to draw upon for support during his lifetime. Where did his father turn to for help in being a father? Was he able to become such an excellent father alone or did he have help?

7. Do you think that West has provided a thorough and accurate statement of the problems that black fathers in America face today? As you respond,

consider his purpose in writing, especially in the second half of the article, the eulogy. Do you think this article is more informative or inspirational?

WRITING ASSIGNMENTS

1. Using Clifton West's eulogy as an example, write a statement praising the accomplishments of one of your parents. If you would prefer, write a statement praising the accomplishments and effects on your life of an important adult (such as a religious leader, a teacher, or someone who has made a difference for you). What qualities do you find admirable in this person? What in his or her example do you try to emulate?
2. Both Barbara Dafoe Whitehead and West make a strong connection between being a good father and being a good husband. Compare and contrast the two essays. Examine specifically what each writer believes makes a good father.
3. Using your library's resources, examine the claims that black men have a harder time fulfilling the traditional, patriarchal role as father. What information can you find on employment, education levels, and social problems that help support West's generalized claims? Do other men, particularly from other minority groups, have similar problems?

GROUP PROJECTS

1. Look up the Bible passage West provides in paragraph 10, 1 Corinthians 13. Divide your class into two (or more) groups; have half of the class apply the statements about love to fathering and have half apply them to mothering. Try to come up with practical rules or guidelines for parenting behavior. For instance, you might apply the first phase of verse 4, "Charity suffereth long, and is kind," to mean that fathers or mothers should not lose patience with children and should count to ten if they feel impatient. Once you have brainstormed separate lists for fathers and mothers, compare them. Do you find any differences?
2. Working together, brainstorm a list of resources or community services that you think would help individual men with their fathering skills. You might list some of the same kinds of resources that West's father had access to, such as a church or a group of men interested in benefiting their communities. You might also be able to recommend some other resources that contemporary young men would find valuable.
3. Research and compile a directory of the different resources available to young fathers in your area. Assign different members of the class to different areas. For instance, one group might contact programs through the YMCA or similar public organizations; another might contact local reli-

gious organizations or investigate noncredit community college course offerings. Compile a description of your findings—including telephone numbers, contact people, and a description of the services offered—for use by your campus's counseling services office.

Pro/Con: Should Same-Sex Marriages Be Legalized?

The next two selections represent contrary views on the issue of gay marriage.

PRO

Let Gays Marry
Andrew Sullivan

Andrew Sullivan is the editor of *New Republic,* a magazine of cultural and political opinion. He is a gay man, a conservative, and a Roman Catholic. His 1996 book, *Virtually Normal: An Argument About Homosexuality,* argues that the best way to tackle antigay prejudice is to shape public laws and policies that extend exactly the same rights and protections to gays as they do to heterosexuals.

This article originally appeared in *Newsweek* in 1996, paired with the William Bennett article, the next essay. In his half of the debate, Sullivan argues that allowing gay men and lesbians to marry is a compassionate and appropriate response to "the most simple, the most natural, the most human instinct in the world."

1 A state cannot deem a class of persons a stranger to its laws," declared the Supreme Court last week. It was a monumental statement. Gay men and lesbians, the conservative court said, are no longer strangers in America. They are citizens, entitled, like everyone else, to equal protection—no special rights, but simple equality.

2 For the first time in Supreme Court history, gay men and women were seen not as some powerful lobby trying to subvert America, but as the people we truly are—the sons and daughters of countless mothers and fathers, with all the weaknesses and strengths and hopes of everybody else. And what we seek is not some special place in America but merely to be a full and equal part of America, to give back to our society without being forced to lie or hide or live as second-class citizens.

3 That is why marriage is so central to our hopes. People ask us why we want the right to marry, but the answer is obvious. It's the same reason anyone wants the right to marry. At some point in our lives, some of us are lucky enough to meet the person we truly love. And we want to commit to that person in front of our family and country for the rest of our lives. It's the most simple, the most natural, the most human instinct in the world. How could anyone seek to oppose that?

4   Yes, at first blush, it seems like a radical proposal, but, when you think about it some more, it's actually the opposite. Throughout American history, to be sure, marriage has been between a man and a woman, and in many ways our society is built upon that institution. But none of that need change in the slightest. After all, no one is seeking to take away anybody's right to marry, and no one is seeking to force any church to change any doctrine in any way. Particular religious arguments against same-sex marriage are rightly debated within the churches and faiths them-selves. That is not the issue here: there is a separation between church and state in this country. We are only asking that when the government gives out *civil* marriage licenses, those of us who are gay should be treated like anybody else.

5   Of course, some argue that marriage is *by definition* between a man and a woman. But for centuries, marriage was *by definition* a contract in which the wife was her husband's legal property. and we changed that. For centuries, marriage was *by definition* between two people of the same race. And we changed that. We changed these things because we recognized that human dignity is the same whether you are a man or a woman, black or white. And no one has any more of a choice to be gay than to be black or white or male or female.

6   Some say that marriage is only about raising children, but we let childless het-erosexual couples be married (Bob and Elizabeth Dole, Pat and Shelley Buchanan, for instance). Why should gay couples be treated differently? Others fear that there is no logical difference between allowing same-sex marriage and sanctioning polygamy and other horrors. But the issue of whether to sanction multiple spouses (gay or straight) is completely separate from whether, in the existing institution be-tween two unrelated adults, the government should discriminate between its citizens.

7   This is, in fact, if only Bill Bennett could see it, a deeply conservative cause. It seeks to change no one else's rights or marriages in any way. It seeks merely to pro-mote monogamy, fidelity and the disciplines of family life among people who have long been cast to the margins of society. And what could be a more conservative project than that? Why indeed would any conservative seek to oppose those very family values for gay people that he or she supports for everybody else? Except, of course, to make gay men and lesbians strangers in their own country, to forbid them ever to come home.

EXPLORING THE TEXT

1. What is the difference between a stranger and a citizen? Between a "pow-erful lobby" and "the sons and daughters" of other people? How do these sets of opposing terms in Sullivan's first paragraphs identify his stance on gay marriage?
2. Why does Sullivan say that gay men and lesbians want to marry—what motivates them? Do heterosexual couples marry for the same motivations as gays?

3. Can you think of other, less idealistic reasons that a man and a woman might want to marry? Based on these other practical (or even shady) reasons that people marry, how slanted do you think Sullivan's description is of motivations for marrying?

4. How does Sullivan anticipate and defend against the possible counterarguments that gay marriages are unnatural? That they are against some religions' teachings?

5. Sullivan uses historical change in paragraph 5 as part of his argument to legalize gay marriage. How is his use of history to support his ideas similar to Barbara Dafoe Whitehead's use of history ("Rethinking Divorce")? How is it different?

6. Why does Sullivan call gay marriage a "deeply conservative cause" (paragraph 7)? That is, what does the label *conservative* mean? Has he adequately proven that this is a conservative issue?

7. What segment of his readership is Sullivan trying to persuade by using the label *conservative*? What connotations does that word have? What other loaded words or phrases does he use in his final paragraph to appeal to these readers?

8. Before you read Sullivan's article, had you thought much about extending the right to marry to gay men and lesbians? Has Sullivan's article changed your mind, swayed you one way or the other, or left you undecided? Discuss the effect, if any, this article has had on your personal beliefs and opinions.

WRITING ASSIGNMENTS

1. Write a letter to a minister, rabbi, or other religious leader. Explain why you think he or she should agree to perform a commitment ceremony, celebrating the long-term partnership of two of your best friends, a gay or lesbian couple. Assume that this religious leader is generally sympathetic to gay people, but has not given much thought to the issues of gay marriage. Use Sullivan's comments about the reasons people want to marry to help you make your case.

2. Gays and lesbians have become more visible on television over the past several years. What images has television presented its viewers? What objections have sponsors or viewers raised to these images? How do the images correspond to Sullivan's claims that gay men and lesbians are just like everyone else? Use your school's library to find newspaper and media trade journals to research this trend.

3. Most of the authors in this chapter have made children an important focus of their arguments about family. Both Sullivan and Bennett write as if gays and lesbians are not parents. Using your school's library to locate both mainstream and gay press resources, research the impact of marriage laws

upon the children of gay parents. You may need to narrow your discussion to topics such as adoption opportunities, child custody or visitation when gay relationships break up, professional evaluations of children's adjustment and well-being in gay families, or similar legal and social concerns.

GROUP PROJECTS

1. Sullivan says that gay and lesbian couples want public recognition of their partnerships. What parts of any marriage are public? Working in small groups, brainstorm a list. Some examples to get you started: a wedding ceremony, tax breaks, spousal health insurance through an employer, formal relationships with in-laws and friends.

2. Will legalizing gay marriage help or harm the social acceptance gay men and lesbians now face in America? What benefits might all gay people receive, whether or not they choose to marry? Do you think that a legal change in marriage will help to change the beliefs of people who now disapprove of homosexuality? Why or why not? Working in small groups, list and discuss the consequences of the change Sullivan suggests and present your findings to classmates in a panel discussion.

3. Working as a team with your school's Internet Web browser, see what information you can find about gay and lesbian marriages. For instance, can you locate organizations that promote the idea of extending marriage? Examples of gay and lesbian commitment ceremonies? Additional arguments to support what Sullivan has written in this article? Once you have assembled a preliminary list of topics, compare lists with other groups. Then, select a narrower topic for each group to research through the Internet. Assemble a list of the ten most important Web sites that your group finds on its topic and prepare a brief description of what Internet users might expect to find at each site.

CON

Leave Marriage Alone
William Bennett

In this article, published next to Sullivan's article in *Newsweek* magazine in 1996, William Bennett explains why he does not believe gay marriages should become public policy. He is especially concerned that such a change would encourage immoral ideas and behavior, among gays and straights alike.

Bennett has served the United States as chairman of the National Endowment for the Humanities and as secretary of education during the Bush administration. He writes about social and domestic issues, in works such as *The Book of Virtues* (1995). He is also cofounder of Empower America, an organization promoting progressive-conservative public policy.

1 There are at least two key issues that divide proponents and opponents of same-sex marriage. The first is whether legally recognizing same-sex unions would strengthen or weaken the institution. The second has to do with the basic understanding of marriage itself.

2 The advocates of same-sex marriage say that they seek to strengthen and celebrate marriage. That may be what some intend. But I am certain that it will not be the reality. Consider: the legal union of same-sex couples would shatter the conventional definition of marriage, change the rules which govern behavior, endorse practices which are completely antithetical to the tenets of all of the world's major religions, send conflicting signals about marriage and sexuality, particularly to the young, and obscure marriage's enormously consequential function—procreation and child-rearing.

3 Broadening the definition of marriage to include same-sex unions would stretch it almost beyond recognition—and new attempts to expand the definition still further would surely follow. On what *principled* ground can Andrew Sullivan exclude others who most desperately want what he wants, legal recognition and social acceptance? Why on earth would Sullivan exclude from marriage a bisexual who wants to marry two other people? After all, exclusion would be a denial of that person's sexuality. The same holds true of a father and daughter who want to marry. Or two sisters. Or men who want (consensual) polygamous arrangements. Sullivan may think some of these arrangements are unwise. But having employed sexual relativism in his own defense, he has effectively lost the capacity to draw any lines and make moral distinctions.

4 Forsaking all others is an essential component of marriage. Obviously it is not always honored in practice. But it is the ideal to which we rightly aspire, and in most marriages the ideal is in fact the norm. Many advocates of same-sex marriage simply do not share this ideal; promiscuity among homosexual males is well known. Sullivan himself has written that gay male relationships are served by the "openness of the contract" and that homosexuals should resist allowing their "varied and complicated lives" to be flattened into a "single, moralistic model." But that "single, moralistic model" has served society exceedingly well. The burden of proof ought to be on those who propose untested arrangements for our most important institution.

5 A second key difference I have with Sullivan goes to the very heart of marriage itself. I believe that marriage is not an arbitrary construct which can be redefined simply by those who lay claim to it. It is an honorable estate, instituted of God and built in moral, religious, sexual and human realities. Marriage is based on a natural teleology, on the different, complementary nature of men and women—and how they refine, support, encourage and complete one another. It is the institution through which we propagate, nurture, educate and sustain our species.

6　　That we have to engage in this debate at all is an indication of how steep our moral slide has been. Worse, those who defend the traditional understanding of marriage are routinely referred to (though not to my knowledge by Sullivan) as "homophobes," "gay-bashers," "intolerant" and "bigoted." Can one defend an honorable, 4,000-year-old tradition and not be called these names?

7　　This is a large, tolerant, diverse country. In America people are free to do as they wish, within broad parameters. It is also a country in sore need of shoring up some of its most crucial institutions: marriage and the family, schools, neighborhoods, communities. But marriage and family are the greatest of these. That is why they are elevated and revered. We should keep them so.

EXPLORING THE TEXT

1. What are the two key issues Bennett says people disagree over in debating gay marriage? What paragraphs does Bennett devote to the first issue? Where does he write about the second? Summarize his stance on these two issues, using one well-written sentence for each.

2. What emotional response does Bennett intend to elicit from readers with the final sentence of paragraph 2? Why is this sentence so long? What is the effect of its length?

3. What is wrong with the different kinds of relationships Bennett describes in paragraph 3? Why do you think Bennett does not explain what he thinks is wrong with them? Does his silence weaken or strengthen his argument?

4. Bennett states that Sullivan's argument lacks "principled ground." What does he mean by this statement? Can you come up with a satisfactory principle that Sullivan might write, allowing gay marriage but prohibiting public recognition and approval of other kinds of relationships?

5. In paragraph 4, Bennett quotes material that Andrew Sullivan has written elsewhere. Do Sullivan's statements actually support promiscuity, as Bennett claims? Has Bennett used Sullivan's words fairly, giving them adequate context and development?

6. What is "the very heart of marriage" (paragraph 5), according to Bennett? What sources does he use to justify his definition of marriage? What counterarguments does Sullivan offer to this definition?

7. What answer do you think Bennett expects to his rhetorical question at the end of paragraph 6: yes or no? What tone and expectations about his readers does Bennett convey in this paragraph? How hopeful is he that his views will be endorsed by his readers?

8. Before you read Bennett's article, what did you think about gay marriage? Did Bennett change any of your ideas or give you material to think about that you had not considered before? Was he successful in persuading you to his point of view, if you did not agree completely with him before?

WRITING ASSIGNMENTS

1. Draft a letter to the same religious figure described in the first writing exercise for the Sullivan article, commenting on the same two friends' desire to have a commitment ceremony. This time, use Bennett's arguments to explain why you think the ceremony is not such a good idea. Keep in mind as you write that a commitment ceremony is not a marriage; it is not binding or legal. Also keep in mind that you love your friends and that your opinions may cause them some pain.

2. Bennett claims that recognizing gay marriages will, among other problems, "send conflicting signals about marriage and sexuality . . . to the young" (paragraph 2). In your opinion, what signals should be sent to young people about marriage and sexuality? What messages does our culture actually send now—especially since we don't always live up to our ideals? What would change about these messages if gay marriage were recognized? Do you agree with Bennett about the changes or not?

3. Bennett claims that marriage is based on "the different, complementary nature of men and women." Many of the authors in this chapter on family also believe that men and women are different in some important ways. Choose one article and examine the stated and implied differences the author believes exist. Based on this information, do you think the author would argue for or against gay marriage? Why or why not?

4. What do other cultures think and do about marriage? Are there different practices, acceptable relationships, taboos, or tolerances for slipups? Using your library's resources in sociology, anthropology, and related social science fields, examine other ideas about marriage. You will want to narrow your research and discussion, either by focusing on a comprehensive overview of one culture or by choosing one aspect to examine among several different cultures. You might even choose to investigate the beliefs and practices of Americans who lived several decades or centuries ago.

GROUP PROJECTS

1. Do you think that Bennett deserves to be called intolerant, bigoted, and homophobic for his views? Divide the class into two (or more) groups to prepare debate responses, with each group taking one side or the other.

2. In paragraph 4, Bennett objects to relationships that deviate from a " 'single, moralistic model.' " Working in small groups, come up with lists of arrangements he might describe this way. Some possibilities: divorced parents who live together for their children's sake; common-law marriages (with no legal or religious sanction); group living arrangements in which two members become romantically involved. Pool your lists with

those generated by classmates. Are all of the possibilities you have listed equally objectionable? Should some be encouraged and others discouraged? Why?

3. Should marriage be a political and public institution, as Sullivan believes? Or should it be a religious and moral institution, as Bennett believes? Or should it share some features of both? List the qualities that marriage draws from each of these realms. Then, divide your class into two debate groups, assigning half the members to argue that marriage should be primarily public and the other half to argue that it should be primarily moral.

4. Design a survey that you will administer anonymously to other members of your class, asking their opinions about gay issues besides marriage. Have one group prepare a set of related questions on a single issue. Some examples might be student activity fees used to fund gay groups on campus, discrimination in housing or employment, or gays in the military. After you have tabulated the results, discuss what you have found. Are there any surprises? Inconsistencies? Hot topic issues?

While the adult crime rate has dropped, juvenile crimes have risen at a disturbing rate since 1990 in both scope and severity. The statistics are frightening. One-quarter of the people arrested for weapons offenses during 1997 were males under the age of 18. Juvenile homicides have quadrupled over the last decade. Likewise, the number of children murdered has increased 82 percent in that same period. Particularly disturbing is the fact that things could get even worse since the number of juveniles approaching the teenage "peak crime years" is greater than it has been in nearly half a century.

The problem is not restricted to any particular population or area. In fact, a survey by the American Medical Association reported that suburban children were just as likely to face assault as urban children. Drug and alcohol use is increasing among youth, leaving parents, teachers, civic leaders, and law enforcement at a loss to stop the escalating problem. But while many argue about how to solve the problem, almost everyone agrees that its roots are deeply embedded in our culture.

How we judge acceptable behavior is determined by our social background and cultural ideology. However, our value system may be sending out mixed messages to teenagers. In the first essay, "The Culture of Violence," Myriam Miedzian provides an overview of our contemporary culture and the kinds of forces that work on the young. In her piece, Miedzian imagines how anthropologists from a remote tribe might view us were they to study various aspects of our popular culture. What, in other words, might they conclude about our value system from the headline-news roundup of daily assaults and murders; or male movie idols, Sylvester Stallone and Arnold Schwarzenegger; or all the mayhem on television and movies; or rock and rap songs advocating violence against women; or video games depicting street warfare? They might conclude we were a society bent on self-destruction.

While the media and music industry are frequently cited as underlying causes of youth violence, the authors of the next selection disagree. Instead, Mike Males and Faye Docuyanan cite rising youth poverty as the reason why juveniles increasingly turn to crime. In "Giving Up on the Young," they explain that the poverty gap motivates children to take what they don't have. Instead of helping such kids, our society locks them away at younger and younger ages—a plan that Males and Docuyanan say is doomed to failure.

The next two pieces look for alternate solutions to early lockup. In their editorial "Putting the Brakes on Juvenile Crime," Ralph C. Martin II and William D. O'Leary explain that early intervention—helping children before they commit criminal acts—is a far better answer than locking them up and throwing away the keys. Instead of focusing on crime and punishment, Martin and O'Leary call on communities to make an "unwavering" and comprehensive commitment to making a difference before problems arise. It is just such individual commitment that is explored by Geoffrey Canada in the next essay. In "Peace in the Streets," the author calls for all communities to band together and effect change. As he illustrates, a single individual has the power to impact youth for the better. One *can* make a difference, especially when one is part of a community working as a unified force.

Two oft-cited gateways to violent crimes are drugs and alcohol. The next piece turns to the home front and growing parental fears that children may be abusing controlled substances. But in her editorial "Johnny, Take Your Drug Test!" Ellen Goodman questions if parental fears are replacing parental trust. Is this Big Brother approach of tracking our children the answer to solving the youth drug problem?

This chapter closes with a pair of opposition pieces—two contrary points of view regarding juvenile punishment. In "Youth Crime Has Changed—And So Must the Juvenile Justice System," Tom Reilly contends that the juvenile court system, established in 1899, is outdated. It is not equipped to handle the kinds of brutal crimes routinely committed by today's youth. We're not dealing with simple juvenile delinquents, but cold-blooded juvenile killers. On the other side are Abbe Smith and Lael E. H. Chester who are fearful of a system that labels young offenders as "predators." Under new legislation, young offenders, of both violent and nonviolent crimes, could be "banished" to adult prisons. Considering what goes on in adult prisons, the authors conclude that treating children as adults is not the answer to juvenile crime.

The Culture of Violence
Myriam Miedzian

Culture shapes behavior and our society's most impressionable members—children—learn what behavior is acceptable and what's unacceptable by watching the activities their culture sponsors. They imitate what they see in the various cultural forms—music, sports, games, drama, and so on—and reason out the principles by which actions are accepted by their community. In an effort to explore the kind of culture our children are being raised in today, Myriam Miedzian creates a hypothetical situation. She imagines what anthropologists from an isolated tribe in Australia would make of contemporary America were they to examine our popular role models, films, leisure time, music, sports, toys, and the content of play activity, as well as other components of our culture. Their conclusions would point to some "deep contradictions and absurdities" of our habits as they ponder the root causes.

Miedzian is the author of *Boys Will Be Boys: How We Encourage Violence in Our Sons and What We Can Do to Stop It* (1991) from which this essay is taken.

1   Anyone who has ever taken a cultural anthropology course is aware that different societies weave different patterns of culture, and that the different threads—religion, music, sports, children's games, drama, work, relations between the sexes, communal values, and so on—that make up the cultural web of a society are usually intricately related.

2   If a tribe's songs and dramas are centered on violence and warfare, if its young boys play war games and violently competitive sports from the earliest age, if its

paintings, sculptures, and potteries depict fights and scenes of battle, it is a pretty sure bet that this is not a peaceful, gentle tribe.

3   Every child in the world is born into a particular culture and "from the moment of his birth the customs into which he is born shape his experience and behaviour," we are told by anthropologist Ruth Benedict.[1] Throughout history people have known this intuitively and so they have been careful to acculturate their children from the youngest age into a pattern of behavior that is acceptable to the group. We have in our own society some very clear and simple examples: Christian groups like the Hutterites and the Amish, or Jewish groups like the Hasidim want their children to grow up to be devoted primarily to religious rather than material values, to be sexually modest and completely chaste before marriage. They share a strong sense of community and commitment to taking responsibility for the well-being of all their members. Among the Hutterites and Amish there is a strong emphasis on non-violence. None of these groups allows their children to participate in the mainstream culture.

4   Sometimes societies develop customs that become highly detrimental to their members. A cultural trait that may be of considerable value in a limited form or that was of value at an earlier point of history is elaborated and continued in a form that is socially deleterious. Ruth Benedict refers to this as the "asocial elaboration of a cultural trait."

5   A prime example is the incest taboos and marital customs of the Kurnai tribe of Australia. Many a student of anthropology has laughed or at least chuckled at Benedict's descriptions. Benedict explains that all human societies have incest taboos, "but the relatives to whom the prohibition refers differ utterly among different peoples."[2] The Kurnai, like many other tribes, do not differentiate "lineal from collateral kin." Fathers and uncles, brothers and cousins, are not distinguished, so that "all relatives of one's own generation are one's brothers and sisters."[3]

6   The Kurnai also have an extreme horror of "brother-sister" marriage. Add to this their strict rule with respect to locality in the choice of a mate and the right of old men to marry the attractive young girls, and a situation is created in which there are almost no mates for young people, especially young men. This does not lead the Kurnai to change their incest taboos or rules of marriage. Quite to the contrary, "they insist upon them with every show of violence."[4]

7   As a result, the usual way for tribe members to marry is to elope. As soon as the villagers get wind of this crime, they set out in pursuit of the newlyweds with the intent to kill them if they catch them. That probably all the pursuers were married in the same way does not bother anyone. Moral indignation runs high. However, if the couple can reach an island traditionally recognized as a safe haven, the tribe may eventually accept them as husband and wife.

8   Cultural webs and irrationalities are simpler and easier to see in small, isolated tribes or small communities than in large industrial societies, but they exist in both.

9   Industrialized societies are made up of different socioeconomic classes, and often different ethnic groups. In a large country like ours, differences in geography and climate affect people. Nevertheless, there are certain aspects of our culture, besides a common language, that are widely shared. Children and adolescents from

coast to coast play with the same toys, see many of the same films and TV shows, listen to the same rock music, play many of the same sports.

10   I suspect that if the Kurnai were to send a few anthropologists over to study contemporary American society, they would be as amused by our irrationalities as we are by theirs.

11   On the one hand, they would find in our Declaration of Independence a deep commitment to life, liberty, and the pursuit of happiness. An examination of the Constitution would reveal that the goals of our government include "justice," "domestic tranquility," and "the general welfare." An examination of contemporary society would reveal that we deplore murder, assault, wife- and child-battering, sexual abuse of children, and rape.

12   On the other hand, our newspaper headlines, our TV news with its daily roundups of murders and rapes, our crime statistics, and the fact that over six hundred thousand of our citizens—mostly male—are in prison would inform them just how deeply these problems afflict us. Having established this strong contradiction between our professed goals and beliefs, and our reality, our Kurnai anthropologists would begin to wonder what we teach our boys that makes them become such violent men. They would ask, "Who are your young boys' heroes, who are their role models?"

13   Rambo, Chuck Norris, Arnold Schwarzenegger, would be high on the list.

14   "Do your boys watch only violent adventure films?"

15   No. They like comedies too, but when they reach adolescence many of them become particularly fond of "slasher" films in which they can watch people being skinned, decapitated, cut up into chunks. Wanting to experience all aspects of our culture, the Kurnai anthropologists would undoubtedly watch a few slasher films. They would find out that the perpetrators are practically all male, and the films frequently center on the victimization of females.

16   "What about the rest of their leisure time, what do your boys do with it?"

17   Our young boys spend about twenty-eight hours a week watching TV. By the time they are eighteen, they have seen an average of twenty-six thousand TV murders, a vast majority of them committed by men.

18   "Do they listen to much music?"

19   They certainly do. They spend billions of dollars a year on records and tapes, not to mention radio and MTV. The Kurnai anthropologists might be advised to turn on MTV to see what the young boys like. They would find that the programming often consists of very angry-looking young men singing lyrics that are hard to make out, but the music sounds as angry as the men look. Women on the shows are often scantily clad, and sometimes it looks as if they are about to be raped.

20   "Can we see the texts of some of these lyrics?"

21   Samples of popular hits might include an album by Poison that reached number three on the Billboard pop charts and has sold over two million copies. Its lyrics include, "I want action tonight . . . I need a hot and I need it fast/*If I can't have her, I'll take her and make her* [my emphasis]."

22   Switching channels from MTV, the Kurnai would find that a considerable amount of American television is devoted to sports. Brawls and fistfights are com-

mon at these events, particularly in hockey but also in baseball and basketball. The main tactics in football, tackling and blocking, look exactly like bodily assault.

23   The anthropologists would find out that our high rates of violent crime have been exacerbated by an ever-growing drug problem. In light of this they would note that drug and alcohol abuse are common among athletes and the heavy metal musicians that many young people admire and emulate.

24   "What about your sons' toys?" the Kurnai might ask next.

25   A trip to the playground or a look under Christmas trees—religious symbols used to commemorate the birth of the deified founder of the nation's leading religion who preached a gospel of love and nonviolence—would reveal that while little girls get dolls and carriages and dollhouses; little boys get guns, "action figures" like GI Joe, and violent space-age toys and games.

26   By now the Kurnai would no doubt have discovered that rates of violence in our society are highest among boys and men raised by single mothers. Being anthropologists they would not be surprised since they would be aware of cross-cultural data indicating that the presence of a caring, involved father decreases the chances of a son being violent.

27   Delving deeper, they would find out that many boys who start out with fathers lose them along the way through divorce. They would hear divorced women, [as well as] social workers, psychiatrists, and other professionals complain bitterly that a large percentage of divorced fathers never or rarely see their children, nor do they make child support payments.

28   Increasingly stunned by the irrationalities of our society, they might inquire of these professionals: In light of the lack of interest of so many of your men in nurturing and taking responsibility for their children, and the subsequent increases in rates of violence and other social problems, why don't you encourage your little boys to become good fathers by buying them dolls and baby carriages and dollhouses? Why don't you encourage them to play house instead of training them to become warriors?

29   "Parents would never stand for that," professionals and parents would explain. "They are much too afraid that their sons might grow up to be gay if they played with 'wimpy' girls' toys."

30   At this point the visiting anthropologist might emit a cry of disbelief. Is it not obvious to these strange people who deplore violence, yet do everything possible to encourage it in their sons, that gay men do not have children? They don't push baby carriages, change diapers, or give bottles to their babies. Only heterosexual men become fathers and do these things. What could be more absurd than to think that little boys will become gay by rehearsing the quintessentially heterosexual role of being a father?[5]

31   Having established the deep contradictions and absurdities of our customs, the Kurnai would look for their origins. They would find that like many warrior societies, we have a long tradition of raising our boys to be tough, emotionally detached, deeply competitive, and concerned with dominance.

32   These traits, they would note, have gotten out of hand. The enormous escalation of violence that Americans are experiencing seems to coincide with the develop-

ment of a vast system of communications technology that has led to the creation of a culture of violence of unprecedented dimensions, much of it directed toward or available to children. Instead of treasuring their children as a precious national resource to be handled with the utmost care, Americans have allowed them to be exploited as a commercial market.

33 How could they let this happen? the Kurnai would wonder. Surely they must understand that one of society's most important tasks, the socialization of the next generation, should not be left in the hands of people whose main concern is financial gain, people who will not hesitate to exploit the basest human tendencies for profit?

34 In their efforts to understand this puzzle they would be helped by their understanding of their own culture. The Kurnai would see that our "laissez-faire" attitude toward our children can be traced to the asocial elaboration of some of our most beneficial and admirable values, just as their absurd marital rules can be traced to originally useful taboos.

35 A system of largely unfettered free enterprise led to the extraordinary economic development of the nation. The subsequent commitment to free enterprise is so deep that the economic exploitation of children is taken for granted. Companies manufacture toys for six-year-olds that encourage reckless violence, sadism, and torture, and few people question their right to do so.

36 The Kurnai would turn next to the First Amendment, the embodiment of the national commitment to free speech.

37 It would not escape their attention that with respect to pornographic and "indecent" material, it has long been acknowledged that the First Amendment cannot apply equally to children and adults. Long-standing laws protect children from such material. That is why there are no Saturday morning pornographic TV programs.

38 For some strange reason, the Kurnai would conclude, these people have blinded themselves to the fact that what makes sense with respect to sex makes at least as much sense with respect to violence. And so they have allowed their children to be raised on tens of thousands of TV murders, detailed depictions of sadistic mutilations on the screen, and song lyrics that advocate rape.

39 What a perfect example of an asocial elaboration, they might exclaim! Everything is justified in terms of free enterprise and free speech, but this freedom as interpreted in present-day society contributes to the nation's enslavement!

40 Don't these Americans see that boys raised in a culture of violence are not free? Their basest, most destructive tendencies are reinforced from the youngest age to the detriment of their altruistic, pro-social tendencies. Then when they commit serious acts of violence they are sent to prison.

41 Don't they see that millions of Americans, especially women and elderly people, live in great fear of being mugged, raped, or murdered? Many are afraid to leave their homes after dark.

42 A survey of national crime statistics published by U.S. government agencies would inform the Kurnai that about twenty thousand Americans a year suffer the greatest loss of freedom. They are deprived of their lives through violent deaths. Their families and friends are permanently deprived of someone they love.

43 How long will it take these people, the exasperated anthropologists might wonder, until they realize that an interpretation of freedom that allows for no restraints with respect to the commercial exploitation of children is self-destructive?

44 The Kurnai would note that in other areas Americans acknowledge there is no such thing as absolute freedom. Ordinances prohibit people from playing loud music in the middle of the night if in doing so they deprive others of sleep. Laws restrict the freedom of chemical companies to dump pollutants into streams and rivers. But when it comes to producing a culture of violence that pollutes the minds of their young and encourages violence, these strange people act as if freedom were an absolute!

Notes

1. Ruth Benedict, *Patterns of Culture* [New York: Mentor Books, 1946 (1934)], p. 18.
2. Ibid., p. 42.
3. Ibid., p. 43.
4. Ibid.
5. I owe this point to Letty Cottin Pogrebin in *Growing Up Free: Raising Your Child in the 80's* (New York: Bantam Books, 1981).

EXPLORING THE TEXT

1. In the first three paragraphs, what connections does Miedzian draw between culture and behavior? How does culture shape the behavior of young people as they learn to become adults in their society?
2. When or how do social customs become obsolete? Why are some customs that are not useful to a society's members still practiced?
3. Who are the Kurnai? How do the Kurnai define "brother-and-sister" relationships? Why does this definition force elopement among young people who wish to marry each other?
4. What kinds of questions do the Kurnai ask about American culture? How are their questions distinguished from the responses Americans give them? What subjects or themes do they seem to be most interested in? Can you think of anything they may have forgotten to ask?
5. In paragraphs 32 and 33, Miedzian identifies a single source for America's problems with violence. What is that source? Do you agree with her explanation for the root cause of violence? Can you think of additional reasons?
6. In paragraphs 34 and 35, what explanation does Miedzian offer (through the Kurnai) about why this destructive attitude has been allowed to create a culture of violence? How does her reason illustrate the general principle she discussed in paragraph 4?
7. This article focuses almost completely on the socialization boys experience as they grow into men. How are girls and women presented in this article?
8. Miedzian's initial discussion of the Kurnai in paragraphs 5–7 makes them seem almost funny. How do her inclusion of a chuckling student and her

word choices convey this tone? Why do you think she uses this tone to begin the article?

9. Why does the author use the Kurnai to investigate violence in America? How would her discussion have been different (more boring, more confrontational, perhaps even unpatriotic) without this storytelling touch? How does this device help a reader who does not know what a cultural anthropologist does?

10. Why does Miedzian have the Kurnai begin their investigation by reading the Declaration of Independence and the Constitution in paragraph 11? What function do these documents play?

11. Do you think that the portrait of how American boys and girls are socialized is overstated? For example, can you think of films showing violent women and gentle men? Male musicians who do not advocate rape? Toys that teach men to love children? How do exceptions to Miedzian's observations help or hinder her argument?

12. What basic assumption does Miedzian make about human nature in paragraph 40? How likely is the average boy (and the average man) to commit a violent act? How important is this assumption to her argument? Does she infer what it is that prevents all men from being insanely violent?

13. Miedzian makes a number of broad generalizations about American culture and behavior. List five examples of generalization. You might start by looking for places where she uses "often" or "usually," or where she refers to averages. Do these generalizations strengthen or weaken her argument?

WRITING ASSIGNMENTS

1. Identify a specific product available to young people today that you believe contributes to violence in America (e.g., a film, toy, or CD with objectionable lyrics). Write a letter to the manufacturer (or producer or artist), explaining why this product is harmful and why it should no longer be made available.

2. Following Miedzian's example of the Kurnai anthropologists, write a description of a social group of at least ten people that you know well. The group may be your dormitory, your family, your church or temple, or another set of people that thinks of itself as a unit and shares rules of conduct and commonly held values. Write as if you are a complete outsider, observing it for the first time and not fully understanding the reasons for what you see. Be sure to look for customs that have outlived their usefulness.

GROUP PROJECT

1. Assume that your group has been given as much money and as many skilled, thoughtful people as you need to make three specific changes

within your community—your city, your college campus, or some other community that you define as yours. Your goal is to eliminate or sharply reduce violence. What specific changes would you make and why would you make them? Be sure to discuss what specific forms of violence you seek to eliminate. Present your report to the class.

Giving Up on the Young
Mike Males and Faye Docuyanan

What makes some young people join violent gangs? What should society do to prevent this choice? In trying to answer these questions, Mike Males and Faye Docuyanan spoke with people who had chosen violence in their youths but who are now working to help young people make better choices. They also relied on carefully assembled statistics to present a picture of youth violence that is very different from the pictures presented in other readings in this chapter.

The authors are social ecology doctoral students at the University of California, Irvine. Males is author of *The Scapegoat Generation: America's War Against Adolescents* (1996). This essay first appeared in the February 1996 issue of *The Progressive*.

1   Madness is the word Stephen Bruner uses to describe the summer of 1992. "The things I did, things I had done to me. . . . Madness." It was the summer after eighth grade. He and his gang Panic Zone hung out where the rural black community of Spencer intersects the southeast Oklahoma City suburb of Midwest City. He rattles off the names of a dozen gangs—Hoover Street, Westside, Candlewood, 6-0—that inhabit the district.

2   For his contribution to the madness, Bruner spent his ninth grade in an Oklahoma juvenile lockup. Now Bruner works as an intern for Wayne Thompson at the Oklahoma Health Care Project in Founder's Tower overlooking the city's opulent northwest side. Thompson himself spent three years in prison in the 1970s at Terminal Island and Lompoc for armed bank robbery on behalf of the San Francisco Black Panther chapter.

3   Madness, Thompson suggests, is "the natural, predictable reaction" of youths to the "larger, hostile adult culture that is anti-youth, particularly anti-African-American youth."

4   Twenty thousand more Oklahoma City children and teenagers live in poverty than a quarter of a century ago. "These kids are at risk of extinction if they depend upon adults to protect them," Thompson says. It is not just parents who fail them, but an adult society increasingly angry and punishing toward its youth. "That is the perception of the young people who are being ground up in this culture and the grinder of the juvenile-justice system. Their perception of their situation is very correct."

5   Today, state after state is imposing harsher penalties on juveniles who run afoul of the law. "The nationwide trend is to get tough on juvenile crime," says Gary Taylor of Legal Aid of Western Oklahoma. Rehabilitation and reintegration into the community are concepts that have already fallen out of fashion for adult criminals. Now they are fast becoming passé for juveniles, as well. Instead of prevention and rehabilitation programs, more prisons are being built to warehouse juveniles along with adults. The trend began in California; it is now sweeping the nation.

6   Juveniles are being waived into adult court at lower and lower ages. In Wisconsin, ten-year-olds can now be tried as adults for murder. Juveniles convicted of drug offenses in adult court receive lengthy mandatory sentences. In California, studies by the state corrections department show that youths serve sentences 60 percent longer than adults for the same crimes. Oklahoma wants to try thirteen-year-olds as adults and petitioned the Supreme Court to allow executions of fourteen- and fifteen-year-olds.

7   And it's not just the states. It's the Clinton Administration, too. *The New York Times* reported in December that "proposals by the Administration would allow more access to juvenile records and give federal prosecutors discretion to charge serious juvenile offenders as adults."

8   In short, we are giving up on human beings at a younger and younger age.

9   Juvenile crime is on the rise. But the reason is not media violence, rap music, or gun availability—easy scapegoats that have little to do with the patterns of violence in real life. Rather, the reason is rising youth poverty.

10   Sensational press accounts make it seem as though juvenile crime is patternless. It is hardly that. Juvenile crime is closely tied to youth poverty and the growing opportunity gap between wealthier, older people and destitute, younger people. Of California's fifty-eight counties, thirty-one with a total of 2.5 million people recorded zero teenage murders in 1993. Central Los Angeles, which has roughly the same number of people, reported more than 200 teen murders.

11   In the thirty-one counties free of teenage killers, the same blood-soaked media and rock and rap music are readily available (more, since white suburban families over-subscribe to cable TV), and guns are easy to obtain. Nor can some "innate" teenage qualities be the cause, since by definition those qualities are as present in youths in areas where violent teenage crime is rare as in areas where it is common.

12   "We see kids from *all* walks of life," says Harry Hartmann, counselor with the L.A. Office of Education. But "the races are skewed to blacks and Hispanics," he acknowledges. Very skewed—six out of seven of those who are arrested for violent juvenile crimes are black or Hispanic. By strange coincidence, that is just about the proportion of the county's youths in poverty who are black or Hispanic.

13   "Poverty in a society of affluence, in which your self-esteem is tied to failure to achieve that affluence," is a more accurate explanation for our uniquely high level of violence, says Gilbert Geiss, a criminologist formerly with the University of California, Irvine. It's not just "poverty, per se."

14   L.A. County is a clear illustration. Its per-capita income is much higher, and its general poverty rate lower, than the United States as a whole. But its youth poverty rate is staggering: 200,00 impoverished adolescents live in the county.

15   L.A. County is home to one in fifteen teenage murderers in the United States. Its vast basin harbors such a bewildering array of gangs and posses that estimates of the number of youths allied with them at any one time are almost impossible to pin down.

16   Jennifer, seventeen, at the Search to Involve Pilipino Americans (SIPA), a local community center, rattles off the names of twenty youth gangs, takes a breath, admits she has left some out. Los Angeles County (population 9 million) has more teen murders than the dozen largest industrial nations outside the United States combined. Of L.A.'s 459 teen murder arrestees in 1994, just twenty-four were white. Blacks and Hispanics predominated, but Asian Americans comprise the fastest-rising group of violent juveniles.

17   "I tried to ask them, 'Why are you in it?'" Jennifer asks. "They don't know. A lot of people regret it after. 'Yeah, that was some stupid shit.' They thought it was so cool." But if stupid, confused kids were the whole problem, why are black kids in Los Angeles a dozen times stupider than white kids? Why are Asians getting stupider faster than anyone else?

18   As youth poverty rises and becomes more concentrated in destitute urban neighborhoods, violence becomes more concentrated in younger age groups.

19   But today's reigning criminal-justice experts—UCLA's James Q. Wilson, Northwestern's James Allen Fox, Princeton's John D'Iulio, former Robert Kennedy aide Adam Walinsky—dismiss poverty as a cause of youth violence. Instead, they talk about an insidious culture of poverty, and they argue relentlessly that only more cops and more prisons will bring down juvenile crime. Instead of proposing more money for alleviating poverty or for crime prevention, they want more law enforcement—at a cost of tens of billions of dollars.

20   Writing in the September 1994 *Commentary,* Wilson calls the growing adolescent population "a cloud" that "lurks . . . just beyond the horizon." It will bring "30,000 more muggers, killers, and thieves than we have now." Wilson downplays poverty, racism, poor schools, and unemployment as "not . . . major causes of crime at all." The real problem, he writes, is "wrong behavior" by a fraction of the population (he pegs it at 6 percent) with bad temperament, concentrated in chaotic families and "disorderly neighborhoods."

21   If more prisons and surer sentences were the solutions to crime and delinquency, California should be a haven where citizens leave doors unlocked and stroll midnight streets unmenaced. California inaugurated the new era of imprisoning juvenile offenders in Ronald Reagan's second term as governor in 1971, and since then the state has incarcerated a higher percentage of its youths than any other state. By 1993, a state corrections study found teenagers served terms nearly a year longer than adults for equivalent offenses.

22   "I tell parents who want to release their kid to the [juvenile-justice] system: he might come out worse than when he went in," says Gilbert Aruyao of SIPA.

23   Eleven hundred new state laws passed during the 1980s set longer, more certain prison terms, especially for juveniles. California's forty-one-prison, 140,000-inmate system is the third-largest in the world; only the United States as a whole and China have larger inmate systems.

24   The Golden State's biggest growth industry is corrections. Seven new prisons opened in California from 1989 to 1994, at a cost of $1.3 billion, to accommodate

16,000 more prisoners; today, they confine 28,000 prisoners. From 1995 through 1996, four new prisons, costing $839 million, will open their doors. There's a new prison built every eight months. Each one is full upon opening.

25   "For that incorrigible 25 percent (of youth offenders), prisons may be the only way to go," says Harry Hartmann of the L.A. Office of Education. "It's really hard for them to change." In California in 1994, 140,000 persons under the age of twenty were arrested for felonies—including one out of five black males, and one in ten Hispanic males ages sixteen through nineteen. If even one-tenth of that number must be imprisoned more or less permanently, the state's minority teenage male population will require four new prisons every year to contain them.

26   As youth poverty mushrooms and the attitudes of the larger society become harsher, the traditional markers of race and class are sliding toward new realignments. "There's still a racial element, sure," says Thompson. "But this has gone beyond race now. There's a larger madness."

27   Says Bruner: "There are white kids in black gangs, blacks in Mexican gangs, Mexicans in white gangs, blacks in white gangs, Asians in black gangs. We don't fight each other that way. It isn't a race thing. It's who's in the 'hood.'"

28   The *1995 Kids Count Factbook* lists 47,000 impoverished children and adolescents in the Oklahoma City metropolitan area—21,000 whites, 13,500 blacks, 4,500 Native Americans, 3,000 Asian Americans, 5,000 Latinos.

29   A November 1995 *Daily Oklahoman* series on the metropolis's exploding poverty reported that these adolescents are increasingly isolated, jammed together in a chain of destitute neighborhoods ringing downtown and extending eastward past the suburbs.

30   "You go to school with them, people ask of this guy you know, 'Is he OK with you, 'cause if he's OK with you, he's OK with me,'" says Bruner. "If you're in a subcultural group, it's no different in society's eyes whether you're in a gang or not. Kids had no choice but to hang with us. Racism is here. You can't run away from it. [But] racism is not just black or white." Nonwhite youths, white youths on the wrong side, "we are all targets."

31   Bruner is training in office management and in television production and editing through Thompson's program. Enough of his friends remain trapped in the justice system. Bruner sees that as surrender. "They didn't get out like I did; now they're up for murder one."

32   Bruner says the system is rigged: "I believe they want to keep me and every other black male and minority male and poor kid in the system permanently, send us all to the penitentiary."

33   In 1988, Oklahoma petitioned the U.S. Supreme Court to execute fourteen- and fifteen-year-olds (and lost only on a 5–4 vote).

34   "Society wants to kill these kids," says Thompson. "The death penalty. Shooting them in the street. If it can't do that, then killing their spirit."

35   Gary Taylor, deputy director of Legal Aid of Western Oklahoma, recounts his agency's efforts to reform a juvenile prison system whose brutality and punitive excesses had been exposed nationally. "Beatings, sexual assaults, hog tying, extreme medical punishments, extreme isolation," said Taylor. "It was kid-kid; it was staff-kid."

36   There was no notion of rehabilitation. San Francisco lawyers for convicted murderer Freddy Lee Taylor investigated his incarceration in the Oklahoma juvenile prison system and found "a concentration-camp environment," attorney Robert Rionda said.

37   Many of these youths were wrongly imprisoned: they had been removed from their homes because their parents were abusive or neglectful, or the youths had committed minor offenses like curfew violations or truancy. Rionda's firm did not have to look hard to find Freddy Taylor's co-inmates: most were now in state prison serving terms for major felonies.

38   "There were many, many kids who were in the system because they were poor and in need of supervision, and they turned them into monsters," Rionda said.

39   In recent years, twice as many Oklahoma youths have been placed in the adult prison system as in the juvenile system. Oklahoma imprisons more of its citizens than any other state except Texas. If forcing youths into the adult prisons and administering harsh punishment is the remedy, Oklahoma, like California, should be a paradise of peace.

40   Yet arrest figures over the last decade show Oklahoma's juvenile violence growing at twice the already alarming national pace.

41   Los Angeles County and Oklahoma City officials stress prevention but note that it is underfunded. The most effective prevention effort by far is to raise fewer children in poverty. However, "reducing child poverty, much less eliminating it, is no longer a paramount priority for either political party," *U.S. News & World Report* pointed out in November 1995.

42   Wayne Thompson in Oklahoma City takes prevention seriously. "We approach juvenile crime as a public-health problem, not a law-enforcement problem," says Thompson. "Intervene, then trace the pathology back to its source." The source inevitably turns out to be "the low social, educational, and economic status of the families and communities" violent youths come from.

43   Thompson's program uses employment training and a variety of family services to reintegrate youths who have already been convicted back into their communities. "We want to empower these young people to change the social and economic circumstances of their lives," he says.

44   An initial evaluation showed that Thompson's program was more effective than law-enforcement approaches in preventing recidivism among delinquent youths as well as preventing younger members of their families from following in their older siblings' footsteps. The clientele served by the program is small—fewer than 100 youths per year.

45   The adults most responsive to Thompson's approach are in the business community, Republicans more than Democrats, he notes. "That's frightening," he says. "The social services, academia, are bound like serfs to the status quo."

46   When he talks to Oklahoma City's business groups, Thompson finds growing concern over the costs of more prisons and "alarm in the white community because the gangs are becoming more integrated." He doesn't push charity or altruism.

47   "I tell them, 'You're going to die in fifteen or twenty years, and you have grandchildren. They're going to have to live with the environment we've created.

And we've created a hellacious environment.' This is not just some teenage rite-of-passage problem. The alienation of young people from the traditional institutions is profound. This is the legacy we're leaving: armed camps. If we don't learn how to share with the people who are now powerless, this culture is ultimately going to acquire the means to bring our society to an end."

EXPLORING THE TEXT

1. Why do you think Males and Docuyanan begin this essay with the quote about madness? How is madness defined in this context? How do the authors use the idea of madness to focus their discussion?

2. The authors quote Wayne Thompson, who claims that the "larger, hostile adult culture . . . is anti-youth" (paragraph 3). What evidence do the authors provide in support of this claim?

3. What evidence do the authors offer to support their claim that poverty is the reason for rising juvenile crime?

4. Make a list of several instances where statistics are used. What do the authors try to accomplish by using these statistics? Are they successful? What is the effect of this choice? Can you think of ways to argue against these statistics?

5. What is significant about the authors' decision to discuss youth violence in Los Angeles and Oklahoma? What are the positive aspects of this choice? What are the negative aspects? To what extent can you generalize on the basis of this information? Explain your answers in detail.

6. Look at the "If . . . then" arguments the authors make in paragraphs 21, 25, and 39 and consider their rhetorical effect. Do they convince you of the point being argued? Do they present any particular problem for readers? Can you argue against them? Discuss your answer in detail.

7. The final paragraph of this article is a long quote from Wayne Thompson, the former gang member who works at the Oklahoma Health Care Project, directed to business groups. Consider what this quote says and how it relates to the argument of this essay overall. Briefly discuss why you think the authors chose to end the essay this way and whether or not you believe this was a good choice.

WRITING ASSIGNMENTS

1. Males and Docuyanan make the claim that the rise in juvenile crime is not due to "media violence, rap music, or gun availability. . . . Rather, the reason is rising youth poverty" (paragraph 9). Look at two (or more) other essays in this chapter and compare the various explanations of rising crime rates. Compare the facts and analyses to the state of your community.

Whose explanation seems to match your community most closely? Do research as necessary and explain your answer in a carefully written essay.

2. This essay presents a very focused argument against the recent trends of building more prisons, exacting longer prison terms, and trying young people as adults. Arguments in favor of these trends are presented in other essays in this chapter, particularly those by Tom Reilly and Abbe Smith and Lael E. H. Chester. Write an essay in which you compare the arguments made in two or more of these essays, as well as the evidence and analysis presented. Whose arguments seem most compelling? Why? What other research should be done to improve the various positions?

GROUP PROJECTS

1. Are Males and Docuyanan correct when they claim that the adult world is "hostile"? Is poverty the primary cause of juvenile crime? What other causes do people identify? Are prisons the best weapon in the war on crime? What other programs does your community offer to reduce juvenile crime? Have members of your group interview people in your community who are somehow involved with juvenile crime issues. Devise a series of questions based on the ideas in this text and ask the same questions of a range of experts: police officers, social service workers, prison and court personnel, youth offenders themselves, victims of youth crime, church leaders, and so on. Write a report on your findings.

2. As a group, consider the use of statistics and authority in this essay and compare it to such use by other authors in this chapter. What "authority" do other authors invoke? Whom does each choose to quote? What numbers are presented? How are they used? Can you argue against the choice of statistics or authorities in any way? Have your group do some research on statistics. What do readers need to know about statistics in order to evaluate an argument most effectively? How should we question statistics? What should we be careful of when we use statistics in our own writing? Prepare a lesson and "teach" the other students in your class how to use and evaluate statistics most effectively.

Putting the Brakes on Juvenile Crime
Ralph C. Martin II and William D. O'Leary

As you might expect, Ralph C. Martin II and William D. O'Leary, district attorney in Boston's Suffolk County and commissioner of Massachusetts' Department of Youth Services, respectively, argue that the best response to rising criminal activity should come from the juvenile justice system. What you might not expect is *how* they believe the system should be involved: They do not advocate harsher penalties or longer sentences. Instead, they argue, the answer must come from earlier intervention, better education, and direct community involvement. Like Mike Males and Faye Docuyanan earlier in this chapter, they describe programs that have been successful in cities across the nation.

This article was originally published in the *Boston Globe* in 1997.

1   Youth violence—it leads the evening news and headlines the morning newspapers. Criminologists tell us that in less than 10 years, there will be a 23 percent increase in the number of 14- to 17-year-old males and a likely corresponding increase in violent juvenile crime.

2   How should we respond? Enforcement? Education? Community Partnerships? We need all these, and more. First, law enforcement, courts, educators and community leaders must be willing to reach beyond their traditional roles and develop an unwavering commitment to education, community supervision, law enforcement and public accountability. Then they must define joint approaches to accomplish those tasks.

3   We need to think of kids as individual atoms—each one capable of energy that can be guided or misguided. Long before a juvenile's first arrest, obvious warning signs are often ignored. For example, most juvenile offenders have a history of truancy. But today, many if not most communities lack the capacity to identify, investigate and intervene with truants. Kids don't receive the swift and direct message that society values their attendance in school.

4   Truancy laws were created upon the belief that education was essential to youths and the well-being of the community. We still hold these values. How then do we get kids to go to school? And how can we expect educators to cope with the myriad problems of truants?

5   First, we should reestablish the role of truant officers. The modern-day truant officer would not only enforce attendance, but also act as a link between parents and the schools, law enforcement, social service agencies and the community.

6   Second, we need a continuum of alternative education. While most students will benefit from improvements to mainstream education, a small but critical percentage need more. We must provide educational environments in which a youth recognizes that the lessons of the street are no match for the knowledge he receives in class.

7   Third, some youths need to be educated in the most structured and supervised settings. These youths are the products of community violence, broken homes, substance abuse and hopelessness. Educators cannot bear the sole brunt of those problems. We should consider developing small regional education and supervision centers that include educators as well as probation, Department of Youth Services and other community staff.

8   Youths need structure, supervision and support to succeed. When they don't receive it, they become "problem" kids. We have to hold parents accountable, but where families don't exist, communities will have to step to the fore.

9   In most cases the void can be filled by civic groups, churches, YMCAs and Boys & Girls Clubs. In other instances we will need law enforcement, juvenile justice and community agencies to collaborate. An active business community can play

a pivotal role. Currently, only a small percentage of corporate leaders provide the resources and environment where kids learn why an education leads to better opportunity. Critical to rebuilding our community is an investment by a much larger proportion of business leaders.

10 Now is the time to study prevention programs, to track kids' movement through them and replicate them when they are successful. Supporting programs like Midnight Baseball, SCORE (a vital school-based conflict resolution program), DARE (Drug Awareness Resistance and Education), and others does not make a public official soft on crime. Yet just as important, prevention programs alone are seldom a sufficient response to violence after it has occurred. Support of prevention programs combined with stiff sanctions for the most resistant juvenile offenders is the most effective crime fighting approach.

11 Community policing and targeted crime control are proving successful from New York to Houston. Local examples include the Safe Neighborhoods Initiatives in Boston and Chelsea, where police, district attorneys and community groups have targeted crime. Through Operation Nightlight, Boston Police and probation staff have worked jointly to enforce probation orders. Similarly, police gang task force staff and DYS apprehension staff have worked successfully to pick up juvenile violators.

12 We have to separate kids from guns. Coordinated federal, state and local interdiction efforts have met with some success. We should explore the use of new technologies, including hand-held metal detectors. With the recent passage of the Brett/Martin bill, there is certainty to both sanctions and treatment for gun-toting youths who now receive a minimum of six months in a DYS facility.

13 Crime hurts real victims and distresses communities. In addition to punishment, treatment and deterrence, we suggest that offenders be accountable for their actions whenever possible. There are many strategies that have been employed, including community service, restitution and victim/offender mediation. For all youths who are found delinquent, restorative sanctions should be added to treatment and supervision.

14 It is essential that the juvenile justice system maintain integrity in the eyes of the public and our youths. While there are no simple solutions, we must develop common-sense approaches that protect the public and reduce crime. Our future is dependent upon the safety of all the neighborhoods, the quality of education that all children receive and the redemption of kids' lives wherever possible.

EXPLORING THE TEXT

1. Martin and O'Leary pinpoint several areas where improvements need to be made. What are these areas? How do their categories help define what they see as the problem of juvenile crime?

2. What reasons do Martin and O'Leary offer for reestablishing the role of the truant officer and truancy laws? What new services should the modern truant officer provide?

3. What is "alternative education" (paragraph 6)? Why do these authors discuss it as a continuum?
4. According to the authors, what are the goals and purposes of prevention programs? Which programs do they cite as noteworthy? What suggestions do they offer to either improve existing programs or create new ones?
5. What role do Martin and O'Leary envision for the business community in helping to reduce juvenile crime?
6. In paragraph 3, what metaphor is used to describe kids? What ideas do you associate with this metaphor? Do you think this comparison is effective?
7. Discuss the organization of this essay. What strategies have the writers used in presenting their argument? In what ways are their strategies effective? Ineffective?

WRITING ASSIGNMENT

1. Martin and O'Leary ignore the causes of juvenile crime and instead focus on solutions to the existing problem. Other authors in this chapter (Myriam Miedzian, for example) focus more on the causes, the reasons why youths turn to crime. Write an essay in which you survey these various approaches, identify the extent to which the arguments overlap, and then propose your own argument for what should be done to reduce juvenile crime.

GROUP PROJECTS

1. As a group research the problem of juvenile crime in your community and/or state. Prepare a report that details the different kinds of crime committed and the frequency of each kind of crime. Also discuss the different kinds (and duration) of sentences meted out. Find the government documents that report these numbers, but also do other kinds of research. Compile your findings and prepare a report.
2. Make a list of various programs (DARE, SCORE, midnight baseball, or others) offered in your community to help prevent juvenile crime—this might require some initial research, though phone calls might be sufficient. Here individual group members choose one program and do research into what the program is, who it targets, how it is run, how effective it is, and so on. Gather information available from the program itself, look for newspaper articles, interview people who run the program, interview young people who have participated in the program, and look for government reports or hearing transcripts that discuss the program. Compile your findings and present a report that discusses the effectiveness of the prevention programs in your community.

Peace in the Streets

Geoffrey Canada

Young people become criminals when they have neither hope nor heroes. Such is the claim of Geoffrey Canada who draws from his experience working with young people in Harlem. In the essay below, he argues that society should not concern itself with punishing youth violence so much as its members should work to prevent the circumstances that encourage it. Thus, he advocates a range of programs that address the needs of young people long before they commit violent or criminal acts, including reduced availability of drugs and handguns, protection from abusive adults, and reduction of violent television programming. What he is arguing for is a safer world for children—and for the rest of us.

Canada is president and CEO of Harlem's Rheedlen Center for Children and Families, is responsible for the Beacon Schools and the Peacemakers program in Harlem, and is East Coast coordinator for the Children's Defense Fund's Black Community Crusade for Children. This selection is from his book, *Fist Stick Knife Gun: A Personal History of Violence in America* (1995).

1   It's a Wednesday night in October and I'm early for my martial arts class in Harlem. I walk into the brightly lit gym and all eyes turn toward me. I'm walking with purpose, quickly and silently. A little boy begins to run over to me and an older student grabs his arm. I see him whispering in the younger boy's ear. I'm sure he's telling him, "You can't talk to him before class." And he's right. I stand in front of my class, looking unhappy and displeased. Everyone wonders who is out of place or not standing up straight. This is part of my act. Finally I begin the class and then I'm lost in the teaching. I'm trying to bring magic into the lives of these kids. To bring a sense of wonder and amazement. I can feel the students losing themselves and focusing on me. They are finally mine. I have them all to myself. I have crowded all the bad things out of their minds: The test they failed, the father who won't come by to see them, the dinner that won't be on the stove when they get home. I've pushed it all away by force of will and magic.

2   This is my time and I know all the tricks. I yell, I scream, I fly through the air with the greatest of ease. And by the time the class is ending my students' eyes are wide with amazement and respect, and they look at me differently. I line them up and I talk to them. I talk to them about values, violence, and hope. I try to build within each one a reservoir of strength that they can draw from as they face the countless tribulations small and large that poor children face every day. And I try to convince each one that I know their true value, their worth as human beings, their special gift that God gave to them. And I hope they will make it to the next class with something left in that reservoir for me to add to week by week. It is from that reservoir that they will draw the strength to resist the drugs, the guns, the violence.

3   My two best students usually walk with me after class and stay with me until I catch a cab. I tell them it's not necessary, but they are there to make sure I get home

all right. What a world. So dangerous that children feel that a second-degree black belt needs an escort to get home safely.

4   This community, like many across this country, is not safe for children, and they usually walk home at night filled with fear and apprehension. But when I walk with them after class they are carefree, as children ought to be. They have no fear. They believe that if anything happens they'll be safe because I'm there. I'll fly through the air and with my magic karate I'll dispatch whatever evil threatens them. When these children see me standing on the corner watching them walk into their buildings they believe what children used to believe, that there are adults who can protect them. And I let them believe this even if my older students and I know different. Because in a world that is so cold and so harsh, children need heroes. Heroes give hope, and if these children have no hope they will have no future. And so I play the role of hero for them even if I have to resort to cheap tricks and theatrics.

5   If I could get the mayors, the governors, and the president to look into the eyes of the 5-year-olds of this nation, dressed in old raggedy clothes, whose jacket zippers are broken but whose dreams are still alive, they would know what I know—that children need people to fight for them. To stand with them on the most dangerous streets, in the dirtiest hallways, in their darkest hours. We as a country have been too willing to take from our weakest when times get hard. People who allow this to happen must be educated, must be challenged, must be turned around.

6   If we are to save our children we must become people they will look up to. We must stand up and be visible heroes. I want people to understand the crisis and I want people to act: Either we address the murder and mayhem in our country or we simply won't be able to continue to have the kind of democratic society that we as Americans cherish. Violence is not just a problem of the inner cities or of the minorities in this country. This is a national crisis and the nation must mobilize differently if we are to solve it.

7   Part of what we must do is change the way we think about violence. Trying to catch and punish people after they have committed a violent act won't deter violence in the least. In life on the street, it's better to go to jail than be killed, better to act quickly and decisively even if you risk being caught.

8   There are, however, things that governments could and should do right away to begin to end the violence on our streets. They include the following:

Create a Peace Officer Corps

9 Peace officers would not be police; they would not carry guns and would not be charged with making arrests. Instead they would be local men and women hired to work with children in their own neighborhoods. They would try to settle "beefs" and mediate disputes. They would not be the eyes and ears of the regular police force. Their job would be to try to get these young people jobs, to get them back into school, and, most importantly, to be at the emergency rooms and funerals where young people come together to grieve and plot revenge, in order to keep them from killing one another.

Reduce the Demand for Drugs

10 Any real effort at diverting the next generation of kids from selling drugs *must* include plans to find employment for these children when they become teenagers. While that will require a significant expenditure of public funds, the savings from reduced hospitalization and reduced incarceration will more than offset the costs of employment.

11   And don't be fooled by those who say that these teenagers will never work for five dollars an hour when they can make thousands of dollars a week. I have found little evidence of this in my years of working with young people. Most of them, given the opportunity to make even the minimum wage, will do so gladly. The problem for many young people has been that they have looked for work year after year without ever finding a job. In some cities more than 40 percent of minority youth who want to work can't find employment.

Reduce the Prevalence of Domestic Violence and Child Abuse and Neglect

12 Too many children learn to act violently by experiencing violence in their homes. Our society has turned a blind eye to domestic violence for so long that the smacking, punching, and beating of women has become almost routine. And in many of the same homes where women are being beaten, the children are being beaten also. Our response as a society has been to wait until the violence has gotten so bad that the woman has to go to a battered-women's shelter (often losing the only place she has to live), or we have to take the abused child from the family. In both cases we break up a family, and common sense tells us this ends up costing us more money than it would have if we had intervened early and kept the family together.

13   The best mode of early intervention for really troubled families is family preservation services—intensive, short-term interventions designed to teach families new coping skills. The family preservation worker spends as much time as needed with a family to ensure that it gets the type of support and skills that it needs to function as a supportive unit rather than a destructive one.

Reduce the Amount of Violence on Television and in the Movies

14 Violence in the media is ever more graphic, and the justification for acting violently is deeply implanted in young people's minds. The movie industry promotes the message that power is determined not merely by carrying a gun, but by carrying a big gun that is an automatic and has a big clip containing many bullets.

15   What about rap music, and especially "gangsta rap"? It is my opinion that people have concentrated too much attention on this one source of media violence. Many rap songs are positive, and some are neither positive nor negative—just kids telling their stories. But there are some rap singers who have decided that their niche in the music industry will be the most violent and vile. I would love to see the record industry show some restraint in limiting these rappers' access to fame and fortune.

16   But by singling out one part of the entertainment industry as violent and ignoring others that are equally if not more violent (how many people have been killed in

movies starring Arnold Schwarzenegger, Sylvester Stallone, and Clint Eastwood?) we will have no impact on reducing violence in this country. The television, movie, and record industries must all reduce the amount of violence they sell to Americans.

Reduce and Regulate the Possession of Handguns

17 I believe all handgun sales should be banned in this country. Recognizing, however, that other Americans may not be ready to accept a ban on handguns, I believe there are still some things we must do.

Licensing

18 Every person who wants to buy a handgun should have to pass both a written test and a field test. The cost for these new procedures should be paid by those who make, sell, and buy handguns.

Insurance

19 Gun manufacturers and dealers should be required to register every handgun they manufacture and sell. This registration would be used to trace guns that wind up being used for crimes, and the manufacturers and dealers should be held liable for damages caused by any gun they manufacture and sell. Individual citizens would be required to carry insurance policies for liability and theft on their handguns, which would increase the pressure on citizens to make sure that their guns were safely locked away.

Ammunition Identification

20 While we are beginning to bring some sane regulations to the handgun industry, we must also begin to make the killing of Americans with handguns less anonymous than it is today. One way to do this is to make all handgun ammunition identifiable. Gun owners should have to sign for specially coded ammunition, the purchase of which would then be logged into a computer. The codes should be etched into the shell casing as well as the bullet itself, and the codes should be designed so that even when a bullet breaks into fragments it can still be identified.

Gun Buy-Backs

21 The federal government, which recently passed a $32 billion crime bill, needs to invest billions of dollars over the next ten years buying guns back from citizens. We now have more than 200 million guns in circulation in our country. A properly cared-for gun can last for decades. There is no way we can deal with handgun violence until we reduce the number of guns currently in circulation. We know that young people won't give up their guns readily, but we have to keep in mind that this is a long-term problem. We have to begin to plan now to get the guns currently in the hands of children out of circulation permanently.

22   The truth of the matter is that reducing the escalating violence will be complicated and costly. If we were fighting an outside enemy that was killing our children at a rate of more than 5,000 a year, we would spare no expense. What happens when the enemy is us? What happens when those Americans' children are mostly black and brown? Do we still have the will to invest the time and resources in saving their lives? The answer must be yes, because the impact and fear of violence has overrun the boundaries of our ghettos and has both its hands firmly around the neck of our whole country. And while you may not yet have been visited by the specter of death and fear of this new national cancer, just give it time. Sooner or later, unless we act, you will. We all will.

EXPLORING THE TEXT

1. As this essay begins, Canada describes his "act" (paragraph 1). How does he define his role? How does he create his persona?
2. According to Canada, why do children need heroes? How would Canada define the word *hero*? What other definitions of hero are common in our culture?
3. How does Canada use pronouns to define the problem of violence in America? How does he use them when he is talking about responsibility for the violence? For the solution? Be sure to point to particular passages in your discussion.
4. Pay particular attention to Canada's tone as evidenced by his choice of words throughout the text. What is his tone? How is it developed? How does the tone affect our response to his argument?
5. Canada begins this essay with a personal anecdote. Do you find this an effective rhetorical strategy? Does it help to make him more credible as an author? Explain your answer.
6. The second half of Canada's article contains a list of things governments should do to end violence. Discuss the effect of this listing strategy. What is the relationship between form and content?
7. Critique Canada's argument. Identify several claims he makes and the support he offers for each claim. Does he provide enough evidence? Is his discussion always logical? Discuss your findings.

WRITING ASSIGNMENTS

1. Canada writes a narrative that positions himself at the center of the solution to the problem of youth violence. Write your own fictive narrative and position yourself as part of the solution. Imagine you are one of the "we" that he enlisted in his fight. Borrow one of his solutions and create a scenario in

which you enact that solution. Describe what you would do, what problems you would expect to confront, and how you would address those problems.
2. Other writers in the chapter, especially Ralph C. Martin II and William D. O'Leary, also offer solutions to the problem of youth violence. Pick one of the solutions proposed in any of these essays and prepare your own argument in favor of that solution. Plan to do research as necessary, including interviews of people working within the juvenile justice system.
3. Many movies on the market present a "hero" who comes into the lives of troubled youths and helps them to make a better life for themselves (e.g., *Dangerous Minds* and *Stand and Deliver*). Watch one such movie and compare that hero with the role Canada has taken on in his dealings with kids. In what ways are the two heroes alike? How are they different? Write an essay in which you analyze the relevance of these two presentations of important "heroes" in the lives of kids.

GROUP PROJECTS

1. Divide your group into two units. Choose one of Canada's proposed solutions and research its viability. Have one unit prepare an argument in favor of the solution and have the other unit prepare an argument in opposition to the proposed solution. Compare information so that each side has a chance to prepare a response to the other side's position. Debate your final arguments in front of your class.
2. Present a report on the qualities and values our culture typically attributes to heroes and compare them to the qualities and values claimed by Canada in his discussion. Each member of your group should spend several days looking at one (different) outlet of the popular media—movies, television dramas (or sitcoms), television news programs, television news magazine programs, newspapers, magazines, and so on. Then come together to compare and categorize your findings and present your final report.

Johnny, Take Your Drug Test!
Ellen Goodman

Kids and drugs is an equation for crime—and one we are all too familiar with in America. But what can parents do to help reduce the sad equation? And when does that help infringe upon the rights and trust of young people? The editorial below was motivated by a new product on the market: an at-home drug-testing kit that parents can use to monitor potential drug abuse by their kids. Though a parent, Goodman lines up on the side of young people: She recognizes the potential violations of privacy that such a test might provoke. Ultimately, she argues that parents must be vigilant and involved, but that they should focus their attention on building a healthy relationship with their children rather than playing parole officers.

Goodman is a widely syndicated, Pulitzer Prize–winning columnist. Collections of her columns have been published in *Keeping in Touch* (1985) and *Making Sense* (1989). This piece was first published in the *Boston Globe* in February 1997.

1   So this is Morning in America, circa 1997.

2   Mom is making breakfast and hurrying 15-year-old Joanna through the before-school ritual: "Honey, don't forget to brush your teeth and take your drug test."

3   Dad jumps up at dawn Saturday to run a pop urine quiz on 17-year-old Johnny for any substance leftovers from last night's party. He accompanies his son into the, uh, collection room with a small plastic vial.

4   These warmhearted little scenes of modern family life may soon become domestic docudramas.

5   At long last and to great public acclaim, the FDA has approved a sample collection kit called "Dr. Brown's Home Drug Testing System." For a mere $30 a pop, or a pee, parents will have the marvelous opportunity to become their own child's parole officer.

6   This product was created out of a chemical mix of parental anxiety, politics, and marketing savvy.

7   Back last fall, a Georgia mother named Sunny Cloud was prevented from marketing a similar home test by the FDA. This reticence created an uproar from politicians. It ended up as part of the family values debate.

8   Not surprisingly, the FDA eventually found a product it could approve, and before spring Dr. Brown will be making house calls. We'll have a mail-order drug test for marijuana, PCP, amphetamines, cocaine, heroin, codeine, and morphine. And a test case for that other ingredient in family life called trust.

9   Trust and teens? Teens and trust? I am told these words go together like mustard and strawberries. I know the statistics that have parents panicking. Some 22 percent of all 12- to 17-year-olds have at least tried marijuana.

10   There are parents who have reason to be suspicious. For these parents, Dr. Brown is a mother's little helper. But what happens to family relationships when every teen-ager becomes a suspect? How do kids feel, and indeed behave, when they are presumed guilty?

11   Americans have been uneasy about adolescents since before we invented the term. But today we have simultaneously let these young people drift out of our line of vision and ordered a crackdown.

12   In the cities, we have begun to impose curfews. In the schools, we have the right to inspect lockers. In the car, we install a speed monitor advertised as "The Teen-ager's Nightmare" to tattletale on how fast they were driving. We even have beepers to keep track of their whereabouts.

13   What happens next? If we can conduct weekly tests for drugs, why not monthly tests for teen pregnancy? Why not have hidden cameras or electronic anklets?

14   Does anyone remember when reading a child's diary was considered a violation of privacy? Or when time and talk were the tools that we depended on to keep tabs?

15   I wonder if Dr. Brown's market share of parents has lost more faith in themselves than in their kids. Baby-boomer parents may have forgotten how much we wanted our parents to trust us, and remember only those times we were untrustworthy.

16   Twenty years ago, high school seniors were twice as likely to smoke marijuana daily as they are now. How many parents have forgotten they survived and remember they were at risk?

17   This generation of parents hasn't merely morphed into the last. Today, parents are more likely to be at work and less likely to be at home. There are newer, scarier pressures. When we feel out of touch these days, it seems that we reach for some remote control. Instead of parental supervision, we are tempted by the tools of surveillance.

18   The irony is that kids in deepest trouble are least likely to volunteer the evidence into their parents' plastic vial. And they are most likely to be estranged.

19   Every one of us crosses the time zone of our kids' adolescence with our eyes open and our fingers crossed. We want to keep them safe and get them out on their own. They want to be emancipated and protected. There's no trickier time.

20   But if there's any hedge against trouble, it's in building a relationship of trust— not blind trust but reasonable trust. And when it's broken, rebuilding it.

21   Ask teen-agers what they want, and when you get through the flak, they want adults who connect, grown-ups who believe in them. They want parents, not parole officers.

22   That is the real home test.

EXPLORING THE TEXT

1. Goodman begins her discussion with an imagined family scenario. Note the roles of the respective family members. Is this view realistic? Utopian? Explain your answer.

2. In paragraph 7, Goodman mentions the "family values debate." Does she offer a definition? Can you offer your own definition of what she's referring to?

3. What, for Goodman, is the difference between supervision and surveillance? Are the two terms synonymous? Is the difference one of degree or kind? Explain your answer.

4. Goodman focuses on certain ethical considerations in her discussion. What ethical issues does she point to and why does she see them as important?

5. In paragraph 9, Goodman quotes a statistic that she says "has parents panicking." Evaluate this statistic. What information does it reveal literally? Why might this statistic make parents panic? Should it?

6. How does Goodman's choice of words throughout this essay establish her tone? What is her attitude toward the material she discusses? Point to several examples in your discussion.
7. Discuss how Goodman positions herself in relation to this debate. When she says "we," to whom is she referring? Does this positioning make her more, or less, credible when she takes the side of teenagers in demanding parents who are "parents, not parole officers" (paragraph 21).

WRITING ASSIGNMENTS

1. Goodman makes a distinction between supervision and surveillance that might be seen to relate to the distinction Ralph C. Martin II and William D. O'Leary make between rehabilitation and incarceration. Write an essay in which you carefully describe these concepts and then compare (or contrast) the issues raised by each author's choice of focus and the distinctions he or she argues.
2. Write an essay in which you discuss Goodman's ideas on the degree and extent to which parents are and should be responsible for the actions of children; likewise, discuss her ideas on the extent to which children are to be held responsible for their own actions. Then compare her ideas on adult and child responsibility to the ideas of another author you've read in this chapter. Discuss how their different ideas about responsibility relate to the solutions they offer.

GROUP PROJECTS

1. Do some historical research on the changing nature of the drug debate. What was being said and written at different times throughout this century? Think back to arguments for and against prohibition in the early part of the century; look to discussions of drugs and juvenile delinquency in the 1940s and 1950s. Look again at the arguments offered in the 1960s and 1970s. Look carefully at the movements that began in the 1980s and continue today. Have different group members research different periods and combine your research and present a report on what has changed, what has remained constant, and what these findings suggest.
2. One recent response to concern about drug use has been the increasing use of drug tests at school and at various work sites. As a group, research the issues surrounding such issues, including the right to privacy and the right against self-incrimination and also issues of reliability, due process, treatment, etc. In other words, look at this problem from the standpoint of

employers (or school administrators), employees (or students), and society at large. Write a report in which you discuss the pros and cons of such testing.

Pro/Con: Punish Juvenile Offenders as Adults

The next two selections represent contrary views on how to deal with young people who commit serious crimes. In the first piece, Tom Reilly argues in the affirmative. The authors of the piece that follows, Abbe Smith and Lael E. H. Chester, disagree.

PRO

Youth Crime Has Changed—And So Must the Juvenile Justice System
Tom Reilly

> Like Ralph C. Martin II whose article appears earlier in this chapter ("Putting the Brakes on Juvenile Crime"), Tom Reilly is a district attorney in Massachusetts. and like Martin, his argument applies nationwide. But Reilly presents a very different view about how the juvenile justice system should deal with increasing—and increasingly violent—juvenile crime. Reilly says that the system is outdated and unable to accommodate certain "predators" who commit brutal crimes, even murder. The only solution is that "cold-blooded" juveniles be tried and sentenced as adults. What do you think?
>
> Reilly's editorial originally appeared in the *Boston Globe* in 1997.

1   On July 1, 1899, the first juvenile court in the United States was established in Cook County, Ill. It represented a dramatic shift in the way the criminal justice system and all of American society dealt with wayward or criminally involved youth. The new court was founded on the principle of "parens patriae"—the idea that children should not be treated as criminals but as wards of the state.

2   Parens patriae encapsulated the view that children were not fully responsible for their conduct and were capable of being rehabilitated. It gave rise to the ongoing practice of terming youthful offenders "delinquents" and not criminals. Parens patriae remains the underlying philosophy of the juvenile justice system in Massachusetts and across the country. Then and now, juvenile court was designed more to protect the child than to punish bad behavior.

3   Until fairly recently, the juvenile justice system served our country and our children reasonably well. Beginning in the 1970s, however, the realities of juvenile crime began to change. Juvenile crime grew more violent and more common, and the

system was unprepared. In recent years those changes have accelerated at an astonishing rate, and time and again the system has proven itself helpless under the crush.

4   Violent juvenile crime is increasing at double the rate of violent crime committed by adults. By the year 2005, the number of teen-agers between the ages of 14 and 17 will increase by 23 percent, and it appears likely that unless we change things now, those soon-to-be-teen-agers will be the most violence prone in history.

5   Our juvenile justice system is outdated, designed to address infractions like truancy and petty theft. These were serious problems a century ago, but they bear no resemblance to the "routine" infractions of the present day: everything from rape to crimes involving guns to cold-blooded murder. In 1996, juveniles are committing brutal crimes with such numbing regularity that it takes the most shocking failures of the juvenile justice system to respond to dramatize the out-of-touch mentality underlying it.

6   It makes no sense to change the system simply to navigate the current wave of public anger. We must instead reform the system to steer clear of the coming storm of violent juvenile crime. Parens patriae need not be fully abandoned. There are and will always be children who make poor choices, who need our help and who can be turned around. However, we cannot ignore reality. Crimes such as murder are serious; they cannot under any circumstances be excused or explained away. Here, hope for rehabilitation is a myth, and public protection must be the priority.

7   How can we possibly treat cold-blooded juvenile killers as "delinquents" and not as the dangerous predators their own actions prove them to be? When a person, any person, brings himself to a point where he deliberately murders another human being, there is no going back. A mere hope for rehabilitation is nothing but a gamble on other people's lives. The public has a right to expect that a killer will never, ever have the chance to kill again. Juveniles accused of murder should be tried as adults and, if convicted, sentenced as adults.

8   For other crimes, determining whether a juvenile can be rehabilitated is problematic under the current system, so conducting the trial first makes sense. Once a determination of guilt has been made and the court has a clear view of the nature of the crime and whether or not a juvenile is dangerous or capable of rehabilitation, then a reasonable decision can be made whether to sentence as a juvenile or as an adult.

9   Even apart from these steps to hold juvenile offenders responsible, other aspects of the juvenile justice system must be reformed to achieve a proper balance between respect and sensitivity toward victims and a juvenile's due process rights. Eliminating "trial de novo" tops the list. Under de novo, a juvenile has the right to be tried first before a judge. If found guilty (or delinquent), the juvenile can simply demand a new trial before a jury, forcing victims to endure a painful ordeal not once, but twice. It's time to put an end to this unfair, wasteful system.

10   The juvenile justice system founded nearly a century ago was in many respects visionary, but ultimately it was a system designed to address the pressing issues of its day. That day is long past. It's time for us to craft a new vision for juvenile justice in Massachusetts, where compassion for the young and common sense about crime coexist. Our new vision should reflect our belief that the system does have a respon-

sibility to protect a child's interests, but our system has an equally important responsibility to protect the public's safety interests.

EXPLORING THE TEXT

1. In the first three paragraphs, Reilly describes a dramatic shift in the history of the juvenile justice system. What is the importance of this shift to his argument?

2. What statistics does Reilly forecast for the future of the juvenile justice system? How does he use these statistics to argue for a change in the juvenile justice system?

3. Reilly remarks, "Our juvenile justice system is outdated" (paragraph 5). What support does he offer for this statement? Do you find this support adequate?

4. What is Reilly's position on the concept of *parens patriae?* Does he want to abandon it? Does he defend its model of rehabilitation?

5. How does Reilly balance the importance of protecting the public safety with the importance of the state's responsibility for the welfare of the child?

6. Reilly makes a clear distinction between "youthful offenders" or "delinquents" (paragraph 2) and criminals or "predators" (paragraph 7). How do these choices in terminology underscore and support his argument? Why is this important? Explain your answer.

7. Consider the language Reilly uses in making this argument. How do words and phrases such as "shocking" (paragraph 5) and "cold-blooded" (paragraphs 5 and 7) define his tone and influence how readers respond to the points he argues?

WRITING ASSIGNMENTS

1. Reilly claims that "the public has a right to expect that a killer will never, ever have the chance to kill again" (paragraph 7). What is he assuming in making this claim? In what ways is his position problematic? Is there a philosophical dilemma that arises from his contention, on the one hand, that young people can be rehabilitated, and, on the other hand, his abandonment of that possibility?

2. Reilly argues that the traditional philosophy of *parens patriae* is no longer sufficient and needs to be modified or even abandoned in certain cases. Write an essay in which you discuss the extent to which Abbe Smith and Lael E. H. Chester's argument against the Violent Youth Predator Act of 1996 "is actually a defense of this *parens patriae.*"

GROUP PROJECTS

1. Reilly describes the practice of "trial de novo," which makes it possible to have two trials rather than one. Not all states, however, allow "trial de novo." Find out how the juvenile justice system works in your community. Working in a group, arrange to interview court personnel, social workers, lawyers, and criminal offenders. Gather statistics on the kinds of crime committed in the past year, as well as the number of offenses. Prepare a report of your findings.

2. Many of the essays in this chapter use statistics to set up or support the arguments being presented by the authors. Assign particular pieces to different group members, and isolate the places in each argument where statistics are used. Write an essay in which you discuss how effectively the statistics are used. You may need to do some research on how statistics can be used to present (and sometimes manipulate) information. Discuss whether your investigation of the statistics affects or changes your understanding of each text.

CON

Cruel Punishment for Juveniles
Abbe Smith and Lael E. H. Chester

For the authors in this essay, calling young offenders "predators" only helps society to forget that they are kids in need of help. Arguing directly against Tom Reilly, Abbe Smith and Lael E. H. Chester claim that treating juveniles as adults and punishing them within the adult justice system constitute "cruel and unusual punishment" forbidden by the U.S. Constitution. Like other authors in this chapter, they rely on their experience with young offenders to frame their views.

Smith is deputy director of the Criminal Justice Institute at Harvard Law School, and Chester is a fellow at that institute. This argument originally appeared in the *Boston Globe* in July 1996.

1 The first time we saw Frankie was in the lock-up of the Cambridge District Court. He was barely 17, baby-faced, nothing but skin and bones, his scrawniness exaggerated by baggy pants.

2 Frankie had spent the night in jail, an adult jail. In Massachusetts, 17 is the age of adulthood for purposes of criminal prosecution. He had been arrested for breaking into the basement of the house from which his best friend's family had just been evicted. His friend wanted to retrieve his punching bag.

3 Frankie didn't know us, but boy was he glad to see us. He managed to hold back tears—there were guys in the cell who were old enough to be his father, and crying was the last thing he wanted to do—but his eyes held a mix of worry, fear and ex-

haustion. You're my lawyers? he asked. Wow, that's good news. And both of my parents are out there in the court room? Gee, I wasn't sure I'd ever see them again.

4   His parents were relieved and furious when the police called the night before, nearly an hour after Frankie was due home. With mixed feelings, they decided that Frankie should spend the night in jail. Maybe it'd teach him a lesson.

5   Maybe.

6   In recent years, there has been an increasing call in the commonwealth and the country to stop "coddling" juveniles in a separate justice system and punish them like adults. Now the call has gone further. We should punish kids with adults.

7   A bill recently introduced by Rep. Bill McCollum, chairman of the House Judiciary Subcommittee on Crime, seeks to end the jailhouse separation of juvenile and adult offenders and allow kids to serve time in adult prisons. Notwithstanding the powerful political rhetoric accompanying its introduction, the strategically entitled "Violent Youth Predator Act of 1996," is not sound social policy.

8   It is wrong to suggest that young offenders are being "coddled" in the juvenile institutions to which more and more are sent. There is simply no funding for small, community-based youth programs built on education, counseling and job training. Whether we call them locked rooms or locked cells, juvenile offenders are already spending time in prison.

9   Subjecting children to punishment with adults defines cruel and unusual punishment. Sexual and physical assault are already prevalent in adult prisons. One can imagine the scale of these offenses if we send in a fresh crop of younger and more vulnerable prey. Given the number of prisoners with HIV (the Journal of the American Medical Association reports the rate of AIDS among incarcerated adults is six times that of the general population), sending children into adult prisons might as well be a death sentence.

10   The truth is that the get-tough approach is being driven by a few highly publicized cases that do not reflect the reality of most juvenile crime. In Massachusetts, juvenile homicides are a tiny percentage of juvenile arrests (there were 14 homicide cases out of 22,000 juvenile arraignments this year). The increased rate of homicides by juveniles nationally is largely due to the proliferation of guns in this country, not the changed nature of children.

11   And yet instead of pushing for a ban on all firearms, Massachusetts lawmakers prefer to increase mandatory minimum sentences for gun-related offenses by adults and juveniles. Instead of banning guns, we banish kids.

12   The federal government has also been in danger of embracing punishment over prevention. Along with doing away with federal and state mandates separating children from adult prisoners, the bill would abolish the Office of Juvenile Justice and Delinquency Prevention, the only federal agency that sponsors research on juvenile violence prevention.

13   We know that the problem of juvenile crime and violence is much more complicated than this angry antichild bill suggests. In the ravaged urban neighborhoods where most violent juvenile crime occurs, there are no clear lines between "good" and "bad" kids. As John Silva, director of safety and security for the Cambridge public schools, has observed: "Good kids have guns . . . there's so much fear. Good

kids who want to go to school and do the right thing—they're afraid of the gangs and the drug dealers; they want to protect themselves and their families. Good kids, bad kids—the categories don't apply anymore."

14   We know much more about the causes of juvenile crime and how to prevent it than a policy which would raze juvenile institutions and send youngsters into adult prisons for more sophisticated training in violent crime and victimization.

15   We also know that, as Robert J. Sampson and John H. Laub pointed out in their groundbreaking 1993 book on juvenile delinquency, "Crime in the Making: Pathways and Turning Points Through Life," most youthful wrongdoers do not become adult criminals. There are important turning points—quality education, well-paid work, stable marriage—that help young offenders become law-abiding adults.

16   The juvenile justice programs that have been shown to work—community-based programs that deal with kids on an individual basis—are hanging by a financial thread. We seem to prefer to make fun of "midnight basketball," the much maligned program in the Clinton crime bill, than acknowledging it makes sense to provide kids with alternatives to the street.

17   Why do we appear to hate our most troubled kids? When we call young lawbreakers "superpredators" and "violent youth predators," we stop thinking of them as kids, or as people. Race and racism help to fuel the anticrime hysteria sweeping the land. When most people think of juvenile crime, they think of young, African-American males, the ones we see hiding their faces on the TV news.

18   By arguing against punishing kids with adults, we are not demeaning the seriousness of violent juvenile crime. Violence perpetrated by juveniles has the same devastating effect on victims as violence perpetrated by adults. Youth violence contributes to community breakdown and causes despair for the families of both victims and perpetrators.

19   But we are talking about kids, many of whom have barely had a childhood on the mean streets of our cities. We are talking about kids, most of whom have been badly hurt themselves.

20   Frankie, the hapless burglar, is a juvenile wrongdoer. The burglary charge makes him a serious juvenile wrongdoer, an accused felon. He is more like most juvenile offenders than these "predators" the politicians are railing about. But if the politicians have their way, children like Frankie could be locked up with experienced adult inmates.

21   His parents regretted leaving Frankie in jail for the night, even though it was only one night and nothing really happened to him. When he was led out into the courtroom for arraignment, he was shackled to an adult detainee. He was held in the dock with seasoned criminals. His parents think that one night in jail killed something in Frankie. Maybe his childhood.

EXPLORING THE TEXT

1. Smith and Chester's intention in this essay is to argue against a pending piece of legislation. What is the bill they oppose? Why are they opposed to it?

2. What is Smith and Chester's version of "the reality of most juvenile crime" (paragraph 10)? What statistics do they offer in support of their version? Are these statistics convincing?

3. How does race play a role in the argument these authors make?

4. What support do the authors provide for their claim that punishing juveniles with adults would constitute "cruel and unusual punishment" (paragraph 9)?

5. Smith and Chester use the pronoun *we* throughout this essay, but who "we" is changes. Who is represented by the "we" in various parts of this text? Why do the authors make this shift? What is the effect of this shift?

6. Why do the authors use the anecdote at the beginning of the text? How does the story influence your response to their argument?

7. Smith and Chester adopt the charged and powerful language of their opponents—"coddled" and "predator," for example. Yet there are places in this piece where Smith and Chester offer their own charged and powerful language against their opponents' position. What are some examples of such language in their own argument?

WRITING ASSIGNMENTS

1. In a previous essay, Tom Reilly argues that certain youthful offenders should be recognized as "predators," an idea that underlies his argument in favor of imprisoning these criminals to protect society. Smith and Chester argue against the idea that some youthful offenders might be considered "predators," stating that they are typically victims themselves (paragraphs 18–19). Write an essay in which you explore "predator" as a metaphor. What ideas are associated with predators? If Reilly or Smith and Chester want us to agree with their arguments (which, of course, they do), how important is it for them to convince us to accept or reject this metaphor?

2. Smith and Chester's essay argues against Reilly's. Which argument do you find most compelling? Why? Write an essay in which you discuss the particular strengths and weaknesses of each argument. What questions might you ask of each author? How would you argue against each essay? What could the authors do to strengthen their arguments?

GROUP PROJECTS

1. Smith and Chester refer to society's attitudes against juvenile offenders (see paragraphs 16 and 17). Working as a group, prepare your own discussion of what attitudes are being presented in a variety of cultural outlets. For one week, read newspapers, watch a wide range of television news programs, listen to radio programs, and survey the covers of various maga-

zines. Write a report that describes how much attention is paid to juvenile crime, what issues are raised, and what solutions are proposed.

2. "Charged language" can be defined as words and phrases that encourage an emotional response in readers or listeners. Smith and Chester use charged language throughout this essay, as do Reilly and the other authors included in this chapter. Find several examples of charged language from among these essays and write an essay that discusses the advantages and disadvantages of the use of "charged language." Does such language make an argument more persuasive? Does it make the argument more credible? What's the difference?

Work: What's in It for Me?

As college students, you have entered a four-year training program for entry into a place where you'll spend the rest of your lives: the working world. Toward that end, you will choose majors that you hope will lead to careers that, in turn, will be both personally and financially rewarding. But what are your expectations of the working world? What do you hope to get out of a job besides a regular paycheck? What might job satisfaction mean to you at this point? And what might be your idea of making it, of achieving success as a professional? These and other questions are explored in the essays in this chapter—questions that you will face upon graduation in a few short years.

Most college graduates choose a profession that they hope will afford them satisfaction on several levels. They also hope that when the time comes, they will have saved enough money to enjoy a well-earned retirement. But this may not be the case, according to Paul Osterman in the opening article, "Getting Started." As Osterman explains, while today's young workforce supports its elders on Social Security, they have little hope of similar support in their own retirement. Young people like yourselves can hardly imagine thinking so far into the future, especially when you haven't even begun a career yet. But Osterman's piece serves as a sober preview of what he sees as a shrinking job market—one where a college degree appears to be losing its worth. As he points out, however, having one is better than having none, and for those with degree and drive, there will always be opportunities for the taking.

Americans today face a different set of problems and priorities than their parents did. For many people a generation or two ago, a job was a job—something that put food on the table, something they looked forward to retiring from. But today's professional men and women expect to find personal fulfillment in their careers and plan to keep working into their sixties and seventies. They spend more time at the office, while trying to juggle families and social obligations. In the next essay, "Having It All," Robert Wuthnow examines a society driven to achieve and often running to catch its breath. He depicts the late 1990s careerist as ever striving to attain the American Dream, but never quite getting there.

The next piece looks at today's youth—a bright eager generation that is entering the job market with a set of expectations so different from that of their parents. In her editorial, "Generation Xers and Their American Dream," Jennifer Singer offers some insights into the changing nature of work for the so-called Generation X. In a society where salaries have decreased and people work longer hours, children born after the baby boom want something else out of life. As Singer explains, they judge their success by different standards from what drove Mom and Dad.

Standards change not just between generations, but within one's own life span. Renee Loth, in her essay "Measuring Success," discusses how our notions of what it means to be successful grow as we do. When we are young, we enter the working world with clear ideas of what "success" means, of what we hope to achieve. But, as Loth points out, experience will change such perceptions as we learn to view the world through older, wiser eyes. There are no absolutes, including what it means to feel fulfilled in the job of life.

This chapter ends with some views that caused a stir when they were first published. In "There's No Place Like Work," Arlie Russell Hochschild challenges the standard impression—and one promoted by the media—that Americans would rather not have to work so much, that they'd rather be home playing with the kids or relaxing in the backyard, that they feel guilty not spending more time with the family. But the reality is, according to Hochschild, that Americans like to work—in fact, they *prefer* to work. At work they feel more appreciated, more fulfilled, less harried. And they know they could always click their shoes and go home—if they had to.

Getting Started
Paul Osterman

How hard is it to break into the job market in your field? Will your education prepare you? Will jobs be available? Will you earn a good wage? Paul Osterman describes our "age of anxiety about jobs" and reports a range of statistics that shed light on how the job market works, what skills are most in demand, and what kinds of jobs people find at entry level. He also considers the different systems in place in Germany and Japan and the ways in which they do a better job of introducing young people into their job markets. Osterman concludes by offering his suggestions on how the American system should be changed. Is your training on the right track? Osterman's ideas might help you to evaluate your own situation and prospects.

Osterman is a professor of human resources and management at the Massachusetts Institute of Technology. This essay was published in *Wilson Quarterly* in the Autumn 1994 issue.

1   We live in an age of anxiety about jobs, and perhaps the greatest anxiety is felt by young people searching for their first employment. All the other dangers and discontents of the world of work—from stagnant wages to insecurity bred by corporate "re-engineering"—seem to form a dark ceiling over those who are putting their feet on the lowest rungs of the ladder. Not only must today's young endure a larger-than-usual share of the uncertainties of starting out, but they must contemplate a future that seems truncated and unpromising. The news media have cast them as an "edgy," cynical, and disheartened "Generation X," the first generation in American history, we are constantly told, that cannot look forward to a future better than its parents had. A staple of the Generation X story is the young person who invested in four years of college and yet finds himself in a job well below what he expected, both in terms of what it demands and what it pays. The *Washington Post* tells of college graduates forced to take unpaid internships because real jobs are unavailable. *Time* says it all in a headline: "Bellboys with B.A.'s."

2   There is a crisis among young people who are trying to get started in life, but it is not quite the crisis that the news media describe and its causes are not quite what one might expect. The facts simply do not support a terribly gloomy view of the immediate prospects for the middle-class, college-educated kids who are generally labeled Generation X. It is true that wage growth, an important part of the escalator of upward mobility, has slowed or ended, and it is far from certain that the old more-

or-less automatic increases will resume. College-educated men aged 25 to 29, for example, earned an average of $28,963 in 1992, roughly the same amount in real dollars as in 1983. (Their female peers, however, improved their earnings by a bit more than 10 percent.) But while average pay may not have increased, college grads still get good jobs, jobs that give them responsibility, decent pay, room for a little creativity, and opportunities for advancement. In the boom years of 1984–86, about 47 percent of newly hired college grads in their twenties landed jobs in top-shelf occupations, as executives, managers, or professionals. The years 1989–91 saw a slight decline, to 45 percent, but this hardly represents a collapse of the job market. And another 40 percent of the 1989–91 crowd landed jobs in other desirable areas: technical work, sales, and administration, including jobs as various as air traffic controller, cashier, stockbroker, and ticket and reservations agent.

3   Slow economic growth has increased the risks facing college graduates and ratcheted up their anxiety. On university campuses a more somber career-oriented atmosphere prevails, shocking the visiting journalists who came of age in sunnier and, some would say, dreamier days. It takes more time and more effort to get a good job, and often the pay is disappointing. Nonetheless these young people are still in relatively good shape.

4   The young people who face true difficulty are those with less education. They are in fact the great majority of young jobseekers. In 1992, only 23 percent of 25- to 29-year-olds had a college degree. Another 48 percent had some college or an associate's degree. Sixteen percent had only a high school diploma, and 13 percent lacked even that. In the past, there was a fairly reliable route that kids without college could follow. After high school and perhaps a year or two of college, they churned through a succession of less-than-desirable jobs before settling down. Instead of learning job skills in school, they went through an extended period of what economists call "labor market adjustment." They might work a string of jobs as retail clerks, construction workers, or unskilled factory hands, punctuated by short spells of more-or-less voluntary unemployment. Then, as now, many twentysomethings were not ready for permanent jobs. They were mainly interested in earning some spending money for an apartment and a car and, perhaps, in having a little fun with their coworkers on the job. Few cared much what kind of job it was.

5   With age, maturity, and new family responsibilities later in their twenties, these people settled down into "adult jobs," but the paths they followed were many and varied. Credentials were less important than personal contacts, and many found their adult jobs through the help of parents, relatives, and friends. The young man who followed his father into a particular factory or mine might not have been typical, but his informal way of getting started was. Uncle Bob might pull some strings for you at the union hall or Mom's best friend might tip you off to an opening in the billing office. This system, if it can be called that, succeeded for most people because jobs were plentiful and because most of the skills workers needed could be learned on the job. Today many young men and women cannot count on either the old routes or the old destinations. The factory likely is silent, the union hall half empty, and the help-wanted ads full of jobs requiring specialized skills. Ready to make the leap into adulthood, these young people find there is no obvious place to land.

6   The system still works for large numbers of high school graduates; most move gradually from "youth jobs" to "adult jobs." The National Longitudinal Survey of Youth, which followed a group of young people between 1979 and 1988, offers a sharper picture of the problem areas. It found that 44 percent of 16- to 19-year-olds worked in wholesale or retail trade, which offers mostly low-paying and high-turnover positions. But by ages 20 to 31 the fraction employed in this sector was down to only 17 percent. Moreover, the study shows steadily growing work commitment among the young people. Only 3.5 percent of the oldest men in the study and four percent of the oldest women were unemployed at the time of the last interview. All of this suggests that the process of integrating the young into the workplace is going fairly well. Yet one also needs to know whether the jobs are steady and whether people are enjoying long stretches without unemployment. Here the news is more troubling. Among employed 29- to 31-year-old high school graduates who did not go to college, more than 30 percent had not been in their position for even a year. Another 12 percent had only one year of tenure. The pattern was much the same for women who had remained in the labor force for the four years prior to the survey. These are adults who, for a variety of reasons—a lack of skills, training, or disposition—have not managed to secure "adult" jobs.

7   For blacks and Latinos, the malfunctioning of the job market has reached a critical stage. In 1993, only 50 percent of young blacks between the ages of 16 and 24 who were not in school even had jobs. Among young Latinos the figure was 59 percent. By contrast, nearly three-quarters of their white counterparts had jobs. (A college degree significantly narrows but does not close the gaps. Ninety percent of white college graduates in the age group were employed, as were 82 percent of the black graduates and 85 percent of the Latinos.)

8   Young people in many other industrialized countries have a lot more help getting started. In Germany, virtually all students except the small number bound for universities spend the last three years of high school in an apprenticeship system that combines part-time schooling with training in factories, labs, and offices. For each of some 400 recognized occupations there is a standardized curriculum that specifies the skills to be taught on the job and the content of schooling. The system is overseen by committees of representatives from government, business, and unions. After formal examinations at the end of high school, new graduates are placed in "adult" jobs, often with the company that trained them.

9   Not all German apprentices can find employment in their field; the Germans, a notoriously well-fed people, joke that they always seem somehow to turn out too many bakers. Yet inculcating the essentials of workplace behavior—be prompt, dress properly, follow instructions—is nearly as important a function of the system as teaching particular skills. The German system has other drawbacks. Women are still "gender tracked" into fields such as hairdressing, and the system can be slow to react to technological change in the workplace. Still the training and placement help German youngsters receive are far superior to what is available to their American peers.

10   In Japan, the process of launching the young into the world of work is not so highly organized as it is in Germany, but it is still far more structured than in the United States. Teachers maintain contacts with employers and play an important

role in placing high school graduates. In Japan, as in Germany, the first job is a giant step into the work world. The years of casual, American-style "job shopping" are virtually unknown in these countries, and especially in Japan the young are expected to remain with their first employer for a long time. Yet if the American system is less orderly, it also provides much more freedom for the individual to experiment and change his or her mind—highly prized qualities that should not be lost in any attempt at reform.

11   Finding a steady job is only half the challenge of getting started. Finding one that pays relatively well is the second, and lately most daunting, hurdle. Pay for college graduates has at least stayed even over the years, but high school graduates and (especially) dropouts have lost a lot of ground. There now exists a huge pay gap between the college educated and their less fortunate peers. Between 1979 and 1991, the real wages of high school dropouts fell more than 20 percent, and the wages of high school graduates without college degrees fell more than 11 percent. People equipped with only a high school degree are finding it increasingly difficult to earn a decent living. According to a recent U.S. Census Bureau report, nearly half of all 18- to 24-year-olds who worked full time in 1992 still had annual incomes below $14,335, the poverty line for a family of four.

12   The labor market is sending a clear signal. While the American way of moving youngsters from high school to the labor market may be imperfect, the chief problem is that, for many, even getting a job no longer guarantees a decent standard of living. More than ever, getting ahead, or even keeping up, means staying in school longer.

13   While many things may have contributed to the erosion of wages over the past two decades, including the oft-cited influxes of cheap immigrant labor and cheap imported goods, the new premium on skills explains much of what has happened. When new technologies are combined with new ways of organizing work, such as team production or total quality management programs, the need for various kinds of skills rises. Today, employees are asked to understand and analyze certain kinds of data, to think about ways to improve the processes and products of the workplace, and to work with others to bring improvements about. No longer is it enough to perform rote tasks on an assembly line.

14   In part, employers are looking for better command of "hard" skills such as math, and the best evidence for this is the fact that they are willing to pay for such hard skills with hard cash. Economists Richard Murnane, John Willett, and Frank Levy recently found that, six years after graduation, members of the high school class of 1986 who had scored in the top third of a standardized math test were earning 16 percent more than those who had scored in the bottom third. In the class of '72, by contrast, top scorers enjoyed an edge of only five percent six years after graduation.

15   This is a graphic illustration of the growth in demand for relatively simple math skills. And they are "relatively simple." Skills of this sort are not out of reach for most people. The question is whether the schools can do a good job of providing them. The answer is a little more textured than the bitter criticisms of political leaders and employers suggest. In fact, there is little reason to believe that schools are

providing worse training than in the past. Scores on the National Assessment of Educational Progress, which declined during the 1970s, generally rose during the 1980s. Kids in most age groups scored slightly higher on most tests at the end of the '80s than they did in the early '70s. High school dropout rates have even improved a bit: In 1972, 16.1 percent of 19- to 20-year-olds lacked a high school diploma and were not enrolled in school. By 1991, that number was down to only 14.3 percent.

16 The real problem appears to be that jobs (and employers) are requiring ever-higher levels of skill, and that the schools, though moving slowly forward, are failing to keep up. Test scores have not declined, but they are not very impressive either. The National Assessment of Educational Progress, for example, offers the depressing claim that 30 percent of young people lack basic literacy skills (e.g., the ability to collect information from different parts of a document) and that 44 percent of 17-year-olds cannot compute with decimals, fractions, and percentages. And while it is nice that dropout rates are not rising, they are still too high, especially among minority groups: 17 percent of young blacks and 36 percent of Latinos are dropouts.

17 Employers, moreover, are not simply looking for technical skills. The workplace of the 1990s, with its team-oriented approach and quality programs, requires people who are able to work cooperatively with others. They need good interpersonal skills. The same is true in the service sector—from fast-food restaurants to airlines—where there is a growing emphasis on pleasing the customer. When asked in a survey conducted by the National Association of Manufacturers why they rejected job applicants (more than one reason could be given), 37 percent of employers cited writing skills and 27 percent cited math skills, but 64 percent cited ability to adapt to the workplace.

18 Thus, despite all the talk of a "deskilled" nation of hamburger flippers, the American labor market is demanding more and more skill. Although unskilled service-sector work has certainly grown, so has the quantity of more demanding work. Indeed, the U.S. Bureau of Labor Statistics projects that between now and 2005 the occupational group with the fastest growth rate will be "professional specialty" jobs—such as engineering, the health-care professions, and teaching—almost all of which require at least some college. Growth in executive, administrative, managerial, and technical occupations will also be faster than average.

19 It is important for those who would fix the American system to put aside utopian thoughts. Getting started will always be a difficult, anxiety-producing experience. Moreover, young people are and will continue to be marginalized in virtually every labor market in the world. Even Germany does this, albeit subtly, by placing them mostly in apprenticeships at small firms, where long-term career prospects are not good. Young people simply lack the skills and maturity of their elders, and in any event it makes sense to reserve most good jobs for people with adult responsibilities.

20 Hearkening to the German example, American policymakers have focused on the need to strengthen links between local school and employers. The Clinton administration's new School to Work Opportunities Act, budgeted at $100 million this year, encourages employers to provide on-the-job training and encourages schools

to reformulate their curricula to include real-world examples that can be used both to motivate and to teach. The new "tech-prep" education, unlike the old vocational education, seeks to give teenagers serious instruction in traditional academic disciplines. The hope is that by appealing to a bigger slice of the teenage population, the low-prestige, second-rate taint of old-fashioned vocational education will be avoided. Making all of this work in the highly decentralized American system will be difficult. Individual school systems must be persuaded to rethink how material is taught. Without strong European-style employers' associations, there has to be firm-by-firm recruitment of "good" employers to train students and hire graduates. Still, the effort is well worth making.

21   Ultimately, however, helping the young find good jobs is more than a matter of tinkering with what happens to teenagers in school and on the job. One of the top requirements in today's job market is schooling beyond high school. This means that increased financial aid to help more youngsters attend college must be a high priority. Likewise, the employment problems of black and Latino youngsters owe much to a daunting array of larger urban ills, from crime to inferior education, for which narrowly focused programs—with the exception of the tiny Job Corps—have been unable to compensate. Overcoming this group's special problems will require large helpings of collective as well as individual ambition and initiative.

EXPLORING THE TEXT

1. The second paragraph begins, "There is a crisis among young people who are trying to get started in life, but it is not quite the crisis that the news media describe and its causes are not quite what one might expect." In what ways does Osterman define the "crisis among young people"? How do the media define this problem?

2. Speaking of college graduates, Osterman says that "these young people are still in relatively good shape" (paragraph 3). Good shape relative to whom? Which young people are not in such good shape? Why?

3. How does race factor into the availability of jobs for young people?

4. Evaluate Osterman's use of statistics in paragraph 6 where he reports and analyzes the National Longitudinal Survey of Youth. What statistics does he initially report? What limitations does he note with regard to these numbers? How does he use different kinds of statistics to provide a more complete analysis of the situation?

5. What lessons does Osterman suggest we might learn from other countries and the ways in which they educate and train young people? What are the limitations of these systems as compared to the American model?

6. Outline this argument, beginning with a clear statement of Osterman's thesis and listing the various points he offers in support of this thesis. Briefly explain whether or not you believe that he has offered sufficient support for his thesis.

7. According to Osterman, what programs are in place to solve the problems he describes? What other solutions ought to be available?

WRITING ASSIGNMENTS

1. In paragraph 15, Osterman states what he believes to be the real problem: the lack of basic literacy and math skills. Analyze the training you have received so far in these areas. What does he define as the basic needs? What has been done to insure that you meet these standards? How much further do you plan to proceed in these disciplines in the years of education remaining to you? Are there any deficiencies? If so, how might you work around them? Discuss your analysis in an essay.
2. Do more extensive research into the education and job training system in Germany or Japan or in another country whose system seems to provide a successful model for educating young people and effectively integrating them into the job market. Compare that system with the U.S. system. Write an essay in which you carefully discuss the advantages and disadvantages of each system and make your own recommendations for how the U.S. system might be improved.

GROUP PROJECTS

1. Osterman briefly discusses problems related to race (paragraph 7) and makes clear that the statistics he discusses aren't necessarily applicable to all young people entering the job market. He does not, however, discuss these discrepancies in great detail. Do your own research and prepare a report in which you more fully consider why the job market can be so different for blacks and Latinos (you might also research the status of other racial groups). Consider why these discrepancies exist, what is being done now (and what has been done in the past) to reduce them, and what should be done in the future. Different members of the group should be responsible for researching one part of this question.
2. Have group members research the programs proposed by the Clinton administration and the laws eventually passed. Has the system been improved since Osterman wrote his report? What changes have been made in the U.S. system since 1992? What changes were voted down? How successful have the changes been? As a group, research in the government documents section of the library and consult transcripts of congressional hearings as well as the texts of laws, regulations, and oversight reports. Gather your findings and write a report recommending what remains to be done.

Having It All
Robert Wuthnow

What is the American Dream? Some describe it simply as the promise of a better life—better than their parents' lives, better than what they set out to make for themselves. But how does that pursuit affect the way people live their daily lives? Or the quality of those lives? In other words, do people push themselves too hard in order to make it? Or perhaps the opposite is true: Are American workers soft, lazy, and spoiled? Is our version of the dream too heavily devoted to luxury and leisure? These are some of the questions Robert Wuthnow raises in his essay as he questions the real quality of American life at work and at home.

Robert Wuthnow is the Gerhard R. Andlinger Professor of Sociology and Director of the Center for the Study of American Religion at Princeton University. He is the author of numerous articles and books on American religion and culture, including *Acts of Compassion* (1994) and, most recently, *Poor Richard's Principle: Recovering the American Dream Through the Moral Dimension of Work, Business, and Money* (1997), from which this essay was excerpted.

1   When Mark Latham graduated from college, he had no idea what he wanted to do next. Like many other young people with talent and good credentials, he decided to maximize his options by getting into something where he could make a lot of money. That meant Wall Street. Within two years, Mark was a successful analyst negotiating leveraged buyouts for a major corporate finance firm. Now, at age 26, he works for another firm arranging financing for huge real estate deals. Handling sales in the $400 million range has become routine. He knows he could become enormously successful if he really tried. He says, "It'd be great to be famous, having everybody wanting to talk to you, going to interesting parties, not having to worry about money, traveling, living in a nice home."

2   But Mark Latham is not so sure this is the life he wants. "Someday, our planet's going to be a speck of dust," he muses, "so what's the point of making a lot of money?" He fears he will spend his whole life trying to fill it up with possessions, only to have someone ask, "Did you really make a difference? Did you give a little more than you took? Or did you just take a lot?" He is no visionary, but he wants to be remembered as a decent person who left the world a little better than he found it.

3   John and Mary Phelps, both at age 30, have achieved a comfortable standard of living compared with most Americans. After finishing his MBA, John moved up the corporate ladder in various finance and marketing positions in Minneapolis. Mary runs her own graphic design business. They own their home and have enough money to buy most of the things they want. Both find their work intellectually stimulating and see a rosy economic future ahead.

4   They do not aspire to the fast track, but even in the driving lane they have discovered more pressure and frustration than they ever imagined. Recently John gave up his marketing position because of sixty-plus hour-weeks, back stabbing, and office politics, only to find himself in a job with grueling deadlines and endless paper-

work. He says he comes home and just screams to relieve the tension. Mary feels the pressure, too, especially when clients insist she work evenings and weekends. She wants to have children but fears she will not have time to be a good mother. Both would like to play a more positive role in their community—developing environmental projects and helping the disadvantaged. They are uncertain whether they will ever realize these dreams.

Rethinking the American Dream

5 Throughout much of our nation's history people pursued the American Dream by trying to attain high-paying jobs, working hard to become materially successful, and striving for an economically comfortable life. But to a growing number of Americans, the life envisioned in this dream is no longer enough. Having moved securely into the professional-managerial class, they want more than simply an above-average standard of living. Working harder just to climb the corporate ladder and acquire more economic resources no longer seems as appealing as it once did. Instead, concerns are being expressed with increasing frequency about the ill effects of working too hard, of subjecting oneself to relentless job pressures, and of becoming focused so single-mindedly on material pursuits that other human values are neglected. People are now reconsidering the benefits of family life, community service, spiritual pursuits, and self-realization, in opposition to the search for material success alone.

6 "The New American Dream," writes family sociologist Arlene Skolnick, "mixes the new cultural freedoms with many of the old wishes—marital and family happiness, economic security, home ownership, education of children."[1] But, she cautions, there are more twists and turns to be faced. In part, this is because economic conditions themselves may provide fewer opportunities than they did in the past. But it is even more a result of uncertainty about what the American Dream should include.

7 Observers assess the current mood with differing emphases but agree that serious rethinking of the American Dream is taking place. Increasingly, writes Graham Hueber of the Gallup Poll, "Americans [are] seeking more personal satisfaction through recreation, family life, friends, religion, and a search for meaning in life—not through work."[2] There is "a great craving," notes a leading business magazine, for a slower pace and the time just to relax and do other things besides work.[3] Finding how to do this might even make our work more productive, counsel the editors of another magazine, because "the human spirit, strangely and wondrously made, always turns out to be a surprise."[4]

8 As the lives of people like Mark Latham, John and Mary Phelps, and millions of others demonstrate, however, economic aspirations and the demands that go with them are seldom easy to escape. In all periods the great sages and social visionaries hoped for a better way. Aristotle predicted a time when people could expend a minimum of energy working, saving most of their time for reflection and pleasure. Centuries later, the explorers who came to American shores envisioned a land of plenty

in which the toil and drudgery of the past could be forgone.[5] But, for all the industrial and technological advancement that has happened since then, these dreams have failed to be realized.

9   Even the more prosperous members of our society find themselves beleaguered to the point of exhaustion with economic commitments. In one sense, they have everything—talent, connections, opportunity, prosperity, freedom from back-breaking labor, the ability to live securely and comfortably—but they clearly want more. Economic well-being is only a means to realizing the other aspirations they hold more dearly. Indeed, it is a means that sometimes gets in the way of these other aspirations. The economic portion of their lives seems to be ever on the move, expansive, demanding, threatening to encroach on every other realm of their lives. And so they struggle to find legitimate ways in which to restrain their economic commitments, still feeling the need to work hard, but also experiencing high levels of stress, periodic burn-out, and the constant desire to achieve greater fulfillment.

10   The ambivalence toward economic commitments that seems to characterize a growing number of middle-class Americans has been expressed well in a recent book by psychologist Sam Keen. Reflecting on his own ambivalence, Keen writes, "I don't know who I would be without the satisfaction of providing for my family, the occasional intoxication of creativity, the warm companionship of colleagues, the pride in a job well done, and the knowledge that my work has been useful to others." Keen's devotion to his work, however, is plagued by unease about the price of this devotion. He adds, "But there is still something unsaid, something that forces me to ask questions about my life that are, perhaps, tragic: In working so much have I done violence to my being? How often, doing work that is good, have I betrayed what is better in myself and abandoned what is best for those I love? How many hours would have been better spent walking in silence in the woods or wrestling with my children?"[6]

11   Such questions of course are not popular in many circles. If there is anything wrong with the American Dream, say the politicians and corporate analysts, it is that most people are not pursuing it hard enough. Sagging productivity, inflated salaries, long lunch breaks, padded expense accounts, lax supervision, too little interest in doing the job well, an education system that provides inadequate training in technical skills—these are the problems. Not a rapacious economic system that extracts too much from its workers. Even to suggest that economic commitments may need to be reined in is to fly in the face of most conventional wisdom. Yet a growing body of evidence demonstrates clearly that the vast majority of Americans who have achieved a comfortable level of economic well-being are experiencing the pressures of work and monetary commitments so acutely that they wonder how to make room for the more basic human values these commitments were once intended to achieve.

Working Harder

12   Long hours on the job signal the first line across which material pursuits embark in their relentless quest for a greater share of our lives. Compared with the Japanese, the American worker has often been made to feel like an outright shirker. Faltering national competitiveness in world markets has been blamed on the U.S. worker tak-

ing too many holidays and vacations, watching too much television, cutting hours, and idling the time away while on the job. The Japanese, critics point out, work longer hours each week and take fewer vacations. Americans also fall behind their German counterparts, apparently valuing free time at the expense of the national economy. These accusations square well with other impressions of American society: that it is devoted increasingly to leisure and relaxation, that the decline of agriculture and heavy industry has led to a more humane life for the average worker, and that the proverbial work ethic nurtured by Puritan strictness has long been on the decline. But portraying the American worker in this manner is to engage in a massive deception.

13   Statistics on the average workweek did register substantial decline (about 10 percent each decade) between 1900 and 1940. Since then, however, the workweek has remained remarkably stable. It does so, moreover, when estimates of holidays, paid vacations, and sick leaves are taken into account. Comparative figures from other countries also show that workers in countries such as Japan and Germany put in about the same number of hours as American workers when actual time in similar-sized companies is considered, and that working hours in many other advanced industrialized countries have been declining in contrast with those in the United States.[7]

14   Labor statistics show that the typical hourly worker in the United States still receives wages for a workweek of approximately forty hours. What these figures mask, however, is the fact that an increasing number of people—who are not paid by the hour—generally work longer. At present, approximately 40 percent of all men in the U.S. labor force put in more than forty hours a week at their jobs—and a quarter put in more than fifty hours. Among women, the figures are still somewhat lower, but at least one woman in five works outside the home more than the standard forty hours. These figures are even higher in professional and managerial occupations and reach the highest levels among married men and women—precisely those whose time is likely to be fullest with other responsibilities, such as childrearing.[8] The fact that many Americans take their work home with them, mulling it over while they watch television or mow the grass, also means that official estimates give a distorted picture. One national study found that one American in three thinks about his or her work a lot outside of the workplace itself.[9] Some evidence also indicates that an increasing share of the American workforce is now *required* to work evenings and weekends, rather than being able to restrict their jobs to the conventional "nine-to-five" working day.[10]

15   The most substantial increase in the typical workweek has come from more and more women participating in the labor force. When the workweek for individual workers is counted, this fact is missed. But for most people, the relevant fact of life is that they and their spouse *both* work now, whereas a generation ago only one spouse was likely to be employed outside the home. In 1950, for instance, only 37 percent of all women between ages 25 and 54 were gainfully employed, meaning that the typical household contributed about forty hours a week to the labor market, or if this 37 percent were averaged in, no more than about fifty-five hours. By comparison, 81 percent of all women in this age-group are now employed, meaning that the typical household involves dual careers, or at least eighty hours a week on the job.[11] When work from all these various sources is taken into consideration, some

estimates suggest that per capita involvement in the labor force may on average be as much as an extra month per year, compared with only two decades ago.[12]

16   As a result, large numbers of the American public complain of having too little time to do anything but work. According to one recent survey, 48 percent of the U.S. labor force say they have too little time to spend with their spouse, and 39 percent say they have too little time for their children. Thirty-two percent of those polled felt they had to spend too much time working.[13] In my survey, 66 percent of the labor force said the statement "I'm working harder than I did five years ago" described themselves very well or fairly well. One person in two (52 percent) said the same about the statement "I wish I could work fewer hours than I do."[14]

17   In another national survey 41 percent complained of having too little time to spend with their families, and three-quarters said they sleep fewer than eight hours a night; indeed, four people in ten sleep only six hours a night or less.[15] And, while many adults may feel this is the only way to get everything done, research is beginning to document its serious negative consequences. As one writer observes, "Evidence is mounting that sleep deprivation has become one of the most pervasive health problems facing the U.S."[16] Many people, it appears, might agree. In my survey, 48 percent said the statement "I should get more sleep than I do" described them very well or fairly well.[17]

8   Despite the fact that leisure time is probably more abundant than it was a century ago, many people are thus pressured to find enough time to relax or pursue any of their other interests. With both spouses working, less time is left over to care for children or engage in community activities. Even with labor-saving devices such as household appliances, and the growing availability of professional services, people find that much of their free time must be spent maintaining these labor-saving devices, traveling to and from work, and doing routine household and personal chores.

19   "The hours are a real pain in the ass," says Jena Forsythe, 29, a New York securities trader who specializes in Japanese equities and bonds. At work every morning by seven-thirty, she spends at least five evenings a week at the office in order to be in contact with her counterparts in Tokyo. In eight years, she has found little time to pursue personal relationships, let alone get married or think about having children. Yet, even without these commitments, she finds it virtually impossible to do the things she needs to do for herself. "Like, this morning I'm thinking, oh my God, I do not have an ironed blouse in my apartment and somehow I've got to figure out how to get my blouses ironed so that I have some clothes!"

20   In the same way that labor statistics have sometimes given a misleading impression of the American workforce, studies of leisure time have also been deceptive, leading many observers to assume that people actually have more free time than ever before, despite their protests to the contrary. But when viewed more closely, these studies indicate how small the segment of American society is that has actually gained greater free time in recent years. Since 1975, for example, leisure time appears to have edged up by as much as two hours a week for the American population as a whole. Yet, when subgroups are examined, this increase turns out to be limited almost entirely to men and women in their fifties and sixties. Among married people with children, there has actually been a decrease in leisure time.[18]

21   With a wife and two daughters, Stuart Cummings, 33, a corporate lawyer in Chicago, is beginning to resent the long hours his job requires. "On a good day," he says, "I'm away from seven to seven, and many nights I don't make it home before my kids go to bed at nine." He says he has trouble accepting this as the way it will be for the next thirty years. But, like many other Americans in high-level professional positions, he sees no immediate way of escaping these requirements.

22   On objective grounds alone, then, it appears that many middle-class people are putting in long hours on the job, despite the fact that prosperity is already relatively widespread among this segment of the population, and that automation and other labor-saving devices seem not to have done much in recent decades to reduce the overall workweek. Some would argue that these conditions have been created by economic laws operating in the marketplace itself. These objective conditions, however, do not fully explain why their subjective correlates take the form they do. Previous generations might well have complained about being physically exhausted from too much work, but the current sense that one has a moral obligation to choose between working and other commitments hinges on much more recent definitions of the self and the social context in which it must function. Without yet trying to make sense of these definitions, we can at least begin to see that understanding the nature of work and the ways in which it might be reconciled more fully with other human aspirations will require us to consider it in relation to broader cultural assumptions involving moral meanings and conceptions of the good.

The Golden Handcuffs

23   One of the reasons why so many Americans find it difficult to cut back on the work they do, according to their own accounts, is that they are caught up in a cycle of lifestyle expectations that leaves them financially dependent on every marginal gain they can possibly earn. Henry David Thoreau once wrote critically of this financial dependence as "golden or silver fetters."[19] But in current management parlance "the golden handcuffs" have evolved into a strategy for cultivating corporate loyalty. Pay people enough, build in fringe benefits, encourage them to lead a lifestyle in keeping with rising economic expectations, and they will have trouble quitting or slowing the pace.

24   Corporate executives seldom have to bend employees' arms to apply these handcuffs, for economic obligations tend to rise during the life course of most individuals. Married couples typically spend more on housing than do singles, and as children enter the picture, housing, food, clothing, and education costs all escalate, usually at a rate equal to or above annual salary increases. Only as they reach their late fifties, do most people begin to feel they can afford to consider such options as working shorter hours in order to have more free time.[20] In my survey, people between the ages of 35 and 49 were particularly subject to financial concerns: 44 percent in this age bracket were trying to save money for children to attend college, 43 percent were paying off credit card debts, 57 percent were saving for retirement, 40 percent were either saving to buy a house or meeting high mortgage payments, and 31 percent were paying for medical bills.[21]

25   American culture is also geared to encourage rising material expectations across the life cycle. Rising costs associated with a growing family may induce greater economic pressures, but so do rising expectations about consumer goods, luxury items, and other material comforts. In one national survey, 56 percent of the respondents age 18 to 34 admitted that their desire to have "nice things" had risen within the past five years, as did 42 percent of those age 35 to 49.[22]

26   The result is that fewer and fewer Americans are able to escape the cycle of working harder to buy more things and to pay the bills for what they have already purchased. Some evidence of this pattern is evident in public opinion polls. In my survey, for example, 69 percent of the U.S. labor force admitted they had more money now than they did five years ago; yet 53 percent said they worry a lot about meeting their financial obligations, and 84 percent wished they had more money than they do.[23]

27   Better evidence comes from economic data themselves. In the last two decades alone, consumer borrowing on charge accounts has risen from $8.7 billion to $20.4 billion—a figure that now comprises approximately 21 percent of U.S. disposable income.[24] Over the same period, bank-card delinquencies have grown steadily.[25] Personal savings have experienced a corresponding decline, putting an increasing number of families at the mercy of short-term swings in the economy; for example, in one survey, half the respondents said they had managed to save less than $3,000, and 40 percent said it would be a "big problem" for them to receive an unexpected bill for $1,000.[26]

28   On balance, the most serious indication of how the golden handcuffs have increased their hold on the American public is probably the fact that household debt, which only a decade ago was 20 percent below the average level of household income, is now 10 percent higher than household income.[27] Much truth, it seems, is borne by the bumper sticker "I owe, I owe, so off to work I go."[28]

29   John Phelps, the Minneapolis businessman, had recently become acutely aware of the golden handcuffs he was wearing. Climbing the corporate ladder, he began to feel he was no longer being true to the values his parents had tried to instill in him; instinctively, he knew he wanted to pursue something else. "I definitely wanted to drop out," he recalls, but he postponed doing it. "They talk about the golden handcuffs in the corporate world where you get the nice benefits and the high pay, and you build a lifestyle around that." He knew he was tied to the corporation by financial necessity. "It's hard to leave," he admits, "no matter what you're thinking."

Notes

1. Arlene Skolnick, *Embattled Paradise: The American Family in an Age of Uncertainty* (New York: Basic Books, 1991), 220.
2. Graham Hueber, "Baby-boomers Seek More Family Time," *The Gallup Poll* (April 7, 1991), 1.
3. Timothy Belknap, "Reeling in a Fly-Fishing Collectible," *Business Week* (June 17, 1991), 116.
4. T. George Harris and Robert J. Trotter, "Work Smarter, Not Harder," *Psychology Today* (March 1989), 33.

5. Others who predicted a time when work would be minimized, freeing humanity for higher pursuits, include Thomas Jefferson, Karl Marx, John Stuart Mill, and John Maynard Keynes; for an overview, see Benjamin K. Hunnicutt, *Work Without End* (Philadelphia: Temple University Press, 1988).

6. Sam Keen, *Fire in the Belly: On Being a Man* (New York: Bantam Books, 1991), 67.

7. Thomas J. Kniesner, "The Full-Time Workweek in the United States," *Industrial and Labor Relations Review* 30 (1976), 3–15; *Business Statistics, 1961–88* (Washington, D.C.: U.S. Department of Commerce, 1989), 51; "ILO Report Predicts Shorter Workweek, Longer Vacations Before End of Century," *Daily Labor Report* (January 18, 1985), 4–5.

8. Susan E. Shank, "Women and the Labor Market: The Link Grows Stronger," *Monthly Labor Review* 111 (1988), 3–8; G. H. Moore and J. N. Hedges, "Trends in Labor and Leisure," *Monthly Labor Review* 94 (1971), 3–11. Polls that attempt to measure the average workweek by asking individuals themselves how much they work contain certain biases but suggest that Americans on the whole are actually working harder than in the recent past. For example, Harris surveys conducted in 1973 and again in 1990 revealed a rise in the average workweek from 40.6 hours to 48.8 hours. Among professionals, people with incomes over $50,000, and those termed "baby boomers," the average was 52 hours, and among small businesspeople 57 hours. These figures are reported in Benjamin K. Hunnicutt, "No Time for God or Family," *Wall Street Journal* (January 4, 1990): A12. Results of a 1991 Gallup survey, though reported in less detail, also indicate that many Americans work more than the standard forty-hour week. Thirty-nine percent reported they work more than forty-five hours in a typical week; one person in eight works more than sixty hours a week. Larry Hugick and Jennifer Leonard, "Job Dissatisfaction Grows; 'Moonlighting' on the Rise," *The Gallup Poll* (September 2, 1991), 10.

9. *The Gallup Poll* (July 1989).

10. According to Hugick and Leonard, "Job Dissatisfaction Grows," 10, the percentage of Americans who say they are regularly scheduled to work evenings and weekends increased from 24 percent in 1989 to 36 percent in 1991.

11. Shank, "Women and the Labor Market."

12. Juliet B. Schor, *The Overworked American: The Unexpected Decline of Leisure* (New York: Basic Books, 1991).

13. Hugick and Leonard, "Job Dissatisfaction Grows," 5.

14. My survey was conducted in February and March 1992, among 2,013 randomly selected adults who were currently working full-time or part-time.

15. "Time at a Premium for Many Americans; Younger People Feel the Pressures Most," *The Gallup Poll* (November 4, 1990).

16. Anastasia Toufexis, "Drowsy America," *Time* (December 17, 1990), 78.

17. Economic Values Survey.

18. John P. Robinson, "Time's Up," *American Demographics* 11 (1989), 33–35.

19. Henry D. Thoreau, *Walden* (Princeton: Princeton University Press, 1973 [1854]), 16.

20. These observations are borne out by figures from the annual Consumer Expenditure Survey conducted by the U.S. Bureau of Labor Statistics; see, for example, Margaret Ambry, "The Age of Spending," *American Demographics* (November 1990), 16–23.

21. Economic Values Survey.

22. Unpublished results from a survey designed by the author and conducted by the George H. Gallup International Institute in November 1990 among a national sample of 1,000 U.S. adults. Fourteen percent of the younger group said having nice things had become less important, as did 21 percent of the older group. Among persons over age 50, having nice things was also more—rather than less—important by a margin of 26 percent to 22 percent.

23. Economic Values Survey. The figures are percentages of the sample who said each statement describes them very well or fairly well.

24. U.S. Bureau of the Census, *Statistical Abstract of the U.S., 1990* (Washington, D.C.: Government Printing Office, 1990), 506.

25. "Credit-Card Delinquencies Growing, Bank Group Says," *Wall Street Journal* (March 13, 1991).

26. "Personal Savings," *Wall Street Journal* (May 23, 1991); Clint Willis, "Americans and Their Money," *Money* (April 1991), 74–76.

27. Robert F. Black, Don L. Boroughs, Sara Collins, and Kenneth Sheets, "Heavy Lifting: How America's Debt Burden Threatens the Economic Recovery," *U.S. News and World Report* (May 6, 1991), 53–61.

28. Keen, *Fire in the Belly,* 52–53, quotes this bumper sticker, adding: "Debt, the willingness to live beyond our means, binds us to the economic system that requires both surplus work and surplus consumption."

EXPLORING THE TEXT

1. What is the traditional definition of the American Dream? Make a list of all that it represents to you, all that you hope for.

2. In what ways does the "'New American Dream'" (paragraph 6) begin to refashion the historical goals?

3. Wuthnow quotes Aristotle and the early explorers of the American continents to present historical views on how we might want to balance work and leisure (paragraph 8). How does this historical perspective relate to the modern problem as he presents it?

4. What does the "conventional wisdom" say about the American Dream? Why do politicians and corporate analysts suggest that it may be failing?

5. How does the author use statistics to combat the "conventional wisdom" that Americans aren't working hard enough?

6. In the same way that Wuthnow deflates the labor statistics, suggesting that they sometimes give a misleading impression about the American workforce, he also suggests that studies of leisure are deceptive. Describe the way in which he makes this argument.

7. What does Wuthnow mean when he refers to "golden handcuffs" (paragraph 23)? What examples does he offer? What is the importance of this image in the context of this argument?

WRITING ASSIGNMENTS

1. What is your definition of the American Dream? How important is money in your version of the dream? What priorities do you give to leisure time? Write an essay in which you compare Wuthnow's ideas and statistics to your own lifestyle choices—and aspirations.

2. Wuthnow refers to "the proverbial work ethic nurtured by Puritan strictness" (paragraph 12). Review the work of some important early writers who presented this idea (e.g., various colonial writings, Benjamin Franklin's *The Way to Wealth,* any book by Horatio Alger). What exactly is this puritan work ethic? How has it been interpreted historically? Think of television programs (and their advertisements) you've watched recently; or, if possible, watch television for an evening and take careful notes on what you see. Using this cultural outlet as your primary source, write an essay in which you discuss the extent to which you see this work ethic perpetuated in American culture today. In what ways do you see it being undermined?

GROUP PROJECTS

1. As a group, watch different movies about the American Dream (i.e., *Death of a Salesman, Wall Street, Field of Dreams*). What arguments do these movies put forth? How might they be comparable to the claims that Wuthnow makes in this essay? Write a report that compares the different (or similar) ideas you uncover.

2. As a group, create a survey to distribute to a range of people. Your purpose in this survey should be to test Wuthnow's ideas by finding out how pervasive they are in society. Carefully review the issues that Wuthnow raises, and the claims he makes about the experiences and attitudes of people in general. Remember to distribute the survey according to gender and to consider race, economic class, education, marital status, and so on as relevant criteria. Ask the same questions of as wide a range of people as possible. Prepare a report on your findings.

Generation Xers and Their American Dream
Jennifer Singer

In the 1960s, the term *generation gap* was often used to describe the gulf between the World War II generation and their children, the Baby Boomers. Jennifer Singer offers a new use for the term: She describes the gulf between members of her generation, the so-called Generation X, and their parents, the Boomers. Just as the Boomers rejected the values and practices of their parents, Singer claims that Xers are rejecting the values and practices of the Boomers. But rather than having different beliefs about the role of the military and the government in people's everyday lives, Singer's generation has different views of the pursuit of its own American Dream. She offers a defense of Generation X—often called "slackers"—and a critique of the greed and careerism of Boomers. Her argument is especially interesting in light of other reports in this chapter, which were written by older authors.

Singer began her own communications firm when she was 25 years old. She published this essay in the *Chicago Tribune* in August 1995.

1   We grew up on Brady Bunch reruns, Reaganomics and Soviet nuclear missile threats. We are Generation X, and according to some in the media and a number of frustrated Baby Boomers, we are big business' greatest disappointment. Some Baby Boomer bosses have labeled my generation self-oriented, cynical and non-committal. In reality, many of us Gen Xers are simply finding our own entrepreneurial solutions to a dramatic restructuring of corporate America.

2   We were born after the post-war baby boom, roughly between 1965 and 1975. There are several titles for us, including Generation X (after a novel by Douglas Coupland), Baby Busters and Twentysomethings. We are also referred to as slackers for our apparent disregard for everything the Yuppies labored for while we were busy watching MTV.

3   I can understand why my generation appears apathetic and lazy. Unlike our Boomer predecessors, some Gen Xers are rejecting the traditional climb up the corporate ladder. We appear to be disloyal to employers when we shun 70-hour work weeks. As a member of Generation X, however, I know well that we are trying to deal with a business world that changed considerably soon after we declared our majors in college.

4   When I graduated from Boston University six years ago, I saw the 1980s promise of making a million dollars on Wall Street by age 30 disappear as quickly as President Bush's helicopter did after his speech to my graduating class. My entire teenage and college years fell into the era of the famous line from the film "Wall Street"—"greed is good." Yet when my classmates and I hit the streets with diplomas in hand at the end of the decade, that upwardly mobile brand of greed was gone. It was lost in a federal deficit that had swelled almost five times its size since my 5th grade class trip to Washington, D.C.

5   Even though Gen Xers are the best-educated generation in U.S. history, many of us couldn't find jobs after graduation. Some went to graduate school to wait out the recession—and are still waiting. Those who were lucky enough to land entry level positions for $17,000 a year (in shrinking 1990 dollars) and to move home, were happy simply to find employment and a nice place to live.

6   In fact, my generation is the largest group to live with our parents as young adults since the Great Depression. Some label our return to the safety of our parents' homes as an avoidance of adulthood. I believe many of us simply can't afford the obligations of adulthood.

7   Before we even left the security of our college dorms, we knew there would be a business world less kind and gentle toward graduates. While we were rushing to macro economics class, IBM—which once declared Big Blue would never have layoffs—let go tens of thousands of loyal employees. Around Homecoming 1987, the

stock market crashed—and the job-for-life crashed with it. We had watched many Baby Boomers dedicate much of their lives to companies that eventually let them go during middle-management layoffs.

8   Like the Woodstock Generation, who rebelled against their parents' pre-Vietnam acquiescence to establishment, many Gen Xers feel as though we have been lead down the garden path. And big business was our tour guide. As a result, Generation X is swinging the pendulum away from the blind corporate careerism we learned about on TV's "Thirtysomething" as teenagers. We are capitalizing on our experience with technology and heeding our affinity toward individualism to take a more entrepreneurial approach to our careers and our lives. Some say Generation X may well be the most entrepreneurial generation in decades. Some believe we are reshaping the American dream.

9   Still, our desire for more quantity time makes us Gen Xers seem lazy. But as the first generation of divorce—some 40 percent of us grew up in homes of divorce or separation—many of us felt neglected while growing up. We don't want to neglect our families or ourselves.

10   So, if your Generation X employees, co-workers and bosses seem to snub traditional corporate procedures, understand that they are not trying to be difficult. Don't confuse a new approach to a rapidly changing business atmosphere with apathy or laziness. Instead, give us some credit for remaining loyal to ourselves at a time when the business world can't. Remember, Boomers, you can still trust anyone under 30.

EXPLORING THE TEXT

1. Singer's argument makes a clear distinction between what she calls Generation X and the Baby Boom generation. Who are the members of each group? In what ways does Singer say they are different from each other? In what ways are they similar?

2. What are the values that Singer attributes to each generation? How have they been shaped?

3. In paragraph 2, Singer refers to the Xers' "apparent disregard for everything the Yuppies labored for." What does she mean? What did they labor for? What, then, are Xers rejecting?

4. Singer claims that Xers are "big business' greatest disappointment" and notes that Xers are commonly called "slackers" and that big business sees her generation as "self-oriented, cynical and non-committal" (paragraph 1). Why does she believe her generation is perceived as such? How does she defend her generation from these charges?

5. What is an entrepreneur? How does this concept relate to Singer's argument? How is it distinct from other attitudes?

6. Singer claims that members of Generation X are reshaping the American Dream. What in your own mind is the American Dream? How does her ar-

gument conform to your understanding of this concept? Does it in any way diverge from it?

7. Do you find Singer's defense of Generation X effective? Do you want more information? What is the significance of the final sentence? How does it affect your response to the argument? Explain your answer in detail.

WRITING ASSIGNMENTS

1. Singer, like Robert Wuthnow ("Having It All") above, addresses the ideas and issues related to the American Dream. Write an essay in which you rely on your own experience to describe and define the American Dream. Go on to consider how your own ideas are similar to or distinct from the ideas presented by each author and the ways in which the authors agree or disagree with each other.

2. Compare Singer's claims with those presented by Osterman earlier in this chapter ("Getting Started"). Do the facts he presents support Singer's claim (paragraph 5) that Generation Xers are the "best educated"? Does her argument seem to satisfy the "anxiety" Osterman claims young people feel? Do her claims hold true for all members of Generation X? Write an essay in which you consider these issues.

GROUP PROJECTS

1. As a group, do some research and evaluate Singer's claims about the success and desirability of entrepreneurship. How many Generation Xers own their own companies? How successful are they? Do they have more (and better) personal time? Are they less careerist and greedy than their parents? Does entrepreneurship really offer a solution to the "anxiety" of Singer's generation? You might want to interview some entrepreneurs, Xers or Boomers, and incorporate their anecdotes and opinions in your discussion. Present your group findings in a report.

2. As a group, interview several Generation Xers, some who have chosen careers in the corporate world and others who have opted for entrepreneurship. Try to identify a diverse assortment of people and careers. Ask them why they made their choices (use Singer's own reasons as points of reference). How many agree with her? How many disagree? What are their reasons? What impact do your interviews have on the extent to which you agree or disagree with Singer's claims? Write a group report on what you discover.

Measuring Success
Renee Loth

The Declaration of Independence describes our inalienable right to "life, liberty and the pursuit of happiness." But what, exactly, is "the pursuit of happiness"? As that document has been interpreted, it often means financial independence and success. When Renee Loth was a college student, she would have agreed. Now that she has entered into the world of work, however, she has redefined the term, and she writes this essay as an argument in support of her more mature definition. Though she never speaks specifically of the American Dream, her ideas provide an interesting counterpoint to ideas presented by the other authors in this chapter.

Loth is a columnist for the *Boston Globe Magazine* where this article first appeared in 1997.

1   Back when I was a callow college student, I devised a neat grid system for what I hoped would be my life's achievements. I could count my life a good one, I thought, if I could attain both success and happiness. So I set about analyzing the component parts of each: Happiness I subdivided into sections labeled health and love; success, I determined, was composed of wealth and fame.

2   Once I actually entered the world of work, however, I learned that success is not so easy to define. For one thing, when I made my simple calculation, I never took into account the joy of creation; the approbation of one's peers; the energy of collaboration; or the sheer satisfaction of a job well done. These are real qualities of success that live outside of wealth or fame.

3   Also, I found that definitions of success are mutable, shifting along with our changing values. If we stick with our chosen fields long enough, we sometimes have an opportunity to meet our heroes, people we thought wildly successful when we were young. A musician friend told me that he spent most of his youth wanting to play like the greats, until he started getting to know some of them. To his surprise, many turned out to be embittered, dulled by drink or boredom, unable to hold together a marriage, or wantonly jealous of others. That's when he realized he wanted to play like himself.

4   Success is defined differently by different people. For some, it is symbolized by the number of buttons on the office phone. For others, it is having only one button— and a secretary to field the calls. Some think the more nights and weekends they spend at the office, the more successful they must be. For others, success is directly proportional to time off.

5   And what about those qualities I did include in my handy grid system? Wealth—beyond what is needed to provide for oneself and one's family, with a little left over for airfare to someplace subtropical in January—turned out to be superfluous. And the little experience I had with fame turned out to be downright scary.

6   Several years ago, I had occasion to appear on a dull but respected national evening television news show. My performance lasted exactly six minutes, and my

name flashed only twice. But when I got home from the live broadcast, my answering machine had maxed out on messages.

7   I heard from a woman I had last seen in Brownie Scouts. I heard from former boyfriends, conspiracy theorists, and celebrity agents. I even got an obscene phone call—what kind of pervert watches PBS?—from someone who might have been an old friend pulling my leg. At least, I hope so.

8   For weeks afterward, I received tons of what an optimist might call fan mail. One fellow insisted that if I froze a particular frame of a political campaign ad I had been discussing, I could see the face of Bill Clinton in the American flag. Somebody sent me a chapter of a novel in progress with a main character disturbingly like me. Several people sent me chain letters.

9   I was relieved when the fickle finger of fame moved on to someone else.

10   When I was young and romanticizing about success, I liked a particular Joni Mitchell lyric: "My struggle for higher achievement and my search for love don't seem to cease." Ah, but the trouble with struggling and searching is that it keeps us in a permanent state of wanting—always reaching for more. The drive to succeed keeps us focused on the future, to the detriment of life in the moment. And the moment is all we ever really have.

11   When I look back at my simplistic little value system, I am a bit chagrined at how absolute I thought life was. But I am also happy to report that the achievements that have come my way are the ones that count. After 20 years of supercharged ambition, I have stumbled upon this bit of wisdom. Who needs wealth and fame? Two out of four ain't bad.

EXPLORING THE TEXT

1. In paragraph 1, Loth recalls the days when she was "a callow college student." What does "callow" mean? How does this particular word choice help to establish both the tone and theme of this essay?

2. How did Loth initially define *happiness*? How did she define *success*? How would you have defined each of these terms before reading Loth's essay? How do you explain these definitions—in other words, what or who helped you form these definitions?

3. How does Loth redefine her early notion of success? Why do you think this happened?

4. What is Loth's definition of *wealth*? To what extent does it remain a part of her revised definition of success? How would you define *wealth*? How important is it to your own definition of success?

5. Loth also changes her definition of *fame* and abandons it as a goal of success. Why does she do this? Why do you think she ever wanted fame? Do you? Why or why not? Explain your answer.

6. With respect to the Joni Mitchell lyric she quotes, Loth says that "the trouble with struggling and searching is that it keeps us in a permanent state of wanting—always reaching for more" (paragraph 10). What does she mean by this? How does it relate to the point of this essay overall?

7. The entire point of this essay is to define words we are already familiar with and which we could easily find in a dictionary, but Loth's purpose is more rhetorically strategic. Why do you think she wrote this essay? What is her point? Do you agree with her? What would her definition of *success* be if she were to write it as it might appear in a dictionary?

WRITING ASSIGNMENTS

1. Write your own essay definition of happiness and/or success. Be sure to employ the same strategies Loth does: Think of your own experience—the things that have made you feel happy or successful—and talk to friends and family to gather their insights and anecdotes.

2. Look at the other essays in this chapter and consider the ways in which they define (either directly or indirectly) happiness and success. Compare the ideas and conclusions of the other authors with those presented by Loth. Write an essay in which you discuss the various ways in which the words are defined; end with your own definition, which should be informed by the differences (and similarities) you have identified among the other essays.

GROUP PROJECTS

1. Since you, too, might be described as "a callow college student," work with a small group of students in your class and devise a series of questions that group members can pose to a number of older and more experienced friends, family, and acquaintances. Don't make the mistake of asking only those people you think are happy and successful (such a judgment would only reflect your own standards). Talk to these people in person, so that you can ask follow-up questions. Take good notes of the responses you receive. Your goal will be to write an essay in which you argue in favor of your group's definition of what success and happiness really mean based on the evidence gathered in your interviews.

2. Find other essays that define happiness and/or success. Consider a number of authors from a range of historical periods and from diverse cultures. Divide the work load among group members. Once each person has gathered, read, and annotated at least three definitions (in the form of essays), com-

pare notes and prepare a report on the ways in which these definitions are similar, are different, or have changed over time.

There's No Place Like Work
Arlie Russell Hochschild

Where are you happiest, at work or at home? If you inherited a fortune, would you quit your job? If you had your choice, would you spend more or less time with your family? What do you want your family life to look like in five years? Why do people work in the first place? These are some basic questions that you will soon face once in the job force. These are also questions that Arlie Russell Hochschild put to scores of people in researching the book from where this essay came. And the answers are disturbing. According to Hochschild, family life in America is suffering seriously from the demanding work schedules of parents and spouses. Worse, many find work preferable to home life in the way it nurtures and stimulates. If Hochschild is right, America has a very serious problem. See if the facts she presents resemble your experience and expectations.

Hochschild, a professor of sociology at the University of California at Berkeley, is the author of *The Second Shift*. This essay has been excerpted from her latest book, *The Time Bind: When Work Becomes Home and Home Becomes Work* (1997).

1   7:40 A.M. when Cassie Bell, 4, arrives at the Spotted Deer Child-Care Center, her hair half-combed, a blanket in one hand, a fudge bar in the other. "I'm late," her mother, Gwen, a sturdy young woman whose shot-cropped hair frames a pleasant face, explains to the child-care workers in charge. "Cassie wanted the fudge bar so bad, I gave it to her," she adds apologetically.

2   "*Pleeese,* can't you take me with you?" Cassie pleads.

3   "You know I can't take you to work," Gwen replies in a tone that suggests that she has been expecting this request. Cassie's shoulders droop. But she has struck a hard bargain—the morning fudge bar—aware of her mother's anxiety about the long day that lies ahead at the center. As Gwen explains later, she continually feels that she owes Cassie more time than she gives her—she has a "time debt."

4   Arriving at her office just before 8, Gwen finds on her desk a cup of coffee in her personal mug, milk no sugar (exactly as she likes it), prepared by a co-worker who managed to get in ahead of her. As the assistant to the head of public relations at a company I will call Amerco, Gwen has to handle responses to any reports that

---

Over three years, I interviewed 130 respondents for a book. They spoke freely and allowed me to follow them through "typical" days, on the understanding that I would protect their anonymity. I have changed the names of the company and of those I interviewed, and altered certain identifying details. Their words appear here as they were spoken. —A. R. H.

may appear about the company in the press—a challenging job, but one that gives her satisfaction. As she prepares for her first meeting of the day, she misses her daughter, but she also feels relief; there's a lot to get done at Amerco.

5 Gwen used to work a straight eight-hour day. But over the last three years, her workday has gradually stretched to eight and a half or nine hours, not counting the E-mail messages and faxes she answers from home. She complains about her hours to her co-workers and listens to their complaints—but she loves her job. Gwen picks up Cassie at 5:45 and gives her a long, affectionate hug.

6 At home, Gwen's husband, John, a computer programmer, plays with their daughter while Gwen prepares dinner. To protect the dinner "hour"—8:00–8:30— Gwen checks that the phone machine is on, hears the phone ring during dinner but resists the urge to answer. After Cassie's bath, Gwen and Cassie have "quality time," or "Q.T.," as John affectionately calls it. Half an hour later, at 9:30, Gwen tucks Cassie into bed.

7 There are, in a sense, two Bell households: the rushed family they actually are and the relaxed family they imagine they might be if only they had time. Gwen and John complain that they are in a time bind. What they say they want seems so modest—time to throw a ball, to read to Cassie, to witness the small dramas of her development, not to speak of having a little fun and romance themselves. Yet even these modest wishes seem strangely out of reach. Before going to bed, Gwen has to E-mail messages to her colleagues in preparation for the next day's meeting; John goes to bed early, exhausted—he's out the door by 7 every morning.

8 Nationwide, many working parents are in the same boat. More mothers of small children than ever now work outside the home. In 1993, 56 percent of women with children between 6 and 17 worked outside the home full time year round; 43 percent of women with children 6 and under did the same. Meanwhile, fathers of small children are not cutting back hours of work to help out at home. If anything, they have increased their hours at work. According to a 1993 national survey conducted by the Families and Work Institute in New York, American men average 48.8 hours of work a week, and women 41.7 hours, including overtime and commuting. All in all, more women are on the economic train, and for many—men and women alike—that train is going faster.

9 But Amerco has "family friendly" policies. If your division head and supervisor agree, you can work part time, share a job with another worker, work some hours at home, take parental leave or use "flex time." But hardly anyone uses these policies. In seven years, only two Amerco fathers have taken formal parental leave. Fewer than 1 percent have taken advantage of the opportunity to work part time. Of all such policies, only flex time—which rearranges but does not shorten work time—has had a significant number of takers (perhaps a third of working parents at Amerco).

10 Forgoing family-friendly policies is not exclusive to Amerco workers. A 1991 study of 188 companies conducted by the Families and Work Institute found that while a majority offered part-time shifts, fewer than 5 percent of employees made use of them. Thirty-five percent offered "flex place"—work from home—and fewer than 3 percent of their employees took advantage of it. And an earlier Bureau of La-

bor Statistics survey asked workers whether they preferred a shorter workweek, a longer one or their present schedule. About 62 percent preferred their present schedule; 28 percent would have preferred longer hours. Fewer than 10 percent said they wanted a cut in hours.

11   Still, I found it hard to believe that people didn't protest their long hours at work. So I contacted Bright Horizons, a company that runs 136 company-based child-care centers associated with corporations, hospitals and Federal agencies in 25 states. Bright Horizons allowed me to add questions to a questionnaire they sent out to 3,000 parents whose children attended the centers. The respondents, mainly middle-class parents in their early 30's, largely confirmed the picture I'd found at Amerco. A third of fathers and a fifth of mothers described themselves as "workaholic," and 1 out of 3 said their partners were.

12   To be sure, some parents have tried to shorten their hours. Twenty-one percent of the nation's women voluntarily work part time, as do 7 percent of men. A number of others make under-the-table arrangements that don't show up on surveys. But while working parents say they need more time at home, the main story of their lives does not center on a struggle to get it. Why? Given the hours parents are working these days, why aren't they taking advantage of an opportunity to reduce their time at work?

13   The most widely held explanation is that working parents cannot afford to work shorter hours. Certainly this is true for many. But if money is the whole explanation, why would it be that at places like Amerco, the best-paid employees—upper-level managers and professionals—were the least interested in part-time work or job sharing, while clerical workers who earned less were more interested?

14   Similarly, if money were the answer, we would expect poorer new mothers to return to work more quickly after giving birth than rich mothers. But among working women nationwide, well-to-do new mothers are not much more likely to stay home after 13 weeks with a new baby than low-income new mothers. . . . A second explanation goes that workers don't dare ask for time off because they are afraid it would make them vulnerable to layoffs. . . . But when I asked Amerco employees whether they worked long hours for fear of getting on a layoff list, virtually everyone said no. . . .

15   Were workers uninformed about the company's family-friendly policies? No. Some even mentioned that they were proud to work for a company that offered such enlightened policies. Were rigid middle managers standing in the way of workers using these policies? Sometimes. But when I compared Amerco employees who worked for flexible managers with those who worked for rigid managers, I found that the flexible managers reported only a few more applicants than the rigid ones. The evidence, however counterintuitive, pointed to a paradox: workers at the company I studied weren't protesting the time bind. They were accommodating to it.

16   Why? I did not anticipate the conclusion I found myself coming to: namely, that work has become a form of "home" and home has become "work." The worlds of home and work have not begun to blur, as the conventional wisdom goes, but to reverse places. We are used to thinking that home is where most people feel the most

appreciated, the most truly "themselves," the most secure, the most relaxed. We are used to thinking that work is where most people feel like "just a number" or "a cog in a machine." It is where they have to be "on," have to "act," where they are least secure and most harried.

17   But new management techniques so pervasive in corporate life have helped transform the workplace into a more appreciative, personal sort of social world. Meanwhile, at home the divorce rate has risen, and the emotional demands have become more baffling and complex. In addition to teething, tantrums and the normal developments of growing children, the needs of elderly parents are creating more tasks for the modern family—as are the blending, unblending, reblending of new stepparents, stepchildren, exes and former in-laws.

18   This idea began to dawn on me during one of my first interviews with an Amerco worker. Linda Avery, a friendly, 38-year-old mother, is a shift supervisor at an Amerco plant. When I meet her in the factory's coffee-break room over a couple of Cokes, she is wearing blue jeans and a pink jersey, her hair pulled back in a long, blond ponytail. Linda's husband, Bill, is a technician in the same plant. By working different shifts, they manage to share the care of their 2-year-old son and Linda's 16-year-old daughter from a previous marriage. "Bill works the 7 A.M. to 3 P.M. shift while I watch the baby," she explains. "Then I work the 3 P.M. to 11 P.M. shift and he watches the baby. My daughter works at Walgreen's after school."

19   Linda is working overtime, and so I begin by asking whether Amerco required the overtime, or whether she volunteered for it. "Oh, I put in for it," she replies. I ask her whether, if finances and company policy permitted, she'd be interested in cutting back on the overtime. She takes off her safety glasses, rubs her face and, without answering my question, explains: "I get home, and the minute I turn the key, my daughter is right there. Granted, she needs somebody to talk to about her day. . . . The baby is still up. He should have been in bed two hours ago, and that upsets me. The dishes are piled in the sink. My daughter comes right up to the door and complains about anything her stepfather said or did, and she wants to talk about her job. My husband is in the other room hollering to my daughter, 'Tracy, I don't ever get any time to talk to your mother, because you're always monopolizing her time before I even get a chance!' They all come at me at once."

20   Linda's description of the urgency of demands and the unarbitrated quarrels that await her homecoming contrast with her account of arriving at her job as a shift supervisor: "I usually come to work early, just to get away from the house. When I arrive, people are there waiting. We sit, we talk, we joke. I let them know what's going on, who has to be where, what changes I've made for the shift that day. We sit and chitchat for 5 or 10 minutes. There's laughing, joking, fun."

21   For Linda, home has come to feel like work and work has come to feel a bit like home. Indeed, she feels she can get relief from the "work" of being at home only by going to the "home" of work. Why has her life at home come to seem like this? Linda explains it this way: "My husband's a great help watching our baby. But as far as doing housework or even taking the baby when I'm at home, no. He figures he

works five days a week; he's not going to come home and clean. But he doesn't stop to think that I work seven days a week. Why should I have to come home and do the housework without help from anybody else?" . . .

22   When Bill feels the need for time off, to relax, to have fun, to feel free, he climbs in his truck and takes his free time without his family. Largely in response, Linda grabs what she also calls "free time"—at work. Neither Linda nor Bill Avery wants more time together at home, not as things are arranged now.

23   How do Linda and Bill Avery fit into the broader picture of American family and work life? Current research suggests that however hectic their lives, women who do paid work feel less depressed, think better of themselves and are more satisfied than women who stay at home. One study reported that women who work outside the home feel more valued at home than housewives do. . . . Many workers feel more confident they could "get the job done" at work than at home. One study found that only 59 percent of workers feel their "performance" in the family is "good or unusually good," while 86 percent rank their performance on the job this way.

24   Forces at work and at home are simultaneously reinforcing this "reversal." The lure of work has been enhanced in recent years by the rise of company cultural engineering—in particular, the shift from Frederick Taylor's principles of scientific management to the Total Quality principles originally set out by W. Edwards Deming. Under the influence of a Taylorist world view, the manager's job was to coerce the worker's mind and body, not to appeal to the worker's heart. The Taylorized worker was de-skilled, replaceable and cheap, and as a consequence felt bored, demeaned and unappreciated.

25   Using modern participative management techniques, many companies now train workers to make their own work decisions, and then set before their newly "empowered" employees moral as well as financial incentives. At Amerco, the Total Quality worker is invited to feel recognized for job accomplishments. Amerco regularly strengthens the familylike ties of co-workers by holding "recognition ceremonies" honoring particular workers or self-managed production teams. Amerco employees speak of "belonging to the Amerco family," and proudly wear their "Total Quality" pins or "High Performance Team" T-shirts, symbols of their loyalty to the company and of its loyalty to them. . . .

26   In a New Age recasting of an old business slogan—"The Customer Is Always Right"—Amerco proposes that its workers "Value the Internal Customer." This means: Be as polite and considerate to co-workers inside the company as you would be to customers outside it. How many recognition ceremonies for competent performance are being offered at home? Who is valuing the internal customer there?

27   Amerco also tries to take on the role of a helpful relative with regard to employee problems at work and at home. The education-and-training division offers employees free courses (on company time) in "Dealing With Anger," "How to Give and Accept Criticism," "How to Cope With Difficult People." At home, of course, people seldom receive anything like this much help on issues basic to family life. . . .

28   If Total Quality calls for "re-skilling" the worker in an "enriched" job environment, technological developments have long been de-skilling parents at home. Over the centuries, store-bought goods have replaced homespun cloth, homemade soap

and homebaked foods. Day care for children, retirements homes for the elderly, even psychotherapy are, in a way, commercial substitutes for jobs that a mother once did at home. Even family-generated entertainment has, to some extent, been replaced by television, video games and the VCR. . . .

29   The one "skill" still required of family members is the hardest one of all—the emotional work of forging, deepening or repairing family relationships. It takes time to develop this skill, and even then things can go awry. Family ties are complicated. People get hurt. Yet as broken homes become more common—and as the sense of belonging to a geographical community grows less and less secure in an age of mobility—the corporate world has created a sense of "neighborhood," of "feminine culture," of family at work. Life at work can be insecure; the company can fire workers. But workers aren't so secure at home, either. Many employees have been working for Amerco for 20 years but are on their second or third marriages or relationships. The shifting balance between these two "divorce rates" may be the most powerful reason why tired parents flee a world of unresolved quarrels and unwashed laundry for the orderliness, harmony and managed cheer of work. People are getting their "pink slips" at home.

30   Amerco workers have not only turned their offices into "home" and their homes into workplaces; many have also begun to "Taylorize" time at home, where families are succumbing to a cult of efficiency previously associated mainly with the office and factory. Meanwhile, work time, with its ever longer hours, has become more hospitable to sociability—periods of talking with friends on E-mail, patching up quarrels, gossiping. Within the long workday of many Amerco employees are great hidden pockets of inefficiency while, in the far smaller number of waking weekday hours at home, they are, despite themselves, forced to act increasingly time-conscious and efficient.

31   The Averys respond to their time bind at home by trying to value and protect "quality time." A concept unknown to their parents and grandparents, "quality time" has become a powerful symbol of the struggle against the growing pressures at home. It reflects the extent to which modern parents feel the flow of time to be running against them. The premise behind "quality time" is that the time we devote to relationships can somehow be separated from ordinary time. Relationships go on during quantity time, of course, but then we are only passively, not actively, wholeheartedly, specializing in our emotional ties. We aren't "on." Quality time at home becomes like an office appointment. You don't want to be caught "goofing off around the water cooler" when you are "at work."

32   Quality time holds out the hope that scheduling intense periods of togetherness can compensate for an overall loss of time in such a way that a relationship will suffer no loss of quality. But this is just another way of transferring the cult of efficiency from office to home. . . .

33   Advertisers of products aimed at women have recognized that this new reality provides an opportunity to sell products, and have turned the very pressure that threatens to explode the home into a positive attribute. Take, for example, an ad promoting Instant Quaker Oatmeal: it shows a smiling mother ready for the office in her square-shouldered suit, hugging her happy son. A caption reads: "Nicky is a

very picky eater. With Instant Quaker Oatmeal, I can give him a terrific hot break-fast in just 90 seconds. and I don't have to spend any time coaxing him to eat it!" Here, the modern mother seems to have absorbed the lessons of Frederick Taylor as she presses for efficiency at home because she is in a hurry to get to work. . . .

34   Children often protest the pace, the deadlines, the grand irrationality of "effi-cient" family life. Children dawdle. They refuse to leave places when it's time to leave. They insist on leaving places when it's not time to leave. Surely, this is part of the usual stop-and-go of childhood itself, but perhaps, too, it is the plea of children for more family time, and more control over what time there is. This only adds to the feeling that life at home has become hard work.

35   Instead of trying to arrange shorter or more flexible work schedules, Amerco par-ents often avoid confronting the reality of the time bind. Some minimize their ideas about how much care a child, a partner or they themselves "really need." They make do with less time, less attention, less understanding and less support at home than they once imagined possible. They *emotionally downsize* life. In essence, they deny the needs of family members, and they themselves become emotional ascetics. If they once "needed" time with each other, they are now increasingly "fine" without it.

36   Another way that working parents try to evade the time bind is to buy them-selves out of it—an approach that puts women in particular at the heart of a contra-diction. Like men, women absorb the work-family speed-up far more than they re-sist it; but unlike men, they still shoulder most of the workload at home. And women still represent in people's minds the heart and soul of family life. They're the ones—especially women of the urban middle and upper-middle classes—who feel most acutely the need to save time, who are the most tempted by the new "time saving" goods and services—and who wind up feeling the most guilty about it. For example, Playgroup Connections, a Washington-area business started by a former executive recruiter, matches playmates to one another. One mother hired the service to find her child a French-speaking playmate.

37   In several cities, children home alone can call a number for "Grandma, Please!" and reach an adult who has the time to talk with them, sing to them or help them with their homework. An ad for Kindercare Learning Centers, a for-profit child-care chain, pitches its appeal this way: "You want your child to be active, tolerant, smart, loved, emotionally stable, self-aware, artistic and get a two-hour nap. Anything else?" It goes on to note that Kindercare accepts children 6 weeks to 12 years old and provides a number to call for the Kindercare nearest you. Another typical service or-ganizes children's birthday parties, making out invitations ("sure hope you can come") and providing party favors, entertainment, a decorated cake and balloons. Creative Memories is a service that puts ancestral photos into family albums for you.

38   An overwhelming majority of the working mothers I spoke with recoiled from the idea of buying themselves out of parental duties. A bought birthday party was "too impersonal," a 90-second breakfast "too fast." Yet a surprising amount of lunchtime conversation between female friends at Amerco was devoted to express-ing complex, conflicting feelings about the lure of trading time for one service or another. . . . Many women dwelled on the question of how to decide where a mother's job began and ended, especially with regard to baby sitters and television.

One mother said to another in the breakroom of an Amerco plant: "Damon doesn't settle down until 10 at night, so he hates me to wake him up in the morning and I hate to do it. He's cranky. He pulls the covers up. I put on cartoons. That way, I can dress him and he doesn't object. I don't like to use TV that way. It's like a drug. But I do it."

39   The other mother countered: "Well, Todd is up before we are, so that's not a problem. It's after dinner, when I feel like watching a little television, that I feel guilty, because he gets too much TV at the sitter's."

40   As task after task falls into the realm of time-saving goods and services, questions arise about the moral meanings attached to doing or not doing such tasks. Is it being a good mother to bake a child's birthday cake (alone or together with one's partner)? Or can we gratefully save time by ordering it, and be good mothers by planning the party? Can we save more time by hiring a planning service, and be good mothers simply by watching our children have a good time? "Wouldn't that be nice!" one Amerco mother exclaimed. As the idea of the "good mother" retreats before the pressures of work and the expansion of motherly services, mothers are in fact continually reinventing themselves.

41   The final way working parents tried to evade the time bind was to develop what I call "potential selves." The potential selves that I discovered in my Amerco interviews were fantasy creations of time-poor parents who dreamed of living as time millionaires.

42   One man, a gifted 55-year-old engineer in research and development at Amerco, told how he had dreamed of taking his daughters on a camping trip in the Sierra Mountains: "I bought all the gear three years ago when they were 5 and 7, the tent, the sleeping bags, the air mattresses, the backpacks, the ponchos. I got a map of the area. I even got the freeze-dried food. Since then the kids and I have talked about it a lot, and gone over what we're going to do. They've been on me to do it for a long time. I feel bad about it. I keep putting it off, but we'll do it, I just don't know when."

43   Banished to garages and attics of many Amerco workers were expensive electric saws, cameras, skis and musical instruments, all bought with wages it took time to earn. These items were to their owners what Cassie's fudge bar was to her—a substitute for time, a talisman, a reminder of the potential self.

44   Obviously, not everyone, not even a majority of Americans, is making a home out of work and a workplace out of home. But in the working world, it is a growing reality, and one we need to face. Increasing numbers of women are discovering a great male secret—that work can be an escape from the pressures of home, pressures that the changing nature of work itself are only intensifying. Neither men nor women are going to take up "family friendly" policies, whether corporate or governmental, as long as the current realities of work and home remain as they are. For a substantial number of time-bound parents, the stripped-down home and the neighborhood devoid of community are simply losing out to the pull of the workplace.

45   There are several broader, historical causes of this reversal of realms. The last 30 years have witnessed the rapid rise of women in the workplace. At the same time, job mobility has taken families farther from relatives who might lend a hand, and made it harder to make close friends of neighbors who could help out. Moreover, as

women have acquired more education and have joined men at work, they have absorbed the views of an older, male-oriented work world, its views of a "real career,"
far more than men have taken up their share of the work at home. One reason
women have changed more than men is that the world of "male" work seems more
honorable and valuable than the "female" world of home and children.

46   So where do we go from here? There is surely no going back to the mythical
1950's family that confined women to the home. Most women don't wish to return
to a full-time role at home—and couldn't afford it even if they did. But equally troubling is a workaholic culture that strands both men and women outside the home.

47   For a while now, scholars on work-family issues have pointed to Sweden, Nor-
way and Denmark as better models of work-family balance. Today, for example, almost all Swedish fathers take two paid weeks off from work at the birth of their children, and about half of fathers and most mothers take additional "parental leave"
during the child's first or second year. Research shows that men who take family
leave when their children are very young are more likely to be involved with their
children as they grow older. When I mentioned this Swedish record of paternity
leave to a focus group of American male managers, one of them replied, "Right,
we've already heard about Sweden." To this executive, paternity leave was a good
idea not for the U.S. today, but for some "potential society" in another place and time.

48   Meanwhile, children are paying the price. In her book "When the Bough
Breaks: The Cost of Neglecting Our Children," the economist Sylvia Hewlett claims
that "compared with the previous generation, young people today are more likely to
"underperform at school; commit suicide; need psychiatric help; suffer a severe eating disorder; bear a child out of wedlock; take drugs, be the victim of a violent
crime." But we needn't dwell on sledgehammer problems like heroin or suicide to
realize that children like those at Spotted Deer need more of our time. If other advanced nations with two-job families can give children the time they need, why
can't we?

EXPLORING THE TEXT

1. Hochschild begins her essay by telling the story of a day in the life of
   Cassie Bell and her parents. In paragraph 18, she tells a second story of
   the Avery family. Why does she tell each story? What kinds of issues
   does each establish? In what ways are the stories similar? How do they
   differ?

2. In paragraph 16, Hochschild says that "work has become a form of 'home'
   and home has become 'work.'" What ideas do we typically associate with
   home? With work? What evidence does she offer in support of this claim?
   Why does she think this shift is so important?

3. What are the two management philosophies Hochschild refers to in this article? How does she relate these philosophies to home management issues?

4. In what ways has corporate America responded to the shifts Hochschild describes? What conflicts are contained within these responses?
5. What does Hochschild say about the changing role of women in American society? In what ways is their role *not* actually changing? How are these concerns important to the argument overall?
6. What is the "potential self"? How does this potential self function in the situations Hochschild describes? How does it contribute to the problem?
7. Consider the rhetorical question Hochschild poses at the end of this essay. Hasn't Hochschild already answered this question in a way? Why then does she pose it here? What does she really see as the problem here? Is her argument convincing?

WRITING ASSIGNMENTS

1. Since many of the ideas Hochschild presents can be related to those discussed in Robert Wuthnow's essay earlier in this chapter ("Having It All"), compare each author's argument. What issues are raised in each article? How do these issues, as presented, compare between articles? In what ways does each author use stories to establish and support her position? Are the stories similar to or different from each other as you move from essay to essay? What similarities and differences can you note in the way each author uses statistics to support his or her claims? Write an essay in which you compare and contrast the arguments and the ways in which each argument is made.
2. Hochschild focuses primarily on the role of women and their particular concerns with regard to work and family time. Do you agree that this is primarily a female issue? What are the roles of men in families? In business? Who, ultimately, is responsible? Why? How do other authors in this chapter make distinctions between these roles (or do they)? Compare these ideas with your own experience. Be sure to consider everyone's perspective on this issue; carefully consider the facts and try to remain objective. When you've gathered enough information, write an essay in which you discuss the evolving roles of men and women in the United States today.

GROUP PROJECTS

1. Hochschild polled many people in preparation for her essay, but her discussion focuses primarily on adult issues. Have members of your group poll children who live in such time-starved families and prepare a response to Hochschild that represents their perspective. In preparing a list of questions, begin with those Hochschild has already posed, but formulate others

based on your group members' understanding of the issues and concerns most relevant to young people.

2. Hochschild's discussion focuses primarily on corporate America. Have members of your group interview a number of people working in a variety of professions and for different kinds of businesses or organizations (don't forget academia). Use these interviews to investigate whether Hochschild's findings hold up when the lives of other kinds of workers are considered. Prepare a report of your findings.

As centuries draw to a close, people seem more aware of the future than at any other time, and they feel predisposed to offer predictions of what's to come. While we'd like to think what we predict will come to pass, history is rife with bad calls. For instance, a hundred years ago, Wilbur Wright, the aviation pioneer, predicted that we would not develop an airplane until the 1950s. Western Union President William Orton rejected Alexander Graham Bell's newly invented telephone as an "electrical toy" that no company would want to manufacture. Others foresaw the automobile as a passing "fad" and tobacco as a "medicinal breakthrough." Perhaps Charles H. Duell, the U.S. commissioner of patents, summed up turn-of-the-century arrogance when he said in 1899, "Everything that can be invented has been invented."

This chapter offers what I hope are some thoughtful futurological glimpses across the next millennial threshold. This chapter opens with noted futurist Gerald Celente who tries his hand at some twenty-first-century predictions. In "Welcome to the Millennium," he envisions a nation with gardens instead of lawns, vitamin counselors, and "aerobic warrior" workout classes. Reacting to the materialism of the twentieth century, he claims, Americans will embrace "voluntary simplicity" in an effort to recapture a calmer, more frugal era.

While the title of the next piece, "America Remains No. 1," seems to predict a hopeful future for America, Ronald Steel presents a very different perspective. He approaches the future with his eye on the political and social changes that may occur in the world. And he envisions a future American landscape that we might not like to be part of.

Steel is not the first to warn us to brace ourselves for what comes next. For years many science fiction and speculative fiction authors have depicted a world where every action was controlled by the government. Perhaps the classic dystopian nightmare is George Orwell's 1948 novel, *1984,* which extrapolated from the totalitarian horrors of World War II, creating a nightmare vision of a world of brainwashed people monitored by faceless government technology called "Big Brother." In the next essay, "Big Brother Is Us," James Gleick speaks to our Orwellian fears that our privacy may be compromised—that we might unknowingly give away a basic constitutional right. Gleick raises the question of where we should draw the line.

The question of medical privacy and genetic testing is addressed by Philip Kitcher in the next article, "Junior Comes Out Perfect." What would happen if we were all genetically tested and some of us learned that we were predisposed to a particular disease? How might our families, employers, and insurance companies respond? Kitcher also explores the possibility of genetically planning our future children. And he raises a disturbing question: Will some races and ethnicities suffer at the hands of genetic testing?

Stanley Crouch's answer would be probably not. In his article "Race Is Over," Crouch extrapolates from a growing racial phenomenon. Since the late 1960s, America has experienced a dramatic increase in interracial marriages. By 1990, according to the census, 2.2 percent of all marriages were interracial. By the year 2000, that number should more than double. Already there are over two million children under age 18 who are of mixed race. And celebrities—golf champ, Tiger Woods (Caucasian, black, Indian, Asian); singer Mariah Carey (black Venezuelan, white); actors,

Johnny Depp (Cherokee, white) and Keanu Reeves (Hawaiian, Chinese, white)—are proving that multiracial is hip. Meanwhile companies like Calvin Klein, Benetton, and Nike are cashing in on the global youth culture as we saw in Chapter 2. As barriers fall and racial intermarriage becomes the norm, some people such as Crouch see a future America when race may be meaningless as color lines blur.

While history continues its relentless march into the future, some things we can still count on, including the power of attraction. In the short story "Mystery Date," A. M. Homes writes of a future featuring pill shops instead of ice cream parlors and home oxygen delivery systems instead of air conditioning. But teenagers will still be teenagers—full of teenage boredom and teenage dreams.

In the next selection, "Where Have All the Causes Gone?" John Meacham laments the lack of unity and bonding between young people today. He says that earlier generations formed common foundations based on common causes such as the Great Depression and World War II. But today's generation does not face unifying national crises. He fears that today's generation won't know what to do when their time comes.

The chapter closes with some fitting observations by essayist Meg Greenfield. Despite changing technology, the dazzling inventions and innovations to come, and our onward rush into the new century, the essence of our humanity remains unchanged, she muses. In "Back to the Future," Greenfield says that after we peel away all the layers, the issues we face and how we deal with them remain the same—because in the future we will be "the same old us."

Welcome to the Millennium
Gerald Celente

As we approach the next century, we bring with us great expectations of advanced technology and mind-boggling invention. Consider the huge advances made in the twentieth century and how in only 100 years they radically changed our world—cars, airplanes, television, antibiotics, laser surgery, and the Internet. We can barely imagine what life will be like in 2100. But maybe we should look to the past as we approach tomorrow. In the following article, Gerald Celente predicts that what was old will be new again. Instead of a future resembling the *Jetsons,* it may be more like *Green Acres.*

Celente, a "trends forecaster," is director of the Trends Research Institute. He is also the author of the nationally syndicated column "Trends in the News," which tracks major social, political, business, and consumer trends. The following article is from Celente's latest book, *Trends 2000: How to Prepare For and Profit from the Changes of the 21st Century* (1997).

1 It's January 1, 2000. The world has just celebrated the greatest New Year's Eve party in recorded history. Even cultures that follow different calendars are reveling in the streets. But unlike New Year's parties past, nobody has waited until December 31 to hit the streets. The celebration has been going full blast since Christmas;

the world has been psyching itself up for this blowout since 1995, when the symptoms of Millennium Fever were first evident.

2   For several years religious fanatics and prophets of doom have been preaching the end of the world. And when you look at the events going on around you on New Year's Day, 2000—civil war in Russia, student revolts in the United States, the threat of nuclear terrorism—there's good reason for fear. But Armageddon hasn't happened. The world hasn't gone up in flames.

3   In fact, there's a strange elation threading through the chaos and disruption. Though the United States and the rest of the world will be going through increasingly troubled times in the immediate future, the first signs of the scientific, artistic, and spiritual renaissance that will shape this new millennium are unmistakable. Those who anticipate and act on the changes taking place will be able to prosper both materially and spiritually. Here are a few trends that will dramatically alter our lives in the coming millennium.

Living the Simple Life

4 Voluntary simplicity, once merely a counterculture ideal, will finally become a reality in the twenty-first century. Simplicity doesn't mean deprivation. Rather, it's old-fashioned Yankee frugality, rediscovered and redesigned for the modern age. Moderation, self-discipline, and spiritual growth will be the personal goals of the future, not material accumulation. As the old saying goes: Use it up, wear it out, make it do, do without. If you don't really need it, it's a luxury. Not that there's anything wrong with luxuries; it's just that we won't confuse them with necessities.

5   In the 1960s, these ideas and goals seemed quaint and cute. In the new century, however, as cost-cutting corporations continue to lay off vast numbers of workers, many people will have to drastically scale back their lifestyles to survive. Call it *in*voluntary simplicity. But downsizing—currently perceived by the government and the media as a grave problem, and by the downsized as a catastrophe—will prove to be a blessing in disguise in the new millennium. Forced into freedom, millions of us will find ways to take control of our lives and do what we've always wanted to do: change careers, start companies of our own, or become work-at-home freelancers. In 1996, 12 percent of downsized workers started their own businesses, double the rate of 1993.

6   One major outgrowth of the voluntary simplicity movement will be our desire to grow as much of our own food as possible. But how many people will be able to do this when relatively few Americans live in rural areas where there's room for the type of extensive garden needed to produce a substantial portion of the year's food?

7   Somewhere around the year 2000, the revelation—and revolution—will come. The lawn! Lawns are everywhere: millions of costly, intensively cared for suburban lawns have been doing nothing but growing grass. But a lawn that's turned into a vegetable patch can produce fresh food.

8   The trend to convert lawns into gardens will have a significant impact not only on the way we eat but also on how we live and feel. It will be one of the keys to living better for less. Billions of dollars formerly spent on lawn care will either be

saved or redeployed into producing fresh food. The American lawn won't disappear entirely, of course. Kids will always romp on them, barbecues will still be held on them. But a significant portion of the nation's arable lawn will be revamped for food production. Just two mature standard fruit trees produce 250 pounds of fruit a year. With millions of downsized or underemployed people struggling to make ends meet, a thousand saved here and a thousand saved there will make a real difference. Even university and corporate campus lawns will be transformed into edible landscapes, providing students and employees with practical, enjoyable, and therapeutic respite from study or work.

Millennium Family Values

9 Practicing voluntary simplicity, of course, will require a redistribution of our priorities, a rethinking of how we spend our days. Most of us will no longer make the false distinction we used to between "quality" time and the rest of the day. All time will be quality time (except for filling out tax forms and that sort of thing). After all, it takes time to cook a good meal, to play with the kids, to sew a ripped skirt that you once would have thrown away.

10 With more of us working and spending our free time at home, it's easy to imagine the model twenty-first-century family as Ozzie and Harriet with laptops. But the Nelson family and their real-life counterparts were the products of the 1950s, a time when unparalleled American prosperity allowed the traditional extended family to fragment. In the new millennium, the multigenerational extended family will come together.

11 Instead of being banished to nursing homes or retirement communities, large numbers of retirees—aging, often ailing, unable to care for themselves or to afford quality care—will move in with their adult children. We'll also see perfectly healthy widowed and divorced parents setting up house alongside their kids—ideally with separate entrances and kitchens to preserve some of the privacy to which we've become accustomed. Family households will sometimes extend to four generations when married or unmarried Generation Xers move back home with their young kids.

12 Whatever the drawbacks of multigenerational families living together, there will be substantial benefits, too. Healthy grandparents will pull their weight as babysitters. This trend is already strong: In 1994, 44 percent of grandparents spent an average of 650 hours—the equivalent of 81 eight-hour days—taking care of their grandchildren. But more than babysitters, grandparents will also function as home educators. They'll be the modern equivalent of tribal elders who were valued and revered in traditional hunter-gatherer societies for their wisdom and experience.

Back to the Boardinghouse

13 The meaning of the word "family" will also broaden beyond that of blood relationships during the twenty-first century. It will come to mean groups of interdependent people—relatives, friends, and neighbors—who share values, goals, responsibilities,

and a long-term commitment to one another and their communities. A number of creative (and sometimes desperate) solutions will be found for a wide spectrum of new economic and social challenges.

14   For example, the 1930s boardinghouse will return in an upgraded version that's designed to meet the needs of modern-day low-income single people. By the year 2010, 31 million people will be living alone. But as disposable incomes continue to fall and the job market tightens, workers of every age will be unable to afford the rents on even studio apartments. While two can live more cheaply than one, ten can live substantially cheaper than two, so boardinghouses will reemerge. They'll provide home-cooked communal meals and a congenial familylike atmosphere, becoming social oases in an increasingly impersonal world.

15   If the revival of boardinghouses represents an effective defensive tactic against economic changes, "cohousing" will be an offensive long-term strategy. First developed in Denmark in 1976, cohousing combines upscale condominium-style accommodations and privacy with the shared responsibilities and amenities of communes.

16   The main difference between cohousing and the twentieth century's standard apartment complex or condo is the sharing, which will be tailored to suit the needs of the individuals involved. Most labor-intensive family duties, including meals, child care, elder care, and even education, will be handled communally to some extent. The result will be considerable savings in time and effort, along with pleasant and productive socializing—at least when the personality mix is right. For example, a typical communal dinner arrangement might find residents cooking and serving about once every two weeks, in exchange for having the remaining 13 dinners cooked and served to them.

What You Hear Is What You See

17 The videophone, meanwhile, will keep us in touch with faraway relatives. Today when we use the phone, we are still communicating by radio. With the addition of the videophone's visual dimension, long-distance communication will be more like television.

18   The psychological and social connections fostered by the videophone will transform human interaction. People experience intensely personal, intimate feelings when they can see the person they're talking to; body language comes into play and a person becomes something more than just a disembodied voice. As self-employment, downsizing, and work decentralization keep more and more people in their homes, face-to-face communication will become increasingly uncommon—and therefore increasingly important.

19   Currently communication industry experts are resisting the videophone idea, pointing to market research that suggests people would rather preserve the comparative anonymity of talking on the telephone. Yet there were similar objections when the telephone answering machine was introduced in the late 1970s. Analysts said that people felt intimidated by the new devices and would not leave messages. In the beginning that was often the case, but today if you call someone and don't get an answering machine to pick up your call, you're probably annoyed. You'll have to call

back—an inconvenience. As for the privacy problem, just as a mute button turns off a television's sound, a "blind" button will protect us from Peeping Toms.

Millennium Health Kit

20 If you read magazines or watched television in the 1980s and 1990s, it looked as if the whole country was running, pumping iron, and doing aerobics. Sales of running and training shoes soared, and millions bought rowing machines or signed up at gyms. A fitness trend had swept the nation.

21 Or so it seemed. In reality, two-thirds of Americans were overweight as the twentieth century came to a close. If you'd conducted supermarket research, you would have seen battalions of out-of-shape people pushing shopping carts filled with Twinkies, soft drinks, salty snacks, cigarettes, candy, and processed frozen entrees. As for those brisk sales of athletic shoes, 90 percent of the people who bought them did so for comfort and fashion rather than for exercise.

22 Nevertheless, the health movement, hyped by fitness-gear manufacturers and ballyhooed by the media, is real. And the fitness trend will gather steam as more and more baby boomers begin "previewing": seeing in their parents' aging what lies in store for them.

23 By the year 2000, getting and staying healthy will no longer be a hobby but a necessity for survival. The health information people need will be available; the difficulty will be distinguishing the gold from the dross. Those who are serious about their millennium resolutions to take better care of themselves will begin by checking into one of the new longevity centers springing up around the country. Longevity centers will be to health what colleges are to education—equal parts spa, health club, hospital, detoxification center, fat farm, and resort. They will be staffed with medical doctors well versed in both state-of-the-art medicine and alternative therapies, as well as nutritionists, acupuncturists, herbalists, chiropractors, and a diverse group of physical, emotional, and spiritual therapists and healers.

24 Another key player will be the vitamin counselor. While vitamins have been available in supermarkets and health food stores for decades, it was only in the early 1990s that it became apparent that no two people have the same nutritional needs. Effective vitamin counseling must be individualized, just like effective medical advice; a person's age, lifestyle, profession, and eating habits must be taken into account. But most mainstream physicians have had little training in nutrition, and we can't expect knowledgeable advice from minimum-wage clerks at health food stores. Vitamin counselors, on the other hand, will be multidisciplinary practitioners; they'll have a solid grounding of medical knowledge but won't need four years of medical school. By the year 2000 they will be on their way to becoming as professionalized and as respected as pharmacists.

25 In an age of intense health awareness, most people will give up their Stair-Masters and stop training for marathons. Hyperactive workouts, while better than nothing, won't be the answer to stress-filled but sedentary lifestyles. Instead, we will integrate our workout routines into our lives. If we haven't given up our lawns altogether, we'll replace our power mowers with high-tech light-

weight push mowers.

26   We'll still use our local gym during the winter and in rainy weather. But instead of doing the usual aerobics, we'll push mowers. And if we're using our lawns to grow food, as most people will be, the physical work of gardening will build bone and muscle.

27   We'll still use our local gym during the winter and in rainy weather. But instead of doing the usual aerobics, we'll consider becoming "aerobic warriors"—learning an aerobic workout that teaches us self-defense techniques. Since we're putting in the physical effort anyway, why not learn something with a practical application?

Coming Attractions

28 Today, against the dark and violent backdrop of late-twentieth-century life, many of the trends that will soon reshape our lives are not yet apparent. But since writers, musicians, painters, and filmmakers are by nature more sensitive than others to shifts in the tempo of the times, these changes will be quickly reflected in the art of the new century. Just as rock and roll replaced swing and ragtime music, a new genre of millennium music will emerge. It will be upbeat without the anger and despair of today's cutting-edge rock and rap. Painting and sculpture will be revolutionized by the incorporation of virtual reality and computer technology. New, friendly styles of architecture will replace the impersonal cookie-cutter tract housing that has been the norm since the 1950s.

29   The return of individuality will spell an end to the multibillion-dollar fashion industry. The bulk of day-to-day apparel will consist of durable mass-produced casual wear. Where appearance matters, the combination of computerization and declining wages will bring custom tailoring back to an affordable price range. The result—personally designed "smartwear"—will bridge the gap between casual and formal: appearance-enhancing but comfortable.

30   Together, these and numerous other trends will help usher in a new renaissance in thought. It will be an era of intense individuality directed toward common goals. And like the European Renaissance of the fourteenth through seventeenth centuries, the global renaissance ahead will be a time of rich intellectual, philosophical, and artistic achievement—a period of genius in the world's history.

EXPLORING THE TEXT

1. Why does Celente think we will adopt "voluntary simplicity" in the next century? What appeal will voluntary simplicity hold for Americans?
2. In our fast-paced hectic world, do you think that Americans will embrace voluntary simplicity? Draw from what you know about the past to predict the future.

3. Do you agree with Celente's prediction that Americans will sacrifice their lawns in favor of raising homegrown produce? Explain your point of view.

4. Are Celente's predictions revolutionary and startling? Or are they predictable?

5. Celente states that we will have more extended families as elderly parents move in with their adult children. On what does he base his assumption? Do you agree with his prediction?

6. Celente claims that we will witness the return of the boardinghouse in the next century. Would you live in a boardinghouse instead of an apartment or dormitory?

7. Review the role of physical fitness in our lives. Do you see this role changing? Apply your view to Celente's predictions.

8. What can we expect from music in the next century? How will trends in music affect other media, such as art and drama?

WRITING ASSIGNMENTS

1. Write a short essay on predictions for the future based on the past. What trends can you forecast? Explain why you think these predictions will come true.

2. Why will Americans embrace "voluntary simplicity"? Examine current cultural trends in our society. Do you see us moving toward simplicity? Why or why not? Discuss what simplicity means to you and how you think you can apply it to your future.

3. Research one of the "old" relics Celente discusses in his article, such as the boardinghouse and the home garden. What appeal did these institutions have for Americans? On what principles were they based? Applying what you learn from your research, write an essay on whether you think these aspects of American life will really return, and why or why not.

GROUP PROJECTS

1. With your group, embark on a cultural investigation. Try to identify three trends for the future that have their roots in the past. Discuss with your group why these trends will develop and then share your predictions with the class.

2. They say that if you just wait long enough, something will become fashionable again. Brainstorm with group members in identifying current trends that are based on things that were popular in the past. Why do you think things "come back"? Present your report to the class.

3. Based on trends in music today, form a musical act with your group. What do you call yourselves and what type of music do you sing and/or play?

Remember that marketing yourselves is as important as your music. Define your style. Why will your group be successful in the next century?

America Remains No. 1
Ronald Steel

Whenever a century draws to a close, people make predictions for the future. Some predictions are full of doom and destruction, while others are full of hope and optimism. In the essay below, Ronald Steel predicts a little of both, arguing that only the United States will possess the power to play the role of "benevolent hegemon."

Steel is a professor of International Affairs at George Washington University. This article appeared in the *New York Times Sunday Magazine* in September 1996.

1 We imagine the past and create the future in its image. People in 1896 got much of the coming century wrong; we are unlikely to do much better. Here is how some of the operating myths of 1996 might collapse:

2 *The Information Age Is Knitting the World Together.* Russians gobble Big Macs. Children in Bangladesh wear Chicago Bulls T-shirts. CNN beams America around the globe, creating a community of news junkies that leaps cultural walls and defies censors. English is the universal language and the Internet the tribune of the people. Now we will all be one. Right?

3 Wrong. The notion of a global village is a product of our self-congratulation and worship of technology. We assume that if everyone sees the same programs they will espouse similar values. And since we provide much of the world's pop culture, won't everyone adopt our values?

4 Unfortunately, it doesn't work that way. When we see our products and images abroad we think of it as Americanization. For others, it is just modernization. Eating pizza and playing soccer doesn't make us Italian, any more than drinking Coke or playing baseball turns the Japanese into Americans. Sometimes the more people know about one another, the more they find to dislike. Take a feuding family. Or a civil war, as in Bosnia or Rwanda, to use a couple of current examples. The telephone doesn't make us love one another. Why should the Internet?

5 *Capitalism Will Always Rule the World.* Today, capitalism is riding high, and Socialism (along with its utopian apotheosis, Communism) has been confined to what Leon Trotsky called the "dustbin of history." Memories are short. Only 50 years ago, socialism was the wave of the future. Britain and France were nationalizing their industries, while backward places like China and India hailed the Soviet Union as a model of fast growth.

6 All that seems bizarre now. Everyone wants to be a capitalist, even former commissars. Capitalism distributes resources efficiently and produces a pile of money, but it always has, along with big booms and bad busts.

7   It was because capitalism destroyed even as it created the Socialist parties were formed in Europe and America a century ago. Capitalism survived because its own excesses were tamed through government intervention: pensions and health insurance for workers, welfare to buy off the poor. Left to its own devices, it periodically spins out of control. Then it goes into the dustbin for a while.

8   *The Refugee Problem Is Manageable.* Everyone knows that the world's population is growing too fast—6 billion today versus 1.5 billion 100 years ago—but hardly anyone wants to deal with it. Thanks to advances in agriculture and medicine, more poor people survive in the impoverished countries where population growth is fastest. But unable to find jobs or live off the depleted land, they swarm into megacities like São Paulo, Lagos and Calcutta. And they spill across borders into richer places like Texas and California, France and Germany. We like to assume that tough immigration laws will stem the tide. They won't. The great migration from the world's slums is only just beginning.

9   *Democracy Will Triumph.* Democracy is infectious and inevitable, or so we believe. It has already come to most of Eastern Europe and Russia, as well as Latin America. Even the Chinese are getting restless. But democracy can mean many things—for some, the liberty to do whatever they please, for others the ability to express opinions freely and to choose their governors. For the 30 million Russians who voted Communist in the recent Presidential elections, it means high living for a few and misery for just about everyone else. And in the fast-growing economic "tigers" of Asia, in societies that put a high premium on order, security and tradition, it suggests anarchy.

10   For democracies to work, they must deliver the goods. Where they fail, the people will turn against them—as the Germans did in 1933 when they voted Hitler into power. Democracy is not easily transplanted; some societies find it disruptive and a threat to traditional values. Its virtue is that the public's voice is heard powerfully. Its weakness is that it can degenerate into demagoguery and anarchy. The whole world does not have to be democratic for us to make our way in it. And it won't be.

11   *China Will Be the Next Superpower.* Of course China will dominate the next century. It's big, industrious and growing fast. What's to stop it? Maybe the Chinese themselves.

12   For centuries China has been the great emerging power and the bogy man of the West. Napoleon warned that when it awoke the world would be sorry. Our own strategists today have found in China a replacement for the Soviet Bear.

13   But this scenario tells us more about ourselves than about China. There will be 300 million to 400 million more Chinese over the next 20 years, yet there is little more arable land. Millions of hungry peasants are fleeing to the cities. Conflicts have broken out between the capital and the provinces, between industrial and agricultural regions and between powerful economic and military factions. The Soviet state disintegrated to the astonishment of virtually every expert. So may China.

14   *The Wretched Will Always Accept Their Lot.* Nobody says this openly, but it is what most governments think. Although we have always had the rich and the poor, the gap between them has been growing. This is particularly true of the United States, where the distribution of wealth is now in a class with Guatemala. Not only

people, but whole countries are growing poorer. Wealth has become so concentrated that 358 billionaires worldwide control assets greater than the combined national incomes of countries with 45 percent of the world's population.

15   The haves assume that nothing much needs to be done about this. They figure that with enough cops, prisons and gated enclaves, the situation will be manageable—Watts won't march on Beverly Hills, or Central Americans on gringoland, or Africans on manicured Europe. Maybe. That's what the rich have always assumed. Sometimes they were right, and sometimes they were sorry.

16   *The Nation-State Is Withering Away.* What is the function of the state today? It feeds atavistic passions, sends it citizens off to wars and interferes with the global market. Surely it will fade in the 21st century, when everyone is joined together by a common language, English, and worships the same god, commerce.

17   Don't bet on it. Nations may merge their economies, but people resist giving up their national identities. The European Union has run into a brick wall of member states that don't want to disappear into a Brussels bureaucracy. The Soviet Union disintegrated, and Yugoslavia splintered into warring ethnic states. People like to belong to a clan. The nation-state, in one form or another, will survive.

18   *The United States Will Decline.* The hardest thing about being on top is staying there. History is a chronicle of great empires that have disappeared in a trail of decaying monuments. Will the United States go the same way?

19   Not soon. Who is to challenge us? Japan is dependent on imported resources and foreign markets. China is a demographic disaster ripe for a return to warlordism. India verges on explosion and anarchy. Brazil has forever been the country of tomorrow. Europe will never be more than a big, and contentious, shopping mall. Russia has always been a phantom giant.

20   What's more, it is asked, why would anyone want to challenge us? The United States is a "benevolent hegemon." We covet no one else's territory, demand no monetary tribute. Rather than exploiting our allies, we are exploited by them: providing security from enemies, insuring access to cheap oil and running up huge trade deficits buying their goods. We are the friendly cop on the beat, and it is in everyone's interest to keep us there.

21   At least so we say, and so we mean. But there are two problems with this picture. First is the predicament of the overextended superpower that puts so much of its wealth into feeding its military and protecting its allies that it fails to keep up economically. Second is the fact that rising nations don't like to take orders, even from the best-intentioned protector. Adolescents want to be, and will be, adults.

22   The United States will remain No. 1 in the foreseeable future. But 2096 is a long time away.

23   *Nothing Will Happen to Knock All Predictions Into a Hat.* In 1896, Americans and Europeans basked in a golden age of prosperity and perpetual progress. They were rich, self-confident and optimistic. Then came 1914 and the war that defied all reason, the war that tore Europe apart, undermined the values of the Victorian age, spawned the Russian Revolution, opened the doors to Fascism and Communism, sowed the seeds of World War II and degenerated into the Holocaust. The world has not been the same since. When the unimaginable happens, and it can, all bets are off.

EXPLORING THE TEXT

1. How does Steel's optimistic title, "America Remains No. 1," compare with what he actually says about America's world role in the future?
2. This entire article is based on the premise that we hold certain assumptions regarding the future. Review Steel's list of assumptions. Do you think we really hold such predictions for the future?
3. What is the tone of this article? How do you think Steel feels about America?
4. Examine the structure of Steel's article. Is this the most effective way to present his ideas?
5. Consider how Steel ends the article. Does such an ending provide adequate closure to his material? Explain your view.
6. According to Steel's predictions, what impact will the poor have on the future of the world?
7. Explain what a nation-state is. Why does Steel feel nation-states will remain in the next century? Why, do you think, we "assume" their decline?
8. Consider Steel's comments about our belief that the world is smaller. Do his comments make sense or could he be missing the point?
9. Many would argue that Steel's world is not one of hope. Are we more likely by nature to be pessimistic about the future? How does our pessimism compare to attitudes in the past?

WRITING ASSIGNMENTS

1. After reading the essay, do you feel optimistic or pessimistic regarding the future? Why? Explain your view in a paper.
2. Look over Steel's essay again. What predictions do you feel were left out? Which predictions do you feel fall short of the mark? Write an essay of your conclusions.
3. In a well-considered essay, discuss why predicting the future is a risky and often ridiculous venture.
4. Think back to when you were 10 years old. What did you think the future would be like when you reached college? What was the basis of your predictions? Discuss how accurate or inaccurate your predictions were.

GROUP PROJECTS

1. Make a list of assumptions about the future your group feels we have "as a nation." Discuss whether you think these assumptions are true. Explain why or why not and share your conclusions with the class.
2. Imagine you are living in 1900. What would you think the next century would bring? Explain the basis for your predictions. Then, with the benefit of hindsight, discuss how your predictions compare with our reality.

3. Together with your group, think of recent movies that are set in the future. Do you think such a world is possible? Discuss your feelings with your group, using logic and reason to defend your position.

Big Brother Is Us
James Gleick

In 1948, George Orwell wrote his classic totalitarian novel *1984,* which describes a world of social and mental control where every movement was monitored and every individual thought forbidden. Under the constant scrutiny of Big Brother, brainwashed humans lived out their miserable lives in a world that would make Gotham City look like Disneyland. The year 1984 came and went uneventfully, and the totalitarian world of television monitors and Thought Police remained but fiction. Or did it?

James Gleick claims that our privacy is not safe and that we are indeed being watched. The government, or anyone else for that matter, can obtain personal information at the touch of a button. Moreover, Gleick maintains, it is our own idea. Gleick is a columnist for the *New York Times Sunday Magazine* where this article appeared in September 1996. Gleick is also the author of the best-selling book, *Chaos: Making a New Science* (1987), and *Genius: The Life and Science of Richard Feyman* (1992).

1 For much of the 20th century, 1984 was a year that belonged to the future—a strange, gray future at that. Then it slid painlessly into the past, like any other year. Big Brother arrived and settled in, though not at all in the way George Orwell had imagined.

2 Underpinning Orwell's 1948 anti-utopia—with its corruption of language and history, its never-ending nuclear arms race and its totalitarianism of torture and brainwashing—was the utter annihilation of privacy. Its single technological innovation, in a world of pig iron and pneumatic tubes and broken elevators, was the telescreen, transmitting the intimate sights and sounds of every home to the Thought Police. BIG BROTHER IS WATCHING YOU. "You had to live—did live, from habit that became instinct—" Orwell wrote, "in the assumption that every sound you made was overheard, and, except in darkness, every movement scrutinized."

3 It has turned out differently. We have had to wait a bit longer for interactive appliances to arrive in our bedrooms. Our telescreens come with hundreds of channels but no hidden cameras. If you want a device with a microphone to record and transmit your voice, you are better off with a multimedia P.C. or, for that matter, a dedicated Internet connection: hook up your camera and turn on the switch that Winston Smith could never turn off. People in large numbers are doing just this: acting out their private lives before online cameras, accessible to the world. Grim though Orwell's vision was, it never encompassed the Dan-O-Cam (H. Dan Smith at work in his office in Fresno, Calif.), the LivingRoom-Cam (watch children and pets at play:

"personal publishing of personal spaces") and scores of similar Internet "cams"—evidence that some citizens of the 21st century, anyway, will not be grieving over their loss of privacy.

4   And yet. . . .

5   Information-gathering about individuals has reached an astounding level of completeness, if not actual malevolence. So has fear of information-gathering, if not among the broad public, at least among those who pay attention to privacy as an issue of law and technology. Hundreds of privacy organizations, newsletters, annual conferences, information clearinghouses, mailing lists and Web sites have sprung into existence—a societal immune-system response.

6   The rapid rise of the Internet surpasses the grimmest forecasts of interconnectedness among all these computer dossiers. Yet it defies those forecasts as well. Strangely enough, the linking of computers has taken place democratically, even anarchically. Its rules and habits are emerging in the open light, rather than behind the closed doors of security agencies or corporate operations centers. It is clear that technology has the power not just to invade privacy but to protect it, through encryption, for example, which will be available to everyone, as soon as the Government steps out of the way. The balance of power has already shifted from those who break codes—eavesdroppers and intelligence agencies—to those who wish to use them. In these closing years of the century, we are setting the laws and customs of a future built on networked communication, giant interlinked data bases, electronic commerce and digital cash. Historians will see our time as a time of transition. But transition to what?

7   "There's a very important and long-term debate taking place right now about technologies of privacy in the next century," says Marc Rottenberg, director of the Electronic Privacy Information Center in Washington. "Privacy will be to the information economy of the next century what consumer protection and environmental concerns have been to the industrial society of the 20th century."

Middle-Class Secrets

8   Privacy is a construct of our age. As a tradition in law, it is young. When Louis D. Brandeis issued his famous opinion in 1928 that privacy is "the right to be let alone—the most comprehensive of rights, and the right most valued by civilized men," he was looking to the future, because he was dissenting; the Supreme Court's majority was upholding the right of the police to tap telephone lines without warrants.

9   "In the beginning, there was no such thing as private life, no refuge from the public gaze and its ceaseless criticism," writes Theodore Zeldin, a social historian, in "An Intimate History of Humanity." He adds, "Then the middle classes began cultivating secrets." In villages and small towns, the secret life was rare. The neighbors knew far more about one's intimacies, from breakfast habits to clandestine affairs, than in any city of the 20th century. One's shield, if a shield was needed, was a formal civility: rules of discourse that discouraged questions about money or sex. The pathological case of the private person was the hermit—hermits, by and large, have disappeared. The word is quaint. In a crowd, we can all be hermits now.

10   "Privacy means seeing only people whom one chooses to see," writes Zeldin. "The rest do not exist, except as ghosts or gods on television, the great protector of privacy."

11   In public opinion surveys, Americans always favor privacy. Then they turn around and sell it cheaply. Most vehemently oppose any suggestion of a national identification system yet volunteer their telephone numbers and mothers' maiden names and even—grudgingly or not—Social Security numbers to merchants bearing discounts or Web services offering "membership" privileges. For most, the abstract notion of privacy suggests a mystical, romantic, cowboy-era set of freedoms. Yet in the real world it boils down to matters of small convenience. Is privacy about Government security agents decrypting your E-mail and then kicking down the front door with their jackboots? Or is it about telemarketers interrupting your supper with cold calls?

12   It depends. Mainly, of course, it depends on whether you live in a totalitarian or a free society. If the Government is nefarious or unaccountable to individuals—or, if you believe it is—the efficient ideal of easy-to-use, perfectly linked and comprehensive national data bases must be frightening indeed. But if, deep down, you feel secure in your relations with the state, then perhaps you are willing to let your guard down: put off till tomorrow your acquisition of that encryption software, send your E-mail in the clear, perhaps even set up an Internet camera at the kitchen table or discuss your sexual history with Oprah.

13   Certainly where other people's privacy is concerned, we seem willing to lower our standards. We have become a society with a cavernous appetite for news and gossip. Our era has replaced the tacit, eyes-averted civility of an earlier time with exhibitionism and prying. Even borderline public figures must get used to the nation's eyes in their bedrooms and pocketbooks. That's no Big Brother watching. It's us.

The Network Knows

14 Like any gossip, we trade information to get information. Over in the advanced research laboratories of the consumer electronics companies, futurists are readying little boxes that they believe you would like to carry around—not just telephones but perfect two-way Internet-connected pocket pals. They could use Global Positioning system satellites so that you always know where you are. They could let the Network know too: then the Network could combine its knowledge of your block-by-block location and your customary 11 A.M. hankering for sushi to beam live restaurant guidance to your pocket pal. Surely you don't mind if the Network knows all this. . . .

15   It knows much more, of course. Here is what exists about you in Government and corporate computers, even if you are not a particularly active (or unlucky) participant in the wired and unwired economy:

- Your health history; your credit history; your marital history; your educational history; your employment history.

- The times and telephone numbers of every call you make and receive.
- The magazines you subscribe to and the books you borrow from the library.
- Your travel history: you can no longer travel by air without presenting photographic identification; in a world of electronic fare cards tracking frequent-traveler data, computers could list even your bus and subway rides.
- The trail of your cash withdrawals.
- All your purchases by credit card or check. In a not-so-distant future, when electronic cash becomes the rule, even the purchases you still make by bills and coins could be logged.
- What you eat. No sooner had supermarket scanners gone on line—to speed checkout efficiency—than data began to be tracked for marketing purposes. Large chains now invite customers to link personal identifying information with the records of what they buy, in exchange for discount cards or other promotions.
- Your electronic mail and your telephone messages. If you use a computer at work, your employer has the legal right to look over your shoulder while you type. More and more companies are quietly spot-checking workers' E-mail and even voice mail. In theory—though rarely in practice—even an on-line service or private Internet service provider could monitor you. "Anyway," advices a Web site at, naturally, paranoia.com, "you should assume that everything you do on line is monitored by your service provider."
- Where you go, what you see on the World Wide Web. Ordinarily Net exploring is an anonymous activity, but many information services ask users to identify themselves and even to provide telephone numbers and other personal information. Once a user does that, his or her activity can be traced in surprising detail. Do you like country music? Were you thinking about taking a vacation in New Zealand? Were you perusing the erotic-books section of the on-line bookstore? Someone—some computer, anyway—probably already knows.

16   Many of these personal facts are innocuous in themselves. Some are essentially matters of public record. What matters is mere efficiency—linkage. Your birth certificate was never private; it was always available to someone willing to stand in line and pay a few dollars to a clerk at town hall. Computers and telephone lines make that a bit more convenient, that's all—but it turns out that proficiency in compilation, sorting and distribution can give sinister overtones to even simple collections of names and addresses. A Los Angeles television reporter recently bought a list of 5,000 children, with ages, addresses and phone numbers, in the name of Richard Allen Davis, the convicted murderer of a 12-year-old girl. The company that sold the list, Metromail, boasts of compiling consumer information on 90 percent of United States households.

17   To David Burnham, the former New York Times reporter who wrote the admonitory "Rise of the Computer State" more than a decade ago, this inexorably more detailed compiling of information about individuals amounted to one thing: surveillance. "The question looms before us," he wrote. "Can the United States continue to flourish and grow in an age when the physical movements, individual purchases, conversations and meetings of every citizen are constantly under surveil-

lance by private companies and Government agencies?" And he added, "Does not surveillance, even the innocent sort, gradually poison the soul of a nation?"

18   Does it? If so, we're like sheep to the slaughter.

Privacy or Anonymity?

19 The right to be left alone—privacy on Brandeis's terms—is not exactly the same as the right to vanish, the right to act in society without leaving traces and the right to assume a false identity. Most privacy experts who have studied the possible futures of electronic money favor versions that allow for the anonymity of cash rather than the traceability of checks and credit cards. That is appealing; we ought to be able to make a contribution to a dissident political organization without fear of exposure.

20   Still, the people with the greatest daily, practical need for untraceable cash are criminals: tax cheats, drug dealers, bribers and extortionists. Most drivers prove willing to use an electronic card to pass through tollbooths without worrying about whether a data base is logging their movements. Yet if cards like these replaced cash altogether, the net around us would unquestionably be drawn a notch tighter—especially if we are lying to our employers or spouses about our whereabouts, or if we are simply planning to take it on the lam, Bonnie and Clyde-style.

21   In a past world of intimate small towns, people could disappear. The mere possibility was an essential aspect of privacy, in Rottenberg's view: "People left those small towns and re-emerged in other towns and created new identities." Could you disappear today: abandon all the computerized trappings of your identity, gather enough cash, vanish without leaving a trail and start life again? Probably not. Certainly, there have never been so many invisible chains to the life you now lead.

22   On the Internet, we are re-creating a small-town world, where people mingle and share news easily and informally. But this time it is just one town. Some of its residents advocate rights not just to passive privacy, the right to be left alone, but to what might be called aggressive privacy: the right to retain anonymity even while acting with force and consequence on a broad public stage.

23   Passive privacy is the kind elegantly described by the Fourth Amendment— "the right of the people to be secure in their persons, houses, papers, and effects, against unreasonable searches and seizures." We do have a lot of papers and effects these days.

24   Aggressive privacy implies much more. Telephone regulatory commissions have listened to arguments that people have a right to remain anonymous, hiding their own numbers when placing telephone calls. On the Internet, surprising numbers of users insist on a right to hide behind false names while engaging in verbal harassment or slander.

25   The use of false on-line identities has emerged as a cultural phenomenon. Those who cannot reinvent a new self in real life can easily do so on line. Sometimes they are experimenting with role playing. Most often, though, as a practical reality, the use of false identity on the Internet has an unsavory flavor: marketers sending junk mail from untraceable sources; speculators or corporate insiders trying to influence stock prices; people violating copyrights or engaging in character assassination.

26   Changing personas like clothing—is that what the demand for privacy will come to mean? It's a game for people who choose a form of existence impossible in the old world, maybe hermits at that, hiding in digitally equipped homes, visiting by telecam. Something has been lost after all, in the rush to modernity: the chance to mingle freely and thoughtlessly in our communities, exposing our faces and brushing hands with neighbors who know what we had for breakfast and will remember if we lie about it.

27   In compensation, our reach is thousands of times longer. We meet people, form communities, make our voices heard with a freedom unimaginable to a small-towner of the last century. But we no longer board airplanes or enter schools and courthouses secure in our persons and effects; we submit, generally by choice, to the most intrusive of electronic searches. In banks, at tollbooths, in elevators, in doorways, alongside highways, near public telephones, we submit to what used to be called surveillance. In Orwell's country, thousands of closed-circuit cameras are trained on public streets—pan, zoom and infrared. Every suitcase bomb in a public park brings more cameras and, perhaps, more digital hermits.

28   We turn those cameras on ourselves. Then we beg for more gossip. We invent diamond-hard technologies of encryption, but we rarely bother to use them. If we want to live freely and privately in the interconnected world of the 21st century— and surely we do—perhaps above all we need a revival of the small-town civility of the 19th century. Manners, not devices: sometimes it's just better not to ask, and better not to look.

EXPLORING THE TEXT

1. Gleick comments that "underpinning Orwell's [book] . . . was the utter annihilation of privacy" (paragraph 2). Most people would argue that our world is nothing like the one in Orwell's bleak novel. We like to think that we have our privacy. After reading Gleick's article, do you feel we truly have our privacy?

2. What does Gleick mean when he states in paragraph 8, "Privacy is a construct of our age"?

3. Gleick notes that before the modern era, people who wanted their extreme privacy went off and became hermits. Hermits withdrew from society and lived in isolation. Now, however, we can be hermits "in a crowd." Explain how this seemingly contradictory statement can be true.

4. In paragraph 11, Gleick states that although Americans covet their own privacy, they "turn around and sell it cheaply." Explain how we willingly "sell" our own privacy.

5. How are we "willing to lower our standards" (paragraph 13) when it concerns other people's privacy?

6. What is Gleick's tone in the article? How do you think he feels about privacy in today's world?

7. Examine the role of manners in regards to privacy. Do you think we have lost our manners or our sense of discretion in today's society?

WRITING ASSIGNMENTS

1. If you are familiar with George Orwell's novel *1984,* try to compare elements from that book to our present society. Can you identify any similarities between that bleak totalitarian state and our own? If so, what are they and how are they disturbing? Or, how are they nothing to worry about after all?
2. Answer Gleick's question about the ability to disappear in today's world. "Could you disappear today: abandon all the computerized trappings of your identity, gather enough cash, vanish without leaving a trail and start life again (paragraph 21)?" Explain your reasoning.
3. Write an essay on the privacy rights of public figures. Do you think individuals in the public eye deserve their privacy or is it something they must forfeit in exchange for public recognition? How has privacy, and the violation of privacy, affected our government?

GROUP PROJECTS

1. Gleick provides a list of things that the government can find out about you. With your group, go over this list and discuss how the accessibility of such information could affect you. How could it affect the future?
2. Discuss the role of manners in today's society. What do you think is the basic principle of manners? Why do we need them? With your group discuss rules of etiquette that you think have declined in recent years but should be revived.

Junior Comes Out Perfect
Philip Kitcher

By the twenty-first century, scientists hope to complete the Human Genome Project. Its goal is to isolate and identify every gene within the 23 pairs of human chromosomes in every human being. As work progresses, we are learning more about genetic diseases and how to identify those people who are susceptible to some genetic mutations that may cause disease. But with this knowledge comes controversy. Shall we all be genetically tested? What will we do if we find out we may have a higher chance of developing a genetic mutation? How will our families and insurance companies respond?

In the following article, Philip Kitcher predicts changes in medical treatment that we may face in the next century. He also explores the impact of genetic foreknowledge on pregnancy in the future. Kitcher is a philosopher of science at the University of California in San Diego and is author of *The Lives to Come: The Genetic Revolution and Human Possibilities* (1996). This article first appeared in the *New York Times* in September 1996.

1   The pace and extent of the genetic revolution makes it tempting to speculate about life at the end of the 21st century. Will sex become completely recreational, with the serious business of reproduction going on in carefully monitored tubes? Will the main form of medical treatment consist of gene therapy, designed to replace defective DNA at the squeeze of a syringe?

2   Probably not. Doubtless in the decades to come gene therapy will become more exact, but unless numerous difficult problems are solved, the possibility of precisely engineering people who carry mutant genes into people who are genetically normal is minute. Yet our understanding of the genetics of human disease does promise to transform medical practice. One hundred years from now, we shall know the molecular structures of virtually all human genes, the functions of a significant percentage of them and the molecular mechanisms at work in a large number of human afflictions. Fantasies aside, the chief novelty of late-21st-century medicine will lie in its powerful ability to predict and prevent.

3   Disease, it should be remembered, even hereditary disease, does not always have to be treated by replacing genes. A proper understanding of how a particular genetic mutation leads to illness or disability can sometimes provide clues about how to put it right, through dietary modifications, medicines or surgery. Looking into the next century, we can foresee a continuum of cases. At one extreme are the diseases for which genetic knowledge will lead to successful treatment. Many biomedical researchers draw inspiration from the case of phenylketonuria, or PKU. Children with PKU carry genes that render them unable to metabolize the amino acid phenylalanine. Left untreated, they build up large amounts of phenylalanine in their cells (and lack sufficient amounts of another amino acid, tyrosine) and become severely mentally retarded. By testing a baby just after birth, however, a doctor can prescribe a diet low in phenylalanine and high in tyrosine that enables an afflicted child to develop normally.

4   At the opposite pole are diseases that, despite enormous molecular insight, we are at a loss to treat. For example, the structure of the crucial protein implicated in sickle-cell anemia has been known for decades, but for almost 40 years (at least), that knowledge inspired no significant improvements in treatment. In between lie diseases like cystic fibrosis, where scientists have made some progress but so far have not achieved total success. Investing in molecular genetic research today is like buying tickets in a huge number of lotteries: we would be exceptionally unfortunate not to win the jackpot in some, but we cannot tell in advance how many prizes we will obtain or exactly what they will be.

5   Given the trajectory of genetic technology, it is fairly easy to envisage what a visit to the doctor may be like in 2096. The patient, let's call her Baby K, has her first checkup when she is an 8-week old fetus. A technician removes a few fetal cells. Several days later, interviews with the doctor and a genetic counselor provide

a detailed picture: a 250-page printout sums up information about the DNA at 50,000 regions of the fetal chromosomes—all those regions whose functions in human development are at last understood.

6   The first pages of the printout are devoted to rare but dreadful disruptions of early development. To their relief, the parents of Baby K learn that she will not suffer tragic neural diseases like Tay-Sachs, neurofibromatosis or Lesch-Nyhan syndrome: at the genetic loci affecting these and hundreds of less familiar diseases, the sequences in the fetal DNA are reassuringly normal. With luck, more common genetic diseases—cystic fibrosis and fragile X syndrome—are also ruled out. Baby K's susceptibility to the major diseases that develop later in life, which depend on numerous environmental variables, is described in probabilistic terms: it turns out she is at average or at low risk for the vast majority of diseases, the principal exceptions being juvenile diabetes and a form of breast cancer that usually develops late in middle age. Fortunately, the molecular underpinnings of these diseases are well understood by the 21st century; by making mild changes in Mrs. K's diet before she gives birth and prescribing medicine to Baby K in early childhood, doctors can reduce Baby K's risk of diabetes to the normal range. As she grows into early adulthood, she will be well advised to receive regular breast-tissue checks.

7   The printout continues with a detailed preview of Baby K's immune system. The sequencing of bacterial and viral genomes began in the 1990's and will be elaborated on a grand scale in the coming decades. The resultant knowledge, combined with enhanced understanding of the workings of the immune system, will surely offer doctors in 2096 new clues for fortifying a young child against infectious diseases: changes in diet perhaps, or a schedule of injections designed to bolster the immune response. Baby K's parents will also learn something about the looks of their child-to-be: brown eyes and curly hair, say, maybe slightly over-average height and slender.

8   The session concludes with a review of the printout's last pages, the "behavioral tendencies." The counselor emphasizes the importance of environmental variables: the probability that Baby K will develop a particular personality trait might vary quite widely. But, thanks in part to advances made in neurochemistry in the late 20th century, Mr. and Mrs. K can learn a few things about their daughter: she does not carry any of the known markers for same-sex preference; there is no reason to think she will have less-than-average intelligence; she is not very likely to be hyperactive or suffer from an attention deficit, and she displays no abnormal propensity for depression. If the K's are particularly fortunate, the only cause for worry might be a possible tendency toward alcohol addiction—another predictive diagnosis stemming from the pioneering investigations of the 1990's and another case in which forewarned is forearmed.

9   The K's leave the interview with a vivid picture of their child and the contours of her life. Genetic testing has issued no guarantee against the ravages of birth trauma, childhood accidents, urban violence, earthquakes or other acts of God. Yet they don't have to worry about many potential threats to their child's well-being, and they have been told how to cope with certain aspects of her genetic inheritance—aspects that, in an earlier era, would have been recognized too late.

10   That is what we can hope genetic technology will bring. But the real value of biomedical research will depend not just on what scientists do but on the ways in

which social policy is framed to make use of their contributions. Even in 2096, the news that genetic counselors deliver will not always be good. The story of Baby K was optimistic partly because her genetic abnormalities could be addressed with preventive strategies. What options will be available for parents and patients, and what pressures will they feel, when problems do not come with solutions?

11   Suppose Baby K's parents had learned she has a propensity for muscular degeneration, which could not be halted, or a tendency to depression, which only crude therapies could treat, or that she would be blind or deaf. Under these circumstances, they would have been let pondering a different group of questions: not the practical details of raising a healthy daughter but wondering whether they should allow the pregnancy to continue. Although the K's cannot ask for a baby engineered to their specifications, they can decide, to some extent—and to a far greater degree than is currently possible—what kinds of children they will have, provided they are prepared to abort fetuses with characteristics at odds with their wishes.

12   So far, the consequences of genetic foreknowledge have been very largely benign. In the past 20 years, prenatal genetic screening has greatly reduced the incidence of Tay-Sachs disease, both in the United States and in many other countries, and the incidence of types of thalassemia (a disease similar to sickle-cell anemia) in various Mediterranean countries where it once was prevalent. All except the most devout opponents of abortion should view these developments as merciful, sparing the parents of a Tay-Sachs child, for example, the anguish of watching an apparently healthy infant degenerate beyond help. By 2096, it will be possible to spread mercy more widely, forestalling births that would have revealed grossly disordered development or would have brought pain without hope of improvement. But it will be possible to do many other things as well—terminate a pregnancy because, say, the fetal genes indicate high risk for a heart attack in middle age, or a predisposition to obesity or blue eyes or a disease that can only be treated at great expense.

13   This is precisely the point at which social pressure comes to bear. We can rest comfortably, I think, in assuming that our descendants will not institute some centrally directed eugenics program. Medicine in 2096 will continue to leave choices in the hands of parents. But reproductive decisions will not be entirely free: compulsory sterilization and the storm-trooper's gun are only the least subtle ways of controlling birth. Thousands, perhaps millions, of women in some parts of the world are already aborting female fetuses because they believe that their daughters, growing up in cultures heavily biased toward males, will not lead healthy and happy lives.

14   American parents of the late–21st century are unlikely to be pressured into aborting a healthy female fetus, but unless there are large social changes, other prejudices could permeate their society. For some, news that their child will be extremely short, obese or learning-disabled will be received with distaste or even revulsion. Many others simply may fear their neighbors' attitudes and believe that a child with one of these characteristics will face an uphill struggle. Knowing the personal and career difficulties confronted by those who are very short or obese, the menial jobs often delegated to school dropouts, otherwise unprejudiced parents may decide, with great reluctance, to end the pregnancy. "It just wouldn't be fair," they may say, "to bring a child like that into a world like this." Intense competition and social inequality already drive middle-class parents to register newborn infants for

elite schools, to select the "right" preschool enrichment programs. Tomorrow, the struggle for advancement may begin in the womb.

15   Genetic discoveries already underscore old prejudices and create new ones. As news reports were hailing the mapping and sequencing of the first genes implicated in breast cancer, women from high-risk families were discovering that the new ability to test had devastating consequences: many who carry abnormal genes at the pertinent loci have found that some insurance companies will not cover prophylactic mastectomies, that insurance coverage abruptly stops, that employers dismiss them. Genetic discrimination has already begun, and it is likely to become more extensive unless measures are taken to protect people whose draw in the genetic lottery has been unlucky. Several states have passed legislation to limit genetic discrimination, but these are only timid and hesitant first steps. Universal health coverage is necessary to protect the 5 to 10 percent of the population who will find themselves uninsurable because of accidents in conception.

16   Far more is required to insure that the reproductive choices made in 2096 are free from harsh constraints. Children born with genetic disabilities not only need the same access to health care and employment as other members of their society; they also need special support that will enable them to realize their potential. Unless prospective parents can rely on tolerance and respect for those who are different, unless they are assured that their community will do what it can to aid the disabled, then the pressure to view reproduction as a process in which the "right" products are stamped with social approval and the "wrong" ones discarded will be irresistible.

17   Baby K will surely exist. The pressing question is: How many Baby K's will there be? In the gloomiest vision of the future, the parents of Baby K are simply privileged members of a callous society. They have access to sophisticated medical testing and the results do not pose any hard choices for them. As middle-class citizens, well-educated and comfortable, they take the standard course of finding out if the fetus is "defective." Their child's place in the meritocracy depends on their doing all they can to produce a "perfect" baby—and, luckily, they receive good news.

18   Economic and genetic differences amplify each other, reinforcing pressure on the affluent to produce only "genetically correct" children. As long as there is a wide difference in social and economic status between those who succeed by the prevailing standards and those who do not, many middle-class parents will feel compelled only to have children who satisfy the genetic requirements for success. At the other social extreme will be people whose genetic misfortunes doom them to unemployment, the people with disabilities whose lives are cramped by inadequate support, those whose limited insurance coverage or minimal education denies them the chance to benefit from the new preventive medicines. Some genetic disabilities, virtually eliminated in the middle class, will persist at significant frequency in this segment of the population, but because they lack any powerful constituency, the disabled will find that services to help them are underfinanced. If we simply extrapolate from today's social attitudes, from the growing inequality between rich and poor, from the merciless individualism and competitiveness characteristic of most affluent societies, it is not farfetched to predict that the medical practices of 2096 will follow suit. Socioeconomic inequalities will turn victims of the quirks of conception into a true genetic underclass.

19   There are brighter possible futures. The K's might come from any stratum of society, from any ethnic group: the resources of preventive medicine would be available to all. Inhabiting a more egalitarian society—in which people with many different characteristics are valued and have productive lives, in which the highly educated surgeon and the manual laborer do not inhabit different economic and social spheres—the K's do not have to measure their child against a standard of "genetic correctness." As they await the detailed report from their doctor, they know that if the news is less than exceptional, they will face a genuine choice: government and community support will help them do the best for their child; prejudice will not sharply constrain the life of a child who is different from the majority.

20   This future is not beyond reach. In recent years, some Mediterranean countries have shown that it is possible to combat thalassemia while retaining a compassionate attitude toward those who are afflicted with it. The incidence of the disease has declined in Sardinia and Cyprus, but those Governments have continued to invest heavily in treatment and support for sufferers so that the crucial blood transfusions that are needed are now much more widely available than before. These countries point a way forward. Prenatal testing need not be a substitute for the costly business of nurturing those born with diseases and disabilities: it can be part of a comprehensive community investment in all citizens.

21   It is not easy, of course, to extend policies that work for small, homogeneous societies to a large, multiethnic nation. But that is the challenge. The tools for probing the human genome give us the responsibility of deciding how much to learn about embryonic lives and what to do with that knowledge. The medicine of the future will be a vivid portrait of our social priorities. The character of our choices will be measured by the number of people who will live the fortunate story of Baby K.

EXPLORING THE TEXT

1. Kitcher asks in the first paragraph of his essay if "sex will become completely recreational." For many people, sex is just that—recreational. Discuss the social role of sex versus the reproductive role. How have our views changed regarding "recreational sex"? Could such changes indeed lead to marginalizing sex as a purely recreational function, leaving "the serious business of reproduction" to the medical laboratory?

2. How could our understanding of genetics change medical practice? What are the extreme of genetic knowledge in medical practice?

3. Review Kitcher's description of Baby K's first checkup. Discuss his views on the social and medical ramifications of this checkup.

4. "Baby engineering" is not yet possible, or probable, and won't be for many years. Yet, with the recent success of cloning experiments and gene replacement therapy, the possibility of determining the genetic makeup of our children does exist in the future. What type of genetic control does the "genetic foreknowledge" Kitcher discusses offer future parents?

5. What exactly does Kitcher mean by "genetic correctness"?

6. How could genetic foreknowledge influence social prejudice?

7. How could genetic testing create even greater disparity between the rich and the poor? How does genetics influence our current economic hierarchy?
8. Kitcher's closing comments include his prediction that "medicine of the future will be a vivid portrait of our social priorities." What does he mean by this statement? How are social priorities and medicine linked?

WRITING ASSIGNMENTS

1. Would you want to know the genetic blueprint of your future child? If you would want to know, explain to what use you would put such knowledge. If you would not want to know, explain why not.
2. Discuss the role you feel genetics has on a person's professional and personal success.
3. Write about what impact the ability to determine a child's genetic makeup could have on future generations. Besides medical benefits or problems, discuss the social ramifications of such power. As Kitcher notes, many families already abort female fetuses in countries where males are more socially valued. What could the long-term ramifications of genetic control have on the world?

GROUP PROJECTS

1. Kitcher notes that "the real value of biomedical research will depend . . . on the ways in which social policy" uses this knowledge (paragraph 10). How does society determine the use of scientific knowledge? Can group members think of any examples where society had a role in the use of medical treatment or directed the use of scientific advances? (For example, consider the controversial "morning after" pill.)
2. Discuss the social ramifications of moving reproduction to the laboratory. With your group, develop a picture of what society would be like in such a world. Share your views with the class.

Race Is Over
Stanley Crouch

As we have seen in previous chapters, our nation has always faced difficulties in race relations. Throughout its history, America has marginalized, cast blame upon, and eyed with suspicion various races. The white Anglo-Saxon Protestant status quo has discriminated against Native Americans, blacks, Asians, Latinos, and even "European brothers" from countries such as Ireland and Italy. Historically, America does not have a very pretty record with regards to race relations. However, barriers of race have been breaking down. It is now illegal to deny work on the basis of race. Racial intermarriage is becoming more common and more socially acceptable. And it is the children of these intermarriages, says Stanley Crouch in this essay, who are literally changing the face of America.

Crouch is the author of several books on race including *Notes of a Hanging Judge: Essays and Reviews* (1990) and *The All-American Skin Game: Or, The Decoy of Race* (1996). This article first appeared in the *New York Times* in September 1996.

1   Even though error, chance and ambition are at the nub of the human future, I am fairly sure that race, as we currently obsess over it, will cease to mean as much 100 years from today. The reasons are basic—some technological, others cultural. We all know that electronic media have broken down many barriers, that they were even central to the fall of the Soviet Union because satellite dishes made it impossible for the Government to control images and ideas about life outside the country. People there began to realize how far behind they were from the rest of the modern world. The international flow of images and information will continue to make for a greater and greater swirl of influences. It will increasingly change life on the globe and also change our American sense of race.

2   In our present love of the mutually exclusive, and our pretense that we are something less than a culturally miscegenated people, we forget our tendency to seek out the exotic until it becomes a basic cultural taste, the way pizza or sushi or tacos have become ordinary fare. This approach guarantees that those who live on this soil a century from now will see and accept many, many manifestations of cultural mixings and additions.

3   In that future, definition by racial, ethnic and sexual groups will most probably have ceased to be the foundation of special-interest power. Ten decades up the road, few people will take seriously, accept or submit to any forms of segregation that are marching under the intellectually ragged flag of "diversity." The idea that your background will determine your occupation, taste, romantic preference or any other thing will dissolve in favor of your perceived identity as defined by your class, livelihood and cultural preferences. Americans of the future will find themselves surrounded in every direction by people who are part Asian, part Latin, part African, part European, part American Indian. What such people will look like is beyond my imagination, but the sweep of body types, combinations of facial features, hair textures, eye colors and what are now unexpected skin tones will be far more common, primarily because the current paranoia over mixed marriages should by then be largely a superstition of the past.

4   In his essay "The Little Man at Chehaw Station," Ralph Ellison described a young "light-skinned, blue-eyed, Afro-American-featured individual who could have been taken for anything from a sun-tinged white Anglo-Saxon, an Egyptian, or a mixed-breed American Indian. . . . " He used the young man as an example of our central problem—"the challenge of arriving at an adequate definition of American cultural identity. . . . " While the youth's feet and legs were covered by riding boots and breeches, he wore a multicolored dashiki and "a black homburg hat tilted at a jaunty angle." For Ellison, "his clashing of styles nevertheless sounded an integrative, vernacular tone, an American compulsion to improvise upon the given."

5   The vernacular tone Ellison wrote of is what makes us improvise upon whatever we actually like about one another, no matter how we might pretend we feel about people who are superficially different. Furthermore, the social movements of minorities and women have greatly aided our getting beyond the always culturally inaccurate idea that the United States is "a white man's country."

6   We sometimes forget how much the Pilgrims learned from the American Indians, or look at those lessons in only the dullest terms of exploitation, not as a fundamental aspect of our American identity. We forget that by the time James Fenimore Cooper was inventing his backwoodsmen, there were white men who had lived so closely to the land and to the American Indian that the white man was, often quite proudly, a cultural mulatto. We forget that we could not have had the cowboy without the Mexican vaquero. We don't know that our most original art-music, jazz, is a combination of African, European and Latin elements. Few people are aware that when the Swiss psychoanalyst Carl Jung came to this country he observed that white people walked, talked and laughed like Negroes. He also reported that the two dominant figures in the dreams of his white American patients were the Negro and the American Indian.

7   Are we destined to become one bland nation of interchangeables? I do not think so. What will fall away over the coming decades, I believe, is our present tendency to mistake something borrowed for something ethnically "authentic." Regions will remain regions and within them we will find what we always find: variations on the overall style and pulsation. As the density of cross-influences progresses, we will get far beyond the troubles the Census Bureau now has with racial categories, which are growing because we are so hung up on the barbed wire of tribalism and because we fear absorption, or "assimilation." We look at so-called "assimilation" as some form of oppression, some loss of identity, even a way of "selling out." In certain cases and at certain times, that may have been more than somewhat true. If you didn't speak with a particular command of the language—or at a subdued volume—you might have been dismissed as crude. If you hadn't been educated in what were considered the "right places," you were seen as some sort of a peasant.

8   But anyone who has observed the dressing, speaking and dancing styles of Americans since 1960 can easily recognize the sometimes startling influences that run from the top to the bottom, the bottom to the top. Educated people of whatever ethnic group use slang and terms scooped out from the disciplines of psychology, economics and art criticism. In fact, one of the few interesting things about the rap idiom is that some rappers pull together a much richer vocabulary than has ever existed in black pop music, while peppering it to extremes with repulsive vulgarity.

9   One hundred years from today, Americans are likely to look back on the ethnic difficulties of our time as quizzically as we look at earlier periods of human history, when misapprehension defined the reality. There will still be squabbling, and those who supposedly speak in the interest of one group or another will hector the gullible into some kind of self-obsession that will influence the local and national dialogues. But those squabbles are basic to upward mobility and competition. It is the very nature of upward mobility and competition to ease away superficial distinctions in the interest of getting the job done. We already see this in the integration of the workplace, in the rise of women and in the increase of corporations that grant spousal-

equivalent benefits to homosexuals because they want to keep their best workers, no matter what they do privately as consenting adults. In the march of the world economy, the imbalances that result from hysterical xenophobia will largely melt away because Americans will be far too busy standing up to the challenges of getting as many international customers for their wares as they can. That is, if they're lucky.

EXPLORING THE TEXT

1. Crouch claims that our notions of race will change in the next century. What are our notions of race?
2. What reasons does Crouch give for why we classify or define in terms of race? Do you agree with his reasoning?
3. Discuss the American desire for the exotic. What other exotic tastes have become social norms in our culture and nation?
4. Couch claims that "definition by racial, ethnic and sexual groups will . . . have ceased to be the foundation of special-interest power" (paragraph 3). On what does he base his claim?
5. What are the implications of the title Crouch selected for his article? What might it mean?
6. Explain what Crouch means in paragraph 6 that Americans are "often quite proudly . . . cultural mulatto[s]."
7. Consider the contributions various races and cultures made to our mainstream culture. For example, what is the role of rap music on music, art, dress, and speech. How can such contributions "conquer" racial and ethnic barriers?

WRITING ASSIGNMENTS

1. Do you think we will become more racially and/or ethnically melded in the next century? Explain your view.
2. Examine your own racial and/or ethnic background. Write about how you identify and define yourself and why.
3. Crouch comments that in the future, "the idea that your background will determine your occupation, taste [or] romantic preference . . . will dissolve" (paragraph 3). Write about how your own ethnicity influenced a decision you made in your life.

GROUP PROJECTS

1. Construct with your group a demographic picture of the future. Try to determine what the face of the nation will look like after another century. Share your vision, and your reasoning, with the rest of the class.

2. With your group, make a list of the things a particular ethnicity or race has contributed to mainstream American culture. Select one ethnicity only. Try to identify their contributions and when these contributions became mainstream. Cite specific examples in media such as music, art, dance, advertising, and television.

Mystery Date
A. M. Homes

As we advance into the next century, we focus on technology and how things will change. But some things, they say, never change. While technology may advance, affairs of the heart will remain fundamentally the same. In the following fictional piece, A. M. Homes describes how teenagers will still be teenagers in the next century, and how an old sixties game like "Mystery Date" can transcend decades.

This story appeared in the *New York Times Sunday Magazine* in September 1996. Homes is the author of a book of short stories, *The Safety of Objects* (1990), and the novel, *The End of Alice* (1996).

1   The rain pat-patters on the roof. Daisy and her friend Vivienne, who is visiting from France for the day, are sprawled on the living-room sofa.

2   "I'm bored," Daisy whines.

3   "Why don't you girls do something?" Daisy's mother asks. "Write a book, make a movie."

4   The girls curl up their noses. "We've done it," Daisy says. "We've done it all before. We want something new, something different."

5   "Nothing is new," Vivienne says. "That is what's so sad."

6   "Well, then, why don't you go up into the attic and see if you can find my old Singer fabric fuser—you know, the textile toaster that presses plastic bottles into cloth. I think I'd like to try and whip up something."

7   "Like what?" Daisy asks.

8   "Never mind what. Just go. Up, up. Go, go." She claps six times hard and fast, as though the slapping of her hands will rouse the lazy girls. It works: at once they are up the stairs and staring at the trapdoor that leads to the attic.

9   "I really like your mother," Vivienne says. "She's so energetic."

10   "She's getting old," Daisy says, touching the panel that opens the trapdoor. "She's 82. She waited until she retired to have me." The door mechanism jams and Daisy has to jump up and grab the ancient dangling cord. She pulls the trapdoor down; a staircase unfolds.

11   "And," Daisy adds, "there are two more embryos in our freezer, a boy and a girl, just waiting until she decides when—I already named them Tom and Emily."

12   "Aaahhh," Vivienne says. "I've never been in an attic before."

13   "Me neither," Daisy says. "This is actually my great-grandmother's house. My whole family has lived in Larchmont for, like, 150 years. We're so incredibly dull."

14   The magic of the attic, the dank, dark, thick and thin smells of must and dust and all that has lived and died, rises up in a cloud that blows over the girls, stealing their words, whisking them back in time. Beneath their feet, the floorboards creak. "It's like a museum," Vivienne says, tiptoeing carefully, "like the lost rooms of the Louvre."

15   "This stuff must be worth trillions," Daisy says, flinging open one trunk after another, all of them loaded with clothing from some place called the Gap.

16   "Can you imagine wearing this?" Vivienne asks, slipping a T-shirt imprinted with the phrase "Just Do It or Die" over her head. "It must be from before they knew it was harmful to have words so close to your skin."

17   "How could they not have known that language causes cancer? It's so obvious."

18   "Look how strange they were," Vivienne says, pointing to the cover of an old magazine featuring a model with a big brown mole above her lip.

19   "I wonder how come she didn't fix that?" Daisy asks.

20   "What a waste of paper," Vivienne says. "This would never be allowed today. Paper is only for toilet tissue and birthday cards."

21   "What are these?" Daisy asks, tilting her head sideways to read a stack of old game boxes. "Chinese Checkers, Monopoly and Risk." She pulls out the box. "Have you heard of Yugoslavia or the U.S.S.R.?"

22   "Vaguely. I think they used to be countries or maybe they're ex-Presidents." Vivienne coughs, waving her hand in front of her face. "Too much antique air."

23   Daisy buzzes her mother via Wrist-Dish Satellite Communicator. "Hey, Mom, are the vents open up here?"

24   "They should be—aren't you getting enough air? The filter probably needs cleaning—I'll turn the oxygen up."

25   "Thanks," Daisy says. She brushes the dust off an old white box. "'Mystery Date. By Milton Bradley. The key to fun. For girls 6–16.'"

26   "Perfecto, we're just 12," Vivienne says. "Do you think it still plays?"

27   *Object: Girls, be ready when your date calls at the door.*

28   Daisy opens the box: a stack of cards, a set of dice, four cardboard girls, a board with a white door in the middle, a big blue question mark.

29   She hands Vivienne the dice. "You go first."

30   "Comment jouer?"

31   "Roll the dice."

32   Vivienne tosses the dice onto the board. Daisy moves Vivienne's marker eight spaces down the board. Vivienne draws a card—the evening gown.

33   "Baahh, I'd never wear that."

34   Daisy takes a turn, moves three and gets a bathing suit. "Do you remember when I went to the Riviera with your cousin Claude? He was awful and he had a giant boiling blister on his chin."

35   "Quoi?"

36   "A huge zit."

37   "French men are horrible," Vivienne says. "I only date boys from other countries. And American boys are so annoying. The moon, the moon, they always want to take you to the moon. Big deal. Going up in a rocket ship."

38   "I like it," Daisy says. "The thrust, the feeling of all that pressure against you, it's exciting."

39   "The first time, yes, but after that, boring."

40   It's Vivienne's turn. This time she gets a pair of skis and shrugs. "What I really want to do is go to the outback." She leans forward, whispering: "Yesterday I let a boy I hardly know take me for a walk in Tuscany. Don't tell anyone. I promised my mother I wouldn't leave the country without letting her know where I was going and yesterday I lied. I said I was visiting Monica in Limoges. Worse yet, his father is a physician and Mama has forbidden me from dating underlings: bankers, lawyers, doctors—nobody trusts them. She wants me to meet a good auto mechanic or an electronics repairman."

41   "What about Donald?" Daisy asks. "He's very Mr. Fix-It."

42   "Ooooff," Vivienne says. "A showoff. He made such a big deal of ordering in Indian food direct from Delhi. I got a parasite and was in hospital for a week."

43   Daisy rolls double fives and goes again: six and three. She's hopping down the game board. "Oh," she says, "oh, I think I've won. It's my turn to go on a mystery date."

44   "Oui, but will he be a 'dream' or a 'dud'?"

45   Daisy carefully turns the small knob that opens the white door and there he is, her mystery date—all grease and grunge, splat and spatter. "Uh-oh, you need the right accessories," she says, disappointed. "All I've got is the bathing suit, but he's not the beach bum."

46   "Well, then, I guess you lose," Vivienne says.

47   Daisy's communicator vibrates and her mother's face fills the screen. "Hello, hello," her mother says. "It's not raining anymore. Come out, come out, wherever you are. Did you find my fabric fuser?"

48   "I forgot to look," Daisy says, embarrassed.

49   "What have you been doing up there?"

50   Daisy stalls, worried that her mother will lecture her about wasting time, being unproductive, et cetera et cetera. "I'm not sure," she says. "We found some old games."

51   "You're playing, how wonderful. That's what I used to do on rainy days. Well, come on down now. I've called a taxi-guard to take you and Vivienne to Ye Olde Pille Pop Shoppe before Vivienne has to catch her plane."

52   "Be right down," Daisy says.

53   The Pop Shoppe is crowded with people needing a little pick-me-up after the foul weather.

54   "Wow, so many base feelings to chose from," Vivienne says. "In France we only have three: light, serious and strawberry ebullience."

55   "Well, when the F.D.A. took over from Baskin-Robbins they put a lot into it—years of research. They have 32 classics, 211 blend-ins, with a special formula every week. "

56   The pharmacist takes Daisy's order—she asks for something in orange, good for energy, with a dash of violet for joy and a hint of cheerination for her temperament.

57   Vivienne orders straight blue, which enhances your view of yourself and makes your hair shiny. As they're waiting for their pills, a boy who looks uncannily like Daisy's mystery date comes in.

58   Vivienne elbows her. "Vite, look, go tell him he's your mystery date."

59   Daisy shakes her head, suddenly shy.

60   "Monsieur," Vivienne calls to the pharmacist. "Pardon, but who is that boy?" The pharmacist aims his lens at the boy, feeding the image into his screen, and the simple statistics folder of Walter Taylor opens—he's top of his lot, with a gold star in thermomolecular theory, and his father is an auto mechanic.

61   "Your dud is a dream," Vivienne says.

62   "Would you like to hear him play the trombone?" the pharmacist asks. "There's a sample on file—he's first chair in the Invisible Band."

63   The girls swallow their pills, washing them down with shot glasses of water. "Thanks."

64   The pharmacist comes out from behind the counter and introduces Daisy to Walter. They shake hands.

65   "This is my friend Vivienne, from France," says Daisy.

66   "Hi," Walter says. "What kind of pill did you pop?"

67   "Blue," Vivienne says. "And you?"

68   "I don't take anything. I like to have my feelings. I just come here to meet people."

69   Vivienne yawns. "Pardon." She checks her watch and turns to Daisy. "It's 3 in the morning in Paris. I should get back."

70   "Hey," Walter says as the girls are leaving. "Are you free tomorrow night? You could come over for dinner. My mom makes a great meatloaf and we could watch some information or something. I live around the corner on Maple Street."

71   "Wow," Daisy says, "that sounds great. I've never been to someone's house for dinner before. But I have to check with my mother first."

72   "Mon Dieu," Vivienne says, rubbing her head as they get into the car. "I shouldn't have had so much blue. I'm feeling a little overinflated."

73   From an open window comes the faint sound of theme music—since 2046 you always hear things from the past. All that has ever been said, or done, is constantly replayed. There is no silence. The girls unconsciously hum along: "He's here, my mystery date. Are you ready? Don't be late, open the door for your mystery date."

74   Daisy gushes, "He's so alive, so human—not like any boy I've ever met."

75   "Oui," Vivienne says. "He is, enfin, finally, something new."

EXPLORING THE TEXT

1. In her story Homes includes many inventions and aspects of life in the future. Identify some of these innovations. Do you think such a future is possible?

2. Vivienne and Daisy stop by Ye Olde Pille Pop Shoppe. Consider the implications of such a store.
3. What social changes occur in the future according to Homes? What has remained essentially unchanged?
4. Identify the underlying message of Homes's story. How do you know what this message is?
5. What is ironic about Homes's ending?

WRITING ASSIGNMENTS

1. Write your own short story about what dating in the future will be like. Think about what it is like for you. You might ask your parents and grandparents what dating was like for them when they were teenagers; then drawing from your family, develop a story about dating in the next century.
2. Identify the underlying message of Homes's story. What is still important in the future? Write an essay about the things you think will remain unchanged in human relationships, no matter how much technology advances.

GROUP PROJECTS

1. With your group discuss dating relationships. Consider how dating has changed in the last 50 years. Do you think it will change significantly in the next 50 years?
2. Make a list of professions that your group considers prestigious. Why do we think of these professions as more important than others? Do you think that prestige associated with employment will change in the future? Explain your reasoning to the class.

Where Have All the Causes Gone?
Jon Meacham

Throughout much of the twentieth century, Americans have been brought together by common causes. Two world wars, financial hardship, and national tragedies have linked people together, transcending gender, age, and social gaps. But according to Jon Meacham, the so-called Generation X—young adults born in the late sixties and early seventies—lacks the unifying national emergencies of their ancestors. In many ways, they are a people without a cause, says Meacham, who believes that such a lack of history could prove dangerous in the future.

Meacham is senior editor at *Newsweek* magazine where this article first appeared in January 1997.

1 Barring unforeseen circumstances, I will have just turned 30 as the next millennium begins. When my grandfather was that age, he had lived through the Depression in the South, enlisted in the navy and spent four years at war in the Pacific; the day the bomb was dropped, he was aboard the USS St. George preparing for the invasion of Japan. One of the first things he did when he returned home to Tennessee was to sire my father, who was born in July 1946. By the time *he* had hit 30, he had watched the civil-rights movement unfold around him and had fought in Vietnam, carrying a 12-gauge shotgun in search-and-destroy missions as part of the Fourth Infantry Division in Pleiku. The toughest combat decision I've ever faced was whether to watch the networks or CNN cover the gulf war.

2 This is a fairly common story. People my age—those born between 1965 and 1976 (there are 40 million of us)—face a history gap. All the Big Causes seem to be settled. The country beat the Depression, defeated Hitler, stared down the Soviets and abolished Jim Crow long before we were on the scene. On one level this is wonderful: we are the beneficiaries of relative peace and prosperity, which beats the hell out of war or economic want. But as the century winds down, there is a sentimental longing for big things to happen. For us, history is a virtual thing, the stuff of A&E "Biography" episodes and downloaded speeches from the Richard Nixon Library Web site. Hollywood, ever sensitive to cultural appetites, is finding a market for our romance with the past: Steven Spielberg, Tom Hanks, Bruce Willis and Arnold Schwarzenegger are all making World War II movies.

3 But multimedia experience is pretty weak compared with what came before us. Every other generation in the 20th century faced common enemies and had cohesive ambitions. In the years after 1900, Theodore Roosevelt sensed a new role for America, and inspired—taunted, really—younger men like his cousin Franklin to embrace the world. TR had tapped into something powerful: many of that generation envied the men who had fought in the Civil War. One, Douglas MacArthur, spent his life trying to match the exploits of his father, Arthur MacArthur, who was 18 when he won the Medal of Honor at Missionary Ridge. Woodrow Wilson gave this generation—FDR, MacArthur, Marshall, Truman, Eisenhower—a moral frame for TR's cult of action. The young officers of World War I became the commanders of World War II. Their troops in the fight against Hitler were men who already understood sacrifice. The Depression had seen to that. Meanwhile, in Washington, FDR was making government sexy. There were the Brain Trusters from Harvard, and Hubert Humphrey quit pharmacy school to do relief work.

4 It was, obviously, a very different country then. Public schools and the draft united the middle class and the poor; money was important, but people from different backgrounds mingled more easily than they do at the end of the century. The famous example is the crew of PT 109. There, John F. Kennedy served with a refrigeration engineer from Macon, Ga., a machinist from Chicago, a Polish immigrant factory worker and a jazz pianist.

5 Even the usually self-indulgent boomers grew up with a sense of connection to real drama. They heard about the great battles from their GI fathers; a frequent playground query in the early 1950s was "What did *your* dad do in the war?" There was the cold war and the great civil-rights struggle. In the White House, LBJ was able to

call on a seemingly limitless faith in government to fight segregation, launch the Great Society and escalate the conflict in Southeast Asia. The boomers marched on Washington, building their own myths, however "countercultural." Then things began to fall apart.

6   That's where we came in: during the falling-apart. The antiwar protests and the crusade for racial equality had all died down; Watergate and malaise were the order of the day. And we tended to be more segregated by class than ever. An increasing number of us went to private schools, and the draft was phased out.

7   The problem is not our willingness to be moved by events, or causes. We love to hug trees, and how else to explain our rallying round the gulf war, or the series of Ribbon Crises, beginning with the yellow sashes of the Iranian hostage debacle to the white ones of Flight 800? The dangerous thing is that without epic scope, every news story becomes a "crisis," and "heroes" come cheap. (Remember Grenada, or Scott O'Grady?) The cumulative effect of such confected moments—and the media's appetite for instant drama never helps—is to trivialize just about everything.

8   Something will ultimately test us. Entitlements could collapse, a derivatives deal may bring down the markets, some rogue nation might fire a missile at Manhattan. Americans are never comfortable for long without a crusade; one is sure to be thrust upon us. Then it will be our turn, and how we do will be the first big story of the millennium.

EXPLORING THE TEXT

1. Meacham writes that "for us, history is a virtual thing" (paragraph 2). What does he mean by this statement? How can history be virtual?

2. Explain how people were more unified in the past. Why do you think a common enemy helped bring people together under the banner of a "common cause"?

3. Define the word *cause*. How does the article seem to identify a cause?

4. In paragraph 5, Meacham comments that after the late sixties, "things began to fall apart." How did things fall apart? Do we truly live in an age without causes and unity?

5. What is the tone of Meacham's article? How does he use elements of sarcasm to express his ideas?

6. Meacham claims that "the media's appetite for instant drama" (paragraph 7) prevents us from unifying in times of crisis. Explain what you think he means by this statement. Do you think it is true?

WRITING ASSIGNMENTS

1. Interview a parent or relative who can remember living through World War II or another military conflict. Did the crisis draw them together with others, and if so, in what ways?

2. Describe a unifying experience of your own. What were the circumstances of your situation and why did it unify you with others? Explore your feelings about the experience. Did it help prepare you for future conflicts? If so, how?

3. Meacham recalls that a common question children asked each other in the 1950s was "what did your dad do in the war?" Write an autobiography of your future life. What will your children say about you? (Or, what would you like them to say?)

4. Many movies featuring events occurring during World War II have hit the big screen in recent years. Watch one such movie and analyze how it depicts civic reaction to common crisis. What brought people together and how did they work for a common cause?

GROUP PROJECTS

1. Make a list of the historical conflicts Meacham describes in his article. Discuss how these common causes unified Americans. How does your group, as a generation who may not remember these conflicts first hand, feel about these periods in history?

2. What issues do we face as a nation today? Are they political, medical, financial, social, intellectual, or religious issues? Identify a few of the problems our society must confront. Discuss with your group whether these issues will unify or divide us or have they already done so?

Back to the Future
Meg Greenfield

With each generation comes new technology—and with it a technological "generation gap." The failure of the older generation to catch up is the foundation for many jokes. One commercial for a VCR boasts that its machine is easy enough for an adult to program. Another ad features two teenagers racing home to prevent their father from using their home computer because he might ruin it. And many young adults simply give up trying to explain to grandparents how e-mail works. But one things remains unchanged: human nature.

Although it may be difficult at times for one generation to relate to the technological advances of another, Meg Greenfield notes below that it's the "same old us" beneath all the shiny new gadgetry. And it's our basic human nature that breaches the generation gap. Her essay first appeared in her *Newsweek* column in January 1997. Greenfield is also the editorial page editor for the *Washington Post*.

1 We are about to be engulfed in futurist talk: new term, new century, new millennium—what will it all be like? Here's one provisional answer: the science/technol-

ogy will be different. Its human manipulators, subjects and beneficiaries won't. Therein lies the enduring story.

2   Sometimes when I am working my clumsy way through the once inconceivable electronic, cordless present I think of my own long-departed parents, when they were young and (they no doubt thought) on the cutting edge of modernity. I interrupt their 1920s courtship—the poky car they considered a new-age marvel, the relatively novel telephone and telegram and radio and movie culture in which they were comfortable and their parents were not, the manner of self-presentation and dress their parents denounced as indecent, and the cockiness with which they considered themselves newly secure in their physical health on the basis of medical advances we now consider primitive. I try to tell them about space stations and the Internet and heart and liver transplants and cell phones and laptops. I say: look, I can sit up here in this airplane, which will get me to Europe in a very few hours, and type a story and file it to an office in Washington and exchange messages and phone calls with people around the world—all right here in my airplane seat. They are agog. But then they make the same mistake social analysts and prophets and visionaries always make. They think that life will have been transformed by these blessings in ways it has not been.

3   Yes, there is a sense—an important one—in which life *has* been transformed from the past in our age, just as it was transformed from an earlier time in theirs. Illness, ignorance and want have obviously not been eliminated. But millions upon millions of people living today, who not all that long ago would have been direly afflicted by all three, will never know them in anything like their once common form, if they know them at all. Better, faster and more are the defining terms of our culture and our condition. I don't see how anyone could doubt that or fail to be awed by the way both physical and intellectual access have been expanded so you can go anywhere and/or learn anything with a speed that only a couple of decades ago, never mind a generation back, would have seemed merely fanciful, sci-fi stuff. And if we know anything, it is that this kind of progression is certain to continue.

4   Such predictions have always been a pretty safe bet. There were Greeks, there were Renaissance figures (of whom Leonardo was but one) and there were 19th-century figures, such as even the poet Tennyson, whose imaginations enabled them to see well beyond the scientific confines of their times. And so of course can we. What is harder to see is a day when human nature and human life on earth will have been commensurately transformed. What I am saying is that the humanists' insights will probably always be more to the point than the imagery of technological marvels yet to be. What Shakespeare uniquely knew about the human mind and heart and the timeless human predicament will be just as apt a millennium or two from now as it is today and was 400 years ago. The uses to which actual, famously fallible people put the newfangled marvels will still be the issue.

5   I think of this when the lawyer-commentators are taking us through the latest permutations of the O.J. case. All the knowledge about DNA, all the supersensitive means of analyzing microscopic traces of blood and hair and all, do not get you past an ancient kind of drama and an equally familiar set of responses to it by accuser and accused. I think of the dear old Newt mess, entangled as it now is in interception

technology, unencrypted cell-phone messages, arguments about which kind of cable connector to which kind of recording device from which kind of scanner went into the notoriously taped phone call.

6   And, above all, I think of the tremendous conflicts in this country over the uses to which the new technologies will be put. These are conflicts riding on moral choices, and the mathematical principle has not been thought of that can resolve them. We fight about who gets the good of the lifesaving device and technique. This can be a fight among equally needy individuals for a scarce resource or a fight between generations about how much one person must pay to extend another's longevity. We fight about where we should put our pooled resources to get the good of the burgeoning knowledge—in space? in bombs? in basic research? We fight about who owns the new knowledge and its fruits, who has proprietary rights, who is entitled to privacy, who should be able to hook up with whom. We fight about what to do when a new scientific blessing, as is so often the case, comes accompanied by a curse—the pesticide or vehicle or energy source that saves and also, simultaneously, sickens or kills. Decked out in our ever newer skills and abilities and seemingly magical potential, facing the glowing screens of our new life, soaring above the earth, bouncing back from a long dreaded and once mortal disease, guess what? It's the same old us.

7   I think it is awfully important to remember this as the rhetoric ascends toward the millennial moment, starting this week and gaining verbal altitude as the turn of the century nears. There are not and never can be any scientific rules whereby we can perfect ourselves the way we can perfect certain objects and processes in the physical world. And in this limitation will always reside our potential glory and our potential shame. It will always be easier to do the scientifically impossible thing (as we contemporaneously think of it) than to do the personally possible but difficult thing—the right thing by ourselves and by others and by the technologically amazing world we have concocted to live in. I believe, in other words, that my seemingly quaint, flapper-age parents, once they got the hang of the gadgetry, would be as at home in this world as we all would be in the super-duper one about to come. So far as its human inhabitants are concerned, we would have seen it all before.

EXPLORING THE TEXT

1. What is Greenfield saying about the generation gap and technology? Will technology always be a part of the generation gap? If so, in what ways?

2. Greenfield notes that "there is a sense . . . in which life has been transformed from the past in our age" (paragraph 3). What does she mean by this statement?

3. What is Greenfield, in essence, saying in paragraph 4 about the things that transcend time? What do you think are the things that transcend time, place, and technology?

4. Consider the examples Greenfield uses concerning the type of moral conflicts we face with technological advances. What moral dilemmas must we deal with as we move into the next century?

5. How can it be "easier to do the scientifically impossible thing" as Greenfield claims in her final paragraph, than to "do the personally possible but difficult thing"?
6. How can technology affect communication between generations?
7. Do you think the older generation will always resist the "advances" of the technology of the younger generation? Explain your reasoning.

WRITING ASSIGNMENTS

1. Drawing from your personal experience, describe an incident where technology created a gap between you and another generation. Describe the circumstances involved and why the gap existed.
2. Greenfield notes that despite the forward march of technology, we are "still the same old us." What elements do we all hold in common, regardless of age? How will these similarities help us communicate despite the gaps created by technology?
3. Discuss with someone from an older generation the technological breakthroughs of their generation. Why were these inventions so important and how did they change lives? Then, connect this "old" technology to your own life. Describe the ways in which the technology of the past affects your life now.

GROUP PROJECTS

1. Discuss with your group the technological advances that make our life easier or more efficient. What things do you identify first? How new are these advances? What other things can you think of that you might have not thought of at first? Did you forget them because they are older or more established innovations? Why do you think you forgot them?
2. How do you think the technology today will affect the advances of tomorrow? Project into the future how a particular "cutting-edge" technology will be used in the next century. Will it be as common to everyday life as the washing machine or the electric light? Will it become obsolete as our needs change as in the case of eight-track tapes and beta video recorders? Discuss your ideas with the group.

Sequencing Assignments: Making New Connections

This book offers a wide range of provocative readings on contemporary subjects that should interest students like you entering the twenty-first century. The very breadth of information in these readings suggests that there are other ways to organize course work beyond the boundaries of individual chapters. What follows are three reading and writing sequences that model other ways to make use of material in this book. These sequences, like the rest of the book, are organized thematically, but the readings have been chosen from chapters throughout. Undoubtedly other selections in the book would fit into any sequence, as add-ons or replacements, so you might want to make use of complementary essays.

Specific goals of sequencing questions:

1. The sequences that follow illustrate that writing is recursive. The sequenced questions not only help you prepare your own reservoir of materials to use in writing formal essays, but they encourage you to keep circling back and forth between your writings in order to produce your best insights.

2. A primary goal is to make sure you recognize that texts are often engaged in a kind of conversation with each other—and with you.

3. Sequenced questions also allow you to complicate your own thinking—that is, to resist the urge to reduce ideas and issues to their simplest elements. They encourage you to consider a variety of approaches to a topic and to see that there can be validity in more than one perspective, including your own.

4. These sequences offer an opportunity for you to recognize how rhetorical modes work as strategies in writing (and reading). The first sequence emphasizes how important *narrative* can be even in academic or persuasive writing, the second sequence focuses primarily on the importance of *definition* as a strategy in presenting various arguments, and the third incorporates each of these strategies, but asks for a distinctly *persuasive* final essay.

5. A final goal is to offer you the opportunity to collaborate—to receive feedback on your work and to offer feedback to peers. A writing classroom is a community of writers, and it would be beneficial for you to bring your questions to class for peer (as well as instructor) input—to see your classmates as resources for working through problems. Writing, after all, is a very public form of communication, so you shouldn't be shy in seeking input.

Sequence 1: Reflections on the Personal

The essays:

> "The Eye of the Beholder," Grace Suh (54–57)
> "The Other Body: Reflections on Difference, Disability and Identity Politics,"
>   Ynestra King (59–63)
> "Amelia Earhart: The Lady Vanishes," Camille Paglia (285–286)
> "Getting to Know About You and Me," Chana Schoenberger (325–327)
> "A Puerto Rican Stew," Esmeralda Santiago (332–334)
> "Mute in an English-Only World," Chang-rae Lee (364–366)

Personal narratives are an excellent place to begin exploring a topic or issue. The classic advice to "write what you know" suggests that drawing upon our own experience allows us not only to reexamine our lives in writing but also to write from a position of authority, adding to our sense of confidence. Drawing on personal experience also allows us to be more vivid and descriptive in our writing and, perhaps most importantly, to flesh out generalizations with examples and details.

The essays you will look at in this sequence use a narrative approach to examine personal experiences that touch upon a variety of issues. In these essays, however, the writers do more than simply tell a story; they shape their experiences in order to explore and articulate a point of view—that is, all these narratives are ultimately persuasive in nature. You may think it is always necessary to use objective evidence such as statistics, scientific studies, or expert opinion to support an argument, but subjective or anecdotal evidence is also widely used in persuasive writing and can be extremely effective in capturing readers' attention and swaying their thinking.

In looking more closely at narrative form, you will be asked to pay special attention to *voice*. Part of your job will be to identify the sound or texture of the various voices in these narratives and to think about how you might more effectively develop your own narrative voice. Later, you will be asked to go one step further and to practice blending your voice with the voices of the authors of those pieces. This ability to *synthesize* multiple voices into one coherent piece of writing that has its own strong voice—your voice—is one of the mot effective writing skills.

1. Establishing Your Voice

All of the writers in this unit talk in one way or another about their experience as outsiders. Before you take another look at what they have to say, explore the issue for yourself:

a. Write a brief narrative about a time in your life when you were left out of a group. Be sure to make clear how and why you were excluded and how it made you feel. Did this experience have any long term-effects on you?

b. Now try looking at the subject from the other side—that is, write a narrative about a time when you excluded someone else. What motivated you to behave in this way? Did you later regret your actions or did you feel justified in your behavior? Do you think it is ever appropriate to exclude others? Why or why not?

c. Combine your two narratives into one piece that reflects on the issue of exclusion. Include examples and/or details from both previous narratives and add any new material you think might be relevant. Come to some kind of conclusion about how exclusion has affected you as well as the people you have known.

2. **Looking at Other Voices**

   Now take a look at what some others have said. In order to examine more closely the voices you hear, describe at least two of the essays from this unit in terms of the following:

   a. How do you see this voice dressed? For instance, is the voice you hear quite formal (wearing a tuxedo, perhaps) or is it quite casual (wearing a T-shirt, jeans, and plastic thongs)? Is this a conventional voice or a daring voice? Does this voice wear big chunky jewelry or does it prefer a plain gold watch? See if you can draw the speaker. As you write your description, be sure to incorporate quotes from the essay that back up the choices you have made.

   b. Now turn back to your writing from the first section in this sequence. Exchange your final essay with a classmate. Do the same exercises (how would this voice be dressed, how would you draw it) on each other's essay. When you get your essay back, read over your partner's comments then write a few paragraphs about what you've learned about your own voice.

3. **Synthesizing Voices**

   This section asks you to combine your own experience and insights with those of the writers listed at the beginning of this unit. In order to do this effectively, you may want to review MLA citation rules so that you can cite from the essays correctly. These questions divide the essays into two groups of three to help keep your discussion focused, but there is room for substitution if other interesting connections occur to you.

   a. Ynestra King, Chana Schoenberger, and Chang-rae Lee all discuss the difficulty of being different in American society. Read (or reread) the essays carefully and respond to the following questions:

      - In a sentence or two, write what you think is the main point of each essay. Do the writers seem to be saying similar things? Where is there common ground? Where do the essays diverge?
      - For each essay, list four or five examples the authors use to support their main ideas.
      - Describe the tone (author's attitude toward the subject) of each piece. List some words or phrases that communicate this attitude.
      - Write a paragraph for each essay describing how the examples and tone contribute to the effectiveness (or ineffectiveness) of the argument.

      Now that you have a good feel for what these articles are saying and how they are saying it, see if you can write an essay that combines the authors' voices with your own. Write an essay that incorporates summary, paraphrasing, or quotes from at least two of the essays. Draw upon your own experience, but feel free to weave in the experiences of King, Schoenberger, and/or Lee where appropriate.

In paragraph 11 of her essay, Chana Schoenberger writes, "Difference, in America, is supposed to be good. We are expected—at least, I always thought we were expected—to respect each other's traditions." Write an essay discussing the issue of how difference is viewed by our society. While Americans often praise the quality of individuality, do we really like difference? Are there some kinds of difference we like and other kinds we are suspicious of, even hostile to? Be sure to draw on your own experience with being different (for inspiration, you may want to return to your first narrative about being excluded).

b. Camille Paglia, Esmeralda Santiago, and Grace Suh all describe their struggles as women to find an identity with which they are comfortable. All these women in some way or another are describing their search for identity. Explore this issue further by responding to the following assignments:

• In a short essay, compare and contrast Suh's and Santiago's essays. Does either woman seem to resolve the conflict she feels about who she is supposed to be? Offer evidence from the text to support your answers.

• Look at the issue of independence in Santiago's and Paglia's essays. Drawing on their examples, write an essay discussing why achieving independence is often more difficult for women than men.

4. Preparing the Final Essay

You have explored some of your own thoughts about outsiders and have familiarized yourself with the ideas and voices of these three writers. It is now time to prepare a formal essay in which you discuss how the search for identity can be compared to a quest—that is, a search or pursuit made in order to find or obtain something. You may want to focus on your own experience with coming to college and how that experience changed and/or reshaped your view of yourself. Or you may want to focus on a period of your life when you sought role models on whom to base your "ideal self." (These role models could be anyone from an older brother or sister or a sports star or a celebrated super model). As in the other assignment, incorporate ideas from at least two of the three essays (Paglia, Santiago, and Suh).

Sequence 2: Images of Power

The essays:

"Redesigning Pocahontas," Gary Edgerton and Kathy Merlock Jackson (232–244)

"Into the Heart of Darkness," Terrence Rafferty (185–191)
"The Masculine Mystique—An Interview of Sylvester Stallone," Susan Faludi
  (218–230)
"John Wayne: America's Favorite Icon," Garry Wills (291–298)
"Xena: She's Big, Tall, Strong—and Popular," Donna Minkowitz (300–304)

Powerful men. What do they look like? How many kinds are there? What about powerful women? How are they similar to powerful men? How are they different? What does the word *powerful* mean to you? What might it mean to other people?

We live in a world of media images that contribute to our understanding of what is beautiful, disgusting, desirable. Through the images they present, popular media *define* how we should look and behave—and how we shouldn't. As influential as these images are, we can accept or reject them by analyzing and challenging the definition behind the constructed image. This reading and writing sequence offers an opportunity for you to consider how other people have defined the word *power* through popular images—and to develop your own definition.

1. Establishing Your Voice

To get started on this topic, set aside one hour to think about the ideas you already have. Work to identify your own opinions and to recall the circumstances that helped you form them. Write out answers to some of the questions below and plan to share your answers with class members.

a. Make a list of powerful female characters you know from television, including as many different kinds as you can. Think of players in the WNBA, but think also of the *Baywatch* lifeguards; think of Murphy Brown but also of the Nanny. Now list the characteristics attributed to each, especially those we associate with the particular kinds of power the women represent. In what ways do these women resemble each other? How are they different? What values do you attribute to each type? What values do others attribute to each?

b. Now make a similar list of powerful males and their attributes. Think of Dr. Mark Green on *ER,* but also of Dr. Mancini on *Melrose Place,* think of professional athletes and the male lifeguards on *Baywatch.* In what ways are they similar or different? What values do they represent?

c. In light of the way these powerful characters are presented to us, what does it mean to be powerful according to our culture? Which characteristics of power are absolute (that is, present in all heroes)? Which vary from one female hero to another? Which vary from one male hero to another? Which are primarily restricted to female or male heroes alone? Write out several paragraphs in which you explore possible answers to these questions.

2. Looking at Other Voices

a. You might think of Sylvester Stallone as a quintessential macho man, as are many of the characters he plays, but reread Susan Faludi's interview with Stallone, "The Masculine Mystique," and make note of the parts of that discussion that focus particularly on issues of power—how it is presented, how it is defined. How important is physical power to Stallone? What distinctions does he make between masculine and feminine? What do you make of his blurring of boundaries between the two? What kinds of power does he discuss? Write out and explain your thoughts on these questions, making reference to particular passages in the text that offer particular insight.

b. Now read Garry Wills's "John Wayne: America's Favorite Icon," and make note of the various parts of this discussion that focus on power—how it is presented, how it is defined, the ways in which it is masculine and/or feminine. Rely on any memories you have of John Wayne film characters and discuss the way that he defined power as well as how his characters presented different (but related) images of powerful men.

c. Compare Sylvester Stallone and his characters to John Wayne and his characters. If you have time, review one or more films by each actor (they are often on cable television or available in town or school libraries) and consider these details in your discussion. Write out an extended definition of how masculine power is constructed by these men and their film roles.

d. Now consider the feminine side. Read "Xena: She's Big, Tall, Strong—and Popular" by Donna Minkowitz and consider the definition of power that this character represents. How important is physical power to Xena? How important is sexual attractiveness? What distinctions are made between masculine and feminine characteristics? What other kinds of power are discussed? Write out and explain your thoughts on these questions.

e. Read "Redesigning Pocahontas" by Gary Edgerton and Kathy Merlock Jackson and compare the considerations that went into the creation of Pocahontas as a powerful female hero with those that went into the creation of Xena. How much of this power is physical? How important are other kinds of power? How are these female characters similar to or distinct from the male characters you read about earlier? Explain your answers.

f. Now read Terrence Rafferty's discussion of the heroes on *The X-Files* series, "Into the Heart of Darkness." If you have a chance, watch or rent an episode and include its details in your discussion. What kinds of power do these characters exhibit? Since one is male and the other female, consider how power is distributed. In what ways is the female hero (Scully) powerful like Xena or Pocahontas? How is her power different? In what ways does she resemble Stallone or Wayne heroes? How is the male hero (Mulder) similar to or different from the other male and female heroes you've considered? Write out your answers and make specific references to details from the text.

3. Synthesizing Voices

At this point, you have compared a wide range of ideas on the way power is defined in popular culture, particularly for men and for women. Take time now to cluster or classify the various components of the definitions, including your own ideas from question 1: What are the various kinds of power presented?

What is masculine power? What is feminine power? What characteristics are common to every powerful character? What differences in value are attached to the various kinds (and characteristics) of power?

4. Preparing the Final Essay

Prepare to write a formal essay in which you explore the construction of different types of power by answering the following question: When we speak of powerful men and powerful women, are we speaking of the same thing? Discuss the ways in which heroic qualities transcend the bodily or physical aspects of power (strength or sexuality)—and the ways in which they don't. Incorporate your own definition of powerful and heroic characters into this discussion, making sure that your definition is firmly supported by detailed evidence and analysis.

Be prepared to share this draft with other students and with your instructor and to incorporate their feedback into your revision(s). To strengthen your argument, make specific references to the texts (quotations, paraphrasing, summary) and properly cite all information you borrow.

Sequence 3: The Politics of Language

The essays:

"Crimes Against Humanity," Ward Churchill (316–323)
"Cultural Baggage," Barbara Ehrenreich (344–346)
"One Nation, One Language, One Ballot," John Silber (351–353)
"What's So American About English?" Andrew Ward (354–356)
"English Plus, Not English Only," Michael E. Dickstein (368–370)
"Race Is Over," Stanley Crouch (550–553)

The essays in this reading and writing sequence offer an opportunity to evaluate arguments presented by various authors about how language defines our American identity and to prepare your own argument in response. You will use skills developed throughout this book and in the previous sequences, but your particular aim here will be to present, finally, a well-considered and persuasive essay in which you take on the issues of how we in the United States use language to form identity in a number of ways.

1. Preparing for the Topic

To get started on this topic, write out answers to the questions below. Plan to share your answers with class members.

a. Think of language and identity on a personal level. Think of the ways you communicate with family or friends or other groups that you are a member of: Do you speak different languages in different groups or different versions of the same language? List certain words or phrases that are unique to certain groups even if English is the primary language. (Think of slang, of phrases used to re-call common experiences, and so on.) Describe these differences in language in detail, then go on to consider the following: How do these differences distin-guish groups from one another? Why might this be important?

b. Now, think of this issue on a more cultural level: Does your family speak En-glish? What are some of the different versions of English that you are familiar with? (Think of people in different professions, from different places, with dif-ferent levels of authority.) What about people who don't speak English or who speak a different version of English: What problems do they encounter? What do you think should be done about these problems? Who should do it?

2. Looking at Other Voices

a. Reread the essay "One Nation, One Language, One Ballot," where John Silber claims that language is one of the most important elements of identity, espe-cially national identity. He says, "Our common language provides the unity that, paradoxically, enables us to understand and cherish our cultural diversity" (paragraph 10). He also says, "America is a nation based on a set of ideas and allegiance to those ideals—it's not based on ethnicity or national origin" (para-graph 11).

   Write out your own understanding of what Silber means by these state-ments. What elements of American culture does he look at to support these claims? Do you find his argument compelling? Can you think of any cultural el-ements he overlooks?

b. Reread Michael Dickstein's "English Plus, Not English Only" and Andrew Ward's essay, "What's So American About English?" Ward claims that "when we talk about language we are really talking about identity, and making English our national language suggests that we are Americans only to the extent to which we know English. But what we should cherish most about America [is] the promise of freedom and justice and opportunity" (paragraph 9). Consider, then, how Dickstein and Ward want us to define "identity" and compare their ideas to Silber's. Write out your analysis.

c. Relying on the information you've gathered so far, read Ward Churchill's piece, "Crimes Against Humanity." Churchill argues that identity often emerges more from the visual images we create or associate with people (or groups of people) than from the language we use to create those images. Write two to three pages in which you summarize those ideas in Churchill's essay that seem to speak to ideas in Silber's and Ward's pieces and then discuss several ways in which the authors agree or disagree among themselves.

d. Finally, read the pieces by Barbara Ehrenreich ("Cultural Baggage") and Stan-ley Crouch ("Race Is Over"). These authors suggest another position in the ar-gument of how identity is determined. As with the earlier authors, they note the important role language can play in creating identity, but their focus moves to the qualities we attach to people as we *talk about* them. How do they make this shift? How do their arguments compare to each other? How do they compare to (or contrast with) the arguments of Silber, Dickstein, Ward, and/or Churchill? How are they different?

3. **Synthesizing Voices**

   Now that you've generated a good deal of prewriting material to help discover your own ideas, blend your views with those of the various authors. How do Silber's ideas relate to your own understanding of how language determines identity? How do Dickstein's and Ward's ideas agree with your own? What about Churchill? Ehrenreich? Crouch? Have they given you new ideas? Do they make you want to rethink any of your ideas? Explain your analysis in detail.

4. **Preparing the Final Essay**

   Write a formal, persuasive essay that answers these questions: What role does language play in forming people's identity? What role should it play?

   Your essay should have a persuasive goal, should consider the range of arguments offered, and should offer your own argument on how best to answer the questions. Your discussion should be informed by the readings and by your own experience. Once you have received peer (and perhaps instructor) feedback on your draft(s), revise it into final form. Be sure to incorporate specific references to the assigned writings (quotations, paraphrasing, summary), and to properly cite all information you borrow.

Credits

Photo Credits

Page 23 Archive Photos/Reuters/Stefano Rellandini; Page 69 Feldman & Associates/Jill Birschbach; Page 128 Courtesy of Mercedes-Benz of North America, Inc., photographer: Steve Hellerstein; Page 130 Courtesy of Smirnoff; Page 132 Courtesy of Sara Lee Intimates; Page 134 Courtesy of Kalis Supernaturals, Inc.; Page 136 Courtesy of Diesel U.S.A., Inc.; Page 138 Courtesy of Consolidated Cigar Corporation; Page 140 Courtesy of Airwalk; Page 142 Courtesy of National Fluid Milk Processor Promotional Board; Page 144 Courtesy of AT&T; Page 146 Courtesy of U.S. Army; Page 148 Archive Photos/Jeff Greenberg; Page 200 Shooting Star International Photo/Scott Harrison; Page 264 SuperStock International; Page 309 Archive Photos/Reuters/Steve Schaefer; Page 349 Feldman & Associates/Jill Birschbach; Page 372 Sipa Press/Bob Strong; Page 407 Everett Collection/Capital Cities/ABC, Inc.; Page 485 SuperStock International; Page 521 SuperStock International; Page 557 Courtesy of NASA

Text Credits

Acosta, Rolando Flores, "Seeking Unity in Diversity," reprinted with permission of *The Wall Street Journal.* Copyright © 1996 Dow Jones & Company, Inc. All rights reserved.

Barnett, Rosalind and Caryl Rivers, "The New Nostalgia," excerpts from "The New Nostalgia" from *She Works He Works* by Rosalind Barnett and Caryl Rivers. Copyright © 1996 by Rosalind Barnett and Caryl Rivers. Reprinted by permission of HarperCollins Publishers, Inc.

Barry, Dave, "No Sale," reprinted by permission of *The Miami Herald* from *No Sale* by Dave Barry. Copyright © 1997 by Dave Barry. Reprinted by permission.

Bayles, Martha, "In Defense of Prime Time," from *The Washington Post,* March 1996. Reprinted by permission.

Bennett, William, "Leave Marriage Alone," from *Newsweek*, June 3, 1996. Copyright © 1996 Newsweek, Inc. All rights reserved. Reprinted by permission.

Borst, Jan, "Relatively Speaking," from *Newsweek,* July 22, 1996. Copyright © 1996 Newsweek, Inc. All rights reserved. Reprinted by permission.

Brotman, Barbara, "Burning Desire to Be Slimmer Is a Slow Suicide," from "Burning Desire to Be Slimmer Is a Slow Suicide" by Barbara Brotman. © Copyrighted Chicago Tribune Company. All rights reserved. Used with permission.

Brubach, Holly, "Heroine Worship," copyright © 1996 by The New York Times Company. Reprinted by permission.

Canada, Geoffrey, "Fist Stick Knife Gun," excerpted from *Fist Stick Knife Gun* by Geoffrey Canada. Copyright © 1995 by Geoffrey Canada. Reprinted by permission of Beacon Press, Boston.

Celente, Gerald, "Trends 2000: How to Prepare for and Profit from the Changes of the 21st Century," reprinted by permission of Warner Books, Inc. New York, U.S.A. From *Trends 2000: How to Prepare for and Profit from the Changes of the 21st Century* by Gerald Celente. Copyright © 1997 by Gerald Celente. All rights reserved.

Churchill, Ward, "Crimes Against Humanity," *Z,* March 1993. Reprinted by permission.

Coontz, Stephanie, "Single Mothers: A Menace to Society?," *Vogue,* December 1994. Reprinted by permission.

Crouch, Stanley, "Race Is Over," copyright © 1996 by The New York Times Company. Reprinted by permission.

Dickstein, Michael E., "Canada's Example Shows Drawback of English Only," from *The Chicago Tribune.* Reprinted by permission.

574

Dornink, Lynn, "Silencing the Feminine," reprinted by permission.

Douglas, Susan, "Remote Control: How to Make a Media Skeptic," from *The Utne Reader.* Reprinted by permission.

Dyson, Esther, "The Internet: If You Don't Love it Leave It," copyright © 1995 by The New York Times Company. Reprinted by permission.

Edgerton, Gary and Kathy Merlock Jackson, "Redesigning Pocahontas," *Journal of Popular Film and Television,* Volume 24, No. 2, 1996. Reprinted with permission of the Helen Dwight Reid Educational Foundation. Published by Heldref Publications, 1319 Eighteenth St., N.W., Washington, D.C. 20036-1802 Copyright © 1996.

Ehrenreich, Barbara, "Cultural Baggage," copyright © 1992 by The New York Times Company. Reprinted by permission.

Ehrenreich, Barbara, "Oh Those Family Values," copyright © 1994 Time, Inc. Reprinted by permission.

Faludi, Susan, "Masculine Mystique, An Interview of Sylvester Stallone," *Esquire*, December 1996. Reprinted by permission.

Fitzpatrick, Michael, "3 for the Stripes," reprinted by permission.

Gaiter, Leonce, "Revolt of the Black Bourgeoisie," copyright © 1994 by The New York Times Company. Reprinted by permission.

George, Lynell, "Gray Boys, Funky Aztecs and Honorary Home Girls," copyright © 1997 *The Los Angeles Times.* Reprinted by permission.

Gilliam, Dorothy, "Breathing Easier with a Rare Film," copyright © 1996 *The Washington Post.* Reprinted with permission.

Gleick, James, "Big Brother Is Us," copyright © 1996 by The New York Times Company. Reprinted by permission.

Goodman, Ellen, "Johnny, Take Your Drug Test," copyright © 1997 The Boston Globe Newspaper Company/Washington Post Writers Group. Reprinted with permission.

Greenfield, Meg, "Back to the Future," *Newsweek*, January 1997. Reprinted by permission.

Hancock, Lynnell, "The Have and Have-Nots," *Newsweek*, February 27, 1995. Copyright © 1995 Newsweek, Inc. All rights reserved. Reprinted by permission.

Hass, Nancy, "Sex and Today's Single-Minded Sitcoms," copyright © 1997 by The New York Times Company. Reprinted by permission.

Hochschild, Arlie Russell, "The Time Bind: When Work Becomes Home and Home Becomes Work," from *The Time Bind: When Work Becomes Home and Home Becomes Work* by Arlie Russell Hochschild, copyright © 1997 by Arlie Russell Hochschild. Reprinted by permission of Henry Holt and Company, Inc.

Homes, A. M., "Mystery Date," copyright © 1996 by A. M. Homes, reprinted with the permission of The Wylie Agency, Inc.

hooks, bell, "Mock Feminism: Waiting to Exhale," excerpt from *Reel to Real: Race, Sex and Class at the Movies* by bell hooks. Published by Routledge Holdings, Inc. Reprinted with permission.

Jago, Carol, "English Only, For the Kids' Sake, *The Los Angeles Times.* Reprinted by permission.

Johnson, Rebecca, "The Body Myth," *Vogue,* September, 1996.

King, Ynestra, "The Other Body: Reflections on Difference, Disability and Identity Politics," *Ms.*, March–April 1993. Reprinted by permission.

Kitcher, Philip, "Junior Comes Out Perfect," copyright © 1996 by The New York Times Company. Reprinted by permission.

Lee, Change-rae, "Mute in an English-Only World," copyright © 1996 by The New York Times Company. Reprinted by permission.

Leo, John, "No-Fault Holocaust," *US News & World Report,* July 30, 1997. Reprinted by permission.

Leonhardt, David and Kathleen Kerwin, "Hey Kids, Buy This!," reprinted from June 30, 1997 issue of *Business Week* by special permission, copyright © 1997 by the McGraw-Hill Companies, Inc.

Letters from Vogue?, "Talking Back," Letter to the Editor, Courtesy *Vogue.* Copyright © 1996 The Condé Nast Publications, Inc.

Reilly, Tom, "Youth Crime Has Changed and so Must the Juvenile Justice System," *The Boston Globe,* 1997. Reprinted by permission.

Rheingold, Howard, "The Virtual Community," from *The Virtual Community,* by Howard Rheingold, (pages 17, 19, 20, 23–27). Copyright © 1993 Howard Rheingold. Reprinted by permission of Addison-Wesley Longman Inc.

Rohter, Larry, "A Legend Grows and so Does an Industry," copyright © 1997 by The New York Times Company. Reprinted by permission.

Romero, D. James, "Believers in Search of Piercing Insight," *Los Angeles Times,* January 29, 1997. Copyright © 1997 *The Los Angeles Times.* Reprinted by permission.

Santiago, Esmeralda, "A Puerto Rican Stew," copyright © 1994 by The New York Times Company. Reprinted by permission.

Schoenberger, Chana, "Getting to Know About You and Me," from *Newsweek,* September 20, 1993. Copyright © 1993 Newsweek, Inc. All rights reserved. Reprinted by permission.

Siegel, Ed, "Where Are the Heroes?," reprinted courtesy of *The Boston Globe.*

Silber, John, "One Nation, One Language, One Ballot," reprinted with permission of *The Wall Street Journal.* Copyright © 1996 Dow Jones & Company, Inc. All rights reserved.

Singer, Jennifer, "Shunning 70-Hour Work Weeks, Generation Xers Are Defining Their Own American Dream," *The Chicago Tribune*, August 9, 1995. Reprinted by permission.

Smith, Abbe and Lael E. H. Chester, "Cruel Punishment for Juveniles," *The Boston Globe,* July 1996. Reprinted by permission.

Steel, Ronald, "America Remains No. 1," copyright © 1996 by The New York Times Company. Reprinted by permission.

Sullivan, Andrew, "Let Gays Marry," From *Newsweek,* June 3, 1996. Copyright © 1996 Newsweek, Inc. All rights reserved. Reprinted by permission.

Talbot, Margaret, "Hasta La Vista," *Vogue,* May 1997. Reprinted by permission.

Tannen, Mary, "Mr. Clean," copyright © 1995 by The New York Times Company. Reprinted by permission.

Twitchell, James B., "But First a Word from Our Sponsor," *The Wilson Quarterly*, Summer 1996. Reprinted by permission.

West, Cornel, "On Black Fathering," copyright © 1996 by Cornel West from *Faith of Our Fathers* by Andre C. Willis. Used by permission of Dutton Signet, a division of Penguin Books USA, Inc.

Whitehead, Barbara Dafoe, "Rethinking Divorce," *The Boston Globe,* February 4, 1997. Reprinted by permission.

Wills, Garry." John Wayne: America's Favorite Icon," from *John Wayne's America* by Garry Wills, copyright © 1997 by Literary Research, Inc. Reprinted by permission of Simon & Schuster.

Wuthnow, Robert, "Poor Richard's Principle," Wuthnow, Robert, "Poor Richard's Principle." Copyright © 1996 by Princeton University Press. Reprinted by permission of Princeton University Press.

Yemma, John, "Innocent and Presumed Ethnic," reprinted courtesy of *The Boston Globe.*

Index of Authors and Titles